T0201392

Theory and Applications of Image Registration

Theory and Applications of Image Registration

Arthur Ardeshir Goshtasby

Registered Offices
John Wiley & Sons, Inc., 111 River Street, Hoboken, NJ 07030, USA

Editorial Office
111 River Street, Hoboken, NJ 07030, USA

For details of our global editorial offices, customer services, and more information about Wiley products visit us at www.wiley.com.

Wiley also publishes its books in a variety of electronic formats and by print-on-demand. Some content that appears in standard print versions of this book may not be available in other formats.

Library of Congress Cataloging-in-Publication Data

Names: Goshtasby, Ardeshir, author.
Title: Theory and applications of image registration / Arthur
    Ardeshir Goshtasby.
Description: Hoboken, NJ : John Wiley & Sons, 2017. | Includes
    bibliographical references and index. | Description based on print version
    record and CIP data provided by publisher; resource not viewed.
Identifiers: LCCN 2017007704 (print) | LCCN 2017012539 (ebook) | ISBN
    9781119171720 (PDF) | ISBN 9781119171737 (ePub) | ISBN 9781119171713
    (cloth)
Subjects: LCSH: Image registration.
Classification: LCC TA1632 (ebook) | LCC TA1632 .T4815 2017 (print) | DDC
    006.6–dc23
LC record available at https://lccn.loc.gov/2017007704

Cover image: © Hayami Yanagisawa / EyeEm/Gettyimages
Cover design by Wiley

Set in 10/12pt WarnockPro by SPi Global, Chennai, India

Printed in the United States of America

10 9 8 7 6 5 4 3 2 1

To my wife Mariko, and my parents Bahram and Firoozeh.

Brief Table of Content

Contents

Contributors

EDGARDO MOLINA received his PhD in computer science from the CUNY Graduate Centre in New York in 2015 and a BS degree in computer science from the Macaulay Honors College at The City College of New York – CUNY in 2005. His research interests are computer vision, human–computer interaction, 3-D visualization, and applications for assistive technologies. He has been cofounder and CEO of Vista Wearable, Inc., developing wearable assistive devices for the visually impaired and providing consulting services to other corporations.

WAI L. KHOO received his PhD in computer science from the Graduate Centre – CUNY in 2016 and BS and MS degrees in computer science at The City College of New York – CUNY in 2009 and 2012, respectively. His research interests include computer vision, multimodal sensing, human–computer interaction, and virtual/augmented reality and also application of computer vision to assistive technology for the visually impaired.

HAO TANG is an assistant professor of computer science at Borough of Manhattan Community College – CUNY. He received a PhD degree in computer science in 2013 from the Graduate Centre – CUNY. He was an adjunct faculty member with The City College of New York and a senior researcher at The City College Visual Computing Research Laboratory. His research interests include 3-D computer modeling, visualization of large-scale scenes, image understanding, and mobile vision navigation, as well as their applications in surveillance, and assistive technology for the visually impaired. His research paper in the International Conference on Multimedia and Expo won the best paper award Finalist.

ZHIGANG ZHU is the Herbert G. Kayser professor of computer science at The City College of New York and the Graduate Center – CUNY. He is also the director of The City College Visual Computing Laboratory (CCVCL). His research interests include 3-D computer vision, multimodal sensing, virtual/augmented reality, video representation, and various applications of assistive technology in environment, robotics, surveillance, and transportation. He has published over 150 technical papers in related fields. He is an associate editor of the Machine Vision Applications Journal and has been technical editor of the ASME/IEEE Transactions on Mechatronics.

Acknowledgments

The satellite images used in this monograph are courtesy of NASA, USGS, Google, and Microsoft Bing; the aerial images are courtesy of Image Registration and Fusion Systems and the Computer Vision Group at Brown University; and the medical images are courtesy of Kettering Medical Center. Results reported in this monograph are from research conducted with funding from NSF, NIH, AFRL, Kettering Medical Center, and the Ohio Board of Regents. The contributions and support of these organizations toward preparation of this monograph are greatly appreciated. The author would like to recognize and thank Edgardo Molina, Wai Lun Khoo, Hao Tang, and Zhigang Zhu, who contributed a key chapter to this monograph. Finally, the author would like to thank Libby Martin for editorial assistance in preparation of this monograph.

A.A.G

About the Companion Website

This book is accompanied by a companion website:

http://www.imgfsr.com/WileyRegistrationBook.html

[If the website cannot be accessed for some reason, contact the author directly at arthur.goshtasby@gmail.com for the online materials relating to the book.]

1

Introduction

The field of image registration came to being even before the advent of digital media. Dressler, in a US patent in 1956 [1], disclosed an electronic image comparison device that could register images recorded on films. By providing the mechanism to translate and rotate one film over the other and by projecting the images to a subtraction device using a half mirror and a full mirror, he provided the means to register and compare images. Circuitry was provided to produce an output at any given time with its amplitude proportional to the degree of match between the images. While observing the amplitude of the output, the user was enabled to interactively register the images.

The first work in digital image registration goes as far back as 1963 in the Ph.D. dissertation of Lawrence Roberts at MIT [2]. By aligning a 2-D projection of a 3-D polyhedral scene to edges of known polyhedral objects, he was able to identify polyhedral objects in the scene via image registration.

Image registration as we know it today came to being by the groundbreaking work of Anuta [3]. Anuta developed an automated method for spatially aligning remote sensing images by the fast Fourier transform.

Image registration is the process of spatially aligning two images of a scene. The alignment process determines the correspondence between points in the images. If the images are taken by the same sensor but at different times, the correspondence process makes it possible to detect changes in the scene occurring between the times the images are obtained [4]. If the images are obtained by different sensors, the correspondence process makes it possible to combine information in the images, creating a richer source of information about the underlying scene [5, 6].

By registering frames in a video captured by a moving camera, it becomes possible to distinguish image differences caused by camera motion from image differences caused by object motion, making it possible to track moving

Theory and Applications of Image Registration, First Edition. Arthur Ardeshir Goshtasby.
© 2017 John Wiley & Sons, Inc. Published 2017 by John Wiley & Sons, Inc.

objects in the video [7]. If the images represent different views of a scene, the correspondence process makes it possible to determine the geometry of the scene [8].

This monograph covers the fundamentals of digital image registration. Only feature-based image registration methods are covered. Although a variety of optimization-based methods have been developed that use image intensities to register images, such methods are often very time consuming and are influenced by image noise. Feature-based methods are more resistant to noise and are computationally very efficient.

Image registration methods that use feature points and feature lines will be covered. Feature points identify locally unique neighborhoods in an image, facilitating the correspondence process. In addition to its location, a feature point may have various feature values, characterizing the neighborhood of the point. Feature points have been referred to as *control points, point landmarks, key points, corners, centroids,* and *tie points* in the literature.

A feature line at the minimum has a position and an orientation. The position of a line is the point on the line closest to the origin. The orientation of a line is the angle the normal to the line makes with the x-axis. These are the parameters used to define a line in polar form. In addition to the position and orientation of a line, the midpoint, length, endpoints, intensities, and gradients along the line can be used as features to describe the line.

The process of spatially aligning two images involves resampling one image to the geometry of the other. The image that is kept unchanged is called the *reference image* and the image that is resampled to the geometry of the reference image is called the *test image*. Reference image has also been called *source image* in the literature, and test image has also been called *target image* and *sensed image* in the literature.

An example of image registration is given in Fig. 1.1. Reference image (a) is a Landsat Multispectral Scanner (MSS) image of Kalkaska County, Michigan,

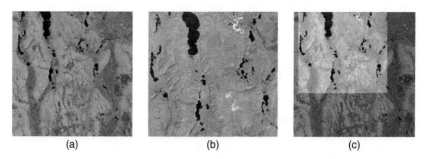

(a)   (b)   (c)

Figure 1.1 (a) A Landsat MSS image and (b) a Landsat TM image of Kalkaska County, Michigan. (c) The TM image is geometrically transformed to spatially align the MSS image. These images are courtesy of the USGS.

and test image (b) is a Landsat Thematic Mapper (TM) image of the same area. These images are courtesy of the US Geological Survey (USGS). The registered image (c) is obtained by geometrically transforming the TM image to spatially align the MSS image. By registering the images, it is possible to fuse information in the images or quantify differences between the images.

In this monograph, coordinates of points in the reference image will be denoted by (x, y), while coordinates of the corresponding points in the test image will be denoted by (X, Y). Image registration involves finding the relation between (x, y) and (X, Y). This relation is called a *transformation model*. A transformation model for registering 2-D images has two components, denoted by f_x and f_y:

$$X = f_x(x, y), \tag{1.1}$$
$$Y = f_y(x, y). \tag{1.2}$$

Functions f_x and f_y represent the x- and the y-components of the transformation. For each point (x, y) in the reference image, f_x and f_y determine the coordinates of the corresponding point (X, Y) in the test image. Therefore, once the components of a transformation model are determined, by scanning the reference image, for each pixel (x, y) there, the location (X, Y) of the same pixel in the test image is determined. Then, the intensity at (X, Y) in the test image is read and saved at (x, y) in a new image called the *resampled image*. The resampled image, therefore, has the geometry of the reference image and the intensities of the test image.

Note that functions f_x and f_y map pixels in the reference image to the corresponding pixels in the test image. This mapping in effect finds intensities in the test image corresponding to the pixels in the reference image. For integer pixel coordinates (x, y) in the reference image, f_x and f_y produce floating-point coordinates (X, Y) in the test image. The integers closest to X and Y are taken as the coordinates of the pixel in the test image corresponding to pixel (x, y). Alternatively, the intensity at location (X, Y) in the test image is estimated from the intensities of pixels surrounding (X, Y) by bilinear interpolation or cubic convolution [9].

1.1 Organization of the Book

This monograph provides theoretical basis and implementation details of methods for finding feature points/feature lines in images, establishing correspondence between the feature points/feature lines, and using the correspondences to compute the parameters of a transformation model to register the images.

Chapter 2 describes a method for determining the orientation of an image. An image containing a nonsymmetric pattern has a preferred orientation.

By determining the orientations of two images and by bringing the images to the same orientation, steps in image registration are simplified.

Chapter 3 discusses methods for identifying locally unique neighborhoods in an image. Centers of locally unique neighborhoods are taken as feature points. Rotation-variant and rotation-invariant methods are described. Rotation-variant methods are suitable for registering images that have the same orientation, and rotation-invariant methods are suitable for registering images that have different orientations.

Chapter 4 covers various line detection methods. Hough transform–based methods find lines among unorganized points, edge-based and curve-based methods find lines among edge contours, and region subdivision-based methods find lines among raw image intensities. Region subdivision-based methods by subdividing an image into regions of similar gradient directions and by fitting a line to each region detect lines.

Chapter 5 discusses the point correspondence problem. Given two sets of points, the problem of finding correspondence between points in the two sets is addressed. Corresponding points are also referred to as *homologous points*. First, clustering methods that use information about the locations of the points to find homologous points are described. Then, methods that use various information in addition to point locations to find homologous points are described. Finally, methods that determine homologous points in images by template matching are described. Geometric constraints and robust estimators that remove outliers from obtained correspondences are also discussed.

The problem of line correspondence is covered in *Chapter 6*. First, formulations that relate the parameters of homologous lines in two images to the parameters of a transformation model registering the images are derived. Then, methods that determine homologous lines in images by line grouping are discussed.

Chapter 7 covers topics relating to nonrigid image registration. Given a set of homologous points in two images of a scene, the problem of finding the parameters of an elastic transformation model to transform the geometry of the test image to the geometry of the reference image is discussed. Various elastic transformation models suitable for nonrigid image registration are described.

While Chapters 2–7 cover methods for the registration of projective images, *Chapter 8* covers methods for the registration of tomographic images. A tomographic image sequence represents a stack of cross-sectional images captured of a 3-D object. In this chapter, after discussing a method for converting a tomographic image sequence into an isotropic volume, methods for rigid and nonrigid registration of isotropic volumes are discussed.

In *Chapter 9*, methods for validating the accuracy of an image registration software are discussed. Specifically, methods that use a gold standard or simulation data to determine the accuracy of an image registration software are discussed. A number of methods that measure registration accuracy in the absence of simulation data or a gold standard are also discussed.

In *Chapter 10*, registration of video images to create panoramas, including stereo panoramas, is discussed. Registration under different camera motions, including pure rotation, pure translation, and general motion, are discussed. The structure of a camera setup to create panoramas in real time with a minimal computational requirement is also described.

Chapter 11 discusses registration of multitemporal images. It is found that feature lines remain more stable than feature points in images of scenes going through natural disasters. Lines representing roads, bridges, and edges of building are hardly affected by storms, flooding, and earthquakes. Fusion of registered images to detect scene changes in multitemporal images is also discussed.

In *Chapter 12*, open problems and research topics in image registration are mentioned. These include rotation-invariant similarity and distance measures for registration of multimodality images, rotation-invariant descriptors for registration of multimodality images, and the relation between parameters of a nonrigid transformation model and parameters of homologous lines in images.

The majority of algorithms discussed in this monograph have been implemented and the software packages producing the results reported in this monograph are made available to the readers as learning tools. The software packages may be downloaded from http://www.imgfsr.com/WileyRegistrationBook.html. *Appendix A* is meant to serve as a user's guide to the software packages.

1.2 Further Reading

Image registration has been an active area of research in image processing and computer vision since early 1970s. Papers on image registration regularly appear in *IEEE Transactions on Pattern Analysis and Machine Intelligence, IEEE Transactions on Image Processing, IEEE Transactions on Geoscience and Remote Sensing, IEEE Transactions on Medical Imaging, Medical Image Analysis, International Journal of Computer Vision, Image and Vision Computing, Pattern Recognition, Pattern Recognition Letters,* and *Computer Vision and Image Understanding* journals.

Surveys of image registration methods [10–18], special issues [19–22], and books on the subject [9, 23–28] also appear in the literature.

References

1 R. Dressler, *Image Matching Apparatus*, US Patent 2,989,890, Filed No. 13, 1956, Patented June 27, 1961.
2 L. G. Roberts, *Machine Perception of Three-Dimensional Solids*, Department of Electrical Engineering, Massachusetts Institute of Technology, 1963.

3 P. E. Anuta, Spatial registration of multispectral and multitemporal digital imagery using fast Fourier transform techniques, *IEEE Transactions on Geoscience Electronics*, **8**(4):353–368, 1970.

4 C. Zhao and A. Goshtasby, Registration of multitemporal aerial optical images using line features, *ISPRS Journal of Photogrammetry and Remote Sensing*, **117**:149–160, 2016.

5 A. Goshtasby and S. Nikolov, Image fusion: advances in the state of the art, *Information Fusion*, **8**:114–118, 2007.

6 F. Maes, D. Loeckx, D. Vandermeulen, and P. Suetens, Image registration using mutual information, in *Handbook of Biomedical Imaging*, Springer, 295–308, 2015.

7 M. Linger and A. Goshtasby, Aerial image registration for tracking, *IEEE Transactions on Geoscience and Remote Sensing*, **53**(4):2137–2145, 2015.

8 O. C. Ozcanli, Y. Dong, J. L. Mundy, H. Webb, R. Hammoud, and V. Tom, A comparison of stereo and multiview 3-D reconstruction using cross-sensor satellite imagery, in *IEEE Conference on Computer Vision and Pattern Recognition Workshops*, 17–25, 2015.

9 A. Goshtasby, *2-D and 3-D Image Registration for Medical, Remote Sensing, and Industrial Applications*, Wiley Press, 2005.

10 W. Crum, T. Hartkens, and D. Hill, Non-rigid image registration: theory and practice, *British Journal of Radiology*, **77**(2):140–153, 2004.

11 M. Holden, A review of geometric transformations for nonrigid body registration, *IEEE Transactions on Medical Imaging*, **27**(1):111–128, 2008.

12 J. A. Schnabel, M. P. Heinrich, B. W. Papież, and Sir J. M. Brady, Advances and challenges in deformable image registration: from image fusion to complex motion modelling, *Medical Image Analysis*, **33**:145–148, 2016.

13 A. Sotiras, C. Davatzikos, and N. Paragios, Deformable medical image registration: a survey, *IEEE Transactions on Medical Imaging*, **32**(7):1153–1190, 2013.

14 P. A. van den Elsen, E. J. D. Pol, and M. A. Viergever, Medical image matching: a review with classification, *IEEE Engineering in Medicine and Biology*, **3**:26–39, 1993.

15 M. A. Viergever, J. A. Maintz, S. Klein, K. Murphy, M. Staring, and J. P. W. Pluim, A survey of medical image registration, *Medical Image Analysis*, **33**:140–144, 2016.

16 L. Zagorchev and A. Goshtasby, A comparative study of transformation functions for nonrigid image registration, *IEEE Transactions on Image Processing*, **15**(3):529–538, 2006.

17 B. Zitova and J. Flusser, Image registration methods: a survey, *Image and Vision Computing*, **21**(11):977–1000, 2003.

18 L. G. Brown, A survey of image registration techniques, *ACM Computing Surveys*, **24**:326–376, 1992.

19 B. Dawant, G. E. Christensen, J. M. Fitzpatrick, and D. Rueckert, *Biomedical Image Registration: 5th International Workshop*, Springer, 2012.

20 J. C. Gee, J. B. Maintz, and M. W. Vannier, *Biomedical Image Registration: 2nd International Workshop*, Springer, 2003.

21 A. Goshtasby and J. Le Moigne, Image registration: an introduction, *Pattern Recognition*, **32**(1):1–2, 1999.

22 A. Goshtasby, L. Staib, C. Studholme, and D. Terzopoulos, Nonrigid image registration, *Computer Vision and Image Understanding*, **89**(2/3):109–113, 2003.

23 A. Goshtasby, *Image Registration: Principles, Tools, and Methods*, Springer, 2012.

24 D. L. G. Hajnal, J. V. Hill, and D. J. Hawkes, *Medical Image Registration*, CRC Press, 2001.

25 J. Le Moigne, N. S. Netanyahu, and R. D. Eastman, *Image Registration for Remote Sensing*, Cambridge University Press, 2012.

26 J. Modersitzki, *Numerical Methods for Image Registration*, Oxford University Press, 2003.

27 J. Modersitzki, *FAIR: Flexible Algorithms for Image Registration*, SIAM, 2009.

28 K. Rohr, *Landmark-Based Image Analysis: Using Geometric and Intensity Models*, Kluwer Academic, Boston, MA, 2001.

2

Image Orientation Detection

2.1 Introduction

Images that are in different orientations are the most difficult to register. Just as we can recognize objects in their upright poses more easily than in upside-down or rotated poses, computer algorithms can more easily locate patches in one image in another if the images are not rotated with respect to each other. To simplify the correspondence process, images have to be brought to the same orientation.

Unless an image contains a perfectly symmetric pattern, it will have a preferred orientation. Images of natural scenes often possess this property. If the preferred orientation of each image can be reliably determined, the images can be brought to the same orientation, simplifying the correspondence process. In the remainder of this chapter, preferred orientation will be referred to as *orientation.*

The orientation of an image depends on the geometric layout of the pattern within the image. If the images to be registered do not have a sufficient overlap, they may have different orientations. Images of a scene captured by different sensors may also have different orientations because the same scene can appear differently in the images. However, when the images are from the same sensor and there is significant overlap between the images, by knowing the orientations of the images, it should be possible to bring both images to the same orientation.

An image's (global) orientation is calculated from the aggregate of its local orientations, and a local orientation is determined from intensity gradients or geometric gradients in a small neighborhood. Since orientation is a geometric property, we will see that geometric gradients provide a more reliable means of estimating it than intensity gradients.

Radiometric and geometric noise can influence estimation of an image's orientation. Radiometric noise is usually zero-mean and can be reduced by image

Theory and Applications of Image Registration, First Edition. Arthur Ardeshir Goshtasby.
© 2017 John Wiley & Sons, Inc. Published 2017 by John Wiley & Sons, Inc.

smoothing. However, geometric noise is not zero-mean, and if not removed, it can adversely influence estimation of an image's orientation.

To compare image orientations computed from intensity gradients and geometric gradients, consider the noise-free image in Fig. 2.1a. The image contains a solid circle with its radius taken in such a way that there would be 360 pixels on the boundary of the circle. Ideally, pixels along the boundary of the circle should produce uniform gradient directions between $0°$ and $359°$. The histogram of intensity gradient directions of pixels with nonzero gradient magnitudes are shown in Fig. 2.1c in red. While there are many pixels with gradient directions that are a multiple of $45°$, there are not any pixels at many other gradient directions.

Denoting the intensity at pixel (x, y) in image I by $I(x, y)$, intensity gradient in x-direction will be $I_x(x, y) = I(x + 1, y) - I(x, y)$, intensity gradient in y-direction will be $I_y(x, y) = I(x, y + 1) - I(x, y)$, intensity gradient magnitude $GM(x, y)$ will be

$$GM(x, y) = \sqrt{I_x^2(x, y) + I_y^2(x, y)} \tag{2.1}$$

and intensity gradient direction $\theta(x, y)$ will be

$$\theta(x, y) = \arctan\left(\frac{I_y(x, y)}{I_x(x, y)}\right). \tag{2.2}$$

By smoothing the image in Fig. 2.1a with a Gaussian filter of standard deviation 3 pixels and calculating the gradient directions at pixels with gradient magnitudes greater than 0.5, the blue histogram of Fig. 2.1c is obtained. A larger number of pixels belong to the blue histogram compared to the red histogram. Although there are no longer strong preferences toward $45°, 135°, 225°$, and $315°$ orientations, there are still strong preferences toward orientations that are a multiple of $90°$.

By increasing the radius of the circle by a factor of 2 so that there will be 720 pixels along the boundary of the circle as shown in Fig. 2.1b, the gradient direction histograms shown in Fig. 2.1d are obtained when using the original image (red) and the image after smoothing with a Gaussian filter of standard deviation 3 pixels (blue). The preference of gradient directions toward angles that are a multiple of $90°$ remains, making global orientation detection from the aggregate of local intensity gradient directions unreliable, even in the absence of radiometric noise. Local orientations determined by intensity gradients are biased toward the horizontal and vertical arrangement of pixels in an image—something that cannot be avoided irrespective of the level of intensity smoothing applied to the image.

A second example demonstrating the unreliable nature of intensity gradients in the estimation of an image's orientation is given in Fig. 2.2. The major axis of the ellipse in Fig. 2.2a makes a $30°$ angle with the horizontal axis. Therefore,

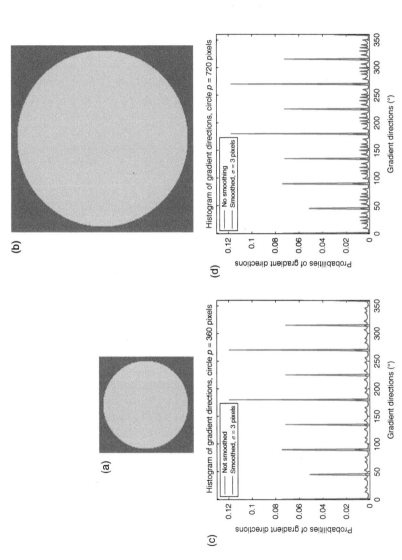

Figure 2.1 (a and b) Solid circles with perimeters 360 and 720 pixels, respectively. The intensity of pixels within the circles is 200, while the intensity of pixels outside the circles is 100. (c and d) Intensity gradient direction histograms of images (a) and (b), respectively, before smoothing (red) and after smoothing with a Gaussian of standard deviation 3 pixels (blue).

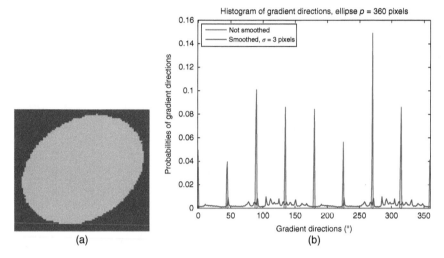

(a) (b)

Figure 2.2 (a) A solid ellipse with its major axis making a 30° angle with the x-axis. (b) Intensity gradient direction histograms of image (a) before smoothing (red) and after smoothing with a Gaussian of standard deviation 3 pixels (blue).

the preferred orientation of the image is clearly 30° or 210°. Nonetheless, when local orientations are calculated using intensity gradients, the histograms shown in Fig. 2.2b are obtained when using the image as is (red) and the image after smoothing with a Gaussian of standard deviation 3 pixels (blue). Before smoothing, strong preferences are observed toward angles that are a multiple of 45°. After smoothing, the preferences are not as strong but are still there. Considering that the intensity gradient direction at a boundary pixel is normal to the boundary contour, the peak intensity gradient direction in this image should be 120° or 300°.

The circle and the ellipse images in these examples are free of radiometric noise. When an image of a scene is captured, radiometric and geometric noises are both present. Radiometric noise is primarily sensor noise, and geometric noise is the displacement of scene points from their true positions after being projected to the discrete image space. Radiometric noise can be reduced by image smoothing; however, geometric noise will not disappear with intensity smoothing and will be present as long as the created image has discrete pixel coordinates.

To reliably determine the orientation of an image, two problems must be solved. First, the image should be converted into a form that is independent of absolute intensities and so insensitive to changes in scene lighting. Second, the digital domain of an image should be taken to a continuous one to remove/reduce geometric noise. To achieve this, the concepts of *geometric gradient* and *geometric smoothing* are introduced.

2.2   Geometric Gradient and Geometric Smoothing

To reduce the effect of sensor noise, an image is smoothed, and to make an image insensitive to changes in scene lighting, image edges rather than image intensities are used. Image edges can be detected by (1) the Canny edge detector [1], (2) zero-crossings of the second derivative intensities [2] followed by the removal of phantom edges [3, 4], (3) functional approximation [5], and (4) one-crossings of intensity ratios [6]. Edges obtained by these methods detect similar structures. Although Canny edge detector will be used below, other edge detectors may be used in the same manner. Canny edges represent pixels in an image where intensity gradient magnitude in the gradient direction becomes locally maximum. Canny edges appear in open and closed contours; they do not appear in structures with branches.

Edges are influenced by the horizontal and vertical arrangement of pixels in an image. To reduce this dependency, the digital domain should be converted into a continuous one by approximating each edge contour by a continuous parametric curve.

Given a sequence of pixels along an edge contour,

$$\mathbf{P} = \{\mathbf{p}_i = (x_i, y_i) : i = 0, \dots, n-1\}, \tag{2.3}$$

the parametric curve approximating the contour takes the form

$$\mathbf{p}(u) = [x(u), y(u)], \tag{2.4}$$

where $x(u)$ and $y(u)$ are the components of the curve, defined in terms of the same parameter u. For the curve to approximate the contour, it is required that

$$\begin{aligned} x(u_i) &\approx x_i, \\ y(u_i) &\approx y_i, \end{aligned} \quad \text{for } i = 0, \dots, n-1. \tag{2.5}$$

In the following, the rational Gaussian (RaG) curve formulation [7] is used for its ability to approximate a curve of a desired smoothness to a sequence of points. The RaG curve approximating the sequence of edge pixels in $\mathbf{P}$ is defined by

$$\mathbf{p}(u) = \sum_{i=0}^{n-1} \mathbf{p}_i g_i(u), \quad u \in [0, n-1], \tag{2.6}$$

where

$$g_i(u) = \frac{G_i(u)}{\sum_{j=0}^{n-1} G_j(u)}, \quad i = 0, \dots, n-1 \tag{2.7}$$

are the basis functions of the curve, and

$$G_i(u) = \exp\left\{-\frac{(u - u_i)^2}{2\sigma^2}\right\} \tag{2.8}$$

is a Gaussian of height 1 and standard deviation σ centered at parameter u_i. Parameters $\{u_i : i = 0, \ldots, n-1\}$ are the nodes of the curve. These are the parameters at which the curve approximates the individual pixels along the edge contour. σ is the smoothness parameter. By increasing it, the curve becomes smoother, and by decreasing it, the curve reproduces more details along the contour.

The equations above are used for an open curve. For a closed curve, Eq. (2.8) is replaced with

$$G_i(u) = \sum_{j=-\infty}^{j=\infty} \exp\left\{ -\frac{[u - (u_i + jn)]^2}{2\sigma^2} \right\}. \qquad (2.9)$$

Since a Gaussian vanishes exponentially from its center point, instead of ∞ in Eq. (2.9), a small number such as 1 or 2 is sufficient. The addition of jn to u_i or subtraction of jn from u_i ensures that at the point where the curve closes, the Gaussians centered at the nodes corresponding to the contour pixels extend over the closing point, producing a continuous and smooth curve everywhere.

Examples of curve fitting in this manner are given in Fig. 2.3. The Canny edges of the circle in Fig. 2.1a and the ellipse in Fig. 2.2a obtained with a Gaussian smoother of $\sigma = 3$ pixels are shown in Fig. 2.3a and b, respectively. The RaG curves approximating the contours are drawn in red over the edge contours.

As σ is increased, the approximating curve smoothes more details along the edge contour, and as σ is decreased, the curve follows the edge contour more closely, reproducing the details. In the following, the σ used in curve fitting is set to 3 pixels or higher. A σ lower than 3 pixels will reproduce geometric noise by closely following pixels along the contour and, therefore, is not recommended.

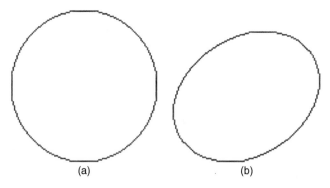

(a)   (b)

Figure 2.3 (a and b) RaG curves (shown in red) approximating the boundary contours of the solid circle in Fig. 2.1a and the solid ellipse in Fig. 2.2a obtained by the Canny edge detector when using a Gaussian smoother of standard deviation 3 pixels.

2.2.1 Calculating Geometric Gradients

The tangent direction θ at a curve point with parameter u is defined by

$$\theta(u) = \arctan\left(\frac{dy(u)}{dx(u)}\right) \tag{2.10}$$

or

$$\theta(u) = \arctan\left(\frac{dy(u)/du}{dx(u)/du}\right). \tag{2.11}$$

Since

$$\frac{dx(u)}{du} = \left.\frac{x(u+\delta u)-x(u)}{\delta u}\right|_{\delta u\to 0}, \tag{2.12}$$

to estimate $dx(u)/du$, $x(u)$ is computed at two very close values of u and their difference is divided by the difference in their u values. That is,

$$\frac{dx(u)}{du} = \frac{x(u+\delta u)-x(u-\delta u)}{2\delta u}. \tag{2.13}$$

Similarly,

$$\frac{dy(u)}{du} = \frac{y(u+\delta u)-y(u-\delta u)}{2\delta u}. \tag{2.14}$$

δu is a very small increment, such as 0.01. With such a small increment in u, the difference between the actual and estimated tangent directions will be negligible considering that θ will be quantized to create the histogram of tangent directions. All tangent directions are changed between 0 and π so that independent of the direction a contour is traced, the same tangent direction is obtained at a point. *The tangent direction $\theta(u_i)$ at point $\mathbf{p}(u_i)$ on the curve approximating contour $\mathbf{P}$ is considered the geometric gradient direction at pixel $\mathbf{p}_i$ on the* contour.

By computing geometric gradient directions along the RaG curve that approximates the circular edge contour in Fig. 2.3a at uniform increments $du = 0.01$ and creating the histogram of the geometric gradient directions, the histogram depicted in red in Fig. 2.4 is obtained. The histogram is almost flat, showing no significant preferred orientation. Due to large linear segments along the contour with angles that are a multiple of $45°$, small bumps are observed at those angles. The bumps will get smaller by increasing the smoothness parameter σ in curve fitting. The histogram of geometric gradient directions for the curve that approximates the elliptic edge contour in Fig. 2.3b is depicted in blue in Fig. 2.4. The peak orientation at $30°$ is obvious.

To determine the curvature value at a curve point, first, $d^2x(u)/du^2$ and $d^2y(u)/du^2$ are estimated from changes in $dx(u)$ and $dy(u)$ over a small change

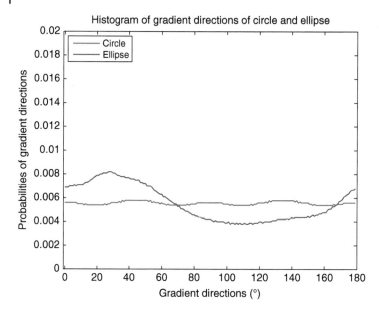

Figure 2.4 The red and blue plots show histograms of tangent directions along curves in Fig. 2.3a and b, respectively.

in u, that is,

$$\frac{d^2x(u)}{du^2} = \frac{dx(u + \delta u) - dx(u - \delta u)}{2\delta u}, \tag{2.15}$$

$$\frac{d^2y(u)}{du^2} = \frac{dy(u + \delta u) - dy(u - \delta u)}{2\delta u}, \tag{2.16}$$

for $\delta u = 0.01$. Note that the difference between the parameters of curve points corresponding to adjacent pixels along a contour is 1. That is, $u_{i+1} - u_i = 1$ for $i = 0, \ldots, n - 2$.

Denoting $dx(u)/du, dy(u)/du, d^2x(u)/du^2$, and $d^2y(u)/du^2$ by x', y', x'', and y'', respectively, the magnitude curvature at the point with parameter u on the curve can be computed from [8]:

$$\kappa = \frac{|x'y'' - y'x''|}{(x'^2 + y'^2)^{3/2}}. \tag{2.17}$$

Since curvature is independent of the coordinate system of the curve or the edge contour it is approximating, it produces the same value at a curve point independent of the location and the orientation of the edge contour in an image.

Examples of image orientation detection by geometric gradients using real images are given in Fig. 2.5. Figure 2.5a shows a Martian rock, and (b) shows its Canny edges. The peak geometric gradient direction of RaG curves with smoothness parameter $\sigma = 3$ pixels fitting the edge contours is found to be 18°,

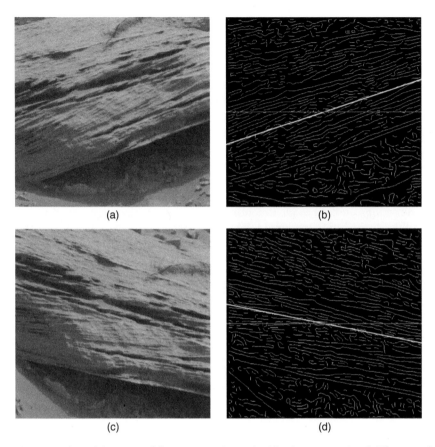

Figure 2.5 (a and c) Images of the same Martian rock with a known rotational difference of 30°. These images are courtesy of NASA. (b and d) Canny edges of images (a) and (c), respectively, obtained when using a Gaussian smoother of standard deviation 3 pixels. Image orientations determined from geometric gradients and intensity gradients are shown with yellow and purple lines, respectively.

shown by the yellow line in Fig. 2.5b. The peak intensity gradient direction for Fig. 2.5a after smoothing with a Gaussian filter of standard deviation 3 pixels is found to be 90°. Since the intensity gradient direction at a pixel along an edge contour is normal to the edge contour, the image orientation obtained by intensity gradient directions will be 0°, as depicted in Fig. 2.5b by the purple line. In order to compare image orientations determined by geometric gradients and intensity gradients, *in all examples given in this chapter, the direction normal to the intensity gradient direction at a pixel is used as the intensity gradient direction there.*

Figure 2.5a represents a small window of a much larger image. By rotating the image by 30° clockwise and taking a window of the same size from the same area, the image in Fig. 2.5c is obtained. Canny edges of this image are shown in Fig. 2.5d. The peak geometric gradient direction is found to be $169°$, shown by the yellow line in this image. The peak intensity gradient direction is found to be $90°$ with the direction normal to it being $0°$, shown by the purple line in Fig. 2.5d. The difference in orientations of the yellow lines in images (b) and (d) is $18° - 169° = -151° \equiv 29°$, because no distinction is made between θ and $\theta \pm \pi$. The true rotational difference between the images is $30°$. The rotational difference between the images estimated by geometric gradients is off by only $1°$.

Figure 2.6a and b shows the RaG curves approximating the edge contours in Fig. 2.5b and d, respectively. Curve points drawn with brighter red are points with higher curvatures. When calculating the histogram of geometric gradient directions, instead of incrementing the histogram bin representing direction θ by 1, the bin is incremented by $1 - \kappa$, where κ is the curvature at the point, after normalizing all curvatures to values between 0 and 1. The process assigns higher values to curve points with lower curvatures, emphasizing straight segments over curved ones. The histograms of geometric gradient directions obtained in this manner for Fig. 2.6a and b are shown in red and blue, respectively, in (c).

In the following experiments, the standard deviation of the Gaussian smoother in the Canny edge detector is set to 3 pixels and the smoothness parameter of RaG curves approximating the edge contours is set to 5 pixels. Also, the tangent direction at a curve point is weighted by $w = 1 - \kappa$, with κ being the curvature value at a curve point after normalizing all curvatures to values between 0 and 1.

2.3 Comparison of Geometric Gradients and Intensity Gradients

To compare the sensitivities of geometric gradients and intensity gradients to variations in intensities and geometry of an image, the intensities and geometry of an image are varied and the stabilities of image orientations determined by the two methods are compared.

Figure 2.7a depicts a Martian scene. This image is courtesy of NASA. The image does not have a strong orientation, but it contains a unique pattern; therefore, it must have a unique orientation. Figure 2.7b shows the image after smoothing with a Gaussian of standard deviation of 2 pixels. The image after addition of Gaussian noise of standard deviation 20 is shown in Fig. 2.7c. If by this addition intensity became less than 0, it was set to 0, and if it became greater than 255, it was set to 255. The image in Fig. 2.7d is obtained by transforming the intensities in Fig. 2.7a by the following nonlinear function:

$$O(x, y) = I(x, y) + 50 \sin(4\pi y / n_r) \cos(4\pi x / n_c). \tag{2.18}$$

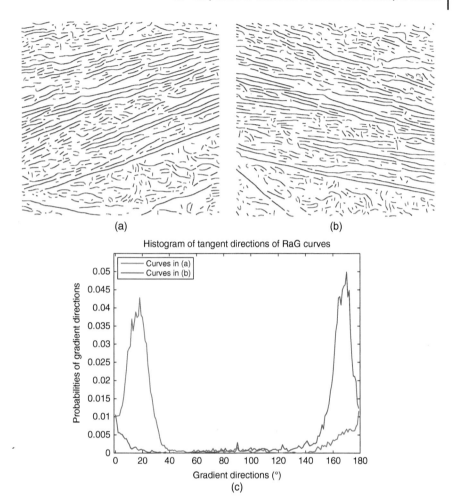

Figure 2.6 (a and b) RaG curves with $\sigma = 3$ approximating the edge contours in Fig. 2.5b and d, respectively. A point with a higher curvature is shown with a higher red intensity. (c) Red and blue plots show histograms of geometric gradient directions or tangent directions of points along curves in (a) and (b), respectively.

$I(x, y)$ is the intensity at (x, y) in Fig. 2.7a and $O(x, y)$ is the intensity at the same location in image (d). Parameters n_r and n_c show the number of rows and the number of columns in the images. Figure 2.7e is obtained by rotating image (a) by 90°. Finally, Fig. 2.7f is obtained by scaling image (a) by 1.5 using bilinear interpolation. Figure 2.7a–f contains the same pattern but have somewhat different intensities or have different orientations and scales. The ability of geometric gradients and intensity gradients in determining the orientations of these images is investigated.

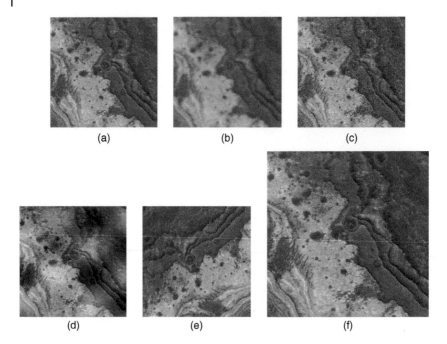

(a)   (b)   (c)

(d)   (e)   (f)

Figure 2.7 (a) An image of a Martian scene. This image is courtesy of NASA. (b) Blurred, (c) noisy, (d) nonlinear intensity mapping, (e) rotated, and (f) scaled versions of image.

Orientations of the images in Fig. 2.7 determined by geometric gradients and intensity gradients are shown by yellow and purple lines, respectively, in Fig. 2.8. The lines in each image pass through the image center and have the orientations obtained from the highest peaks in the histograms computed from geometric gradient directions and intensity gradient directions. The orientations estimated by geometric gradients and intensity gradients are listed in Table 2.1. While geometric gradients assign an orientation to an image that represents the orientation of the pattern, the orientation assigned to an image by intensity gradients is more representative of the arrangement of pixels in the image than the orientation of the pattern. Due to preferences toward angles that are a multiple of 45° by intensity gradients, when a pattern with a strong orientation does not appear in an image, the orientation assigned to the image will be a multiple of 45°.

Blurring, noise, and change in scene lighting hardly affect estimation of an image's orientation by geometric gradients. By performing computations in the continuous domain, geometric gradients make the orientation detection process independent of the horizontal and vertical arrangement of pixels in an image. Geometric gradients assign an orientation to the pattern in an image independent of the way the pattern is pixelated.

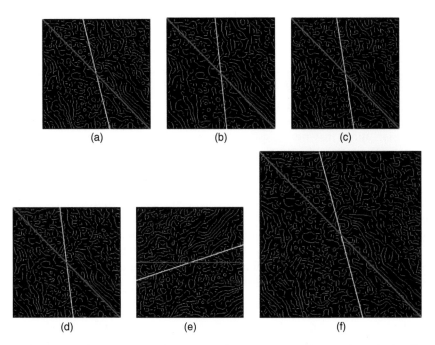

Figure 2.8 (a)–(f) Canny edges of images (a)–(f) in Fig. 2.7. Image orientations obtained by geometric gradients and intensity gradients are shown by yellow and purple lines, respectively.

Table 2.1 Orientations of images (a)–(f) in Fig. 2.8 estimated by geometric gradients (θ_{gg}) and intensity gradients (θ_{ig}).

Figure 2.8	θ_{gg}	θ_{ig}
(a)	104	135
(b)	96	135
(c)	99	135
(d)	97	135
(e)	16	0
(f)	105	135

2.4 Finding the Rotational Difference between Two Images

Now that we have a method for determining the orientation of an image, we can use it to determine the rotational difference between two images and rotate one image to the orientation of the other. Once the images are in the same orientation, the correspondence process becomes much easier, simplifying the registration process.

If the pattern appearing in two images has a strong preferred orientation, the difference in the peak gradient directions of the images is sufficient to find the rotational difference between the images. However, when the pattern appearing in the images does not have a strong orientation, information only about the peak orientations may not be sufficient to determine the rotational difference between the images, and information about all orientations may be needed to robustly find the rotational difference between the images.

Sometimes, the images to be registered may not contain exactly the same scene parts. A part of a scene visible in one image may be hidden in the other image due to occlusion or by falling outside the view. When the scene pattern does not contain a strong orientation or the overlap between the images is not large enough, the peak orientation determined in one image may not be the same peak orientation in the other image. By using all gradient directions rather than only the peak gradient direction in each image, the rotational difference between the images can be more reliably determined.

To compare two gradient direction histograms, one histogram is shifted cyclically over the other, and at each shift position, the Euclidean distance between the histograms is determined, and the shift position producing the smallest Euclidean distance is used as the rotational difference between the images. Govindu and Shekhar [9] show that the shift amount producing the smallest Euclidean distance between two histograms provides the maximum likelihood estimation of the translational difference between the histograms and, thus, shows the maximum likelihood rotational difference between the images the histograms are computed from.

Denoting the gradient direction histograms of two images by $H_1(\theta)$ and $H_2(\theta)$, the Euclidean distance between the histograms when the second histogram is cyclically shifted over the first by θ_i is

$$D(\theta_i) = \left\{ \sum_{j=0}^{m-1} [H_1(\theta_j) - H_2(\theta_j + \theta_i)]^2 \right\}^{\frac{1}{2}}, \qquad (2.19)$$

where m is the number of bins in each histogram. In our case, $m = 180$. By varying i from 0 to 179 and computing the Euclidean distance D, the shift value producing the smallest distance measure is determined and used as the rotational difference between the images. Note that cyclic shifting of H_2 with respect to H_1 implies that when $\theta_j + \theta_i \geq m$, $H_2(\theta_j + \theta_i - m)$ is taken as the value for $H_2(\theta_j + \theta_i)$.

Although discrete angles may be acceptable when determining the orientation of an image, it may not be sufficient when determining the rotational difference between two very large images. An error of a single degree can result in displacement of a few to several pixels when registering the images.

To determine the subdegree rotational difference between two images, assuming the minimum distance between two histograms when using the Euclidean norm is θ, we fit a quadratic curve to $[(\theta - 1), D(\theta - 1)]$, $[\theta, D(\theta)]$, $[(\theta + 1), D(\theta + 1)]$, find the location of the minimum in the curve, and use that as the rotational difference between the images with subdegree accuracy.

The histograms of geometric gradient directions of images (a)–(f) in Fig. 2.8 are shown in Fig. 2.9. Computing the subdegree rotational difference between histogram (a) and histogram (b) by shifting histogram (b) over histogram (a) and finding the shift amount where the Euclidean distance between the histograms becomes minimum, we find the rotational difference of image (b) with respect to image (a) be 179.7° or −0.3°. Similarly, we find image (c) to be rotated with respect to image (a) by 0.2°, image (d) to be rotated with respect to image (a) by 0.1°, image (e) to be rotated with respect to image (a) by 90.0°, and image (f) to be rotated with respect to image (a) by 179.7° or −0.3°. Use of all bins in histograms of geometric gradient directions provides a more robust means of determining the rotational difference between two images when compared to the use of only histogram bins corresponding to the peak orientations.

2.5 Performance Evaluation

In this section, reliability, accuracy, and computational complexity of geometric gradients in image orientation detection are evaluated.

2.5.1 Reliability

To ascertain the ability of geometric gradients in determining the orientation of various types of images, experiments were carried out using aerial images (Fig. 2.10), close-range images captured from different camera views (Fig. 2.11), images with perspective differences (Fig. 2.12), images with radiometric as well as structural differences (Fig. 2.13), images with scale and rotational differences (Fig. 2.14), and images from different sensors (Fig. 2.15).

Edges detected in the images in Figs 2.10–2.15 are shown in Figs 2.16–2.21, respectively. Edges in color images are obtained by the method outlined in [6, 10]. Peak tangent directions obtained from the edges in images (a) and (b) in Fig. 2.16 are 15° and 19°, drawn with yellow lines in the images. By matching the gradient direction histograms of the images, image (b) is found to be rotated with respect to image (a) by 3.2°. The preferred orientations determined for these images by intensity gradients were both 0°, shown by purple lines in the images. Due to the horizontal and vertical preferences of intensity gradients, direction 0° has been selected for both images.

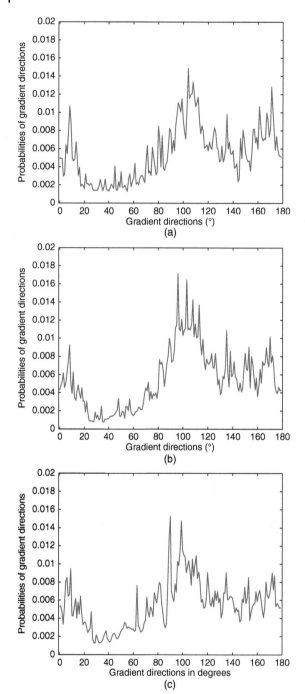

Figure 2.9 (a)–(f) Histograms of geometric gradient directions of images (a)–(f) in Fig. 2.8.

Figure 2.9 (*Continued*)

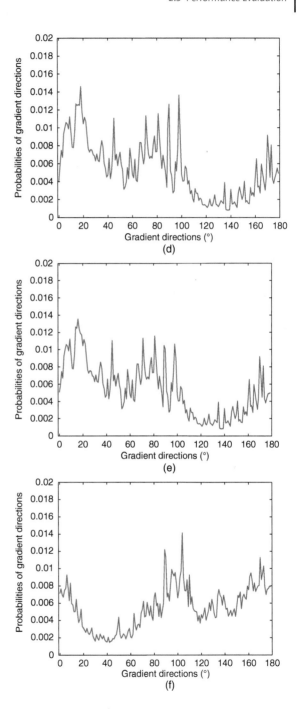

(d)

(e)

(f)

Figure 2.10 (a and b) Aerial images taken from different views of a suburban area.

Figure 2.11 (a and b) Images of a garden scene captured from different views.

Figure 2.12 (a and b) Images captured of a historical building from different views.

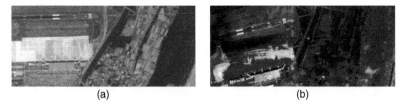

(a)   (b)

Figure 2.13 (a and b) Aerial images of the Sendai International Airport taken before and after the grand tsunami of 2011. These images are courtesy of Google Maps.

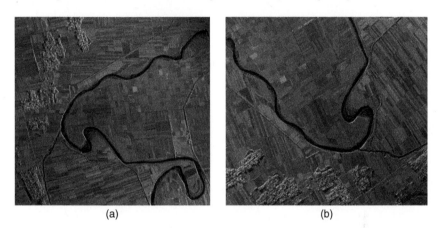

(a)   (b)

Figure 2.14 (a and b) Radar images of a relatively flat agricultural area captured in different flight paths. Image (b) is artificially scaled to introduce scale difference between images. These images are courtesy of Radarsat-1.

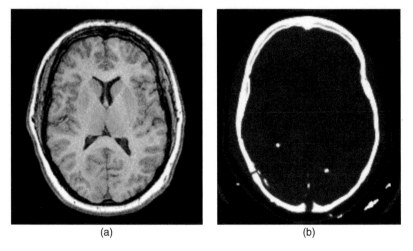

(a)   (b)

Figure 2.15 (a and b) Corresponding axial slices from registered MR and CT brain volumes. These images are courtesy of Kettering Medical Center.

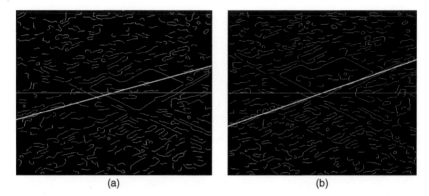

(a) (b)

Figure 2.16 (a and b) Canny edges of aerial images (a) and (b) in Fig. 2.10 and the orientations detected by geometric gradients (yellow) and intensity gradients (purple).

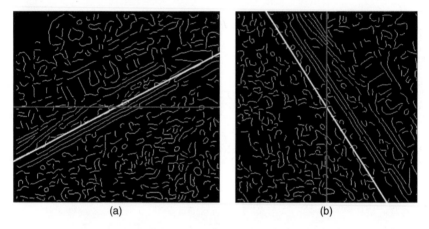

(a) (b)

Figure 2.17 (a and b) Canny edges of the garden scene images (a) and (b) in Fig. 2.11. The orientations detected for these images by geometric gradients and intensity gradients are shown with yellow and purple lines, respectively.

The peak orientations determined for the garden scene images in Fig. 2.11 are shown in Fig. 2.17. The peak orientations determined by geometric gradients are 27° and 123° for images (a) and (b), respectively. These peak orientations are shown with yellow lines in the images. By matching the histograms of geometric gradient directions, image (b) is found to be rotated with respect to image (a) by 96.4°. The peak orientations determined from the histograms of intensity gradient directions in images (a) and (b) are found to be 0° and 90°, respectively. Peak orientations determined by the intensity gradients are shown with purple lines in these images.

Large perspective differences exist between images (a) and (b) in Fig. 2.12. The orientations determined from geometric gradients of the edge images

(a)   (b)

Figure 2.18 (a and b) Canny edges of the historical building images (a) and (b) in Fig. 2.12. The orientations detected by geometric gradients and intensity gradients are shown with yellow and purple lines, respectively.

(a)   (b)

Figure 2.19 (a and b) Canny edges of the before and after tsunami images (a) and (b) in Fig. 2.13. The orientations detected by geometric gradients and intensity gradients are shown by yellow and purple lines, respectively.

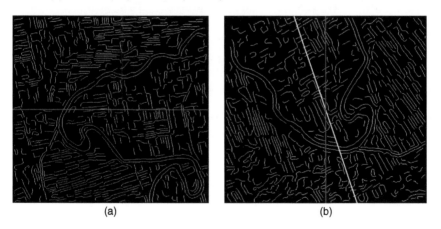

(a)   (b)

Figure 2.20 (a and b) Canny edges of the radar images (a) and (b) in Fig. 2.14. The orientations detected by geometric gradients and intensity gradients are shown with yellow and purple lines, respectively. The yellow line in (a) is hidden by the purple line and, thus, is not visible.

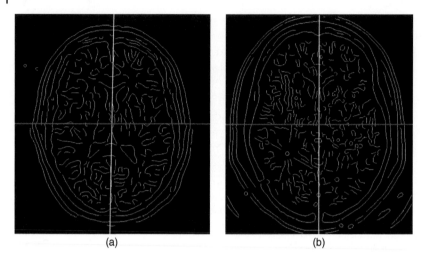

(a)   (b)

Figure 2.21 (a and b) Canny edges of the MR and CT brain slices in Fig. 2.15. The orientations determined by geometric gradients and intensity gradients are shown with yellow and purple lines, respectively.

depicted in Fig. 2.18 are 10° and 4°, respectively. By matching the histograms of geometric gradient directions, image (b) is found to be rotated with respect to image (a) by 173.5° or −6.5°. The orientations determined from the histograms of intensity gradient directions are 90° and 0°, shown with purple lines in Fig. 2.18.

Figure 2.13a and b not only have very different colors due to change in ground cover, there are also considerable structural changes in the scene caused by destructions from tsunami. Examining the images we see, however, that certain scene structures remain unchanged. Such structures are the airport's runway, the nearby streets, and waterways. Peak orientations obtained from edge images (a) and (b) in Fig. 2.19 are 12° and 179°, respectively. The process has assigned the same orientation to the scene independent of the image differences. Through histogram matching, image (b) is found to be rotated with respect to image (a) by 13.2°. The orientations computed from intensity gradient directions are found to be both 0°, shown by purple lines in the images.

Figure 2.14 has rotational and scaling differences. The geometric gradient direction peaks calculated from the edge images in Fig. 2.20 are 0° and 109°. These orientations are shown with yellow lines in the images. By matching the gradient direction histograms of the images, image (b) is found to be rotated with respect to image (a) by 109.2°. The orientations determined from the peaks in the intensity gradient direction histograms of the images are 0° and 90°. These orientations are shown with purple lines in the images. 0° orientation is detected by both methods for image (a), resulting in the yellow and purple lines coinciding. The yellow line is drawn first, and then the purple line is drawn, covering the yellow line in this image.

Finally, the orientations of the MR and CT brain images shown in Fig. 2.15 are calculated. In spite of considerable intensity differences between the images, edges in both images as shown in Fig. 2.21 represent similar anatomical structures. Although local details in some brain areas are different, both images share major structures, representing the skull and the brain boundary. The peak orientations determined from geometric gradient directions of edges in MR and CT images are 89° and 90°. The rotational difference between the images determined by histogram matching is 0.1°. The orientations detected by intensity gradient directions for both images are 0°. There appears to be a larger number of small horizontal edge segments in these images. However, when the edges are weighted by their inverse curvatures, directions belonging to longer low-curvature segments get emphasized, resulting in the vertical direction shown in Fig. 2.21.

2.5.2 Accuracy

To determine the accuracy of the orientations determined from geometric gradients, simulation data were used. Using image (a) in Fig. 2.22 as the base, images (b)–(d) were created by rotating the base image clockwise by 30°, 60°, and 90°. Knowing the orientation in (a), the accuracy of the method in determining the orientations in (b)–(d) is determined.

The orientations determined for images (a)–(d) in Fig. 2.22 by geometric gradients are 90°, 60°, 30°, and 1°, respectively. These angles are shown with yellow lines in the respective images. Even though the images have somewhat different contents, the detected orientations are within a degree of true orientations.

To determine the sensitivity of accuracy to noise, uniformly distributed zero-mean noise of amplitudes from 10 to 255 were added to the images in Fig. 2.22 to obtain new images. The case with noise amplitude of 255 is shown in Fig. 2.23. If by adding noise to intensity the intensity became less than 0, it was set to 0, and if the intensity became greater than 255, it was set to 255. Noise was added to three color components independently. The orientations detected in these noisy images were within a degree. Therefore, orientations detected in these images are not sensitive to zero-mean noise. This is attributed to the inherent smoothing involved in edge detection and curve fitting employed by the method.

The above limited evaluation shows some of the characteristics of orientation detection by geometric gradients. Generally, it is required to evaluate a method against a perspecified class of images. However, to determine the true accuracy of a method a gold standard is needed. In the absence of a gold standard, simulation data of the kind shown in Figs 2.22 and 2.23 may be used to measure the method's accuracy and determine its sensitivity to noise.

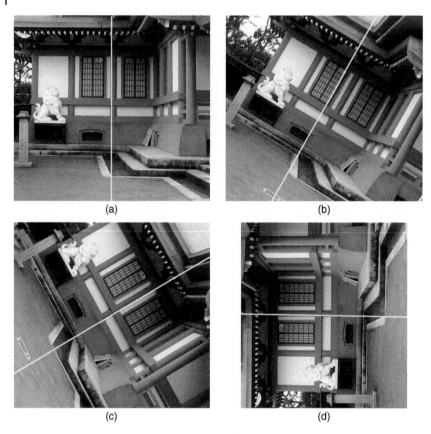

Figure 2.22 (a) An outdoor scene image, (b)–(d) The outdoor scene image rotated clockwise by 30°, 60°, and 90°. The yellow line in each image shows the detected orientation.

2.5.3 Computational Complexity

The computational complexity of image orientation detection by geometric gradients is a linear function of the number of pixels in an image and the number of edges detected in the image.

Since an image that has a strong orientation will not change its orientation by changing its size, reducing the size of the image is not expected to greatly change the detected orientation. Figure 2.24a–d depicts the Canny edges of the image in Fig. 2.5a and the Canny edges of the same image after reducing its size by factors of 2, 4, and 8. The orientations obtained for images (a)–(d) in Fig. 2.24 are 18°, 14°, 13°, and 18°, respectively. Very similar orientations are obtained for different resolutions of the same image. When an image has a strong orientation, lowering its resolution or size will not change its orientation greatly. Reducing the scale of an image by factors of 2, 4, and 8 will reduce the

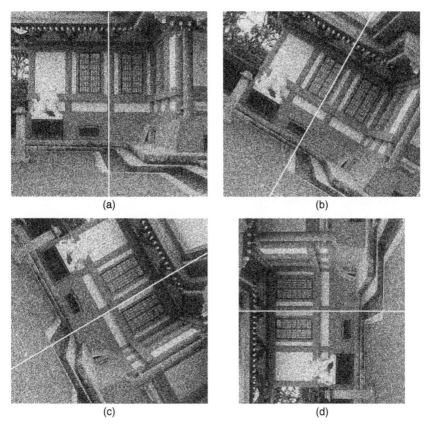

Figure 2.23 (a)–(d) Images (a)–(d) in Fig. 2.22 with added zero-mean uniform noise of amplitude 255. The detected orientations are shown with yellow lines in the images.

computational requirements of orientation detection by geometric gradients by factors of 4, 16, and 64, respectively.

Results from images (a)–(d) in Fig. 2.24 suggest that shorter edge/curve segments have very little effect on an estimated orientation and it is primarily the longer segments that determine the orientation of an image. By keeping the scale of an image unchanged but using only the longest half of the edge contours, a speed-up factor of 2 is obtained without significantly influencing the detected orientation. Edge images (e)–(h) in Fig. 2.24 progressively contain fewer shorter segments. The orientations determined for the images are 19°, 19°, 20°, and 19°, respectively. Therefore, the longer segments in an image primarily determine the orientation of the image.

In the discussions above, the RaG curve formulation was used to convert digital contours into continuous curves. Other parametric curves, such as B-splines [11], can be used in the same manner. If B-spline curves are used, the curves

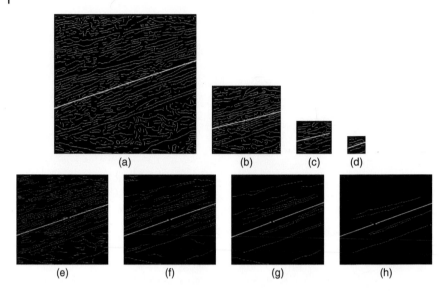

Figure 2.24 (a)–(d) Canny edges of the Martian rock in Fig. 2.5a and the peak orientations determined by geometric gradient directions as the image scale is reduced by factors of 2, 4, and 8. (e)–(h) Increasingly shorter edge segments are ignored when calculating the orientation.

should be of degree 3 or higher to provide curvature continuity and enable calculation of curvatures everywhere along a curve. With the RaG formulation, it is possible to fit curves of a desired smoothness to edge contours in an image by simply choosing an appropriate smoothness parameter σ. If B-spline curves are used, the smoothness of the curves is controlled by the degree of the curves. While the σ in a RaG curve can be varied continuously, the degree of a B-spline curve can be varied only discretely. Nonetheless, similar results are possible by both RaG and B-spline curves, with B-spline being a factor of 2–3 faster than RaG. Figure 2.25 compares RaG curves of smoothness $\sigma = 3$ pixels and B-spline curves of degree 3 when approximating the edge contours in Fig. 2.24e.

2.6 Registering Images with a Known Rotational Difference

Once the rotational difference between reference and test images is determined, the test image can be rotated to the orientation of the reference image. Rotation should be with respect to the image center to minimize parts of the image falling outside the view as a result of the rotation.

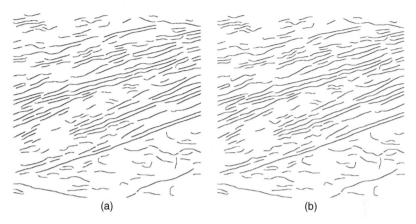

(a)   (b)

Figure 2.25 Approximating the edge contours in Fig. 2.24e by (a) RaG curves of smoothness $\sigma = 3$ and (b) B-spline curves of degree 3.

If (X, Y) are the coordinates of a point in the test image and (X', Y') are the coordinates of the same point after rotating the image by θ about its center, and assuming (X_c, Y_c) are the coordinates of the center of the test image, the relation between points in the test image before and after rotation can be written as

$$
\begin{bmatrix} X' - X_c \\ Y' - Y_c \\ 1 \end{bmatrix} = \begin{bmatrix} \cos\theta & \sin\theta & 1 \\ -\sin\theta & \cos\theta & 1 \\ 0 & 0 & 1 \end{bmatrix} \begin{bmatrix} X - X_c \\ Y - Y_c \\ 1 \end{bmatrix} \tag{2.20}
$$

or

$$
\mathbf{P}'_c = R(\theta)\mathbf{P}_c, \tag{2.21}
$$

where $\mathbf{P}_c$ and $\mathbf{P}'_c$ are homogeneous coordinates of a point in the test image before and after rotation. Note that these coordinates are measured with respect to the image center. Letting $\mathbf{T} = [X_c \quad Y_c \quad 1]^t$, where t denotes transpose, the relation between points in the test image before and after rotation can be written as

$$
\mathbf{P}' = R(\theta)(\mathbf{P} - \mathbf{T}) + \mathbf{T}, \tag{2.22}
$$

where $\mathbf{P} = [X \ Y \ 1]^t$ and $\mathbf{P}' = [X' \ Y' \ 1]^t$.

If coordinates of points in the reference image are denoted by (x, y) or in homogeneous coordinates by $\mathbf{p} = [x \ y \ 1]^t$, and if the transformation model to register the rotated test image to the reference image is found to be $\mathbf{f}$, then

$$
\mathbf{P}' = \mathbf{f}\mathbf{p}. \tag{2.23}
$$

From (2.22) and (2.23), we conclude

$$
\mathbf{f}\mathbf{p} = R(\theta)(\mathbf{P} - \mathbf{T}) + \mathbf{T}, \tag{2.24}
$$

or

$$\mathbf{P} = R(-\theta)(\mathbf{fp} - \mathbf{T}) + \mathbf{T}. \tag{2.25}$$

Equation (2.25) shows the relation between a point $\mathbf{p}$ in the reference image and the corresponding point $\mathbf{P}$ in the original test image. Although $\mathbf{f}$ shows the transformation obtained for registering the rotated test image to the reference image, Eq. (2.25) shows the relation between the original reference and the original test images. For each point $\mathbf{p}$ in the reference image, Eq. (2.25) finds the coordinates of the corresponding point $\mathbf{P}$ in the original test image. This makes it possible to resample the original test image to the geometry of the reference image pixel by pixel.

It should be mentioned that if the estimated rotational difference between two images is off by a few to several degrees, the image reorientation step described in this chapter can still help the registration process. The transformation $\mathbf{f}$ determined by a registration method includes the residual rotation. Therefore, any inaccuracy in estimation of the rotational difference between images becomes a part of $\mathbf{f}$ that is determined by a registration method. Many registration methods can tolerate small rotational differences between images although they may fail under larger rotational differences.

To tell whether a computed rotational difference between two images is correct or not, the rotational difference between the images can be determined at different resolutions of the images and if similar results are obtained, it can be concluded that the estimated rotational difference is highly likely to be correct. If inconsistent results are obtained, the true rotational difference between the images cannot be determined with sufficient certainty and a method that can register images independent of their rotational difference should be used.

2.7 Discussion

Knowledge about the rotational difference between two images facilitates registration of the images. Although rotationally invariant measures, such as invariant moments [12], can be used to find homologous neighborhoods in images independent of the rotational difference between the images, such measures depend on intensities and intensity gradients that may vary from one image to another. Moreover, rotationally invariant measures are small in number and computationally expensive when compared to measures that are not rotationally invariant.

Local image descriptors have been developed [13–16] that first rotate a local neighborhood based on its orientation and then determine features of the neighborhood. These descriptors are often centered at dark or bright blobs that do not have a strong orientation. Use of intensity gradients that are biased toward horizontal and vertical directions are often unable to determine the true orientation of blob-like neighborhoods in images.

If the rotational difference between two images can be reliably determined, both images can be brought to the same orientation, making it possible to find homologous neighborhoods in the images without the use of rotation-invariant descriptors. By bringing two images into the same orientation, steps in image registration can be simplified.

Geometric gradients are not as sensitive to changes in scene lighting and sensor characteristics compared to intensity gradients; therefore, geometric gradients can describe the geometry of an image more precisely than intensity gradients can.

To minimize the influence of geometric noise on calculated local and global orientations in an image, digital noise in the image should be reduced by converting edge contours in the image into continuous curves, determining tangent directions along the curves, and mapping the directions back to the digital contours before computing the orientations. Intensities and, to a lesser degree, intensity gradients are influenced by scene lighting and sensor noise. Also, because intensity gradients are dependent on an image's scan direction, they are influenced by factors other than the image's content. Consequently, geometric gradients provide a more reliable means of encoding geometric information in an image than intensity gradients.

The difference in the orientation of two images can be determined once the orientation of each image is calculated. If the scene pattern appearing in two images does not possess a strong orientation, it is more reliable to use information about all gradient directions than information about only the peak gradient directions when calculating the rotational difference between the images.

Experiments on images with varying degrees of intensity and geometric differences show that histograms of tangent directions obtained by fitting smooth curves to image edges carry sufficient information to determine the rotational difference between the images and simplify steps in image registration discussed in the remainder of this book.

2.8 Further Reading

Methods on image orientation detection have used (1) intensity gradients, (2) spatial frequency characteristics of intensities, and (3) principal axes of intensities.

Intensity gradient direction at pixel (x, y) in an image is defined by Eq. (2.2). Errors in estimation of gradient directions have been of concern since very early in image processing and computer vision [17, 18]. O'Gorman [19] quantified this error for step edges using intensities in square neighborhoods. Davies [20] noticed that edge operators that use circular masks produce more accurate gradient directions than edge operators that use square masks. It was observed that errors emerge when the profile of intensities in a neighborhood deviates from being planar and become worst at step edges. Among the 3 × 3 gradient operators tested, Sobel was found to estimate gradient directions most accurately [20]. To estimate local gradient directions accurately, Wilson and Bhalerao [21] developed a filter kernel that determined the gradient direction of a 3 × 3 neighborhood by minimizing an error criterion.

Desolneux et al. [22] found gray-level quantization as the major source of inaccuracy in the calculation of gradient directions. To estimate local gradient directions more accurately, they suggested reconstructing and using the original signal from its quantized version via Shannon interpolation. Although this method is still influenced by sensor noise and changes in scene lighting, it provides a means to remove/reduce geometric noise and is perhaps the method closest to that described in this chapter.

Le Pouliquen et al. [23] suggested the use of complementary gradient and valleyness masks to estimate local orientations in an image. A gradient mask was used to find orientations at edges, a valleyness mask was used to find gradient directions at crests and valleys, and a combination of the two masks was used to estimate gradient directions everywhere else in the image.

Knowing that local orientations obtained by intensity differencing are sensitive to noise, Jiang [24] used sum of intensities horizontally and vertically within a square neighborhood to estimate the local orientation of the neighborhood. It is argued that since addition has an averaging effect, it reduces noise and thus produces local orientations that are less sensitive to noise compared to methods that find local orientations from intensity differences.

To determine the orientation of a neighborhood, Kass and Witkin [25] estimated the gradient direction at the center of the neighborhood by (1) convolving the neighborhood with a difference-of-Gaussian filter, (2) finding the derivatives of the convolved neighborhood with respect to x and y, and (3) calculating the direction of maximum intensity change from the derivatives.

To determine the orientation of a neighborhood, Rao and Schunck [26] smoothed the neighborhood with a Gaussian filter, calculated gradient directions at pixels in the neighborhood, and used the peak gradient direction within the neighborhood as the orientation of the neighborhood. A coherence measure was associated with the calculated orientation, showing the degree of agreement between the estimated orientation before and after smoothing.

Freeman and Adelson [27] used two first-derivative Gaussian basis filters to calculate the gradient direction at each pixel. This is the same as smoothing the image with a Gaussian filter, finding the derivatives of the smoothed image with respect to x and y, and using the derivatives to find the gradient direction locally.

Gorkani and Picard [28, 29] used the basis filters of Freeman and Adelson to calculate the orientation of an image. They found that if instead of the sum of gradient magnitudes in a given orientation the number of pixels in that orientation is used, a more reliable estimation to the orientation will be obtained. Yiu [30] used the orientation detection of Gorkani and Picard [28] to distinguish indoor images from outdoor images.

Knowing that images that have rotational differences produce modulus Fourier transform images that are rotated with respect to each other by the same amount, De Castro and Morandi [31] used the rotational difference between the modulus Fourier transforms of two images as the rotational difference between the images.

Noticing that when the modulus Fourier transforms of two images are rotated with respect to each other produce polar images that are translated with respect to each other, Reddy and Chatterji [32] used phase correlation to determine the translational difference between the polar quantization of modulus Fourier transform images and then from the obtained translation computed the rotational difference between the images.

Neupauer and Powell [33, 34] used a modified Morlet wavelet to determine the orientation of an image. Morlet wavelet in its original form [35] is a complex-valued wavelet that has directionally dependent real and imaginary parts but has isotropic magnitude. Neupauer and Powell modified the Morlet wavelet to have directionally dependent real and imaginary parts and anisotropic magnitude. The authors showed that the orientation of an image determined by the anisotropic Morlet wavelet matches well with the orientation observed by humans. This wavelet model was later combined with a filtering method to detect both primary and secondary orientations in an image [36].

Treating an image as a rigid body that is made up of pixels with masses that are equal to their intensities, the rigid body representing a nonsymmetric image has a unique axis known as the axis of minimum inertia [37, 38]. The axis of minimum inertia has been used as the orientation of an image to register images with rotational differences [39]. Since there are more pixels horizontally and vertically within a circular region than in any other direction, this method is also biased toward horizontal and vertical directions.

To calculate the local orientation of a neighborhood, Bigün and Granlund [40] used intensities in the neighborhood and the axis of least gradient inertia as the local orientation of the neighborhood. In a similar procedure, van Vliet and Verbeek [41] calculated the square gradient matrix of a neighborhood, determined the eigenvalues and eigenvectors of the inertia matrix, and took the direction of the smaller eigenvector as the orientation of the neighborhood.

Most recently, Yi et al. [42] used the Siamese networks [43] to learn various local orientations. Then, the orientation of a neighborhood was chosen from among learned orientations.

A number of methods have tried to improve estimation of an image's local or global orientation by intensity smoothing. Intensity smoothing is effective when dealing with radiometric noise, but as demonstrated in Figs 2.1 and 2.2, intensity smoothing cannot remove geometric noise. To remove or reduce geometric noise, the geometric smoothing described in this chapter should be used.

References

1 J. Canny, A computational approach to edge detection, *IEEE Transactions on Pattern Analysis and Machine Intelligence*, **8**(6):679–698, 1986.

2 D. Marr and E. Hildreth, Theory of edge detection, *Proceedings of the Royal Society of London Series B*, **207**:187–217, 1980.

3 J. J. Clark, Authenticating edges produced by zero-crossing algorithms, *IEEE Transactions on Pattern Analysis and Machine Intelligence*, **11**(1):43–57, 1989.

4 F. Ullupinar and G. Medioni, Refining edges detected by a LoG operator, *Computer Vision, Graphics, and Image Processing*, **51**:275–298, 1990.

5 R. M. Haralick, Ridges and valleys on digital images, *Computer Vision, Graphics, and Image Processing*, **22**:28–38, 1983.

6 A. Goshtasby, *2-D and 3-D Image Registration for Medical, Remote Sensing, and Industrial Applications*, Wiley Press, 2005.

7 A. Goshtasby, Geometric modeling using rational Gaussian curves and surfaces, *Computer-Aided Design*, **27**(5):363–375, 1995.

8 M. E. Mortenson, *Geometric Modeling*, Industrial Press, 2006.

9 V. Govindu and C. Shekhar, Alignment using distributions of local geometric properties, *IEEE Transactions on Pattern Analysis and Machine Intelligence*, **21**(10):1031–1043, 1999.

10 D. Di Zenzo, A note on gradient of a multi-image, *Computer Vision, Graphics, and Image Processing*, **33**:116–125, 1986.

11 K. Höllig and J. Hörner, *Approximation and Modeling with B-Splines*, SIAM, 2013.

12 S. Theodoridis and K. Koutroumbas, *Pattern Recognition*, Fourth Edition, Academic Press, 2009.

13 J. Liang, Z. Liao, S. yang, and Y. Wang, Image matching based on orientation-magnitude histograms and global consistency, *Pattern Recognition*, **45**:3825–3833, 2012.

14 K. Liu, H. Skibbe, T. Schmidt, T. Blein, K. Palme, T. Brox, and O. Ronneberger, Rotation-invariant HOG descriptors using Fourier analysis in polar and spherical coordinates, *International Journal of Computer Vision*, **106**:342–364, 2014.

15 D. Lowe, Distinctive image features from scale-invariant keypoints, *International Journal of Computer Vision*, **60**:91–110, 2004.

16 K. Mikolajczyk and C. Schmid, A performance evaluation of local descriptors, *IEEE Transactions on Pattern Analysis and Machine Intelligence*, **27**:1615–1630, 2005.

17 M. J. Brooks, Rationalizing edge detectors, *Computer Graphics and Image Processing*, **8**:277–285, 1978.

18 R. M. Haralick, Edge and region analysis for digital image data, *Computer Graphics and Image Processing*, **12**:60–73, 1980.

19 F. O'Gorman, Edge detection using Walsh functions, *Artificial Intelligence*, **10**:215–223, 1978.

20 E. R. Davies, Circularity—a new principle underlying the design of accurate edge orientation operators, *Image and Vision Computing*, **2**(3):134–142, 1984.

21 R. Wilson and A. H. Bhalerao, Kernel designs for efficient multiresolution edge detection and orientation estimation, *IEEE Transactions on Pattern Analysis and Machine Intelligence*, **14**(3):384–390, 1992.

22 A. Desolneux, S. Ladjal, L. Moisan, and J.-M. Morel, Dequantizing image orientation, *IEEE Transactions on Image Processing*, **11**(10):1129–1130, 2002.

23 F. Le Pouliquen, J.-P. Da Costa, C. Germain, and P. Baylou, A new adaptive framework for unbiased orientation estimation in texture images, *Pattern Recognition*, **38**:2031–2046, 2005.

24 X. Jiang, Extracting image orientation feature by using integration operator, *Pattern Recognition*, **40**:705–717, 2007.

25 M. Kass and A. Witkin, Analyzing oriented patterns, *Computer Vision, Graphics, and Image Processing*, **37**:362–385, 1987.

26 A. R. Rao and B. G. Schunck, Computing oriented texture fields, *CVGIP: Graphical Models and Image Processing*, **53**(2):157–185, 1991.

27 W. T. Freeman and E. H. Adelson, The design and use of steerable filters, *IEEE Transactions on Pattern Analysis and Machine Intelligence*, **13**(9):891–906, 1991.

28 M. M. Gorkani and R. W. Picard, Texture orientation for sorting photos "at a glance", *IEEE International Conference on Pattern Recognition*, Vol. **1**, 459–464, 1994.

29 R. W. Picard and M. Gorkani, Finding perceptually dominant orientations in natural textures, *Spatial Vision*, **8**(2):221–253, 1994.

30 E. C. Yiu, *Image classification using color cues and texture orientation*, Master's Thesis, Department Electrical Engineering and Computer Science, MIT, 1996.

31 E. De Castro and C. Morandi, Registration of translated and rotated images using finite Fourier transforms, *IEEE Transactions on Pattern Analysis and Machine Intelligence*, **9**(5):700–703, 1987.

32 B. S. Reddy and B. Chatterji, An FFT-based technique for translation, rotation and scale invariant image registration, *IEEE Transactions on Image Processing*, **5**(8):1266–1271, 1996.

33 R. M. Neupauer and K. L. Powell, A fully-anisotropic Morlet wavelet to identify dominant orientation in a porous medium, *Computers & Geosciences*, **31**:465–471, 2005.

34 R. M. Neupauer, K. L. Powell, X. Qi, D. H. Lee, and D. A. Villhauer, Characterization of permeability anisotropy using wavelet analysis, *Water Resources Research*, **42**:1–13, 2006.

35 J. P. Antoine, P. Carrette, R. Murenzi, and B. Piette, Image analysis with two-dimensional continuous wavelet transform, *Signal Processing*, **31**:241–272, 1993.

36 L. Watkins, R. M. Neupauer, and G. P. Compo, Wavelet analysis and filtering to identify dominant orientations of permeability anisotropy, *Mathematical Geosciences*, **41**:643–659, 2009.

37 B. K. P. Horn, *Robot Vision*, The MIT Press, Cambridge, MA, p. 432, 1986.

38 S. K. Parui and D. D. Majumder, A new definition of shape similarity, *Pattern Recognition Letters*, **1**(1):37–42, 1982.

39 L. K. Arata, A. P. Dhawan, J. P. Broderick, M. F. Gaskil-Shipley, A. V. Levy, and N. D. Volkow, Three-dimensional anatomical model-based segmentation of MR Brain images through principal axes registration, *IEEE Transactions on Biomedical Engineering*, **42**(11):1069–1077, 1995.

40 J. Bigün and G. H. Granlund, Optimal orientation detection of linear symmetry, in *Proceedings of International Conference on Computer Vision (ICCV)*, 433–438, 1987.

41 L. J. van Vliet and P. W. Verbeek, Estimators for orientation and anisotropy in digitized images, in *Proceedings of the First Conference on Advanced School for Computing and Imaging*, 442–450, 1995.

42 K. M. Yi, Y. Verdie, P. Fua, and V. Lepetit, Learning to assign orientations to feature points, in *Proceedings of IEEE Conference on Computer Vision and Pattern Recognition*, 107–116, 2016.

43 J. Bromley, I. Guyon, Y. LeCun, E. Sackinger, and R. Shah, Signature verification using a Siamese time delay neural network, *International Journal of Pattern Recognition and Artificial Intelligence*, **7**(4), 1993.

3

Feature Point Detection

3.1 Introduction

To register two images, there is a need to find a transformation model that can transform the geometry of one image to resemble the geometry of the other. To find a suitable transformation model, a set of locally unique points is selected from each image, correspondence is established between points in the images, and from the coordinates of corresponding (homologous) points, the parameters of the transformation model to register the images are determined.

As local geometric differences between the images increase, a larger number of homologous points is required to account for the increased geometric differences between the images. So that sufficient homologous points are obtained to compute the parameters of a transformation model, there is a need to find a sufficiently large number of feature points in each image.

This chapter discusses various methods for detecting feature points in an image. A feature point represents the center of a dark or bright spot/blob, the point of intersection of two or more straight edges, the point of locally maximum curvature along an edge contour, or the center of a unique neighborhood in an image.

Various methods for detecting feature points in an image have been reported. These methods typically identify neighborhoods where a particular image property becomes locally maximum or minimum.

Depending on the type of images being registered, one property may be more appropriate than other properties. For instance, if the images being registered are rotated with respect to each other, a property that is rotation invariant is appropriate. Choosing the right property is critical in finding a sufficient number of homologous points in the images.

In spite of possible radiometric and geometric differences between two images, we would like to detect the same scene points in the images. Therefore, the method used to detect feature points in images should be insensitive to global radiometric and geometric differences between the images. A method

Theory and Applications of Image Registration, First Edition. Arthur Ardeshir Goshtasby.

that can find many of the same scene points in two images is said to be highly repeatable.

Image differences can be geometric, radiometric, or a combination of both. Examples of geometric differences are rotation, scaling, affine, and perspective distortions caused by the view-angle difference between the cameras capturing the images. These differences are global. If the geometric difference between two images varies locally, rotation, scaling, affine, and perspective differences will be local. Radiometric differences between two images can be due to changes in scene lighting or differences in the characteristics of the sensors capturing the images. In the following sections, various image properties/features suitable for detecting highly repeatable feature points in images with possible radiometric and geometric differences are discussed.

3.2 Variant Features

Often the images to be registered have only very small radiometric and geometric differences. Homologous neighborhoods in such images have very similar radiometric and geometric properties. For instance, consecutive frames in a video captured by a slowly moving camera of a static scene have very small radiometric and geometric differences. Therefore, the properties to be maximized or minimized do not have to be invariant to geometric and radiometric changes. We are after image features that can find neighborhoods with very similar geometries and intensities. Among variant image features used in feature point detection are central moments and uniqueness.

3.2.1 Central Moments

Considering a small $n \times n$ window centered at (x_0, y_0) in gray-scale image $I(x, y)$, the central moment of order pq of the window is defined by [1]

$$\mu_{pq}^I(x_0, y_0) = \sum_{x=x_0-n/2}^{x_0+n/2} \sum_{y=y_0-n/2}^{y_0+n/2} (x - x_0)^p (y - y_0)^q I(x, y), \qquad (3.1)$$

where p and q are nonnegative integers. The moments are computed with respect to the center of the window and within a square window in order not to favor the x-coordinates more than or less than the y-coordinates when detecting points.

$\mu_{00}^I(x_0, y_0)$ shows the sum of intensities within the window centered at (x_0, y_0) in gray-scale image $I(x, y)$. By locating the extrema of $\mu_{00}^I(x_0, y_0)$ while moving the center of the window within the image, locally bright and dark blobs will be identified. The process will detect textureless spots in an image, which may not be very useful when finding homologous neighborhoods in images. To detect more distinct neighborhoods in an image, instead of intensity I in Eq. (3.1), intensity gradient magnitude I_g calculated from

$$I_g(x,y) = \{I_x^2(x,y) + I_y^2(x,y)\}^{\frac{1}{2}} \qquad (3.2)$$

is used, where $I_x(x,y) = I(x+1,y) - I(x,y)$ is gradient in the x-direction and $I_y(x,y) = I(x,y+1) - I(x,y)$ is gradient in the y-direction at (x,y). Therefore,

$$\mu_{pq}^{I_g}(x_0,y_0) = \sum_{x=x_0-n/2}^{x_0+n/2} \sum_{y=y_0-n/2}^{y_0+n/2} (x-x_0)^p (y-y_0)^q I_g(x,y) \qquad (3.3)$$

is used to measure the central moment of order pq of an $n \times n$ window centered at (x_0,y_0) in an image where pixel values show intensity gradient magnitudes. Note that use of intensity gradient magnitudes rather than intensities in Eq. (3.3) makes the process insensitive to global intensity differences between the images being registered.

The moment of order 00 will not be used because it is independent of x and y and will not contain information about the geometric layout of intensities within a window. Higher-order moments can be used to characterize the pattern appearing in a neighborhood. By finding image locations where the moment of a required order assumes locally maximum or minimum values, a network of points will be obtained. Such points will be centered at highly detailed neighborhoods, facilitating the correspondence process. The order and the magnitude of moments at a point can be used as features to find initial homologous points in the images. Incorrect homologous points can then be identified and removed by a robust estimator, discussed in Chapter 5.

For a color image, the intensity gradient magnitude is replaced with color gradient magnitude. If $r(x,y)$, $g(x,y)$, and $b(x,y)$ are the red, green, and blue components of color at pixel (x,y), we will locate the extrema of

$$\mu_{pq}^{C_g}(x_0,y_0) = \sum_{x=x_0-n/2}^{x_0+n/2} \sum_{y=y_0-n/2}^{y_0+n/2} (x-x_0)^p (y-y_0)^q C_g(x,y) \qquad (3.4)$$

to find the feature points, where

$$C_g(x,y) = \{r_x^2(x,y) + r_y^2(x,y) + g_x^2(x,y) + g_y^2(x,y) + b_x^2(x,y) + b_y^2(x,y)\}^{\frac{1}{2}} \qquad (3.5)$$

is the color gradient magnitude at (x,y), $r_x(x,y) = r(x+1,y) - r(x,y)$, and $r_y(x,y) = r(x,y+1) - r(x,y)$ are red gradients in the x- and y-directions, respectively. Similarly green and blue gradients at (x,y) are calculated.

The computational complexity of central moments for a window of size $n \times n$ pixels is on the order of n^2 multiplications at each pixel in an image. Therefore, determining points in an image of size $M \times N$ pixels requires on the order of MNn^2 multiplications.

            (a)   (b)

            (c)   (d)

Figure 3.1 (a and b) Gray-scale images of an artwork, and (c and d) color images of an outdoor scene taken from slightly different views. The 50 strongest points in each image obtained by central moments of order $pq = 11$ are shown. Red points show local maxima and blue points show local minima of the central moments. Yellow and light blue points in conjugate images are the red and blue points in the images that show the same scene points. They are the homologous points.

Figure 3.1 shows a pair of gray-scale images and a pair of color images. The images in each pair have been obtained from slightly different views of a static scene. When letting $p = 1$ and $q = 1$, 13,207, 13,111, 10,829, and 11,036 points are detected in images (a)–(d), respectively. In each image, the 50 points with the highest magnitude central moments are selected and shown. Points depicted in red represent local maxima, while points shown in blue represent local minima of the calculated central moments. Red points in conjugate images that represent the same scene point are shown in yellow and blue points in conjugate images that represent the same scene point are shown in light blue. The points in yellow and light blue are the homologous points. Overall, 22 homologous points are obtained in images (a) and (b) and 10 homologous points are obtained in images (c) and (d).

Windows of size 15×15 pixels were used to obtain these points. To avoid detection of very close points, the points are ordered according to their strengths from the strongest to the weakest in a list. Then, starting from top of the list, for each point that is visited, points below it in the list that are within distance 15 pixels of it are removed. Then, from among the points remaining in the list, the first 50 points are returned.

The images are not smoothed before calculating the moments. Smoothing blurs image details and reduces distinctiveness of detected points. Since the central moments described above represent the sum of weighted image gradients, the summation process reduces the effect of noise. However, since the gradient process enhances noise, if an image is known to be noisy, it should be smoothed before determining its gradients.

Smoothing the images in Fig. 3.1 with a Gaussian filter of standard deviation 1 pixel reduced the number of detected points in images (a)–(d) to 1505, 1577, 787, and 799, respectively. The number of points identifying the same scene points from among the 50 highest magnitude central moments, however, remained the same in these images. For images (a) and (b), the number of homologous points appearing among the 50 strongest points reduced from 22 to 20, while in images (c) and (d) they increased from 10 to 13.

Increasing the window size to 35×35 pixels reduced the number of detected points to 4827, 4630, 6374, and 6442, in images (a)–(d), respectively. Increasing the window size reduced the number of homologous points in these images. The number of homologous points obtained in images (a) and (b) reduced from 22 to 20, whereas for images (c) and (d) reduced from 10 to 8. By increasing the window size, homologous neighborhoods become more dissimilar due to the view-angle difference between the images. When neighborhoods are smaller, homologous neighborhoods in the images become more similar, producing more homologous points.

The image pairs in Fig. 3.1 have small local radiometric and geometric differences due to the small change in the view angle of the camera capturing the images. Radiometric difference is reduced when using intensity gradients and color gradients instead of raw intensities and raw colors. When corresponding neighborhoods in two images appear the same, a locally minimum/maximum central moment in a neighborhood in one image is expected in the corresponding neighborhood in the conjugate image.

If a central moment becomes locally minimum/maximum at a pixel in an image and the neighborhood of the pixel appears differently in the conjugate image, the same point may not be detected in the conjugate image. The more similar the geometries of homologous neighborhoods are in two images, the higher will be the number of homologous points in the images. Therefore, central moments $\mu_{pq}^{I_g}$ and $\mu_{pq}^{C_g}$ are most effective when used to detect feature points in images with insignificant geometric differences, such as consecutive frames in a video captured by a slow-moving camera.

3.2.2 Uniqueness

To locate unique neighborhoods in an image, Moravec [2] determined intensity variances horizontally and vertically at a pixel, and if both variances were sufficiently high, the neighborhood centered at the pixel was considered unique and used as a feature point. The variance horizontally at a pixel is measured by the mean squared intensity differences of small windows to the left and to the right of the pixel. Similarly, the variance vertically at the pixel is determined from the mean squared intensity differences of windows above and below the pixel. Of the two variances, the smaller is taken to represent the uniqueness at the pixel.

To avoid detection of points along diagonal lines, in addition to using variances horizontally and vertically, we will also use variances diagonally. The mean squared intensity differences of an $n \times n$ window centered at (x_0, y_0) and windows centered at $(x_0 + in, y_0 + jn)$ are determined, where i and j can assume values -1, 0, and 1 but not both simultaneously 0 (Fig. 3.2). The smallest of the eight variances is then taken to represent the uniqueness measure at the pixel.

Uniqueness is calculated at all pixels in an image, creating a matrix of uniqueness values (Fig. 3.2). Entries with locally peak values are then identified and used as feature points. Note that no points will be detected within the narrow bands of width $3n/2$ pixels of the four image borders because variances cannot be calculated there. To limit the number of detected points, the required number of points that have the largest locally maximum variances and are apart by at least n pixels from other points are identified and used as feature points.

To determine the variance at pixel (x_0, y_0) in a color image, variances of red, green, and blue bands are calculated at the pixel and the variances are added to obtain the color variance at the pixel. Overall, 2625, 2559, 2515, and 2591 points are detected in images (a)–(d) in Fig. 3.1 using 15×15 windows. The

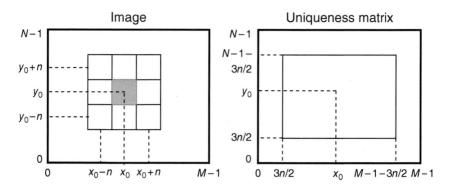

Figure 3.2 To determine the local uniqueness at (x_0, y_0) in an image, variances of the window centered at (x_0, y_0) and the eight surrounding windows are determined. The minimum of the eight variances is then considered the uniqueness at (x_0, y_0) and saved in the uniqueness matrix at (x_0, y_0).

(a)   (b)

(c)   (d)

Figure 3.3 (a)–(d) Points in images (a)–(d) in Fig. 3.1 that represent centers of the 50 most unique neighborhoods in the images. Homologous points are shown in yellow.

points centered at the 50 most unique neighborhoods are shown in Fig. 3.3. Ten of the points detected in images (a) and (b) and eight of the points detected in images (c) and (d) show the same scene points and represent homologous points. Homologous points are shown in yellow, while other points are shown in red.

As variance is sensitive to noise, when noise is present, images should be appropriately smoothed before calculating the variances. For the images shown in Fig. 3.1, smoothing reduced the number of detected feature points, and it did not increase the number of homologous points from among 50 unique points detected in each image. Increasing the window size also reduced the number of points, and it did not increase the number of homologous points. Increasing the window size actually reduced the number of homologous points in these images because the images have been taken from different views. Although some homologous neighborhoods have the same geometry, some other homologous neighborhoods have different geometries caused by occlusion and perspective differences.

When using a uniqueness measure that is calculated from variances in eight directions, the measure becomes invariant to rotations that are a multiple of 45°. Since two images are rarely rotated by a multiple of exactly 45°, the uniqueness measure is suitable when the images have very small to no rotational differences, such as consecutive frames in a video captured by a slow-moving camera. Round blobs in an image that have the size of the window tend to produce high variances in eight directions and will be detected as points. By changing the window size, different sized blobs in an image can be detected.

Computation of uniqueness at each pixel in an image when using windows of size $n \times n$ is on the order of n^2 multiplications. Determining the variance between two windows requires less computation than finding the central moment at a window of the same size, but since eight variances are calculated at each pixel, computation of uniqueness at a pixel requires the same time as that of a central moment at the pixel. Therefore, it takes on the order of MNn^2 multiplications to find feature points in an image of size $M \times N$ pixels and windows of size $n \times n$ pixels by uniqueness.

3.3 Invariant Features

The images to be registered may have geometric and/or radiometric differences. Geometric differences can be rotational, scaling, affine, projective, or nonlinear differences. Radiometric differences can be due to changes in scene lighting and/or differences in sensor characteristics.

Rotational and scaling differences can be handled relatively easily since shape information is not changed. Affine, projective, and nonlinear differences are more difficult to handle because they change the shapes of image regions. If the differences are locally small and the neighborhoods used to detect the points are also small, geometric differences between homologous neighborhoods in images can be approximated by a combination of rotation and scaling.

Intensity differences between two images caused by changes in scene lighting can be reduced if intensity gradients rather than raw intensities are used. Differences in sensor characteristics are more difficult to handle because the differences can be nonlinear. If the mapping function that relates the intensities of two images can be determined, it can be used to convert the intensities of one image into those of the conjugate image before finding the feature points. These issues are discussed in more detail next.

3.3.1 Rotation-Invariant Features

Feature points that are independent of an image's orientation can be determined using intrinsic properties, such as curvature, that are independent of the image's coordinate system. Rotation- invariant features can also be obtained using features that are normalized with respect to rotation, such as invariant moments. The responses of a rotationally symmetric operator, such as the Laplacian of Gaussian (LoG), to an image can be used to detect rotation-invariant feature points. In addition, properties within a circular region that do not depend on the orientation of the region, such as entropy, can be used to detect rotation-invariant feature points in an image. In this section, feature point detection using the LoG operator, entropy, and invariant moments are described. Also, a variant of the LoG-based point detector known as scale-invariant feature transform (SIFT) is described.

3.3.1.1 Laplacian of Gaussian (LoG) Detector

The Laplacian of gray-scale image $I(x, y)$ at location (x, y) is $I_{xx}(x, y) + I_{yy}(x, y)$, where $I_{xx}(x, y)$ is the second- derivative intensity in x-direction at (x, y) and $I_{yy}(x, y)$ is the second-derivative intensity in y-direction at (x, y). In the digital domain, Laplacian is approximated by

$$L(x, y) = I(x - 1, y) + I(x + 1, y) + I(x, y - 1) + I(x, y + 1) - 4I(x, y).$$

(3.6)

Since second-derivative intensities emphasize noise, to reduce the effect of noise, an image is first smoothed with a Gaussian filter and then its derivatives are determined. Smoothing an image with a Gaussian filter and then finding its Laplacian is the same as convolving the image with the LoG. The LoG operator is defined by

$$
\begin{aligned}
\text{LoG} &= \frac{\partial^2 G(x, y)}{\partial x^2} + \frac{\partial^2 G(x, y)}{\partial y^2}, \\
&= \frac{\partial^2 G(x)}{\partial x^2} G(y) + \frac{\partial^2 G(y)}{\partial y^2} G(x).
\end{aligned}
$$

(3.7)

The LoG operator is rotationally symmetric as shown in Fig. 3.4a. It has a symmetric negative part (Fig. 3.4b) that is surrounded by a symmetric positive part (Fig. 3.4c). The sum of the values in the positive part is the same as that in the negative part, implying that when the operator is convolved with an image, the result will be the difference of the weighted sums of intensities inside a circular region and the weighted sum of intensities outside the circular region.

As the LoG operator is moved over an image, the convolution result will change. The LoG of the image becomes locally maximum at a pixel that is the center of a dark spot, and it becomes locally minimum when the pixel represents the center of a bright spot. By locating local extrema of the LoG of an image, centers of dark and bright spots in the image can be identified.

Due to the circular nature of the LoG operator, theoretically, the operation is independent of the orientation of an image. However, in a digital image, because there are fewer pixels diagonally than horizontally or vertically in a circular region, the operator will have some dependency on image orientation. Within

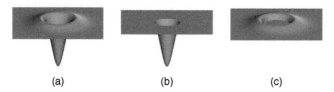

Figure 3.4 (a) The Laplacian of Gaussian operator and its (b) negative and (c) positive parts.

a certain error tolerance, however, the operator can be considered rotationally invariant.

The LoG operator can be approximated by the difference of two Gaussians. The best approximation to the LoG operator of standard deviation σ is obtained from the difference of Gaussians (DoGs) of standard deviations σ and 1.6σ [3]. More specifically,

$$\text{DoG} = \frac{1.6[G(1.6\sigma) - G(\sigma)]}{\sigma^2}. \tag{3.8}$$

The Laplacian operator is described for a gray-scale image. Therefore, this operator can find points in only gray-scale images. Points detected in the penny images in Fig. 3.5 by the LoG operator of $\sigma = 2.3$ pixels (windows of size 15×15 pixels) are shown. Overall, 722 points are detected in images (a) and 721 points are detected in image (b). The extrema corresponding to the highest 50 LoG magnitudes are shown. Points representing local minima are shown in blue, while points representing local maxima are shown in red.

Blue points identify centers of bright spots/blobs while red points identify centers of dark spots/blobs in an image. If blue points in images (a) and (b) show the same scene point, both points are painted with light blue, while if red points in the image show the same scene point, they are painted with yellow. Among the 50 points detected in images (a) and (b), 16 represent the same scene points and so represent homologous points.

Points detected by the LoG operator do not always represent round blobs. They can represent elongated and branching structures as shown in Fig. 3.5. Such points are easily influenced by noise and change in scene lighting.

The response of the LoG operator to a circular blob reaches a peak when the size of the negative part of the LoG matches the size of the blob. The relation between the scale σ of the LoG and the diameter D of the blob is $D = 2\sqrt{2}\sigma$ [4]. The LoG of scale σ detects blobs of diameters smaller than and larger than $2\sqrt{2}\sigma$ also. Therefore, this point detector is invariant to small changes in scale/resolution of an image when dealing with circular blobs. When a point represents an elongated blob, changing the scale/resolution of the image

(a)   (b)

Figure 3.5 (a and b) Two images of a penny taken from different views by a camera. Points detected in the images by the LoG operator of size 15 × 15 pixels are shown. Points in red show local maxima, points in blue show local minima, points in yellow show corresponding local maxima, and points in light blue show corresponding local minima.

may change the shape of the blob, breaking it into pieces or merging it with a neighboring blob and resulting in different points.

Although, theoretically, 2-D Gaussians and LoGs extend to infinity in all directions, in practice, because a Gaussian approaches 0 exponentially, it is only necessary to consider a window of size $n \times n$ pixels centered at a LoG of standard deviation σ where $n = 6\sigma + 1$. For example, when $\sigma = 2$ pixels, the window representing the LoG operator will be 13 × 13 pixels.

If the LoG is replaced by its approximating DoG, the DoG of an image can be computed from the difference of two Gaussian smoothed images. Because a 2-D Gaussian smoothing can be achieved by a 1-D Gaussian smoothing horizontally followed by a 1-D Gaussian smoothing vertically, it takes $2n$ multiplications to determine the 2-D Gaussian smoothing at each image pixel. However, since n is usually small, 1-D smoothing does not result in a considerable saving compared to 2-D smoothing. Therefore, overall, the computational complexity of point detection by the LoG operator is on the order of MNn^2 multiplications when using an image of size $M \times N$ pixels and windows of size $n \times n$ pixels, where $n = 6\sigma + 1$ and σ is the standard deviation of the LoG.

3.3.1.2 Entropy

Entropy measures information content, and by locally maximizing it, most informative neighborhoods in an image can be identified. If $p(i)$ is the probability that when a pixel is randomly selected in an image window it will have intensity i, and if intensities in a window vary between 0 and 255, the entropy of the window is computed from

$$E = -\sum_{i=0}^{255} p(i)\log_2 p(i). \tag{3.9}$$

To obtain the probability density of intensities in a window, first the histogram of the intensities is obtained. Denoting the ith bin in the histogram by $H(i)$, which shows the number of pixels in the window with intensity i, and assuming the window is of size $n \times n$ pixels, then

$$p(i) = \frac{H(i)}{n^2}, \text{for } i = 0, \dots, 255. \tag{3.10}$$

Since pixel locations are not used in the calculation of $p(i)$, the entropy of a window will not change by rearranging its pixels or by rotating all pixels with respect to the window centered by the same amount. Therefore, entropy is a rotationally invariant feature. Feature point detection using image entropy is proposed by Kadir and Brady [5].

To produce meaningful probabilities from which an entropy is computed, the window used to calculate a histogram should be sufficiently large. If 256 different intensities appear in an image, the window should contain at least 256 pixels. As the window size is increased, however, computation time increases, and if two images have small local intensity or geometric differences, by increasing the window size, differences between homologous windows increase. When homologous windows in two images do not contain the same scene parts, a locally peak entropy in one image may not produce a locally peak entropy in another image, resulting in points that do not correspond.

To reduce the influence of intensity and geometric differences between images on determination of homologous points, windows are taken small and range of intensities in the images is reduced. For instance, when using windows of size 15×15 pixels, intensities in 0–255 are linearly mapped to 0–63. By doing so in the images in Fig. 3.5, overall, 386 points are obtained in image (a) and 397 points are obtained in image (b). Points representing the 50 highest entropies are shown in Fig. 3.6, of which 19 (shown in yellow) correspond to each other. Increasing the window size to 25×25 pixels and using the original intensities (histograms with 256 bins), only four corresponding points are obtained.

Point detection by entropy can be applied to color images also. The entropy of a color window is the sum of the entropies of its color bands. Locally maximum entropies of the color images in Fig. 3.7 using windows of size 15×15 pixels, after mapping the red, green, and blue color values to 0–63 are shown. Overall, 308 points are detected in image (a) and 298 points in image (b). The points representing the highest 50 locally maximum entropies are shown. Sixteen of the 50 detected points (shown in yellow) identify the same scene points and are considered homologous points.

(a)   (b)

Figure 3.6 (a and b) Points representing locally maximum entropies of images (a) and (b) in Fig. 3.5 when using windows of size 15 × 15 pixels and intensities in the range 0–63. Points in the images showing the same scene points (homologous points) are shown in yellow.

(a)   (b)

Figure 3.7 (a and b) Images of a garden scene taken at different camera orientations. Points in the images representing the highest 50 locally maximum entropies when using windows of size 15 × 15 pixels and color components in the range 0–63 are shown. Homologous points are shown in yellow.

3.3.1.3 Invariant Moments

The central moment of order pq of gray-scale image I within a window of size $n \times n$ centered at (x_0, y_0) was described by Eq. (3.1). Hu [1], by combining various central moments, created moments that are invariant to the orientation of the pattern within the window. These rotationally invariant moments are as follows:

$$\phi_1 = (\mu_{20} + \mu_{02}), \tag{3.11}$$

$$\phi_2 = (\mu_{20} - \mu_{02})^2 + 4\mu_{11}^2, \tag{3.12}$$

$$\phi_3 = (\mu_{30} - 3\mu_{12})^2 + (3\mu_{21} - \mu_{03})^2, \tag{3.13}$$

$$\phi_4 = (\mu_{30} + \mu_{12})^2 + (\mu_{21} + \mu_{03})^2, \tag{3.14}$$

$$\begin{aligned}
\phi_5 = &(\mu_{30} - 3\mu_{12})(\mu_{30} + \mu_{12}) \\
&\times [(\mu_{30} + \mu_{12})^2 - 3(\mu_{21} + \mu_{03})^2] \\
&+ (3\mu_{21} - \mu_{03})(\mu_{21} + \mu_{03}) \\
&\times [3(\mu_{30} + \mu_{12})^2 - (\mu_{21} + \mu_{03})^2],
\end{aligned} \tag{3.15}$$

$$\begin{aligned}
\phi_6 = &(\mu_{20} - \mu_{02})[(\mu_{30} + \mu_{12})^2 - (\mu_{21} + \mu_{03})^2] \\
&+ 4\mu_{11}(\mu_{30} + \mu_{12})(\mu_{21} + \mu_{03}),
\end{aligned} \tag{3.16}$$

$$\begin{aligned}
\phi_7 = &(3\mu_{21} - \mu_{03})(\mu_{30} + \mu_{12}) \\
&\times [(\mu_{30} + \mu_{12})^2 - 3(\mu_{21} + \mu_{03})^2] \\
&- (\mu_{30} - 3\mu_{12})(\mu_{21} + \mu_{03}) \\
&\times [3(\mu_{30} + \mu_{12})^2 - (\mu_{21} + \mu_{03})^2].
\end{aligned} \tag{3.17}$$

The window is required to be circular because square and rectangular windows cannot contain the same image pattern when they are rotated with respect to each other by angles that are not a multiple of 90°.

Using intensity gradients at pixels within a window of size $n \times n$, the central moment of order pq of the window was described by Eq. (3.3), and using color gradients at the pixels, it was described by Eq. (3.4) for a color image.

Use of intensity gradients instead of intensities and color gradients instead of colors makes point detection less dependent on raw intensities and colors and helps to detect more homologous points in images with global radiometric differences. Since gradients enhance noise, to make the process less sensitive to noise, an image should be smoothed before calculating its gradients.

By maximizing ϕ_2 using images (a) and (b) in Fig. 3.5, after the images are smoothed with a Gaussian filter of standard deviation 1 pixel and using windows of size 15×15 pixels, 386 points are obtained in image (a) and 384 points are obtained in image (b). The points representing the highest 50 ϕ_2 are shown in Fig. 3.8 in red or yellow. Points in yellow represent the same scene points and, thus, are homologous points. There are 19 homologous points in the images.

Instead of ϕ_2, other invariant moments can be used to detect different sets of points. Different invariant moments capture different local geometric properties of an image, thus, produce different points.

To show results on color images, the garden images (a) and (b) in Fig. 3.7 were used after smoothing with a Gaussian filter of standard deviation 1 pixel. Overall, 336 points are obtained in image (a) and 316 points in image (b) when using

(a)   (b)

Figure 3.8 (a and b) Feature points detected in images (a) and (b) in Fig. 3.5 by maximizing ϕ_2. Points in yellow identify the same scene points and so represent homologous points. Points in red are those without a correspondence. There are 19 homologous points in the images.

(a)   (b)

Figure 3.9 (a and b) Points detected in images (a) and (b) in Fig. 3.7 by maximizing ϕ_2 when using windows of size 15 × 15 pixels. Twenty homologous points are obtained in the images. Homologous points are shown in yellow.

windows of size 15 × 15 pixels. Points representing the locally peak ϕ_2 that have the highest 50 values are shown in Fig. 3.9. Twenty of the points detected in these images show the same scene points and represent homologous points. Homologous points are shown in yellow, while the remaining points are shown in red.

The computation of ϕ_2 in a window of size $n \times n$ requires on the order of n^2 multiplications. Therefore, finding feature points in an image of size $M \times N$ by an invariant moment using windows of size $n \times n$ pixels requires on the order of MNn^2 multiplications.

3.3.2 SIFT: A Scale- and Rotation-Invariant Point Detector

The SIFT [6] estimates the scale and orientation of a neighborhood before determining whether the neighborhood qualifies for a feature point or not. The SIFT point detector extends the LoG detector by determining the scale of the LoG at each neighborhood in such a way to maximize the LoG response there.

To speed up computation of LoG at different scales, the LoG operator is approximated by a DoG [6, 7]. To determine the feature points in an image, first a stack of images representing the smoothed versions of the image at increasingly higher scales is created. Smoothing is achieved via Gaussian convolution. Starting from a small scale, such as 1 pixel, the scale of the Gaussian filter is increased by a factor of $\sqrt{2}$ until the maximum desired scale is reached.

Therefore, an image is smoothed with Gaussians of $\sigma = 1, \sqrt{2}, 2, 2\sqrt{2}, 4,$ and so on up to the desired scale. From the difference of adjacent Gaussian smoothed images, another stack of images is created approximating the LoG of the image at different scales. If the scale ratio of the Gaussian smoothing at adjacent slices was 1.6, by subtracting adjacent smoothed images, a stack of images closely resembling LoG images would be obtained. Nevertheless, a scale ratio of $\sqrt{2}$ seems sufficiently close to 1.6 to detect blobs of different sizes in an image.

A pixel is considered a feature point if it assumes a locally minimum or a locally maximum value in scale space. That is, pixel (x, y) is considered a feature point if it takes a locally extremum value at (x, y) in the spatial domain as well as in scale represented by σ.

If (x, y) is the center of a blob of diameter $D = 2\sqrt{2}\sigma$ in an image, the blob is expected to be detected at scale σ by SIFT. If the image is scaled by a factor of s, the center of the same blob is expected to be detected at scale $s\sigma$ by SIFT. Therefore, SIFT detects centers of blobs in an image independent of the scale/resolution of the image. Because DoG and LoG have similar properties, just like feature points detected by LoG, feature points detected by DoG or by SIFT are rotation invariant. Therefore, feature points detected by SIFT are scale and rotation invariant.

Similar to the LoG point detector, the SIFT point detector works only on gray-scale images. If the given image is color, the luminance component of the image may be used to find the points. Using image (a) in Fig. 3.5 and image (b) in the same figure after scaling it by a factor of 0.75, the SIFT detector found 1656 points in image (a) and 1000 points in the scaled image (b). Points representing

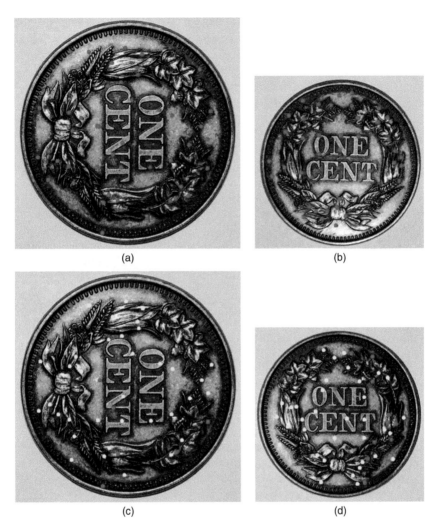

(a)

(b)

(c)

(d)

Figure 3.10 (a and b) SIFT points detected in image (a) of Fig. 3.5 and image (b) of the same figure after scaling by a factor of 0.75. (c) Same as (a). (d) SIFT points detected in image (a) after rotating it by 90° and scaling it by 0.75. Points in yellow in (c) and (d) represent homologous points. These results are obtained with the SIFT software made publicly available by Lowe [6].

the centers of the 50 largest blobs detected in the images are shown in Fig. 3.10. Note that these images have rotational and scaling differences.

None of the points detected in images (a) and (b) in Fig. 3.10 represent the same scene point because SIFT points represent local extrema of the second derivative of an image in scale space and the location of an extremum shifts with change in local intensity gradient. When a local extremum belongs to an elongated or branching structure, the location of the extremum could move by a small change in local intensities, as is the case in images (a) and (b) in Fig. 3.10.

If local intensity differences between two images are negligible, many of the same SIFT points are expected in the images independent of the scale and orientation of the images. Taking image (a) in Fig. 3.5, rotating it by 90° and reducing its scale by a factor of 0.75, and obtaining the SIFT points, the points shown in Fig. 3.10d are obtained. The SIFT points detected in the image in Fig. 3.10a are again shown in Fig. 3.10c. Thirty-six out of the 50 points shown in Fig. 3.10c and d represent the same scene points. This shows that many of the same SIFT points are expected in two images of a scene taken from the same view independent of the scale and orientation of the images as long as local intensity differences do not exist between the images.

If two images of a scene have local intensity differences, the same SIFT points may not be detected in the images, especially when the images contain very few circular blobs. If the images represent man-made scenes, due to the abundance of corners in the images, methods that detect corner points in images should be used. Corner detectors by using information in very small neighborhoods detect points that are less sensitive to intensity differences between images than the SIFT point detector.

3.3.3 Radiometric-Invariant Features

Many point detectors use intensity derivatives rather than raw intensities to characterize local neighborhoods in images. Intensity derivatives reduce the sensitivity of a method to radiometric changes. Among the methods in this category, the Harris corner detector [8], which uses first-derivative intensities, and the Hessian corner detector [9], which uses second-derivative intensities, are described. Although these point detectors are not scale invariant, they are rotation invariant and so they can be used to detect homologous points in images that are rotated with respect to each other.

3.3.3.1 Harris Corner Detector
Given gray-scale image I, and assuming $I(x, y)$ is the intensity, $I_x(x, y)$ is the gradient in x-direction, and $I_y(x, y)$ is the gradient in y-direction at (x, y), the square gradient matrix [10, 11] defined by

$$N(x, y) = \begin{bmatrix} \overline{I_x^2(x, y)} & \overline{I_x(x, y)I_y(x, y)} \\ \overline{I_y(x, y)I_x(x, y)} & \overline{I_y^2(x, y)} \end{bmatrix} \tag{3.18}$$

is calculated at each pixel in the image. Since gradients emphasize noise, usually an image is smoothed before finding its gradients. Let us suppose the standard deviation of the Gaussian used to smooth an image before finding its gradients is σ_1.

The overlines in Eq. (3.18) imply averaging each entry of the matrix within a small window centered at (x, y). A small window is typically a 7×7 or a 9×9 neighborhood. This smoothing can be achieved faster by creating an image N_{11} with its entry (x, y) showing $I_x^2(x, y)$, an image N_{22} with its entry (x, y) showing $I_y^2(x, y)$, and an image N_{12} with its entry (x, y) showing $I_y(x, y)I_x(x, y)$. Note that by knowing $I_x(x, y)$ and $I_y(x, y)$ at each pixel, these three images can be quickly created. Also note that the upper-right and the lower-left entries of matrix N are the same. Therefore, image N_{12} provides values for both the upper-right and the lower-left entries of matrix N at each pixel location (x, y).

Images N_{11}, N_{22}, and N_{12} are then smoothed by averaging values within small $n \times n$ windows. Alternatively, smoothing can be achieved by convolving each of the images by a Gaussian filter of standard deviation $\sigma_2 = (n - 1)/6$.

After smoothing images N_{11}, N_{22}, and N_{12}, values at (x, y) in the images are used as values for the upper-left, lower-right, upper-right, and lower-left entries of $N(x, y)$. A fourth image is created denoted by $R(x, y)$ with its entry (x, y) computed from the determinant and trace of $N(x, y)$:

$$R(x, y) = \text{Det}[\mathbf{N}(x, y)] - h\text{Tr}^2[\mathbf{N}(x, y)]. \tag{3.19}$$

$\text{Det}(x, y)$ and $\text{Tr}(x, y)$ denote the determinant and the trace of matrix $\mathbf{N}(x, y)$, and h is a small number such as 0.05.

Usually $\sigma_2 \geq \sigma_1$. σ_1 is chosen based on the noise level in the given image, and σ_2 is chosen sufficiently large to avoid the detection of weaker points near stronger ones. Increasing σ_1 and/or σ_2 will decrease the number of detected points. An image entry (x, y) where $R(x, y)$ is sufficiently large and locally maximum represents a point where a large number of pixels within the window centered at (x, y) have high gradients in directions normal to each other. Such neighborhoods typically represent corners where two straight edges normal to each other meet. For that reason, strong Harris points represent corners in an image.

The Harris point detector was originally designed to detect both edges and corners. Analysis of $R(x, y)$ over variations of parameter h reveals that h can assume values between 0 and 0.25; when $h = 0$ only points are detected and when $h = 0.25$ only edges are detected.

Rohr [12] found that $\text{Det}(\mathbf{N})/\text{Tr}(\mathbf{N})$ is one of the principal invariants of matrix $\mathbf{N}$ and that the other principal invariant of $\mathbf{N}$ is $\text{Det}(\mathbf{N})$. By maximizing $\text{Det}(\mathbf{N})$, points of least uncertainty in an image are detected. Note that Rohr points are the same as the Harris points when $h = 0$.

Harris points are theoretically invariant of an image's orientation. However, due to the dependency of image gradients on image orientation, as discussed in Chapter 1, detected points will have some dependency on image orientation. Since Harris points represent corners in an image and corners are defined locally, detected points will not be sensitive to small changes in the scale of an image. Therefore, changing the scale/resolution of an image slightly will not

(a) (b)

Figure 3.11 (a and b) Harris corners detected in images (a) and (b) in Fig. 3.5 when letting $\sigma_1 = \sigma_2 = 1.5$ pixels and $h = 0.05$. Homologous points are shown in yellow.

change the detected corners significantly. For this reason, not only are Harris corners insensitive to changes in scene lighting, they are not very sensitive to the orientation and small scale changes.

Using the penny images in Fig. 3.5 and letting $\sigma_1 = \sigma_2 = 1.5$ pixels and $h = 0.05$ when calculating the entries of matrix $\mathbf{N}(x, y)$, 595 points were detected in image (a) and 584 points were detected in image (b). The points representing the 50 locally highest R values in each image are shown in Fig. 3.11. Overall, 15 of the 50 points (shown in yellow) represent the same scene points.

For a color image, matrix $\mathbf{N}$ is replaced with the following [13]:

$$\mathbf{N}_c = \begin{bmatrix} \overline{R_x^2 + G_x^2 + B_x^2} & \overline{R_x R_y + G_x G_y + B_x B_y} \\ \overline{R_x R_y + G_x G_y + B_x B_y} & \overline{R_y^2 + G_y^2 + B_y^2} \end{bmatrix}, \tag{3.20}$$

where R, G, and B imply the red, green, and blue bands of a color image and subscripts x and y denote gradients in x- and y-directions.

When using the color images in Fig. 3.7, 650 points are obtained in image (a) and 652 points are obtained in image (b). The 50 strongest points detected in the images are shown in Fig. 3.12. Of the 50 points, 34 (shown in yellow) represent the same scene points. These points are obtained when letting $\sigma_1 = \sigma_2 = 1.5$ pixels, and $h = 0.05$.

The computational complexity of the Harris corner detector when using windows of size $n \times n$ in an image of size $M \times N$ pixels is on the order of MNn^2 multiplications. At each pixel in the image, there is a need to calculate the square matrix N, which requires on the order of n^2 multiplications.

(a)   (b)

Figure 3.12 (a and b) Harris corners detected in the garden scene images in Fig. 3.9 when letting $\sigma_1 = \sigma_2 = 1.5$ pixels, and $h = 0.05$. Homologous points are shown in yellow.

3.3.3.2 Hessian Corner Detector

A corner detector based on the Hessian matrix is described by Beaudet [9]. The Hessian matrix of gray-scale image $I(x, y)$ at pixel (x, y) is defined by

$$\mathbf{H}(x, y) = \begin{bmatrix} I_{xx}(x, y) & I_{xy}(x, y) \\ I_{xy}(x, y) & I_{yy}(x, y) \end{bmatrix}. \tag{3.21}$$

Image locations where the absolute value of the determinant of $\mathbf{H}(x, y)$:

$$\text{Det}(x, y) = I_{xx}(x, y)I_{yy}(x, y) - I_{xy}^2(x, y) \tag{3.22}$$

becomes locally maximum are taken as corners. Treating the intensity value at (x, y) as the height of the surface approximating the image intensities, Nagel [14] has shown that the determinant of the Hessian matrix at (x, y) is proportional to the Gaussian curvature of the surface at (x, y). Hessian points, therefore, detect points in an image where Gaussian curvature of the surface approximating the intensities becomes locally maximum.

Since second-derivative intensities used in the calculation of $\mathbf{H}(x, y)$ are sensitive to noise, it is suggested to smooth the image before calculating the Hessian matrix. Because Gaussian curvature is an intrinsic property of the approximating surface, theoretically, detected points will be independent of the orientation and scale of the surface. In practice, however, digital noise, which cannot be removed by image smoothing, can affect detected points, making them somewhat dependent on the orientation and scale of the image. The Hessian matrix is defined only for gray-scale images; therefore, this method can detect feature points in only gray-scale images.

The Hessian corners detected in the penny images in Fig. 3.5 are shown in Fig. 3.13. To obtain these points, the images are first smoothed with a Gaussian

(a)   (b)

Figure 3.13 (a and b) The 50 strongest Hessian corners detected in images (a) and (b) in Fig. 3.5. Points in yellow show the homologous points.

of standard deviation $\sigma = 1.5$ pixels and then the second- derivative intensities are calculated. Overall, 851 points are detected in image (a) and 861 points are detected in image (b). Points representing the highest 50 values of "Det" in each image are shown in Fig. 3.13. There are 14 points (shown in yellow) in the images that represent the same scene points.

The computational complexity of point detection by the Hessian matrix for an image of size $M \times N$ is on the order of MNn^2 multiplication, where $n = 6\sigma + 1$, and σ is the standard deviation of the Gaussian filter used to smooth the image before calculating its second derivatives.

3.4 Performance Evaluation

Performance measures important in a feature point detector are *repeatability*, *positional accuracy*, and *speed*. Repeatability measures the ability of a method in detecting the same scene points in images taken under different lighting conditions and/or different camera vantage points of a scene. A highly repeatable method is one that detects the same scene points in different images of the scene.

Positional accuracy relates to the localization error of detected points. Measurement of accuracy requires knowledge about true positions of detected points. This is usually not available. If points detected in the images result in an accurate registration, detected points are considered accurate. Otherwise, at least some of the points are not accurately localized. To determine the accuracy of a feature point detector, a reference image is transformed with a known transformation to obtain a test image. Feature points are then detected

(a)   (b)

Figure 3.14 (a and b) Two images with the same geometry but different intensities. These images are of dimensions 380 × 380 pixels.

in the images. By knowing the true relation between homologous points in the images, the accuracy of each pair of homologous points detected by the method is determined.

Eight different point detectors were discussed in this chapter. To compare the performances of these methods under radiometric differences, the images shown in Fig. 3.14 are used. These images are registered within a pixel accuracy.

The parameters used to obtain the points by the methods described in the preceding sections were used to detect points in the images in Fig. 3.14. Since the images are registered within a pixel accuracy, homologous points are expected to have similar coordinates. Two points in the images falling within a distance of 5 pixels of each other are considered homologous points when calculating repeatability. Average distance between homologous points is then used to measure the positional error of the detected points. Finally, the time required by each method to find 50 points in both images is used to compare the speeds of the methods. The performance measures obtained for the eight methods when using the images in Fig. 3.14 are summarized in Table 3.1.

The reason for determining these performance measures using only the 50 strongest points rather than all points is that in a real application only a subset of the points is often used. Not knowing which points in two images correspond to each other, the larger the number of detected points, the larger will be the percentage of outliers. There is a higher likelihood for the stronger points in the images to correspond compared to the weaker ones. To avoid detection of very close points, once a point is detected, all weaker points within distance n pixels of it are removed, where information within $n \times n$ pixels is used to compute image properties from which the feature points are detected. When

Table 3.1 Performance measures of central moments, uniqueness, LoG, entropy, invariant moments, SIFT, Harris corners, and Hessian corners.

Method	REP	ERR	SEC	Method	REP	ERR	SEC
Central moments	0.42	1.35	2.28	Uniqueness	0.30	3.09	2.85
LoG extrema	0.32	2.48	7.10	Entropy	0.14	3.26	1.76
Invariant moments	0.30	1.24	4.07	SIFT	0.36	2.14	2.32
Harris corners	0.30	1.55	1.23	Hessian corners	0.32	2.54	4.18

REP denotes repeatability, which is the ratio of scene points detected in both images and the number of detected points (50 in this case), ERR denotes positional error and shows the average distance between homologous points in images after rigid registration, and SEC shows computation time in seconds for finding 50 points in each image on a Windows PC with a Core i7 processor.

letting $n = 15$, there will be no ambiguity in finding homologous points in the images if homologous points after registration are required to be within 5 pixels of each other.

Examining the results in Table 3.1, we see that highest repeatability is obtained by central moments followed by SIFT. Highest positional accuracy is obtained by invariant moments followed by central moments. Harris corner detector has the fastest speed followed by entropy.

Among the point detectors tested, central moments provide the overall best performance. It has the best repeatability, the second lowest positional error, and the third highest computational speed. The Harris corner detector follows next with a high repeatability, a low positional error, and the fastest computational speed.

The method based on entropy is the least repeatable for not using the adjacency relation between pixels in a window, losing geometric information within the neighborhood of a point. It uses probability density of intensities in a neighborhood that could easily change by a slight blurring or change in scene lighting.

It is interesting to note that although the SIFT detector has produced the second highest repeatability when using the images in Fig. 3.14, it produced no homologous points when using images (a) and (b) in Fig. 3.10. Because these images do not contain well-defined circular blobs, the obtained points represent centers of elongated and branching bright and dark regions that can break or change shape when rotating or scaling the image. Therefore, when the images have rotational and/or scaling differences and the images do not contain circular blobs, the SIFT detector should be avoided. On the other hand, if the images are of the same scale and orientation and/or the images contain round blobs, the SIFT detector can find abundant and accurately positioned points in the images.

Rarely two images of a scene do contain the same radiometry and geometry. Different levels of noise can be present in the images, the images may have been obtained at different distances to the scene and from different views, and lighting and other environmental factors could be different when capturing the images. Under these variations, a feature point detector is required to detect the same scene points in the images.

The methods discussed in this chapter (except for entropy) can detect 30–40% of the same points in the images in Fig. 3.14. From 50 points detected in each image, 15–20 homologous points are obtained, which are sufficient to at least globally register the images. Once the images are globally registered, attempts can be made to find more homologous points in the images and register the images more accurately.

Eight different feature point detectors were discussed. The detector based on central moments depends on the orientation and scale of an image, but because it uses intensity gradients rather than intensities, it is insensitive to global intensity changes. Methods based on LoG, entropy, and invariant moments do not depend on the orientation of an image, and LoG and invariant moments for using intensity derivatives are not sensitive to global radiometric changes.

The SIFT detector is designed to be independent of the scale and orientation of an image, and for using intensity derivatives approximated by the DoG operator, it is expected to be insensitive to global radiometric changes. Harris and Hessian detectors are rotation invariant by design, and for using intensity derivatives, they are insensitive to global radiometric changes.

The performance measures reported in Table 3.1 are for using the images in Fig. 3.14. Although the images have locally large radiometric difference, they have very similar geometries. If a feature point detector is to be used to register image with more complex geometric differences, the detector should be tested against such images.

If the images to be registered have local geometric differences, since the form of the transformation model to register the images is not known, homologous points in the images cannot be used to measure the localization accuracy of the points. In such a situation, simulation data created by a known transformation model should be used to measure the various performance measures.

Starting from a reference image, a test image can be created with an appropriate transformation model. Selecting feature points in the reference image, the locations of the homologous feature points can be estimated in the test image using the known transformation. The number of feature points detected in the test image that are within a threshold distance of the points predicted by the transformation model can then be used to determine the repeatability of the detector. The obtained homologous points can then be used to determine the accuracy of a detector, which can be considered the average distance between the detected homologous points in the test image and the homologous points predicted by the transformation model.

3.5   Further Reading

Feature points have been referred to as *control points, interest points, key points, anchor points, corner points, landmarks,* and *tie points* in the literature. The majority of point detectors can be categorized into corner detectors [8, 10, 12 15–27] and blob detectors [6, 7, 28–33]. Corner detectors use intensity derivatives in the square gradient matrix, and blob detectors use intensity derivatives computed by the LoG or its approximation DoG operator.

Many other point detectors have appeared in the literature. A number of detectors start with image edges and find unique points along edge contours based on different criteria [34–38]. These methods, similar to gradient-based methods, are not sensitive to changes in scene lighting and to changes in the orientation and scale of an image. Because the methods work with only image edges representing a fraction of pixels in an image, they are among computationally efficient point detectors. On the other extreme are methods that work with image intensities [39–44] and are sensitive to radiometric changes.

Points can represent geometric features other than corners and blobs. A number of methods create models of the geometric objects to be detected in an image and provide the means to search for the models through various matching and search techniques [45–56] or by pattern recognition methods [57–63]. Some methods detect neighborhoods of a desired property from responses to various oriented filters [64, 65]. Centroids of image regions have been used as points also [66]. Region centroids are not only invariant of an image's orientation, they are also invariant of the image's scale. Therefore, they are useful in registration of images with rotational and scaling differences.

Some point detectors are psychologically inspired and detect points representing centers of symmetric neighborhoods [67–74]. These methods are usually computationally intensive but can produce rotationally invariant and highly repeatable points in some images. Li et al. [75] detect points that are locally asymmetric to increase correspondence accuracy.

Although most images are in color, most point detectors work with gray-scale images. Measuring the color distinctiveness of a neighborhood by its information content, van de Weijer et al. [76] developed a method for detecting points in a color image by maximizing local color distinctiveness. Other point detectors that take advantage of color information in an image are described by Montesinos et al. [13] and Heidemann [77].

Point detection has been studied and evaluated extensively. Reviews, evaluations, and comparisons of the methods can be found in [78–88].

References

1 M. K. Hu, Visual pattern recognition by moment invariants, *IEEE Transactions on Information Theory,* **8**:179–187, 1962.

2 H. P. Moravec, Rover visual obstacle avoidance, in *Proceedings of International Joint Conference on Artificial Intelligence*, 785–790, 1981.

3 D. Marr and E. Hildreth, Theory of edge detection, *Proceedings of the Royal Society of London Series B*, **207**:187–217, 1980.

4 D. Blostein and N. Ahuja, A multiscale region detector, *Computer Vision, Graphics, and Image Processing*, **45**:22–41, 1989.

5 T. Kadir and J. M. Brady, Scale, saliency and image description, *International Journal of Computer Vision*, **45**(2):83–105, 2001.

6 D. Lowe, Distinctive image features from scale-invariant keypoints, *International Journal of Computer Vision*, **60**:91–110, 2004.

7 D. G. Lowe, Object recognition from local scale-invariant features, in *Proceedings of International Conference on Computer Vision*, **2**:1150–1157, 1999.

8 C. Harris and M. Stephens, A combined corner and edge detector, in *Proceedings of the 4th Alvey Vision Conference (AVC88)*, University Manchester, 147–151, 1988.

9 P. R. Beaudet, Rotationally invariant image operators, in *Proceedings of International Conference on Pattern Recognition*, 579–583, 1978.

10 W. Förstner, A feature based correspondence algorithm for image matching, in *International Archives of the Photogrammetry, Remote Sensing*, **26**:150–166, 1986.

11 W. Förstner and E. Gülch, A fast operator for detection and precise location of distinct points, corners and centers of circular features, in *Intercommission Conference on Fast Processing of Photogrammetric Data*, Interlaken, Switzerland, 281–305, 1987.

12 K. Rohr, Extraction of 3D anatomical point landmarks based on invariance principles, *Pattern Recognition*, **32**:3–15, 1999.

13 P. Montesinos, V. Gouet, and R. Deriche, Differential invariants for color images, in *Proceedings of the 14th International Conference on Pattern Recognition*, Vol. **1**, 838–840, 1998.

14 H. H. Nagel, Displacement vectors derived from second order intensity variations in image sequences, *Computer Vision, Graphics, and Image Processing*, **21**:85–117, 1983.

15 S. Ando, Image field categorization and edge/corner detection from gradient covariance, *IEEE Transactions on Pattern Analysis and Machine Intelligence*, **22**(2):179–190, 2000.

16 Y. Bastanlar and Y. Yardimci, Corner validation based on extracted corner properties, *Computer Vision and Image Processing*, **112**:243–261, 2008.

17 M. Brown, R. Szeliski, and S. Winder, Multi-image matching using multi-scale oriented patches, in *Proceedings of IEEE Conference on Computer Vision and Pattern Recognition*, Vol. **1**, 510–517. Also see Microsoft Research Technical Report MSR-TR-2004-133, 2005.

18 L. Calvet, P. Gurdjos, C. Griwodz, and S. Gasparini, Detection and accurate localization of circular fiducials under highly challenging conditions, in

Proceedings of IEEE Conference on Computer Vision and Pattern Recognition, 562–570, 2016.

19 G. Carneiro and A. D. Jepson, Phase-based local features, in *European Conference on Computer Vision*, Copenhagen, Denmark, 282–296, 2002.

20 M. Loog and F. Lauze, The improbability of Harris interest points, *IEEE Transactions on Pattern Analysis and Machine Intelligence*, **32**(6):1141–1147, 2010.

21 K. Mikolajczyk and C. Schmid, Indexing based on scale invariant interest points, in *Proceedings of International Conference on Computer Vision*, 525–531, 2001.

22 K. Mikolajczyk and C. Schmid, Scale and affine invariant interest point detectors, *International Journal of Computer Vision*, **60**(1):63–86, 2004.

23 J. A. Nobel, Finding corners, in *Proceedings of the 3rd Alvey Vision Conference*, Cambridge, England, 267–274, 1988.

24 K. Rohr, Localization properties of direct corner detectors, *Journal of Mathematical Imaging and Vision*, 4:139–150, 1994.

25 J. Shi and C. Tomasi, Good features to track, in *Proceedings of IEEE Conference on Computer Vision and Pattern Recognition*, Seattle, WA, pp. 593–600, 1994.

26 C. Tomasi and T. Kanade, Shape and Motion from Image Streams: A Factorization Method—Part 3, Technical Report CMU-CS-91-132, April 1991.

27 Z. Zheng, H. Wang, and E. K. Teoh, Analysis of gray level corner detection, *Pattern Recognition Letters*, **20**:149–162, 1999.

28 A. E. Abdel-Hakim and A. A. Farag, CSIFT: a SIFT descriptor with color invariant characteristics, *Proceedings of IEEE Conference on Computer Vision and Pattern Recognition*, **2**:1978–1983, 2006.

29 H. Bay, T. Tuetelaars, and L. van Gool, SURF: speeded up robust features, in *Proceedings of European Conference on Computer Vision*, also in *Computer Vision and Image Understanding*, **110**:346–359, 2006.

30 J. L. Crowley and A. C. Parker, A representation for shape based on peaks and ridges in the difference of low pass transform, *IEEE Transactions on Pattern Analysis and Machine Intelligence*, **6**(2):156–170, 1984.

31 T. Lindeberg, Feature detection with automatic scale selection, *International Journal of Computer Vision*, **30**(92):79–116, 1998.

32 A. Mukherjee, M. Velez-Reyes, and B. Roysam, Interest points for hyperspectral image data, *IEEE Transactions on Geoscience and Remote Sensing*, **47**(3):748–760, 2009.

33 H. Voorhees and T. Poggio, Detecting textons and texture boundaries in natural images, in *1st International Conference on Computer Vision*, 250–258, 1987.

34 D. J. Beymer, Finding junctions using the image gradient, in *Proceedings of IEEE Conference on Computer Vision and Pattern Recognition*, Maui, HI, 1991; also see MIT AI Lab Memo No. 1266, December 1991.

35 B. K. P. Horn, The Binford-Horn Line-finder, MIT Artificial Intelligence Laboratory AI Memo No. 285, July 1971, revised December 1973.

36 F. Mokhtarian and R. Suomela, Robust image corner detection through curvature scale space, *IEEE Transactions on Pattern Analysis and Machine Intelligence*, **20**(12):1376–1381, 1998.

37 P.-L. Shui and W.-C. Zhang, Corner detection and classification using anisotropic directional derivative representations, *IEEE Transactions on Image Processing*, **22**(8):3304–3218, 2013.

38 X. Xie, R. Sudhakar, and H. Zhuang, Corner detection by a cost minimization approach, *Pattern Recognition*, **26**:1235–1243, 1993.

39 S. C. Bae, S. Kweon, and C. D. Yoo, COP: a new corner detector, *Pattern Recognition Letters*, **23**:1349–1360, 2002.

40 I. Kweon and T. Kanade, Extracting topologic terrain features from elevation maps, *CVGIP: Image Understanding*, **59**(2):171–182, 1994.

41 E. Rosten and T. Drummond, Machine learning for high-speed corner detection, in *European Conference on Computer Vision*, 430–443, 2006.

42 E. Rosten, R. Porter, and T. Drummond, Faster and better: a machine learning approach to corner detection, *IEEE Transactions on Pattern Analysis and Machine Intelligence*, **32**(1):105–119, 2010.

43 S. M. Smith and J. M. Brady, SUSAN—a new approach to low level image processing, *International Journal of Computer Vision*, **23**(1):45–78, 1997.

44 T. Tuytelaars and L. Van Gool, Wide baseline stereo matching based on local, affinely invariant regions, *11th British Machine Vision Conference*, University of Bristol, UK, 412–425, 2000.

45 S. Baker, S. K. Nayar, and H. Murase, Parametric feature detection, *International Journal of Computer Vision*, **27**(1):27–50, 1998.

46 S. J. Cooper and L. Kitchen, Early jump-out corner detectors, *IEEE Transactions on Pattern Analysis and Machine Intelligence*, **15**(8):823–828, 1993.

47 E. R. Davies, Application of the generalized Hough transform to corner detection, *IEE Proceedings*, **135**(1):49–54, 1988.

48 X. Fan, H. Wang, Z. Luo, Y. Li, W. Hu, and D. Luo, Fiducial facial point extraction using a novel projective invariant, *IEEE Transactions on Image Processing*, **24**(3):1164–1177, 2015.

49 X. Li, T. Wu, and R. Madhavan, Correlation measure for corner detection, in *Proceedings of IEEE Conference on Computer Vision and Pattern Recognition*, 643–646, 1986.

50 G. Olague and B. Hernández, A new accurate and flexible model based multi-corner detector for measurement and recognition, *Pattern Recognition Letters*, **26**(1):27–41, 2005.

51 K. Paler, J. Föglein, J. Illingworth, and J. V. Kittler, Local ordered grey levels as an aid to corner detection, *Pattern Recognition*, **17**(5):535–543, 1984.

52 W. A. Perkins and T. O. Binford, A corner finder for visual feedback, Stanford Artificial Intelligence Laboratory, Memo AIM-214, Computer Science Department, Report No. CS-386, 1973.

53 K. Rohr, Modelling and identification of characteristic intensity variations, *Image and Vision Computing*, **10**:66–76, 1992.

54 K. Rohr, Recognizing corners by fitting parametric models, *International Journal of Computer Vision*, **9**(3):213–230, 1992.

55 A. Singh and M. Shneier, Grey level corner detection: a generalization and a robust real time implementation, *Computer Vision, Graphics, and Image Processing*, **51**(1):54–59, 1990.

56 E. Vincent and R. Laganière, Detecting and matching feature points, *Journal of Visual Communication & Image Representation*, **16**:38–54, 2005.

57 M. Banerjee, M. K. Kundu, and P. Mitra, Corner detection using support vector machines, in *Proceedings of International Conference on Pattern Recognition (ICPR)*, Vol. **2**, 819–822, 2004.

58 W.-C. Chen and P. Rockett, Bayesian labeling of corners using a grey-level corner image model, in *IEEE International Conference on Image Processing*, Vol. **1**, 687–690, 1997.

59 P. Dias, A. Kassim, and V. Srinivasan, A neural network based corner detection method, in *IEEE International Conference on Neural Networks*, Perth, Australia, Vol. **4**, 2116–2120, 1995.

60 Y.-S. Lee, H.-S. Koo, and C.-S. Jeong, A straight line detection using principal component analysis, *Pattern Recognition Letters*, **27**:1744–1754, 2006.

61 L. Trujillo, G. Olague, R. Hammoud, and B. Hernandez, Automatic feature localization in thermal images for facial expression recognition, in *2nd Joint IEEE International Workshop on Object Tracking and Classification in and Beyond the Visible Spectrum (OTCBVS)*, in conjunction with CVPR2005, Vol. **3**, 14–20, 2005.

62 L. Trujillo and G. Olague, Using evolution to learn how to perform interest point detection, *Int'l Conf. Pattern Recognition*, Hong Kong, China, 211–214, 2006.

63 L. Trujillo and G. Olague, Synthesis of interest point detectors through genetic programming, in *Genetic and Evolutionary Computation Conference*, Seattle, WA, 887–894, 2006.

64 M. Felsberg and G. Sommer, Image features based on a new approach to 2-D rotation invariant quadrature filters, in *Computer Vision –ECCV 2002, Lecture Notes in Computer Science*, A. Heyden, G. Sparr, M. Nielsen, and P. Johansen (Eds.), Springer, Vol. **2350**, 369–383, 2002.

65 L. Rosenthaler, F. Heitger, O. Kubler, and R. van Heydt, Detection of general edges and keypoints, in *Proceedings of European Conference on Computer Vision*, 78–86, 1992.

66 A. Goshtasby, G. Stockman, and C. Page, A region-based approach to digital image registration with subpixel accuracy, *IEEE Transactions on Geoscience and Remote Sensing*, **24**(3):390–399, 1986.

67 B. Johansson and G. Granlund, Fast selective detection of rotational symmetries using normalized inhibition, in *Proceedings of the 6th European Conference on Computer Vision*, Vol. **1**, 871–887, 2000.

68 P. Kovesi, Detection of interest points using symmetry, in *Proceedings of the 3rd International Conference on Computer Vision*, 62–65, 1990.

69 G. Loy and A. Zelinsky, A fast radial symmetry transform for detecting points of interest, in *7th European Conference on Computer Vision*, 358–368, 2002.

70 H.-H. Oh and S.-I. Chien, Exact corner location using attentional generalized symmetry transform, *Pattern Recognition Letters*, **23**(11):1361–1372, 2002.

71 D. Reisfeld, H. Wolfson, and Y. Yeshurun, Detection of interest points using symmetry, in *Proceedings of the 3rd International Conference on Computer Vision*, Osaka, Japan, 62–65, 1990.

72 D. Reisfeld, H. Wolfson, and Y. Yeshurun, Context-free attention operators: the generalized symmetry transform, *International Journal of Computer Vision*, **14**(2):119–130, 1995.

73 G. Sela and M. D. Levine, Real-time attention for robotic vision, *Real-Time Imaging*, **3**:173–194, 1997.

74 B. Takács and H. Wechsler, A dynamic and multiresolution model of visual attention and its application to facial landmark detection, *Computer Vision and Image Understanding*, **70**(1):63–73, 1998.

75 Q. Li, J. Ye, and C. Kambhamettu, Interest point detection using imbalance oriented selection, *Pattern Recognition*, **41**:672–688, 2008.

76 J. van de Weijer, T. Gevers, and A. D. Bagdanov, Boosting color saliency in image feature detection, *IEEE Transactions on Pattern Analysis and Machine Intelligence*, **28**(1):150–156, 2006.

77 G. Heidemann, Focus-of-attention from local color symmetries, *IEEE Transactions on Pattern Analysis and Machine Intelligence*, **26**(7):817–847, 2004.

78 F. Fraundorfer and H. Bischof, Evaluation of local detectors on nonplanar scenes, in *Proceedings of the 28th Workshop of the Austrian Association for Pattern Recognition*, 125–132, 2004.

79 S. Gauglitz, T. Höllerer, and M. Turk, Evaluation of interest point detectors and feature descriptors for visual tracking, *International Journal of Computer Vision*, **94**:335–360, 2011.

80 A. Goshtasby, *Image Registration: Principles, Tools, and Methods*, Springer, 2012.

81 A. Heyden and K. Rohr, Evaluation of corner extraction schemes using invariance methods, in *Proceedings of the 13th International Conference on Pattern Recognition (ICPR '96)*, Vienna, Austria, Vol. **1**, 895–899, 1996.

82 F. Mokhrarian and F. Mohanna, Performance evaluation of corner detectors using consistency and accuracy measures, *Computer Vision and Image Understanding*, **102**:81–94, 2006.

83 P. Moreels and P. Perona, Evaluation of features detectors and descriptors based on 3D objects, in *Proceedings of International Conference on Computer Vision*, Vol. **1**, 800–807, 2005.

84 P. K. Rajan and J. M. Davidson, Evaluation of corner detection algorithms, in *IEEE Proceedings of the 21st Southeastern Symposium on System Theory*, pp. 29–33, 1989.

85 C. Schmid and R. Mohr, Local gray-value invariants for image retrieval, *IEEE Transactions on Pattern Analysis and Machine Intelligence*, **19**(5):530–535, 1997.

86 C. Schmid, R. Mohr, and C. Bauckhage, Comparing and evaluating interest points, in *International Conference on Computer Vision*, 230–235, 1998.

87 C. Schmid, R. Mohr, and C. Bauckhage, Evaluation of interest point detectors, *International Journal of Computer Vision*, **37**(2):151–172, 2000.

88 T. Tuytelaars and K. Mikolajczyk, Local invariant feature detectors: a survey, *Foundations and Trends in Computer Graphics and Vision*, **3**(3):177–280, 2007.

4

Feature Line Detection

Similar to feature points, feature lines are geometric features that are resistant to radiometric changes and are useful in image registration. A line is defined by its orientation and its distance to the origin. A line in an image has endpoints; therefore, it is more precisely a line segment. Although the position and orientation of a line can be determined with a relatively high accuracy, the endpoints of a line displace due to noise and imaging view angle and so do not represent reliable features for image registration.

In addition to image registration, which is our main focus, lines can be used to detect vanishing points in an image [1, 2], calibrate multicamera systems [3], compress image data [4], navigate autonomous robots [5], establish correspondence between images of a scene [6–8], and recover the 3-D geometry of a scene from homologous lines in multiview images [9].

Literature on line detection is rich, starting with a method described by Hough in a US patent in 1962 [10]. To detect lines among a set of points in an image, Hough observed that if the image plane is treated like the xy-plane, point (x, y) on line $y = mx + b$ maps to a line in the mb parameter space, and all points on line $y = mx + b$ map to lines in the mb space that pass through point (m, b). By representing the mb space by an accumulator array, counting the number of lines that pass though each entry of the array, and identifying locally peak entries, the parameters of lines in the image are determined.

The line detection method of Hough works well when the lines have small slopes. For nearly vertical lines, since the slopes of the lines become very large, a very large accumulator is required to find the lines, which may not be possible to allocate.

To avoid use of very large accumulator arrays in the method of Hough, the points are processed twice: once using them as they are to find lines with slopes between -1 and 1, and another time using them after switching the x and y coordinates of the points. If a line with slope m' and y-intercept b' is obtained after switching the x and y coordinates of the points, the slope m and the y-intercept b of the line with the original x and y coordinates will be $m = 1/m'$ and $b = -b'/m'$.

Theory and Applications of Image Registration, First Edition. Arthur Ardeshir Goshtasby.
© 2017 John Wiley & Sons, Inc. Published 2017 by John Wiley & Sons, Inc.

Duda and Hart [11] suggested using the polar equation of lines instead of the slope and y-intercept equation of lines when finding lines among points. The polar equation of a line is $\rho = x \cos \theta + y \sin \theta$. A point in the xy space corresponds to a sinusoid in the $\rho\theta$ parameter space and all points on line $\rho = x \cos \theta + y \sin \theta$ produce sinusoids that pass through point (ρ, θ) in the parameter space. By representing the $\rho\theta$ parameter space by an accumulator array, drawing a sinusoid in the $\rho\theta$ space for each edge point in the xy space, and counting the number of sinusoids that pass through each array entry, locations of the peak counts in the array are then used to determine the parameters of the lines in the xy space.

By representing the mb or $\rho\theta$ parameter space by an accumulator array, drawing a line in the mb space or a sinusoid in the $\rho\theta$ space for each point in the xy space, counting the number of lines or sinusoids that pass through each array entry, and finding locally peak entries, the parameters of lines in the xy space are estimated. Methods that find lines in an image in this manner are known as Hough transform–based methods.

Hough transform–based methods do not use the connectivity between the points to find the lines; they only use the coordinates of the points. There are methods that use the connectivity between the points to find the lines. These methods start with an edge image and by tracing each edge contour find straight segments, and approximate each segment by a line or line segment. The origin of these methods can be traced back to the work of Bellman [12], approximating a continuous curve by a polygon in least-squares fashion. Pavlidis and Horowitz [13] adapted Bellman's method to the digital domain, approximating each edge contour by a sequence of lines in such a way that the maximum distance between the contour and the approximating lines stayed below a required a distance tolerance.

A number of methods subdivide an image into regions with different gradient directions and find a line within each region. The origin of these methods can be traced back to the work of Roberts [14], reducing an image into a collection of line segments from which a polyhedral scene could be interpreted.

In the following sections, details of well-known line detection methods in the literature are provided. The characteristics of the methods are examined and their performances are compared quantitatively and qualitatively. To measure the performances quantitatively, synthetic images containing known lines are used, and to evaluate the performances qualitatively, various natural images of man-made scenes are used.

The synthetic images used in the experiments are shown in Fig. 4.1. Figure 4.1a shows an image of dimensions 821×821 pixels. All straight edges in this image pass through the image center: $(410, 410)$. Lines with various orientations are included in the image to determine the ability of a line detector to find different line orientations. Intensities are assigned to pixels in the image in such a way that lines with different gradient magnitudes are obtained. Some

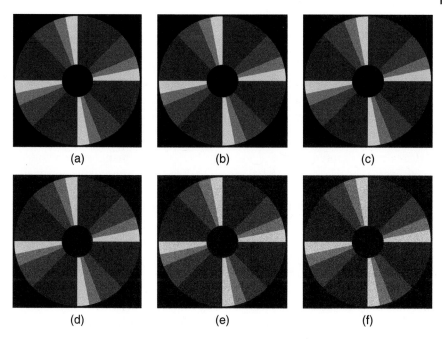

Figure 4.1 (a) A synthetically generated image with known straight edges. (b)–(f) Same as (a) but with added uniformly distributed zero-mean noise of amplitudes 5, 10, 20, 30, and 40, respectively. These images are of dimensions 821 × 821 pixels.

methods use gradient directions and gradient magnitudes at the points to find the lines.

Points in an image can be represented by

$$x = r \cos \alpha + x_c, \tag{4.1}$$

$$y = r \sin \alpha + y_c, \tag{4.2}$$

where (x_c, y_c) are the coordinates of the image center, which is considered the coordinate system origin, and r is the distance of point (x, y) to the origin determined from

$$r = \sqrt{(x - x_c)^2 + (y - y_c)^2}. \tag{4.3}$$

The angle of the line connecting pixel (x, y) to the image center (x_c, y_c) with the x-axis is computed from

$$\alpha(x, y) = \arctan\left(\frac{y - y_c}{x - x_c}\right). \tag{4.4}$$

Intensity I is assigned to pixel (x, y) in the image in Fig. 4.1a by calculating α at the pixel using Eq. (4.4) and looking up the corresponding intensity in the following table:

$\alpha(x, y)$	$I(x, y)$	$\alpha(x, y)$	$I(x, y)$	
if $0 \le \alpha < \pi/16$	200	if $\pi/2 \le \alpha < 9\pi/16$	200	
if $\pi/16 \le \alpha < \pi/8$	100	if $9\pi/16 \le \alpha < 5\pi/8$	100	(4.5)
if $\pi/8 \le \alpha < \pi/4$	50	if $5\pi/8 \le \alpha < 3\pi/4$	50	
if $\pi/4 \le \alpha < \pi/2$	25	if $3\pi/4 \le \alpha < \pi$	25	

When $\pi \le \alpha < 2\pi$, intensities are assigned to pixels by letting $\alpha = \alpha - \pi$. After calculating intensities of pixels in the image in this manner, intensities of pixels inside the disc of radius 100 are set to 0 and intensities of pixels outside the disc of radius 400 are also set to 0 to obtain the image shown in Fig. 4.1a. This image, therefore, contains straight edges of length 300 pixels, all passing through the image center at angles

$$0, \pi/16, \pi/8, \pi/4, \pi/2, 9\pi/16, 5\pi/8, 3\pi/4, \pi,$$
$$17\pi/16, 9\pi/8, 5\pi/4, 3\pi/2, 25\pi/16, 13\pi/8, 7\pi/4. \tag{4.6}$$

Not only are lines with different gradient directions created, lines with different gradient magnitudes are also created.

Uniformly distributed zero-mean noise of amplitudes 5, 10, 20, 30, and 40 are generated and added to image (a) to obtain images (b)–(f) in Fig. 4.1, respectively. More specifically, to obtain image (b), random numbers between −5 and 5 are generated and added to the intensities of pixels in (a). If by this addition, an intensity becomes less than 0, it is set to 0, and if it becomes greater than 255, it is set to 255. Similarly, images (c)–(f) are created.

Some methods only use the edge locations to find the lines. To produce data for such methods, the Canny edges [15] of the images in Fig. 4.1 are determined using a Gaussian smoother of standard deviation 2 pixels. Very weak edges are then removed to obtain the edge images shown in Fig. 4.2.

The measures used to evaluate the performances of various line detectors are true positive rate (TPR), false positive rate (FPR), average directional error (ADE), average positional error (APE), average line length (ALL), and computation time (TME). There are 16 line segments in the images in Fig. 4.1 or 4.2. If a line detector finds n lines, of which m are correct, the remaining $n - m$ lines will be false. Therefore, TPR $= m/16$ and FPR $= (n- m)/n$. A line is considered correctly detected if it passes within 5 pixels of the image center and its orientation is within 5° of the directions shown in (4.6).

From among the correctly detected lines, the average distance to the image center is taken as APE. Also, the average absolute difference between angles of detected lines and their true angles is used as ADE. Average length of correctly detected lines is denoted by ALL. Finally, the time in seconds (TME) an algorithm takes to find lines in an image on a Windows PC with a CORE i7 processor is used to measure the speed of the method.

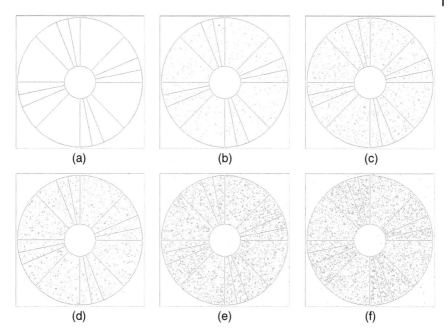

Figure 4.2 (a)–(f) Canny edges of images (a)–(f) in Fig. 4.1 when using a Gaussian smoother of standard deviation 2 pixels and removing the weaker edges.

4.1 Hough Transform Using Polar Equation of Lines

Given a set of points:

$$\mathbf{P} = \{\mathbf{p}_i : i = 1, \dots, N\}, \tag{4.7}$$

where $\mathbf{p}_i = (x_i, y_i)$, we would like to find the lines hidden among the points.

Treating the image space as the Cartesian coordinate system with the origin at the image center, the polar equation of a line in the image space can be written as

$$\rho = x \cos \theta + y \sin \theta. \tag{4.8}$$

Parameter ρ shows the distance of the line to the origin, and parameter θ shows the angle between the normal to the line and the x-axis.

Steps involved in line detection by the Hough transform using the polar equation of lines are as follows. A represents an accumulator array, D is the diameter of the image, $R = D/2$, n represents the number of points that are within a small distance tolerance dr of the line with parameters (ρ, θ), $n_{\min}$ is the minimum number of points required on a detected line, and $d\rho$ and $d\theta$ represent distances between adjacent entries in the accumulator array in ρ and θ directions, respectively. Parameters ρ, $d\rho$, dr, and R are in pixels and parameters θ and $d\theta$ are in degrees. Parameter θ varies between $0°$ and $180°$. No distinction is made between lines with directions θ and $\theta + \pi$ as no information about intensity gradient directions at the points is used.

Algorithm 4.1   Line detection by the Hough transform using the polar equation of lines

---

1. Initialize entries of array $A[R/d\rho, 180/d\theta]$ to 0.
2. For $\rho = 0$ to $R - 1$ by $d\rho$ and $\theta = 0$ to $180 - 1$ by $d\theta$:
   - 2.1. Let $n = 0$.
   - 2.2. For $k = 0, \ldots, N - 1$;
     - 2.2.1. Calculate $d = (x_k - x_c) \cos\theta + (y_k - y_c) \sin\theta - \rho$.
     - 2.2.2. If $|d| \le dr$, increment n by 1.
   - 2.3. Save n in $A[\rho/d\rho, \theta/d\theta]$.
3. Find local peaks in array A that are greater than or equal to n_{min}. If (ρ_i, θ_i) are the indices of a peak, the parameters of the line forming it are $(\rho_i d\rho, \theta_i d\theta)$ and the count at the peak shows the number of points in the xy space that belong to the line. To determine the points that have contributed to peak (ρ_i, θ_i), for $k = 0, \ldots, N - 1$ calculate distance $d_k = (x_k - x_c) \cos(\theta_i d\theta) + (y_k - y_c) \sin(\theta_i d\theta) - \rho_i d\rho$ and if $|d_k| \le dr$ add (x_k, y_k) to the list of points belonging to the line.

To find possible line segments within a detected line, identify connected segments that contain n_{min} or more points and fit a line to points within each segment by the least-squares method.

Note that Algorithm 4.1 does not use gradient directions at the points. It only uses the coordinates of the points to find the lines. As a result, the detected lines will not be directed. We will later add directions to the detected lines by examining the intensity gradient direction at the center of each line segment.

Rather than drawing a sinusoid in the accumulator array for each point in the xy space, for each accumulator array entry, the number of points that produce sinusoids passing through the entry is found. An accumulator array is selected small enough to produce clear peaks but large enough not to merge peaks belonging to nearby parallel lines.

The location of a peak within the accumulator array can be determined more accurately by fitting biquadratic function

$$F(\rho, \theta) = a\theta^2 + b\rho^2 + c\theta\rho + d\theta + e\rho + f \tag{4.9}$$

to the ρ and θ values corresponding to the indices of the 3×3 entries centered at the peak together with values at the entries, and finding parameters $a - f$ of the function by the least-squares method. Knowing the coefficients of function F, the location of the analytic peak can be determined by finding the partial derivatives of F with respect to ρ and θ, setting them to 0, and solving the two equations for ρ and θ. Doing so, we find that the analytic peak is at

$$\theta = \frac{2bd - ce}{c^2 - 4ab},$$ (4.10)

$$\rho = -\frac{2a\theta + d}{c}.$$ (4.11)

The number and the quality of lines detected in an image by Algorithm 4.1 depend on four parameters: $d\rho$, $d\theta$, dr, and n_{min}. As $d\rho$, $d\theta$, and dr are increased, the method becomes more tolerant of digital noise, but that may merge lines with similar ρ and/or θ parameters. As these parameters are decreased, the lines become more distinct, but the process can become sensitive to digital noise and miss some lines by breaking them into smaller segments. Parameter n_{min} represents the lower limit on the value at a peak to declare a line there. Note that a detected line may contain many line segments with possibly some isolated points that accidentally fall on the path of the line.

Figure 4.3a–f shows the lines detected using the edge images in Fig. 4.2 by Algorithm 4.1 when letting $n_{min} = 50$ pixels, $dr = 2$ pixels, $d\rho = 2$ pixels, and $d\theta = 2°$, respectively. The detected lines are overlaid with the original edge images of Fig. 4.2 to enable visual evaluation of the detected lines. Note that only the edge points in Fig. 4.2 are used to detect the lines. Correctly detected lines are shown in green, while incorrectly detected lines are shown in red.

The performance measures of Algorithm 4.1 when using the images in Fig. 4.2 are summarized in Table 4.1. Measures TPR, ADE, and APE remain about the same under increasing noise amplitude because the edges representing the lines are among the provided edges; however, measures FPR and TME increase with increasing noise level due to the increase in the number of

Table 4.1 Performance measures of line detection by Algorithm 4.1 when using the edge images of Fig. 4.2 and letting $n_{min} = 50$ pixels, $d\rho = 2$ pixels, $dr = 2$ pixels, and $d\theta = 2°$.

Figure 4.3	TME	TPR	FPR	ADE	APE	ALL
(a)	0.51	0.69	0.00	0.94	0.95	292
(b)	0.68	0.69	0.08	0.70	0.95	279
(c)	0.94	0.63	0.17	0.75	0.92	284
(d)	1.05	0.63	0.23	0.90	1.04	268
(e)	1.82	0.50	0.56	1.05	0.95	247
(f)	2.08	0.75	0.57	1.02	1.03	172

TME, computation time in seconds; TPR, true positive rate; FPR, false positive rate; ADE, average directional error; APE, average positional error; and ALL, average line length.

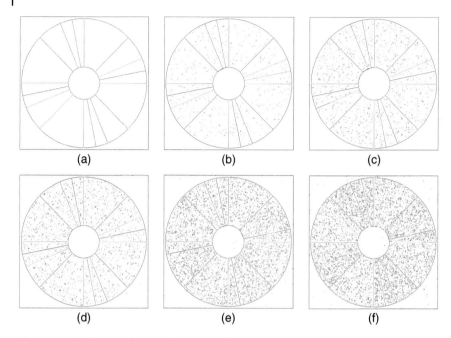

Figure 4.3 (a)–(f) Lines detected in Fig. 4.2a–f, respectively, by Algorithm 4.1 when letting $n_{min} = 50$ pixels, $dr = 2$ pixels, $d\rho = 2$ pixels, and $d\theta = 2°$. Correctly detected lines are shown in green, while incorrectly detected lines are shown in red.

points to be processed. Finally, as noise level is increased, ALL decreases due to fragmentation of the edge contours.

The computational complexity of Algorithm 4.1 is on the order of MN, where $M = (R/d\rho)(360/d\theta)$ is the number of entries in the accumulator array and N is the number of edge pixels from which the lines are detected. Increasing $d\rho$ and $d\theta$ will decrease TME, but that can merge some lines together. Decreasing $d\rho$ and $d\theta$ will detect more distinct lines; however, decreasing these parameters too much may detect multiple lines for each true line in the image due to digital noise that displaces points from their true positions along edge contours.

4.2 Hough Transform Using Slope and *y*-Intercept Equation of Lines

The slope and *y*-intercept equation of a line is

$$y = mx + b. \tag{4.12}$$

Parameter m shows the slope and parameter b shows the *y*-intercept. A point (x, y) in the image space maps to a line in the mb parameter space, and all points on the line with parameters m and b produce lines in the mb space that pass through point (m, b). To detect lines in the xy image space, the parameter space is represented by an accumulator array with all entries initially set to 0. Then, for each point in the xy space, a line is drawn in the mb space, incrementing array entries that fall on the line by 1. After processing all points in the xy space, indices of locally peak entries in the accumulator array are used to estimate the parameters of lines in the xy space.

Given the set of points in (4.7), the following algorithm finds the slope m and y-intercept b of each line present among the points. A is the accumulator array counting the number of lines that pass through each entry (m, b) in the discrete parameter space, parameter n_{min} is the minimum number of points required on a detected line, D is the diameter of the image, $R = D/2$, dm and db are distances between adjacent accumulator entries in m and b directions, respectively, and n counts the number of lines that go through an array entry. dr is the maximum distance allowed between a point and a line to consider the point a part of the line. The distance of point (x, y) to the line with parameters (m, b) is computed from

$$d = \frac{|y - mx - b|}{\sqrt{1 + m^2}}. \tag{4.13}$$

Algorithm 4.2 Line detection using the slope and y-intercept equation of lines

---

This algorithm detects lines with slopes between -1 and 1.

1. Initialize entries of array $A[180/dm + 1, D/db + 1]$ to 0.
2. For $M = -90$ to 90 by dm and $b = -R$ to R by db:
   2.1. Let $n = 0$.
   2.2. For $k = 0, \ldots, N - 1$;
       2.2.1. Calculate $d = |y_k - (M/90)x_k - b|/\sqrt{1 + (M/90)^2}$.
       2.2.2. If $d \le dr$, increment n by 1.
   2.3. Save n in $A[(M + 90)/dm, (b + R)/db]$.
3. Find peaks in A with counts greater than or equal to n_{min}. A peak at $(M_i/dm, b_i/db)$ determines line $y = m_i x + b_i$, where $m_i = \frac{M_i}{90}$, and the count at the peak shows the number of points belonging to the line.
4. To identify points that belong to line with parameters (m_i, b_i), for $k = 0, \ldots, N - 1$, find $d_k = |y_k - (M_i/90)x_k - b_i|/\sqrt{1 + (M_i/90)^2}$ and if $d_k \le dr$ add (x_k, y_k) to the list of points belonging to the line.

To identify possible line segments within a detected line, find connected segments containing n_{min} or more points and fit a line to the points by the least-squares method.

To detect lines in an image with slopes less than -1 or greater than 1, switch the x and y coordinates of the points before passing them to Algorithm 4.2. For each obtained slope m'_i and y-intercept b'_i, calculate $m_i = 1/m'_i$ and $b_i = b'_i/m'_i$. Note that when $m'_i = 0$, the equation of the line will be $x = b'_i$.

Once parameters m and b of a line are found from a peak in the accumulator array, the parameters can be determined more accurately by fitting biquadratic function

$$f(m, b) = Am^2 + Bb^2 + Cmb + Dm + Eb + F \qquad (4.14)$$

to the m and b values corresponding to the indices of the 3×3 entries centered at the peak together with their values by the least-squares method. After finding parameters A through F of function f, the analytic location of the peak is determined by finding the partial derivatives of f with respect to m and b, setting them to 0, and solving for m and b. Doing so, we find

$$m = \frac{2BD - CE}{C^2 - 4AB},$$
$$b = -\frac{2Am + D}{C}. \qquad (4.15)$$

If the lines are obtained after switching the x and y coordinates of the points, in the aforementioned equations, obtained m will actually be m' and obtained b will actually be b'. Once the analytic location of a peak in the $m'b'$ space is found, the analytic location of the peak in the mb space can be computed from $m_i = 1/m'_i$ and $b_i = b'_i/m'_i$, again noticing that if $m'_i = 0$, the equation of the line representing the peak will be $x = b'_i$.

The lines detected in the edge images in Fig. 4.2 by Algorithm 4.2 when letting $dm = 2$, $db = 2$, $dr = 2$ pixels, and $n_{\min} = 50$ pixels are shown in Fig. 4.4. The performance measures of Algorithm 4.2 in this example are summarized in Table 4.2. The results are better than those for Algorithm 4.1 but at about four times the TME. The increased TMEs are for calling Algorithm 4.2 twice, once to detect lines with slopes between -1 and 1 and another time for finding lines with slopes less than -1 or greater than 1. Increased TMEs are also for using a somewhat larger accumulator array.

Algorithm 4.2 finds more lines, increasing both TPR and FPR rates compared to Algorithm 4.1. Increased TPR is desirable, but increased FPR is not. Although the positional accuracies (APE) of Algorithm 4.2 are about the same as those for Algorithm 4.1, the ADEs of Algorithm 4.2 are lower than those for Algorithm 4.1.

The computational complexity of Algorithm 4.2 is on the order of MN, where $M = (180/dm)(D/db)$ is the size of the accumulator array and N is the number of points from which the lines are detected. TME linearly increases with increase in M and N.

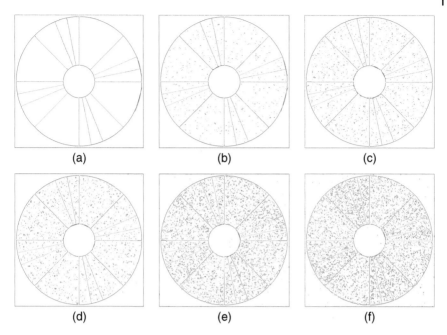

Figure 4.4 (a)–(f) Lines detected in the edge images in Fig. 4.2 by Algorithm 4.2 when letting $n_{min} = 50$, $dm = 2$, $db = 2$ pixels, and $dr = 2$ pixels. Correctly detected lines are shown in green, while incorrectly detected lines are shown in red.

Table 4.2 Performance measures of Algorithm 4.2 when detecting the lines in Fig. 4.4.

Figure 4.4	TME	TPR	FPR	ADE	APE	ALL
(a)	2.40	1.00	0.20	0.46	0.85	291
(b)	3.17	1.00	0.20	0.56	0.91	215
(c)	4.13	1.00	0.33	0.55	1.05	209
(d)	4.71	0.81	0.46	0.58	0.97	229
(e)	8.13	0.69	0.59	0.58	0.91	237
(f)	9.20	0.75	0.68	0.50	1.04	175

TME, computation time in seconds; TPR, true positive rate; FPR, false positive rate; ADE, average directional error; APE, average positional error; and ALL, average line length.

Although line detection methods in the literature have used either the polar or the slope and y-intercept equation of lines, lines can be represented in parametric form also. Next, a method that uses the parametric equation of lines to find lines among a set of points is described.

4.3 Line Detection Using Parametric Equation of Lines

Given a line segment with endpoints (x_1, y_1) and (x_2, y_2), any point on the line satisfies

$$x = (x_2 - x_1)t + x_1, \qquad (4.16)$$

$$y = (y_2 - y_1)t + y_1. \qquad (4.17)$$

Parameter t is shared by the x and y components of the line.

By taking two points randomly from among the given points and hypothesizing a line through them, the correctness of the hypothesis can be verified by finding the number of other points that also fall on the line. A point (x, y) is considered to be on the line passing through points (x_1, y_1) and (x_2, y_2) if

$$\left| \frac{x - x_1}{x_2 - x_1} - \frac{y - y_1}{y_2 - y_1} \right| \leq \Delta t. \qquad (4.18)$$

Δt is a small error tolerance measured in terms of the parameter of the line, which can be made a function of the distance between points (x_1, y_1) and (x_2, y_2):

$$\Delta t = \frac{d}{\sqrt{(x_2 - x_1)^2 + (y_2 - y_1)^2}}. \qquad (4.19)$$

d is a small distance such as 1 or 2 pixels. Shorter lines are influenced by the digital inaccuracy of its endpoints more than longer lines; therefore, a larger tolerance is used for a shorter line segment. After randomly selecting points (x_1, y_1) and (x_2, y_2), other points falling on the line are identified and removed from the set and the process is repeated until the set becomes empty or lines of a desired length no longer exist among the points remaining in the set.

In the following algorithm, N is the number of points in point set $\mathbf{P}$, n_{min} is the minimum number of points on a detected line, and Δt (computed from Eq. (4.19)) is the maximum allowed difference between parameter t calculated

---

Algorithm 4.3   Line detection using the parametric equation of lines

---

1. If $N < n_{min}$, stop. Otherwise, empty list $\mathbf{L}$ and let $n = 0$.
2. Move two distinct points randomly selected from point set $\mathbf{P}$ to list $\mathbf{L}$, decrement N by 2, let $n = 2$, and denote the points by (x_1, y_1) and (x_2, y_2).
3. For $k = 0, \ldots, N - 1$:
   3.1. Let $x = x_k$ and $y = y_k$ and calculate t from (4.16) and (4.17) and denote them by t_x and t_y, respectively. Then, if $|t_x - t_y| \leq \Delta t$, move (x_k, y_k) to $\mathbf{L}$, increment n by 1, and decrement N by 1.
4. If $n < n_{min}$, return points in $\mathbf{L}$ back to $\mathbf{P}$, increment N by n, let $n = 0$, and go to Step 2. Otherwise, declare the points in $\mathbf{L}$ a line and go to Step 1.

---

by the x-component Eq. (4.16) and the y-component Eq. (4.17) of points on a detected line. $\mathbf{L}$ is a list containing the points belonging to a line, and n is the number of points in $\mathbf{L}$.

In Step 4, when a line is declared, points in list $\mathbf{L}$ are ordered according to their t parameters. Assuming points with the smallest and largest parameters are (x_i, y_i) and (x_j, y_j), the points are reparametrized by letting the parameter at (x_i, y_i) be 0 and the parameter at (x_j, y_j) be 1. Then, the points are reordered in the list according to their parameter values. This makes it possible to identify various line segments on a detected line. If the parametric distance between adjacent points in the ordered list is greater than a small tolerance δt, a gap is detected between the points and the two points are considered the endpoints of different line segments.

To find δt, since we do not know which points on a line are connected and which ones are not, we scan the line from $t = 0$ to $t = 1$ and find the shortest parametric distance between two points: t_0. Then, $\delta t = w t_0$, where w is the largest gap in pixels allowed between points within a line segment. Parameter δt will be the largest gap in parameters of adjacent points on a line segment. This mechanism allows small gaps to appear within a detected line segment.

The lines detected in the edge images in Fig. 4.2 when letting $n_{\min} = 50$ pixels and $d = 1$ pixel in Eq. (4.19) are shown in Fig. 4.5. To partition a detected line into line segments, parameter $w = 5$ was used.

When a pair of randomly selected points fall near each other, the accuracy of the line they represent may not be high. Therefore, if the randomly selected points are closer than $n_{\min}/2$, new random points are selected. Also, when randomly selected points are apart by more than one-fourth the diameter of the image, point selection is repeated because the probability that the randomly selected points belong to the same line decreases quadratically with increased distance between the points.

The performance measures corresponding to the results shown in Fig. 4.5 are summarized in Table 4.3. The method has been able to find all lines in the noise-free and low-noise images in Fig. 4.2. The lines detected by Algorithm 4.3 are generally longer than those obtained by Algorithms 4.1 and 4.2.

Finally, it should be mentioned that after removing the longer lines from the set of points, points remaining in the set may not contain lines of a desired length and the process may continue indefinitely without detecting a line. To avoid such a situation, in Step 4 of the algorithm, the number of iterations that the algorithm has gone through without finding a line is checked, and whenever the maximum allowed number of iterations is reached without finding a line, the algorithm is stopped. The computation times reported in Table 4.3 are for stopping the algorithm when no lines are detected within 1000 iterations.

The computational complexity of the method is a quadratic function of the number of lines. Assuming all points belong to some lines, all lines are of the same length, and there are l lines among the points, when the first random

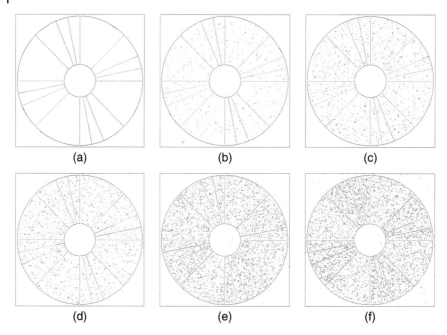

Figure 4.5 Lines detected in the edge images in Fig. 4.2 by Algorithm 4.3 when letting $n_{min} = 50$ pixels and $d = 1$ pixel.

Table 4.3 Performance measures of Algorithm 4.3 when detecting lines in the images in Fig. 4.2 using $n_{min} = 50$ pixels and $d = 1$ pixel.

Figure 4.5	TME	TPR	FPR	ADE	APE	ALL
(a)	0.03	1.00	0.33	0.08	0.96	275
(b)	0.11	1.00	0.26	0.04	0.95	281
(c)	0.23	1.00	0.00	0.08	0.99	279
(d)	0.34	0.94	0.00	0.06	1.02	219
(e)	1.41	0.75	0.00	0.07	1.0	271
(f)	1.60	0.37	0.00	0.06	1.02	257

TME, computation time in seconds; TPR, true positive rate; FPR, false positive rate; ADE, average directional error; APE, average positional error; and ALL, average line length.

point is selected that belongs to a line, the likelihood that the second random point will belong to the same line is $1/l$. Therefore, on average, l iterations will be needed to find two points that belong to the same line. If l lines are present among the points, the computational complexity of Algorithm 4.3 will be proportional to l^2. If overall N points are given, once a pair of points is selected, there is a need to process all the points to find those that fall on the line with a required error tolerance. Therefore, the computational complexity of Algorithm 4.3 is on the order of Nl^2.

4.4 Line Detection by Clustering

Clustering-based methods use gradient directions and/or gradient magnitudes at the points in addition to the coordinates of the points to detect lines. In a method described by Dudani and Luk [16], the histogram of gradient directions is determined, and the histogram is partitioned at the valley between the modes to group the points into subsets, each containing points with approximately the same gradient direction.

A 1-D accumulator array is then used to subdivide points within each subset into smaller subsets, each containing points that belong to lines of approximately the same distance to the origin. Using the (x, y) coordinates of a point and its gradient direction θ, $\rho = (x - x_c) \cos \theta + (y - y_c) \sin \theta + R$ is calculated, where (x_c, y_c) are the coordinates of the image center, also used as the coordinate system origin, and R is half the diameter of the image. The ρ calculated for each point is quantized to obtain a digital number, showing an entry of the 1-D accumulator array, which is incremented by 1.

After processing points of approximately the same gradient direction θ, the contents of the accumulator array, which is treated like a histogram, is partitioned at the valley between the peaks and a line is fitted to points within each histogram mode by the least-squares method. Inui et al. [17] suggested using least median of squares [18] instead of least squares to reduce the effect of outliers in line fitting.

Kyrki and Kälviäinen [19] performed clustering in the Hough space. A 2-D accumulator array is used to represent the $\rho\theta$ parameter space. The entries of the array are initially set to 0. Then, the gradient direction θ and the coordinates (x, y) of a point are used to calculate the distance ρ of the line passing through (x, y) and making angle $\pi/2 + \theta$ with the x-axis. Entry (ρ, θ) of the array is then incremented by the gradient magnitude of point (x, y). After processing all points, peaks in the array are used to determine the parameters of the lines.

An algorithm based on the method of Kyrki and Kälviäinen [19] is described as follows. In addition to the coordinates of points, gradient directions and gradient magnitudes at the points are used. Denoting the coordinates of the kth point by (x_k, y_k) and the gradient magnitude and gradient direction at the point by g_k and θ_k, this algorithm finds the polar equations of the lines. Parameter θ varies in the range $[0, 359]$ degrees. A represents the accumulator array quantizing the $\rho\theta$ parameter space, $R = D/2$, and D is the diameter of the image. $d\rho$ and $d\theta$ show distances between adjacent array entries in ρ and θ directions, and $n_{\min}$ is the minimum number of points required on a detected line.

Algorithm 4.4   Line detection by clustering

---

1. Initialize entries of array $A[R/d\rho, 360/d\theta]$ to 0.
2. For $k = 0, \ldots, N - 1$:
   2.1. Calculate $\rho_k = |(x_k - x_c) \cos \theta_k + (y_k - y_c) \sin \theta_k|$.
   2.2. Increment $A[\rho_k/d\rho, \theta_k/d\theta]$ by g_k.
3. Find peaks in the accumulator array, and from the coordinates of each peak, determine parameters (ρ, θ) of the line.

In Step 3, if $A[i, j]$ is a peak, $\rho = i \times d\rho$ and $\theta = j \times d\theta$. More accurate parameters can be determined by calculating ρ and θ at 3×3 entries centered at the peak and using the obtained ρ and θ values as well as the counts at the entries to find more accurate (ρ, θ) parameters at the peak by a process similar to that outlined in Section 4.1.

To find different line segments within a detected line, connected segments containing n_{min} or more points are identified and a line is fitted to points within each segment by the least-squares method.

To find lines among edges in Fig. 4.2a, gradient magnitudes and gradient directions at the edges are determined using the original intensity image (Fig. 4.1a). The intensity image is smoothed with a Gaussian of standard deviation 2 pixels before finding its gradient magnitudes and gradient directions. Algorithm 4.4 finds the lines depicted in Fig. 4.6a using the edge locations as well as gradient magnitudes and gradient directions at the edges. Similarly, lines in edge images (b)–(f) in Fig. 4.2 are detected and shown in Fig. 4.6b–f, respectively. The parameters of Algorithm 4.4 finding the lines are $n_{min} = 50$ pixels, $d\rho = 2$ pixels, and $d\theta = 2°$.

Since gradient directions vary between 0 and 2π, lines can be given directions in such a way to keep the brighter side of an edge always to the right of the edge. Therefore, use of gradient directions at the edges makes it possible to detect more unique lines in an image than when gradient directions are not available.

The performance measures of this algorithm when using the edge images in Fig. 4.2, calculating gradient directions and gradient magnitudes at the edges in the corresponding intensity images in Fig. 4.1, and letting $n_{min} = 50$, $d\rho = 2$ pixels, and $d\theta = 2°$ are shown in Table 4.4. Due to digital noise when gradient directions are not a multiple of 90°, some of the nonvertical and nonhorizontal lines are fragmented. Edges with gradient directions that are a multiple of 90° do not contain such errors and are detected in their entirety.

Overall, the quality of lines detected by Algorithm 4.4 are inferior to those obtained by Algorithms 4.1–4.3. The main reason for this is inaccuracies in gradient directions caused by the horizontal and vertical arrangement of pixels in an image (see Chapter 2), biasing some directions over others, and consequently displacing some peaks, missing some true peaks, while detecting some false peaks.

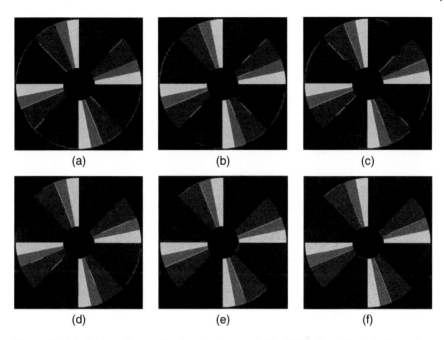

Figure 4.6 (a)–(f) Lines detected in the edge images in Fig. 4.2 by Algorithm 4.4 when using gradient directions and gradient magnitudes at the edges computed in the corresponding intensity images in Fig. 4.1. The parameters of the algorithm used to find these are $n_{min} = 50$ pixels, $d\rho = 2$ pixels, and $d\theta = 2°$. Correctly detected lines are shown in green, while incorrectly detected lines are shown in red.

Table 4.4 Performance measures of Algorithm 4.4 when using the edge images in Fig. 4.2 and the gradient directions and gradient magnitudes computed from the intensity images in Fig. 4.1 and letting $d\rho = 2$ pixels, $d\theta = 2°$, and $n_{min} = 50$ pixels.

Figure 4.6	TME	TPR	FPR	ADE	APE	ALL
(a)	0.14	0.88	0.70	0.28	0.94	232
(b)	0.16	0.75	0.74	0.29	0.89	193
(c)	0.15	0.94	0.77	0.53	1.01	162
(d)	0.16	0.88	0.75	0.93	1.06	123
(e)	0.20	0.75	0.80	1.07	0.87	128
(f)	0.20	0.75	0.76	1.14	1.04	117

TME, computation time in seconds; TPR, true positive rate; FPR, false positive rate; ADE, average directional error; APE, average positional error; and ALL, average line length.

The computational complexity of Algorithm 4.4 is much lower than those of Algorithms 4.1 and 4.2, and for high noise levels lower than that of Algorithm 4.3. This is because the clusters are formed by going through the points once. This computation is on the order N, the number of given points. Searching for the peaks depends on the size of the accumulator array, which is $(R/d\rho)(360/d\theta)$, R being half the diameter of the image. Therefore, the computational complexity of Algorithm 4.4 is on the order of $N + M$, where N is the number of given points and M is the size of the accumulator array.

4.5 Line Detection by Contour Tracing

The methods discussed so far detect lines among unorganized points in an image without knowledge about the connectivity between the points. Often the points represent pixels along edge contours. A number of methods use the connectivity between the points to identify sequences of points, each of which could represent a line.

A method described by Pavlidis and Horowitz [13] traces an edge contour and fits a line to the visited pixels. Whenever the maximum distance between the visited pixels and the approximating line becomes greater than a prespecified value, the visited pixels are replaced with the approximating line. The process is repeated on remaining pixels on the edge contour until all pixels along the contour are processed. Similarly, other edge contours are processed and replaced with line segments.

A line detection algorithm based on the contour tracing and subdivision method of Pavlidis and Horowitz [13] is described as follows. The algorithm receives a sequence of n pixels along an edge contour $\mathbf{p} = \{\mathbf{p}_k : k = 0, \ldots, n-1\}$, where $n > 1$ and $\mathbf{p}_k = (x_k, y_k)$. It then approximates the contour by a sequence of lines in such a way that the maximum distance between each contour segment and the approximating line stays within a required distance tolerance of d pixels. A line is declared whenever the contour segment producing it contains $n_{\min}$ or more pixels. *start* and *end* are pointers used to show the first pixel and the last pixel along the contour that is being approximated by a line segment.

The lines detected in the images in Fig. 4.2 by this algorithm when letting $n_{\min} = 50$ pixels and $d = 2$ pixels are shown in Fig. 4.7. The detected lines are generally longer than those detected by Algorithms 4.1–4.4.

The performance measures of Algorithm 4.5 on the edge images in Fig. 4.2 are summarized in Table 4.5. As noise level is increased, since the edge contours become more fragmented, fewer longer lines are obtained. This reduction in the number of detected lines keeps the ADE, APE, and ALL relatively unchanged under various noise levels. Increase in noise level, however, reduces the TPR and FPR measures. Reduction in FPR is desired, but reduction in TPR is not.

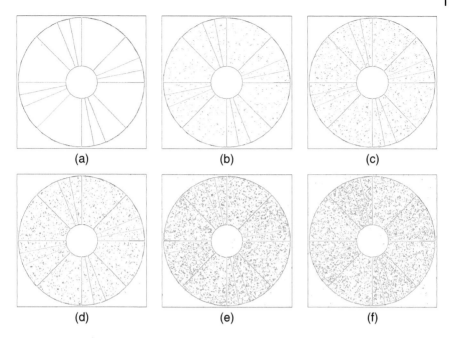

Figure 4.7 (a)–(f) Lines detected in the images in Fig. 4.2 by Algorithm 4.5 when letting $n_{min} = 50$ pixels and $dr = 2$ pixels. Correctly detected lines are shown in green while incorrectly detected lines are shown in red.

Algorithm 4.5   Line detection by contour tracing

This algorithm finds lines in one edge contour.

1. Let *start* $= 0$ and *end* $= 1$.
2. If *end* $\geq n - 1$, fit a line to the pixels from *start* to *end* by the least-squares method and go to Step 7. Otherwise, continue.
3. Fit a line to the sequence of pixels from *start* to *end* by the least-squares method.
4. Find the maximum distance d_{max} of pixels along the contour from *start* to *end* to the line.
5. If $d_{max} \leq d$, increment *end* by 1 and go to Step 2. Otherwise, break the contour at *end* $- 1$, fit a line to the points from *start* to *end* $- 1$ by the least-squares method, and if the length of the line is equal to or greater than n_{min}, keep it; otherwise, discard it.
6. If *end* $\geq n - 1$ exit program. Otherwise, let *start* $=$ *end*, *end* $=$ *start* $+ 1$, and go to Step 2.
7. If the length of the line is equal to or greater than n_{min}, keep it; otherwise, discard it.

Table 4.5 Performance measures of Algorithm 4.5 when finding lines in the edge images in Fig. 4.2 using parameters n_{min} = 50 pixels and dr = 2 pixels.

Figure 4.7	TME	TPR	FPR	ADE	APE	ALL
(a)	0.11	1.00	0.61	0.50	1.12	279
(b)	0.25	0.88	0.64	1.00	1.13	235
(c)	0.41	0.88	0.67	1.02	1.13	235
(d)	0.53	0.81	0.63	1.05	1.14	253
(e)	1.00	0.75	0.58	1.10	0.97	269
(f)	1.14	0.75	0.50	1.12	0.95	268

TPR, true positive rate; FPR, false positive rate; ADE, average directional error; APE, average positional error; ALL, average line length; and TME, computation time.

The contour tracing method does not require intensity or gradient information at the edges. It starts from an edge image and approximates each edge contour by a sequence of line segments with a required error tolerance. The method has the disadvantage of requiring edge contours that can be traced. If the provided edges are disconnected or adjacency relation between the points is not available, this algorithm cannot be used to detect the lines.

The computational complexity of Algorithm 4.5 depends on the number of provided edge pixels. It also depends on the number of detected lines. As n_{min} or dr is increased, fewer line segments are detected, requiring fewer least-squares estimation. Therefore, the computational complexity of Algorithm 4.5 is a linear function of the number of edges and the number of detected lines.

Natural images contain radiometric and digital noise. Radiometric noise, which is primarily sensor noise, can be reduced by smoothing the image in the spatial or temporal domain. Digital noise is caused by the discrete nature of pixel coordinates, displacing projected scene points by up to half a pixel. When a straight edge in the scene appears horizontal, vertical, or diagonal, it creates a straight line; however, when a straight edge in the scene projects to a line in the image plane that has an orientation other than a multiple of $45°$, it breaks into a combination of line segments. Such digital errors contribute to the positional and directional accuracies of detected lines.

To reduce digital noise in an edge contour, the digital domain of the edge contour is taken to a continuous one, replacing each edge contour by a smooth and continuous curve. Similar to image smoothing that is done to reduce radiometric noise, curve fitting is done to reduce digital noise. Next, a line detector is described that replaces an edge contour by a smooth curve and identifies straight segments within the curve.

4.6   Line Detection by Curve Fitting

A curve of zero curvature in a scene becomes a digital line when projected to the image plane. The imaging process reduces a continuous curve into a discrete sequence of pixels, all of which may not fall exactly on the projection of the curve to the image plane. Deviation of a digital line from its true projection depends on a number of factors, including the orientation of the camera capturing the image. To reduce the degradations caused by the imaging process, a method is described here that converts the digital domain to a continuous one, reducing the digital degradations caused by image acquisition.

To detect line segments within an edge contour, the contour is represented by a continuous curve and the curve is partitioned into segments that have zero or very low curvatures. Consider an edge contour $\mathbf{p}$ that represents a sequence of n pixels:

$$\mathbf{p} = \{\mathbf{p}_k : k = 0, \dots, n-1\}, \tag{4.20}$$

where $\mathbf{p}_k = (x_k, y_k)$ is the kth pixel along the contour. To reduce digital noise in the edge contour, it is approximated by a smooth curve. A parametric curve formulation is chosen for this purpose for its ability to represent a very long and complex contour by a single curve. The parametric curve approximating a sequence of pixels in 2-D has two components, both of which are a function of the same parameter u:

$$\mathbf{p}(u) = (x(u), y(u)). \tag{4.21}$$

For the curve to closely approximate pixels along a contour, it is required that

$$\begin{aligned} x(u_k) &\approx x_k, \\ y(u_k) &\approx y_k, \end{aligned} \quad \text{for } k = 0, \dots, n-1. \tag{4.22}$$

The rational Gaussian (RaG) curve formulation [20, 21] will be used to represent $x(u)$ and $y(u)$ for its ability to smooth a desired level of noise in the edge contour. A RaG curve approximating the sequence of points $\mathbf{p}$ is defined by

$$\mathbf{p}(u) = \sum_{k=0}^{n-1} \mathbf{p}_k g_k(u), \quad u \in [0, n-1], \tag{4.23}$$

where

$$g_k(u) = \frac{G_k(u)}{\sum_{j=0}^{n-1} G_j(u)}, \quad k = 0, \dots, n-1 \tag{4.24}$$

are the basis functions of the curve and $G_k(u)$ is a Gaussian of height 1 and standard deviation σ centered at u_k:

$$G_k(u) = \exp\left\{ -\frac{(u - u_k)^2}{2\sigma^2} \right\}. \tag{4.25}$$

$u_k = k$ is the kth node of the curve, for $k = 0, \ldots, n - 1$. The nodes of a curve are the parameter values at which the curve approximates the pixels along the contour. σ is the smoothness parameter. By increasing it, the curve becomes smoother, reducing more digital noise, and by decreasing it, the curve gets closer to the contour, reproducing more details along the contour.

The aforementioned equations are for an open curve. For a closed curve, Eq. (4.25) should be replaced with

$$G_k(u) = \sum_{j=-\infty}^{j=\infty} \exp\left\{ -\frac{[u - (u_k + jn)]^2}{2\sigma^2} \right\}. \tag{4.26}$$

Since a Gaussian approaches 0 exponentially away from its center point, in practice, instead of ∞ in Eq. (4.26), a small number such as 1 is sufficient. The addition of n to u_k or subtraction of n from u_k ensures that, at the point where the curve closes, the Gaussians extend over the closing point, producing a continuous and smooth curve. Note that for an open RaG curve, parameter u varies between 0 and $n - 1$, while for a closed curve, it varies between 0 and n with the curve points at $u = 0$ and $u = n$ coinciding and producing a closed curve. Open and closed RaG curves are infinity differentiable, so they have a very high degree of continuity everywhere.

The tangent direction ϕ at a curve point with parameter u is computed from

$$\phi(u) = \arctan\left[\frac{dy(u)}{dx(u)} \right], \tag{4.27}$$

$$= \arctan\left[\frac{dy(u)/du}{dx(u)/du} \right]. \tag{4.28}$$

Since

$$\frac{dx(u)}{du} = \frac{x(u + \delta u) - x(u)}{\delta u}\bigg|_{\delta u \to 0}, \tag{4.29}$$

to estimate $dx(u)/du$, $x(u)$ is calculated at two very close values of u and their difference is divided by the difference in their u values. That is, $dx(u)/du$ is estimated from

$$\frac{x(u + \delta u) - x(u - \delta u)}{2\delta u}. \tag{4.30}$$

Similarly $dy(u)/du$ is estimated from

$$\frac{y(u + \delta u) - y(u - \delta u)}{2\delta u}. \tag{4.31}$$

Typically, $\delta u = 0.01$. With such a small increment in u, the difference between the actual and estimated tangent directions will be negligible. Note that the difference between parameters of curve points approximating adjacent pixels on a contour is 1. That is, $u_{k+1} - u_k = 1$ for $k = 0, \ldots, n - 2$.

Similarly, $d^2x(u)/du^2$ and $d^2y(u)/du^2$ are estimated from changes in $dx(u)$ and $dy(u)$, respectively, under a small change in u, that is,

$$\frac{d^2x(u)}{du^2} \approx \frac{dx(u + \delta u) - dx(u - \delta u)}{2\delta u}, \tag{4.32}$$

$$\frac{d^2y(u)}{du^2} \approx \frac{dy(u + \delta u) - dy(u - \delta u)}{2\delta u}, \tag{4.33}$$

for $\delta u = 0.01$.

Denoting $dx(u)/du$, $dy(u)/du$, $d^2x(u)/du^2$, and $d^2y(u)/du^2$ by $x'(u)$, $y'(u)$, $x''(u)$, and $y''(u)$, respectively, the magnitude curvature at a curve point with parameter u is computed from [22]:

$$\kappa(u) = \frac{|x'(u)y''(u) - y'(u)x''(u)|}{[x'(u)^2 + y'(u)^2]^{3/2}}. \tag{4.34}$$

Total bending between two points with parameters u_1 and u_2 along a curve can be measured from the angle between the tangents at the points:

$$B(u_1, u_2) = \phi(u_2) - \phi(u_1). \tag{4.35}$$

Curvatures along a curve generally decrease as σ is increased. Therefore, as a curve with a larger σ is fitted to points along an edge contour, a smoother curve is obtained, producing lower curvature values. Figure 4.8 shows RaG curves fitting to the edge contours in Fig. 4.2a for $\sigma = 1, 2$, and 3 pixels. Points with higher curvatures are shown in a brighter red. The reason for straight edges at angles $\pi/16$, $9\pi/16$, $17\pi/16$, and $25\pi/16$ appearing red in Fig. 4.8a is because a very small $\sigma = 1$ pixel is used. At such a small σ, the curve closely follows the pixels, reproducing digital noise and creating high curvatures locally. By increasing σ, the effect of digital noise gradually disappears.

Starting from one end of a curve and moving along the curve, whenever total bending reaches 0.1 radians, the point is considered the end of one segment and the start of another segment. By partitioning the curves in Fig. 4.8a–c in this manner, the segments depicted in Fig. 4.9a–c are obtained. When $\sigma = 1$ pixel, lines in directions $\pi/16$, $9\pi/16$, $17\pi/16$, and $25\pi/16$, as well as lines in directions $\pi/8$, $5\pi/8$, $9\pi/8$, and $13\pi/8$, are segmented into small pieces delimited by green points. This happens because pixels along a contour in these directions do not fall exactly on a line but rather fall near a line, and the curve is simply trying to follow the pixels and reproduce relatively high curvatures at some pixels. When σ is increased to 2 or 3 pixels, the curves smooth digital noise, producing smaller curvatures. Segments with total bending less than or equal to 0.1 radians that are longer than 100 pixels are delimited by blue points in these figures and are the detected line segments.

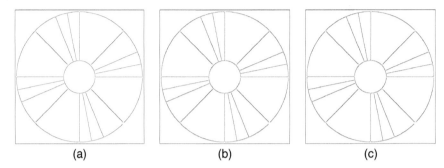

Figure 4.8 (a)–(c) RaG curves approximating the edge contours in Fig. 4.2a when $\sigma = 1, 2$, and 3 pixels, respectively. A curve point with a higher curvature is shown in a brighter red.

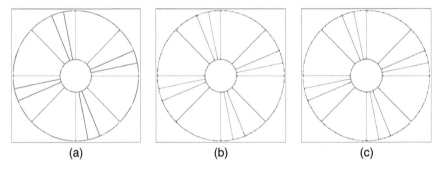

Figure 4.9 (a)–(c) Segmentation of the curves in Fig. 4.8a–c into segments with total bending equal to 0.1 rad (5°). Curve segments of length 100 pixels or longer are delimited by blue points in these figures and are the detected line segments.

An algorithm that approximates an edge contour $\mathbf{p} = \{\mathbf{p}_k : k = 0, \ldots, n-1\}$, where $\mathbf{p}_k = (x_k, y_k)$ is the kth pixel along the contour, by a RaG curve and partitions the curve into segments, each with a required total bending e radians, is given in what follows. $n_{\min}$ is the length of the shortest segment to be kept. $B(u_1, u_2)$ denotes the total bending along the curve from u_1 to u_2.

Note that Algorithm 4.6 finds lines within one edge contour. Therefore, if an image contains m edge contours, this algorithm should be called m times to find all lines in the image.

Algorithm 4.6 has three parameters: (1) smoothness parameter σ in curve fitting, (2) bending tolerance e radians in a detected line, and (3) minimum length $n_{\min}$ in a detected line segment. These parameters can be selected by taking into consideration the characteristics of the given image and the required properties of the detected lines. For a noisier image, a larger smoothness parameter should be used to reduce noisy details along the edge contours. A larger bending tolerance produces longer lines, but that decreases the positional and directional accuracies of detected line segments. If line segments shorter than a required length are not useful in an application, the minimum length parameter can be set accordingly to ensure that line segments shorter than the required length are not detected. If all lines are to be detected in an image, this parameter should be set to 2.

Algorithm 4.6 Line detection by curve fitting

This algorithm finds lines in one edge contour.

1. If $n < n_{min}$, exit. The contour is too short to contain a line.
2. Fit a RaG curve to points along the contour according to Eq. (4.23).
3. Find curvature $\kappa(u)$ at $u = 0, \ldots, n - 1$.
4. Let $u_1 = 0$.
5. Starting from $u = u_1$, if $\kappa(u) > e$ let $u_1 = u + 1$ and go to Step 5. Otherwise, increase u by 1 and calculate total bending $B(u_1, u)$ until either $B(u_1, u) > e$ or $u = n - 1$. If $B(u, u_1) > e$, let $u_2 = u - 1$, and declare a line segment with endpoints $\mathbf{p}(u_1)$ and $\mathbf{p}(u_2)$. Then, let $u_1 = u$ and go to Step 5. If $u = n - 1$, declare the portion of the curve between parameters u_1 and $u = n - 1$ the last line segment.
6. Among the detected line segments identify those with lengths equal to or greater than n_{min} pixels and report them as the line segments in the edge contour.

The line detection results of Algorithm 4.6 on the edge images in Fig. 4.2 when letting $\sigma = 5$ pixels, $n_{min} = 50$ pixels, and bending tolerances $e = 5°$ are shown in Fig. 4.10.

The performance measures of Algorithm 4.6 for the results depicted in Fig. 4.10 are given in Table 4.6. While the TPR measure of Algorithm 4.6 is only slightly higher than that of Algorithm 4.5, the FPR measure is considerably lower than that of Algorithm 4.5. This shows that the lines detected by Algorithm 4.6 are more likely to represent true lines than lines detected by Algorithm 4.5. Moreover, we see that the lines detected by Algorithm 4.6 are generally more accurately positioned and directed and are longer than the lines detected by Algorithm 4.5.

The performance measures of Algorithm 4.6 are stable under varying levels of noise. This can be attributed to the curve-fitting process that reduces digital noise among pixels along edge contours. This is a unique ability of line detection by curve fitting when compared to other line detection methods.

The computational complexity of Algorithm 4.6 is a linear function of the number of edge pixels in an image as the curve fitting and curvature calculations are a linear function of pixels along a contour. This algorithm is slower than Algorithms 4.1 and 4.2, and while it is slower than Algorithms 4.3 and 4.5 when noise level is low, it is faster than Algorithms 4.3 and 4.5 when noise level is high. The clustering-based Algorithm 4.4 is the fastest of all algorithms discussed so far.

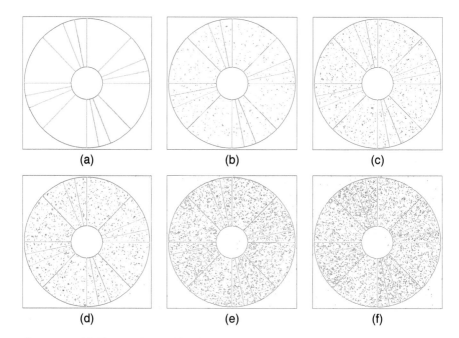

(a) (b) (c)

(d) (e) (f)

Figure 4.10 (a)–(f) Lines detected by Algorithm 4.6 in the edge images in Fig. 4.2 when letting $\sigma = 5$ pixels, $n_{min} = 50$ pixels, and $e = 5°$. Correctly detected lines are shown in green, while incorrectly detected lines are shown in red.

Table 4.6 Performance measures of Algorithm 4.6 when detecting lines in Fig. 4.10a–f using parameters $n_{min} = 50$ pixels and $e = 5°$.

Figure 4.6	TME	TPR	FPR	ADE	APE	ALL
(a)	0.61	1.0	0.0	0.45	0.92	285
(b)	0.53	0.94	0.17	0.72	0.97	233
(c)	0.54	1.0	0.19	0.77	1.04	213
(d)	0.60	0.81	0.19	0.33	0.93	269
(e)	0.45	0.75	0.37	0.42	1.00	269
(f)	0.48	0.75	0.14	0.46	0.99	285

TME, computation time in seconds; TPR, true positive rate; FPR, false positive rate; ADE, average directional error; APE, average positional error; and ALL, average line length.

4.7 Line Detection by Region Subdivision

Region subdivision-based methods find line segments within small regions and then combine the segments into longer ones. The first such method was described by Roberts [14]. Gradient magnitudes in an image are calculated and pixels with gradient magnitudes below a threshold value are marked as the background. From among the nonbackground pixels, a dominant gradient direction is calculated within each 4×4 window, and adjacent windows with dominant directions within $\pi/8$ are merged to create larger regions. Then, a line is fitted to each region by the least-squares method and the endpoints of the segment falling inside the region are determined. Finally, line segments with similar parameters that have sufficiently close endpoints are connected to create longer lines.

Burns et al. [23] described a region subdivision method that first marks pixels with gradient magnitudes below a threshold value as the background. Then, it forms regions from among nonbackground pixels by connecting adjacent pixels that have similar gradient directions. Next, a plane is fitted to the coordinates and intensities of pixels in a region and the intersection of that plane with a horizontal plane at a height equal to the average intensity of pixels in the region is determined. Finally, the projection of the line obtained from the intersection of the planes to the image plane is determined and used as the line representing the region.

Algorithm 4.7   Line detection by region subdivision

---

1. Smooth image I with a Gaussian of standard deviation σ pixels to obtain image $\tilde{I}$.
2. Find the gradient magnitude and gradient direction of $\tilde{I}$ at each pixel to create gradient magnitude image $\tilde{G}_m$ and gradient direction image $\tilde{G}_d$.
3. Set gradient magnitudes below g_t in $\tilde{G}_m$ to 0. These pixels represent the background.
4. Find connected regions from among nonbackground pixels. Remove regions containing fewer than n_{min} pixels by setting their gradient magnitudes in $\tilde{G}_m$ to 0.
5. For each connected region remaining in $\tilde{G}_m$:
   5.1. Create histogram H of gradient directions weighted by gradient magnitudes, smooth H to obtain $\tilde{H}$, and find peaks of $\tilde{H}$.
   5.2. For each obtained peak θ_m:
      5.2.1. Find pixels in the region with gradient direction $\theta_m \pm d\theta$, and if n_{min} or more pixels are found, fit a line to them by weighted least squares using gradient magnitudes at the pixels as the weights.

Steps of an algorithm following the line detection method of Burns et al. [23] are given in Algorithm 4.7. I is the provided intensity image and σ is the standard deviation of the Gaussian filter used to smooth the image. Parameter g_t is the gradient magnitude threshold value below which image pixels are considered a part of the background. H is an array with $360/d\theta$ entries representing the histogram of gradient directions of a region with bins of size $d\theta$ degrees. n_{min} is the minimum required length of a detected line.

As parameter σ is increased, noise among the edge directions is reduced. As σ is reduced, the gradient directions become more localized, reproducing more noise. Inaccuracies in gradient directions due to digital noise cause some pixels belonging to a line to be assigned to regions for different lines. The histogram of gradient directions in Step 5.1 is appropriately smoothed to avoid detection of noisy peaks. In the following experiments, a 1-D Gaussian of standard deviation 1 is used to smooth the gradient direction histogram H.

In Step 5.2.1, if gradient direction peak θ is between $45°$ and $135°$ or between $225°$ and $315°$, since gradient direction is normal to the line to be detected, the slope of the line is expected to fall between -1 and 1. In that case, line $y = mx + b$ is fitted to the pixels in the connected region with gradient directions between $\theta - d\theta$ and $\theta + d\theta$. Assuming pixels $\{(x_i, y_i) : i = 0, \dots, n-1\}$ belong to the region under consideration, the parameters of the line fitting to pixels in the region by the least-squares method will be

$$m = \frac{\sum_{i=0}^{n-1} x_i y_i - \frac{1}{n} \sum_{i=0}^{n-1} x_i \sum_{i=0}^{n-1} y_i}{\sum_{i=0}^{n-1} x_i^2 - \frac{1}{n}(\sum_{i=0}^{n-1} x_i)^2}, \tag{4.36}$$

$$b = \frac{1}{n} \sum_{i=0}^{n-1} y_i - \frac{m}{n} \sum_{i=0}^{n-1} x_i. \tag{4.37}$$

The endpoints of a computed line are determined by first identifying pixels with the smallest and largest x coordinates within the region and then computing the y coordinates of the endpoints by substituting the x coordinates into $y = mx + b$ and solving for y.

When gradient direction peak θ is found to be between $-45°$ ($315°$) and $45°$, or between $135°$ and $225°$, the slope of the line to be detected will be either less than -1 or greater than 1. In that case, the x and y coordinates of the points are switched, the equations of the lines are determined, and the endpoints of the lines are determined as described earlier. Finally, the x and the y coordinates of the endpoints are switched back to obtain the line segments in the original image. Computation in this manner avoids working with very large positive and negative numbers when calculating the m and b parameters for vertical or nearly vertical lines.

Note that the weighted least squares line fitting step in the algorithm replaces the step in the method of Burns et al. [23] that fits a plane to pixel intensities

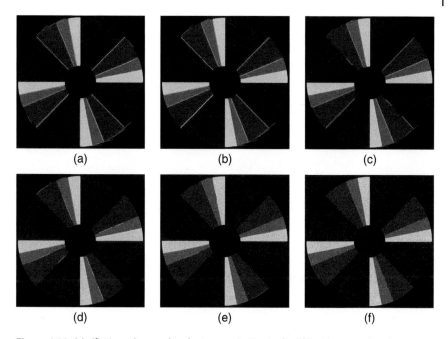

Figure 4.11 (a)–(f) Lines detected in the images in Fig. 4.1 by Algorithm 4.7 when letting $n_{min} = 50$ pixels, $g_t = 1$, $d\theta = 3°$, and $\sigma = 3$ pixels. Correctly detected lines are shown in green, while incorrectly detected lines are shown in red.

in a region by weighted least squares, the weights being gradient magnitudes at the pixels, and finding the intersection of that plane with another plane that represents the average intensity of pixels in the region.

The lines detected by Algorithm 4.7 when using the images in Fig. 4.1 and letting $g_t = 1$, $\sigma = 3.0$ pixels, and $d\theta = 3°$ are shown in Fig. 4.11. These parameters were determined interactively to produce overall highest TPR. Digital noise in the calculation of gradient direction can sometimes result in two regions with slightly different gradient directions at the two sides of an edge. An example is shown in Fig. 4.11a. Two very close lines (shown in red and green) are detected at approximately 225° angle, one of which is redundant.

The performance measures of Algorithm 4.7 for the lines detected in Fig. 4.11 are summarized in Table 4.7. Although this algorithm is one of the fastest tested, its TPR measures are slightly better than those of the clustering-based Algorithm 4.4 and Hough transform Algorithm 4.1 when noise is low, but it is worse than all other algorithms when noise is high. Its FPR measures are better than those of clustering-based Algorithm 4.4 and edge tracing and subdivision-based Algorithm 4.5, but they are worse than those of all other algorithms. Obtained line lengths are better than those of Algorithm 4.4, but are worse than those of all other algorithms.

Table 4.7 Performance measures of Algorithm 4.7 when using images (a)–(f) in Fig. 4.1 and letting n_{min} = 50 pixels, g_t = 1, $d\theta$ = 3°, and σ = 3 pixels.

Figure 4.11	TME	TPR	FPR	ADE	APE	ALL
(a)	0.22	1.0	0.41	0.80	1.63	285
(b)	0.19	0.94	0.35	1.16	1.55	269
(c)	0.17	0.94	0.40	0.85	2.05	205
(d)	0.15	0.75	0.43	1.14	1.88	160
(e)	0.15	0.50	0.56	0.82	2.17	148
(f)	0.32	0.44	0.50	0.73	1.56	131

TME, computation time in seconds; TPR, true positive rate; FPR, false positive rate; ADE, average directional error; APE, average positional error; and ALL, average line length.

Determining the best parameters of a line detector can be a difficult task. von Gioi et al. [24–26], using the segment validation method of Desolneux [27], developed a method for finding the best parameters of the line detection method of Burns et al. [23] by minimizing the number of false detections. They also reduced the effect of digital noise by reducing the scale of the image slightly (by 80%). In addition, they ordered pixels in a region according to their gradient magnitudes and formed a line starting from the highest gradient pixel and gradually using lower gradient pixels until a well-defined line was obtained. Implementation of this refined region subdivision method is referred to as Algorithm 4.8 in the following discussions.

All results reported for Algorithm 4.8 are obtained from the software made publicly available by von Gioi et al. [28]. Results reported on Algorithms 4.1–4.7 are those obtained from software developed by closely following the steps in the respective algorithms described in the preceding sections.

Lines detected in the images in Fig. 4.1 by Algorithm 4.8 are shown in Fig. 4.12 and the obtained performance measures are summarized in Table 4.8. This algorithm produces very good results when the images contain either no noise or very little noise. The best results are obtained for images (a) and (b) when compared with the results of most algorithms; however, at higher noise levels, the performance measures of the algorithm fall quickly, becoming worse than the performance measures of Algorithm 4.7.

Computational complexities of Algorithms 4.7 and 4.8 are both a linear function of the number of pixels in an image. Determination of nonbackground pixels in an image requires computation of image gradients at all pixels, which is a linear function of the number of pixels in the image. Subdivision of nonbackground pixels into different regions and fitting a line to pixels within each region is linear function of the number of nonbackground pixels. If one-third of pixels in an image represent the nonbackground pixels, the computational

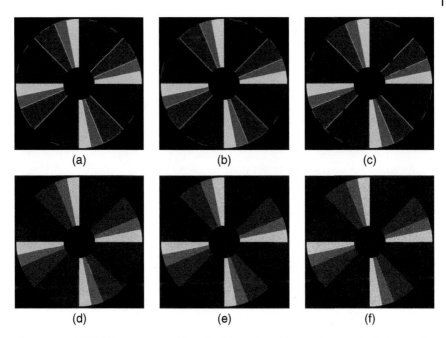

Figure 4.12 (a)–(f) Line segments of lengths 50 pixels and longer detected in the images in Fig. 4.1 by Algorithm 4.8. Correctly detected lines are shown in green, while incorrectly detected lines are shown in red.

Table 4.8 Performance measures of Algorithm 4.8 when using the images in Fig. 4.1.

Figure 4.12	TME	TPR	FPR	ADE	APE	ALL
(a)	0.06	1.0	0.56	0.10	0.96	297
(b)	0.08	1.0	0.59	0.12	0.98	296
(c)	0.09	1.0	0.64	0.54	1.32	150
(d)	0.12	0.50	0.50	0.73	1.10	149
(e)	0.17	0.25	0.33	0.81	0.92	83
(f)	0.19	0.25	0.20	0.10	1.48	68

Only line segments of lengths 50 pixels and longer are used in the calculation of the performance measures. TME, computation time in seconds; TPR, true positive rate; FPR, false positive rate; ADE, average directional error; APE, average positional error; and ALL, average line length.

complexities of Algorithms 4.7 and 4.8 will still be a linear function of the number of pixels in the image.

4.8 Comparison of the Line Detection Algorithms

In the preceding sections, the performance measures of eight line detection algorithms were determined on a set of synthetically generated images. In this section, these performance measures will be compared to determine the strengths and weaknesses of the algorithms. Also, the quality of lines detected by the algorithms in natural images will be compared.

4.8.1 Sensitivity to Noise

To compare the TPRs of Algorithms 4.1–4.8, the TPR values in Tables 4.1–4.8 at different noise levels are plotted in Fig. 4.13a. At low noise levels, the parametric-line-based Algorithm 4.3, the curve fitting-based Algorithm 4.6, and the region subdivision based Algorithm 4.8 are the best performers. At high noise levels, the contour tracing and subdivision-based Algorithm 4.5 and the curve-fitting-based Algorithm 4.6 coincide to produce the highest TPR, followed by the Hough transform using the slope and y-intercept equation of lines Algorithm 4.2. Considering all noise levels, Algorithm 4.6 is the best followed by Algorithms 4.3 and 4.2.

Similarly, the FRP measures of the algorithms reported in Tables 4.1–4.8 are plotted in Fig. 4.13b. At very low noise levels, the Hough transform–based Algorithms 4.1 and 4.2, the curve-fitting-based Algorithm 4.6, and the parametric-line-based Algorithm 4.3 are the best performers. At high levels of noise, Algorithm 4.3 is the best followed by Algorithm 4.6. Considering all noise levels, Algorithm 4.3 is the best followed by Algorithm 4.6. By focusing on identifying points that fall on a line, Algorithm 4.3 avoids detecting false lines. By reducing/removing digital noise among edges via curve fitting, Algorithm 4.6 avoids fragmentation of edge contours and creation of false lines.

4.8.2 Positional and Directional Errors

In the performance measures reported earlier, a line is considered correctly detected if its distance to the image center is less than or equal to 5 pixels. The average distance of correctly detected lines to the image center is then used as the positional error of an algorithm since all true lines should pass through the image center.

Assuming the equation of a detected line is $ax + by + c = 0$, the distance of the line to image center (x_c, y_c) is computed from

$$E(d) = \frac{|ax_c + by_c + c|}{\sqrt{a^2 + b^2}}. \tag{4.38}$$

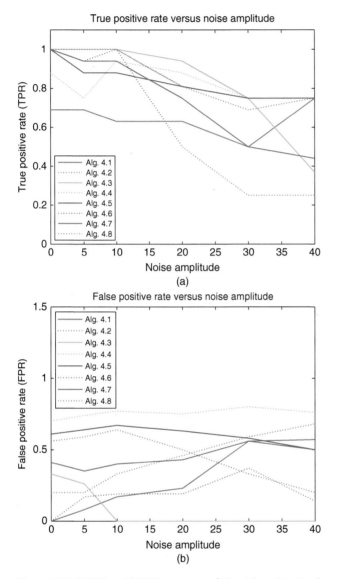

Figure 4.13 (a) TPR and (b) FPR measures of Algorithms 4.1–4.8 when using the images in Fig. 4.1 and/or images in Fig. 4.2, as needed.

Then, the average of $E(d)$ for correctly detected lines in an image by an algorithm is used to measure the positional error of the algorithm for that image.

The positional errors of the eight line detectors under different noise levels are depicted in Fig. 4.14a. The region subdivision-based Algorithm 4.7 has

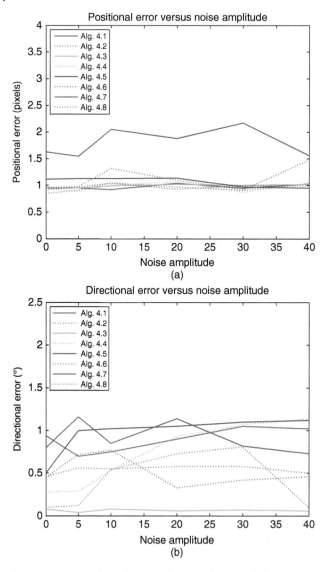

Figure 4.14 (a) Positional and (b) directional errors of Algorithms 4.1–4.8 when using the images in Fig. 4.1 and/or in Fig. 4.2, as needed.

the highest positional error. Although the region subdivision-based Algorithm 4.8 has an improved positional error compared to Algorithm 4.7, its positional error is still worse than those of the other six algorithms. This can be attributed to fitting a line to pixels in a region created from noisy gradient directions.

The directional errors of Algorithms 4.1–4.8 are plotted in Fig. 4.14b. The parametric-line-based Algorithm 4.3 produces the lowest directional errors under all noise levels. This can be attributed to hypothesizing a line from two distant points, finding other points that fall sufficiently close to the line, and fitting a line to only those points by the least-squares method. By filtering out points that are not sufficiently close to a hypothesized line, the process reduces directional error.

4.8.3 Length Accuracy

Some methods detect only a part of a line while others detect entire lines. It is required to detect lines as completely as possible. Knowing that all true lines in the images in Figs 4.1 and 4.2 are of length 300 pixels, the average length of correctly detected lines by each algorithm is used to characterize the length accuracies of the line detectors.

The ALL determined for each algorithm under different noise levels is depicted in Fig. 4.15a. The least-squares-based Algorithm 4.5, the curve-fitting-based Algorithm 4.6, and the parametric- line-based Algorithm 4.3 detect the most complete lines under all noise levels, while the region subdivision-based Algorithms 4.7 and 4.8 and the clustering based Algorithm 4.4 produce the shortest lines under high noise levels.

4.8.4 Speed

The TMEs of the algorithms are depicted in Fig. 4.15b. The TMEs of the Hough transform–based Algorithms 4.1 and 4.2 are the highest. The TMEs in these algorithms increase with increasing noise due to increase in the number of points to be processed. The TME of the parametric-line-based Algorithm 4.3 also increases with the increase in noise level as more random point pairs need to be tested to find a point pair that falls on a sufficiently long line. The region subdivision-based Algorithms 4.7 and 4.8 are the fastest, with the improved region subdivision Algorithm 4.8 being somewhat faster than the original region subdivision Algorithm 4.7.

Although the region subdivision-based Algorithms 4.7 and 4.8 have low accuracy measures under high levels of noise, under low levels of noise, their accuracy measures are comparable to those of other methods, and because they are the fastest among the algorithms tested, they are most suitable in applications where the images are not noisy and speed is of critical importance.

4.8.5 Quality of Detected Lines

To determine the quality of lines detected by Algorithms 4.1–4.8 in images of man-made scenes, the images shown in Fig. 4.16 and the respective edge images in Fig. 4.17 are used. Dimensions of images (a)–(d) are 1063 × 848, 1111 × 753,

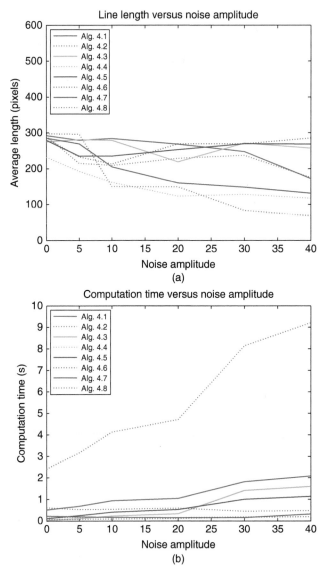

Figure 4.15 (a) Length accuracies and (b) computational times of Algorithms 4.1–4.8 when using the images in Fig. 4.1 and/or in Fig. 4.2, as needed.

749×670, and 966×474 pixels, respectively. The images contain very little sensor noise and represent man-made structures with a large number of straight edges. Algorithms 4.1–4.8 were used to detect lines in the images. The parameters used for each algorithm were those used to detect lines in the synthetically generated images in Fig. 4.1 or the edge images in Fig. 4.2.

(a) (b) (c) (d)

Figure 4.16 (a) A hotel building, (b) a bridge with side rails, (c) a high-rise building, and (d) the US Capitol used in the experiments.

The lines detected in the hotel image of Fig. 4.16a or its edge image in Fig. 4.17a by Algorithms 4.1–4.8 are shown in Fig. 4.18. Most lines are detected by Algorithm 4.2, but a close examination of the detected lines reveals that some of the lines are not accurately positioned and oriented. The same is true for some of the lines detected by Algorithm 4.1. These are Hough transform–based algorithms that use peaks in the accumulator arrays to detect lines, and for short line segments the peaks do not accurately represent the positions and orientations of the lines. The lines detected by Algorithms 4.5 and 4.6 are relatively accurately positioned and oriented, although these methods miss some of the shorter line segments due to edge fragmentation by the algorithms. Algorithms 4.7 and 4.8 find the longer lines but miss the shorter ones due to subdivision of some of the regions into fragments that produce line segments shorter than 50 pixels.

Some of the edge contours in the bridge edge image in Fig. 4.17b are parallel and very close to each other. The edge contours contain considerable digital noise, although the respective intensity image (Fig. 4.16b) contains very little sensor noise. Algorithms 4.1–4.4 do not use the adjacency relation between pixels along an edge contour, rather they use the edges as independent points. Algorithms 4.1, 4.2, and 4.4 use accumulator arrays to find lines; therefore, they merge peaks belonging to close parallel lines into a new peak, detecting a single

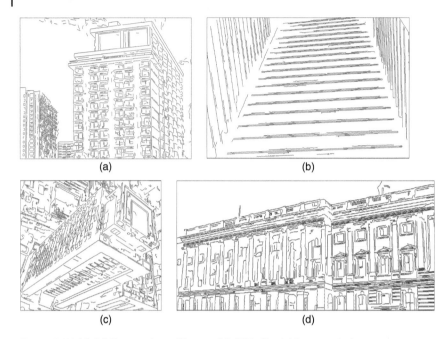

Figure 4.17 (a)–(d) Canny edges of images (a)–(d) in Fig. 4.16, respectively.

line for multiple lines. Algorithm 4.3 does not use an accumulator array, and so it does not merge lines, but it misses some lines and breaks lines with orientations that are not a multiple of $45°$ into smaller segments due to increased digital noise. Algorithms 4.5 and 4.6 detect the most lines by using the adjacency relation between points along a contour. The region-based Algorithms 4.7 and 4.8 detect some of the lines near the image center due to high contrast, but they miss all lines on the left and right rails due to low contrast. These results are depicted in Fig. 4.19.

Lines detected in the high-rise image of Fig. 4.16c or its edge image of Fig. 4.17c by Algorithms 4.1–4.8 are shown in Fig. 4.20. Algorithms 4.1, 4.2, and 4.4 detect many lines, although some of the shorter ones are not accurately positioned and oriented. Algorithm 4.3 misses many lines, but the ones it finds are accurately positioned and oriented. Algorithms 4.5 and 4.6 find many accurately positioned and oriented lines. The region subdivision-based Algorithms 4.7 and 4.8 miss many lines and fragment some of the longer lines.

Finally, the result of line detection by Algorithms 4.1–4.8 when using the image of the US Capitol in Fig. 4.16d or its edge image in Fig. 4.17d are shown in Fig. 4.21. Similar conclusions can be reached from these images. The contour tracing and subdivision-based Algorithm 4.5 and the curve-fitting-based Algorithm 4.6 produce the largest number of lines among all algorithms. Moreover,

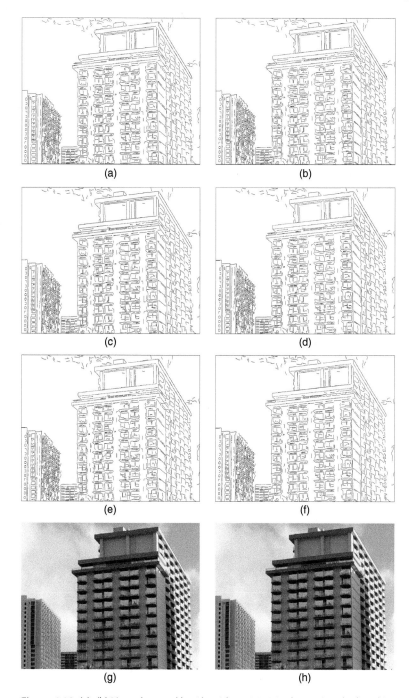

(a)

(b)

(c)

(d)

(e)

(f)

(g)

(h)

Figure 4.18 (a)–(h) Lines detected by Algorithms 4.1–4.8 when using the hotel image in Fig. 4.16a and/or Fig. 4.17a, as needed.

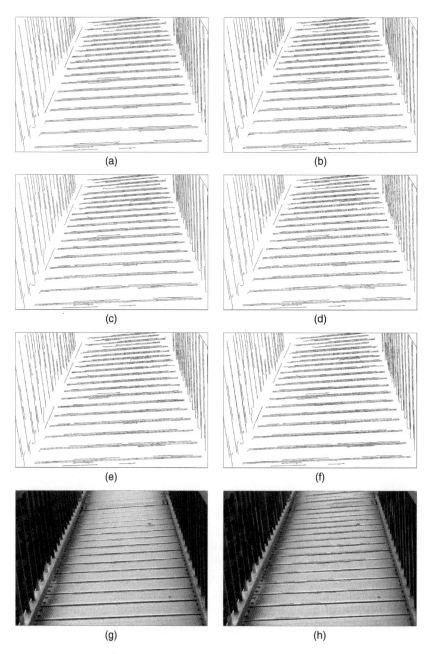

(a)

(b)

(c)

(d)

(e)

(f)

(g)

(h)

Figure 4.19 (a)–(h) Lines detected by Algorithms 4.1–4.8 in the image of Fig. 4.16b and/or image of Fig. 4.17b, as needed.

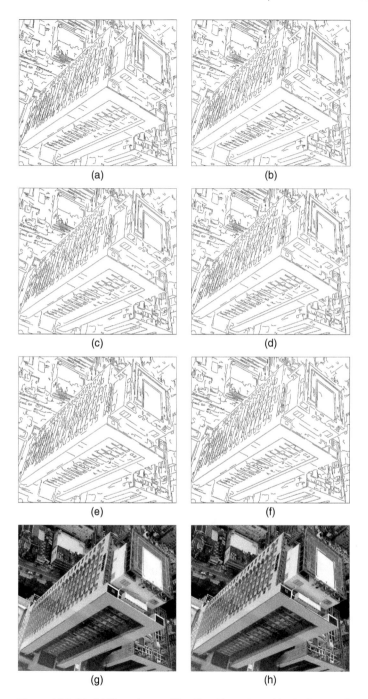

(a)

(b)

(c)

(d)

(e)

(f)

(g)

(h)

Figure 4.20 (a)–(h) Lines detected by Algorithms 4.1–4.8 in the image of Fig. 4.16c and/or Fig. 4.17c, as needed.

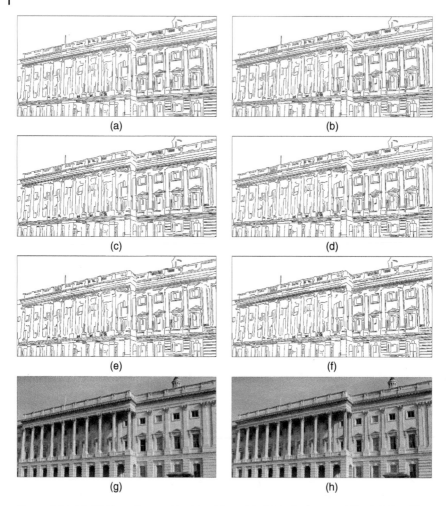

Figure 4.21 (a)–(h) Lines detected by Algorithms 4.1–4.8 in the image of Fig. 4.16d and/or Fig. 4.17d, as needed.

the lines detected by these algorithms are longer than lines detected by other algorithms.

From the experimental results obtained using synthetic and real images, the line detection characteristics of Algorithms 4.1–4.8 can be summarized as follows:

1. Line detection methods based on the Hough transform (Algorithms 4.1 and 4.2) are the slowest. Although the TPRs of these methods are relatively high, the detected lines are generally shorter than they should be.

2. The region-based methods (Algorithms 4.7 and 4.8) are the fastest among the algorithms tested, but their positional and directional errors are higher than those of most other methods.

3. The positional and directional errors of the parametric-line-based Algorithm 4.3 are the lowest among the methods tested, but it misses more lines than others.

4. The clustering-based Algorithm 4.4 is relatively fast and detects many complete lines but only when an image is not noisy. Under noise, its various performance measures drop quickly.

5. Algorithms 4.1–4.3 can find lines among unorganized points, and, therefore, they can be used to find lines among image edges as well as among point sets generated by various scientific and engineering applications. The clustering-based Algorithm 4.4 can use unorganized points, but it requires gradient directions and gradient magnitudes at the points. The contour tracing-based Algorithm 4.5 and the curve-fitting-based Algorithm 4.6 use the connectivity information between edge pixels to find the lines.

6. While Algorithms 4.1–4.6 require preprocessing of an image to find the edges from which lines are detected, Algorithms 4.7 and 4.8 do not require preprocessing of an image and can find lines directly from intensity images.

In the preceding discussions, no mention was made of color images. If lines are to be detected in a color image using one of Algorithms 4.1–4.6, the color edges of the image can be determined [29, 30] and used to find the lines. If lines are to be detected using Algorithm 4.7 or 4.8, the luminance component of the color can be used to find the lines.

4.9 Revisiting Image Dominant Orientation Detection

In Chapter 2, a method for determining the dominant orientation of an image and a method for determining the rotational difference between two images using geometric gradients were described. In this section, the same problems are solved using line directions.

If the scene under consideration contains straight edges, the edges will appear as lines in the images of the scene. If correspondence can be established between a pair of lines in images captured under orthographic projection, the rotational difference between the images can be determined. Any homologous line pair will produce the same rotational difference.

If lines in an image are represented in polar form, the lines can be mapped to points in the polar space. For example, line

$$\rho = x \cos(\theta) + y \sin(\theta) \tag{4.39}$$

in the image space maps to point (ρ, θ) in the polar space. If the image is rotated by $\Delta\theta$ to obtain a new image with coordinates (x_1, y_1), the line in Eq. (4.39) will change to

$$\rho_1 = x_1 \cos(\theta + \Delta\theta) + y_1 \sin(\theta + \Delta\theta) \tag{4.40}$$

in the new image. This line maps to point $(\rho_1, \theta + \Delta\theta)$ in the polar space. Compared to (ρ, θ), we see that rotating an image by $\Delta\theta$ results in translation of the point corresponding to it in the polar space by $(\Delta\rho, \Delta\theta)$.

To determine the dominant orientation of an image, lines in the image are mapped to points in the polar space, and points in the polar space are projected to the θ axis to eliminate $\Delta\rho$. The projection of points in the polar space to the θ axis produces a histogram. The location of the highest peak in the histogram determines the dominant orientation of the image.

To determine the rotational difference between two images, the distance between the locations of the highest peaks in the histograms of the images is used as the rotational difference between the images. Therefore, if the location of the highest peak in the histogram obtained from the reference image is at θ_r and the location of the highest peak in the histogram obtained from the test image is at θ_t, we can conclude that the test image is rotated with respect to the reference image by $\Delta\theta = \theta_t - \theta_r$.

If a dominant peak does not exist in either of the images, instead of the difference of the locations of highest peaks in the histograms of line directions in the images, the histogram obtained from the test image is cyclically shifted over the histogram obtained from the reference image and the shift amount where the two histograms overlap the most is determined and used as the rotational difference between the images.

To demonstrate estimation of the rotational difference between two images using line directions, the Mars rock images shown in Fig. 4.22a and b are used. These images are courtesy of NASA. Directed lines detected in the images are also shown. The tip of a line is shown by a yellow dot. Among the line detection methods discussed earlier, Algorithms 4.1–4.3, 4.5, and 4.6 find line directions in the range 0–180° for not using intensity gradients at the edge points. Algorithms 4.4, 4.7, and 4.8 use intensity gradients and so can determine line directions in the range 0–360°.

When lines in an image are detected by Algorithms 4.1–4.3, 4.5, and 4.6, the lines can be given directions in the range 0–360° by checking the gradient direction at the center of each line segment. A detected line direction θ determined by these methods will be left as is or changed to $\pi + \theta$ to ensure that the right side of a line always appears brighter than its left side.

This is demonstrated in Fig. 4.22. There are 258 lines in Fig. 4.22a and 273 lines in Fig. 4.22b. The lines are detected by Algorithm 4.5. Therefore, detected line directions are in the range 0–180°. By extending the directions to 0–360° using intensity gradient direction at the center of each line, the directed lines shown in Fig. 4.22 are obtained.

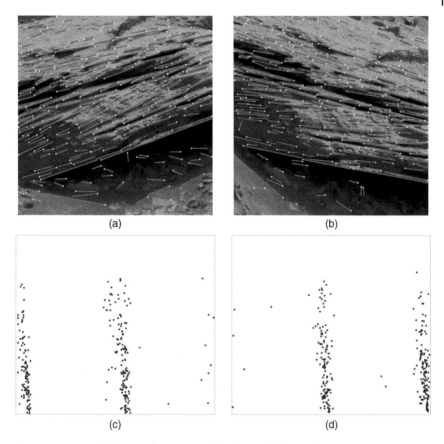

Figure 4.22 (a and b) Two rock images and the detected directed lines. (c and d) Points in the polar spaces of images (a) and (b).

After mapping the lines in each image to the polar space, the point sets shown in Fig. 4.22c and d are obtained. Horizontal axis shows θ and vertical axis shows ρ.

Projecting the points in the polar space to the horizontal (θ) axis, the histograms shown in Fig. 4.23a and b are obtained. Figure 4.23c shows overlaying of histogram a (red) and cyclic translation of histogram b (green) to best match histogram a. Rather than adding 1 to histogram bin θ, the length of the line in the image the point belongs to is added to the bin. This way, longer line segments influence the computed rotational difference between two images more than shorter line segments.

Taking the location of the most dominant peak in a histogram as the dominant orientation of its image, the dominant orientations in Fig. 4.22a and b are found to be 20° and 350°, respectively. Therefore, image (b) is rotated with respect to image (a) by 350° − 20° = 330° or −30°.

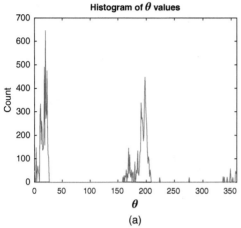

(a)

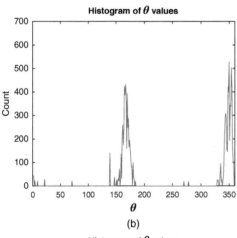

(b)

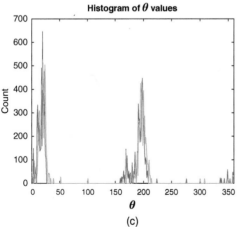

(c)

Figure 4.23 (a and b) Histograms of θ values in the polar spaces depicted in Fig. 4.22c and d. (c) The red histogram is the same as histogram (a) while the green histogram is a cyclic translation of histogram (b) by 30°.

If two nadir-view images of a scene are available, that is, if the images can be related by a similarity transformation, the rotational difference between the images can be determined unambiguously using line directions in the images. However, if the images represent off-nadir-view images of a scene, depending on the view angles of the camera capturing the images, a locally peak direction θ in one image can appear at $\theta \pm 180°$ in another image due to reflection of some vanishing points with respect to the image center, shifting the location of the highest peak in the direction histogram by $180°$. This subject is discussed further in Chapter 6 when covering vanishing points.

4.10   Further Reading

The Hough transform–based line detection method of Duda and Hart [11] is referred to as the standard Hough transform (SHT) line detection method in the literature. The weaknesses of line detection by SHT have been pointed out by Asano and Kawamura [31]. Some peaks in the accumulator array may result from noisy points and points belonging to various lines that intersect the detected line. Means to avoid noisy peaks have been explored by Furukawa and Shinagawa [32], as well as by Vindo et al. [33].

The length of a line segment detected by the Hough transform is difficult to determine because an obtained endpoint may represent a point on another line that intersects the path of a detected line. Li et al. [34] suggested discarding a detected line if the distance between its endpoints was much larger than the number of points on the line. Characteristics of line detection by the Hough transform using the polar equation of lines have been studied by Asano and Katoh [35], providing strategies for its effective implementation. If gradient magnitudes at the edge points are available, O'Gorman and Clowes [36] suggested incrementing accumulator array entries by gradient magnitudes at the points. In this way, stronger edges that are more likely to belong to a line play a bigger role in detecting the line than weaker edges that may be due to noise.

To reduce the effect of noisy and accidental points on a line, methods subdividing the image domain into regions, detecting line segments within each region by the Hough transform, and combining the detected segments into longer ones have been proposed [37–40]. After detecting lines within each region, lines from adjacent regions with similar parameters are merged to create longer lines. Isolated segments that are shorter than a prespecified length are considered noisy segments and discarded.

The characteristics of line detection by the Hough transform when using the slope and y-intercept equation of lines have been studied by Xu et al. [41] and Cha et al. [42]. To speed up line detection by the Hough transform, in a method known as *randomized Hough transform* (RHT), Xu et al. [41] selected point pairs randomly, calculated line parameters, and incremented the accumulator entry corresponding to the parameters of the line by 1. The process is repeated until the count in an entry reaches a prespecified value, showing a high likelihood that a line with the parameters of the entry exists among the points. The points lying on the line are then identified and removed from the set of points, and the process is repeated to detect additional lines from remaining points in the set.

Hare and Sandler [43] compared the performances of RHT and SHT, finding that when a small number of lines is present in an image, RHT is faster and produces fewer false lines than does SHT. However, when a large number of lines is present in an image, RHT produces more false lines than does SHT. To reduce false peaks by RHT, Shen et al. [44] suggested using gradient directions at the points to group the points into subsets of different gradient directions and selecting point pairs within the same group when incrementing accumulator entries. Use of gradient directions in selecting point pairs to increment accumulator entries creates sharper peaks and identifies lines that are more likely to exist in an image. The process is the same as clustering the points according to their gradient directions and then determining lines from points within each cluster by RHT.

Rather than selecting point pairs randomly, in a method known as *probabilistic Hough transform* (PHT) [45], a random subset of the points is selected and used in SHT to detect the lines. PHT has been found to achieve a considerably higher speed than SHT but at the cost of missing some of the smaller line segments. Shaked et al. [46] provided a means to take the sample size adaptively to avoid missing lines. In a method known as *progressive PHT* [47, 48], after processing each point, if the count for an entry reached a prespecified value, a line is declared. Kiryanti et al. [49] compared the performances of RHT and PHT in line detection, finding that RHT performs better than PHT in low noise images while PHT performs better than RHT in noisy and low-quality images.

In a variant of RHT known as *connective RHT* (CRHT), after a random point is selected, a window is centered at the point, a line is fitted to the pixels connected to the center point, and if the error in line fitting is smaller than a prespecified value, the entry of the accumulator array corresponding to the parameters of the line is incremented by 1 [50]. In CRHT, therefore, a sequence of points along an edge contour contributes to a line that is likely to exist rather than a possible unlikely line defined by two random points in RHT. The accumulator array obtained by CRHT, therefore, contains well-defined and sharper peaks than peaks in the accumulator array created by RHT.

In a method known as the *extended CRHT* (ECRHT), small gaps are allowed between points within the line-fitting window [19]; therefore, points in a window that are within a prespecified distance of each other are considered connected and a line is fitted to them. Because a larger number of points in a window participate in determining the line parameters, more well-defined peaks are obtained.

When drawing a sinusoid in the $\rho\theta$ space for each point in the xy space, because of the discrete nature of the parameter space, the sinusoid rarely passes through the centers of the cells that are incremented. Ji and Haralick [51] suggested dropping a Gaussian at uniformly spaced points along a sinusoid, finding the contribution of the Gaussian at each affecting cell, and incrementing each cell based on the contributions of the Gaussians. Bonci et al. [52] developed a maximum-likelihood line detector based on this Gaussian idea.

Fernandes and Oliveira [53] partitioned an edge contour into small segments and incremented array entries with ellipsoidal Gaussian weights computed from uncertainties of ρ and θ of points within a segment. Chao et al. [54], by using the chain-code information along a contour, determined the orientation θ at each contour pixel and incremented the accumulator entry satisfying θ and the coordinates of the pixel. By not incrementing array entries that are not likely to fall on a line with direction θ, sharp peaks are created in the accumulator array.

Rather than mapping a point in the xy space into a sinusoid in the $\rho\theta$ space, Sewisy [55] suggested mapping the point to a circle in the same xy space. The process is known as circle transform (CT) and is based on the observation that if point $\mathbf{p}_0 = (x_0, y_0)$ is the point on a line closest to the origin, then any circle passing through a point $\mathbf{p} = (x, y)$ on the line and the origin $\mathbf{o} = (0, 0)$ with diameter $\mathbf{op}$ will pass through point $\mathbf{p}_0$. Therefore, if xy is considered the accumulator array and for each point $\mathbf{p}$ in the image space, a circle is drawn with diameter $\mathbf{op}$, after drawing circles for all points in the image, a high count will be obtained at entry (x_0, y_0). If multiple lines are present in an image, by processing all points, multiple peaks will be formed in the accumulator array, each corresponding to a line. El Mejdani et al. [56] compared the performances of line detection by CT, SHT, and RHT, finding that the peaks produced by CT are more distinct than the peaks produced by SHT or by RHT.

Deans [57] showed that a special case of Radon transform shares many properties of the Hough transform and, therefore, can be used in line detection. Ho et al. [58] and Zheng and Shi [59] developed fast algorithms for calculating Radon transform, making line detection by Radon transform practical.

A number of clustering-based line detection methods have appeared in the literature. A clustering method described by Leavers et al. [60] determines for a pixel (x_i, y_i) along an edge contour parameter

$$\theta = \arctan\left(\frac{x - x_i}{y_i - y}\right) \tag{4.41}$$

using other pixels (x, y) along the same contour and clusters the resultant θ values. If (x_i, y_i) is truly on a long straight segment, a peak is obtained at the θ representing the angle of the line with the x-axis. Parameter ρ of the line is then determined by the least-squares method. By removing the contour pixels contributing to a detected line and repeating the process on the remaining pixels along the contour, other lines are detected. If point (x_i, y_i) is not on a long straight segment, a dominant peak will not be obtained.

Krishnapuram and Freg [61] and Barni and Gualtieri [62] added a postprocessing step to the clustering- based line detection method of Dudani and Luk [16], merging lines that have sufficiently close parameters. Clustering validity is then performed to determine whether or not a line segment is present among the points in a subset. Yu et al. [63], through a connected component analysis, merged line segments using their gradient directions to create longer line segments.

Various methods for detecting lines among edge contours have been proposed also. A method that determines points belonging to a line by the least-squares method is described by Wall and Danielsson [64]. In this method, an edge contour is traced and a line is fitted to the pixels visited thus far. The area between the contour and the line is determined and divided by the length of the line to obtain the area per unit line length. Whenever the area per unit length becomes larger than a prespecified value, the contour segment traced so far is replaced with the line approximating the points. The process is repeated until all pixels along the contour are processed. The same is repeated for other contours.

Bellman [12] developed an algorithm based on dynamic programming that segments a contour into a sequence of n line segments in such a way as to achieve least-squares error between the contour and the approximating line segments. Gluss [65] solved the same problem by treating the approximation error as information loss and, by minimizing the information loss, minimized approximation error in line fitting.

Chen et al. [66] and Wan and Ventura [67] solved the problem of approximating a digital curve (contour) by a polygon in two steps. Knowing the number of segments required in the approximating polygon, in the first step, the vertices of the polygon are placed at corner points along the contour. Then, the vertices are iteratively repositioned in such a way to minimize the sum of squared distances between the contour and the polygon. Hong and Li [68] achieved the same by dynamic programming.

A relatively small number of region subdivision-based line detection methods have appeared in the literature. A method described by Princen et al. [38] subdivides an image into regions and detects a line within each region by the Hough transform. Lines from adjacent regions with similar parameters are merged into longer lines and the process is repeated in a hierarchical manner until a region covering the entire image is obtained. A similar approach is described by Yacoub and Jolion [39] using a different region subdivision and merging method when going up the hierarchy.

A number of line detection methods have appeared in the literature that do not fall into any of the categories described earlier. Lu et al. [69] created a chain code of an edge contour, identifying corners within the contour, and segmenting the contour at the corners. Linear segments are then recognized from their chain codes. Etemadi [70] started with 2-pixel segments and merged adjacent segments as long as the merged segments satisfied the requirements for a line until no more merging was possible. Segments shorter than a threshold length were then discarded.

Guru et al. [71] centered a window at each edge, calculated the covariance matrix of the edges connected to the center edge, and if the smaller eigenvalue was sufficiently small, considered the corresponding eigenvector the direction of the line passing through the center edge in the window. Line segments with similar directions from adjacent windows were merged to create longer lines. In a similar method, Beumier [72] calculated the moment of inertia of points connected to the center of the window and if the moment was sufficiently small, the axis of minimum inertia was used as the line approximating the points.

Ding and Wang [73] partitioned a contour into segments by locating corners along the contour, found the eigenvalues and eigenvectors of each segment, and declared a segment a line if the smaller of the eigenvalues was sufficiently small. Liu et al. [74] used the first axis in the principal component analysis (PCA) of a local point set in an image as the major axis of the local point set. Lee et al. [75] further demonstrated use of PCA in detecting global lines in an image.

Mattavelli et al. [76] formulated the problem of line detection as one of partitioning an inconsistent linear system into consistent subsystems, the solution of each being a line.

Through wavelet transform and multiresolution analysis at three levels, Wang et al. [77] detected lines. First, line information at low resolution to mid resolution was used to produce intermediate lines. The intermediate lines were then used at high resolution to find the final lines. A line that appeared from low to high resolution was considered robust and kept. Multiple disconnected lines at high resolution that mapped to a single line at low resolution were merged to create a longer line.

Shimamura et al. [78] developed a genetic algorithm [79] that assigned the same label to points falling on or near a line. Then they used RANSAC [80] to identify all points in the image that belonged to the same line. Zheng et al. [81] developed a trainable hidden Markov model based on Vitebri decoding to find parallel lines in an image.

References

1 J.-C. Bazin, Y. Seo, C. Demonceaux, P. Vasseur, K. Ikeuchi, I. K. Kweon, and M. Pollefeys, Globally optimal line clustering and vanishing point estimation in Manhattan world, in *Proceedings of IEEE Conference on Computer Vision and Pattern Recognition*, 1063–6919, 2012.

2 B. Li, K. Peng, X. Ying, and H. Zha, Vanishing point detection using cascaded 1D Hough transform from single images, *Pattern Recognition Letters*, **33**:1–8, 2012.

3 B. W. He, X. L. Zhou, and Y. F. Li, A new camera calibration method from vanishing points in a vision system, *Transactions of the Institute of Measurement and Control*, **33**(7):806–822, 2011.

4 P. Fränti, E. I. Ageenko, H. Kälviäinen, and S. Kukkonen, Compression of line drawing images using Hough transform for exploiting global dependencies, in *Proceedings of the Joint Conference on Information Sciences*, 433–436, 1998.

5 P. Kahn, L. Kitchen, and E. M. Riseman, A fast line finder for vision-guided robot navigation, *IEEE Transactions on Pattern Analysis and Machine Intelligence*, **12**(11):1098–1102, 1990.

6 O. A. Aider, P. Hoppenot, and E. Colle, A model-based method for indoor mobile robot localization using monocular vision and straight-line correspondences, *Robotics and Autonomous Systems*, **52**:229–246, 2005.

7 C. X. Ji and Z. P. Zhang, Stereo match based on linear feature, in *Proceedings of International Conference on Pattern Recognition*, 875–878, 1988.

8 C. Schmid and A. Zisserman, The geometry and matching of lines and curves over multiple views, *International Journal of Computer Vision*, **40**(3):199–233, 2000.

9 E. Guillou, D. Meneveaux, E. Maisel, and K. Bouatouch, Using vanishing points for camera calibration and coarse 3-D reconstruction from a single image, *The Visual Computer*, **16**:396–410, 2000.

10 P. V. C. Hough, *Method and means for recognizing complex patterns*, U.S. Patent 3,069,654, Dec. 18, 1962.

11 R. O. Duda and P. E. Hart, Use of the Hough transform to detect lines and curves in pictures, *Communications of the ACM*, **15**(1):11–15, 1972.

12 R. Bellman, On the approximation of curves by line segments using dynamic programming, *Communications of the ACM*, **4**(6):284, 1961.

13 T. Pavlidis and S. L. Horowitz, Segmentation of plane curves, *IEEE Transactions on Computers*, **23**(8):860–870, 1974.

14 L. G. Roberts, *Machine Perception of Three-Dimensional Solids*, Department of Electrical Engineering, Massachusetts Institute of Technology, June 1963.

15 J. Canny, A computational approach to edge detection, *IEEE Transactions on Pattern Analysis and Machine Intelligence*, **8**(6):679–698, 1986.

16 S. A. Dudani and A. L. Luk, Locating straight-line edge segments on outdoor scenes, *Pattern Recognition*, **10**:145–157, 1978.

17 K. Inui, S. Kaneko, and S. Igarashi, Robust line fitting using LMedS clustering, *Systems and Computers in Japan*, **34**(14):92–100, 2003.

18 P. J. Rousseeuw and A. M. Leroy, *Robust Regression and Outlier Detection*, John Wiley & Sons, New York, 1987.

19 V. Kyrki and H. Kälviäinen, Combination of local and global line extraction, *Real-Time Imaging*, **6**:79–91, 2000.

20 A. Goshtasby, Design and recovery of 2-D and 3-D shapes using rational Gaussian curves and surfaces, *International Journal of Computer Vision*, **10**(3):233–256, 1993.

21 A. Goshtasby, Geometric modeling using rational Gaussian curves and surfaces, *Computer-Aided Design*, **27**(5):363–375, 1995.

22 M. E. Mortenson, *Geometric Modeling*, Industrial Press, 2006.

23 J. B. Burns, A. R. Hanson, and E. M. Riseman, Extracting straight lines, *IEEE Transactions on Pattern Analysis and Machine Intelligence*, **8**(4):425–455, 1986.

24 R. G. von Gioi, J. Jakubowicz, and G. Randall, Multisegment detection, in *Proceedings of IEEE International Conference on Image Processing*, Vol. **2**, 253–256, 2007.

25 R. G. von Gioi, J. Jakubowicz, J.-M. Morel, and G. Randall, On straight line segment detection, *Journal of Mathematical Imaging and Vision*, **32**:313–347, 2008.

26 R. G. von Gioi, J. Jakubowicz, J.-M. Morel, and G. Randall, LSD: a fast line segment detector with a false detection control, *IEEE Transactions on Pattern Analysis and Machine Intelligence*, **32**(4):722–732, 2010.

27 A. Desolneux, L. Moisan, and J. M. Morel, Meaningful alignments, *International Journal of Computer Vision*, **40**(1):7–23, 2000.

28 R. G. von Gioi, J. Jakubowicz, J.-M. Morel, and G. Randall, LSD: a line segment detector, *Image Processing On Line*, **2**:35–55, 2012.

29 M. A. Ruzon and C. Tomasi, Color edge detection with the compass operator, in *IEEE Conference on Computer Vision and Pattern Recognition*, Vol. **2**, 160–166, 1999.

30 P. E. Trahanias and A. N. Venetsanopoulos, Color edge detection using vector order statistics, *IEEE Transactions on Image Processing*, **2**(2):259–264, 1993.

31 T. Asano and Y. Kawamura, Algorithmic considerations on the computational complexities of digital line extraction problem, *Systems and Computers in Japan*, **31**(14):80–89, 2000.

32 Y. Furukawa and Y. Shinagawa, Accurate and robust line segment extraction by analyzing distribution around peaks in Hough space, *Computer Vision and Image Understanding*, **92**:1–25, 2003.

33 V. V. Vindo, S. Chaudhury, S. Ghose, and J. Mukherjee, A connectionist approach for peak detection in Hough space, *Pattern Recognition*, **25**(10):1253–1264, 1992.

34 H. F. Li, D. Pao, and R. Jayakumar, Improvements and systolic implementation of the Hough transformation for straight line detection, *Pattern Recognition*, **22**(6):697–706, 1989.

35 T. Asano and N. Katoh, Variants for the Hough transform for line detection, *Computational Geometry*, **6**:231–252, 1996.

36 F. O'Gorman and M. B. Clowes, Finding picture edges through colinearity of feature points, *IEEE Transactions on Computers*, **25**(4):449–486, 1976.

37 K. Murakami and T. Naruse, High-speed line detection method using Hough transform in local area, *Systems and Computers in Japan*, **32**(10):22–30, 2001.

38 J. Princen, J. Illingworth, and J. Kittler, A hierarchical approach to line extraction, in *Proceedings of Computer Vision and Pattern Recognition Conference*, 92–97, 1989.

39 S. B. Yacoub and J.-M. Jolion, Hierarchical line extraction, *IEE Proceedings – Vision, Image, and Signal Processing*, **142**(1):7–14, 1995.

40 Y. Zhang and R. Webber, A windowing approach to detecting line segments using Hough transform, *Pattern Recognition*, **29**(2):255–263, 1996.

41 L. Xu, E. Oja, and P. Kultanen, A new curve detection method: randomized Hough transform (RHT), *Pattern Recognition Letters*, **11**:331–338, 1990.

42 J. Cha, R. H. Cofer, and S. P. Kozaitis, Extended Hough transform for linear feature detection, *Pattern Recognition*, **39**:1034–1043, 2006.

43 A. R. Hare and M. B. Sandler, General test framework for straight-line detection by Hough transforms, in *Proceedings of IEEE International Symposium on Circuits and Systems*, 239–242, 1993.

44 X. Shen, J. Zhang, S. Yu, L. Meng, and K.-L. Du, An improved sampling strategy for randomized Hough transform based line detection, in *Proceedings of International Conference on Systems and Informatics*, 1874–1877, 2012.

45 N. Kiryanti, Y. Eldar, and A. M. Bruckstein, Probabilistic Hough transform, *Pattern Recognition*, **24**(4):303–316, 1991.

46 D. Shaked, O. Yaron, and N. Kiryanti, Deriving stopping rules for the probabilistic Hough transform by sequential analysis, *Computer Vision and Image Understanding*, **63**(3):512–526, 1996.

47 C. Galambos, J. Matas, and J. Kittler, Progressive probabilistic Hough transform for line detection, in *Proceedings of Computer Vision and Pattern Recognition Conference*, Vol. **1**, 554–560, 1999.

48 J. Matas, C. Galambos, and J. Kittler, Robust detection of lines using the progressive probabilistic Hough transform, *Computer Vision and Image Understanding*, **78**:119–137, 2000.

49 N. Kiryanti, H. Kälaviäinen and S. Alaoutinen, Randomized or probabilistic Hough transform: unified performance evaluation, *Pattern Recognition Letters*, **21**:1157–1164, 2000.

50 H. Kälviäinen and P. Hirvonen, An extension to the randomized Hough transform exploiting connectivity, *Pattern Recognition Letters*, **18**:77–85, 1997.

51 Q. Ji and R. M. Haralick, An improved Hough transform technique based on error propagation, in *Proceedings of IEEE International Conference on Systems, Man, and Cybernetics*, Vol. **5**, 4653–4658, 1998.

52 A. Bonci, T. Leo, and S. Longhi, A Bayesian approach to the Hough transform for line detection, *IEEE Transactions on Systems, Man, and Cybernetics Part A: Systems and Humans*, **35**(6):945–955, 2005.

53 L. A. F. Fernandes and M. M. Oliveira, Real-time line detection through an improved Hough transform voting scheme, *Pattern Recognition*, **41**:299–314 2008, also see the corrigendum to this article in *Pattern Recognition*, 41:2964, 2008.

54 L. Chao, W. Zhong, and L. Lin, An improved HT algorithm on straight line detection based on freeman chain code, in *2nd International Conference on Image and Signal Processing*, 1–4, 2009.

55 A. A. Sewisy, Graphical techniques for detecting lines with the Hough transform, *International Journal of Computer Mathematics*, **79**:49–64, 2002.

56 S. El Mejdani, R. Egli, and F. Dubeau, Straight-line detectors: description and comparison, *Pattern Recognition*, **41**:1845–1866, 2008.

57 S. R. Deans, Hough transform from the Radon transform, *IEEE Transactions on Pattern Analysis and Machine Intelligence*, **3**(2):185–188, 1981.

58 C. G. Ho, R. C. D. Young, C. D. Bradfield, and C. R. Chatwin, A fast Hough transform for the parametrisation of straight lines using Fourier methods, *Real-Time Imaging*, **6**:113–127, 2000.

59 L. Zheng and D. Shi, Advanced Radon transform using generalized interpolated Fourier method for straight line detection, *Computer Vision and Image Understanding*, **115**:152–160, 2011.

60 V. F. Leavers, D. Ben-Tzvi, and M. B. Sandler, A dynamic combinatorial Hough transform for straight lines and circles, in *Proceedings of the Alvey Vision Conference*, 163–168, 1989.

61 R. Krishnapuram and C.-P. Freg, Fitting an unknown number of lines and planes to image data through compatible cluster merging, *Pattern Recognition*, **25**(4):385–400, 1992.

62 M. Barni and R. Gualtieri, A new possibilistic clustering algorithm for line detection in real world imagery, *Pattern Recognition*, **32**:1897–1909, 1999.

63 W. P. Yu, G. W. Chu, and M. J. Chung, A robust line extraction method by unsupervised line clustering, *Pattern Recognition*, **32**:529–546, 1999.

64 K. Wall and P.-E. Danielsson, A fast sequential method for polygonal approximation of digitized curves, *Computer Vision, Graphics, and Image Processing*, **28**:220–227, 1984.

65 B. Gluss, A line segment curve-fitting algorithm related to optimal encoding of information, *Information and Control*, **5**:261–267, 1962.

66 J.-M. Chen, J. A. Ventura, and C.-H. Wu, Segmentation of planar curves into circular and line segments, *Image and Vision Computing*, **14**:71–83, 1996.

67 W. Wan and J. A. Ventura, Segmentation of planar curves into straight-line segments and elliptical arcs, *Graphical Models and Image Processing*, **59**(6):484–494, 1997.

68 J.-H. Hong and J. T. Li, A dynamic programming approach for fitting digital planar curves with line segments and circular arcs, *Pattern Recognition Letters*, **22**:183–197, 2001.

69 G.-Q. Lu, L.-G. Xu, and Y.-B. Li, Line detection based on chain code detection, in *IEEE International Conference on Vehicular Electronics and Safety*, 98–103, 2005.

70 A. Etemadi, Robust segmentation of edge data, in *Proceedings of International Conference on Image Processing and its Applications*, 311–314, 1992.

71 D. S. Guru, B. H. Shekar, and P. Nagabhushan, A simple and robust line detection algorithm based on small eigenvalue analysis, *Pattern Recognition Letters*, **25**:1–13, 2004.

72 C. Beumier, Straight line detection using moment of inertia, in *Proceedings of IEEE International Conference on Industrial Technology*, 1753–1756, 2006.

73 W. Ding and W. Wang, A novel line detection algorithm based on endpoint estimation, in *6th International Congress on Image and Signal Processing*, 400–404, 2013.

74 Z.-Y. Liu, K.-C. Chiu, and L. Xu, Strip line detection and thinning by RPCL-based local PCA, *Pattern Recognition Letters*, **24**:2335–2344, 2003.

75 Y.-S. Lee, H.-S. Koo, and C.-S. Jeong, A straight line detection using principal component analysis, *Pattern Recognition Letters*, **27**:1744–1754, 2006.

76 M. Mattavelli, V. Noel, and E. Amaldi, A new approach for fast line detection based on combinatorial optimization, *Proceedings of International Conference on Image Analysis and Processing*, 168–173, 1999.

77 J. Wang, T. Ikenaga, S. Goto, K. Kunieda, K. Iwata, H. Koizumi, and H. Shimazu, A new multiscale line detection approach for aerial image with complex scene, in *Proceedings of Circuits and Systems Conference*, 1968–1971, 2006.

78 T. Shimamura, M. Hashimoto, T. Fujiwara, T. Funahashi, and H. Koshimizu, Multiple straight line detection based on labeling of pixels by Genetic algorithm, in *17th Korea-Japan Joint Workshop on Frontiers of Computer Vision*, 1–5, 2011.

79 D. E. Goldberg, *Genetic Algorithms in Search, Optimization, and Machine Learning*, Addison Wesley, 1989.

80 M. A. Fischler and R. C. Bolles, Random sample consensus: a paradigm for model fitting with applications to image analysis and automated cartography, *Communications of the ACM*, **24**(6):381–395, 1981.

81 Y. Zheng, H. Li, and D. Doermann, A parallel-line detection algorithm based on HMM decoding, *IEEE Transactions on Pattern Analysis and Machine Intelligence*, **27**(5):777–792, 2005.

5

Finding Homologous Points

5.1 Introduction

Finding homologous points in two images of a scene is the first step in determining the parameters of a transformation model that will ultimately register the images. Homologous points are found either by detecting feature points in each image separately and then finding the correspondence between the feature points, or by detecting feature points in the reference image and then locating the same feature points in the test image by template matching. The former method is used when the images are in the same modality and the latter method is used when the images are in different modalities.

In this chapter, various methods for finding homologous points in two images of a scene are described. When a set of points in each image is given and it is required to find correspondence between the points, the problem becomes one of point pattern matching and is covered in Section 5.2. If the type of transformation model relating the points is known, the parameters of the transformation can be determined by clustering [1] or random sample consensus (RANSAC) [2]. These topics are covered in Sections 5.2.1 and 5.2.2.

If each point is associated with a set of features (a descriptor) that characterizes the neighborhood of the point, an initial set of homologous points is obtained by matching the features/descriptors of the points. Possible incorrect homologous points are then identified and removed by RANSAC. To obtain similar descriptors for homologous points, the images must be of the same modality so that homologous neighborhoods exhibit similar properties. Example image descriptors that can be used to find initial correspondence between feature points in images of a scene are described in Section 5.3.

If the images are in different modalities, it is unlikely that the feature points detected in the images show the same scene points. In such a situation, feature points are detected in the reference image and the same feature points are searched for in the test image using an appropriate similarity or distance measure. The process is known as template matching and is covered

Theory and Applications of Image Registration, First Edition. Arthur Ardeshir Goshtasby.
© 2017 John Wiley & Sons, Inc. Published 2017 by John Wiley & Sons, Inc.

in Section 5.6. Various similarity and distance measures used in template matching are discussed in Sections 5.4 and 5.5.

5.2 Point Pattern Matching

In point pattern matching, two sets of points

$$\mathbf{p} = \{\mathbf{p}_i : i = 1, \ldots, m\}; \quad \mathbf{P} = \{\mathbf{P}_i : i = 1, \ldots, n\} \tag{5.1}$$

are given and it is required to find the correspondence between the points. In 2-D, $\mathbf{p}_i = (x_i, y_i)$ and $\mathbf{P}_i = (X_i, Y_i)$. Point set $\mathbf{p}$ represents points in the reference image, and point set $\mathbf{P}$ represents points in the test image. Some points in $\mathbf{p}$ could be missed in $\mathbf{P}$ and some points in $\mathbf{P}$ could be missed in $\mathbf{p}$. Homologous points can be found only for those points that appear in both sets.

Due to digital and radiometric noise, as well as various image distortions, points in each image could be displaced from their true positions by a few to several pixels. It is assumed that errors in point positions are generally much smaller than distances between points in each point set.

It is also assumed that the type of the transformation model relating the two point sets is known, although the parameters of the transformation model are not known. The simplest transformation is *translation*. Denoting coordinates of points in the reference image by (x, y) and coordinates of points in the test image by (X, Y), when the images are translated with respect to each other, the relation between homologous points in the point sets can be written as

$$X = x + t_x, \tag{5.2}$$
$$Y = y + t_y. \tag{5.3}$$

By translating points in point set $\mathbf{p}$ by (t_x, t_y), the homologous points in point set $\mathbf{P}$ will be obtained.

Adjacent frames in a video of a relatively flat scene that is captured by a moving camera can be related by this transformation. Under translation, not only distances between points and angles between lines remain unchanged, orientations of lines remain unchanged.

Consider an image of a scene captured by an aircraft from a very high altitude at nadir view and another image of the same scene captured at nadir view from the same altitude while the aircraft is pointing in a different direction. The two images will have translation and rotation differences. Homologous points in such images are related by a *rigid* or *Euclidean transformation*:

$$X = x\cos(\theta) - y\sin(\theta) + t_x, \tag{5.4}$$
$$Y = x\sin(\theta) + y\cos(\theta) + t_y. \tag{5.5}$$

By rotating points in set **p** by θ and translating them by (t_x, t_y), homologous points in set **P** are obtained. Under the rigid transformation, distances between points and angles between lines remain unchanged.

If the images are taken from the same altitude of a scene at nadir view but at different zoom levels, the transformation model relating the geometries of the images is known as the *similarity transformation*:

$$X = s[x \cos(\theta) - y \sin(\theta)] + t_x, \tag{5.6}$$
$$Y = s[x \sin(\theta) + y \cos(\theta)] + t_y. \tag{5.7}$$

By rotating points in **p** by θ, then scaling them by s, and finally translating them by (t_x, t_y), the homologous points in **P** are obtained. Similarity transformation does not preserve distances between points, but it preserves angles between lines.

If the images of a flat scene are obtained from off-nadir views and from afar, coordinates of homologous points in the images will be related by the *affine transformation*:

$$X = ax + by + c, \tag{5.8}$$
$$Y = dx + dy + f. \tag{5.9}$$

Under the affine transformation, angles are not preserved, but parallel lines remain parallel. The images, in addition to having translation, rotation, and scaling differences, will have shearing differences.

In affine transformation, parameters of the X-component transformation are independent of parameters of the Y-component transformation. Note that relation between images with translation, rotation, scaling, and shearing differences can be written as

$$\begin{bmatrix} 1 & 0 & t_x \\ 0 & 1 & t_y \\ 0 & 0 & 1 \end{bmatrix} \begin{bmatrix} \cos\theta & -\sin\theta & 0 \\ \sin\theta & \cos\theta & 0 \\ 0 & 0 & 1 \end{bmatrix} \begin{bmatrix} s & 0 & 0 \\ 0 & s & 0 \\ 0 & 0 & 1 \end{bmatrix} \begin{bmatrix} 1 & \alpha & 0 \\ \beta & 1 & 0 \\ 0 & 0 & 1 \end{bmatrix} \tag{5.10}$$

or

$$\begin{bmatrix} s(\cos\theta - \beta \sin\theta) & s(\alpha \cos\theta - \sin\theta) & t_x \\ s(\sin\theta + \beta \cos\theta) & s(\alpha \sin\theta + \cos\theta) & t_y \\ 0 & 0 & 1 \end{bmatrix}. \tag{5.11}$$

This shows that the components of the transformation defined by Eq. (5.11) are dependent on each other because parameters s and θ are shared by both components of the transformation.

Comparing transformation matrix (5.11) to the equations of the affine transformation given by Eqs (5.8) and (5.9), we find

$$a = s(\cos\theta - \beta \sin\theta), \tag{5.12}$$
$$b = s(\alpha \cos\theta - \sin\theta), \tag{5.13}$$

$$c = t_x, \tag{5.14}$$

$$d = s(\sin\theta + \beta\cos\theta), \tag{5.15}$$

$$e = s(\alpha\sin\theta + \cos\theta), \tag{5.16}$$

$$f = t_y. \tag{5.17}$$

If the cameras capturing images of a scene are not very far from the scene but the scene is flat, points in the images of the scene will be related by a *2-D projective transformation* also known as *homography*. The coordinates of homologous points in images related by a homography satisfy the following relations:

$$X = \frac{ax + by + c}{gx + hy + 1}, \tag{5.18}$$

$$Y = \frac{dx + ey + f}{gx + hy + 1}. \tag{5.19}$$

The only property that is preserved under the projective transformation is colinearity. That is, a line segment in the scene is mapped to a line segment in its images. Similarly, a line segment in an image remains a line segment after transformation by a homography, although the length and orientation of the line may change.

Table 5.1 shows the invariant properties of images related by various transformation models and the number of unknown parameters in each transformation. The homography transformation preserves colinearity; the affine transformation, in addition to colinearity, preserves parallelism; the similarity transformation preserves angles in addition to parallelism and colinearity; the rigid transformation preserves all properties of the similarity transformation plus distances; and translation, in addition to preserving all properties of the rigid transformation, preserves image orientation.

The problem to be solved in point pattern matching is as follows. Given two sets of 2-D points, as shown in (5.1), and knowing the type of transformation relating the points, we would like to determine the parameters of

Table 5.1 Invariant properties and the number of unknown parameters of various transformation models used in registration of images of flat scenes.

Transformation function	Invariant properties	Unknowns
Translation	Orientations, distances, and angles	2
Rigid	Distances and angles	3
Similarity	Angles	4
Affine	Parallelism	6
Homography	Colinearity	8

the transformation. The transformation models considered in point pattern matching are those listed in Table 5.1.

If the point patterns are related by an unknown nonlinear transformation, homologous points in the images are determined by template matching, described in Section 5.6.

5.2.1   Parameter Estimation by Clustering

If two point sets are related by a transformation with a small number of parameters, first the independent parameters are determined one at a time and then the remaining parameters are determined. For example, if the images are related by a rigid transformation, since the parameters to be determined are translation and rotation, and rotation is independent of translation but translation is dependent on rotation, first rotation is determined and then translation is found.

Suppose points $\mathbf{p}_1$ and $\mathbf{p}_2$ are selected from set $\mathbf{p}$, and points $\mathbf{P}_1$ and $\mathbf{P}_2$ are selected from set $\mathbf{P}$ (Fig. 5.1). If these points truly correspond, the angle θ between lines connecting the points will be the same as the rotational difference between the point sets. If there are many homologous points in the point sets, there will be many homologous lines in the point sets that produce the same angle θ. All homologous point pairs from the point sets produce angles that are the same as the rotational difference between the point sets. Point pairs from the two sets that do not correspond produce random angles. Therefore, if a histogram is created of angles between lines connecting random point pairs in the point sets, a peak will appear at the angle representing the rotational difference between the point sets.

The following algorithm determines the rotational difference θ between the point sets given in (5.1) by clustering. H is a histogram with 360 bins, with bin θ

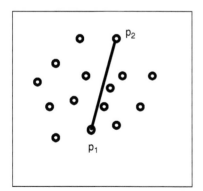
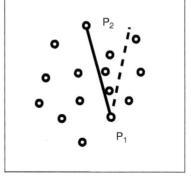

Figure 5.1 When two point sets are related by a rigid transformation, the angle between homologous lines $\mathbf{p}_1\mathbf{p}_2$ and $\mathbf{P}_1\mathbf{P}_2$ determines the angle between the point sets. The dashed line in the right point set is parallel to line $\mathbf{p}_1\mathbf{p}_2$ in the left point set.

showing the number of line pairs from the two sets that make angle θ. t counts the number of line pairs tested so far, and t_m is the number of line pairs to be tested before finding the histogram's most dominant peak.

Since the point sets are related by a rigid transformation, distances between homologous point pairs in the point sets will be about the same. If the distance between the point pair selected in set $\mathbf{p}$ divided by the distance between the point pair selected in set $\mathbf{P}$ is between $1 - \epsilon$ and $1 + \epsilon$, the angle θ between the lines is determined and $H(\theta)$ is incremented. Otherwise, new point pairs are selected from the two sets and the process is repeated. ϵ is a small error tolerance, such as 0.1. By ignoring point pairs from the two sets that have different distances, the process avoids entering angles that are not likely to represent the true rotational difference between the point sets to the histogram, sharpening the peak at the true rotational difference between the point sets.

Algorithm 5.1a   Determining rotational difference between two point sets by clustering

---

1. Allocate an integer array H with 360 entries and initialize all entries to 0. Also, let $t = 0$.
2. Select a pair of points in set $\mathbf{p}$ and denote them by $\mathbf{p}_1$ and $\mathbf{p}_2$ and select a pair of points in set $\mathbf{P}$ and denote them by $\mathbf{P}_1$ and $\mathbf{P}_2$.
3. If $1 - \epsilon < \frac{\|\mathbf{p}_1 - \mathbf{p}_2\|}{\|\mathbf{P}_1 - \mathbf{P}_2\|} < 1 + \epsilon$, find angle θ required to rotate line $\mathbf{p}_1\mathbf{p}_2$ to have the same orientation as line $\mathbf{P}_1\mathbf{P}_2$ and go to Step 4. Otherwise, go to Step 2.
4. Increment $H[\theta]$ by 1. Also, increment t by 1 and if $t \geq t_m$, go to Step 5; otherwise, go to Step 2.
5. If the highest count in histogram H appears at entry $\hat{\theta}$, return $\hat{\theta}$ as the most likely rotational difference between the point sets.

If the angle line $\mathbf{p}_1\mathbf{p}_2$ makes with the x-axis is θ_p and the angle line $\mathbf{P}_1\mathbf{P}_2$ makes with the X-axis is θ_P, in Step 3, $\theta = \theta_P - \theta_p$. Measuring angles in this manner allows the rotational difference between the point sets to vary between 0 and 2π.

Since the lines are not directed, if line $\mathbf{p}_1\mathbf{p}_2$ matches line $\mathbf{P}_1\mathbf{P}_2$, then line $\mathbf{p}_2\mathbf{p}_1$ also matches line $\mathbf{P}_1\mathbf{P}_2$. Therefore, if $\theta < \pi$ is the true rotational difference between the point sets, a peak will also be observed at $\theta + \pi$ with about the same height. This ambiguity will be removed later by choosing the angle that produces a stronger peak when determining the translational difference between the point sets.

If there are m points in $\mathbf{p}$ and n points in $\mathbf{P}$ and if half of the points in $\mathbf{p}$ also appear in $\mathbf{P}$, on average, every two points that are randomly selected in $\mathbf{p}$ will have one correspondence in $\mathbf{P}$. If four points are selected in $\mathbf{p}$, on average, two of the points will have correspondences in $\mathbf{P}$.

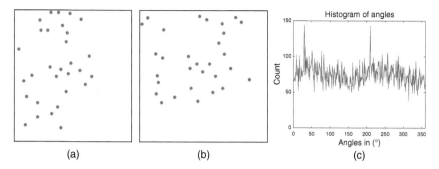

Figure 5.2 (a) Points in set 1. (b) Points in set 2. (c) Histogram of the angular difference of lines created by randomly selecting a point pair in each set. Peaks of about the same height are obtained at 30° and 210°.

When a point pair is selected in **p** that also appears in **P**, for each point in **p**, there will be a need to test n points in **P** to find its correspondence, and to find two points in **P** that correspond to two points in **p**, n^2 point pairs in **P** need to be tested. Therefore, the number of point pairs in the images to be tested to find a pair of homologous points is $4n^2$. To find $m/4$ homologous points in the point sets, Steps 2–5 must be repeated mn^2 times. This shows that $t_m = mn^2$. Using the point sets depicted in Fig. 5.2a and b, the histogram shown in (c) is obtained when letting $t_m = mn^2$. The histogram shows two strong peaks at 30° and 210°.

After finding θ, one can determine parameters t_x and t_y one at a time or jointly by clustering using equations

$$t_x = X - x\cos\theta - y\sin\theta, \tag{5.20}$$
$$t_y = Y + x\cos\theta - y\cos\theta. \tag{5.21}$$

Selecting a point from each point set and assuming they correspond, parameters t_x and t_y can be determined from Eqs (5.20) and (5.21). Points that truly correspond will produce the same translation parameters, and points that do not correspond will produce translation parameters that randomly fill the parameter space. Selecting random points from the point sets, determining translation parameters t_x and t_y, and recording the results in a 2-D histogram, a peak will start to emerge after a sufficient number of iterations.

Considering a 2-D histogram of dimensions $D \times D$ where $D = 2d + 1$ and d is the larger of the number of rows and the number of columns in the test image. This allows t_x and t_y to vary between $-d$ and d. The following algorithm provides the steps needed to find the translational difference between two point sets with a known rotational difference. T is a 2-D histogram of size $D \times D$, t is a counter showing the number of random points from each set tested thus far, and t_m is the number of random points from each set to be tested before finding the translation parameters from the created histogram.

Algorithm 5.1b   Finding the translational difference between two point sets by clustering

---

1. Initialize all entries of 2-D histogram T of dimensions $(2d + 1) \times (2d + 1)$ to 0. Also, let $t = 0$.
2. Select a point randomly from $\mathbf{p}$ and a point randomly from $\mathbf{P}$, and denote them by (x, y) and (X, Y), respectively.
3. Determine t_x and t_y from Eqs (5.9) and (5.10) and, if $-d \le t_x < d$ and $-d \le t_y < d$, increment $T[t_x + d, t_y + d]$ by 1. Otherwise, go to Step 2.
4. Increment t by 1 and if $t < t_m$, go to Step 2. Otherwise, if the location of the histogram peak is (t_1, t_2), return $t_x = t_1 - d$ and $t_y = t_2 - d$ as the translation of the test point set after it is rotated by θ determined by Algorithm 5.1a with respect to the reference point set.

If there are m points in $\mathbf{p}$ and n points in $\mathbf{P}$ and if about half of the points in $\mathbf{p}$ appear in $\mathbf{P}$, on average, every other point selected in $\mathbf{p}$ will exist in $\mathbf{P}$. If a point is selected in $\mathbf{p}$ that has a correspondence in $\mathbf{P}$, to select the homologous point in $\mathbf{P}$, it requires on average testing of n points in $\mathbf{P}$. Therefore, on average, $2n$ points must be tested before finding a single homologous point pair. To obtain a peak that is formed from $m/4$ points in $\mathbf{p}$, overall $mn/2$ iterations will be needed. This shows that we must let $t_m = mn/2$ in Algorithm 5.1b.

Using the point sets shown by (a) and (b) in Fig. 5.2 and the rotational differences shown by the two peaks in Fig. 5.2c, two histograms are obtained as shown in (a) and (b) in Fig. 5.3. A clear peak is obtained at $(4, -2)$ in (a) for using $\theta = 30°$, while no clear peak is observed in (b) when using $\theta = 210°$. Therefore, $\theta = 30°$ is taken as the rotation and $(4, -2)$ is taken as the translation of the test point set with respect to the reference point set. Overlaying of the points using the obtained translation and rotation parameters is shown in

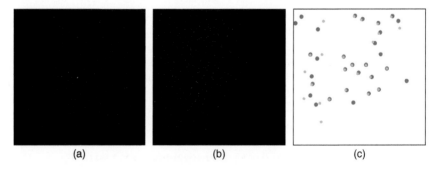

(a)   (b)   (c)

Figure 5.3 The translation histograms when using (a) $\theta = 30°$ and (b) $\theta = 210°$. Higher counts are shown brighter. (c) Rigid transformation of points in $\mathbf{p}$ (shown in green) using the obtained translation and rotation parameters and points in $\mathbf{P}$ (shown in red).

Fig. 5.3c. More accurate parameters can be determined by least squares or a robust estimator discussed in Section 5.7.

Point pattern matching by clustering is most effective when the point sets are shifted with respect to each other or are related by a rigid transformation. When the point sets are related by the similarity transformation, determination of the scale difference between the point sets becomes a challenge because the scale is usually a small floating point number that can assume any value, and coming up with a proper histogram to quantize scale is not obvious. For point sets related by similarity, affine, or projective transformations, a more suitable approach for determining the unknown parameters of the transformation model is RANSAC [2], discussed next.

5.2.2 Parameter Estimation by RANSAC

In the RANSAC paradigm, all parameters of a transformation are determined simultaneously. The process consists of a hypothesis step and a verification step. In the hypothesis step, an appropriate number of points from each set is selected and the points are assumed to correspond. Then, from the corresponding points the parameters of the transformation model are determined. In the verification step, the number of other points in the two sets that also correspond with the obtained transformation are determined and if the number is sufficiently high, the hypothesized transformation is considered correct. Otherwise, the hypothesis and verification steps are repeated until either a transformation is found that is supported by a sufficiently large number of points in the two sets or the maximum number of iterations is reached.

If the point sets are related by a similarity transformation, a pair of points is selected from each set. Denoting the points selected from set $\mathbf{p}$ by $\mathbf{p}_1$ and $\mathbf{p}_2$ and the points selected from set $\mathbf{P}$ by $\mathbf{P}_1$ and $\mathbf{P}_2$, first, the scale of set $\mathbf{P}$ with respect to the scale of set $\mathbf{p}$ is determined from $s = \frac{\|\mathbf{P}_1 - \mathbf{P}_2\|}{\|\mathbf{p}_1 - \mathbf{p}_2\|}$. Rotation θ of $\mathbf{P}$ with respect to $\mathbf{p}$ is determined from the angle of lines $\mathbf{P}_1 \mathbf{P}_2$ with the X-axis minus the angle of line $\mathbf{p}_1 \mathbf{p}_2$ with the x-axis. Knowing the scale and rotation parameters, the translation of $\mathbf{P}$ with respect to $\mathbf{p}$ is determined from

$$t_x = X - s[x \cos(\theta) - y \sin(\theta)], \tag{5.22}$$

$$t_y = Y - s[x \sin(\theta) + y \cos(\theta)]. \tag{5.23}$$

If the point pairs selected randomly from the point sets truly correspond, the parameters s, θ, t_x, and t_y obtained from them map many points in $\mathbf{p}$ to the homologous points in $\mathbf{P}$. Therefore, for each point (x, y) in $\mathbf{p}$, the coordinates of the homologous point $(\hat{X}, \hat{Y})$ in $\mathbf{P}$ are determined using Eqs (5.6) and (5.7), and if $(\hat{X}, \hat{Y})$ falls sufficiently close to a point with coordinates (X, Y) in $\mathbf{P}$, point (x, y) is considered corresponding to point (X, Y). If a sufficiently large number of homologous points is obtained, parameters s, θ, t_x, and t_y are considered parameters of the similarity transformation model relating the coordinates of points in **p** to the coordinates of homologous points in **P**.

Two points are considered sufficiently close if they are within a few to several pixels of each other depending on noise level among the points. If the points are very accurately positioned, the distance tolerance can be as small as 1 or 2 pixels. If there is noise among detected points, a distance tolerance of up to several pixels may be allowed to find homologous points in the point sets.

If half of the points in **p** appear in **P** and RANSAC must find 50% of the homologous points, it implies that correspondence must be obtained for 25% of points in **p**. Therefore, if **p** contains 32 points, there is a need to find 8 homologous points before stopping the algorithm.

An algorithm that finds the parameters of a similarity transformation to relate the coordinates of homologous points in the point sets in (5.1) is described as follows. Parameter δ shows the maximum distance between a point in set **p** after it is transformed with the hypothesized transformation and a point in set **P** to consider them homologous points. Parameter t shows the number of hypotheses generated thus far, t_m shows the maximum number of hypotheses that can be afforded to find the transformation parameters, q shows the number of homologous points found thus far, and $u = q/m$ is the fraction of points in **p** that should fall within the required distance tolerance δ of points in **P** to declare success in estimation of the transformation parameters.

Algorithm 5.2 Finding homologous points in point sets related by the similarity transformation by RANSAC

---

1. Let $t = 0$ and $q = 0$.
2. Select a pair of points from **p** and denote them by $\mathbf{p}_1$ and $\mathbf{p}_2$. Also, select a pair of points from **P** and denote them by $\mathbf{P}_1$ and $\mathbf{P}_2$.
3. Find $s = \frac{\|\mathbf{P}_1 - \mathbf{P}_2\|}{\|\mathbf{p}_1 - \mathbf{p}_2\|}$ and let θ be the angle $\mathbf{P}_1 \mathbf{P}_2$ makes with the X-axis minus the angle $\mathbf{p}_1 \mathbf{p}_2$ makes with the x-axis. Then, using the midpoints of $\mathbf{p}_1 \mathbf{p}_2$ and $\mathbf{P}_1 \mathbf{P}_2$ as homologous points, find t_x and t_y from Eqs (5.22) and (5.23).
4. For $i = 1, \ldots, m$:
   - 4.1. Using coordinates of point $\mathbf{p}_i$ as (x, y) in Eqs (5.2) and (5.3), find the coordinates of the transformed point and denote it by $(\hat{X}, \hat{Y})$.
   - 4.2. For $j = 1, \ldots, n$, find the distance of point $\mathbf{P}_j = (X_j, Y_j)$ to point $(\hat{X}, \hat{Y})$ and denote the distance by d_j. Let $d_k = \min_{j=1}^{n} \{d_j\}$.
   - 4.3. If $d_k < \delta$, increment q by 1, and if $q/m \geq u$, return s, θ, t_x, t_y as the parameters of the transformation.
5. Increment t by 1 and if $t < t_m$, let $q = 0$ and go to Step 2. Otherwise, report failure.

If half of the points in **p** are present in **P**, the probability that when a point is selected in **p** it appears in **P** is 1/2, and the probability that when a point randomly selected in **P** corresponds to the point in **p** is $1/n$. Therefore, the probability that when a point is randomly selected in each set they correspond is $w = \frac{1}{2n}$, and the probability that when two points are randomly selected from each set the points correspond is w^2. Therefore, the probability that one or both of the two points in a selection do not correspond is $1 - w^2$, and the probability that after selecting r pairs of points from each point set none of the pairs correspond is $(1 - w^2)^r$. This shows that the probability p that after randomly selecting r point pairs from the point sets at least one of the pairs correspond is $p = 1 - (1 - w^2)^r$, from which we find

$$r = \frac{\log(1-p)}{\log(1-w^2)}, \tag{5.24}$$

$$= \frac{\log(1-p)}{\log(1-\frac{1}{4n^2})}. \tag{5.25}$$

r is the number of times point pairs must be randomly selected from the point sets so that with probability p at least one of the selected pairs correspond. For example, when $n = 50$, the number of point pairs that must be selected to ensure that with probability $p = 0.99$ at least one of the selected pairs correspond is $r = 46{,}049$. This is a very large number of iterations considering that the point sets are relatively small.

Using the point sets depicted in Fig. 5.4a and b, each containing 50 points, and letting $p = 0.99$, and $\delta = 4$ pixels, RANSAC found the parameters of the similarity transformation to be $s = 0.75$, $\theta = 330.46°$, $t_x = 0.80$ pixels, and $t_y = -1.24$ pixels for mapping points in **p** to the space of **P**. Running the program again, parameters $s = 0.77$, $\theta = 32.83°$, $t_x = 2.77$ pixels, and $t_y = -2.16$ pixels are obtained. Running the program one more time, parameters $s = 0.73$, $\theta = 331.04°$, $t_x = 1.62$ pixels, and $t_y = -1.63$ pixels are obtained. Mapping points in **p** to the space of **P** using the transformation parameters obtained in the three cases, the results depicted in Fig. 5.4c–e are obtained. Due to the random nature of selected points, different results are obtained by RANSAC with $\delta = 4$ pixels and $u = 0.25$.

Because the noise level among the points and the percent of overlap between the point sets are unknown, it may not be possible to select appropriate values for parameters δ and u. Decreasing the distance tolerance δ to 3 pixels, the parameters of the transformation are found to be $s = 0.74$, $\theta = 330.28°$, $t_x = -1.0$ pixels, and $t_y = -1.92$ pixels, resulting in the mapping shown in Fig. 5.4f. Increasing δ to 6 pixels finds parameters that do not satisfactorily map points in **p** to points in **P**.

The transformation parameters determined by RANSAC are not optimal. If we do not halt RANSAC after finding an acceptable transformation

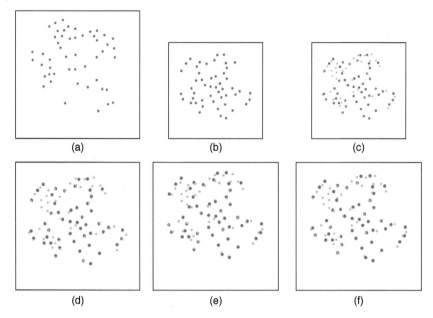

Figure 5.4 (a and b) Point sets **p** and **P**, each containing 50 points, respectively. (c)–(e) Mapping points in **p** to the space of **P** by the similarity transformation with parameters determined by RANSAC when running the program three times with the same parameters $\delta = 4$ pixels and $u = 0.25$. (f) The homologous points obtained when letting $\delta = 3$ pixels and $u = 0.25$. Points in **P** are shown in red, and points in **p** after transformation with the obtained similarity transformation are shown in green.

and continue selecting points from the point sets and estimating new transformations, it is possible to find a transformation that can find more homologous points in the point sets than previously known. In contrast, the transformation parameters determined by clustering are optimal and further increase in the number of iterations is not likely to noticeably change the estimated parameters.

The procedure for finding the affine parameters by RANSAC is similar to that for finding the similarity parameters, except that in affine three points are selected from each point set. If only half of the points in **p** appear in **P**, on average, for every eight point triples selected in **p**, there will be a corresponding triple in **P**. To find a triple in **P** that corresponds to the triple in **p**, on average, $8n^3$ triple of points in **P** needs to be tested. This is a very large number of tests when n is large.

When two point sets are related by a homography defined by Eqs (5.18) and (5.19), since there are eight unknown parameters, four homologous points need to be substituted into Eqs (5.18) and (5.19) to produce eight linear equations from which the eight unknowns can be computed. This, on average, needs to be repeated $16n^4$ times to find four homologous points in the two sets from which the eight unknown parameters of the transformation can be determined.

When n is small, such as 20, the computations may be manageable. However, when $n > 20$, the computations may become prohibitive. In such a situation, subsets of the points are used in RANSAC to find the parameters of the transformation. If half of points in **p** appear in **P**, and if each point set contains 200 points, a subset of 20 randomly selected points from each set will contain, on average, 10 homologous points, which will be sufficient to find the transformation parameters. If RANSAC fails on a subset, another subset from one or both sets can be selected and the process can be repeated until transformation parameters are determined that are supported by a sufficiently large number of points in the two sets.

A very large number of subsets may need to be selected to find three or four point combinations from the two sets that truly correspond when half or fewer points in **p** appear in **P**. To select point combinations from the two sets that correspond with a high likelihood, first, initial correspondence is established between points in the point sets using information about the neighborhoods of the points. Then, when a combination of two, three, or four points is selected in **p**, the corresponding points in **P** will be known from the initial correspondences. Although some of the initial correspondences may be incorrect, there will be correspondences that will be correct. If half of the initial correspondences are correct, a combination of points in **p** can be obtained that have correct correspondences in **P** using a relatively small number of iterations.

Suppose each point in the two point sets has an associating feature vector describing the neighborhood of the point within the image it came from. Then, the correspondence to each point in **p** can be assumed the point in **P** that has the most similar feature vector. The initial homologous points obtained in this manner may contain incorrect and duplicate correspondences, but if the majority of the correspondences is correct, the parameters of an affine or homography to match points in two point sets can be determined with a relatively small number of iterations.

To find homologous points in large point sets that are related by affine or homography, first, a means to extract a set of features for each point from the associating image is required. This is discussed in Section 5.3. Then, a means to calculate the similarity or distance between two feature vectors is needed. Similarity and distance measures are discussed in Sections 5.4 and 5.5. Homologous points in images can be determined by template matching also. Template matching is discussed in Section 5.6. Template matching makes it possible to find homologous points in multimodality images. Finally, knowing an initial set of homologous points, use of a robust estimator to ignore the incorrect and inaccurate homologous points and use only the accurate ones to find the parameters of the transformation model is discussed in Section 5.7.

5.3 Point Descriptors

A feature point identifies a locally unique neighborhood in an image. A small patch centered at a feature point contains information about the neighborhood of the point. Information within the patch may be expressed as a vector of features and used as the descriptor for the point.

Features extracted from a patch can represent the statistical, geometric, algebraic, radiometric, spatial, and/or spectral properties of the patch. Since the objective in feature extraction is to find homologous points in images, it is important that similar features are produced for patches centered at homologous points in images.

There are a number of obstacles in finding similar features in homologous patches. If the images are in different scales, first, the sizes of homologous patches should be taken in such a way that they contain the same parts of the scene. Images often contain noise and have radiometric differences caused by changes in scene lighting or camera parameters. If the images represent different views of a scene, a circular patch in one image may not appear circular or even elliptic in another image of the scene.

Following are some general rules to follow when choosing image features and descriptors to find correspondence between feature points in images.

1. When the images have similar radiometric and geometric properties, for example, representing nadir-view aerial images of a scene taken from the same altitude by the same camera, the images can be related by a rigid transformation. Many descriptors, including intensity histogram [3], scale-invariant feature transform (SIFT) descriptor [4], and gradient location and orientation histogram (GLOH) descriptor [5] can be used to find homologous points in the images.

2. When the images have similar radiometric properties but have different geometries, for example, representing off-nadir views of a relatively flat scene by a camera, the geometries of the patches can be related by an affine transformation. Affine-invariant descriptors [6–8] can be used to find homologous points in such images.

3. When the images are geometrically similar but have radiometric differences, the images may have been obtained by the same camera under different lighting conditions, or by cameras with different sensor characteristics. Region boundaries and their intrinsic properties are among the features effective in establishing correspondence between such images. Often straight boundary segments remain straight in such images and can be used to establish correspondence between the images. In such a situation, instead of homologous points homologous lines are used to find the transformation parameters. The process to find homologous lines in images is described in Chapter 6.

4. If feature points are known in the images and the images have about the same scale and orientation, intensities within patches of the same size centered at the points can be used as their descriptors to find correspondence between the points. Various similarity and distance measures suitable for matching image patches in the same modality and in different modalities are discussed in Sections 5.4 and 5.5.

5.3.1 Histogram-Based Descriptors

Consider a circular window centered at a feature point. The color or intensity histogram of the window is a rotationally invariant vector that describes the intensity/color distribution within the window. Swain and Ballard [3] used the color histogram of an image to characterize the color distribution of the image. Image histograms are insensitive to small changes in imaging view angle, occlusion, and scale. Therefore, this descriptor is to be used when the point sets/images have about the same scale but are rotated with respect to each other. The rotational invariance property of the histogram, which is its strength, is also its weakness. Two images of the same scene could produce very different histograms if the images are taken under different lighting conditions and, although rare, images of two different scenes can produce very similar histograms.

A color image with red (R), green (G), and blue (B) components has a 3-D histogram. When the patch under consideration is small, the obtained histogram will be sparse, making histogram matching unreliable. In such a situation, each color component, which is normally in the range [0,255], is mapped to a smaller range, such as [0,7]. Since this quantization can cause two very similar colors to be mapped to different bins in the histogram, rather than letting the color at a pixel contribute to a single histogram bin, a Gaussian is centered at the histogram bin corresponding to its color, contributing to different histogram bins by amounts inversely proportional to their distances to the bin representing the center of the Gaussian. Assuming $G_\sigma(R, G, B)$ is a 3-D Gaussian of standard deviation σ centered at bin (R, G, B) within the 3-D histogram, the image histogram is then calculated from

$$H(R, G, B) = \sum_x \sum_y G_\sigma(R(x, y), G(x, y), B(x, y)), \tag{5.26}$$

where $(R(x, y), G(x, y), B(x, y))$ denote (R, G, B) color components at pixel (x, y). The sum is over all pixels in a circular window of a given radius centered at a feature point. Note that G_σ does not have to be quantized to discrete values. Rather, floating-point values can be used in the calculation of the histogram. The standard deviation of the Gaussian is typically a small value, such as 1.

Other color coordinates can be used in the same manner to create a color histogram. If the images are obtained under different lighting conditions, *RGB* color coordinates can be transformed into *Lab* or *Luv* color coordinates

[9], dropping the luminance component L and creating a 2-D histogram that characterizes the chromaticity of the neighborhood.

Similarity between two color histograms is determined from their intersection. Given histograms H_1 and H_2, their intersection at entry (R, G, B) is defined by [3]

$$D(R, G, B) = \min\{H_1(R, G, B), H_2(R, G, B)\};$$
(5.27)

and the intersection of the histograms is defined by

$$I(H_1, H_2) = \sum_R \sum_G \sum_B D(R, G, B).$$
(5.28)

To obtain a similarity measure that is independent of the radius of the windows used in matching, the aforementioned measure is normalized with respect to the window size. If the circular windows centered at the points under consideration contain N pixels, normalization is achieved by

$$S(H_1, H_2) = \frac{I(H_1, H_2)}{N}.$$
(5.29)

This normalized similarity measure will be between 0 and 1. The closer S is to 1, the more similar will be the color distributions of the windows under consideration.

If the images are in gray scale, the histograms will be 1-D, simplifying the calculations.

5.3.2 SIFT Descriptor

As was discussed in Section 3.3.2, SIFT points represent centers of dark and bright blobs in an image. If the blobs are round, positions of SIFT points remain stable under rotation and scale and can be used as robust points. However, round blobs are not very distinctive, making it difficult to distinguish them from other blobs. SIFT points that belong to elongated or branching blobs are distinctive, but their centers may displace due to fragmentation/merging of regions under changes in scale and so are not stable.

If a small number of points are required for a particular vision task, the limited information available within nearly round blobs may be sufficient to distinguish them from each other and can be used to find initial homologous points in the images.

The SIFT detector assigns a scale to each detected point, which is the standard deviation of the Laplacian of Gaussian (LoG) operator, or its approximating difference of Gaussians (DoG) that produces the highest response at the point. We know that the response of a LoG of standard deviation σ to a circular region of diameter D becomes maximum when $D = 2\sqrt{2}\sigma$ [10]. Knowing σ, a square region of side D centered at the point is selected and information within the region is used to describe the neighborhood of the point. Therefore, if the image is scaled by a factor of s, it is anticipated that the diameter of the blob under consideration will scale by a factor of s also. As a result, the standard deviation of the LoG (or its equivalent DoG) operator producing the highest response will be $s\sigma$. For circular blobs at least, the SIFT detector correctly finds the scale of the neighborhood of a point.

The orientation of a SIFT point is taken to be the dominant orientation of the neighborhood of the point. Intensity gradient directions of pixels within a square window of side D pixels centered at the feature point are determined and grouped into 36 different directions. A weight is assigned to each pixel within a group that is inversely proportional to its distance to the window center and proportional to its gradient magnitude. Then, the weights of pixels within each group are added together to obtain the strength of the direction represented by the group. Finally, the direction of the strongest group is taken to represent the dominant orientation of the neighborhood of the SIFT point.

After determining the scale σ and orientation θ of the neighborhood of a SIFT point, a square window of side $D = 2\sqrt{2}\sigma$ pixels is taken centered at the point. The square window is subdivided into 4×4 subwindows. The gradient directions within each subwindow are grouped into eight directions and the number of pixels contributing to each group is determined. This produces eight numbers for each subwindow, collectively producing $8 \times 16 = 128$ numbers, which are then arranged in a prespecified order in a vector and used as the descriptor for the neighborhood of the SIFT point.

To have a meaningful SIFT descriptor, the neighborhood of a SIFT point should be at least 16×16 pixels in order to obtain 4×4 subwindows, each of size 4×4 pixels. This shows that SIFT descriptors are most effective when the scale of a SIFT point is at least 6 pixels. SIFT points with smaller scales require use of very small neighborhoods, not containing sufficient information to distinguish them from other points in an image.

To make SIFT descriptors rotation invariant, after finding the dominant orientation of the neighborhood of a SIFT point, the square window centered at the SIFT point is oriented in such a way that the x-axis of the window aligns with the dominant orientation of the neighborhood. This is demonstrated in Fig. 5.5a. The neighborhood is then subdivided into 4×4 subwindows (Fig. 5.5b), and a weighted gradient direction histogram with eight bins is calculated within each subwindow and the histograms are combined to create a rotation-invariant descriptor for the SIFT point. If the image gradient direction at a pixel within a subwindow is θ and the dominant orientation of the window is θ_0, the same pixel is given gradient direction $\theta - \theta_0$ within the subwindow when calculating the gradient direction histogram there.

A SIFT descriptor is a vector of 128 numbers, encoding rotation-invariant gradient information in the neighborhood of the associating SIFT point. To make a descriptor independent of the size (scale) of the neighborhood, the 128-dimensional feature vector is normalized to a unit vector.

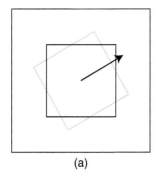 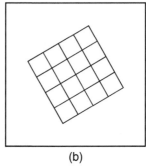

(a)   (b)

Figure 5.5 (a) The black square indicates the window centered at a SIFT point and the gray square indicates the square window used to calculate the descriptor at the point. (b) The selected window is subdivided into 4 × 4 subwindows, histogram of weighted gradient directions within each subwindow is calculated, and the histograms are combined to produce a descriptor for the SIFT point.

Since gradient direction is a function of scale, an area with small texture elements may have quite different gradient directions than the same area at a higher scale. However, when the images have small scale differences, using gradient information to describe a neighborhood may be sufficient to find some homologous points in the images. Gradient information rather than intensity information is used to make the descriptors less sensitive to changes in scene lighting.

Pixel dimensions in medical and remote sensing images are usually known. This makes it possible to resample one image to the scale of the other. When images have the same scale, descriptors can be generated for windows of the same size when looking for homologous points in the images.

In spite of the popularity of SIFT descriptors, the matching rate of SIFT descriptors is not very high. Giving higher weights to gradient directions with higher gradient magnitudes when describing the neighborhood of a SIFT point is not well justified. A scene pattern is formed from various radiances and lower image intensities do not make parts of the pattern with lower radiances less important. When gradients of a pattern are calculated, again, lower gradient magnitudes do not make them less important than higher gradient magnitudes. Making parts of a pattern with higher gradient magnitudes more important than other parts of the pattern is distorting information in a neighborhood, and there is no evidence that such modifications/distortions improve recognition rate.

Although in template matching, giving higher weights to intensities closer to the template center has been shown to improve match rating, the same does not hold when matching windows centered at SIFT points. A SIFT point identifies the center of a dark or a bright blob. The neighborhood of a SIFT point is usually homogenous in intensity, and giving gradient directions closer to the center of the window higher weights simply enhances noise and distorts information in the window. After an image is smoothed to reduce the effect of noise, gradient directions without any weighting encode true gradient information in a window and is a more accurate representation of the neighborhood of a SIFT point than weighting gradient directions according to their gradient magnitudes or their distances to the SIFT point.

Weighting the number of pixels in a particular gradient direction higher when gradient magnitudes are higher or when they are closer to the window center, artificially increases/decreases the number of pixels in that gradient direction. The weighting process changes the true number of pixels in each gradient direction and is not a true representation of the window being described. When it comes to finding correspondence between feature points in images using their descriptors, the more accurately the descriptors represent the contents of windows centered at the points, the higher is expected to be the match rating between the points. The weighting process blurs information in the neighborhoods of the points, making the descriptors less distinct and causing windows centered at the points more similar than they really are. The weighting process in effect increases the number of false correspondences.

When matching points using their descriptors, it has been suggested [4] to take those correspondences that produce a high match rating, and the second-highest match rating is significantly lower than the highest match rating. However, when dealing with hundreds of feature points in each image, often the highest and the second-highest match ratings are very close. For that reason, there is a need to make the descriptors as distinct as possible to increase the distance between the highest and the second-highest match ratings, and that implies avoiding weights that blur information in the neighborhoods of the feature points and make dissimilar neighborhood more similar than they really are.

5.3.3 GLOH Descriptor

Rather than encoding information within a square window, Mikolajczyk and Schmid [5] encoded information within a circular window to a descriptor named GLOH.

To create a GLOH descriptor for a feature point, a circular window of radius 15 pixels is centered at the point. The window is subdivided into three concentric circular regions of radii 6, 11, and 15 pixels (Fig. 5.6). The two outer regions are then angularly subdivided into 8 sectors, creating 17 regions overall. If the images are in different scales and the scales of the images are known, the sizes of the circular regions in the images are taken proportional to their scales. If the scale ratio between the images is not known, the local scale estimated by SIFT is used to select the size of the window.

The concentric circular regions in a GLOH descriptor are subdivided with respect to the dominant orientation of the neighborhood. Then, gradient

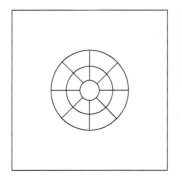

Figure 5.6 The circular window centered at a feature point is subdivided into a log-polar grid of 17 subwindows in the GLOH descriptor. Gradient directions in each subwindow are grouped into 16 directions, producing a descriptor with $17 \times 16 = 272$ values.

directions are determined with respect to the dominant direction within each of the 17 subregions and grouped into 16 directions. Therefore, assuming the dominant orientation of a window is θ_0 and the gradient direction at a pixel is θ, both measured in radians, the pixel is assigned to group $16(\frac{\theta-\theta_0}{2\pi})$.

The number of pixels within each subwindow contributing to each of the 16 directions is determined, producing, $17 \times 16 = 272$ numbers overall, arranged in a vector in a prespecified order. All vectors obtained in an image are then subjected to principal component analysis (PCA), taking the coefficients of the 128 largest eigenvectors as the descriptor for the window.

Image descriptors are often constructed from elements of the same type, encoding one type of information about a neighborhood. To capture various types of information about a neighborhood, either a combination of different descriptors should be used [11] or a descriptor that is composed of different types of features is required. Next, a descriptor that is composed of features capturing complementary information about a neighborhood is described.

5.3.4 Composite Descriptors

If there is a need to find homologous points in images that are rotated with respect to each other, the descriptors associated with the points should be rotation invariant. There are many image features that are rotation invariant and can be made a part of a composite descriptor. Examples of rotation-ally invariant features are invariant moments, cornerness measures, power spectrum features, differential features, and spatial domain features.

5.3.4.1 Hu Invariant Moments
Seven Hu invariant moments of orders two and three [12] were described in Section 3.3.1.3. Any number of the invariant moments can be made a part of a rotationally invariant composite descriptor.

5.3.4.2 Complex Moments
Complex moments are defined by [13]

$$C_{pq} = \sum_x \sum_y (x + jy)^p (x - jy)^q f(x, y), \tag{5.30}$$

where (x, y) are the coordinates of a pixel with intensity $f(x, y)$ at the neighborhood under consideration. Complex moments can also be defined by

$$C_{pq} = \sum_x \sum_y r^{p+q} e^{j(p-q)\theta} f(x, y), \tag{5.31}$$

where $r = \sqrt{x^2 + y^2}$ and $\theta = \tan^{-1}(y/x)$ are the polar coordinates of pixel (x, y). Note that under this definition, C_{qp} becomes the complex conjugate of C_{pq}. Rotating a circular window counterclockwise about its center by ϕ will change the pqth order moment from C_{pq} to $C_{pq}e^{-j(p-q)\phi}$. Therefore, rotating a circular window about its center will only change the phases of the complex moments there without changing the magnitudes of the moments. Since C_{pq} is the complex conjugate of C_{qp},

$$L_{pq}^1 = C_{pq} C_{qp} \tag{5.32}$$

will be real values and rotation invariant. Note that we get about half as many rotationally invariant complex moments of a particular order. This is because $L_{pq}^1 = L_{qp}^1$.

To obtain features invariant to image contrast and image scale, Abo-Zaid et al. [14] normalized complex moments as follows:

$$L_{pq}^2 = C_{pq}^n = C_{pq} \left[\frac{1}{C_{00}} \left(\frac{C_{00}}{C_{11}} \right)^{(p+q)/2} \right], \tag{5.33}$$

where C_{pq}^n is the normalized complex moment of order (p, q), and C_{pq} is the complex moment of order (p, q) computed when the circular window is centered at the origin. The term inside the brackets shows normalization with respect to contrast and scale of the image. Therefore, since $C_{pq} C_{qp}$ is translation and rotation invariant,

$$L_{pq}^3 = C_{pq}^n C_{qp}^n \tag{5.34}$$

will be invariant to translation, rotation, scale, and contrast. Any combination of features L^1–L^3 can be made a part of a composite descriptor for a neighborhood.

5.3.4.3 Cornerness Measures

The Hessian matrix of a small window f centered at (x, y) is defined by

$$H(x, y) = \begin{bmatrix} f_{xx}(x, y) & f_{xy}(x, y) \\ f_{xy}(x, y) & f_{yy}(x, y) \end{bmatrix}, \tag{5.35}$$

where f_{xx} denotes intensity second derivative with respect to x, f_{yy} denotes intensity second derivative with respect to y, and f_{xy} denotes intensity derivatives with respect to both x and y. Beaudet [15] considered the determinant of the Hessian matrix

$$\det[H(x, y)] = f_{xx}(x, y) f_{yy}(x, y) - f_{xy}^2(x, y) \tag{5.36}$$

a cornerness measure and then used locations where the cornerness measure became maximum as feature points. It has been shown [16, 17] that if image intensities are considered height values, treating an image as a surface, the determinant of the Hessian matrix at a pixel is proportional to the Gaussian curvature of the surface at the pixel. That is,

$$\det[H(x,y)] = \frac{1}{1+f_x^2(x,y)+f_y^2(x,y)}\kappa_{max}(x,y)\kappa_{min}(x,y),$$ (5.37)

where κ_{max} and κ_{min} represent the principal curvatures of the surface at (x,y).

Kitchen and Rosenfeld [18] defined a cornerness measure from a combination of image first and second derivatives:

$$k(x,y) = \frac{f_{xx}(x,y)f_y^2(x,y)+f_{yy}(x,y)f_x^2(x,y)}{f_x^2(x,y)+f_y^2(x,y)} - \frac{2f_{xy}(x,y)f_x(x,y)f_y(x,y)}{f_x^2(x,y)+f_y^2(x,y)}.$$ (5.38)

They then selected image locations where this measure became locally maximum as feature points. Wang and Brady [19, 20] after normalizing the cornerness measure of Kitchen and Rosenfeld by

$$\kappa(x,y) = \frac{k(x,y)}{[f_x^2(x,y)+f_y^2(x,y)]^{1/2}},$$ (5.39)

took locations where $\kappa(x,y)$ became locally maximum as feature points. Cornerness measures $\det[H(x,y)]$, $k(x,y)$, and $\kappa(x,y)$ can be used as rotation-invariant features to describe the neighborhood of a feature point.

5.3.4.4 Power Spectrum Features

If $F(u,v)$ is the discrete Fourier transform (DFT) of $f(x,y)$ and $F^*(u,v)$ is the complex conjugate of $F(u,v)$, the power spectrum $\phi(u,v)$ of a window can be defined by

$$\phi(u,v) = F(u,v)F^*(u,v) = ||F(u,v)||^2.$$ (5.40)

Since the angular variation of $||F||^2$ depends on the direction of the pattern within window f, and since values of $||F||^2$ at different distances to the 0 frequency show the presence of objects of different sizes, $||F||^2$ calculated angularly and within various rings can be used to characterize the spatial characteristics of objects in the window. Power spectrum features were first used by Bajcsy [21] to characterize textures in an image.

Letting $r = \sqrt{u^2+v^2}$ and $\theta = \tan^{-1}(v/u)$, annular-ring sampling geometry, defined by [22, 23]

$$P_1(r_0,\delta r) = \sum_r \sum_\theta ||F(r,\theta)||^2,$$ (5.41)

where $r_0 - \delta r \leq r < r_0 + \delta r$ and $0 \leq \theta < 2\pi$ is invariant to image rotation because it is independent of parameter θ.

Letting $s_{uv} = \|F(u,v)\|^2$ and $p_{uv} = s_{uv}/\sum_u \sum_v s_{uv}$, entropy within the frequency domain can be calculated from [24]

$$P_2 = -\sum_u \sum_v p_{uv} \log p_{uv}. \tag{5.42}$$

P_2 can be used as a rotationally invariant feature and made a part of a rotationally invariant descriptor.

5.3.4.5 Differential Features

Letting $\bar{f}(x,y)$ represent a Gaussian filtered intensity at (x,y) in image f, and denoting the derivatives of the smoothed image in x and y directions at (x,y) by $\bar{f}_x(x,y)$ and $\bar{f}_y(x,y)$, respectively, and second derivatives at (x,y) by $\bar{f}_{xx}(x,y), \bar{f}_{xy}(x,y)$, and $\bar{f}_{yy}(x,y)$, the following measures represent rotationally invariant features at (x,y) [25]:

$$D_1(x,y) = \bar{f}(x,y), \tag{5.43}$$

$$D_2(x,y) = \{\bar{f}_x^2(x,y) + \bar{f}_y^2(x,y)\}^{\frac{1}{2}}, \tag{5.44}$$

$$D_3(x,y) = \bar{f}_{xx}(x,y) + \bar{f}_{yy}(x,y), \tag{5.45}$$

$$D_4(x,y) = \{2\bar{f}_x(x,y)\bar{f}_y(x,y)\bar{f}_{xy}(x,y) - \bar{f}_x^2(x,y)\bar{f}_{yy}(x,y) - \bar{f}_y^2(x,y)\bar{f}_{xx}(x,y)\}/ \{\bar{f}_x^2(x,y) + \bar{f}_y^2(x,y)\}^{3/2}, \tag{5.46}$$

$$D_5(x,y) = \{\bar{f}_x(x,y)\bar{f}_y(x,y)(\bar{f}_{yy}(x,y) - \bar{f}_{xx}(x,y)) + \bar{f}_{xy}\{\bar{f}_x^2(x,y) - \bar{f}_y^2(x,y)\}/ \{\bar{f}_x^2(x,y) + \bar{f}_y^2(x,y)\}^{3/2}. \tag{5.47}$$

Features $D_1 - D_5$ are called smoothed intensity, gradient magnitude, Laplacian, isophote curvature, and flowline curvature of smoothed intensity, respectively [25]. After image smoothing, the intensity derivatives of various degrees are obtained by convolving Gaussian derivatives of various degrees with an image, combining both image smoothing and intensity derivative into one operation. By changing the standard deviation of the Gaussian smoother, derivatives of an image at various resolutions can be obtained, creating derivative-based features at different resolutions.

5.3.4.6 Spatial Domain Features

Features can also be calculated from the raw image intensities. These include [26]:

1. *Deviation from mean*: The average absolute difference between intensities in a circular window f and the mean intensity of the window is computed from

$$S_1(x, y) = \frac{1}{N} \sum_x \sum_y |f(x, y) - \bar{f}|, \tag{5.48}$$

where $\bar{f}$ is the mean intensity of the window and N is the number of pixels in the window.

2. *Absolute center contrast*: The average absolute difference between intensities in circular window f and intensity at window center f_c is computed from

$$S_2(x, y) = \frac{1}{N} \sum_x \sum_y |f(x, y) - f_c|, \tag{5.49}$$

where N is the number of pixels in the window.

3. *Center contrast*: The average difference between intensities in circular window f and the intensity at window center f_c is computed from

$$S_3(x, y) = \frac{1}{N} \sum_x \sum_y (f(x, y) - f_c), \tag{5.50}$$

where N is the number of pixels in the window.

4. *Average local contrast*: The average of absolute difference between intensities of adjacent pixels in circular window f is defined by [26]

$$S_4(x, y) = \frac{1}{N} \sum_x \sum_y \frac{1}{M} \sum_{x'} \sum_{y'} |f(x, y) - f(x', y')|, \tag{5.51}$$

where (x', y') represents a pixel adjacent to (x, y) and N is the number pixels in the window. Each pixel is considered to have $M = 8$ neighbors except at window boundary where a pixel has $M < 8$ neighbors.

5. *Dominant intensity*: The dominant intensity in a circular window is obtained from

$$S_5 = \max_k \{H(k)\}, \tag{5.52}$$

where $H(k)$ is the number of pixels with intensity k in the window.

These features are rotation invariant if they are calculated within circular windows. They describe various properties of local neighborhoods. Many other rotationally invariant image features can be used to create rotationally invariant descriptors.

No mention was made of color features in the preceding sections. Descriptors for color images can be created by appending the descriptors for the individual color components. Therefore, the descriptor for an RGB window will be the concatenation of the descriptor for the red band, the descriptor for the green band, and the descriptor for the blue band.

While histogram-based, SIFT, and GLOH descriptors are vectors of magnitude 1, if each is normalized to have a mean of 0, the correlation coefficient (CC) between two descriptors can be used as the similarity of the neighborhoods the descriptors represent. Because features in composite descriptors can be of different types with vastly different dynamic ranges, it is necessary to normalize each feature so that it has a mean of 0 and variance of 1 using all descriptors in an image.

Suppose N feature points are detected in an image, a composite descriptor is associated with each point, and each descriptor contains n features. Let us denote the ith descriptor by

$$\mathbf{v}_i = \{f_i^j : j = 1, \ldots, n\}, \quad i = 1, \ldots, N, \tag{5.53}$$

then, to normalize the features, we first find the mean and variance of each feature:

$$\mu_j = \frac{1}{N} \sum_{i=1}^{N} f_i^j, \tag{5.54}$$

$$\sigma_j^2 = \frac{1}{N} \sum_{i=1}^{N} (f_i^j - \mu_j)^2, \tag{5.55}$$

and then replace f_i^j with $\hat{f}_i^j = (f_i^j - \mu_j)/\sigma_j$.

Denoting two normalized composite descriptors by $\hat{\mathbf{v}}_i$ and $\hat{\mathbf{v}}_k$, the similarity between the descriptors can be measured using the correlation (cosine of the angle) between them:

$$\hat{\mathbf{v}}_i \cdot \hat{\mathbf{v}}_k = \sum_{j=1}^{n} \hat{f}_i^j \hat{f}_k^j. \tag{5.56}$$

The higher the correlation value, the more similar the feature vectors will be. Therefore, given a normalized feature vector $\hat{\mathbf{v}}_i$ in the reference image, we need to find the normalized feature vector $\hat{\mathbf{v}}_k$ in the test image such that it produces the highest correlation with $\hat{\mathbf{v}}_i$.

As an example, consider creating a descriptor composed of 10 features: two Hu moments of order 2 (Eqs (3.11) and (3.12)), a Hu moment of order 3 (Eq. (3.14)), a normalized complex moment invariant of order 11 and a normalized complex moment invariant of order 22 (Eq. (5.34)), a cornerness measure (Eq. (5.36)), a frequency domain entropy (Eq. (5.42)), a response to LoG of standard deviation 2 pixels and a response to LoG of standard deviation 4 pixels (Eq. (5.45)), and a center contrast (Eq. (5.50)).

Suppose the reference image (a) and the test image (b) shown in Fig. 5.7 are available. These Landsat images are courtesy of NASA. Fifty points detected by the Harris corner detector (Section 3.3.3.1) in the images are also shown. A circular window of radius 15 pixels is centered at each point and the 10

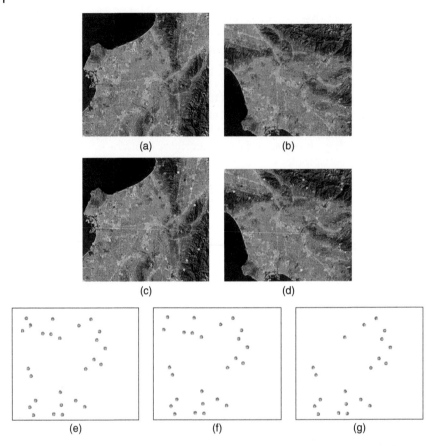

Figure 5.7 (a and b) Reference and test images, each containing 50 feature points. These images are courtesy of NASA. (c and d) Initial homologous points obtained by matching the composite descriptors of the points. Homologous points are shown with the same color. (e)–(g) 26, 25, and 20 final homologous points obtained by RANSAC when using rigid, similarity, and affine transformation models, respectively. Points in the reference image after being mapped to the test image are shown in green, while points in the test image are shown in red.

aforementioned features are computed. The features are normalized so each has a mean of 0 and a variance of 1. For each point $\mathbf{p}_i$ with descriptor D_i, the descriptor D_j in the test image most similar to D_i is determined and point $\mathbf{P}_j$ is considered corresponding to point $\mathbf{p}_i$. Initial homologous points obtained in this manner are shown with the same color in images (c) and (d) in Fig. 5.7.

Some of the initial homologous points are incorrect, but there are some correct homologous points that make it possible to find a transformation model to at least approximately align the images. Approximate alignment

Table 5.2 Computation times of RANSAC in finding rigid, similarity, and affine transformation parameters between the feature points in images (a) and (b) in Fig. 5.7 when (A) starting with the initial homologous points shown in (c) and (d) in Fig. 5.7, (B) finding the homologous points directly without use of the initial homologous points, and (C) finding the homologous points without the initial homologous points, but using only half the feature points in each image.

Method	Rigid	Similarity	Affine
(A) With initial homologous points	0.546	0.390	9.391
(B) Without initial homologous points	0.225	10.672	180.470
(C) Same as (B) but using half of points	0.194	4.740	55.802

The times are in seconds, measured on a Windows PC with a CORE i7 processor.

makes it possible to find more homologous points in the images and register the images more accurately.

The amount of time saved in image registration by using initial homologous points can be significant. Table 5.2 compares the computation times required to register images (a) and (b) in Fig. 5.7 with and without the initial homologous points. First row shows the computation time needed to register the images using the initial homologous points, and the second row shows registering the images without knowledge of the initial homologous points. The third row shows registering the images without the initial homologous points but using only half of the points in each set. The final correspondences obtained by RANSAC when using these initial correspondences under rigid, similarity, and affine constraints are shown in (e)–(g) in Fig. 5.7.

The time required to compute composite descriptors for all points in both images was 0.423 s. Considering this time, we see that no particular advantage is gained by using descriptors to find the rigid transformation between these point sets, but considerable time is saved in the case of similarity and affine transformations when using descriptors to find the initial homologous points and then using RANSAC to separate the correct from the incorrect homologous points and to find the transformation parameters from the correct homologous points.

It is interesting to note that by simply reducing the sizes of the point sets, computations can be reduced by a factor of 2–3 when finding the parameters of the similarity and affine transformations.

Image descriptors are useful when the images to be registered are obtained by the same sensor. When the images are obtained by different sensors, intensities of corresponding pixels in the images represent different properties at a scene point and, therefore, the rotation-invariant descriptors described earlier cannot find homologous points in the images. For images in different modalities, template matching using an appropriate similarity or distance measures can be used to find homologous points in the images. Template matching can be used to find homologous points in images in the same modality also. Various similarity and distance measures used in template matching are described next.

5.4 Similarity Measures

Given two sequences of numbers, $\mathbf{x} = \{x_i : i = 1, \ldots, n\}$ and $\mathbf{y} = \{y_i : i = 1, \ldots, n\}$, we would like to determine the dependency between the sequences. Each number can be considered a feature value where all features are of the same type. If the sequences depend on each other, they vary together. If each sequence represents intensities in a template when scanned in raster order, by determining the similarity between the sequences, we will determine the similarity between the templates. Following are some of the popular similarity measures used in template matching.

5.4.1 Correlation Coefficient

Pearson correlation, also known as correlation coefficient (CC), between sequences $\mathbf{x}$ and $\mathbf{y}$ is defined by [27]

$$CC = \frac{\sum_{i=1}^{n}(x_i - \bar{x})(y_i - \bar{y})}{\left\{ \sum_{i=1}^{n}(x_i - \bar{x})^2 \right\}^{\frac{1}{2}} \left\{ \sum_{i=1}^{n}(y_i - \bar{y})^2 \right\}^{\frac{1}{2}}}, \tag{5.57}$$

where $\bar{x} = \frac{1}{n}\sum_{i=1}^{n}x_i$ and $\bar{y} = \frac{1}{n}\sum_{i=1}^{n}y_i$.

Dividing the numerator and denominator of the right-hand side of Eq. (5.57) by n, we obtain

$$CC = \frac{\frac{1}{n}\sum_{i=1}^{n}(x_i - \bar{x})(y_i - \bar{y})}{\left\{ \frac{1}{n}\sum_{i=1}^{n}(x_i - \bar{x})^2 \right\}^{\frac{1}{2}} \left\{ \frac{1}{n}\sum_{i=1}^{n}(y_i - \bar{y})^2 \right\}^{\frac{1}{2}}}, \tag{5.58}$$

which shows the sample covariance over the product of sample standard deviations. Equation (5.58) can also be written as

$$CC = \frac{1}{n}\sum_{i=1}^{n} \left(\frac{(x_i - \bar{x})}{\sigma_x} \right) \left(\frac{(y_i - \bar{y})}{\sigma_y} \right) \tag{5.59}$$

or

$$CC = \frac{1}{n}\bar{\mathbf{x}}^t\bar{\mathbf{y}}, \tag{5.60}$$

where vectors $\bar{\mathbf{x}}$ and $\bar{\mathbf{y}}$ represent vectors $\mathbf{x}$ and $\mathbf{y}$ after being normalized with respect to their means and standard deviations, and t denotes transpose.

CCs vary between -1 and 1. The case $CC = 1$, called *perfect positive correlation*, occurs when $\bar{\mathbf{x}}$ and $\bar{\mathbf{y}}$ perfectly coincide, and the case $CC = -1$, called the *perfect negative correlation*, occurs when $\bar{\mathbf{x}}$ and the negative of $\bar{\mathbf{y}}$ perfectly coincide.

If $\mathbf{x}$ and $\mathbf{y}$ represent the intensities in templates in two images of a scene obtained under different lighting conditions and corresponding intensities in the images are linearly related, a high similarity will be obtained. When images are in different modalities so that corresponding intensities are nonlinearly related, perfectly matching templates may not produce sufficiently high CCs, resulting in mismatches. Therefore, Pearson correlation is suitable when determining the similarity between templates in same modality images.

5.4.2   Minimum Ratio

If template $\mathbf{y}$ is a noisy version of template $\mathbf{x}$ and if the amplitude of noise is proportional to signal strength, then by letting $r_i = \min\{y_i/x_i, x_i/y_i\}$, measure

$$\mathrm{MR} = \frac{1}{n} \sum_{i=1}^{n} r_i \quad . \tag{5.61}$$

will determine the dependency between $\mathbf{x}$ and $\mathbf{y}$. When noise is not present, r_i will be equal to 1 and so will MR. When $\mathbf{x}$ and $\mathbf{y}$ do not depend on each other, y_i/x_i and x_i/y_i will be quite different, one becoming much smaller than the other. As a consequence, when the sum of the smaller ratios is calculated, it will become much smaller than 1. Therefore, the closer MR is to 1, the more similar the templates will be. Since ratios of intensities are considered in the calculation of the similarity measure, noise that varies with image intensities will have a smaller effect on the calculated similarity than measures that use the difference of intensities to calculate similarity.

Although resistant to noise, minimum ratio is sensitive to intensity differences between images and, therefore, is not suitable for matching images of a scene captured under different lighting conditions or with different sensors. However, if the images are obtained under the same lighting conditions and by the same sensor, such as stereo images or frames in a video, it should do well.

Computation of minimum ratio requires only a small number of simple operations at each pixel. Therefore, its computational complexity is on the order of n.

5.4.3   Spearman's ρ

A similarity measure that relates to the Pearson correlation coefficient is the Spearman's rank correlation or Spearman's Rho [28]. If image intensities do not contain ties when they are ordered from the smallest to the largest, then by replacing the intensities with their ranks and calculating the Pearson CC between the ranks, Spearman's rank correlation will be obtained. This is equivalent to calculating [23]

$$\rho = 1 - \frac{6 \sum_{i=1}^{n} [R(x_i) - R(y_i)]^2}{n(n^2 - 1)}, \tag{5.62}$$

where $R(x_i)$ and $R(y_i)$ represent ranks of x_i and y_i in templates **x** and **y**, respectively. To eliminate possible ties among discrete intensities in a template, the images are smoothed with a Gaussian of a small standard deviation, such as 1 pixel, to produce unique floating-point intensities. Compared to r, ρ is less sensitive to outliers and, thus, less sensitive to impulse noise and occlusion. It is also less sensitive to nonlinear intensity difference between images than Pearson correlation.

Computationally, ρ is much slower than r, primarily due to the need to order intensities in **x** and **y**, which requires on the order of $n\log_2 n$ comparisons. Therefore, if the images do not contain impulse noise or occluding parts, and intensities in the images are related linearly, no gain in accuracy is made by matching templates in the images using ρ instead of r. However, under impulse noise, occlusion, and nonlinear intensity difference between images, the additional computational cost of template matching using ρ rather than r is justifiable.

5.4.4   Ordinal Measure

Suppose intensities in a template are replaced by their ranks from 1 to n, where n is the number of pixels in the template. Suppose no ties exist among the intensities. Since ties are possible when using discrete intensities, to remove ties, the image is convolved with a Gaussian of a small standard deviation, such as 1 pixel. This will maintain image details while removing ties by converting the intensities from integers to floats. Assuming $R(x_i)$ is the rank of intensity x_i in template **x** and $R(y_i)$ is the rank of intensity y_i in template **y**, we first compute

$$D_i = \sum_{j=1}^{i} I[n + 1 - R(x_i) > R(y_i)], \tag{5.63}$$

where $I[E] = 1$ if E is true and $I[E] = 0$ if E is false. Then, the ordinal measure (OM) between sequences **x** and **y** is obtained from [29]

$$OM = \frac{\max_i(D_i)}{n/2}. \tag{5.64}$$

5.4.5   Correlation Ratio

Correlation ratio (CR) is a similarity measure that determines the degree at which **y** is a single-valued function of **x** [30]. To find the CR between templates **x** and **y**, for entries in **x** with intensity i, intensities at the corresponding entries in **y** are found. If mapping of intensities from **x** to **y** is unique, this mapping will be a single-valued function; however, if an intensity in **x** corresponds to many intensities in **y**, the mapping will not be unique. If intensities in **y** are a single-valued function of intensities in **x** with a small amount of zero-mean noise, a narrow band will appear centered at the single-valued function. The standard deviation of intensities in $\mathbf{y}$ that corresponds to each intensity i in $\mathbf{x}$ can be used to measure the width of the band at intensity i:

$$\sigma_i = \left\{ \frac{1}{n_i} \sum_{x_i} (\mathbf{y}[x_i] - m_i)^2 \right\}^{\frac{1}{2}}, \tag{5.65}$$

where x_i shows an entry in $\mathbf{x}$ with intensity i, $\mathbf{y}[x_i]$ shows the intensity at the corresponding entry in $\mathbf{y}$, and n_i is the number of entries in $\mathbf{x}$ with intensity i. m_i is the mean of intensities in $\mathbf{y}$ corresponding to intensity i in $\mathbf{x}$. σ_i measures the scatter of intensities in $\mathbf{y}$ that map to intensity i in $\mathbf{x}$. Therefore, average scatter over all intensities in $\mathbf{x}$ will be

$$\sigma_m = \frac{1}{256} \sum_{i=0}^{255} \sigma_i, \tag{5.66}$$

and variance of σ_i for $i = 0, \ldots, 255$ will be

$$D^2 = \left\{ \frac{1}{n} \sum_{i=0}^{255} (n_i \sigma_i^2) \right\}, \tag{5.67}$$

where $n = \sum_{i=0}^{255} n_i$. Then, CR of $\mathbf{y}$ on $\mathbf{x}$ is defined by

$$\text{CR}_{yx} = \sqrt{1 - D^2}. \tag{5.68}$$

CR_{yx} lies between 0 and 1 and $\text{CR}_{yx} = 1$ only when $D = 0$, showing no variance in intensities of $\mathbf{y}$ when mapped to intensities of $\mathbf{x}$, which implies a unique mapping from $\mathbf{x}$ to $\mathbf{y}$.

Given sequences $\mathbf{x}$ and $\mathbf{y}$ of size n pixels, the steps to calculate the CR between the images can be summarized as follows:

1. For $i = 0, \ldots, 255$, find entries in $\mathbf{x}$ that have intensity i. Suppose there are n_i such entries.
2. If x_i is an entry in $\mathbf{x}$ that has intensity i, find the intensity at the corresponding entry in $\mathbf{y}$. Let this intensity be $\mathbf{y}[x_i]$. Note that there are n_i such intensities.
3. Find the average of such intensities: $m_i = \frac{1}{n_i} \sum_{x_i} \mathbf{y}[x_i]$.
4. Find the variance of intensities in $\mathbf{y}$ corresponding to intensity i in $\mathbf{x}$: $\sigma_i^2 = \frac{1}{n_i} \sum_{x_i} (\mathbf{y}[x_i] - m_i)^2$.
5. Finally, calculate the CR from $\text{CR}_{yx} = \sqrt{1 - \frac{1}{n} \sum_{i=0}^{255} n_i \sigma_i^2}$.

As the variance of intensities in $\mathbf{y}$ that map to each intensity in $\mathbf{x}$ decreases, the CR between $\mathbf{x}$ and $\mathbf{y}$ increases. This property makes CR suitable for comparing images that have considerable intensity differences, or when the intensities of one image are related to the intensities of the other by some linear or nonlinear function. By combining CC and CR, we can determine the linearity of intensities in $\mathbf{x}$ when mapped to intensities in $\mathbf{y}$. The measure that quantifies this linearity is $(CR^2 - CC^2)$ [31] with the necessary condition for linearity being $CR^2 - CC^2 = 0$ [32].

5.4.6 Shannon Mutual Information

Mutual information as a dependency measure was introduced by Shannon [33] and later generalized by Gel'fand and Yaglom [34]. The generalized Shannon mutual information (SMI) is defined by [35, 36]:

$$\text{SMI} = \sum_{i=0}^{255} \sum_{j=0}^{255} p_{ij} \log_2 \frac{p_{ij}}{p_i p_j}, \tag{5.69}$$

where p_{ij} is the probability that corresponding entries in **x** and **y** have intensities i and j, respectively, and shows the value at entry (i,j) in the joint probability density (JPD) of the templates. p_i is the probability of intensity i appearing in template **x** and is the sum of entries in the ith column in the JDP of the templates, and p_j is the probability of intensity j appearing in template **y** and is the sum of entries in the jth row of the JPD of the templates.

Equation (5.69) can also be written as follows:

$$\text{SMI} = \sum_{i=0}^{255} \sum_{j=0}^{255} p_{ij} \log_2 p_{ij}$$

$$- \sum_{i=0}^{255} p_i \log_2 p_i - \sum_{j=0}^{255} p_j \log_2 p_j, \tag{5.70}$$

where

$$p_i = \sum_{j=0}^{255} p_{ij} \tag{5.71}$$

and

$$p_j = \sum_{i=0}^{255} p_{ij}. \tag{5.72}$$

Therefore, letting

$$E_i = - \sum_{j=0}^{255} p_j \log_2 p_j, \tag{5.73}$$

$$E_j = - \sum_{i=0}^{255} p_i \log_2 p_i, \tag{5.74}$$

and

$$E_{ij} = - \sum_{i=0}^{255} \sum_{j=0}^{255} p_{ij} \log_2 p_{ij}, \tag{5.75}$$

we get

$$\text{SMI} = E_i + E_j - E_{ij}, \tag{5.76}$$

which defines mutual information as the difference between the sum of Shannon marginal entropies and the joint entropy. Further insights into the working of mutual information is provided by Tagare and Rao [37], and means to improve the matching performance of mutual information using geometric and spatial information is described by Woo et al. [38].

SMI is a powerful measure for determining the similarity between templates in multimodality images, but it is sensitive to noise. As noise in one or both images increases, dispersion in the JDP of templates being matched increases, reducing the mutual information between perfectly matching templates and causing possible mismatches.

When calculating the mutual information of templates $\mathbf{x}$ and $\mathbf{y}$, the implied assumption is that the templates represent random and independent samples from two distributions. This condition of independency is often violated because x_i and x_{i+1} depend on each other, and y_i and y_{i+1} depend on each other. As a result, calculated mutual information is not accurate and not reflective of the dependency between $\mathbf{x}$ and $\mathbf{y}$.

The computational complexity of SMI is proportional to $256^2 + n$ because creation of the JPD of two images of size n pixels takes on the order of n additions, and calculation of E_{ij} takes on the order of 256^2 multiplications and logarithm evaluations.

5.4.7 Tsallis Mutual Information

If instead of Shannon entropy (SE), Tsallis entropy (TE) is used to calculate the mutual information, Tsallis mutual information (TMI) will be obtained [39]. TE of order q for a discrete probability distribution $\{p_{ij} : i,j = 0, \dots, 255\}$ with $0 \le p_{ij} \le 1$ and $\sum_{i=0}^{255} \sum_{i=0}^{255} p_{ij} = 1$ is defined by [40]

$$\text{TE}_q = \frac{1}{(q-1)} \left(1 - \sum_{i=0}^{255} \sum_{j=0}^{255} p_{ij}^q \right), \tag{5.77}$$

where q is a floating-point number. As q approaches 1, TE approaches SE. TE_q is positive for all values of q and is convergent for $q > 1$ [41, 42]. In the case of equiprobability, TE_q is a monotonic function of the number of intensities i and j in the images [43]. Tsallis mutual information is defined by [39, 44]

$$\text{TMI}_q = \text{TE}_q^i + \text{TE}_q^j + (1-q)\text{TE}_q^i \text{TE}_q^j - \text{TE}_q, \tag{5.78}$$

where

$$\text{TE}_q^i = \frac{1}{q-1} \sum_{j=0}^{255} p_{ij}(1 - p_{ij}^{q-1}) \tag{5.79}$$

and

$$\text{TE}_q^j = \frac{1}{q-1} \sum_{i=0}^{255} p_{ij}(1 - p_{ij}^{q-1}). \tag{5.80}$$

The performance of TMI in image registration varies with parameter q. Generally, the larger the q is, the less sensitive measure TMI_q will be to outliers. The optimal value of q, however, is image dependent. In registration of functional MR images, Tedeschi et al. [45] found the optimal value for q to be 0.7.

Computationally, TMI is more expensive than SMI due to power computations. When the problem is to locate a template inside an image iteratively, Martin et al. [46] found that a faster convergence speed can be achieved by TMI than by SMI due to its steeper slope of the similarity measures in the neighborhood of the peak.

5.4.8 F-Information

The divergence or distance between the joint distribution and the product of the marginal distributions of two templates can be used to measure the similarity between the templates. A class of divergence measures that contains mutual information is the *F*-information or *F*-divergence. *F*-information measures include [47, 48]

$$I_\alpha = \frac{1}{\alpha(\alpha - 1)} \left(\sum_{i=0}^{255} \sum_{j=0}^{255} \frac{p_{ij}^\alpha}{(p_i p_j)^{\alpha-1}} - 1 \right), \tag{5.81}$$

$$M_\alpha = \sum_{i=0}^{255} \sum_{j=0}^{255} |p_{ij}^\alpha - (p_i p_j)^\alpha|^{\frac{1}{\alpha}}, \tag{5.82}$$

$$\chi^\alpha = \sum_{i=0}^{255} \sum_{j=0}^{255} \frac{|p_{ij} - p_i p_j|^\alpha}{(p_i p_j)^{\alpha-1}}. \tag{5.83}$$

I_α is defined for $\alpha \neq 0$ and $\alpha \neq 1$ and it converges to Shannon information as α approaches 1 [47]. M_α is defined for $0 < \alpha \leq 1$, and χ^α is defined for $\alpha > 1$. Pluim et al. [48] have found that for the proper values of α, these divergence measures can register multimodality images more accurately than SMI.

Computationally, *F*-information is costlier than SMI. This is because in addition to calculating the JPD of the images, it requires multiple power computations for each JPD entry. The computational complexity of *F*-information is still proportional to $256^2 + n$ and, therefore, is a linear function of n but with higher coefficients when compared to SMI.

5.5   Distance Measures

5.5.1   Sum of Absolute Differences

Sum of absolute differences (SAD), also known as L_1 norm and Manhattan norm, is one of the oldest distance measures used to compare images and templates. Given sequences $\mathbf{x} = \{x_i : i = 1, \ldots, n\}$ and $\mathbf{y} = \{y_i : i = 1, \ldots, n\}$ representing intensities in two templates when scanned in raster order, the sum of absolute intensity differences between the templates is defined by

$$\text{SAD} = \sum_{i=1}^{n} |x_i - y_i|. \tag{5.84}$$

If templates $\mathbf{x}$ and $\mathbf{y}$ are from images obtained by the same sensor and under the same lighting conditions, and if the sensor has a very high signal-to-noise ratio, this simple measure can produce matching results that are as accurate as those produced by more expensive measures. For instance, images in a video sequence or stereo images obtained under low noise levels can be effectively matched using this measure.

Computation of SAD requires determination of n absolute differences and n additions for templates of size n pixels. Barnea and Silverman [49] suggested ways to further speed up the computations by abandoning a match early in the computations when there is evidence that a correct match is not likely. Coarse-to-fine and two-stage approaches have also been proposed as means to speed up this distance measure in template matching [50, 51].

5.5.2   Median of Absolute Differences

At the presence of salt-and-pepper or impulse noise, sum or average of absolute intensity differences produces an exaggerated distance measure. To reduce the effect of impulse noise on a calculated sum or average of absolute differences, the median of absolute differences (MAD) is used. MAD is defined by

$$\text{MAD} = \text{median}_{i=1}^{n} |x_i - y_i|. \tag{5.85}$$

Although salt-and-pepper noise considerably affects SAD, its effect on MAD is minimal. Calculation of MAD involves finding the absolute intensity differences of corresponding pixels in templates, ordering the absolute differences, and taking the median value as the distance measure. In addition to impulse noise, this measure is effective in determining distance between templates containing occluded regions. These are regions that are visible in only one of the templates. For example, in stereo images, they appear in areas where there is a sharp change in scene depth. Effectiveness of MAD in the matching of templates in stereo images has been demonstrated by Chambon and Crouzil [52, 53]. This is a robust measure that does not change at the presence of up to 50% outliers [54, 55].

Computationally, MAD is much slower than SAD. In addition to requiring computation of n absolute differences, it requires ordering the absolute differences, which is on the order of $n\log_2 n$ comparisons; therefore, the computational complexity of MAD is on the order of $n\log_2 n$.

5.5.3 Square Euclidean Distance

Square Euclidean distance, also known as sum of squared differences (SSD) and square L_2 norm, measures the distance between two sequences from [56]

$$\text{SSD} = \sum_{i=1}^{n} (x_i - y_i)^2. \tag{5.86}$$

Compared to SAD, SSD emphasizes larger intensity differences between $\mathbf{x}$ and $\mathbf{y}$ and is one of the popular measures in stereo matching. Compared to CC, this measure is more sensitive to the magnitude of intensity difference between templates; therefore, it will produce poorer results than CC when used in the matching of templates in images of a scene taken under different lighting conditions.

The computational complexity of SSD is close to that of SAD. After finding the difference of corresponding intensities in $\mathbf{x}$ and $\mathbf{y}$, SAD finds the absolute of a difference while SSD squares the difference; therefore, the absolute-value operation in SAD is replaced with a multiplication in SSD.

5.5.4 Intensity-Ratio Variance

If intensities in one template are a scaled version of intensities in another template, the ratio of intensities at homologous pixels when measured at all locations will be a constant. If two templates are in images obtained by a camera at different exposure levels, this measure can be used to effectively determine the distance between them. Letting $r_i = (x_i + \epsilon)/(y_i + \epsilon)$, where ϵ is a small number, such as 1 to avoid division by 0, intensity-ratio variance (IRV) is defined by [57]

$$\text{IRV} = \frac{1}{n} \sum_{i=1}^{n} (r_i - \bar{r})^2, \tag{5.87}$$

where

$$\bar{r} = \frac{1}{n} \sum_{i=1}^{n} r_i. \tag{5.88}$$

Although it is invariant to scale difference between intensities in templates, this measure is sensitive to additive intensity changes, such as noise. The computational complexity of IRV is on the order of n as it requires computation of a ratio at each pixel and determination of the variance of the ratios.

5.5.5 Rank Distance

This measure is defined in terms of the sum of absolute differences of rank-ordered intensities in two templates. Given templates $\mathbf{x} = \{x_i : i = 1, \ldots, n\}$ and $\mathbf{y} = \{y_i : i = 1, \ldots, n\}$, intensity x_i is replaced with its rank $R(x_i)$ and intensity y_i is replaced with its rank $R(y_i)$. To reduce or eliminate ties among the ranks in a template, the underlying image is smoothed with a Gaussian of a small standard deviation, such as 1 pixel. The rank distance (RD) between $\mathbf{x}$ and $\mathbf{y}$ is defined by

$$\text{RD} = \frac{1}{n^2} \sum_{i=1}^{n} |R(x_i) - R(y_i)|. \tag{5.89}$$

Since $0 \leq |R(x_i) - R(y_i)| \leq n$, RD will be between 0 and 1. The smaller the RD between two templates, the more similar the templates will be. RD works quite well in images that are corrupted with impulse noise or contain occlusion. In addition, RD is insensitive to white noise if noise magnitude is small enough not to change the ranks of intensities in an image. Furthermore, RD is insensitive to bias and gain differences between intensities in images just like other OMs.

RD is one of the fastest OMs as it requires only a subtraction and a sign check at each pixel once ranks of the intensities are determined. The major portion of the computation time is spent on ranking the intensities in each template, which is on the order of $n\log_2 n$ comparisons for a template of size n pixels; therefore, the computational complexity of RD is on the order of $n\log_2 n$.

5.5.6 Shannon Joint Entropy

Entropy represents uncertainty in an outcome. The larger the entropy, the more informative an outcome will be. Joint entropy represents uncertainty in joint outcomes. The dependency of joint outcomes determines the joint entropy. The higher the dependency between joint outcomes, the lower the uncertainty will be and, thus, the lower the entropy will be. When joint outcomes are independent, uncertainty will be the highest, producing the highest entropy. Joint entropy is calculated from the JPD of the templates being matched. Assuming p_{ij} represents the probability that intensities i and j appear at homologous pixels in the templates, Shannon joint entropy (SJE) is defined by [33, 58]

$$\text{SJE} = -\sum_{i=0}^{255} \sum_{j=0}^{255} p_{ij} \log_2 p_{ij}. \tag{5.90}$$

Similar to mutual information, the performance of joint entropy quickly falls with increased noise. The measure, however, remains relatively insensitive to intensity differences between images and, thus, is suitable for comparing multimodality images.

The computational complexity of joint entropy is on the order of $256^2 + n$. It requires on the order of n comparisons to prepare the JDP and it requires on the order of 256^2 multiplications and logarithm evaluations to calculate the joint entropy from the obtained JPD.

5.5.7 Exclusive *F*-Information

Information exclusively contained in templates **x** and **y** when observed jointly is known as exclusive *F*-information (EFI). EFI(**x,y**) is related to SJE(**x,y**) and SMI(**x,y**) by [59]

$$\text{EFI}(\mathbf{x,y}) = \text{SJE}(\mathbf{x,y}) - \text{SMI}(\mathbf{x,y}). \tag{5.91}$$

Since SMI can be computed from SE and SJE [47],

$$\text{SMI}(\mathbf{x,y}) = \text{SE}(\mathbf{x}) + \text{SE}(\mathbf{y}) - \text{SJE}(\mathbf{x,y}), \tag{5.92}$$

we obtain

$$\text{EFI}(\mathbf{x,y}) = 2\text{SJE}(\mathbf{x,y}) - \text{SE}(\mathbf{x}) - \text{SE}(\mathbf{y}). \tag{5.93}$$

The larger the EFI between templates **x** and **y**, the more dissimilar the templates will be.

5.6 Template Matching

A template is a part of an image that we would like to find in another image. It can be an image patch or a shape in the form of a contour or a curve. By taking a template centered at each feature point in reference and test images and by finding the correspondence between the templates, homologous feature points will be obtained in the images.

In Section 5.3, use of descriptors to find homologous points in images was discussed. In this section, circular windows centered at the feature points are used as templates and, by matching templates in the images, homologous feature points are identified in the images.

The images used in template matching should be in the same scale. If the scales of the images are known, one image can be resampled to the scale of the other. Although templates can have any shape, if they are circular, the matching process will treat all directions similarly, and when the images are rotated with respect to each other, templates with coinciding centers will contain the same scene parts. When images are rotated with respect to each other by an unknown angle, it is not possible to contain the same scene parts in two rectangular windows with coinciding centers.

Given a template from the reference image, if no information about the location of the matching template in the test image is available, the template needs to be searched over the entire test image. This can be very time consuming, and to speed up the process, coarse-to-fine and multistage strategies have been proposed. If some information about the location of the matching template is available, a search can be carried out accordingly. For instance, in stereo images, given a template in one image, a search is carried out only along the corresponding epipolar line in the conjugate image [60].

There are two main factors to consider in template matching: (1) the choice of the similarity/distance measure and (2) the search strategy for the correspondences. The similarity/distance measure is chosen by taking the properties of the reference and test images into consideration. Various similarity/distance measures suitable for template matching were discussed in Sections 5.4 and 5.5.

Search strategies in template matching include (1) coarse-to-fine matching, (2) multistage matching, (3) rotationally invariant matching, and (4) Gaussian-weighted matching.

5.6.1 Coarse-to-Fine Matching

The idea behind coarse-to-fine matching is to reduce the resolution of the images sufficiently to enable determination of approximate match positions. Then, use images at a higher resolution to refine the match positions, and repeat the process until correspondence is found in the images at the highest resolution.

The coarse-to-fine search strategy is depicted in Fig. 5.8. The reference and test images at the bottom level (Level 0) represent the images at the highest resolution. The resolution of both images is reduced by a factor of 2 to obtain

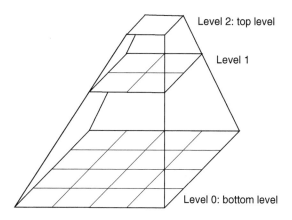

Figure 5.8 An image pyramid created for coarse-to-fine matching.

Level 2: top level

Level 1

Level 0: bottom level

images at Level 1. If the images are still large, the resolution of the images is reduced by a factor of 2 to obtain images at Level 2.

Small templates are selected at the top level in the reference image and searched for in the test image at the same level. If the best match position of the template in the test image is (x, y), when going down the pyramid by one level, the best match position will be somewhere near $(2x, 2y)$. Therefore, to localize the search at one level below the top, the search is performed within a 3×3 neighborhood centered at $(2x, 2y)$.

It is possible for the second best match at Level i to be the best match at Level $i - 1$; therefore, instead of searching at lower levels only for the best match position found at Level i, a small percentage, such as 5%, of best match locations at Level i is searched at Level $i - 1$, until the search is completed at the highest resolution at Level 0.

Note that at the bottom level where template is the largest and takes the most time, only a small percentage of the locations is searched. The time spent in higher levels is generally much smaller than the time spent at Level 0 because the search space is considerably reduced. Therefore, coarse-to-fine template matching can save considerable computation time. Note that because not all locations at the highest resolution are searched, the possibility that the obtained best match being a false match exists.

5.6.2 Multistage Matching

The image smoothing involved in creating lower-resolution images in coarse-to-fine matching changes image properties, and for highly textured images, change in properties could result in poor matches. To search the images at their original resolutions, first, a portion of a template from the reference image is searched in the test image to find the likely match positions. Then, search is repeated at a small percentage (such as the 10%) of the highest matches using a larger portion of the template, and the process is repeated until, at the last stage, the entire template is searched in the test image at most likely locations.

The multistage search strategy is depicted in Fig. 5.9. First, using a small portion of a template in the reference image search is carried out over the entire test image. The n_1 highest match-rating locations are identified, shown in the darker shade in Fig. 5.9a. Using a larger portion of the template, a search is made among the n_1 locations, and $n_2 < n_1$ of the best match locations are identified, shown in the darker shade in Fig. 5.9b. Finally, a search is made among the n_2 locations using the entire template to find the best match position of the template within the test image, shown by a dot in Fig. 5.9c. A two-stage template search based on CC has been described in [61].

If circular templates are used, a small circular portion of each template is used in the search. For example, if the radius of templates in the reference image is

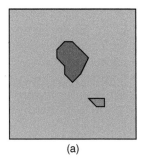 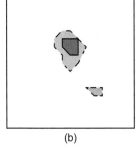 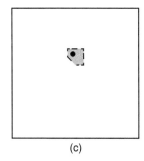

(a)   (b)   (c)

Figure 5.9 Finding the best match position of a template from the reference image in the test image using a three-stage template matching process.

30 pixels, in stage 1 in Fig. 5.9a, the center circular region of radius 10 pixels of the template is used to find likely match positions in the test image. In stage 2 in Fig. 5.9b, the center circular region of radius 20 pixels of the template is used to narrow down the search, and in stage 3 in Fig. 5.9c, the entire template is searched in the test image within the shaded area to find the best match position for the template.

5.6.3   Rotationally Invariant Matching

The match rating between two templates is determined using a similarity or a distance measure. The templates are assumed to be the same size and cover the same scene area. Once corresponding circular neighborhoods are identified in the images, their centers are used as homologous points. Often, the rotational difference between the images to be registered can be determined through the dominant orientation detection method discussed in Chapter 2. In such a situation, the test image is first resampled to the orientation of the reference image and then template matching is performed.

Often the scale difference between two images can be determined from their pixel dimensions. To register the images, the main problem then becomes one of finding the translational and rotational differences between the images. To find corresponding templates in rotated images, either the rotational difference between the images is determined and one image is resampled to the orientation of the other, or a rotationally invariant similarity/distance measure is used to match the templates.

When the images are in the same modality but are rotated with respect to each other by θ, homologous templates with coinciding centers will be rotated with respect to each other by θ also. Rotational difference between the images can be determined from the difference in their dominant orientations. Knowing the rotational difference between the images, the rotational difference between templates in the images will be known.

When the templates to be matched have strong dominant orientations, correcting the orientation of one template with respect to the orientation of other before matching is helpful; however, when matching templates that do not have strong dominant orientations, information about the dominant orientations of templates will not be useful in matching them. Therefore, to find a set of initial corresponding templates in images that are rotated with respect to each other, template matching should be limited to templates that have strong dominant orientations.

Intensity histograms and gradient magnitude histograms of circular windows do not depend on the orientations of the windows; therefore, the histograms themselves or features that are computed from them can be used to measure the similarity/distance between rotated templates.

Rotationally invariant features, similar to those used to compose rotationally invariant descriptors, can be used to match rotated templates. A rotationally invariant template-matching method using normalized invariant moments is described in [62]

5.6.4 Gaussian-Weighted Template Matching

If the match rating is to be determined between two perfectly aligned templates, all pixels within the template are equally important and should be treated the same; however, if the templates being matched are slightly rotated with respect to each other, the farther a pixel in a template is from its center, the more it will be displaced from its true position. Therefore, pixels father away from the center of templates are given smaller weights when calculating the match rating.

If the templates being matched have small rotational differences and a rotation-invariant similarity/distance measure is not used to determine their match rating, the farther a pixel is from the center of the templates, the less influence it should have on the computed match rating between the templates. To reduce the geometric difference between templates with small rotational differences, adaptive windows that vary in size have been used [63]. To reduce the effect of rotational difference between templates in computation of match rating, intensities within the templates are multiplied by weights that are inversely proportional to their distances to the template center. A Gaussian decreases in value as its distance to the center of the Gaussian increases and, therefore, can be used to reduce the effect of small rotational differences between templates when computing their match rating [64].

Assuming the radius of a template is R, and a 2-D Gaussian of height 1 and standard deviation σ is centered at the template, the Gaussian weight at distance r to the center of the template will be

$$G(r) = \exp\left\{-\frac{r^2}{2\sigma^2}\right\}. \tag{5.94}$$

σ is a function of R and should be set to a value between $R/2$ and R when determining the similarity/distance between templates of radius R.

When multiplying intensities in a template by weights that decrease with increasing distance to the template's center, intensities of pixels away from the centers of the templates being matched become more similar. As the range of pixel intensities away from template centers decreases, less information about pixels away from the template centers is used to distinguish the templates from each other. This has the same effect as using smaller templates.

It should be mentioned that Gaussian weighting of intensities works when the images are in the same modality and distance measures such as L_1 norm or square L_2 norm are used to match them. When the images are in different modalities so that a measure such as mutual information or joint entropy is needed to match the templates, Gaussian weights should be applied when calculating the joint histogram of the templates.

To determine the match rating between two templates in different modalities, if intensities of pixels at location (x, y) in the templates are i and j, entry (i, j) of the joint histogram is incremented by 1. When using Gaussian weights, instead of adding 1 to entry (i, j) in the histogram, the Gaussian weight evaluated at (x, y) is added to entry (i, j). In this manner, pixels that are farther from the template centers play a smaller role in the created joint histogram and will have a smaller influence in a calculated similarity/distance measure.

It should be mentioned that although Gaussian weighting increases the true-positive rate, it also increases the false-positive rate by making templates more similar than they really are. Therefore, if the presence of false positives among the true positives is a problem that is very costly to the process, templates should be kept as distinct as possible by not changing their intensities based on their distances to the template center or weighting their intensities with Gaussian weights when calculating the similarity/distance between the templates.

5.6.5 Template Matching in Different Modality Rotated Images

Since it is rare to detect the same feature points in images in different modalities, when the given images are in different modalities, feature points are detected in the reference image and they are searched for in the test image by template matching. When the images are rotated with respect to each other, for each template centered at a point in the reference image, the template must be searched for in the test image at different orientations. This amounts to considerable computation, making template matching in rotated images in different modalities impractical.

Images of a scene taken by different sensors may have considerable intensity differences because they measure different scene properties, but since both images represent the same scene structure, if the images are reduced to edges, some of the edge structures in images will be similar. Areas of homogeneous property in one modality frequently appear homogeneous in another modality, sharing some of the same boundary edges. Therefore, if dominant orientations are detected using region boundaries as demonstrated in Chapter 2, the dominant orientation of each image may be found and from that the rotational difference between the images can be determined.

Once the rotational difference between the images is determined, template matching can be carried out by shifting a template from the reference image over the test image and, by using a similarity/distance measure suitable for multimodality images, such as mutual information or joint entropy, the locations in the test image where templates from the reference image best match can be determined. Centers of matching templates can then be used as initial homologous points in a RANSAC-based algorithm to separate correct homologous points from incorrect ones.

An example demonstrating these steps is given in Fig. 5.10. Image (a) shows a color composite Landsat image covering an area over Phoenix, Arizona, and image (b) shows a thermal infrared image of the same area. These images are of dimensions 543×425 pixels and 533×423 pixels, respectively, and are courtesy of the US Geological Survey. There are homogeneous areas in the color image that appear homogeneous in the thermal image, producing similar region boundaries. These similar region boundaries contribute to the same dominant orientation in the images.

In order to use mutual information as the similarity measure in template matching, the color image is replaced with its luminance component shown in Fig. 5.10c. The difference in dominant orientations of the luminance and thermal images is found to be $-11°$. Knowing this rotational difference between the images, the reference image is rotated to the orientation of the test image so a template in the reference image can be searched for in the test image by regular template matching.

Thirty points detected in the luminance image are shown in Fig. 5.10c. Templates of radius 25 pixels are taken centered at the points and searched for in the infrared image. Coarse-to-fine template matching at three levels is used. The images at the top level (Level 2) are 136×106 pixels and 158×106 pixels. Each template in the reference image is then searched for in the test image by mutual information. A best match position (x, y) at Level 2 is then searched within a 3×3 neighborhood centered at $(2x, 2y)$ in Level 1, and the best match position in Level 1 is searched for in the same manner within a 3×3 neighborhood in Level 0. Therefore, once the best match position for a template is found at Level 2, finding the best match positions at Levels 1 and 0 requires very little computation.

Note that if the images are related by a rigid transformation, after correcting the rotation of one image with respect to the other, all homologous templates will have about the same translational difference. Therefore, if the same

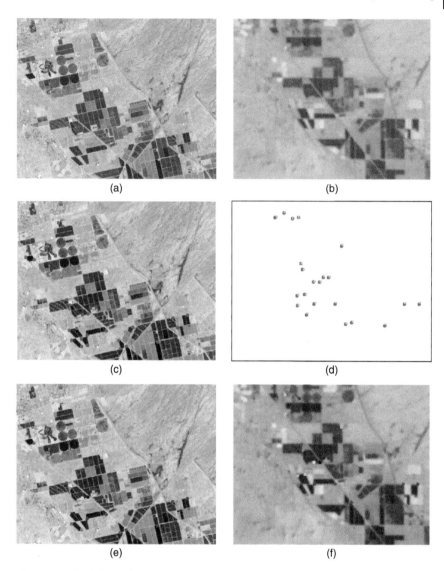

Figure 5.10 (a) Color and (b) thermal infrared images of an area over Phoenix, Arizona. These images are courtesy of the US Geological Survey. (c) Luminance component of image (a). Also shown are 30 feature points in the image. (d) Transformation of points in (c) with the translation and rotation parameters obtained by template matching (green) and the corresponding points in the test image obtained by template matching (red). The centers of corresponding templates in images (c) and (b) obtained by template matching are shown by points with the same color in (e) and (f).

translational difference is observed among a small number of matches, such as five, a search for templates from the reference image can be carried out within small neighborhoods of anticipated match positions within the test image to find the remaining homologous points. The likelihood that five incorrect matches produce the same translational difference is very small.

In the example in Fig. 5.10, template matching required 26.428 s on a Windows PC with a CORE i7 processor to find rotation parameter $-11°$ and translation parameters $(-58, -78)$. Rotation parameter is determined from the difference in the dominant orientations of the images. Translation parameters are set to those most frequently occurring in template matching. Whenever the most frequently occurring translation reaches a prespecified value such as 5, the most frequent translation will be used as the translation at the top level for all templates, which will then be refined in lower levels by the course-to-fine search strategy.

Template centers in the reference image after rotation by $-11°$ with respect to the image center and translation by $(-58, -78)$ are shown in green. The matching template centers in the test image are shown in red in Fig. 5.10d. The process has found 23 homologous points in the images. After finding the translational and rotational differences between the images, if after transformation by the obtained rigid transformation a point in the reference image falls within the distance tolerance of a point in the test image, they are considered homologous points. Otherwise, they are considered mismatches and are removed. The homologous points obtained in this manner are shown in Fig. 5.10e and f.

The transformation parameters determined by template matching are approximate. Since homologous points obtained by template matching may be incorrect or displaced with respect to each other due to noise, view-angle difference between images, or other factors, registration using the parameters obtained by template matching or RANSAC may not result in an accurate registration. RANSAC simply produces a subset of homologous points that meet a required error tolerance. Some homologous points will be more accurate than others. Some of the homologous points may be incorrect due to use of a large error tolerance when finding homologous points in the images.

The next task in the process is to find accurate transformation parameters from homologous points, some of which may be inaccurate or incorrect. The process is known as robust parameter estimation and is discussed next.

5.7 Robust Parameter Estimation

The general problem to be solved in robust estimation is as follows. Given n homologous points in two images of a scene,

$$\{\mathbf{p}_i, \mathbf{P}_i : i = 1, \dots, n\}, \tag{5.95}$$

where $\mathbf{p}_i = (x_i, y_i)$ and $\mathbf{P}_i = (X_i, Y_i)$, we would like to find the parameters of a transformation model with two components f_x and f_y that satisfy

$$
\begin{aligned}
X_i &\approx f_x(x_i, y_i), \\
Y_i &\approx f_y(x_i, y_i),
\end{aligned} \quad i = 1, \ldots n. \tag{5.96}
$$

If the components of the transformation are independent of each other, their parameters can be determined separately. In such a situation, it is assumed that

$$
\{(x_i, y_i, F_i) : i = 1, \ldots, n\} \tag{5.97}
$$

is given and we are required to find the parameters of function f in such a way that

$$
F_i \approx f(x_i, y_i), \quad i = 1, \ldots, n. \tag{5.98}
$$

By letting $F_i = X_i$, the estimated function will represent f_x and by letting $F_i = Y_i$, the estimated function will represent f_y. If the two components of a transformation are dependent, such as the components of a projective transformation, both components should be estimated simultaneously.

Function f can be considered a single-valued surface that approximates the 3-D points given in (5.97). If the points are on or near the surface to be estimated, f will approximate the surface closely. However, if outliers are present so that some points fall far away from the surface to be estimated, f may be quite different from the true surface. The role of a robust estimator is to find the surface/model parameters accurately, even in the presence of outliers.

When a component of the transformation is represented by a polynomial, we have

$$
f = \mathbf{x}^t \mathbf{a}, \tag{5.99}
$$

where $\mathbf{a} = \{a_1, \ldots, a_m\}$ are the m unknown parameters of f and $\mathbf{x}$ is a vector with m components, each a function of x and y. For instance, when f represents a component of the affine transformation, we have

$$
f = a_1 x + a_2 y + a_3, \tag{5.100}
$$

so $\mathbf{x}^t = [x \ y \ 1]$ and $\mathbf{a}^t = [a_1 \ a_2 \ a_3]$. When f represents a quadratic function, we have

$$
f = a_1 x^2 + a_2 y^2 + a_3 xy + a_4 x + a_5 y + a_6, \tag{5.101}
$$

so $\mathbf{x}^t = [x^2 \ y^2 \ xy \ x \ y \ 1]$ and $\mathbf{a}^t = [a_1 \ a_2 \ a_3 \ a_4 \ a_5 \ a_6]$.

When the observations given by (5.97) are contaminated, the estimated parameters will contain errors. Substituting (5.97) into (5.99) and rewriting it to include errors at the observations, we obtain

$$
F_i = \mathbf{x}_i^t \mathbf{a} + e_i; \quad i = 1, \ldots, n, \tag{5.102}
$$

where e_i is the error associated with F_i. This is the estimated positional error in a component of the ith feature point in the test image. Not knowing which homologous points are correct and which ones are not, an estimator finds the surface/model parameters in such a way to minimize a desired error measure between the given data and the estimated surface/model.

If all homologous points are correct but some are inaccurate, and the errors have a zero mean and normal distribution, the ordinary least squares (OLS) is known to be the best estimator [65]. When errors have a long-tailed distribution, often caused by outliers, OLS performs poorly. In such a situation, a robust estimator that reduces or eliminates the influence of outliers on estimated parameters is required. In the following sections, after reviewing the OLS estimator, popular robust estimators are described.

5.7.1 Ordinary Least-Squares Estimator

Letting x_{ij} represent the jth element of $\mathbf{x}$ when evaluated at the ith point, Eq. (5.102) can be written as

$$F_i = \sum_{j=1}^{m} x_{ij} a_j + e_i, \quad i = 1, \dots, n. \tag{5.103}$$

Assuming the error at a point is independent of errors at other points and the errors have a normal distribution, the OLS estimator finds the parameters of the model by minimizing the SSD between the points and the model:

$$R = \sum_{i=1}^{n} r_i^2, \tag{5.104}$$

where

$$r_i = F_i - \sum_{j=1}^{m} x_{ij} a_j. \tag{5.105}$$

Residual r_i can be considered an estimate of the actual error e_i at the ith point. If the components of a transformation depend on each other, the squared residual at the ith point will be

$$r_i^2 = \left(X_i - \sum_{j=1}^{m_x} x_{ij} a_j \right)^2 + \left(Y_i - \sum_{j=1}^{m_y} x_{ij} b_j \right)^2, \tag{5.106}$$

where $\{a_j : j = 1, \dots, m_x\}$ are the parameters describing the x-component transformation, and $\{b_j : j = 1, \dots, m_y\}$ are the parameters describing the y-component transformation. When the two components of a transformation model are interdependent, some parameters appear in both components. For instance, in the case of the projective transformation, we have

$$X = \frac{a_1x + a_2y + a_3}{a_7x + a_8y + 1}, \tag{5.107}$$

$$Y = \frac{a_4x + a_5y + a_6}{a_7x + a_8y + 1}, \tag{5.108}$$

or

$$a_7xX + a_8yX + X = a_1x + a_2y + a_3, \tag{5.109}$$

$$a_7xY + a_8yY + Y = a_4x + a_5y + a_6, \tag{5.110}$$

so the squared distance between the ith point and the transformation model will be

$$r_i^2 = (a_7x_iX_i + a_8y_iX_i + X_i - a_1x_i - a_2y_i - a_3)^2$$
$$+ (a_7x_iY_i + a_8y_iY_i + Y_i - a_4x_i - a_5y_i - a_6)^2. \tag{5.111}$$

The linear parameters $a_1, \ldots, a_8$ are estimated by minimizing the sum of such squared distances or residuals.

If R is the sum of squared residuals, to find the parameters that minimize R, the gradient of R with respect to each parameter is set to 0 and the obtained system of linear equations is solved. For example, a component of an affine transformation ($m = 3$) is determined by solving

$$\frac{\partial R}{\partial a_1} = -2 \sum_{i=1}^{n} x_i(F_i - a_1x_i - a_2y_i - a_3) = 0,$$

$$\frac{\partial R}{\partial a_2} = -2 \sum_{i=1}^{n} y_i(F_i - a_1x_i - a_2y_i - a_3) = 0,$$

$$\frac{\partial R}{\partial a_3} = -2 \sum_{i=1}^{n} (F_i - a_1x_i - a_2y_i - a_3) = 0, \tag{5.112}$$

which can be written as

$$\begin{pmatrix} \sum_{i=1}^{n} x_i^2 & \sum_{i=1}^{n} x_iy_i & \sum_{i=1}^{n} x_i \\ \sum_{i=1}^{n} x_iy_i & \sum_{i=1}^{n} y_i^2 & \sum_{i=1}^{n} y_i \\ \sum_{i=1}^{n} x_i & \sum_{i=1}^{n} y_i & n \end{pmatrix} \begin{pmatrix} a_1 \\ a_2 \\ a_3 \end{pmatrix} = \begin{pmatrix} \sum_{i=1}^{n} x_iF_i \\ \sum_{i=1}^{n} y_iF_i \\ \sum_{i=1}^{n} F_i \end{pmatrix}. \tag{5.113}$$

In matrix form, this can be written as

$$\mathbf{A}^t\mathbf{A}\mathbf{X} = \mathbf{A}^t\mathbf{b}, \tag{5.114}$$

where $\mathbf{A}$ is an $n \times 3$ matrix with $A_{i1} = x_i$, $A_{i2} = y_i$, and $A_{i3} = 1$; $\mathbf{b}$ is an $n \times 1$ array with $b_i = F_i$; and $\mathbf{X}$ is a 3×1 array of unknowns. Generally, when f is a function of m variables, A_{ij} represents the partial derivative of f with respect to the jth parameter when evaluated at the ith point.

We see that (5.114) is the same as left-multiplying both sides of equation

$$\mathbf{AX} = \mathbf{b} \tag{5.115}$$

by $\mathbf{A}^t$, and (5.115) is an overdetermined system of equations for which there is no exact solution. Therefore, OLS finds the solution to this overdetermined system of linear equations in such a way that the sum of squared residuals obtained at the data points becomes minimum.

If Eq. (5.114) has full rank m, its solution will be

$$\hat{\mathbf{X}} = (\mathbf{A}^t\mathbf{A})^{-1}\mathbf{A}^t\mathbf{b}. \tag{5.116}$$

Matrix $\mathbf{A}^\dagger = (\mathbf{A}^t\mathbf{A})^{-1}\mathbf{A}^t$ is known as The pseudo-inverse of $\mathbf{A}$ [66, 67]. Therefore,

$$\hat{\mathbf{X}} = \mathbf{A}^\dagger\mathbf{b}. \tag{5.117}$$

The OLS estimator was developed independently by Gauss and Legendre. Although Legendre published the idea in 1805 and Gauss published it in 1809, records show that Gauss had been using the method since 1795 [68]. It has been shown that if (1) data represent random observations from a model with linear parameters, (2) errors at the points have a normal distribution with a mean of zero, and (3) the variables are independent, then the parameters determined by OLS represent the best linear unbiased estimation (BLUE) of the model parameters [65]. Linear independence requires that the components of $\mathbf{x}$ be independent of each other. An example of dependence is x^2 and xy. This implies that when least squares is used to find parameters of functions such as (5.101) with $\mathbf{x}$ containing interdependent components, the obtained parameters may not be BLUE.

OLS fails in the presence of outliers. A single outlier can drastically change the estimated parameters. The notion of *breakdown point* ε^*, introduced by Hampel [69] is the smallest fraction of outliers that can change the estimated parameters drastically. In the case of OLS, $\varepsilon^* = 1/n$.

Since points with smaller residuals are more likely to represent correct homologous points than points with larger residuals, one way to reduce the estimation error is to give lower weights to points that are farther from the estimated model. This is the method of weighted least squares (WLS), discussed next.

5.7.2 Weighted Least-Squares Estimator

The WLS estimator gives lower weights to points with higher magnitude residuals. The weights are intended to reduce the influence of outliers that are far from the estimated surface/model. It has been shown that OLS produces the BLUE of the model parameters if all residuals have the same variance [70]. It has also been shown that when the observations contain different uncertainties or variances, least-squares error is reached when the square residuals are normalized by the reciprocals of the residual variances [71]. If σ_i^2 is the variance of the ith observation, by letting $w_i = 1/\sigma_i$, we can normalize the residuals by replacing $\mathbf{x}_i$ with $w_i\mathbf{x}_i$ and f_i with w_if_i. Therefore, letting $A'_{ij} = A_{ij}w_i$ and $b'_i = b_iw_i$, Eq. (5.114) converts to

$$\mathbf{A'}^t\mathbf{A'}\mathbf{X} = \mathbf{A'}^t\mathbf{b'}, \tag{5.118}$$

producing the least-squares solution

$$\mathbf{X} = (\mathbf{A'}^t\mathbf{A'})^{-1}\mathbf{A'}^t\mathbf{b'}. \tag{5.119}$$

If variances at the sample points are not known, w_i is set inversely proportional to the magnitude of residual at the ith observation. That is, if

$$r_i = F_i - \mathbf{x}_i\hat{\mathbf{a}}, \quad i = 1, \ldots, n, \tag{5.120}$$

then

$$w_i = \frac{1}{|r_i| + \varepsilon}, \quad i = 1, \ldots, n. \tag{5.121}$$

ε is a small number, such as 0.01, to avoid division by zero.

Since the weights depend on estimated errors at the points, better weights can be obtained by improving the estimated parameters. If (5.120) represents residuals calculated using the model obtained by OLS and if denoting the initial model by $f_0(\mathbf{x})$, the residuals at the $(k + 1)$st iteration can be estimated from the model obtained at the kth iteration:

$$r_i^{(k+1)} = F_i - f_k(\mathbf{x}_i); \quad i = 1, \ldots, n. \tag{5.122}$$

The process of calculating the weights and the process of improving the model parameters are interconnected. From the residuals, weights at the points are calculated, and using the weights, the model parameters are estimated. The residuals are recalculated using the refined model and the process is repeated until the sum of square weighted residuals calculated in an iteration is not noticeably lower than that obtained in the preceding iteration.

If some information about the uncertainties of homologous points is available, the initial weights can be calculated using that information. This enables the initial model parameters to be estimated by WLS rather than by OLS, achieving a more accurate initial model. For instance, if a point in each image has an associating feature vector, the distance between the feature vectors of the ith homologous points can be used as $|r_i|$ in (5.121). The smaller the distance between the feature vectors of homologous points, the more likely it will be that the correspondence is correct and, thus, the smaller will be the correspondence uncertainty.

The main objective in WLS estimation is to provide a means to reduce the influence of outliers on the estimation process. Although weighted mean can reduce the influence of distant outliers on estimated parameters, it does not diminish their influence. To completely remove the influence of distant outliers on the estimated parameters, rather than using the weight function of (5.121), a weight function that cuts off observations farther away than a certain distance to the estimated surface is required. An example of a weight function with this characteristic is

$$
w_i = \begin{cases} \frac{1}{|r_i|+\epsilon} & |r_i| \leq r_0, \\ 0 & |r_i| > r_0, \end{cases}
\tag{5.123}
$$

where r_0 is the required distance threshold to identify and remove the distant outliers.

5.7.3 Least Median of Squares Estimator

The least median of squares (LMS) estimator finds the model parameters **a** by minimizing the median of squared residuals [72]:

$$
\min_{\hat{a}} \{ \text{med}_i(r_i^2) \}.
\tag{5.124}
$$

When the residuals have a normal distribution with a mean of zero and when $m \geq 2$ parameters are to be estimated, the breakdown point of the LMS estimator is [72]

$$
\epsilon^* = \frac{1}{n} \left(\left\lfloor \frac{n}{2} \right\rfloor - m + 2 \right).
\tag{5.125}
$$

As n approaches ∞, the breakdown point of the estimator approaches 0.5.

By minimizing the median of squares, the process in effect minimizes the sum of squares of the smallest $\lfloor n/2 \rfloor$ absolute residuals. Therefore, first, the parameters of the model are estimated by OLS or a more robust estimator. Then, points that produce the $\lfloor n/2 \rfloor$ smallest magnitude residuals are identified and used in OLS to estimate the parameters of the model. The process is repeated until the median of squared residuals reaches a minimum.

5.7.4 Least Trimmed Squares Estimator

The least trimmed squares (LTS) estimator [73] is similar to the LMS estimator, except that it uses fewer than half of the smallest squared residuals to estimate the parameters. LTS estimates the parameters by minimizing

$$
\sum_{i=1}^{h} (r^2)_{i:n},
\tag{5.126}
$$

where $(r^2)_{i:n}$ implies the ith smallest squared residual among the ordered list of n squared residuals, $m \leq h \leq n/2 + 1$ and $(r^2)_{i:n} \leq (r^2)_{j:n}$, when $i < j$. The process initially estimates the parameters of the model by OLS or a more robust estimator. It then orders the residuals and identifies points that produce the h

smallest residuals. Those points are then used to estimate the parameters of the model. The squared residuals are recalculated using all points and ordered. The process of selecting points and calculating and ordering the residuals is repeated. The parameters obtained from the points producing the h smallest residuals are taken as estimates to the model parameters in each iteration. The process is stopped when the hth smallest squared residual reaches a minimum.

The breakdown point of the LTS estimator is [73]

$$
\epsilon^* = \begin{cases} (h - m + 1)/n & \text{if} \quad m \le h < \left\lfloor \frac{n+m+1}{2} \right\rfloor, \\ (n - h + 1)/n & \text{if} \quad \left\lfloor \frac{n+m+1}{2} \right\rfloor \le h \le n. \end{cases}
\tag{5.127}
$$

When n is not very large and if the number of parameters m is small, by letting $h = n/2 + 1$, we see that the breakdown point of this estimator is close to 0.5. When n is very large, by letting $h = n/2$, we see that irrespective of m a breakdown point close to 0.5 is achieved. Note that due to the ordering need in the objective function, each iteration of the algorithm requires on the order of $n\log_2 n$ comparisons.

When the ratio of correct homologous points and all homologous points falls below 0.5, the parameters initially estimated by OLS may not be accurate enough to produce squared residuals that, when ordered, will place correct homologous points before the incorrect ones. Therefore, the obtained ordered list may contain a mixture of correct and incorrect homologous points from the very beginning. When the majority of homologous points is correct and there are no distant outliers and the residuals are ordered, more correct homologous points appear at and near the beginning of the list. This enables points with smaller squared residuals to be selected, allowing more correct homologous points to participate in the estimation process and ultimately producing the optimal solution.

5.7.5 Rank Estimator

A rank (R) estimator ranks the residuals and, by using the ranks of the residuals rather than their actual values, reduces the influence of very distant outliers [74]. By assigning weights to the residuals through a scoring function, the breakdown point of the estimator can be increased up to 0.5. Using a fraction α of the residuals in estimating the parameters of the model, Hossjer [75] reduced the influence of the $1 - \alpha$ largest magnitude residuals in parameter estimation. It is shown that a breakdown point of 0.5 can be achieved by letting $\alpha = 0.5$.

If R_i is the rank of the ith largest magnitude residual $|r_i|$ from among n residuals and if $b_n(R_i)$ is the score assigned to the ith largest magnitude residual from a score generating function, then the objective function to minimize is

$$
\frac{1}{n} \sum_{i=1}^{n} b_n(R_i) r_i^2,
\tag{5.128}
$$

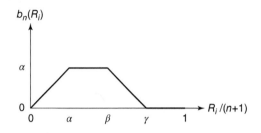

$b_n(R_i)$

α

0

$0 \quad \alpha \quad \beta \quad \gamma \quad 1$

$R_i/(n+1)$

Figure 5.11 Plot of the scoring
function of (5.130).

which can be achieved by setting its gradient to zero and solving the obtained system of linear equations,

$$\sum_{i=1}^{n} b_n(R_i) r_i x_{ik} = 0, \quad k = 1, \ldots, m. \tag{5.129}$$

This is, in effect, a WLS estimator where the weight of the residual at the i point is $b_n(R_i)$.

The scoring function can be designed to assign decreasing scores to increasing residuals from a point and to assign a score of 0 to a percentage of the largest magnitude residuals. For example, consider the scoring function depicted in Fig. 5.11 with $0 < \alpha \le \beta \le \gamma \le 1$,

$$b_n(R_i) = \begin{cases} R_i/(n+1), & \text{if } R_i/(n+1) \le \alpha, \\ \alpha, & \text{if } \alpha < R_i/(n+1) \le \beta, \\ \alpha[\gamma - R_i/(n+1)]/(\gamma - \beta), & \text{if } \beta < R_i/(n+1) \ge \gamma, \\ 0, & \text{if } R_i/(n+1) > \gamma. \end{cases} \tag{5.130}$$

This scoring function discards the 100γ percent of the points that produce the largest magnitude residuals. By discarding such points, the process removes the outliers. Hössjer [75] has shown that if the scoring function is nondecreasing, the process has a single global minimum. However, if the scoring function decreases in an interval, there may be more than one minima, and if the initial parameters estimated by OLS are not near the final parameters, the R estimator may converge to a local minimum that is not the global minimum.

To summarize, estimation by a rank estimator involves the following steps:

1. Design a scoring function.
2. Estimate the model parameters by OLS or a more robust estimator and calculate the residuals.
3. Let initial weights at all points be $1/n$.
4. Rank the points according to the magnitude of the weighted residuals.
5. Find the score at each point using the scoring function, and let the score represent the weight at the point.
6. Find the model parameters by the WLS estimator.
7. Estimate the new residuals at the points. If a minimum is reached in the sum of weighted square residuals, stop. Otherwise, go to Step 4.

An example usage of the estimators described above is given next. Images (a) and (b) in Fig. 5.12 are the reference and test images to be registered. These are Landsat 5 images covering an area over Southern California. Thirty feature points are available in each image, shown by red dots. Using the color histogram of a circular window of radius 25 pixels centered at a point as the descriptor for the point (Section 5.3.1), the initial homologous points shown in images (c) and (d) are obtained. Homologous points are shown with the same color. Some initial homologous points are correct, but some are incorrect. Using the initial homologous points and the affine transformation model, RANSAC found affine parameters $a = 1.024, b = -0.171, c = 26.799, d = 0.193, e = 0.9465,$ and $f = -44.021$ when using a distance tolerance of $\delta = 5$ pixels.

Figure 5.12e shows the reference image points (shown in green) after being mapped to the space of the test image with the obtained affine transformation. Points in the test image are shown in red. The process has found 11 homologous points from among 30 points in the images when using a distance tolerance of $\delta = 5$ pixels by RANSAC. The coordinates of the 11 homologous points obtained in this manner are listed in Table 5.3.

For each point (x, y) in the reference image, the homologous point (X, Y) is found in the test image using the obtained affine transformation. The intensity/color at (X, Y) is read and saved at (x, y) in a new image that has the size of the reference image. In this manner, the test image is resampled to an image that has the geometry of the reference image but the intensities/colors of the test image. The resampled test image obtained in this manner is shown in Fig. 5.12f. Figure 5.13a shows overlaying of the resampled test image (f) and the reference image (a) in Fig. 5.12. Registration error is quite large away from the homologous points.

The solution found by RANSAC is usually not optimal. RANSAC returns the parameters of the transformation that match a required minimum number of feature points in the images by a prespecified tolerance. It does not find the transformation that matches the most points in the images, and it does not find a transformation that produces a minimum error measure.

The transformation found by RANSAC can be used as an initial transformation and its parameters can be gradually refined by a robust estimator until the minimum is reached in an error measure. Using the homologous points shown in Table 5.3 and using the various robust estimators discussed earlier, the registration results shown in Fig. 5.13b–f are obtained.

The root-mean-squared error (RMSE) obtained in each case is shown in Table 5.4. These are root-mean-squared distances between points in the test image and the homologous points in the reference image after being mapped to the space of the test image with the estimated affine transformation by different estimator. All errors are below a pixel, producing the registration results depicted in Fig. 5.13b–f. The registration results obtained by various estimators are visually indistinguishable.

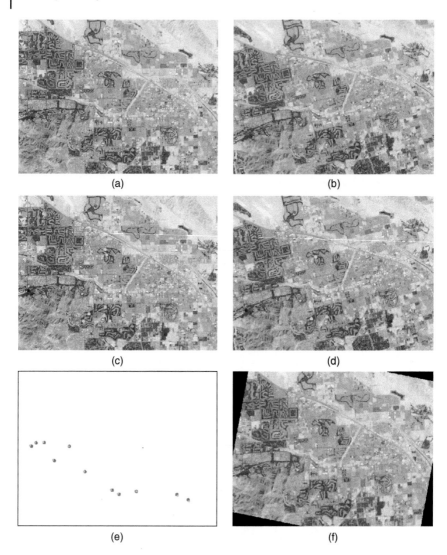

(a)

(b)

(c)

(d)

(e)

(f)

Figure 5.12 (a and b) Landsat images of Southern California. These images are courtesy of NASA. Thirty points are available in each image, shown in red. (c and d) Initial homologous points obtained by matching the color histograms at the points. (e) Points in the test image (red) and points in the reference image (green) after being mapped to the space of the test with the affine transformation obtained by RANSAC. (f) Transformation of the test image with the obtained affine transformation.

Table 5.3 Coordinates of homologous points in reference image (a) and test image (b) in Fig. 5.12 obtained by RANSAC when using the initial homologous points computed by matching the color histograms of templates of radius 25 pixels centered at the points.

i	x_i	y_i	X_i	Y_i	i	x_i	y_i	X_i	Y_i
1	48	267	34	215	7	182	163	187	144
2	263	81	285	82	8	313	78	334	90
3	423	43	450	81	9	451	22	482	67
4	63	272	47	224	10	85	269	69	225
5	153	243	142	215	11	246	96	266	93
6	103	213	99	175	–	–	–	–	–

The homologous points determined by RANSAC in Fig. 5.12 do not contain outliers. The positional errors between the homologous points are small and usually have a zero mean. Therefore, all robust estimators perform at about the same level as the OLS.

To compare the robust estimators at the presence of outliers, the initial homologous points shown in images (c) and (d) in Fig. 5.12 are used. The coordinates of the initial homologous points are listed in Table 5.5. These homologous points are obtained by matching the color histograms at the points. Some of the homologous points are incorrect, but there are sufficient correct homologous points that a robust estimator should be able to detect, remove, and find the parameters of the transformation from the remaining homologous points.

Using the coordinates of homologous points shown in Table 5.5, the various estimators produced the results depicted in Fig. 5.14. The only satisfactory results are obtained by the LMS and the LTS estimators. The RMSE measures are shown in the rightmost column in Table 5.4.

OLS is affected the most by the outliers. WLS has given smaller weights to homologous points that produce larger residuals. This reduces the effect of the outliers, but it does not remove them. The RMSE measure listed in Table 5.4 for WLS is actually the weighted RMSE and that is why it is much smaller than that obtained by OLS. Comparing registration results by OLS and WLS in Fig. 5.14a and b, we see that the registration result by WLS is not any better than that by OLS. The rank estimator with the scoring function shown in Fig. 5.11 when $\alpha = 0.25$, $\beta = 0.50$, and $\gamma = 0.75$ is capable of ignoring some of the outliers, but the influence of other outliers has remained, and for using WLS on the remaining homologous points, it has failed to register the images satisfactorily.

The results by LMS and LTS estimators are remarkable, not only because they are able to ignore a large number of outliers, but also because they produce a subpixel RMSE. Given 30 homologous points in the images, it takes 5 μs to find the histogram descriptors at the points and find initial homologous points, and it takes 6 μs to remove the outliers and find the affine parameters from the

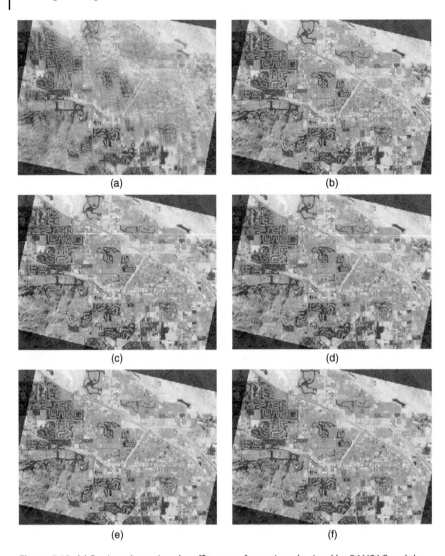

Figure 5.13 (a) Registration using the affine transformation obtained by RANSAC and the homologous points shown in Fig. 5.12e. Registration using the homologous points shown in Fig. 5.12e and the parameters of the affine transformation obtained by (b) ordinary least squares, (c) weighted least squares, (d) least median of squares, (e) least trimmed squares when using 25% smallest residuals, and (f) rank estimator with the scoring function shown in Fig. 5.11 using $\alpha = 0.25$, $\beta = 0.50$, and $\gamma = 0.75$.

Table 5.4 Root-mean-squared errors of various estimators when using the homologous points obtained by RANSAC in Table 5.3 and the initial homologous points in Table 5.5 obtained by matching the descriptors of the points (without RANSAC).

Estimator	RMSE with RANSAC	RMSE without RANSAC
OLS	0.531	96.442
WLS	0.531	0.959
LMS	0.227	0.881
LTS	0.227	0.398
Rank	0.531	12.188

Table 5.5 Coordinates of homologous points depicted in images (c) and (d) in Fig. 5.12.

i	x_i	y_i	X_i	Y_i	i	x_i	y_i	X_i	Y_i
1	491	331	451	377	16	203	101	222	88
2	48	267	34	215	17	216	382	156	361
3	254	15	291	16	18	451	22	482	67
4	419	64	441	101	19	315	29	85	128
5	263	81	222	88	20	85	269	69	225
6	423	43	450	81	21	305	217	142	215
7	63	272	47	224	22	187	81	222	88
8	45	164	54	114	23	72	379	234	260
9	29	165	37	111	24	249	280	234	260
10	253	265	234	260	25	523	164	520	221
11	153	243	142	215	26	223	147	517	28
12	103	213	99	175	27	19	365	234	260
13	79	171	85	128	28	263	248	285	82
14	182	163	187	144	29	246	96	266	93
15	313	78	334	90	30	250	120	266	93

remaining homologous points on a Windows PC with an CORE i7 processor. The process, therefore, lends itself to real-time registration of frames in a video sequence.

If half of the homologous points are incorrect, by letting $\gamma = 0.75$ in the rank estimator, up to half of the incorrect homologous points are ignored. Since a single outlier can break the OLS and WLS estimators, when using WLS on remaining homologous points in the rank estimator, the presence of a single incorrect correspondence can break the estimator. LMS also cannot handle more than 50% outliers. Only LTS can handle more than 50% outliers.

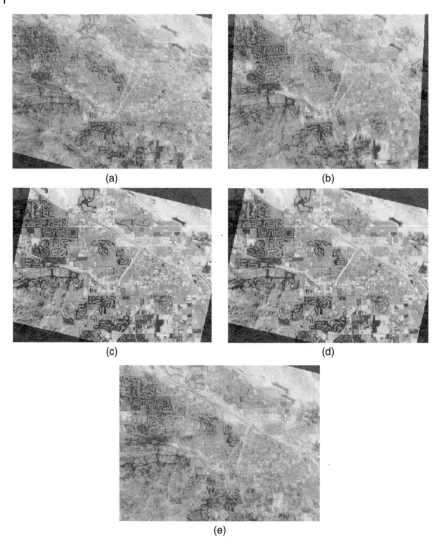

(a)

(b)

(c)

(d)

(e)

Figure 5.14 (a)–(e)Registration of images (a) and (b) in Fig. 5.12 using the homologous points shown in images (c) and (d) in the same figure by (a) ordinary least squares, (b) weighted least squares, (c) least median of squares, (d) least-trimmed squares, and (e) rank estimator with the score function of Fig. 5.11.

When a data set is known to contain more than 50% outliers, a safe way to handle the situation is to use the RANSAC and a robust estimator together. Use RANSAC to remove many of the outliers, then use a robust estimator to ignore the remaining outliers, and find the transformation parameters from the remaining homologous points. This is discussed in more detail next.

5.8   Finding Optimal Transformation Parameters

If more than half of the initial homologous points are known to be incorrect, at least some of the incorrect homologous points should be removed by RANSAC before using them in a robust estimator. To determine the transformation parameters that maximize the number of homologous points, use the homologous points obtained by RANSAC to find the transformation parameters by a robust estimator. Then, using the obtained transformation find new homologous points, and repeat the process of determining the homologous points and finding the transformation parameters until the maximum is reached in the number of homologous points. This often requires a few to several iterations.

An example is given in Fig. 5.15. Images (a) and (b) are aerial images of a relatively flat suburban area. One hundred points are detected in each image. Initial homologous points are obtained by matching color histograms of circular regions of radius 25 pixels centered at the points. The initial homologous points are shown in images (c) and (d). Homologous points are shown with the same color.

Due to a relatively small overlap between the images, many points detected in image (a) do not appear in image (b) and vice versa. Since the initial homologous points find a correspondence for each point in image (a), a single point in image (b) may be assigned to multiple points in image (a), only one of which can be correct. There are many incorrect homologous points (outliers) in this example, but there are sufficient correct homologous points for RANSAC to eliminate most if not all of the outliers.

Registration of the images using the affine parameters obtained by RANSAC is shown in Fig. 5.15e. The registration is approximate, as the obtained parameters are not optimal. The transformation does not produce minimum RMSE at homologous points. Using the homologous points obtained by RANSAC in the LMS estimator, the newly obtained affine transformation registered the images as shown in Fig. 5.15f. The combination of RANSAC and robust estimator can be very effective when registering images with noisy points and inaccurate and incorrect correspondences. To achieve the same, Olsson et al. [76] used convex programming.

5.9   Performance Evaluation

Two performance measures are important in a correspondence algorithm: speed and accuracy. Speed is determined from the computational complexity of the algorithm, which can be determined from the steps in the algorithm. In the preceding sections, computational complexities of the correspondence algorithms were provided. In this section, measurement of the accuracy of a correspondence algorithm is discussed.

(a)   (b)

(c)   (d)

(e)   (f)

Figure 5.15 (a and b) Aerial images of a relatively flat suburban area. These images are courtesy of Image Registration and Fusion Systems. One hundred feature points are detected in each image. (c and d) Initial homologous points obtained by matching color histograms of circular regions centered at the points. Homologous points are shown with the same color. Registration of the images with the affine transformation obtained by (e) RANSAC and (f) the LMS estimator when starting with the homologous points obtained by RANSAC.

Consider the reflectance and infrared images in Fig. 5.16a and b. Fifty points are detected in the reflectance image and the points are located in the infrared image by template matching using mutual information as the similarity measure. Twenty-four of the points in the reflectance image appear in the infrared image as shown in Fig. 5.16c and d.

Registration of the images by an affine transformation with the parameters determined by the OLS estimator is depicted in Fig. 5.16e, and registration of the images using the same homologous points with parameters determined by the LMS estimator is depicted in Fig. 5.16f. The mutual information between registered images within their overlap areas is 0.298 when using OLS and is 0.292 when using LMS. In this case, because OLS uses all homologous points to find the affine parameters, it produces a slightly better registration compared to LMS, which uses only half of the homologous points. Visually, the two registrations are indistinguishable.

If the images from which the points are obtained are not available, but the true homologous points are known, the results obtained by a correspondence algorithm can be compared to known homologous points to measure the accuracy of the algorithm.

Suppose N points are available in the reference image, of which $M \leq N$ also appear in the test image; therefore, the number of true homologous points is M. Suppose a correspondence algorithm finds N_1 homologous points, of which M_1 are correct and the remaining $M_2 = N_1 - M_1$ are incorrect; therefore, the number of true positives is $\text{TP} = M_1$ and the number of false positives is $\text{FP} = M_2$. This shows that the number of homologous points missed, or the false negative is $\text{FN} = M - M_1$. The number of points in the reference image without a correspondence in the test image is $N - M$, and considering that $\text{FP} = M_2$, the number of true negatives will be $\text{TN} = N - M - M_2$. These measures are shown in the confusion matrix in Fig. 5.17.

Some of the performance measures of the correspondence algorithm are

$$\text{TPR} = \frac{\text{TP}}{\text{TP} + \text{FN}} = \frac{M_1}{M}, \tag{5.131}$$

$$\text{FNR} = \frac{\text{FN}}{\text{TP} + \text{FN}} = \frac{M - M_1}{M}, \tag{5.132}$$

$$\text{FPR} = \frac{\text{FP}}{\text{FP} + \text{TN}} = \frac{M_2}{N - M}, \tag{5.133}$$

$$\text{TNR} = \frac{\text{TN}}{\text{FP} + \text{TN}} = \frac{N - M - M_2}{N - M}, \tag{5.134}$$

$$\text{ACC} = \frac{\text{TP} + \text{TN}}{\text{TP} + \text{FN} + \text{FP} + \text{TN}} = \frac{M_1 + N - M - M_2}{N}. \tag{5.135}$$

For example, if $N = 50$ points are available in the reference image, of which 30 also appear in the test image, then $M = 30$. If an algorithm finds 25 homologous points, of which 20 are correct and 5 are incorrect, then $M_1 = 20$

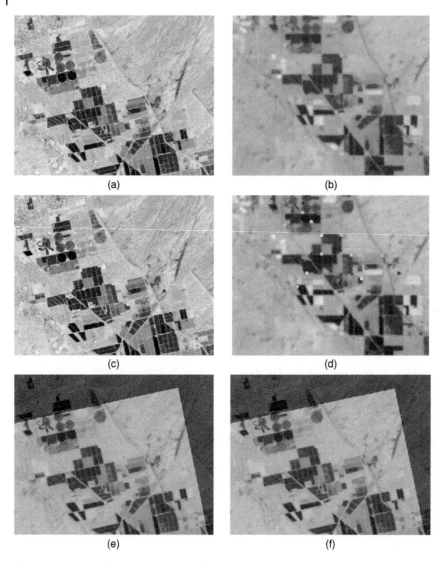

(a)

(b)

(c)

(d)

(e)

(f)

Figure 5.16 (a) A reflectance image and (b) an infrared image of an area over Phoenix, Arizona. These images are courtesy of the US Geological Survey. Fifty points are detected in the reflectance image. Template matching has found correspondence to 24 of the points in the infrared image. Homologous points in the images are shown in (c) and (d) with the same color. (e and f) Registration of the images by the affine transformations obtained by the OLS and LMS estimators, respectively.

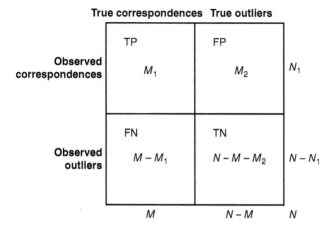

True correspondences True outliers

	True correspondences	True outliers	
Observed correspondences	TP M_1	FP M_2	N_1
Observed outliers	FN $M - M_1$	TN $N - M - M_2$	$N - N_1$
	M	$N - M$	N

Figure 5.17 Confusion matrix of a correspondence algorithm. N is number of points in the reference image, M is the number of true homologous points, N_1 is the number of observed homologous points, M_1 is the number of observed homologous points that are correct, and M_2 is the number of observed homologous points that are incorrect.

and $M_2 = 5$. Knowing these values, we find TPR $= 20/30$, FNR $= 10/30$, FPR $= 5/20$, TNR $= 15/20$, and ACC $= 35/50$. Therefore, the accuracy of the correspondence algorithm is $35/50$ or 0.7.

The accuracy of a correspondence algorithm can be determined using simulation data. The points detected in an image can be used as points in the reference image. Points in the test image can be obtained by transforming the reference points by an appropriate transformation model. The transformation model should represent the kind of transformation relating the geometries of the images to be registered.

Once a set of homologous points is determined in the images, a percentage of points in the test image can be randomly selected and removed. The removed points will contribute to false negatives. The same number of points can be randomly generated and added to the test image. These points will contribute to false positives. After finding homologous points in the images by an algorithm, by knowing the homologous points that are correct and the homologous points that are incorrect, and by finding the homologous points that have been missed by the algorithm, the correspondence accuracy of the algorithm can be determined from formula (5.135).

5.10   Further Reading

RANSAC and outlier removal: The topic of point pattern matching has been studied extensively in computer vision. When the type of transformation relating feature points in the images is known, RANSAC is a preferred method for finding the homologous points and estimating the parameters of the transformation [2]. The computational complexity of RANSAC increases rapidly with the number of unknown parameters of the transformation, the number of points in each point set, and the percentage of outliers. Various methods to speed up RANSAC have been developed throughout the years [77–92].

When the geometric relation between two images is not known or the images have local geometric differences, spatial order has been suggested as a means to detect and remove the outliers [93]. By requiring corresponding points to have the same order when projected to a line but allowing distances between adjacent points to vary, it becomes possible to detect and remove the outliers, facilitating determination of homologous points in the images at the presence of local geometric differences between the images.

Graph-based correspondence algorithms: Many point correspondence algorithms based on graph theory have been proposed. When the point sets are related by a rigid or a similarity transformation and the percentage of outliers is very small, graphs formed from the points, such as minimum-spanning tree, convex hull, or triangulation of the points, produce many similar subgraphs that can be used to find homologous points [94–106].

Spectral-graph-theory-based correspondence algorithms: A number of correspondence algorithms analyze the singular values or eigenvalues of proximity matrices obtained from the points to find homologous points. These algorithms are known as spectral graph theory algorithms [107–117]. Spectral graph algorithms find homologous points in point sets by capturing the global similarity between the point sets.

Correspondence algorithms using the epipolar constraint: A group of algorithms find homologous points in stereo images using the epipolar constraint [118–121].

Other correspondence algorithms: Other algorithms that find homologous points in point sets use vector field consensus [122]; distance preserving hashes [123]; textural similarity [124], feature learning [125]; structure from motion principle [126]; best-buddies count number of pairs of points in the point sets where each point is the nearest neighbor of the other [127]; exclusion principle in Gestalt theory [128]; matching orientation histograms [129], local color distributions [130]; expectation maximization [131]; minimization of an energy function [132]; inlier rate estimation [133]; relaxation matching [134–138]; and integer quadratic programming [139].

Local image descriptors: In addition to the SIFT, GLOH, and histogram-based descriptors discussed in this chapter, histogram of oriented gradients (HOG) [140, 141], rotation-invariant feature transform (RIFT) [142], speeded-up robust features (SURF) [143], dense descriptor (DAISY) [144], binary robust invariant scalable keypoint descriptors (BRISK) [145], binary robust independent elementary features (BRIEF) [146] and its oriented fast version

(ORB) [147], fast retina keypoint descriptor (FREAK) [148], derivative-based scale-invariant feature detector with error resilience (D-SIFER) [149], global point signature (GPS) [150], heat kernel signature (HKS) [151], wave kernel signature (WKS) [152, 153], binary online learned descriptor (BOLD) [154], geodesic invariant feature (GIF) [155], shape context [156], orientation-magnitude histogram [157], orientation codes [158], complementary feature detector [159], filtering responses [5, 160–163], and moment-based descriptors [164–168] have been used to characterize the neighborhood of a point. Learning descriptors and their uses in matching is addressed by Trzcinski et al. [169] and Wohlhart and Lepetit [170], and the evaluation and comparison of descriptors is reported by Gauglitz et al. [171].

While the aforementioned descriptors contain information about the neighborhood of a feature point at a single resolution, at the presence of noise and other image degradations, inclusion of information at multiple resolutions in a descriptor should provide a more robust means of finding homologous points in images at the presence of noise and geometric distortions. A needle descriptor developed by Lotan and Irani [172] encodes information about the neighborhood of a feature point at multiple resolutions in the descriptor for the feature point. The neighborhood at the highest resolution contains the high contrast but covers a smaller area of the scene. The neighborhood of the same feature point at a lower resolution has a lower contrast but covers a larger area of the scene. The descriptor has been shown to find more homologous points in noisy images than descriptors that contain information at a single resolution about the neighborhood of a feature point. Yang et al. [173] contain information about different resolutions of a neighborhood in the descriptor for the neighborhood by using the differences between SIFT descriptors at two scales.

Another descriptor that encodes information at multiresolutions of a neighborhood using a Gaussian hierarchy is described by Matsukawa et al. [174]. A neighborhood is approximated by a set of Gaussian distributions, each showing the appearance of the neighborhood at a resolution. The set of Gaussians in the neighborhood is then represented by another Gaussian distribution. Information about the mean and covariance of intensities of the neighborhood is included in the descriptor for the neighborhood. The descriptor has been shown to be, in particular, effective in describing and detecting pedestrians in an image.

Similarity measures: In addition to the similarity measures discussed in this chapter, Tanimoto measure [175], asymmetric correlation [176], stochastic sign change [177, 178], deterministic sign change [179], Kendall's Tau [180–182], greatest deviation [183], ranked order statistics [184], census transform [185, 186], Rényi mutual information [187], α-mutual information [188], and contextual conditioned mutual information [189] may be used to find the similarity between images or templates. A tone-mapping method to compensate for nonlinear intensity difference between images before cross-correlation template matching [190], and similarity learning mechanisms for efficient image matching [191, 192] and image segmentation [193] have been proposed. Škerl et al. [194] have evaluated various similarity measures for rigid registration of multimodality images.

Distance measures: In addition to the distance measures discussed in this chapter, median square difference [195], normalized SSD [196], incremental sign change [197], and intensity mapping ratio variance [198] may be used to find the distance or dissimilarity between images or templates. Comparing different similarity and distance measures, Holden et al. [199] found joint entropy producing the lowest overall registration error in registration of serial images.

Robust estimators: Among the robust estimators not discussed in this chapter are weighted total least squares or WLTS estimator [200], maximum-likelihood or M estimator [201–204], scale or S estimator [204, 205], and repeated median or RM estimator [206], which may also be used to determine the parameters of a transformation model from homologous points containing outliers.

References

1 G. Stockman, S. Kopstein, and S. Benett, Matching images to models for registration and object detection via clustering, *IEEE Transactions on Pattern Analysis and Machine Intelligence*, 4(3):229–241, 1982.

2 M. A. Fischler and R. C. Bolles, Random sample consensus: a paradigm for model fitting with applications to image analysis and automated cartography, *Communications of the ACM*, 24(6):381–395, 1981.

3 M. J. Swain and D. H. Ballard, Color indexing, *International Journal of Computer Vision*, 7(1):11–32, 1991.

4 D. Lowe, Distinctive image features from scale-invariant keypoints, *International Journal of Computer Vision*, 60:91–110, 2004.

5 K. Mikolajczyk and C. Schmid, A performance evaluation of local descriptors, *IEEE Transactions on Pattern Analysis and Machine Intelligence*, 27:1615–1630, 2005.

6 C. Cui and K. N. Ngan, Global propagation of affine invariant features for robust matching, *IEEE Transactions on Image Processing*, 22(7):2876–2888, 2013.

7 K. Mikolajczyk, T. Tuytelaars, C. Schmid, A. Zisserman, J. Matas, F. Schaffalitzky, T. Kadir, and L. V. Gool, A comparison of affine region detectors, *International Journal of Computer Vision*, 65(1):43–72, 2005.

8 J. M. Morel and G. Yu, ASIFT: a new framework for fully affine invariant image comparison, *SIAM Journal on Imaging Sciences*, 2:438–469, 2009.

9 F. W. Billmeyer Jr., and M. Saltzman, *Principles of Color Technology*, Second Edition, John Wiley & Sons, New York, 63–64, 1981.

10 D. Blostein and N. Ahuja, A multiscale region detector, *Computer Vision, Graphics, and Image Processing*, **45**:22–41, 1989.

11 K.-J. Hsu, Y.-Y. Lin, and Y.-Y. Chuang, Robust image alignment with multiple feature descriptors and matching-guided neighborhoods, in *Proceedings of IEEE Conference on Computer Vision and Pattern Recognition*, 1921–1930, 2015.

12 M. K. Hu, Visual pattern recognition by moment invariants, *IEEE Transactions on Information Theory*, **8**:179–187, 1962.

13 Y. S. Abu-Mostafa and D. Psaltis, Recognitive aspects of moment invariants, *IEEE Transactions on Pattern Analysis and Machine Intelligence*, **6**(6):698–706, 1984.

14 A. Abo-Zaid, O. Hinton, and E. Horne, About moment normalisation and complex moment descriptors, in *Proceedings of the 4th International Conference on Pattern Recognition*, 399–407, 1988.

15 P. R. Beaudet, Rotationally invariant image operators, in *Proceedings of International Conference on Pattern Recognition*, 579–583, 1978.

16 R. Deriche and G. Giraudon, Accurate corner detection: an analytical study, in *Proceedings of the 3rd International Conference on Computer Vision*, Osaka, Japan, 66–70, 1990.

17 H. H. Nagel, Displacement vectors derived from second order intensity variations in image sequences, *Computer Vision, Graphics, and Image Processing*, **21**:85–117, 1983.

18 L. Kitchen and A. Rosenfeld, *Gray Level Corner Detection*, Technical Report #887, Computer Science Center, University of Maryland, 1980. Also in *Pattern Recognition Letters*, **1**:95–102, 1982.

19 H. Wang and M. Brady, A practical solution to corner detection, in *Proceedings of the 5th International Conference on Image Processing*, Vol. **1**, 919–923, 1994.

20 H. Wang and M. Brady, Real-time corner detection algorithm for motion estimation, *Image and Vision Computing*, **13**(9):695–703, 1995.

21 R. Bajcsy, Computer description of textured surfaces, in *Proceedings of the 3rd International Journal Conference on Artificial Intelligence*, 572–579, 1973.

22 C. R. Dyer and A. Rosenfeld, Fourier texture features: suppression of aperture effects, *IEEE Transactions on Systems, Man, and Cybernetics*, **6**:703–705, 1976.

23 R. W. Conners and C. A. Harlow, A theoretical comparison of texture algorithms, *IEEE Transactions on Pattern Analysis and Machine Intelligence*, **2**(3):204–222, 1980.

24 M. E. Jernigan and F. D'Astous, Entropy-based texture analysis in the spatial frequency domain, *IEEE Transactions on Pattern Analysis and Machine Intelligence*, **6**(2):237–243, 1984.

25 B. M. ter Haar Romeny, L. M. J. Florack, A. H. Salden, and M. A. Viergever, High order differential structure of images, in *13th International Conference on Information Processing in Medical Imaging*, 77–93, 1993.

26 P. Gong and P. J. Howarth, An assessment of some small window-based spatial features for land-cover classification, in *International Conference on Geoscience and Remote Sensing Symposium*, Vol. **4**, 1668–1670, 1993.

27 K. Pearson, Contributions to the mathematical theory of evolution, III, Regression, heredity, and panmixia, *Philosophical Transactions of the Royal Society of London, Series A: Mathematical, Physical and Engineering Sciences*, **187**:253–318, 1896.

28 C. Spearman, The proof and measurement of association between two things, *The American Journal of Psychology*, **15**(1):72–101, 1904.

29 N. Bhat and S. K. Nayar, Ordinal measures for image correspondence, *IEEE Transactions on Pattern Analysis and Machine Intelligence*, **20**(4):415–423, 1998.

30 K. Pearson, Mathematical contributions to the theory of evolution, XIV, On the general theory of skew correlation and non-linear regression, in *Drapers' Company Research Memoirs, Biometric Series, II*, Dulau and Co., London, 54–pages, 1905.

31 A. R. Crathorne, Calculation of the correlation ratio, *Journal of the American Statistical Association*, **18**(139):394–396, 1922.

32 J. Blakeman, On tests for linearity of regression in frequency distributions, *Biometrika*, **4**(3):332–350, 1905.

33 C. E. Shannon, *The Mathematical Theory of Communication*, C. E. Shannon and W. Weaver (Eds.), University of Illinois Press, Urbana, IL, 29–125, 1949, reprint 1998.

34 I. M. Gel'fand and A. M. Yaglom, Calculation of the amount of information about a random function contained in another such function, *American Mathematical Society Translations*, **2**(12):199–246, 1959.

35 T. E. Duncan, On the calculation of mutual information, *SIAM Journal Applied Mathematics*, **19**(1):215–220, 1970.

36 F. Maes, D. Vandermeulen, and P. Suetens, Medical image registration using mutual information, *Proceedings of the IEEE*, **91**(10):1699–1722, 2003.

37 H. D. Tagare and M. Rao, Why does mutual-information work for image registration? A deterministic explanation, *IEEE Transactions on Pattern Analysis and Machine Intelligence*, **37**(6):1286–1296, 2015.

38 J. Woo, M. Stone, and J. L. Prince, Multimodal registration via mutual information incorporating geometric and spatial context, *IEEE Transactions on Image Processing*, **24**(2):757–768, 2015.

39 M. P. Wachowiak, R. Smolikova, G. D. Tourassi, and A. S. Elmaghraby, Similarity metrics based on nonadditive entropies for 2D-3D multimodal biomedical image registration, in *Medical Imaging Conference, Proceedings of SPIE*, Vol. **5032**, 1090–1100, 2003.

40 C. Tsallis, Possible generalization of Boltzmann-Gibbs statistics, *Journal of Statistical Physics*, **52**:479–487, 1988.

41 L. Borland, A. R. Plastino, and C. Tsallis, Information gain within nonextensive thermostatistics, *Journal of Mathematical Physics*, **39**(12):6490–6501, 1998.

42 G. A. Raggio, Properties of q-entropies, *Journal of Mathematics and Physics*, **36**(9):4785–4791, 1995.

43 R. J. V. dos Santos, Generalization of Shannon's theorem of Tsallis entropy, *Journal of Mathematics and Physics*, **38**(8):4104–4107, 1997.

44 N. Cvejic, C. N. Canagarajah, and D. R. Bull, Information fusion metric based on mutual information and Tsallis entropy, *Electronics Letters*, **42**(11):626–627, 2006.

45 W. Tedeschi, H.-P. Müller, D. B. de Araujo, A. C. Santos, U. P. C. Neves, S. N. Erné, and O. Baffa, Generalized mutual information fMRI analysis: a study of the Tsallis q parameter, *Physica A*, **344**:705–711, 2004.

46 S. Martin, G. Morison, W. Nailon, and T. Durrani, Fast and accurate image registration using Tsallis entropy and simultaneous perturbation stochastic approximation, *Electronics Letters*, **40**(10):595–597, 2004.

47 I. Vajda, *Theory of Statistical Evidence and Information*, Kluwer Academic Publishers, Dordrecht, 309, 1989.

48 J. P. W. Pluim, J. B. A. Maintz, and M. A. Viergever, F-information measures in medical image registration, *IEEE Transactions on Medical Imaging*, **23**(12):1506–1518, 2004.

49 D. I. Barnea and H. F. Silverman, A class of algorithms for fast digital image registration, *IEEE Transactions on Computers*, **21**(2):179–186, 1972.

50 A. Rosenfeld and G. J. Vanderburg, Coarse-fine template matching, *IEEE Transactions on Systems, Man, and Cybernetics*, **7**(2):104–107, 1977.

51 G. J. Vanderburg and A. Rosenfeld, Two-stage template matching, *IEEE Transactions on Computers*, **26**:384–393, 1977.

52 S. Chambon and A. Crouzil, Dense matching using correlation: new measures that are robust near occlusions, in *Proceedings of the British Machine Vision Conference*, Vol. **1**, 143–152, 2003.

53 S. Chambon and A. Crouzil, Similarity measures for image matching despite occlusions in stereo vision, *Pattern Recognition*, **44**:2063–2075, 2011.

54 H. L. Harter, Nonuniqueness of least absolute values regression, *Communications in Statistics - Theory and Methods*, **A6**(9):829–838, 1977.

55 P. J. Rousseeuw and A. M. Leroy, *Robust Regression and Outlier Detection*, John Wiley & Sons, New York, 1987.

56 R. O. Duda, P. E. Hart, and D. G. Stork, *Pattern Classification*, Second Edition, Wiley-Interscience Publishing, New York, 2001.

57 R. P. Woods, S. R. Cherry, and J. C. Mazziotta, Rapid automated algorithm for aligning and reslicing PET images, *Journal of Computer Assisted Tomography*, **16**:620–633, 1992.

58 A. Rényi, *Probability Theory*, American Elsevier Publishing, North Holland, Amsterdam, 1970.

59 N. F. Rougon, C. Petitjean, and F. Preteux, Variational non-rigid image registration using exclusive f-information, in *Proceedings of International Conference on Image Processing*, Los Alamitos, CA, 703–706, 2003.

60 R. Hartley and A. Zisserman, *Multiple View Geometry in Computer Vision*, Second Edition, Cambridge Press, 2006.

61 A. Goshtasby, S. Gage, and J. Bartholic, A two-stage cross-correlation approach to template matching, *IEEE Transactions on Pattern Analysis and Machine Intelligence*, **6**(3):374–378, 1984.

62 A. Goshtasby, Template matching in rotated images, *IEEE Transactions on Pattern Analysis and Machine Intelligence*, **7**(3):338–344, 1985.

63 M. Okutomi and T. Kanade, A locally adaptive window for signal matching, *International Journal of Computer Vision*, **7**(2):143–162, 1992.

64 L. Nalpantidis, G. Ch. Sirakoulis, and A. Gasteratos, *A dense stereo correspondence algorithm for hardware implementation with enhanced disparity selection*, in *Artificial Intelligence: Theories, Models and Applications. SETN 2008, Lecture Notes in Computer Science*, J. Darzentas, G. A. Vouros, S. Vosinakis, and A. Arnellos (Eds.), Springer, Berlin, Heidelberg, Vol. **5138**, 365–370, 2008.

65 H. Abdi, Least squares, in *The Sage Encyclopedia of Social Sciences Research Methods*, M. Lewis-Beck, A. Bryman, and T. Futing (Eds.), Sage, Thousand Oaks, CA, 1–4, 2003.

66 G. Golub and W. Kahan, Calculating the singular values and pseudo-inverse of a matrix, *SIAM Journal on Numerical Analysis, Series B*, **2**(2):205–224, 1965.

67 R. Penrose, A generalized inverse for matrices, *Mathematical Proceedings of the Cambridge Philosophical Society*, **51**(3):406–413, 1955.

68 H. L. Seal, Studies in the history of probability and statistics XV: the historical development of the Gauss linear model, *Biometrika*, **54**(1&2):1–24, 1967.

69 F. R. Hampel, A general qualitative definition of robustness, *The Annals of Mathematical Statistics*, **42**(6):1887–1896, 1971.

70 F. W. McElroy, A necessary and sufficient condition that ordinary least-squares estimators be best linear unbiased, *Journal of the American Statistical Association*, **62**(320):1302–1304, 1967.

71 A. C. Aitken, On least squares and linear combinations of observations, *Proceedings of the Royal Society of Edinburgh*, **55**:42–48, 1935.

72 P. J. Rousseeuw, Least median of squares regression, *Journal of the American Statistical Association*, **79**(388):871–880, 1984.

73 P. J. Rousseeuw and M. Hubert, Recent developments in PROGRESS, *Lecture Notes on L_1–Statistical Procedures and Related Topics*, **31**:201–214, 1997.

74 L. A. Jaeckel, Regression coefficients by minimizing the dispersion of the residuals, *The Annals of Mathematical Statistics*, **43**(5):1449–1458, 1972.

75 P. Hossjer, Rank-based estimates in the linear model with high breakdown point, *Journal of the American Statistical Association*, **89**(425):149–158, 1994.

76 C. Olsson, O. Enqvist, and F. Kahl, A polynomial-time bound for matching and registration with outliers, in *Proceedings of IEEE Conference on Computer Vision and Pattern Recognition*, 2008.

77 D. Capel, An effective bail-out test for RANSAC consensus scoring, in *Proceedings of the British Machine Vision Conference*, 629–638, 2005.

78 M. Cho, J. Sun, O. Duchenne, and J. Ponce, Finding matches in a Haystack: a max-pooling strategy for graph matching in the presence of outliers, in *Proceedings of IEEE Conference on Computer Vision and Pattern Recognition*, 2091–2098, 2014.

79 O. Chum, J. Matas, and J. Kittler, Locally optimized RANSAC, in *Pattern Recognition. DAGM 2003, Lecture Series in Computer Science*, B. Michaelis and G. Krell (Eds.), Springer, Berlin, Heidelberg, Vol. **2781**, 236–243, 2003.

80 O. Chum and J. Matas, Matching with PROSAC–progressive sample consensus, in *Proceedings of Computer Vision and Pattern Recognition*, Vol. **1**, 220–226, 2005.

81 O. Chum and J. Matas, Optimal randomized RANSAC, *IEEE Transactions on Pattern Analysis and Machine Intelligence*, **30**(8):1472–1482, 2008.

82 J. A. Denton and J. R. Beveridge, An algorithm for projective point matching in the presence of spurious points, *Pattern Recognition*, **40**:586–595, 2007.

83 A. Hast, J. Nysjö, and A. Marchetti, Optimal RANSAC - towards a repeatable algorithm for finding the optimal set, *Journal of WSCG*, **21**(1):21–30, 2012.

84 E. Hsiao, A. Collet, and M. Hebert, Making specific features less discriminative to improve point-based 3D object recognition, in *International Conference on Computer Vision and Pattern Recognition*, 2653–2660, 2010.

85 K. Lebede, J. Matas, and O. Chum, Fixing the locally optimized RANSAC, in *Proceedings of the British Machine Vision Conference*, 1–11, 2012.

86 J. Matas and O. Chum, Randomized RANSAC with Td,d test, *Image and Vision Computing*, **22**(10):837–842, 2004.

87 D. Nister, Preemptive RANSAC for live structure and motion estimation, in *Proceedings of International Conference on Computer Vision*, Vol. **1**, 199–206, 2003.

88 B. Tordoff and D. W. Murray, Guided sampling and consensus for motion estimation, in *Proceedings of European Conference on Computer Vision*, 82–98, 2002.

89 P. Torr and A. Zisserman, MLESAC: a new robust estimator with application to estimating image geometry, *Computer Vision and Image Understanding*, **78**(1):138–156, 2000.

90 P. B. van Wamelen, Z. Li, and S. S. Iyengar, A fast expected time algorithm for the 2-D point pattern matching problem, *Pattern Recognition*, **37**:1699–1711, 2004.

91 X. Wang and X. Zhang, Point pattern matching algorithm for planar point sets under Euclidean transform, *Journal of Applied Mathematics*, **2012**(1):1–12, 2012.

92 W. Zhang and J. Košecká, Generalized RANSAC framework for relaxed correspondence problems, in *Proceedings of International Symposium 3D Data Processing, Visualization, and Transmission*, 2006.

93 L. Talker, Y. Moses, and I. Shimshoni, Using spatial order to boost the elimination of incorrect feature matches, in *Proceedings of IEEE Conference on Computer Vision and Pattern Recognition*, 1809–1817, 2016.

94 M. Bansal and K. Daniilidis, Correspondence for disparate image matching, in *IEEE Conference on Computer Vision and Pattern Recognition*, 2802–2809, 2013.

95 R. C. Bolles, Robust feature matching through maximal cliques, in *SPIE Conference on Imaging Applications for Automated Industrial Inspection and Assembly*, Vol. **182**, 140–149, 1979.

96 C. Bron and J. Kerbosch, Algorithm 547: finding all cliques of an undirected graph, *Communications of the ACM*, **16**:(9):575–577, 1973.

97 R. A. Dwyer, A faster divide-and-conquer algorithm for constructing Delaunay triangulations, *Algorithmica*, **2**:137–151, 1987.

98 A. Goshtasby and G. C. Stockman, Point pattern matching using convex hull edges, *IEEE Transactions on Systems, Man, and Cybernetics*, **15**(5):631–637, 1985.

99 M. Izadi and P. Saeedi, Robust weighted graph transformation matching for rigid and nonrigid image registration, *IEEE Transactions on Image Processing*, **21**(10):4369–4382, 2012.

100 H. Jiang, T.-P. Tian, and S. Sclaroff, Scale and rotation invariant matching using linearly augmented trees, *IEEE Transactions on Pattern Analysis and Machine Intelligence*, **37**(12):2558–2572, 2015.

101 V. Kolmogorov and R. Zabih, Computing visual correspondence with occlusions using graph cuts, in *Proceedings of International Conference on Computer Vision*, 508–515, 2001.

102 D. Lavine, B. A. Lambird, and L. N. Kanal, Recognition of spatial point patterns, *Pattern Recognition*, **16**(3):289–295, 1983.

103 Z. Liu, J. An, and Y. Jing, A simple and robust feature point matching algorithm based on restricted spatial order constraints for aerial image registration, *IEEE Transactions on Geoscience and Remote Sensing*, **50**(2):514–527, 2012.

104 M. R. Sabuncu and P. Ramadge, Using spanning graphs for efficient image registration, *IEEE Transactions on Image Processing*, **17**(5):788–797, 2008.

105 E. Serradel, M. A. Pinheiro, R. Sznitman, J. Kybic, F. Moreno-Noguer, and P. Fua, Non-rigid graph registration using active testing search, *IEEE Transactions on Pattern Analysis and Machine Intelligence*, **37**(3):625–638, 2015.

106 C. T. Zhan Jr.,, An algorithm for noisy template matching, in *Information Processing 74*, North-Holland Publishing, 698–701, 1974.

107 M. Carcassoni and E. R. Hancock, Point pattern matching with robust spectral correspondence, in *IEEE Conference on Computer Vision and Pattern Recognition*, Vol. **1**, 649–655, 2000.

108 M. Carcassoni and E. R. Hancock, Spectral correspondence for point pattern matching, *Pattern Recognition*, **36**:193–204, 2003.

109 F. R. K. Chung, *Spectral Graph Theory*, Second Edition, American Mathematical Society, Providence, RI, 1–22, 1997.

110 M. Leordeanu and M. Hebert, A spectral technique for correspondence problems using pairwise constraints, in *Proceedings of International Conference on Computer Vision*, Vol. **2**, 1482–1489, 2005.

111 M. Pilu, A direct method for stereo correspondence based on singular value decomposition, in *IEEE Conference on Computer Vision and Pattern Recognition*, 261–266, 1997.

112 S. Sclaroff and A. P. Pentland, Model matching for correspondence and recognition, *IEEE Transactions on Pattern Analysis and Machine Intelligence*, **17**(6):545–561, 1995.

113 G. L. Scott and H. C. Longuet-Higgins, An algorithm for associating the features of two images, *Proceedings of the Royal Society of London Series B*, **244**:21–26, 1991.

114 L. S. Shapiro and J. M. Brady, Feature-based correspondence: an eigenvector approach, *Image and Vision Computing*, **10**(5):283–288, 1992.

115 G. W. Stewart, On the early history of the singular value decomposition, *SIAM Review*, **35**(4):551–566, 1993.

116 S. Umeyama, An eigendecomposition approach to weighted graph matching problems, *IEEE Transactions on Pattern Analysis and Machine Intelligence*, **10**(5):695–703, 1988.

117 G. X. Zhao, B. Lu, and J. Tang, Using eigen-decomposition method for weighted graph matching, in *Proceedings of Intelligent Computing 3rd International Conference on Advanced Intelligent Computing Theories and Applications, Lecture Notes in Computer Science*, Vol. **4681**, 1283–1294, 2007.

118 M. Antunes and J. P. Barreto, SymStereo: stereo matching using induced symmetry, *International Journal of Computer Vision*, **109**:187–208, 2014.

119 L. Cheng and T. Caelli, Bayesian stereo matching, *Computer Vision and Image Understanding*, **106**:85–96, 2007.

120 A. K. Jain and T. Q. Nguyen, Discriminability limits in spatio-temporal stereo block matching, *IEEE Transactions on Image Processing*, **23**(5):2328–2340, 2014.

121 M. G. Mozerov and J. van de Weijer, Accurate stereo matching by two-step energy minimization, *IEEE Transactions on Image Processing*, **24**(3):1153–1163, 2015.

122 J. Ma, J. Zhao, J. Tian, A. L. Yuille, and Z. Tu, Robust point matching via vector field consensus, *IEEE Transactions on Image Processing*, **23**(4):1706–1721, 2014.

123 C. Yeo, P. Ahammad, and K. Ramchandran, Coding of image feature descriptors for distributed rate-efficient visual correspondences, *International Journal of Computer Vision*, **94**:267–281, 2011.

124 V. Ila, R. Garciam, X. Cufi, and J. Batlle, Interest point characterization through textural analysis for rejection of bad correspondences, *Pattern Recognition Letters*, **26**:1587–1596, 2005.

125 R. Memisevic, Learning to relate images, *IEEE Transactions on Pattern Analysis and Machine Intelligence*, **35**(8):1829–1846, 2013.

126 W. Hartmann, M. Havlena, and K. Schindler, Predicting matchability, in *Proceedings of IEEE Conference on Computer Vision and Pattern Recognition*, 9–16, 2014.

127 T. Dekel, S. Oron, M. Rubinstein, S. Avidan, and W. T. Freeman, Best-buddies similarity for robust template matching, in *Proceedings of IEEE Conference on Computer Vision and Pattern Recognition*, 2021–2029, 2015.

128 J. Lezama, J.-M. Morel, G. Randall, and R. G. von Gioi, A contrario 2D point alignment detection, *IEEE Transactions on Pattern Analysis and Machine Intelligence*, **37**(3):499–512, 2015.

129 F. Bellavia, D. Tegolo, and C. Valenti, Keypoint descriptor matching with context-based orientation estimation, *Image and Vision Computing*, **32**:559–567, 2014.

130 B. Georgescu and P. Meer, Point matching under large image deformations and illumination changes, *IEEE Transactions on Pattern Analysis and Machine Intelligence*, **26**(6):674–688, 2004.

131 J. Man, H. Zhou, J. Zhao, Y. Gao, J. Jiang, and J. Tian, Robust feature matching for remote sensing image registration via locally linear transforming, *IEEE Transactions on Geoscience and Remote Sensing*, **53**(12):6469–6481, 2015.

132 S. T. Birchfield, B. Natarajan, and C. Tomasi, Correspondence as energy-based segmentation, *Image and Vision Computing*, **25**:1329–1340, 2007.

133 R. Litman, S. Korman, A. Bronstein, and S. Avidan, Inverting RANSAC: global model detection via inlier rate estimation, in *Proceedings of IEEE Conference on Computer Vision and Pattern Recognition*, 5243–5251, 2015.

134 O. Choi and I. S. Kweon, Robust feature point matching by preserving local geometric consistency, *Computer Vision and Image Understanding*, **113**:726–742, 2009.

135 A. Goshtasby and C. V. Page, Image matching by a probabilistic relaxation labeling process, in *Proceedings of the 7th International Conference on Pattern Recognition*, Vol. **1**, 307–309, 1984.

136 J.-H. Lee and C.-H. Won, Topology preserving relaxation labeling for nonrigid point matching, *IEEE Transactions on Pattern Analysis and Machine Intelligence*, **33**(2):427–432, 2011.

137 S. Ranade and A. Rosenfeld, Point pattern matching by relaxation, *Pattern Recognition*, **12**(4):269–275, 1980.

138 A. Stefanidis and P. Argouris, Relaxation matching for georegistration of aerial and satellite imagery, in *Proceedings of International Conference on Image Processing*, Vol. **5**, 449–452, 2007.

139 B. Jiang, J. Tang, B. Luo, and L. Lin, Robust feature point matching with sparse model, *IEEE Transactions on Image Processing*, **23**(12):5175–5186, 2014.

140 N. Dalal and B. Triggs, Histograms of oriented gradients for human detection, in *IEEE Conference on Computer Vision and Pattern Recognition*, 886–893, 2005.

141 K. Liu, H. Skibbe, T. Schmidt, T. Blein, K. Palme, T. Brox, and O. Ronneberger, Rotation-invariant HOG descriptors using Fourier analysis in polar and spherical coordinates, *International Journal of Computer Vision*, **106**:342–364, 2014.

142 S. Lazebnik, C. Schmid, and J. Ponce, Sparse texture representation using local affine regions, *IEEE Transactions on Pattern Analysis and Machine Intelligence*, **27**(8):1265–1278, 2005.

143 H. Bay, T. Tuetelaars, and L. van Gool, SURF: speeded up robust features, in *Proceedings of European Conference on Computer Vision*, also in *Computer Vision and Image Understanding*, **110**:346–359, 2006.

144 E. Tola, V. Lepetit, and P. Fua, DAISY: an efficient dense descriptor applied to wide-baseline stereo, *IEEE Transactions on Pattern Analysis and Machine Intelligence*, **32**(5):815–830, 2010.

145 S. Leutenegger, M. Chli, and R. Y. Siegwart, BRISK: binary robust invariant scalable keypoints, in *Proceedings of IEEE International Conference on Computer Vision*, 2548–2555, 2011.

146 M. Calonder, V. Lepetit, C. Strecha, and P. Fua, BRIEF: binary robust independent elementary features, in *European Conference on Computer Vision*, 2010.

147 E. Rublee, V. Rabaud, K. Konolige, and G. Bradski, ORB: an efficient alternative to SIFT and SURF, in *Proceedings of IEEE International Conference on Computer Vision*, 2564–2571, 2011.

148 A. Alahi, R. Ortiz, and P. Vandergheynst, FREAK: fast retina keypoint, in *IEEE Conference on Computer Vision and Pattern Recognition*, 2012.

149 P. Mainali, G. Lafruit, K. Tack, L. Van Gool, and R. Lauwereins, Derivative-based scale invariant image feature detector with error resilience, *IEEE Transactions on Image Processing*, 23(5):2380–2391, 2014.

150 R. Rustamov, Laplace-Beltrami eigenfunctions for deformation invariant shape representation, in *Proceedings of Symposium Geometry Processing*, 225–233, 2007.

151 J. Sun, M. Ovsjanikov, and L. Guibas, A concise and provably informative multi-scale signature based on heat diffusion, *Computer Graphics Forum*, 28(5):1383–1392, 2009.

152 M. Aubry, U. Schlickewei, and D. Cremers, The wave kernel signature: a quantum mechanical approach to shape analysis, in *Proceedings of IEEE International Conference on Computer Vision Workshops*, 1626–1633, 2011.

153 R. Litman and A. M. Bronstein, Learning spectral descriptors for deformable shape correspondence, *IEEE Transactions on Pattern Analysis and Machine Intelligence*, 36(1):171–180, 2014.

154 V. Balntas, L. Tang, and K. Mikolajczyk, BOLD: binary online learned descriptor for efficient image matching, in *Proceedings of IEEE Conference on Computer Vision and Pattern Recognition*, 2367–2375, 2015.

155 Y. Liu, P. Lasang, and M. Siegel, Geodesic invariant feature: a local descriptor in depth, *IEEE Transactions on Image Processing*, 24(1):236–248, 2015.

156 S. Belongie, J. Malik, and J. Puzicha, Shape matching and object recognition using shape contexts, *IEEE Transactions on Pattern Analysis and Machine Intelligence*, 24(4):509–522, 2002.

157 J. Liang, Z. Liao, S. yang, and Y. Wang, Image matching based on orientation-magnitude histograms and global consistency, *Pattern Recognition*, 45:3825–3833, 2012.

158 F. Ullah and S. Kaneko, Using orientation codes for rotation-invariant template matching, *Pattern Recognition*, 37:201–209, 2004.

159 T. Dickscheid, F. Schindler, and W. Förstner, Coding images with local features, *International Journal of Computer Vision*, 94:154–174, 2011.

160 A. Baumberg, Reliable feature matching across widely separated views, in *IEEE Conference on Computer Vision and Pattern Recognition*, Vol. 1, 774–781, 2000.

161 G. Carneiro and A. D. Jepson, Phase-based local features, in *European Conference on Computer Vision*, Copenhagen, Denmark, 282–296, 2002.

162 L. Florack, B. ter Haar Romeny, J. Koenderink, and M. Viergever, General intensity transformations and second order invariants, in *Proceedings of the 7th Scandinavian Conference on Image Analysis*, 338–345, 1991.

163 C. Schmid and R. Mohr, Local gray-value invariants for image retrieval, *IEEE Transactions on Pattern Analysis and Machine Intelligence*, **19**(5):530–535, 1997.

164 Z. Chen and S.-K. Sun, "A Zernike moment phase-based descriptor for local image representation and matching," *IEEE Transactions on Image Processing*, **19**(1):205–219, 2010.

165 W.-Y. Kim and Y.-S. Kim, Robust rotation angle estimator, *IEEE Transactions on Pattern Analysis and Machine Intelligence*, **21**(8):768–773, 1999.

166 V. Mohan, P. Shanmugapriya, and Y. Venkataramani, Object recognition using image descriptors, in *Proceedings of International Conference on Computing, Communication and Networking*, 1–4, 2008.

167 A. Sit and D. Kihara, Comparison of image patches using local moment invariants, *IEEE Transactions on Image Processing*, **23**(5):2369–2379, 2014.

168 L. van Gool, T. Moons, and D. Ungureanu, Affine/photometric invariants for planar intensity patterns, in *Proceedings of European Conference on Computer Vision*, 642–651, 1996.

169 T. Trzcinski, M. Christoudias, and V. Lepetit, Learning image descriptors with Boosting, *IEEE Transactions on Pattern Analysis and Machine Intelligence*, **37**(3):597–610, 2015.

170 P. Wohlhart and V. Lepetit, Learning descriptors for object recognition and 3D pose estimation, in *Proceedings of IEEE Conference on Computer Vision and Pattern Recognition*, 3109–3118, 2015.

171 S. Gauglitz, T. Höllerer, and M. Turk, Evaluation of interest point detectors and feature descriptors for visual tracking, *International Journal of Computer Vision*, **94**:335–360, 2011.

172 O. Lotan and M. Irani, Needle-match: reliable patch matching under high uncertainty, in *Proceedings of IEEE Conference on Computer Vision and Pattern Recognition*, 439–448, 2016.

173 T.-Y. Yang, Y.-Y. Lin, and Y.-Y. Chuang, Accumulated stability voting: a robust descriptor from descriptors of multiple scales, in *Proceedings of IEEE Conference on Computer Vision and Pattern Recognition*, 327–335, 2016.

174 T. Matsukawa, T. Okabe, E. Suzuki, and Y. Sato, Hierarchical Gaussian descriptor for person re-identification, in *Proceedings of IEEE Conference on Computer Vision and Pattern Recognition*, 1363–1372, 2016.

175 S. Theodoridis and K. Koutroumbas, *Pattern Recognition*, Fourth Edition, Academic Press, 2009.

176 E. Elboher and M. Werman, Asymmetric correlation: a noise robust similarity measure for template matching, *IEEE Transactions on Image Processing*, **23**(8):3062–3073, 2013.

177 A. Venot, J. F. Lebruchec, J. L. Golmard, and J. C. Roucayrol, An automated method for the normalization of scintigraphic images, *Journal of Nuclear Medicine*, **24**:529–531, 1983.

178 A. Venot and V. Leclerc, Automated correction of patient motion and gray values prior to subtraction in digitized angiography, *IEEE Transactions on Medical Imaging*, **3**:179–186, 1984.

179 A. Venot, J. Y. Devaux, M. Herbin, J. F. Lebruchec, L. Dubertret, Y. Raulo, and J. C. Roucayrol, An automated system for the registration and comparison of photographic images in medicine, *IEEE Transactions on Medical Imaging*, **7**(4):298–303, 1988.

180 J. D. Gibbons, *Nonparametric Methods for Quantitative Analysis*, Second Edition, American Science Press, Columbus, OH, 298, 1985.

181 M. G. Kendall, A new measure of rank correlation, *Biometrika*, **30**:81–93, 1938.

182 G. S. Shieh, A weighted Kendall's tau statistic, *Statistics & Probability Letters*, **39**:17–24, 1998.

183 R. A. Gideon and R. A. Hollister, A rank correlation coefficient, *Journal of the American Statistical Association*, **82**(398):656–666, 1987.

184 R. B. Tennakoon, A. Bab-Hadiashar, Z. Cao, and M. de Bruijne, Nonrigid registration of volumetric images using ranked order statistics, *IEEE Transactions on Medical Imaging*, **33**(2):422–432, 2014.

185 R. Zabih and J. Woodfill, Non-parametric local transforms for computing visual correspondence, in *Proceedings of European Conference on Computer Vision*, 151–158, 1994.

186 H. Hirschmüller and D. Scharstein, Evaluation of stereo matching costs on images with radiometric differences, *IEEE Transactions on Pattern Analysis and Machine Intelligence*, **31**(9):1582–1599, 2009.

187 A. Rényi, On measures of entropy and information, in *Proceedings of the Fourth Berkeley Symposium on Mathematical Statistics Probability*, University of California Press, Berkeley, CA, Vol. **1**, 547–561, 1961; also available in *Selected Papers of Alfréd Rényi*, **2**:525–580, 1976.

188 H. Rivaz, Z. Karimaghaloo, and D. L. Collins, Self-similarity weighted mutual information: a new nonrigid image registration metric, *Medical Image Analysis*, **18**:341–358, 2014.

189 H. Rivaz, Z. Karimaghaloo, and D. L. Collins, Nonrigid registration of ultrasound and MRI using contextual conditioned mutual information, *IEEE Transactions on Medical Imaging*, **33**(3):708–725, 2014.

190 Y. Hel-Or, H. Hel-Or, and E. David, Matching by tone mapping: photometric invariant template matching, *IEEE Transactions on Pattern Analysis and Machine Intelligence*, **36**(2):317–330, 2014.

191 J. Masci, M. M. Bronstein, A. M. Bronstein, and J. Schmidhuber, Multimodal similarity-preserving hashing, *IEEE Transactions on Pattern Analysis and Machine Intelligence*, **36**(4):824–830, 2014.

192 F. Yan and K. Mikolajczyk, Deep correlation for matching images and text, *Proceedings of IEEE Conference on Computer Vision and Pattern Recognition*, 3441–3450, 2015.

193 D. Teney, M. Brown, D. Kit, and P. Hall, Learning similarity metrics for dynamic scene segmentation, in *Proceedings of IEEE Conference on Computer Vision and Pattern Recognition*, 2084–2093, 2015.

194 D. Škerl, B. Likar, and F. Pernuš, A protocol for evaluation of similarity measures for rigid registration, *IEEE Transactions on Medical Imaging*, **25**(6):779–791, 2006.

195 Z.-D. Lan and R. Mohr, Robust matching by partial correlation, in *Proceedings of the 6th British Machine Vision Conference*, 651–660, 1995.

196 G. D. Evangelidis and E. Z. Psarakis, Parametric image alignment using enhanced correlation coefficient maximization, *IEEE Transactions on Pattern Analysis and Machine Intelligence*, **30**(10):1858–1865, 2008.

197 S. Kaneko, I. Murase, and S. Igarashi, Robust image registration by increment sign correlation, *Pattern Recognition*, **35**(10):2223–2234, 2002.

198 D. L. G. Hill, D. J. Hawkes, N. A. Harrison, and C. F. Ruff, A strategy for automated multimodality image registration incorporating anatomical knowledge and image characteristics, in *Proceedings of the 13th International Conference on Information Processing in Medical Imaging*, 182–196, 1993.

199 M. Holden, D. L. G. Hill, E. R. E. Denton, et al., Similarity measures for 3-D serial MR brain image registration, *IEEE Transactions on Medical Imaging*, **19**(2):94–102, 2000.

200 T. Wu, Y. Ge, J. Wang, A. Stein, Y. Song, Y. Du, and J. Ma, A WLTS-based method for remote sensing imagery registration, *IEEE Transactions on Geoscience and Remote Sensing*, **53**(1):102–116, 2015.

201 F. R. Hampel, The influence curve and its role in robust estimation, *Journal of the American Statistical Association*, **69**(346):383–393, 1974.

202 P. J. Huber, Robust regression: asymptotics, conjectures and Monte Carlo, *The Annals of Statistics*, **1**(5):799–821, 1973.

203 P. J. Huber, *Robust Statistics*, John Wiley & Sons, New York, 1981.

204 P. Rousseeuw and V. Yohai, Robust regression by means of S-estimators, in *Robust and Nonlinear Time Series Analysis, Lecture Notes in Statistics*,

J. Franke, W. Hördle, and R. D. Martin (Eds.), Springer-Verlag, New York, Vol. **26**, 256–274, 1984.

205 P. J. Rousseeuw and C. Croux, Alternatives to the median absolute deviation, *Journal of the American Statistical Association*, **88**(424):1273–1283, 1993.

206 A. F. Siegel, Robust regression using repeated medians, *Biometrika*, **69**(1):242–244, 1982.

6

Finding Homologous Lines

6.1   Introduction

If images are to be registered using lines, the parameters of the transformation
model registering the images should be determined from the parameters of the
lines. Steps to register images using feature lines are similar to those using feature points. First, correspondence is established between lines in the images.
By knowing a number of homologous lines in the images, the parameters of a
transformation model are determined. Finally, the test image is resampled to
the geometry of the reference image with the obtained transformation.

The problem to be addressed in this chapter is as follows. Given a set of lines
$\{l_i: i = 1, \ldots, m\}$ in the reference image and a set of lines $\{L_j: j = 1, \ldots, n\}$ in
the test image, we would like to determine the correspondence between the
lines. This correspondence makes it possible to determine the parameters of a
transformation model that can register the images. It is understood that some
lines appearing in one image may be missed in another image, and homologous
lines may have different endpoints.

In the following sections, after relating the transformation parameters for
registration of two images to the parameters of homologous lines in the images,
methods for determining homologous lines in images of a scene are described.
Then, examples of image registration using homologous lines in images are
given.

6.2   Determining Transformation Parameters
from Line Parameters

If two images are to be registered using homologous lines, it is required that
lines in one image appear as lines in another image. The relation between such
images is described by a *2-D projective transformation*, also known as *homography*. Treating images as Cartesian coordinate spaces and denoting a point in the

Theory and Applications of Image Registration, First Edition. Arthur Ardeshir Goshtasby.
© 2017 John Wiley & Sons, Inc. Published 2017 by John Wiley & Sons, Inc.

reference image by $\mathbf{p} = (x, y)$ and the same point in the test image by $\mathbf{P} = (X, Y)$, the homography relating the coordinates of homologous points in the images can be written as

$$X = \frac{h_0 x + h_1 y + h_2}{h_6 x + h_7 y + 1}, \tag{6.1}$$

$$Y = \frac{h_3 x + h_4 y + h_5}{h_6 x + h_7 y + 1}. \tag{6.2}$$

Points (x, y) and (X, Y) in Cartesian coordinates can be written in homogeneous coordinates by $[x \ \ y \ \ 1]^t$ and $[X \ \ Y \ \ 1]^t$, respectively, where t denotes transpose. Points $[x \ \ y \ \ 1]^t$ and $[X \ \ Y \ \ 1]^t$ do not include points at infinity and that will not be a problem because an image has a limited domain. For points at infinity, the third coordinate value will be 0.

The homography relation in homogeneous coordinates can be written as

$$\begin{bmatrix} XW \\ YW \\ W \end{bmatrix} = \begin{bmatrix} h_0 & h_1 & h_2 \\ h_3 & h_4 & h_5 \\ h_6 & h_7 & 1 \end{bmatrix} \begin{bmatrix} x \\ y \\ 1 \end{bmatrix} \tag{6.3}$$

or

$$W\mathbf{P} = \mathbf{H}\mathbf{p}. \tag{6.4}$$

W is an unknown scaling parameter that can be eliminated by dividing XW by W and YW by W.

If $ax + by + 1 = 0$ is a line in the reference image in Cartesian coordinates, the same line in homogenous coordinates can be written as

$$[a \ \ b \ \ 1] \begin{bmatrix} x \\ y \\ 1 \end{bmatrix} = 0 \tag{6.5}$$

or

$$\mathbf{l}^t \mathbf{p} = 0. \tag{6.6}$$

Similarly, line $AX + BY + 1 = 0$ in the test image in Cartesian coordinates can be written in homogeneous coordinates by

$$[A \ \ B \ \ 1] \begin{bmatrix} X \\ Y \\ 1 \end{bmatrix} = 0 \tag{6.7}$$

or

$$\mathbf{L}^t \mathbf{P} = 0. \tag{6.8}$$

Left-multiplying both sides of Eq. (6.4) by $\mathbf{L}^t$, we obtain

$$W\mathbf{L}^t \mathbf{P} = \mathbf{L}^t \mathbf{H}\mathbf{p} \tag{6.9}$$

or

$$L^tP = W^{-1}L^tHp. \tag{6.10}$$

Since from Eq. (6.8) we know that the left-hand side of Eq. (6.10) is 0, this implies that the right-hand side of Eq. (6.10) should also be 0. Therefore,

$$W^{-1}L^tHp = 0. \tag{6.11}$$

Since $l^tp = 0$ according to Eq. (6.6), from Eq. (6.11) we conclude that

$$W^{-1}L^tH = l^t. \tag{6.12}$$

Equation (6.12) shows the relation between parameters of homologous lines in two images and parameters of the homography relating the geometries of the images. Equation (6.12) can also be written as

$$W^{-1}[A \ B \ 1] \begin{bmatrix} h_0 & h_1 & h_2 \\ h_3 & h_4 & h_5 \\ h_6 & h_7 & 1 \end{bmatrix} = [a \ b \ 1] \tag{6.13}$$

or

$$W^{-1}(Ah_0 + Bh_3 + h_6) = a, \tag{6.14}$$
$$W^{-1}(Ah_1 + Bh_4 + h_7) = b, \tag{6.15}$$
$$W^{-1}(Ah_2 + Bh_5 + 1) = 1. \tag{6.16}$$

By dividing Eqs (6.14) and (6.15) by Eq. (6.16) to eliminate W^{-1}, we obtained two equations

$$Ah_0 - aAh_2 + Bh_3 - aBh_5 + h_6 = a, \tag{6.17}$$
$$Ah_1 - bAh_2 + Bh_4 - bBh_5 + h_7 = b, \tag{6.18}$$

between the transformation parameters and the parameters of homologous lines in the images. Knowing a minimum of four homologous lines in the images, the homography parameters can be determined. No more than two of the lines can be parallel. This is analogous to use of homologous points in finding the homography parameters where no more than two of the points can be colinear.

After finding the homography parameters, for each point (x, y) in the reference image, the homologous point (X, Y) in the test image can be determined from Eqs (6.1) and (6.2). The intensity at (X, Y) is then read and saved at (x, y) in a new image that has the intensities of the test image and the geometry of the reference image.

If the images are related by an *affine transformation*, the relation between the coordinates of homologous points in the images can be written in Cartesian coordinates as

$$X = f_0x + f_1y + f_2, \tag{6.19}$$
$$Y = f_3x + f_4y + f_5. \tag{6.20}$$

In homogenous coordinates, this relation can be written as

$$\begin{bmatrix} XW \\ YW \\ W \end{bmatrix} = \begin{bmatrix} f_0 & f_1 & f_2 \\ f_3 & f_4 & f_5 \\ 0 & 0 & 1 \end{bmatrix} \begin{bmatrix} x \\ y \\ 1 \end{bmatrix}. \tag{6.21}$$

Following the steps used to determine homography parameters from line parameters, we find the relation between the affine parameters and the parameters of homologous lines to be

$$Af_0 - aAf_2 + Bf_3 - aBf_5 = a, \tag{6.22}$$

$$Af_1 - bAf_2 + Bf_4 - bBf_5 = b. \tag{6.23}$$

The parameters of three homologous lines in reference and test images are needed to find the affine transformation to register the images. No two lines in each image should be parallel.

When the images are related by a similarity transformation, since $f_3 = -f_1$ and $f_4 = f_0$, Eqs (6.22) and (6.23) become

$$Af_0 - Bf_1 - aAf_2 - aBf_5 = a, \tag{6.24}$$

$$Bf_0 + Af_1 - bAf_2 - bBf_5 = b. \tag{6.25}$$

Equations (6.24) and (6.25) contain four unknown parameters: f_0, f_1, f_2, and f_5. It appears that two homologous lines should be sufficient to find the four unknown parameters of the similarity transformation; however, use of two homologous lines is not sufficient to find the scale ratio between the images. To find the scale ratio between two images, three homologous lines are required. Three equations are created using the parameters of three homologous lines in either (6.24) or (6.25). The fourth equation is created from the equation not used and the parameters of one of the homologous lines. Two out of the three lines can be parallel when finding the similarity transformation parameters. Distances between parallel lines in the images contain information about the scale ratio between the images.

If the images are related by a rigid transformation, since the images are in the same scale and the only unknowns are the rotation and translation parameters, it is easier to use the polar equation of lines where a line is defined by its orientation and its distance to the origin: $x \cos \alpha + y \sin \alpha = \rho$. Parameter α shows the angle of the normal to the line with the x-axis and parameter ρ shows the distance of the line to the origin. This line can be more generally written as

$$a'x + b'y + c' = 0, \tag{6.26}$$

where $a' = \cos \theta, b' = \sin \theta$, and $c' = -\rho$. Note that a line in the form of Eq. (6.26) requires that $\sqrt{a'^2 + b'^2} = 1$. In homogenous coordinates, this line can be written as

$$[a'\ b'\ c'] \begin{bmatrix} x \\ y \\ 1 \end{bmatrix} = 0 \tag{6.27}$$

or

$$\mathbf{l}'^t \mathbf{p} = 0. \tag{6.28}$$

Similarly, line $A'X + B'Y + C' = 0$ in the test image, where $\sqrt{A'^2 + B'^2} = 1$, can be written in homogenous coordinates by

$$[A'\ B'\ C'] \begin{bmatrix} X \\ Y \\ 1 \end{bmatrix} = 0 \tag{6.29}$$

or

$$\mathbf{L}'^t \mathbf{P} = 0. \tag{6.30}$$

If two images are related by a rigid transformation, denoting rotation of the test image with respect to the reference image by θ and translation of the rotated test image with respect to the reference image by (t_x, t_y), the rigid transformation relating the geometries of the images can be written as

$$X = x \cos \theta - y \sin \theta + t_x, \tag{6.31}$$
$$Y = x \sin \theta + y \cos \theta + t_y. \tag{6.32}$$

Renaming $\cos \theta$ by f_0, $-\sin \theta$ by f_1, t_x by f_2, and t_y by f_3, we can write Eqs (6.31) and (6.32) as

$$X = xf_0 + yf_1 + f_2, \tag{6.33}$$
$$Y = -xf_1 + yf_0 + f_3, \tag{6.34}$$

or in homogenous coordinates as

$$\begin{bmatrix} X \\ Y \\ 1 \end{bmatrix} = \begin{bmatrix} f_0 & f_1 & f_2 \\ -f_1 & f_0 & f_3 \\ 0 & 0 & 1 \end{bmatrix} \begin{bmatrix} x \\ y \\ 1 \end{bmatrix} \tag{6.35}$$

or

$$\mathbf{P} = \mathbf{F}\mathbf{p}. \tag{6.36}$$

Note that there is no scaling parameter W in Eq. (6.35) or in Eq. (6.36). This is because under rigid transformation the reference and test images have the same scale. By left-multiplying both sides of Eq. (6.36) by $\mathbf{L}'^t$, we obtain

$$\mathbf{L}'^t \mathbf{P} = \mathbf{L}'^t \mathbf{F} \mathbf{p}. \tag{6.37}$$

Since according to (6.30) the left-hand side of (6.37) is 0, it means that the right-hand side of (6.37) should also be 0 . Therefore,

$$L'^t Fp = 0. \qquad (6.38)$$

Using the result of Eq. (6.28) in Eq. (6.38), we obtain

$$L'^t F = l'^t \qquad (6.39)$$

or

$$[A' \ B' \ C'] \begin{bmatrix} f_0 & f_1 & f_2 \\ -f_1 & f_0 & f_3 \\ 0 & 0 & 1 \end{bmatrix} = [a' \ b' \ c'], \qquad (6.40)$$

which shows the relation between the rigid transformation parameters and the parameters of homologous lines in the images.

From Eq. (6.40), we obtain the following three equations:

$$A'f_0 - B'f_1 = a', \qquad (6.41)$$
$$A'f_1 + B'f_0 = b', \qquad (6.42)$$
$$A'f_2 + B'f_3 + C' = c'. \qquad (6.43)$$

Equations (6.41) and (6.42) both show relations between f_0 and f_1 and the line parameters, one of which is redundant. Therefore, one of them along with Eq. (6.43) can be used to find parameters f_0, f_1, f_2, and f_3 of the rigid transformation from the parameters of two homologous lines in the images. To ensure that $f_0^2 + f_1^2 = 1$, after calculating the four parameters, each is divided by $\sqrt{f_0^2 + f_1^2}$.

If the test image is only translated with respect to the reference image, homologous lines in the images have the same orientation. Therefore, if line $L' = [A' \ B' \ C']^t$ in the test image corresponds to line $l' = [a' \ b' \ c']^t$ in the reference image, we have $A' = a'$ and $B' = b'$ and the equations of homologous lines in the images will be

$$a'X + b'Y + C' = 0, \qquad (6.44)$$
$$a'x + b'y + c' = 0. \qquad (6.45)$$

Subtracting (6.45) from (6.44), we obtain

$$a'(X - x) + b'(Y - y) + C' - c' = 0 \qquad (6.46)$$

or

$$a't_x + b't_y + C' - c' = 0. \qquad (6.47)$$

Relation (6.47) shows that a line in the reference image and its correspondence in the test image cannot uniquely determine the translation parameters. Therefore, two nonparallel homologous lines in the images are required to determine the translation parameters.

Table 6.1 The number of homologous lines required to find the parameters of various transformation models for the registration of images of planar scenes is shown in the middle column. The equations to be used to find the transformation parameters from homologous line parameters are shown in the right column.

Transformation model	Number of homologous lines required	Equation(s) to use
Translation	2	(6.48)
Rigid	2	(6.42) and (6.43)
Similarity	3	(6.24) and (6.25)
Affine	3	(6.22) and (6.23)
Homography	4	(6.17) and (6.18)

Due to noise, since homologous lines in images that are translated with respect to one another may not be exactly parallel, instead of Eq. (6.47), the following equation is used to find the translation parameters.

$$\frac{a' + A'}{2} t_x + \frac{b' + B'}{2} t_y + C' - c' = 0. \tag{6.48}$$

Table 6.1 summarizes the number of homologous lines required to determine the parameters of various transformation models to register two images of a planar scene. No two lines in either image should be parallel when determining the translation, rigid, or affine parameters, and no three lines should be parallel when determining the homography parameters.

6.3 Finding Homologous Lines by Clustering

Determination of homologous lines in two images of a planar scene by clustering is practical only when the transformation model used to register the images has a small number of parameters. Given a set of lines in the reference image and a set of lines in the test image, in this section, a clustering algorithm to determine the rigid transformation parameters is described.

Equations (6.42) and (6.43) show the relation between the parameters of a rigid transformation and the parameters of homologous lines in the images. The rotation parameter $\theta = \arctan(f_1/f_0)$ is estimated by clustering the rotational difference between a randomly selected line in the reference image and a randomly selected line in the test image. Knowing the rotation parameter, the translation parameters are determined by clustering parameters f_2 and f_3 computed from Eq. (6.43) by using two randomly selected nonparallel lines in the images.

6.3.1 Finding the Rotation Parameter

The angle of rotation of the test image with respect to the reference image will be a value between 0 and 2π; therefore, a 1-D array with 360 entries is created to record angles of lines in the test image with respect to lines in the reference image. The entries of the array are initially set to 0. A directed line is randomly selected from each image, and the angle θ of the line in the test image with respect to the line in the reference image is determined, and the entry θ of the array is incremented by 1. When randomly selected lines correspond, they produce the same angle, and when randomly selected lines do not correspond, they produce angles that randomly fall between 0 and 2π. If the process is repeated sufficiently, a peak will appear in the histogram at the angle representing the rotational difference between the images.

The following algorithm describes the steps needed to find the rotation of the test image with respect to the reference image. Parameter h_1 is the minimum height of a peak needed for its location to be taken as the rotational difference between the images, and parameter h_2 is the minimum difference needed between a peak and the entries at its left and right sides in the histogram to consider the peak robust enough to be useful.

Algorithm 6.1a   Finding the rotation parameter using lines

Given directed lines $\{l'_i : i = 1, \ldots, m\}$ in the reference image and directed lines $\{L'_j : j = 1, \ldots, n\}$ in the test image, this algorithm finds rotation θ of the test image with respect to the reference image. In the following, $l'_i = [a'\ b'\ c']$, $L'_j = [A'\ B'\ C']$, $\hat{\theta}$ is the location of the highest peak in the histogram, and h_n is the height of the highest peak. When the highest peak in the histogram is higher than h_1 and also greater than values at its both sides by h_2, a peak is declared. t shows the number of iterations completed so far, and t_m is the maximum number of iterations without finding an acceptable peak before declaring failure.

1. Allocate a 1-D array with 360 entries and initialize all entries to 0. Also, let $h_n = 0$ and $t = 0$.
2. Select a random line l' from the reference image and a random line L' from the test image, and increment t by 1.
3. Find angle θ of L' with respect to l'. Then, increment entry θ of the histogram by 1. If the value at entry θ in the histogram is h, then if $h \geq h_1$ and h is greater than entries to its left and right sides by h_2, go to Step 4. Otherwise, if $t \geq t_m$ let $\theta = \hat{\theta}$ and go to Step 4. If $t < t_m$ and $h > h_n$, let $h_n = h$, $\hat{\theta} = \theta$, and go to Step 2.
4. Return θ as the rotation of the test image with respect to the reference image.

Note that the line detector used to find the lines should produce a value between 0 and 2π for the angle of a line (or its normal) with the x-axis. If the detected lines are not directed so that parameter θ varies between 0 and π, when parameter θ is determined from Algorithm 6.1a, the actual rotation of the test image with respect to the reference could be $\theta + \pi$.

If lines in all directions appear in an image with about the same likelihood, Algorithm 6.1a will find the rotational difference between the images. However, when the majority of lines appearing in the images have a few different directions, and especially when there is limited overlap between the images, the dominant orientation obtained from the lines in the reference image may not be the same as that obtained from the lines in the test image, causing Algorithm 6.1a to fail. This is because many lines that do not truly correspond will produce a common rotational angle, creating a false peak and estimating a wrong rotational difference.

If the reference and test images have about the same number of lines, that is, if $m \approx n$ and assuming about half of the lines in each image are outliers, when a line is selected in the reference image the probability that the line is also present in the test image is $1/2$ and when a line is randomly selected in the test image, the probability that it corresponds to the line selected in the reference image is $1/n$. Therefore, when a line is randomly selected in each image, the probability that they correspond is $w = \frac{1}{2n}$. This shows that when a line is randomly selected from each image, the probability that they do not correspond is $(1 - w)$.

After k tries, the probability that none of the lines randomly selected from the images correspond is $(1 - w)^k$, and after k tries the probability that at least one of the lines randomly selected from the images corresponds is $p = 1 - (1 - w)^k$. This shows that the number of tries required for a randomly selected line in each image to correspond with probability p is

$$k = \frac{\log(1 - p)}{\log(1 - w)}, \tag{6.49}$$

$$= \frac{\log(1 - p)}{\log\left(1 - \frac{1}{2n}\right)}. \tag{6.50}$$

When $n = 25$ and $p = 0.99$, we find $k = 227$. Equation (6.50) can be used to calculate the maximum number of iterations t_m needed in Algorithm 6.1a to find a pair of homologous lines in the images. Since the minimum height required at the highest peak is h_1, $t_m = h_1 k$ iterations will be required to obtain a peak that is sufficiently high to determine the rotational difference between the images. For example, when $h_1 = 10$ and $h_2 = 1$, we find $t_m = 10 \times 227 = 2270$.

6.3.2 Finding the Translation Parameters

The translation parameters f_2 and f_3 of a rigid transformation are determined from Eq. (6.43). Parameter f_2 shows translation in x-direction, which can vary from $-w$ to w, with w being the width of the test image. Parameter f_3 shows translation in the y-direction and can vary from $-h$ to h, with h being the height of the test image. Assuming d is the larger of w and h, an array of size $(2d + 1) \times (2d + 1)$ is used to find the translation of the test image with respect to the rotated reference image. The steps of an algorithm that finds the translation parameters in this manner are as follows.

Algorithm 6.1b Finding the translation parameters using lines

---

Knowing the rotation θ of the test image with respect to the reference image determined by Algorithm 6.1a, this algorithm finds the translation of the test image with respect to the rotated reference image. $\mathbf{h}_l$ shows the location of the highest peak within a 2-D histogram that records various translation parameters obtained from random line pairs in the images, and h_n shows the height of the highest peak. Parameters t and t_m are the same as those used in Algorithm 6.1a.

1. Allocate a 2-D array of size $(2d + 1) \times (2d + 1)$ and initialize all entries to 0. Also, let $h_n = 0$ and $t = 0$.
2. If a line $\mathbf{l}'$ in the reference image makes angle θ_r with the x-axis, find line $\mathbf{L}'$ in the test image that makes angle θ_t with the x-axis and θ_t is closest to $\theta_r + \theta$ among all lines in the test image, consider $\mathbf{l}'$ and $\mathbf{L}'$ initial homologous lines. This step, in effect, establishes initial correspondence between lines in the images.
3. Select a pair of lines $\mathbf{l}'_1$ and $\mathbf{l}'_2$ randomly from the reference image, suppose lines $\mathbf{L}'_1$ and $\mathbf{L}'_2$ in the test image correspond to them as determined by Step 2, and increment t by 1.
4. Letting $\mathbf{l}'_1$ and $\mathbf{l}'_2$ correspond to $\mathbf{L}'_1$ and $\mathbf{L}'_2$, determine parameters f_2 and f_3 from Eq. (6.43). If f_2 and f_3 are both between $-d$ and d, increment entry $(f_2 + d, f_3 + d)$ of the histogram by 1 and go to Step 5. Otherwise, if $t \geq t_m$, let $\mathbf{h}_l = (f_2, f_3)$ and go to Step 6. If $t < t_m$, go to Step 3.
5. If the count at $(f_2 + d, f_3 + d)$ is h, then if $h \geq h_1$ and h is greater than histogram entries surrounding the peak by at least h_2, let $\mathbf{h}_l = (f_2, f_3)$ and go to Step 6. Otherwise, if $h > h_n$, let $h_n = h$, $\mathbf{h}_l = (f_2, f_3)$, and go to Step 3.
6. Return $\mathbf{h}_l$ as the translation of the test image with respect to the reference image after it is rotated by θ, determined by Algorithm 6.1a.

Similar to Algorithm 6.1a, Algorithm 6.1b can succeed only when lines in all directions appear in the images. If lines appearing in the images are clustered into a few directions, even when Algorithm 6.1a correctly finds the rotational difference between the images, Algorithm 6.1b could fail because the translation amount to align most lines may not be the correct translational difference between the images, especially when the images contain many parallel lines and have limited overlap.

In Algorithm 6.1b, when two lines are randomly selected from the reference image, the probability that the selected lines appear in the test image is 1/4. This is when half of the lines in each image are considered outliers. Assuming $m \approx n$ and $\sqrt{n}$ out of n homologous lines initially obtained in Step 2 of Algorithm 6.1b are correct and letting $w = 1/\sqrt{n}$, the probability that when two lines are randomly selected from the reference image they are associated with initial homologous lines that are correct is $w^2/4$, and the probability that the two lines randomly selected from the reference image do not have correspondences in the test image is $1 - w^2/4$.

If line pairs are randomly selected from the images k times, the probability that none of the line pairs represent correct homologous lines is $(1 - w^2/4)^k$. Therefore, the probability that after k tries at least one of the line pairs in the reference image represents a correct initial correspondence is $p = 1 - (1 - w^2/4)^k$. The number of iterations required to obtain one line pair in the reference image that corresponds to a line pair in the test image with probability p is

$$k = \frac{\log(1-p)}{\log\left(1 - \frac{w^2}{4}\right)}, \tag{6.51}$$

$$= \frac{\log(1-p)}{\log\left(1 - \frac{1}{4n}\right)}. \tag{6.52}$$

For example, when $n = 25$ and $p = 0.99$, we find $k = 458$. Letting $h_1 = 10$ and $h_2 = 1$, we find $t_m = h_1 k = 4580$ in Algorithm 6.1b.

If Algorithms 6.1a and 6.1b succeed in finding the transformation parameters, determination of correspondence between lines in the images becomes straightforward. Each line in the reference image is transformed with the obtained transformation and the line best matching it in the test image is identified. If the match rating between best matched lines is sufficiently high, the best matched lines are considered homologous lines. An algorithm that finds the correspondence between lines in two images in this manner under rigid transformation is described next.

Algorithm 6.1c Finding homologous lines in images related by a rigid transformation

---

Having determined the rigid transformation parameters $\theta, t_x,$ and t_y from m lines in the reference image and n lines in the test image by Algorithms 6.1a and 6.1b, this algorithm finds the correspondence between the lines. ε_θ is the maximum rotational difference, ε_t is the maximum translation radially, and ε_d is the maximum distance between the midpoint of a line in the test image after it is transformed by the obtained rigid transformation and the midpoint of a line in the reference image.

1. For each line $[a'\ b'\ c']^t$ in the reference image, repeat Steps 2–5.
2. If normal to line $[a'\ b'\ c']^t$ makes angle $\theta_1 = \arctan(b'/a')$ with the x-axis, find line $[A'\ B'\ C']^t$ in the test image where the normal to it makes angle $\theta_2 = \arctan(B'/A')$ with the x-axis and where $\delta\theta = |\theta_1 + \theta - \theta_2|$ is the smallest among all lines in the test image.
3. If $\delta\theta \geq \varepsilon_\theta$, there is no correspondence to line $[a'\ b'\ c']^t$. Otherwise, continue testing the validity of lines $[a'\ b'\ c']^t$ and $[A'\ B'\ C']^t$ as homologous lines.
4. Since homologous lines must satisfy Eq. (6.43), determine whether the lines satisfy $|A't_x + B't_y + C' - c'| < \varepsilon_t$. If they do not, line $[a'\ b'\ c']^t$ does not have a correspondence. Otherwise, continue validating the correspondence.
5. Among all lines in the test image that pass the test in Step 4, choose the one with its midpoint closest to the midpoint of line $[a'\ b'\ c']^t$, and if the distance between the midpoints of the lines is within ε_d, report it as the line corresponding to $[a'\ b'\ c']^t$.

An example of line correspondence by Algorithms 6.1a–6.1c is given in Fig. 6.1. The reference and test images along with their lines are shown in (a) and (b), respectively. These are aerial images of the Dayton International Airport, courtesy of Google Maps and Microsoft Bing. The rigid parameters corresponding to the peak histogram entries obtained from Algorithms 6.1a and 6.1b produce the registration shown in (c). The reference image is shown in yellow and the transformed test image is shown in blue. Because many lines are appearing parallel to the runway, the translation parameters corresponding to the peak histogram entry in Algorithm 6.1b do not represent the correct translational difference between the images. More lines align with an incorrect translation than with the correct one.

Although the highest peak in the histogram in Algorithm 6.1a correctly determines the rotation of the test image with respect to the reference image, the histogram peak in Algorithm 6.1b does not identify the correct translation parameters. The 2-D translation histogram of Algorithm 6.1b is shown in Fig. 6.1d. There are many peaks in the histogram with high values, one of which represents the correct translation of the test image with respect to the reference image.

When segments shorter than 30 pixels are discarded and only the longer segments as shown in Fig. 6.2a and b are used, the registration shown in Fig. 6.2e is obtained. Again, the reference image is shown in yellow and the transformed

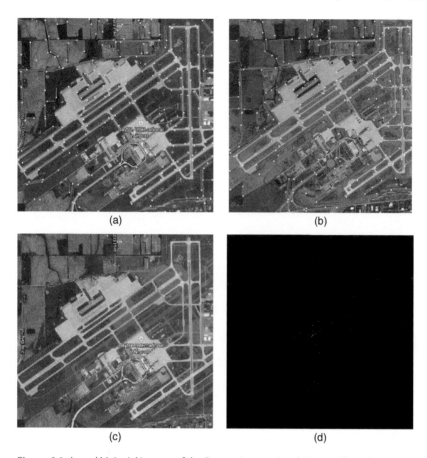

Figure 6.1 (a and b) Aerial images of the Dayton International Airport. These images are courtesy of Google Maps and Microsoft Bing, respectively. (c) Registration of the images by Algorithms 6.1a and 6.1b. (d) The translation histogram created by Algorithm 6.1b while matching random line pairs in the images.

test image is shown in blue. The registration is not very accurate due to the discrete nature of the estimated rigid parameters, but it is accurate enough to produce the homologous lines shown in Fig. 6.2c and d when letting $\varepsilon_\theta = 5°, \varepsilon_t = 5$ pixels, and $\varepsilon_d = 50$ pixels. Homologous lines are shown with the same color. By reducing the number of parallel lines, the likelihood of false peaks forming in the histograms is reduced.

The weakness of clustering is that parameters resulting from most line matches are selected without verification of the correctness of the obtained parameters. Due to the random nature of the line selection process, a correct set of parameters may be obtained when running the program once, but when running the program again on the same images, the correct parameters may

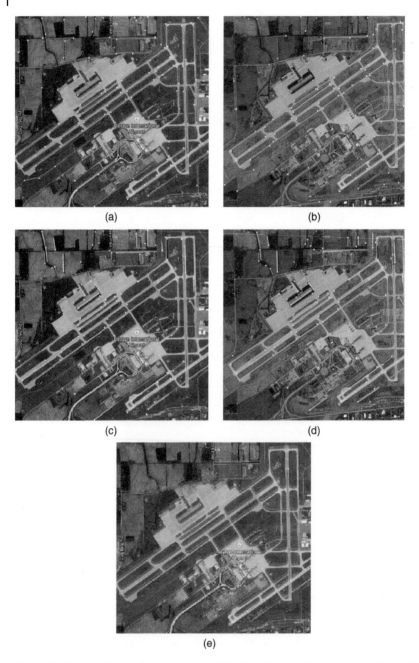

Figure 6.2 (a and b) Same as images (a) and (b) in Fig. 6.1 except for using only lines that are 30 pixels or longer. (c and d) Homologous lines obtained by Algorithm 6.1c are shown with the same color. (e) Registration of the images using the transformation parameters obtained by Algorithms 6.1a and 6.1b.

be missed. Steps to determine the number of homologous lines obtained from the estimated parameters are required in Algorithms 6.1a and 6.1b, and if sufficient homologous lines are not obtained, the process needs to be repeated to reestimate the parameters. This verification step should be repeated until the estimated parameters produce a sufficiently high number of homologous lines in the images.

Rather than adding a verification step to the clustering-based correspondence algorithm, we can use a RANSAC-based algorithm [1], which already has a built-in verification step, to find homologous lines in images.

6.4   Finding Homologous Lines by RANSAC

In a RANSAC paradigm, a hypothesis is formed from minimal information in images and the correctness of the hypothesis is verified using additional information in the images. To find correspondence between lines in two images under a required transformation model, a sufficient number of lines are selected from each image and transformation parameters are estimated from them. The correctness of the estimated (hypothesized) parameters is then verified using other lines in the images.

Without knowledge about homologous lines in the images, RANSAC may require a very large number of iterations before arriving at a hypothesis that is supported by other lines in the images. Therefore, if no knowledge about homologous lines in the images is available, RANSAC is practical only when the transformation model has a very small number of parameters.

In this section, determination of rigid transformation parameters from line parameters by RANSAC is described. Given directed lines $\{l'_i: i = 1, \dots, m\}$ in the reference image and directed lines $\{L'_j: j = 1, \dots, n\}$ in the test image, we would like to find parameters θ, t_x, and t_y of a rigid transformation to register the images and also to find homologous lines in the images.

Algorithm 6.2   Finding rigid transformation parameters by RANSAC

Parameter h_1 is the minimum number of homologous lines that should satisfy a hypothesized transformation model to consider the transformation correct. Parameter t shows the number of hypotheses generated so far, and t_m is the maximum number of consecutive hypotheses not supported by at least h_1 homologous lines before declaring failure.

1. Let $t = 0$.
2. Select lines l'_1 and l'_2 randomly from the reference image. Also, select lines L'_1 and L'_2 randomly from the test image and assume l'_1 corresponds to L'_1 and l'_2 corresponds to L'_2. Also, increment t by 1.

3. Using the two homologous lines, determine the rigid transformation parameters by solving Eqs (6.42) and (6.43). Suppose the rigid transformation parameters obtained as a result are θ, t_x, and t_y.
4. From the obtained rigid transformation find h, the number of lines in the images that correspond, using Algorithm 6.1c.
5. If $h > h_1$, go to Step 6. Otherwise, if $t \geq t_m$, go to Step 7. If $t < t_m$, go to Step 2.
6. Return parameters θ, t_x, and t_y and the h homologous lines.
7. Report failure. Transformation parameters could not be found within t_m iterations.

Parameter t_m of Algorithm 6.2 can be computed as follows. If the images contain about the same number of lines, that is, $m \approx n$, and about half of the lines in each image are outliers, when selecting a line randomly from the reference image, the probability that the line will be present in the test image is 1/2. If a line selected in the reference image is present in the test image, the probability that a line randomly selected in the test image correspond to it is $1/n$. Therefore, when a line is randomly selected from each image, the probability that the lines correspond is $w = \frac{1}{2n}$, and when two lines are randomly selected from the images, the probability that both correspond is w^2.

This shows that the two lines randomly selected from the images will not correspond to each other with probability $1 - w^2$. If line pairs are randomly selected in the images k times, the probability that none of the selected line pairs correspond is $(1 - w^2)^k$. Therefore, the probability that at least one of the k selections contain a homologous line pair is $1 - (1 - w^2)^k$. If we want this probability to be p, the number of iterations required to obtain a homologous pair with probability p is

$$k = \frac{\log(1-p)}{\log(1-w^2)}, \tag{6.53}$$

$$= \frac{\log(1-p)}{\log\left(1 - \frac{1}{4n^2}\right)}. \tag{6.54}$$

For example, when $n = 25$ and $p = 0.99$, we find $k = 11{,}511$. This is a very large number of iterations considering there is a relatively small number of lines in the images. RANSAC quickly becomes impractical as n increases even under the simple rigid transformation. RANSAC, however, finds correct homologous lines in the images with probability p because the returned parameters are verified to be supported by many other lines in the images.

Using images (a) and (b) in Fig. 6.2 with the detected lines, RANSAC was able to find the homologous lines shown in images (a) and (b) in Fig. 6.3. The registration obtained from the rigid transformation parameters estimated by Algorithm 6.2 is shown in Fig. 6.3c.

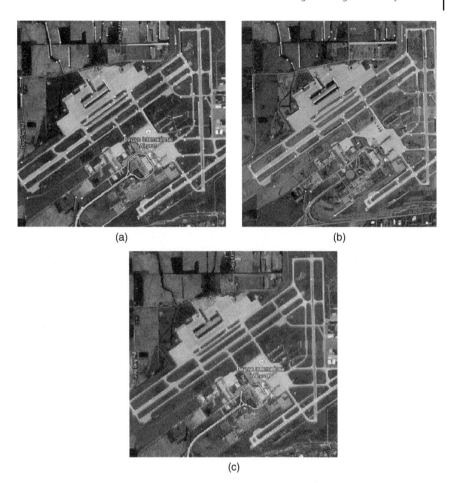

(a)   (b)

(c)

Figure 6.3 (a and b) Homologous lines obtained by Algorithm 6.2 under the rigid transformation model and when using the lines shown in images (a) and (b) in Fig. 6.2. Homologous lines are shown with the same color. (c) Registration of the images using the obtained rigid transformation.

Due to the random nature of RANSAC, different results may be obtained by running Algorithm 6.2 twice. Since RANSAC stops hypothesis generation whenever a hypothesis produces the required number of homologous lines, the result shown in Fig. 6.3c is obtained when letting $h_1 = m/4$. Therefore, in the example in Fig. 6.3, whenever correspondence was found for at least 1/4 of the lines in the reference image, the process was stopped.

Algorithm 6.2 is considerably slower than Algorithm 6.1. Having no knowledge of homologous lines in images, RANSAC may need to test a very large number of line pairs in the images before hitting a pair of homologous lines.

To speed up the correspondence process, either the number of lines in each image must be reduced or an initial set of homologous lines in the images must be determined. Next, two methods are described that group lines in the images into subsets so that hypotheses can be generated using a small subset of lines in each image. Using the transformation parameters obtained from a small set of homologous lines in the images, through an iterative process, the remaining homologous lines in the images are determined.

6.5 Line Grouping Using Local Image Information

When a line belongs to the boundary between two homogenous regions, the line is hardly affected by changes in camera parameters. The same line will be detected at a wide range of resolutions. However, when regions on the two sides of a line are highly detailed, changing the resolution of the image slightly can break the line into pieces, displace the line, or not detect it. Spatial properties of regions on the two sides of a line determine whether a line will remain stationary, break, or disappear under a change in image resolution.

The stability of a line under changes in image resolution can be used to group the lines. Lines in homologous groups in images, therefore, will show lines that have neighborhoods with similar spatial properties. Since many homologous lines have neighborhoods that have similar spatial properties, by matching lines within homologous groups, wasteful hypotheses that are not likely to find the transformation parameters are avoided.

An example demonstrating this idea is given in Fig. 6.4. Reducing the resolution/scale of image (a) by factors of 2, 4, 8, 16, and 32, the lines shown in green, blue, yellow, purple, and light blue are obtained (Fig. 6.4b). Lines at half resolution are obtained by reducing the image to half its size, detecting the lines, and scaling the coordinates of the endpoints of the lines by a factor of 2. Similarly, lines at other resolutions are obtained. Lines at lower resolutions are shown wider so that coinciding lines at different resolutions can be viewed simultaneously.

Some lines persist under considerable changes in image resolution, while others disappear or new lines emerge when changing the resolution. Starting from lines obtained at the highest resolution, each line is tracked from the highest to the lowest resolution until it disappears from the image. Lines that appear at the highest resolution are put in group 0, lines in group 0 that appear at half the resolution are moved from group 0 to group 1. Lines in group 1 that also appear at 1/4 the resolution are moved to group 2. Lines in group 2 that also appear at 1/8 the resolution are moved to group 3. Lines in group 3 that also appear at 1/16 the resolution are moved to group 4. Finally, lines in group 4 that appear at 1/32 the resolution are moved to group 5.

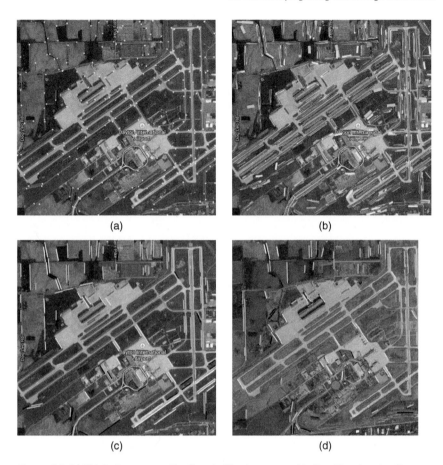

Figure 6.4 (a) This is the same as the Google Map image used in Fig. 6.2a, showing lines detected in an image at full resolution. (b) Lines detected in the same image at reduced resolutions. (c) Grouping of lines in (a) using information in (b). Lines persisting from the highest resolution to resolutions reduced by factors of 2, 4, 8, 16, and 32 are shown in red, green, blue, yellow, purple, and light blue, respectively. (d) Grouping of lines in the Microsoft Bing image of Fig. 6.2b in the same manner.

The grouping of lines in Fig. 6.4b in this manner is shown in Fig. 6.4c. Lines in groups 0, 1, 2, 3, 4, and 5 are shown in red, green, blue, yellow, purple, and light blue, respectively. Algorithm 6.1c is used to determine whether a line persists from group i to group $i + 1$ for $i = 0$ to 4. Parameters $\theta = 0$, $t_x = 0$, and $t_y = 0$ are assumed in Algorithm 6.1c because the lines being compared are from the same image.

The grouping shown in Fig. 6.4c is for the lines in Fig. 6.2a. The grouping obtained for the lines in Fig. 6.2b are shown in Fig. 6.4d. When comparing the groupings obtained in Fig. 6.4c and d, we see that many homologous lines belong to the same group, and for homologous lines that do not appear in the same group, they most likely appear in adjacent groups.

Grouping of lines in this manner makes it possible to match lines in the images that have similar spatial properties. Matching lines within homologous groups enables a reduction in the number of lines used to generate the hypothesis needed to find the transformation parameters. An algorithm is described here that finds the transformation parameters for the registration of two images by matching subsets of lines in images obtained by line grouping.

Algorithm 6.3   Finding homologous lines by line grouping

This algorithm finds homologous lines in two images by grouping the lines according to their spatial properties, and matching lines in the same group in images by RANSAC.

1. Group lines in the images based on their spatial properties. Suppose lines at l levels (from 0 to $l-1$) are obtained, and suppose there are n_i lines at level i, for $0 \leq i < l$.
2. Let $i = l - 1$.
3. Find homologous lines in the images at level i using Algorithm 6.2.
4. If Algorithm 6.2 can successfully find the transformation parameters, go to Step 5. Otherwise, decrement i by 1. If $i < 0$, go to Step 6. Otherwise, go to Step 3.
5. Return the obtained transformation parameters and the homologous lines.
6. Report failure. Transformation parameters could not be found by matching lines in homologous groups using Algorithm 6.2.

A line at level 0 is one that appears only at full resolution, and a line at level $0 < i < l$ is one that appears from full resolution to resolution i. An image at resolution i is obtained by reducing the image's dimensions by a factor of 2^i.

If the images under consideration contain an insufficient number of lines in a group for Algorithm 6.3 to succeed, rather than matching lines at level i in Step 3, lines at levels i and higher may be matched to reduce the chances of failure. This will, in effect, combine lines in groups i and higher into the same group when matching lines in the images.

Matching is performed starting with lines that persist over a wide range of resolutions. These are the most stable lines, which are not affected by blurring or image acquisition parameters. Groups at higher levels (lower resolutions) contain fewer lines when compared to groups at lower levels (higher resolutions); therefore, if sufficient homologous lines exist in the images, RANSAC will be able to find the transformation parameters more quickly by first matching smaller groups of stable lines in the images.

The amount of time saved by grouping lines and matching lines within groups can be substantial. For example, on a Windows PC with a Core i7 processor, RANSAC took 142.21 s to find correspondence between lines in images (a) and (b) in Fig. 6.2, while only 4.04 s were needed to do the same by grouping the lines as depicted in images (c) and (d) in Fig. 6.4 and matching lines within the same group. The time required to group lines in each image into six groups is 0.70 s.

6.6 Line Grouping Using Vanishing Points

When projected to the image plane, parallel lines in the scene merge at a point known as the *vanishing point*. When an image of a planar scene is captured, groups of parallel lines in the scene form vanishing points that fall on a line known as the *vanishing line* [2]. The normal to the vanishing line of a planar scene determines the direction normal to the scene. The orientation of planar patches in a scene can be found if two or more vanishing points within each patch can be found [3–5].

In this section, after a short review of vanishing point detection methods, implementation of one vanishing point detection method is detailed and its use in line grouping is demonstrated.

Vanishing point detection methods either search the image space or transform the image space to another space and search the transformed space for vanishing points. The polar space and the Gaussian sphere are among the most widely used transformed spaces.

6.6.1 Methods Searching the Image Space

Vanishing points appearing inside the image domain are generally easier to detect than vanishing points falling outside the image domain due to the reduced search space. To find the most dominant vanishing point in an image, an accumulator array the size of the image is taken and all entries of the array are initially set to 0. Then, for each line in the image, a line is drawn in the accumulator array, incrementing array entries falling on the line by 1. After all lines in the image are processed, the entry in the accumulator containing the highest count is used as the location of the most dominant vanishing point in the image [6].

If we denote an image's coordinate system origin by O and the vanishing point to be determined by V, a normal from O to any line passing through V will fall on the circle with diameter OV [7]. If lines in an image define a single vanishing point, the problem of finding the vanishing point V in the image becomes one of finding a circle that passes through O and approximates points obtained from the intersection of lines from O normal to the lines. Vanishing point V

will be the point on the circle opposing point O. This property is demonstrated by Thales' theorem and has been used to detect vanishing points in an image [8, 9].

6.6.2 Methods Searching the Polar Space

To find vanishing points in an image, lines in the xy image space are mapped to points in the $\rho\theta$ polar space. If all lines in the xy space intersect at vanishing point (x_0, y_0), the same lines when mapped to the polar space fall on sinusoid

$$\rho = x_0 \cos\theta + y_0 \sin\theta. \tag{6.55}$$

This mapping enables converting the problem of finding a vanishing point in the image space to one of finding a sinusoid in the polar space [10]. While the xy space is infinite, the $\rho\theta$ space is finite. Lines in the image space forming a vanishing point will have ρ parameters that fall between 0 and half the diameter of the image and will have θ parameters that fall between 0 and 2π. This transformation from xy to $\rho\theta$ makes it possible to find vanishing points outside the image domain with the same ease as finding vanishing points inside the image domain. The parameters of the optimal sinusoid fitting points in the polar space are determined by the least-squares fit of the sinusoid in Eq. (6.55) to points in the polar space [11].

6.6.3 Methods Searching the Gaussian Sphere

To find vanishing points in an image, the image space is mapped to a sphere of radius 1, known as the *Gaussian sphere* [12]. Considering a Gaussian sphere at the lens center, rays connecting the lens center to points on a line in the image plane intersect the sphere along a great circle. Lines intersecting at a vanishing point in the image plane create great circles that intersect at a point on the Gaussian sphere. This point of intersection on the Gaussian sphere is the same as the intersection of the ray from the lens center to the vanishing point with the sphere. This shows that a vanishing point obtained from the intersection of lines in the image plane maps to a point on the Gaussian sphere, which is at the intersections of great circles obtained from the lines [3, 13].

A point **P** on the Gaussian sphere can be represented by two angles (ϕ, θ) as shown in Fig. 6.5. Angle ϕ is the elevation, varying between $-\pi/2$ and $\pi/2$, and angle θ is the azimuth, varying between 0 and 2π. To find vanishing points using the Gaussian sphere, line intersections in the image space are mapped to the Gaussian sphere and locally peak intersections are located. One way to find locally peak intersections on the Gaussian sphere is to map the Gaussian sphere points to a 2-D accumulator array and find locally peak entries in the array [14].

Figure 6.5 The relation between the Gaussian sphere and the image plane. The Gaussian sphere is centered at the camera lens center O. The image plane is normal to the camera optical axis. The optical axis of the camera intersects the image plane at piercing point (x_0, y_0).

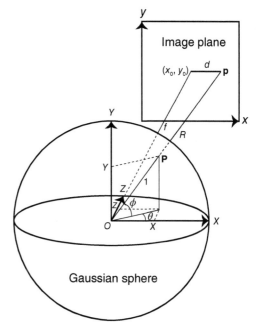

Gaussian sphere

6.6.4 A Method Searching Both Image and Gaussian Sphere

The power of Gaussian sphere–based methods is in the ability of the methods to detect distant as well as nearby vanishing points in the same manner. The geometric relation between the image plane and the Gaussian sphere is shown in Fig. 6.5. The Gaussian sphere is a sphere of radius 1 centered at O, the camera lens center. The X- and Y-axes of the camera coordinate system are parallel to the image's x- and y-axes, respectively, and the camera's Z-axis is normal to the image plane. The distance between the lens center and the image plane is f, the focal length of the camera.

Points on the Gaussian sphere can be represented by angular coordinates (ϕ, θ) or by Cartesian coordinates (X, Y, Z). The relation between (ϕ, θ) and (X, Y, Z) can be written as

$$Y = \sin \phi, \tag{6.56}$$

$$X = \cos \phi \cos \theta, \tag{6.57}$$

$$Z = \cos \phi \sin \theta. \tag{6.58}$$

A point $\mathbf{p} = (x, y)$ in the image plane has coordinates $(x - x_0, y - y_0, f)$ in the camera coordinate system, where (x_0, y_0) are the coordinates of the camera's piercing point in the image plane (Fig. 6.5). If the distance of point $\mathbf{p}$ to the lens center is R, a sphere of radius R centered at O will pass through point $\mathbf{p}$. Point $(x - x_0, y - y_0, f)$ on the sphere of radius R centered at O has angular coordinates (ϕ, θ), which are the same as the angular coordinates of point $\mathbf{p}$ when projected to the Gaussian sphere centered at $\mathbf{O}$. The relation between $(x - x_0, y - y_0, f)$ and (ϕ, θ) can be written as

$$y - y_0 = R \sin \phi, \tag{6.59}$$

$$x - x_0 = R \cos \phi \cos \theta, \tag{6.60}$$

$$f = R \cos \phi \sin \theta. \tag{6.61}$$

Denoting the distance of point $\mathbf{p} = (x, y)$ to piercing point (x_0, y_0) by $d = \{(x - x_0)^2 + (y - y_0)^2\}^{\frac{1}{2}}$, we find $R = \{d^2 + f^2\}^{\frac{1}{2}}$ or $R = \{(x - x_0)^2 + (y - y_0)^2 + f^2\}^{\frac{1}{2}}$. The angular coordinates (ϕ, θ) of the point on the Gaussian sphere corresponding to image point $\mathbf{p} = (x, y)$ can be determined from Eqs (6.59)–(6.61):

$$\phi = \sin^{-1}\left(\frac{y - y_0}{R}\right), \tag{6.62}$$

$$\theta = \tan^{-1}\left(\frac{f}{x - x_0}\right). \tag{6.63}$$

Note that when $x = x_0$, $\theta = \pi/2$.

Angles ϕ and θ depend on the focal length f and the location of the piercing point (x_0, y_0). Focal length f is in pixel units and (x_0, y_0) is the point in the image where the optical axis of the camera intersects the image plane. Therefore, a partially calibrated camera with known focal length and piercing point is needed to relate points in the image to points on the Gaussian sphere. Methods for finding these parameters through a calibration process are detailed in [15–17].

If the camera capturing an image is uncalibrated, but it is of sufficient quality to be approximated by a pinhole camera, vanishing points can be detected without the camera parameters. In a pinhole camera, the piercing point is at the image center and the focal length simply determines the size/resolution of the image without any effect on its geometry. Changing focal length f will simply change the area of the Gaussian sphere mapped to the image domain. Otherwise, f has no effect on the location of a detected vanishing point in the image plane.

Since the infinite xy plane is mapped to the lower hemisphere of the Gaussian sphere, a smaller f will map the image domain to a larger area on the Gaussian lower hemisphere, and that will increase the detection accuracy of vanishing points inside the image domain. A larger f will map the image domain to a smaller area on the Gaussian lower hemisphere, consequently devoting a larger area on the Gaussian lower hemisphere to areas outside the image domain. This increases the accuracy of vanishing points detected outside the image domain. Therefore, even when the focal length of the camera capturing an image is known, the focal length used in the calculations may be appropriately decreased/increased when detecting vanishing points inside/outside

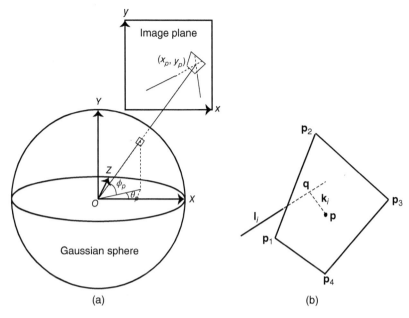

Figure 6.6 (a) A hypothesized vanishing point $\mathbf{p} = (x_p, y_p)$ is mapped to the Gaussian sphere and a small region centered at the point on the Gaussian sphere is mapped back to the image plane, creating a quadrilateral region that contains $\mathbf{p}$. (b) A line $\mathbf{l}_i$ in the image is considered belonging to vanishing point $\mathbf{p}$ if it passes through the quadrilateral and intersects the line from $\mathbf{p}$ and normal to it (line $\mathbf{k}_j$) at a point $\mathbf{q}$ inside the quadrilateral.

the image domain to increase the localization accuracy of detected vanishing points.

To determine a proper value for parameter f, two lines are randomly selected from among the given lines in a RANSAC paradigm [1], the intersection of the lines $\mathbf{p} = (x_p, y_p)$ is determined, and the intersection point is hypothesized a vanishing point (Fig. 6.6a). Parameter f is then set equal to $d + \alpha$, where d is the distance of point $\mathbf{p}$ to the piercing point. The addition of $\alpha \geq 1$ to d is to ensure that when $d = 0$, focal length will not be 0.

The sphere centered at $\mathbf{O}$ and passing though $\mathbf{p}$ has angular coordinates (ϕ_p, θ_p) determined from Eqs (6.62) and (6.63) by letting $x = x_p$ and $y = y_p$. Note that the angular coordinates obtained from point $\mathbf{p}$ in the sphere of radius R is the same as the angular coordinates of point $\mathbf{p}$ when projected to the Gaussian sphere. Therefore, to determine the number of lines in the image that support the hypothesis that point $\mathbf{p}$ is a vanishing point, a small area centered at (ϕ_p, θ_p) on the Gaussian sphere is mapped back to the image plane and the number of lines passing through the region is used to identify the lines that belong to vanishing point $\mathbf{p}$.

To find lines in the image that support the hypothesis that $\mathbf{p}$ is a vanishing point, spherical coordinates $(\phi_p - d\phi, \theta_p - d\theta)$, $(\phi_p - d\phi, \theta_p + d\theta)$, $(\phi_p + d\phi, \theta_p + d\theta)$, and $(\phi_p + d\phi, \theta_p - d\theta)$ on the Gaussian sphere are mapped to the image plane using Eqs (6.59) and (6.60) to obtain points $\mathbf{p}_1 = (x_1, y_1)$, $\mathbf{p}_2 = (x_2, y_2)$, $\mathbf{p}_3 = (x_3, y_3)$, and $\mathbf{p}_4(x_4, y_4)$, respectively. The quadrilateral defined by the four points in the image plane defines the region inside which the lines forming vanishing point $\mathbf{p}$ pass. To find lines that pass through quadrilateral $\mathbf{p}_1\mathbf{p}_2\mathbf{p}_3\mathbf{p}_4$ (Fig. 6.6b), since point $\mathbf{p} = (x_p, y_p)$ is inside the quadrilateral, for each line $\mathbf{l}_i$ with equation $a_i x + b_i y + c_i = 0$, where $a_i^2 + b_i^2 = 1$, line $\mathbf{k}_i$ normal to it and passing through $\mathbf{p}$ is determined. The equation of this line is $b_i(x - x_p) - a_i(y - y_p) = 0$. Thus, the intersection point $\mathbf{q} = (x_q, y_q)$ of lines $\mathbf{l}_i$ and $\mathbf{k}_i$ is found, which will be at

$$x_q = b_i^2 x_p - a_i b_i y_p - a_i c_i, \tag{6.64}$$

$$y_q = a_i^2 y_p - a_i b_i x_p - b_i c_i. \tag{6.65}$$

If points $\mathbf{p}$ and $\mathbf{q}$ are on the same side of the lines defining the four sides of quadrilateral $\mathbf{p}_1\mathbf{p}_2\mathbf{p}_3\mathbf{p}_4$, line $\mathbf{l}_i$ is considered to belong to vanishing point $\mathbf{p}$. In such a case, point $\mathbf{q}$ is mapped to the sphere of radius R passing through point $\mathbf{p}$ using Eqs (6.62) and (6.63). Since the Gaussian sphere and the sphere of radius R centered at $\mathbf{O}$ share the same angular coordinates, the process will, in effect, find angular coordinates of points on the Gaussian sphere corresponding to points in the image plane.

If a sufficiently large number of points such as $\mathbf{q}$ map to the Gaussian sphere within the region centered at (ϕ_p, θ_p), it is concluded that a vanishing point exists at or near $\mathbf{p}$. Assuming n' points: $\{(\phi_j, \theta_j): j = 1, \ldots, n'\}$ fall within the solid angle defined by $(\phi_p - d\phi, \theta_p - d\theta)$, $(\phi_p - d\phi, \theta_p + d\theta)$, $(\phi_p + d\phi, \theta_p + d\theta)$, and $(\phi_p + d\phi, \theta_p - d\theta)$, the average of such spherical coordinates is determined and used as the refined location of the vanishing point on the Gaussian sphere.

Note that the aforementioned procedure does not consider all lines passing through the quadrilateral lines that belong to vanishing point $\mathbf{p}$. If a line that passes through the quadrilateral intersects the line normal to it from $\mathbf{p}$ outside the quadrilateral, the line is not considered to be supporting vanishing point $\mathbf{p}$. Lines passing near the corners of the quadrilateral intersect lines normal to them from $\mathbf{p}$ outside the quadrilateral and are not considered to be lines supporting point $\mathbf{p}$.

Since a hypothesized vanishing point that receives sufficient support from lines in the image may not be at its optimal location, some lines contributing to it could be missed when selecting the search space centered at the hypothesized vanishing point. To improve the location of a hypothesized vanishing point and also to improve the number of lines that contribute to the vanishing point, once a refined vanishing point is obtained, it is considered a newly hypothesized vanishing point and the process is repeated to identify lines previously missed and recalculate a more refined location for the vanishing point. The refinement process is repeated until the number of lines contributing to the vanishing point reaches a maximum.

If a hypothesized vanishing point does not receive sufficient support from lines in an image, another pair of lines is selected and the process is repeated until either a vanishing point with sufficient support is found or the maximum number of iterations is reached. If a vanishing point is found, lines contributing to it are removed from the given lines and the process is repeated to find other possible vanishing points from the remaining lines.

Note that if the spherical region defined by $(\phi - d\phi, \theta - d\theta)$, $(\phi - d\phi, \theta + d\theta)$, $(\phi + d\phi, \theta + d\theta)$, and $(\phi + d\phi, \theta - d\theta)$ contains a part of the great circle in the XY plane, the quadrilateral in the xy space corresponding to it will contain points at infinity. The method is, therefore, capable of detecting vanishing points in an image appearing anywhere from the image center to infinity in all directions.

The following algorithm summarizes the steps to be followed to find the vanishing points and the lines belonging to each, thereby grouping lines in an image into subsets, each containing lines that belong to the same vanishing point.

Algorithm 6.4 Searching for vanishing points in image and Gaussian-sphere spaces

---

Given a set of lines, $S_1 = \{l_i = (a_i, b_i, c_i): i = 1, \ldots, N\}$, in an image, where l_i is described by $a_i x + b_i y + c_i = 0$ and $a_i^2 + b_i^2 = 1$, this algorithm finds the vanishing points in the image. $d\phi$ is the maximum deviation in elevation and $d\theta$ is the maximum deviation in azimuth between two points on the Gaussian sphere to consider them belonging to the same vanishing point. S_2 is the set of lines contributing to a vanishing point, S_3 is the set of candidate vanishing points obtained from the lines in S_2, and n_2 and n_3 are indices of S_2 and S_3. S_4 is the set of final vanishing points detected in the image and n_4 is the index of S_4. t_m is the maximum number of iterations to be performed without finding a vanishing point before exiting the program, and t counts the iterations. Finally, q is the minimum number of lines required to form a detected vanishing point.

1. If $N < q$, exit the program. There are not sufficient lines in the image to form a vanishing point. Otherwise, create empty lists S_2, S_3, and S_4 and let $n_2 = 0$, $n_3 = 0$, and $n_4 = 0$. Also, let $t = 0$.
2. Move two randomly selected lines l_j and l_k from S_1 to S_2, decrement N by 2, and increment n_2 by 2. Also, find the intersection of the two lines, (x_p, y_p).
3. Find angular coordinates (ϕ_p, θ_p) corresponding to (x_p, y_p) using Eqs (6.62) and (6.63), and save the obtained coordinates (ϕ_p, θ_p) in S_3 and increment n_3 by 1.

4. Map angular coordinates $(\phi_p - d\phi, \theta_p - d\theta)$, $(\phi_p - d\phi, \theta_p + d\theta)$, $(\phi_p + d\phi, \theta_p + d\theta)$, and $(\phi_p + d\phi, \theta_p - d\theta)$ on the Gaussian sphere to the xy plane using Eqs (6.59)–(6.61), denoting them by $\mathbf{p}_1 = (x_1, y_1)$, $\mathbf{p}_2 = (x_2, y_2)$, $\mathbf{p}_3 = (x_3, y_3)$, and $\mathbf{p}_4 = (x_4, y_4)$, respectively.

5. For $i = 1, \ldots, N$:

   5.1. Find the point on line l_i closest to (x_p, y_p) from Eqs (6.64) and (6.65) and denote it by (x_q, y_q).

   5.2. If (x_q, y_q) is inside polygon $\mathbf{p}_1 \mathbf{p}_2 \mathbf{p}_3 \mathbf{p}_4$, move line l_i from S_1 to S_2, decrement N by 1, and increment n_2 by 1. Also, find the spherical coordinates of (x_q, y_q) from Eqs (6.62) and (6.63), and save the coordinates in S_3, and increment n_3 by 1.

6. If $n_2 < q$, lines l_j and l_k do not produce a vanishing point; increment t by 1 and if $t < t_m$ return lines in S_2 to S_1, empty list S_3, increment N by n_2, let $n_2 = 0$ and $n_3 = 0$, and go to Step 2. If $t = t_m$, report the vanishing points in S_4, if any, and exit the program. Otherwise, if $t < t_m$ and $n \geq q$, go to Step 7.

7. Find the average of angular coordinates in S_3 as the refined location of the vanishing point on the Gaussian sphere and denote it by (ϕ_n, θ_n). Then determine the xy coordinates of the vanishing point in the image space, (x_n, y_n), using the obtained (ϕ_n, θ_n) in Eqs (6.59) and (6.60).

8. Save (x_n, y_n) in S_4, increment n_4 by 1, empty lists S_2 and S_3, let $n_2 = 0$, $n_3 = 0$, and $t = 0$, and if $N \geq q$, go to Step 2. Otherwise, report the vanishing points in S_4 and exit the program.

In Steps 2 and 3, after hypothesizing a vanishing point at (x_p, y_p) in the image plane, to increase angular resolution of a vanishing point on the Gaussian sphere, distance d of the hypothesized vanishing point to the image center is determined, and f is set to $d + 1$. The addition of 1 is to ensure that when $d = 0$ the image plane will still be outside the Gaussian sphere. Then, parameter R and spherical coordinates (ϕ, θ) of the hypothesized vanishing point are determined. In case the hypothesized vanishing point is at infinity, we find $\theta = 0$ or $\theta = \pi$ depending on the sign of $\phi = \arctan(y_p/x_p)$. Note that when $x_p = 0$, $\phi = \pi/2$ or $-\pi/2$ depending on the sign of y_p.

In Step 7, since points in S_3 belong to one cluster, the cluster center determined by averaging angular coordinates in S_3 is taken as a refined location for the hypothesized vanishing point. Note that locating a vanishing point on the Gaussian sphere in this manner does not require the use of an accumulator array.

The lines contributing to vanishing point (x_n, y_n) in Step 8 are in S_2. Further improvement to the location of the vanishing point and the lines that contribute to it can be achieved by considering the vanishing point (x_n, y_n) in Step 8 as the hypothesized vanishing point (x_p, y_p) in Step 2 and repeating Steps 3–7. This will find a further refined location for the vanishing point and detect the set of lines contributing to it.

If an image contains N lines and n vanishing points, once a line belonging to a vanishing point is selected, on average, it takes on the order of n iterations to select a second line that belongs to the same vanishing point. Once a vanishing point is hypothesized, it takes on the order of N operations to determine the lines that support the hypothesized vanishing point. Therefore, it takes on the order of nN operations to find a vanishing point and the lines associated with it, which means it takes on the order n^2N operations to find all vanishing points and the associated lines. Finally, it takes t_m iterations, each on the order of N' operations, to stop the process after failing to find a vanishing point. N' is the number of lines remaining after removing all lines contributing to the n detected vanishing points. Usually, $N' \ll N$. Overall, Algorithm 6.4 requires on the order of $t_m N' + n^2 N$ operations to find n vanishing points in an image containing N lines.

Parameter t_m depends on the number of lines contributing to a vanishing point. If w is the ratio of lines belonging to a vanishing point and the total number of lines in an image, the probability that two randomly selected lines both belong to the same vanishing point is w^2. This means, the probability that two selected lines both do not belong to the same vanishing point is $1 - w^2$. If random line pairs are selected t_m times, the probability that all selections do not belong to the same vanishing point is $(1 - w^2)^{t_m}$. The probability that at least one of the t_m iterations contain a pair that belong to the same vanishing point is

$$p = 1 - (1 - w^2)^{t_m} \tag{6.66}$$

from which we find

$$t_m = \frac{\log(1 - p)}{\log(1 - w^2)}. \tag{6.67}$$

If there are three vanishing points in an image and one-fourth of the lines do not belong to any vanishing point (they are outliers), we find $w = (1 - 1/4)/3 = 1/4$. This is when each vanishing point is formed by approximately the same number of lines. Therefore, w can be estimated from information about the number of vanishing points in an image and information about the outliers. If we want to find a vanishing point with probability 0.999 after t_m iterations, from Eq. (6.67) we find $t_m = 107$.

Algorithm 6.4 has three free parameters: q, $d\phi$, and $d\theta$. Parameter q is a user-specified threshold value that shows the minimum number of lines required to define a vanishing point. This parameter is used to avoid detection of noisy and false vanishing points. Parameters $d\phi$ and $d\theta$ take the same value and define the search area on the Gaussian sphere for a vanishing point. The smaller $d\phi$ and $d\theta$ are, the more focused the search will be, and the larger these parameters are, the more tolerant the algorithm will be to noise among the lines.

Parameter q itself depends on parameters $d\phi$ and $d\theta$. If the lines are noisy and a larger $d\phi$ and $d\theta$ is needed to make the process more tolerant to noise, a larger q should be taken. This is because a larger value for $d\phi$ and $d\theta$ will require a larger area on the Gaussian sphere to be mapped to the image space, creating a larger quadrilateral that covers more lines in the image space.

6.6.5 Measuring the Accuracy of Detected Vanishing Points

It is important that a detected vanishing point represents a true vanishing point. It is also important that the lines associated with a vanishing point truly belong to that vanishing point. When the endpoints of a line contain up to a pixel positional error, a vanishing point detected within the image domain can be displaced by a few to several pixels from its true position depending on the image size. Some lines that truly belong to a distant vanishing point could pass hundreds of pixels away from the vanishing point due to digital noise and inaccuracy in line detection.

To determine the accuracy of detected vanishing points, consider the images in Fig. 6.7 with the red lines showing the lines from which the vanishing points must be detected. Suppose a vanishing point detector has found one vanishing point in the image, as shown in Fig. 6.8a as a red dot near the top of the image. The lines contributing to the vanishing point are shown in red, while the remaining lines are shown in black.

Figure 6.7 An image of a bicycle path and walkway. This image is courtesy of Image Registration and Fusion Systems. Lines detected in the image are also shown.

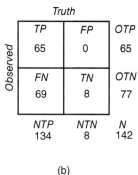

	Truth		
Observed	TP 65	FP 0	OTP 65
	FN 69	TN 8	OTN 77
	NTP 134	NTN 8	N 142

(a) (b)

Figure 6.8 (a) An algorithm has found a vanishing point near the top of the image. The lines supporting the vanishing point are shown in red. Lines in black are those not assigned to any vanishing point. (b) The confusion matrix of the algorithm for detecting the vanishing point and the line assignment shown in (a).

There are $N = 142$ lines in the image in Fig. 6.7. The method has assigned 65 of them to the detected vanishing point, leaving 77 lines unassigned; therefore, the *observed true positive* (OTP) $= 65$ and the *observed true negative* (OTN) $= 77$. Examining the image visually, we see that all lines are correctly assigned to the vanishing point. Thus, the OTP is the *actual true positive* (TP) $= 65$. There are no false assignments; therefore, $FP = 0$.

The lines in Fig. 6.7 actually belong to three orthogonal vanishing points. Only the vanishing point inside the image has been detected by this algorithm, missing the two distant vanishing points. Among the 77 unassigned lines, 69 are visually verified to belong to two other vanishing points; therefore, $FN = 69$. There are eight lines in the image that are considered noise and do not belong to any of the vanishing points. They are the true negatives: $TN = 8$. These results are summarized in the confusion matrix in Fig. 6.8b.

In this example, the *true positive rate* (TPR) is

$$TPR = \frac{TP}{NTP} = \frac{65}{134} = 0.49, \tag{6.68}$$

the *true negative rate* (TNR) is

$$TNR = \frac{TN}{NTN} = \frac{8}{8} = 1.0, \tag{6.69}$$

and the *false positive rate* (FPR) is

$$FPR = \frac{FP}{NTN} = \frac{0}{8} = 0.0. \tag{6.70}$$

Figure 6.9 Vanishing points detected in the image in Fig. 6.7 by Algorithm 6.4. Lines belonging to the same vanishing point are shown in the same color.

Therefore, the *accuracy (ACC)* [18] of the method producing the result in Fig. 6.8a is

$$ACC = \frac{TP + TN}{N} = \frac{65 + 8}{142} = 0.51. \tag{6.71}$$

Letting $q = N/10$ and $d\phi = d\theta = 5°$, Algorithm 6.4 produced the line assignments shown in Fig. 6.9 for the image in Fig. 6.7. Three orthogonal vanishing points are obtained in the image. Lines belonging to the same vanishing point are shown with the same color. The line assignment accuracy of Algorithm 6.4 in this example is 0.99.

Orthogonal vanishing points are identified as follows. If the angular coordinates of a vanishing point are (ϕ, θ), the XYZ coordinates of the same point on the Gaussian sphere can be calculated from Eqs (6.56)–(6.58). Denoting the three spherical points obtained from the three vanishing points by $v_1 = (X_1, Y_1, Z_1)$, $\mathbf{v}_2 = (X_2, Y_2, Z_2)$, and $v_3 = (X_3, Y_3, Z_3)$, vectors $\mathbf{v}_1$, $\mathbf{v}_2$, and $\mathbf{v}_3$ will be mutually orthogonal if $\mathbf{v}_1 \cdot \mathbf{v}_2 \approx 0$, $\mathbf{v}_1 \cdot \mathbf{v}_3 \approx 0$, and $\mathbf{v}_2 \cdot \mathbf{v}_3 \approx 0$. Alternatively, if $|\det(\mathbf{v}_1, \mathbf{v}_2, \mathbf{v}_3)| \approx 1$, the three vectors will be mutually orthogonal. Detection of orthogonal vanishing points by finding three lines that when projected to the Gaussian sphere form mutually orthogonal vectors is described by Zhang et al. [19].

Additional results by Algorithm 6.4 when using the same parameters ($q = 10$, $d\phi = 5°$, and $d\theta = 5°$) are shown in Fig. 6.10. Four vanishing points are obtained in image (a) with the lines belonging to the four vanishing points colored in red, green, blue, and yellow. There are 153 lines in the image, all assigned correctly, although some lines are not assigned. Line assignment accuracy in

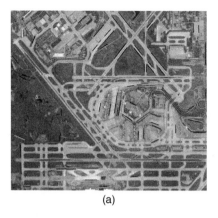 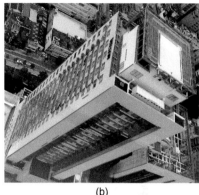

(a)   (b)

Figure 6.10 (a) In an aerial image of the O'Hare International Airport four vanishing points are detected by Algorithm 6.4. This image is courtesy of Google Maps. (b) Orthogonal vanishing points detected in the image of a high-rise building and its surroundings by Algorithm 6.4. This image is courtesy of Image Registration and Fusion Systems. Lines belonging to a vanishing point are shown in the same color. Line assignment accuracy in (a) is 0.96, while that in (b) is 0.93.

this image is 0.96. Three orthogonal vanishing points are obtained in image (b). The lines contributing to the three vanishing points are shown in red, green, and blue. Line assignment accuracy in this image is 0.93.

6.6.6 Discussion

Our focus in this chapter is on registering images of a flat scene using a global transformation model; therefore, we are not concerned with orthogonal vanishing points. When two images are to be registered by a composite of local transformation models, then orthogonal vanishing points may be useful in identifying homologous neighborhoods in images.

The main objective in vanishing point detection is to subdivide lines in an image into small groups so that matching can be performed between small groups of lines. Consider the lines in images (a) and (b) in Fig. 6.2. By grouping the lines according to their vanishing points, the groups shown in Fig. 6.11 are obtained. Lines in the same group are painted with the same color. Red, green, and blue show progressively smaller groups. For these images, due to considerable overlap between them, homologous lines belong to homologous groups when groups are numbered according to their sizes.

As the area of overlap between two images of a scene decreases in size, the likelihood that lines in group i in one image appear in group $i - 1$ or in group $i + 1$ in another image increases. For that reason, if the correspondence to a line in group i in the reference image is not found in group i in the test image, it is

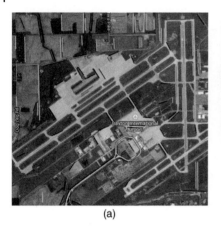 

(a)   (b)

Figure 6.11 (a and b) Grouping of lines in images (a) and (b) in Fig. 6.2 using the vanishing points detected in the images by Algorithm 6.4. Three vanishing points are obtained in both (a) and (b). The lines belonging to the same vanishing in an image are shown in the same color.

possible that the corresponding line appears in group $i - 1$ or in group $i + 1$ in the test image.

To determine the rigid transformation between two images, minimum two homologous lines are required. Since the two lines selected in each image cannot be parallel and lines in a group are either parallel or nearly parallel, the two lines selected from an image should be selected from different groups. Therefore, if lines are selected from groups i_1 and i_2 in the reference image, first an attempt is made to match them to lines in groups i_1 and i_2 in the test image. If a winning hypothesis is not obtained after the required number of iterations, lines in adjacent groups in the test image are tested against the lines in the reference image.

The two largest groups in images (a) and (b) in Fig. 6.11 correspond to each other. By taking the first random line from the largest group in each image and taking the second random line from the second largest group in each image, assuming the two lines correspond, determining the rigid transformation parameters, and finding the number of other lines in the images that correspond according to Algorithm 6.1c, the homologous lines shown in Fig. 6.12 are obtained.

The number of iterations required to find a homologous line pair in the images from which the rigid transformation parameters can be calculated with a sufficient confidence is given in Eq. (6.54). When $n = 25$, up to 11,511 iterations are needed to find a winning hypothesis with 0.99 probability. By grouping the lines, n decreases. Therefore, if the number of lines in each group reduces to 10, the number of iterations required to obtaining a

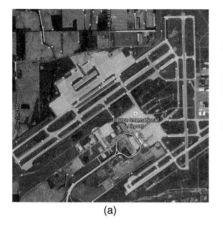 

(a)   (b)

Figure 6.12 (a and b) The homologous lines obtained by RANSAC when matching lines in the two largest groups (red and green) in Fig. 6.11a and b. Homologous lines are shown in the same color.

winning hypothesis reduces to 1840. This is considerably lower than the 11,511 iterations required when $n = 25$.

To register two images by an affine transformation, the correspondence between three lines in the images must be found. The number of iterations required to find three homologous lines in two images with probability p is

$$t_m = \frac{\log(1 - p)}{\log\left(1 - \frac{1}{8n^3}\right)}. \tag{6.72}$$

By grouping lines in an image and assuming there are $n = 10$ lines in a group, we find that $t_m = 36{,}839$ iterations are required for the registration to succeed with probability $p = 0.99$. This is a very large number of iterations, making RANSAC impractical. For the process to be practical when using affine or homography, either the number of lines in each group should be further reduced or an initial set of homologous lines in the images must be determined.

When the images to be registered have about the same scale and the view-angle difference between the images is not large, an initial correspondence can be established between lines in the images using the rigid transformation model. Images that are related by an affine transformation can be registered locally by a rigid transformation when allowing a larger error tolerance in registration. The homologous lines obtained via a rigid transformation can then be used to find affine parameters to register the images more accurately.

The obtained affine transformation can be used to find more homologous lines, and the process of finding the affine parameters from homologous lines and determining more homologous lines from the newly obtained affine transformation can be repeated until no additional homologous lines can be found.

If the images truly register by a homography, from the homologous lines obtained by an affine transformation, the parameters of a homography are determined, and again, the process of finding homologous lines and refining the homography parameters is repeated until a maximum is reached in the number of homologous lines.

An example demonstrating this process is given in Fig. 6.13. Images (a) and (b) are of dimensions 507×499 and 423×361 and show different views of a quilt artwork hanging on a wall. The images ideally register with a homography transformation due to view-angle difference between the images. Starting with a rigid transformation, RANSAC finds 15 initial homologous lines as shown in Fig. 6.13c and d. Homologous lines are shown with the same color. Registration of the images using the rigid transformation obtained by RANSAC is shown in the overlaid image in Fig. 6.13e. The overlaid image is created by taking the red band of the transformed test image and the green and blue bands of the reference image. In areas where the images register well, the original color of the quilt is reproduced. In areas where the images do not register well, double images are obtained. The light blue border areas in the overlaid image show areas in the reference image that are out of view in the test image.

Generating hypotheses using the 15 initial homologous lines obtained under rigid transformation and verifying each hypothesis using all lines in the images, 18 homologous lines are obtained as shown in (f) and (g), producing the registration shown in (h). The rigid transformation model cannot register the images well due to the view-angle difference between the images.

Using the 18 initial homologous lines obtained by rigid transformation in RANSAC again, but this time using affine transformation, the number of homologous lines increases from 18 to 43, as shown in (i) and (j), with the resultant registration shown in (k).

Using the 43 homologous lines obtained under the affine transformation in RANSAC again, this time using the homography transformation, the number of homologous lines increases to 44 as shown in (l) and (m) and produces the registration shown in (n). Root-mean-squared error (RMSE) in the registration results depicted in (e), (h), (k), and (n) are 2.78, 1.74, 1.31, and 0.53 pixels, respectively. Although the number of homologous lines did not increase much from affine to homography, the registration error decreased considerably. This shows that homography is a better transformation model than affine or rigid when registering these images.

Assuming n_c homologous lines are obtained in the images, registration RMSE is calculated using the following formula:

$$\text{RMSE} = \sqrt{\frac{1}{2n_c} \sum_{i=1}^{n_c} \left(d_{i_1}^2 + d_{i_2}^2 \right)}, \tag{6.73}$$

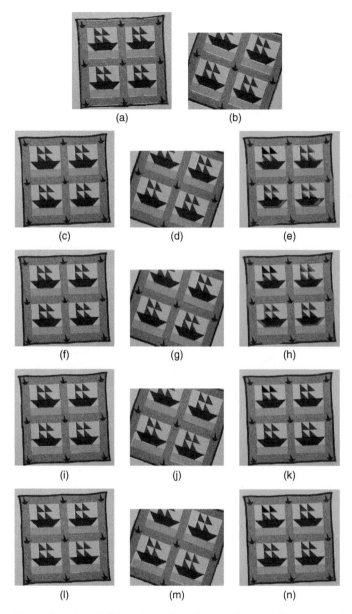

Figure 6.13 (a and b) Two views of a quilt artwork on a wall. Lines in red, green, and blue indicate lines belonging to different vanishing points (groups). (c and d) 15 initial homologous lines obtained by RANSAC when matching lines within individual groups. Homologous lines are shown with the same color. (e) Registration of the images using the initial rigid transformation. (f and g) 18 homologous lines obtained under rigid transformation when starting with the 15 initial homologous lines, and (h) the resultant registration. (i and j) 43 homologous lines obtained by affine transformation, and (k) the resultant registration. (l and m) 44 homologous lines obtained by homography, and (n) the resultant registration.

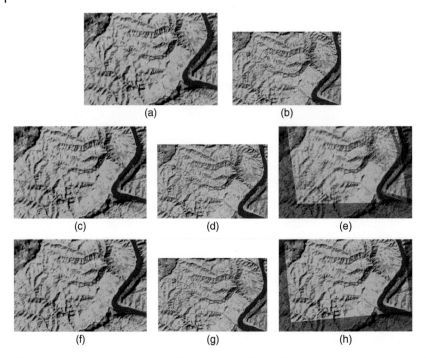

Figure 6.14 (a) A Landsat 5 image of a terrain over China obtained on September 24, 1993 and (b) a Landsat 8 image of the same terrain obtained on September 15, 2013. These images are courtesy of NASA. Lines in the images grouped according to their vanishing points are also shown. (c and d) 28 initial homologous lines are obtained by RANSAC when matching lines within individual groups under the rigid transformation model, and (e) the resultant registration. (f and g) 71 homologous lines are obtained by RANSAC when using the initial homologous lines to generate the hypotheses and using all lines in the images to verify the correctness of the hypotheses. (h) The resultant registration.

where d_{i_1} and d_{i_2} are normal distances of the endpoints of line $\mathbf{l}_i$ in the reference image after it is transformed with the obtained transformation to the corresponding line in the test image.

Methods that use lines to register images are not limited to images of man-made scenes where straight edges are abundant and explicit, they can be used to register images of natural scenes as long as some common line segments appear in the images. Figure 6.14a shows a Landsat 5 image of a terrain taken somewhere over China on September 24, 1993, and Fig. 6.14b shows an image of the same terrain taken by Landsat 8 on September 15, 2013. These images are courtesy of NASA.

There are 272 lines in Fig. 6.14a and 170 lines in Fig. 6.14b. Lines belonging to the same group are shown with the same color. By matching lines within corresponding groups, RANSAC under the rigid transformation model was able to find 28 initial homologous lines in the images depicted in Fig. 6.14c and d. Homologous lines are shown with the same color in these images. Most of the initial homologous lines are correct; however, there is a small number of incorrect homologous lines. The resultant initial registration is shown in Fig. 6.14e.

Using the initial homologous lines to generate hypotheses by RANSAC and using all lines in the images to verify the correctness of a hypothesis, the homologous lines shown in Figs. 6.14f and 6.14g are obtained. Overall, 71 homologous lines are obtained, producing the registration shown in Fig. 6.14h. The registration RMSEs obtained in Figs. 6.14e and 6.14h are 2.40 pixels and 0.79 pixels, respectively.

6.7 Robust Parameter Estimation Using Homologous Lines

In Chapter 5, we saw that when RANSAC is used to find homologous points in images, improved transformation parameters will be obtained over those determined by RANSAC if least squares or a robust estimator is used to determine the transformation parameters from the homologous points obtained by RANSAC. When using lines, experiments show that least squares worsens registration accuracy. This is because lines belonging to a vanishing point all have either the same or very similar orientations.

As evidenced early in this chapter, parallel lines cannot be used to determine the transformation parameters, and nearly parallel lines produce inaccurate transformation parameters. Removing parallel and nearly parallel lines from images considerably reduces the number of lines used in least squares, defeating the purpose of using least squares to estimate the transformation parameters. If least squares worsens the registration result of RANSAC, the same is true when using a robust estimator to estimate the transformation parameters because a robust estimator itself depends on least squares to determine the residuals, which are then ranked and used to distinguish accurate homologous lines from inaccurate ones.

The inability to use least squares and robust estimators to improve the transformation parameters obtained by RANSAC is a drawback of homologous lines when compared to homologous points. To overcome this weakness, one may consider using the intersections of lines as points and use the points to register the images.

Intersections of homologous lines in images, however, may produce inaccurate homologous points. If two line segments are close to each other and make an angle between 30° and 90°, accurately positioned and oriented lines produce accurately positioned intersections. However, if line segments are far from each other or the angle between them is less than 30°, their point of intersection may not be accurate due to the presence of digital noise in images.

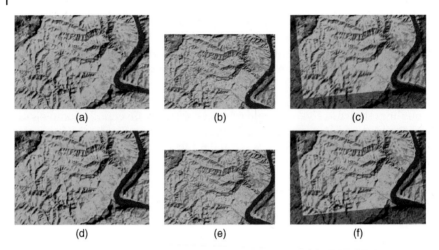

Figure 6.15 (a and b) 64 homologous points within the image domain obtained from the intersections of 72 homologous lines in the images. (c) Registration of images (a) and (b) when using the 64 homologous points by the least median of squares estimator. (d), (e) 34 homologous points obtained in the images by selecting 100 Harris points in each image and finding the correspondence between them by RANSAC under the rigid transformation. (f) Registration of the images using the 34 homologous points with the least median of squares estimator.

To demonstrate this, an example is given in Fig. 6.15. Images (a) and (b) show intersections of homologous lines in images (f) and (g), respectively, in Fig. 6.14. For each line in the reference image, intersections of all lines in the test image with it are determined. If the intersection closest to the midpoint of the line is within the image domain, it is used as a point. Once points are obtained from intersections of lines in the reference image, intersections obtained from homologous lines in the test image are used as the homologous points. Sixty-four homologous points are obtained from 71 homologous lines in images (a) and (b) in Fig. 6.15 in this manner.

Visual examination of the obtained homologous points reveals that although some homologous points are accurate, some are not. Registering the images with the least-squares method produces a registration RMSE of 9.55 pixels. The least median of squares estimator reduces this error to 3.02 pixels. This registration is shown in Fig. 6.15c. In this case, using intersections of homologous lines as homologous points has increased registration error when compared to registering the images with homologous lines.

The question that remains to be answered is whether registration error using lines is better or worse than registration using points. For example, in Fig. 6.15, if points were selected instead of lines, what would the registration RMSE be?

To find the answer to this question experimentally, 100 points are detected in each image, as shown in images (d) and (e) in Fig. 6.15. From among 100 points in each image, RANSAC was able to find correspondence between 34 of them under the rigid transformation model. Using least squares to register the images, registration RMSE of 1.91 pixels was obtained. Using least median of squares estimator, the RMSE reduced to 1.87 pixels. Registration of the images using the 34 homologous points by the least median of squares is shown in Fig. 6.15f. This result is not as good as that shown in Fig. 6.14h, which was obtained using homologous lines, producing an RMSE of 0.79 pixels.

The conclusion to be reached from this experiment is that, when using lines to register images, although least squares or a robust estimator cannot be used to improve upon the result obtained by RANSAC, the obtained result may already be better than that obtained when using points and computing the transformation parameters by the least squares or a robust estimator.

6.8 Revisiting Image Dominant Orientation Detection

To determine the dominant orientation of an image, in Chapter 2 geometric gradients and in Chapter 4 line directions were used. In this chapter, vanishing points are used to determine the dominant orientation of an image.

Although the location of a vanishing point depends on the camera view angle, when camera is far from the scene, the same parallel lines in the scene contribute to the same vanishing point in an image of the scene independent of the view angle of the camera. When camera is far from the scene, parallel lines in the scene project to nearly parallel lines in an image of the scene, creating distant vanishing points.

Calling the vanishing point obtained from the largest number of lines in an image the *dominant vanishing point*, the direction obtained by connecting the image center to the dominant vanishing point defines a unique direction that does not depend on the camera view angle and can be used to define an affine-invariant dominant orientation for an image. Therefore, as long as the scene possesses a dominant orientation and the camera is sufficiently far from the scene, directions of dominant vanishing points in images of the scene can be used to bring the images into the same orientation.

This is demonstrated in an example in Fig. 6.16. Images (a) and (b) are off-nadir-view images of a local airport taken from different camera views. These images are courtesy of the Computer Vision Group at Brown University. The direction of the dominant vanishing point in each image is shown by a yellow line passing through the image center. Reorienting image (b) to the orientation of image (a) using the dominant orientations of the images obtained from the dominant vanishing point in each image, the image shown in (c) is obtained. Images (a) and (c) are overlaid in (d) to enable visual evaluation of

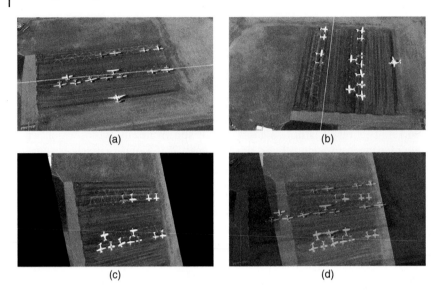

Figure 6.16 (a and b) Two off-nadir-view images of a local airport with the dominant orientation in each image obtained from the orientation of the image's dominant vanishing point. The dominant orientation of each image is shown by a yellow line passing through the image center. (c) Reorientation of image (b) so its dominant orientation aligns with that of image (a). (d) Overlaying of images (a) and (c).

the result. Bringing images of a scene taken from different views into the same orientation simplifies many image analysis tasks, including template matching, which plays a critical role in image registration.

If a nadir-view image of a scene produces a dominant vanishing point that is at infinity, when two images of the same scene are obtained at opposing angles, the obtained vanishing points will be at opposing sides of the origin. Therefore, the rotational difference between two images obtained from the dominant vanishing points of the images could be off by π.

6.9 Further Reading

Although usefulness of lines in image registration has been demonstrated [20–25], very little work on automatic registration of images using lines exists in the literature. The main difficulty has been in determining the correspondence between lines in the images.

Krüger [26] selected two random lines from each image, considered them corresponding to each other, and used their endpoints as homologous points to determine the parameters of a homography to register the images. After transforming lines in the test image with the obtained homography, if the degree of overlap between lines in the images was sufficiently high, the computed homography was considered correct and used to register the images. Rather than using the degree of overlap between lines, Volegov and Yurin [27] used the average color difference of pixels around homologous lines to determine the correctness of a computed homography.

Determination of correspondence between lines in images by clustering was introduced by Stockman et al. [28] using rigid transformation and later extended to affine transformation by others [29–31].

References

1 M. A. Fischler and R. C. Bolles, Random Sample Consensus: a paradigm for model fitting with applications to image analysis and automated cartography, *Communications of the ACM*, **24**(6):381–395, 1981.

2 A. Tai, J. Kittler, M. Petrou, and T. Windeatt, Vanishing point detection, in *British Machine Vision Conference*, 109–118, 1992.

3 S. T. Barnard, Interpreting perspective images, *Artificial Intelligence*, **21**:435–462, 1983.

4 E. Riberir and E. R. Hancock, Improved orientation estimation for texture planes using multiple vanishing points, *Pattern Recognition*, **33**:1599–1610, 2000.

5 R. S. Weiss, H. Nakatani, and E. M. Riseman, An error analysis for surface orientation from vanishing points, *IEEE Transactions on Pattern Analysis and Machine Intelligence*, **12**(12):1179–1185, 1990.

6 H. Nakatani and T. Kitahashi, Determination of vanishing point in outdoor scene, *Transactions on IECE of Japan*, **64**(5):387–388, 1981.

7 W. Gander, G. H. Golub, and R. Strebel, Least-squares fitting of circles and ellipses, *Bit*, **34**:558–578, 1994.

8 C. Bräuer-Burchardt and K. Voss, Robust vanishing point determination in noisy images, in *Proceedings of the 15th International Conference on Pattern Recognition*, Vol. 1, 559–562, 2000.

9 M. Kalantari, F. Jung, and J. Guedon, Precise, automatic and fast method for vanishing point detection, *The Photogrammetric Record*, **24**(127):246–263, 2009.

10 J. R. Kender, Shape from texture: an edge aggregation transform that maps a class of textures into surface orientation, in *Proceedings of the 6th International Conference on Artificial Intelligence*, 475–480, 1979.

11 V. Cantoni, L. Lombardi, M. Porta, and N. Sicard, Vanishing point detection: representation analysis and new approaches, *Proceedings of the 11th International Conference on Image Analysis and Processing*, 90–94, 2001.

12 B. K. P. Horn, *Robot Vision*, The MIT Press, Cambridge, MA, 432, 1986.

13 S. T. Barnard, Method for interpreting perspective images, in *Proceedings of the Image Understanding*, 193–203, 1982.

14 M. J. Magee and J. K. Aggarwal, Determining vanishing points from perspective images, *Computer Vision, Graphics, and Image Processing*, **26**:256–267, 1984.

15 R. Orghidan, J. Salvi, M. Gordan, C. Florea, and J. Batlle, Structured light self-calibration with vanishing points, *Machine Vision and Applications*, **25**:489–500, 2014.

16 M. Pollefeys, R. Koch, and L. Van Gool, Self-calibration and metric reconstruction in spite of varying and unknown intrinsic camera parameters, *International Journal of Computer Vision*, **32**(1):7–25, 1999.

17 H. Wildenauer and A. Hanbury, Robust camera self-calibration from monocular images of Manhattan worlds, in *Proceedings of Computer Vision and Pattern Recognition*, 2831–2838, 2012.

18 T. Fawcett, An introduction to ROC analysis, *Pattern Recognition Letters*, **27**:861–874, 2006.

19 L. Zhang, H. Lu, X. Hu, and R. Koch, Vanishing point estimation and line classification in a Manhattan world with a unifying camera model, *International Journal of Computer Vision*, **117**:111–130, 2016.

20 E. Coiras, J. Santamaria, and C. Miravet, A segment-based registration technique for visual-infrared images, *Optical Engineering*, **39**:282–289, 2000.

21 A. F. Habib and R. I. Alruzouq, Line-based modified iterated Hough transform for automatic registration of multi-source imagery, *The Photographic Record*, **19**(105):5–21, 2004.

22 Y. Li, R. L. Stevenson, and J. D. Gai, Line segment based image registration, in *SPIE Proceedings of Visual Communications and Image Processing*, 68221H-1–8, 2008.

23 C. Li and W. Shi, The generalized-line-based iterative transformation model for imagery registration and rectification, *IEEE Transactions on Geoscience and Remote Sensing*, **11**(8):1394–1398, 2014.

24 T. Long, W. Jiao, G. He, and W. Wang, Automatic line segment registration using Gaussian mixture model and expectation-maximization algorithm, *IEEE Journal of Selected Topics in Applied Earth Observation and Remote Sensing*, **7**(5):1688–1699, 2014.

25 W. Shi and A. Shekar, The line based transformation model (LBTM) for image-to-image registration of high-resolution satellite image data, *International Journal of Remote Sensing*, **27**(14):3001–3012, 2006.

26 W. Krüger, Robust and efficient map-to-image registration with line segments, *Machine Vision and Applications*, **13**:38–50, 2001.

27 D. B. Volegov and D. V. Yurin, Preliminary coarse image registration by using straight lines found on them for constructing super resolution mosaics and 3D scene recovery, *Programming and Computer Software*, **34**(5):279–293, 2008.

28 G. Stockman, S. Kopstein, and S. Benett, Matching images to models for registration and object detection via clustering, *IEEE Transactions on Pattern Analysis and Machine Intelligence*, **4**(3):229–241, 1982.

29 A. Habib and D. Kelley, Automatic relative orientation of large scale imagery over urban areas using modified iterated Hough transform, *Photogrammetry & Remote Sensing*, **56**:29–41, 2001.

30 J. Tang, X. Yang, C. Liu, and X. Wu, Image registration based on fitted straight lines of edges, in *Proceedings of the 6th World Congress on Intelligent Control and Automation*, 9782–9785, 2006.

31 K. Wang, T. Shi, G. Liao, and Q. Xia, Image registration using a point-line duality based line matching method, *Journal of Visual Communication and Image Representation*, **24**:615–626, 2013.

7

Nonrigid Image Registration

7.1 Introduction

Rigid registration involves determining the translational and rotational differences between two images, so the images can be aligned as rigid bodies. If the images, in addition to translational and rotational differences, have scale and shearing differences, an affine transformation is required to register them. If the images represent different views of a planar scene, a homography transformation is required to register them. Images with local geometric differences require a nonlinear or elastic transformation to register them. Nonrigid registration is the process of elastically transforming the geometry of the test image to resemble the geometry of the reference image, so the images can be spatially aligned.

Rigid, affine, and homography transformations were discussed in Chapter 5. These transformations provide the global geometric constraint needed by RANSAC (Section 5.2.2) to find homologous points in the images. If the type of transformation relating the geometries of two images is not known, the constraint required by RANSAC to find homologous points in the images will not be available, making correspondence by RANSAC impossible.

Nonrigid image registration requires solutions to two problems: (1) Determination of a set of homologous points or homologous lines in the images and (2) determination of an elastic transformation model from the homologous points/lines that can accurately map points/lines in the test image to the corresponding points/lines in the reference image.

In the following sections, methods for determining the correspondence between feature points in images with local geometric differences are discussed, various elastic transformation models useful in registration of such images are described, and examples of nonrigid registration using various natural images are given. Discussions in this chapter are limited to homologous points. Use of homologous lines in nonrigid registration is discussed in Chapter 12.

Theory and Applications of Image Registration, First Edition. Arthur Ardeshir Goshtasby.
© 2017 John Wiley & Sons, Inc. Published 2017 by John Wiley & Sons, Inc.

7.2   Finding Homologous Points

If no information about the geometric relation between two images is available, homologous points in the images are determined via coarse-to-fine matching. This involves reducing the resolution of the images sufficiently, so nonlinear geometric differences between the images become negligible. Homologous points are found in the images at the lowest resolution by RANSAC using rigid, affine, or homography constraint. Obtained homologous points are then tracked from low to highest resolution to find homologous points in the original images.

To speed up RANSAC, initial/putative correspondences are obtained by template matching. Templates are selected centered at feature points in the reference image and the templates are searched for in the test image using an appropriate similarity or distance measure. Note that template matching requires that the images have about the same orientation and scale. Details of these methods are provided as follow.

7.2.1   Coarse-to-Fine Matching

If two images have nonlinear geometric differences, the relation between the images can be modeled by a global transformation and a number of local transformations. The global transformation will primarily determine the global scaling and rotational differences between the images, and the local transformations will determine geometric differences between homologous neighborhoods in the images.

Consider the image pyramid shown in Fig. 7.1 and suppose a pyramid such as this is created for each image. The image at the bottom of a pyramid is the image at the highest resolution and the image at the top of the pyramid is the

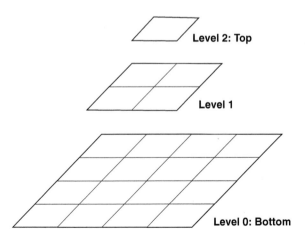

Figure 7.1 An image pyramid showing an image at three resolutions.

image at the lowest resolution. By registering the top-level reference and test images, the transformation to globally align the images will be obtained.

Figure 7.1 shows an image pyramid with three levels. If the highest resolution image at Level 0 in the pyramid is of dimensions $M \times N$, the image above it at Level 1 will be of dimensions $M_1 \times N_1$, where $M_1 = M/2$ and $N_1 = N/2$, and the image at Level 2 will be of dimensions $M_2 \times N_2$, where $M_2 = M_1/2 = M/2^2$ and $N_2 = N_1/2 = N/2^2$.

Given an image at Level 0, the intensity of a pixel in the image at Level 1 is obtained from the average of intensities of pixels within a 2×2 window in the image at Level 0. More specifically, the intensity at pixel (x, y) in the image at Level 1 is obtained from the average of intensities of pixels at $(2x, 2y)$, $(2x + 1, 2y), (2x, 2y + 1), (2x + 1, 2y + 1)$ in the image at Level 0. In this manner, the image at Level $i + 1$ in a pyramid is created from the image at Level i, for $i \geq 0$.

Image pyramids are created for the reference image and test image similarly. Therefore, if an image pyramid with L levels is created for the reference image, an image pyramid with L levels is created for the test image. Images at the top level are registered using a global transformation, such as rigid, affine, or homography, as discussed in Chapter 5. For example, if homography is used and (x, y) and (X, Y) are the coordinates of homologous points in the reference and test images at the top level, we can write

$$X = (ax + by + c)/(gx + hy + 1), \tag{7.1}$$

$$Y = (dx + ey + f)/(gx + hy + 1). \tag{7.2}$$

x and X represent reference and test image columns, increasing from left to right, and y and Y represent reference and test image rows, increasing from bottom to top. If we scale the images by a factor of s to obtain new images with coordinates (x', y') and (X', Y'), since

$$x' = sx, \quad y' = sy, \quad X' = sX, \quad Y' = sY, \tag{7.3}$$

by finding x, y, X, Y from x', y', X', Y' using Eq. (7.3) and substituting them into Eqs (7.1) and (7.2), relations between (x', y') and (X', Y') will be obtained in terms of parameters a–h of the transformation obtained at the top level:

$$X' = (ax' + by' + cs) \Big/ \left(\left(\frac{g}{s}\right)x' + \left(\frac{h}{s}\right)y' + 1 \right), \tag{7.4}$$

$$Y' = (dx' + ey' + fs) \Big/ \left(\left(\frac{g}{s}\right)x' + \left(\frac{h}{s}\right)y' + 1 \right). \tag{7.5}$$

In Fig. 7.1, the images at Level 1 are subdivided into four equal blocks, with each block being the size of the image at Level 2. Knowing the global homography at Level 2 computed from Eqs (7.1) and (7.2), the global homography at Level 1 is estimated using Eqs (7.4) and (7.5). This transformation will bring the images at Level 1 into approximate alignment. By substituting the coordinates of the four corners of a block in the reference image into Eqs (7.4) and (7.5), the coordinates of the corners of the homologous block in the test image at Level 1 will be obtained. The correspondence between points within homologous blocks is then determined by RANSAC using homography as the transformation model.

From the homologous points obtained in homologous blocks in reference and test images, a homography is calculated relating the geometries of homologous blocks at Level 1. The gradual change in the geometry of the test image to resemble the geometry of the reference image is depicted in Fig. 7.2. The homography transformation registering the images at the top level primarily determines the global rotational and scaling differences between the images. Transformations obtained between homologous blocks at lower levels represent local adjustments needed in addition to the global transformation to account for the local geometric differences between the images. As the resolution of the images is increased, more local refinements are needed to account for larger local geometric differences between the images.

Going from a block at one level to blocks below it at one lower level is the same as going from the image at the top level to the four blocks below it. Therefore, once the procedure to match points in blocks at the top level and the blocks below the top level is worked out, the same procedure can be used to match points within homologous blocks at any level, and by tracking image blocks within the pyramids from coarse to fine, correspondence can be established between points within homologous blocks in the images at any level, including the original images at the bottom level.

Once the transformation relating the images at the top level is determined, homologous points in the images at one lower level can be determined very quickly because the four corners of homologous blocks within the images can be determined from the transformation obtained at one higher level. By combining the global homography obtained at the top level and the local

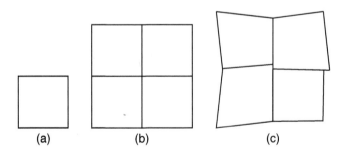

(a) (b) (c)

Figure 7.2 (a) The test image at Level 2 after registration with the reference image at Level 2. (b) Test image at Level 1 after transformation with the approximate transformation obtained at Level 2. (c) Blocks within the test image at Level 1 after transformation with local homographies obtained from homologous points within homologous blocks in the images at Level 1.

homographies obtained at lower levels, local homographies relating homologous blocks in images at any level can be determined. By tracking image blocks from low to high resolution, homologous points within the images can be tracked from low to high resolution. The homologous points obtained from blocks at the bottom level are merged to produce homologous points in the original images. This method is expected to be particularly effective when the images are very large and they have smoothly varying geometric differences.

Note that as the resolution of images in a pyramid increases, some of the blocks covering homogeneous areas in the scene may not produce sufficient points to enable computation of local homographies at a level. In such a situation, identity is used as the local homography. This will, in effect, use the transformation computed for homologous blocks at Level $i + 1$ to relate the geometries of homologous blocks below them at level i for $i \geq 0$.

Steps in the coarse-to-fine correspondence algorithm are summarized next. Homography is used to find correspondence between points in images at the lowest resolution. Homography is also used to find correspondence between points in homologous blocks at higher resolutions. For images with small view-angle differences, instead of homography, affine or rigid transformation may be used in the same manner to represent the local and global transformations.

Algorithm 7.1   Coarse-to-fine matching

Given a reference image and a test image obtained by the same sensor and also given a set of points in the reference image $\{\mathbf{p}_i = (x_i, y_i): i = 1, \dots, N_1\}$ and a set of points in the test image $\{\mathbf{P}_i = (X_i, Y_i): i = 1, \dots, N_2\}$, this algorithm finds homologous points in the images by coarse-to-fine matching.

1. If correspondence can be established between points in the images by a homography (Eqs (7.1) and (7.2)), return the homologous points and exit the program. Otherwise, let $L = 0$ and save the reference and test images at the bottom of the reference and test pyramids, respectively.
2. Reduce the resolution of the images at Level L by a factor of 2 and increment L by 1. If sufficient points cannot be found in either of the images, report failure and exit the program. If correspondence can be established between points in the images by homography H_0 defined by Eqs (7.1) and (7.2), go to Step 3. Otherwise, go to Step 2.
3. Resample the test image at Level $L - 1$ using transformation H_1 defined by Eqs (7.4) and (7.5).
4. Find the correspondence between points within homologous blocks in the images at Level $L - 1$ and let H_{ij} be the homography that relates homologous points in block ij in the images. If homologous blocks do not produce sufficient homologous points, let $H_{ij} = H_1$. Otherwise, let $H_{ij} = H_{ij}H_1$. H_{ij} now

shows the geometric relation between block ij in the reference and block ij in the test images at Level $L - 1$.

5. Decrement L by 1 and for each block ij in the reference image at Level L, let H_{ij} be H_0, the transformation defined by Eqs (7.1) and (7.2), and resample block ij in the test image using transformation H_1 defined by Eqs (7.4) and (7.5). If $L = 0$, go to Step 6. Otherwise, go to Step 4.

6. Find homologous points in homologous blocks at the bottom level by RANSAC and return the combined homologous points.

Steps 1 and 2 of Algorithm 7.1 create the image pyramids and Steps 3–5 find homologous points in the images in a coarse-to-fine fashion. In Step 6, correspondence is established between points in the images at the highest resolution. Points at the highest resolution are the points initially provided. The algorithm, in effect, approximately aligns the images at the bottom level so that correspondence can be established between points within corresponding reference and test neighborhoods. By knowing the correspondence between neighborhoods/blocks in the images, correspondence is only needed between a small number of points within corresponding blocks. The coarse-to-fine strategy not only avoids wasteful matches but also reduces the likelihood of false matches.

Note that the transformation model relating corresponding blocks in images at each level except the top is composed of two transformations: a global transformation that is obtained at one higher level and an adjustment to it obtained using information in the images at that level. As the resolution of the images is increased, corresponding blocks represent smaller areas in the scene. At the bottom level, the blocks are sufficiently small so that corresponding blocks in the images can be considered representing flat scene areas. This makes it possible to use a homography transformation by RANSAC to find corresponding points within corresponding blocks in the images.

An example of point correspondence by Algorithm 7.1 is given in Fig. 7.3. Images (a) and (b) represent multitemporal optical images of an urban area. These images are courtesy of the USDA. 500 points detected in each image by the Harris corner detector (Section 3.3.3.1) are shown. Due to scene changes, some points detected in one image do not appear in the other; however, there are scene areas that have not changed, producing similar points. Algorithm 7.1 has found 226 homologous points in the images. Homologous points are shown in the same color in images (a) and (b). Points in black are those without a correspondence and are considered outliers.

By registering the images using the local homographies computed at the bottom level in Algorithm 7.1, the registration shown in Fig. 7.3c is obtained. To visualize misregistration or changes that have occurred in the scene between the times the images were obtained, a color image is created (Fig. 7.3d) with its

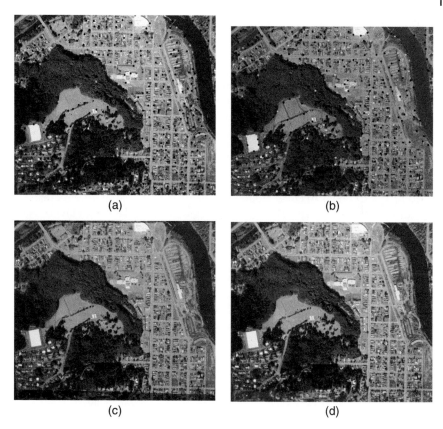

Figure 7.3 (a and b) Multitemporal optical aerial images, courtesy of USDA. 500 points are detected in each image and correspondence is established between the points by Algorithm 7.1. The algorithm has found 226 homologous points in the images. Homologous points are shown with the same color. Points without a correspondence are shown in black. (c) Registration of the images by the local homographies obtained by Algorithm 7.1. (d) Fusion of the registered images to show local misregistration or scene changes occurring between the times the images are obtained.

green and blue bands showing the reference image and its red band showing the resampled test image. Small red regions in this image show the scene changes. The bluish color of the fused image is due to differences in scene lighting when capturing the images.

Algorithm 7.1 subdivides the images into rectangular blocks and finds a local homography, relating the geometries of corresponding blocks. If corresponding neighborhoods in the images can be related by an affine transformation, after finding correspondence between points in the images at the top level, points in the reference image are triangulated. By knowing the corresponding points in the test image, corresponding triangles in the test image will be obtained.

By knowing homologous triangular regions in the images at Level L and by connecting the midpoints of the triangle edges to subdivide each triangle into four, correspondence between each of the smaller triangles in the images will be known. From the vertices of homologous triangular regions in the images at Level L, the approximate homologous triangle vertices at one lower level is estimated by simply multiplying the coordinates of the vertices by two.

Once (approximate) homologous triangular regions in images at Level $L - 1$ are determined, points falling within new homologous triangles at Level $L - 1$ are identified and correspondence is established between them. The affine transformation obtained from the homologous points within homologous triangles is used to refine triangular regions in the test image. By gradually sub-dividing the triangles to cover smaller scene areas at the same time increasing the resolution of the images, homologous regions are tracked from low to high resolution. The homologous points obtained within homologous triangles at the bottom level are then combined to obtain the overall homologous points in the images.

If a pair of homologous regions at Level L are found to match with an affine transformation, after a triangle at Level $L - 1$ is subdivided into four, if points within a homologous triangle pair are found not to correspond by an affine, the transformation obtained at Level L is used to relate the triangles. The process closely follows that of Algorithm 7.1, except for using triangular regions and affine transformation rather than rectangular regions and homography.

Tracking of triangles from coarse to fine is demonstrated in Fig. 7.4. Suppose Fig. 7.4a shows the triangulation obtained for the points in the test image at the top level. A similar triangulation exists in the reference image. The test triangle vertices at one level below the top are determined by multiplying the coordinates of the test triangle vertices at the top level by two. This is shown in Fig. 7.4b. Triangles below the top level in the reference image

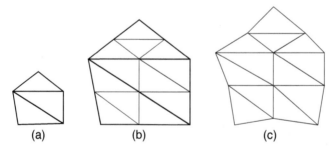

(a)   (b)   (c)

Figure 7.4 (a) Triangulation of points in the test image at the top level. (b) Estimation of triangle vertices at the level below the top in the test image using the triangle vertices at the top level, and subdivision of the triangles. (c) Reestimation of the triangle vertices in the test image at one level below the top from the affine transformations obtained from homologous points within homologous triangles.

are obtained similarly. By finding correspondence between points within corresponding triangles, a new affine transformation is computed for each pair of corresponding triangles.

Using the affine transformations obtained by matching points within corresponding triangles in the images at one level below the top and using the vertices of triangles in the reference image, the new vertices of corresponding triangles can be determined in the test image, as shown in Fig. 7.4c. The process is repeated while going down the pyramids until triangles at the bottom level are reached and an affine transformation is computed from corresponding points within corresponding triangular regions in the images. Note that a minimum of three corresponding points in corresponding triangles is required to find the affine parameters.

In [1, 2], a Voronoi diagram rather than triangulation was used to divide the image domain into small regions so that local transformations could be determined to represent the local geometric differences between the images. The Voronoi diagram and Delaunay triangulation [3, 4] of a set of points are duals of each other. A Delaunay triangulation of a set of points is a triangulation where none of its points fall inside the circumcircles of the triangles.

Given a Voronoi diagram of a set of points, the Delaunay triangulation of the points is obtained by determining the intersections of lines passing through the midpoints of triangle edges and normal to them. Each triangle vertex becomes the center of a Voronoi region. Image pixels within a Voronoi region are closer to the triangle vertex representing the region than to any other triangle vertex. Conversely, given a Voronoi diagram of a set of points, the Delaunay triangulation of the points is obtained by connecting the centers of the Voronoi regions that share an edge.

7.2.2 Correspondence by Template Matching

Images of a scene captured by different sensors have nonlinear radiometric differences. Rarely the same feature points are detected in images captured by different sensors. To find homologous points in multisensor or multimodality images, points are detected in the reference image, and templates centered at the points are searched in the test image by template matching using an appropriate similarity or distance measure.

Various similarity and distance measures suitable for template matching were discussed in Sections 5.4 and 5.5. Since similarity and distance measures used in template matching are not rotation and scale invariant, template matching is limited to images that have the same local scale and orientation.

To make template matching insensitive to the local geometric differences between two images, templates are taken small enough so that the geometric difference between matching templates will be negligible. To make the similarity or distance measure between two templates less dependent on their local geometric difference, a higher weight is assigned to pixels nearer to the template center than to pixels farther away.

Consider a circular template of radius r centered at feature point (x_0, y_0) in the reference image and a circular template of the same radius centered at a point (X_0, Y_0) in the test image. To determine whether point (X_0, Y_0) in the test image corresponds to point (x_0, y_0) in the reference image, templates centered at the points are compared. Suppose the intensity at (x, y) in the reference template is $i(x, y)$ and the intensity at the same location in the test template is $I(X, Y)$. Also, suppose the average intensity of pixels in the reference template is i_0 and the average intensity of pixels in the test template is I_0.

If the images are in the same modality, the correlation of intensities in the templates can be used to measure the similarity/distance between the templates. Correlation is calculated by adding term $(i(x, y) - i_0)(I(X, Y) - I_0)$, which is computed at corresponding locations (x, y) and (X, Y) in the templates. In order for pixels closer to the template center to have a higher influence on the calculated similarity than pixels farther away, the terms are multiplied by a monotonically decreasing weight function that is centered at the template. If a Gaussian is used as the weight function and assuming the template is of radius r and is centered at (x_0, y_0), term $(i(x, y) - i_0)(I(X, Y) - I_0)$ is multiplied by

$$G_r(x, y) = \exp\left\{-\frac{(x - x_0)^2 + (y - y_0)^2}{2r^2}\right\}. \tag{7.6}$$

$G_r(x, y)$ is a Gaussian of height 1 and standard deviation r centered at (x_0, y_0).

If the images are in different modalities, to measure the similarity/distance between templates in the images, measures such as mutual information or joint entropy are required. These measures use the joint histogram or the joint probability density (JPD) of corresponding intensities in the templates to find the similarity/distance between the templates. For a similarity/distance measure calculated from JPD to depend more on intensities of pixels closer to the template center than to intensities of pixels farther away, if intensities of corresponding pixels (x, y) and (X, Y) in the templates are i and I, rather than adding 1 to entry (i, I) in the joint histogram, entry (i, I) in the histogram is incremented by $G_r(x, y)$. This will make pixels closer to the template center influence the obtained JPD more than pixels farther from the template center.

If the centers of a reference template and a test template correspond but the templates have scale, rotation, or nonlinear geometric differences, corresponding pixels in the templates farther from the template center will fall farther apart than corresponding pixels that are closer to the template center. Gaussian weighting reduces the effect of geometric differences between the templates when calculating the similarity/distance between the templates.

Local geometric differences between images can be further reduced by reducing the resolution of the images. After finding corresponding templates in the

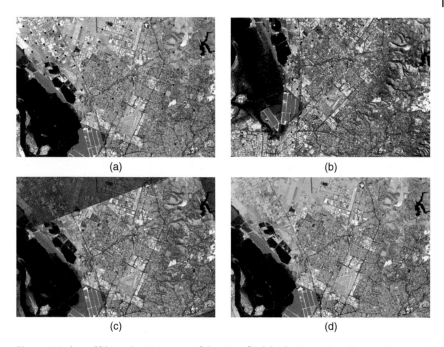

Figure 7.5 (a and b) Landsat 8 images of the city of Adelaide, Australia, taken on January 4, 2015 and on August 29, 2014, respectively. 200 points are detected in the reference image by the Harris corner detector. Correspondence is found for 157 of the reference points in the test image by a coarse-to-fine template-matching process. Corresponding points are shown in the same color in the images. Points appearing in only one of the images are shown in black. Registration of the images using the correspondences by the least median of squares (LMS) estimator and the homography transformation is shown in (c) and fusion of the registered images is shown in (d). Regions in orange/red in the fused image show land-cover changes resulting from change in season. Some changes caused by human activity are also visible.

images at low resolution, the correspondences can be tracked from low to high resolution to find corresponding templates at high resolution.

An example of point correspondence by template matching in this manner is given in Fig. 7.5. Images (a) and (b) represent Landsat 8 images of the city of Adelaide in Australia, taken on January 4, 2015 and on August 29, 2014, respectively. These images are courtesy of the US Geological Survey. Considerable land-cover changes have occurred in some areas in the scene due to change of season.

Rotational difference between the images is determined using their dominant orientations (Chapter 2) and the test image is rotated to the orientation of the reference image. Then, 200 Harris corners (Section 3.3.3.1) are detected in the reference image and the correspondences are searched in the rotated test image by template matching using correlation coefficient (Section 5.4.1) as the similarity measure in a coarse-to-fine fashion. Only those correspondences producing a correlation coefficient greater than 0.6 are kept and the rest are discarded. As the correlation coefficient decreases, the likelihood of a mismatch increases. Scene areas that have changed due to change in season result in corresponding image areas that have radiometric differences. Such areas produce low correlation values and may produce incorrect or inaccurate correspondences.

The coarse-to-fine template-matching process has found correspondence to 157 of the 200 points in the reference image. Points in the upper-left corner in the reference image do not have correspondences in the test image because they are outside the viewing area of the test image. Points falling inside regions that have gone through radiometric changes have also not produced correspondences due to low correlation values.

Registration of the Adelaide images by the least median of squares (LMS) estimator (Section 5.7.3) when using homography as the transformation model is shown in Fig. 7.5c. The LMS estimator has the ability to ignore up to half of the correspondences that are incorrect or inaccurate. Changes occurring in the scene between August 29, 2014 and January 4, 2015 are shown in the fused image in Fig. 7.5d. Areas of no change have the color of the reference image, while areas of change appear in orange/red in the fused image.

The coarse-to-fine strategy speeds up template matching by limiting search in higher resolutions. Knowing homologous points within homologous blocks at Level L, the determination of homologous points in images at Level $L - 1$ requires search in very small neighborhoods. For example, if points (x, y) and (X, Y) in the reference and test images correspond at Level L, point $(2x, 2y)$ in the reference image at Level $L - 1$ will be at $(2X \pm 1, 2Y \pm 1)$ in the test image. Therefore, once homologous points are found at the top level, homologous points at lower levels can be determined quickly.

If the images to be registered are rotated with respect to each other, before carrying out template matching, the rotational difference between the images must be determined and the test image must be resampled to the orientation of the reference image. The orientation detection method described in Chapter 2 can be used for this purpose when the images are in the same modality. If the images are in different modalities but some of the region boundaries in the images are the same, the process may still work. The rotational difference between images (a) and (b) in Fig. 7.5 was determined in this manner, and image (b) was rotated to the orientation of image (a) before carrying out template matching.

An example of multimodal image registration where the images are rotated with respect to each other is given in Fig. 7.6. Reference image (a) shows an area over Phoenix, Arizona, and test image (b) is a thermal infrared (IR) image of the same area. These images are courtesy of the US Geological Survey. First, the rotational difference between the images is determined from the

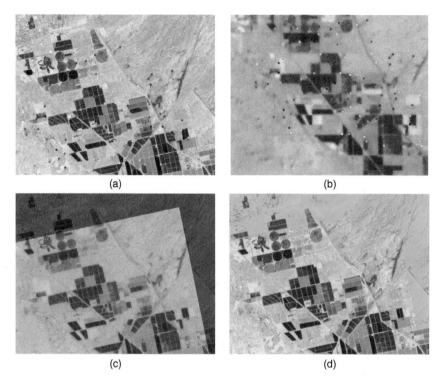

(a)   (b)

(c)   (d)

Figure 7.6 (a and b) Reflectance and thermal IR images of an area over Phoenix, Arizona. These images are courtesy of the US Geological Survey. 200 points are detected in (a) and correspondence is found for 156 of them by the described coarse-to-fine template matching process using mutual information as the similarity measure. (c) Registration of the images by the LMS estimator and the homography transformation model using the 156 homologous points. (d) Fusion of the registered images.

difference in the dominant orientations of the images. The test image is then rotated with respect to its center to the orientation of the reference image. Two hundred points are detected in the reference image by the Harris corner detector. By template matching using mutual information as the similarity measure, homologous points were found in the test image. The mutual information obtained for each correspondence was divided by the largest mutual information obtained among all correspondences to normalize the similarity measures to values between 0 and 1. Only those homologous points that had a normalized mutual information greater than or equal to 0.6 were kept and the rest were discarded.

By discarding homologous points with low similarity measures, the likelihood of an incorrect or inaccurate correspondence is reduced. The obtained homologous points are shown with the same color in images (a) and (b) in

Fig. 7.6. Points shown in black are those without a correspondence. Using the 156 homologous points and homography as the transformation model, and relying on the LMS estimator to remove the inaccurate and incorrect correspondences, the registration shown in Fig. 7.6c is obtained. Fusion of the registered images is shown in Fig. 7.6d. The green and blue bands of the fused image are from the reference image and the red band of the fused image is from the resampled test image.

7.3   Outlier Removal

Incorrect homologous points (outliers) are a major problem in image registration. When the images are related by a simple transformation, such as rigid or affine transformation, RANSAC (Section 5.2.2) or a robust estimator (Section 5.7) can separate inliers from outliers and determine the transformation parameters from the inliers. When the transformation model relating the images is complex, the global constraint RANSAC and robust estimator need to find the transformation parameters will not be available.

In Sections 7.2.1 and 7.2.2, coarse-to-fine approaches to the correspondence problem were discussed. The approaches start with low-resolution images that can be related by a rigid or affine transformation and gradually increase the resolution of the images while guiding the search in small neighborhoods to avoid false homologous points (outliers) entering the process.

The coarse-to-fine process not only reduces the likelihood of obtaining false homologous points but also speeds up the correspondence process. However, when the images have local geometric differences, the likelihood that some outliers remain among homologous points exists. In this section, a more general approach to the problem of outlier removal is discussed.

Consider the images in Fig. 7.7, representing two views of a fossil tree trunk that has been cut at the top. Because of sharp and unknown geometric differences between the images around the cut area, RANSAC and robust estimators are not effective in removing the outliers.

Suppose finding 2000 feature points in each image and finding the initial correspondence between the points using the composite descriptor (Section 5.3.4). The process finds 1142 initial homologous points in the images as shown in Fig. 7.8. Homologous points are shown with the same color in the images. Many of the homologous points are correct, but there are many incorrect ones. Next, an algorithm that removes outliers from among the initial homologous points using local affine constraints is described. The algorithm assumes that corresponding small neighborhoods in the images can be related by an affine transformation.

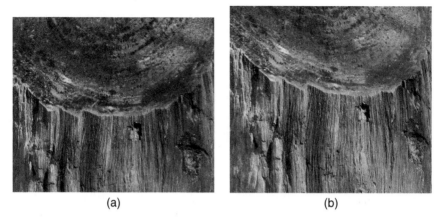

(a)   (b)

Figure 7.7 (a and b) Images taken from different views of a fossil tree truck cut at the top.

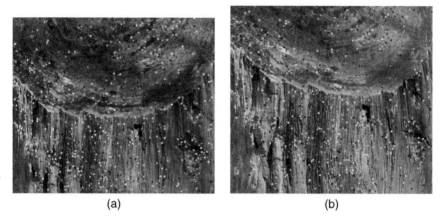

(a)   (b)

Figure 7.8 (a and b) Initial homologous points obtained by matching the image descriptors associated with the points. Homologous points are shown with the same color.

Algorithm 7.2   Outlier removal using local affine constraint

---

Given a set of initial homologous points $\{(x_i, y_i), (X_i, Y_i) : i = 1, \dots, N\}$ in two images of a scene, this algorithm removes the outliers using local affine constraint.

1. For $i = 1, \dots, N$ repeat Steps 1.1–1.4.
    1.1. Find $n - 1$ points closest to (x_i, y_i) in the reference image. Knowing that point (x_i, y_i) in the reference image is likely to correspond to point (X_i, Y_i) in the test image, this will produce n likely homologous points in the images.

1.2. Find an affine transformation $(X = ax + by + c, Y = dx + ey + f)$ from the n initial homologous points by a robust estimator, such as the LMS estimator (Section 5.7.3).

1.3. Let $E_{x_i} = X_i - ax_i - by_i - c, \quad E_{y_i} = Y_i - dx_i - ey_i - f$, and compute $E_i = \sqrt{E_{x_i}^2 + E_{y_i}^2}$.

1.4. If E_i is sufficiently large, declare the initial correspondence $(x_i, y_i), (X_i, Y_i)$ an outlier and remove it. Otherwise, keep the correspondence.

2. Repeat Step 1 on the surviving homologous points until no additional outliers can be found.

In Step 1.4, if the LMS estimator is used to find the affine parameters and the median error is E_m, then when $E_i > E_m$ and E_i is larger than a few pixels, the homologous pair $\{(x_i, y_i)(X_i, Y_i)\}$ is considered incorrect and removed. Otherwise, the homologous pair is considered correct and kept.

If more than 50% of the initial homologous points are false, some outliers will still remain after going through Steps 1.1–1.4 of Algorithm 7.2. To make sure that no outliers remain among the remaining homologous points, Steps 1.1–1.4 are repeated on the homologous points surviving the outlier removal until the process cannot detect any additional outliers. This may take from a few to several iterations.

Using the initial homologous points shown in Fig. 7.8 and the LMS estimator with $n = 30$, and considering the ith homologous pair an outlier if $E_i > E_m$ and $E_i > 3$ pixels, the final homologous points shown in Fig. 7.9 are obtained. From

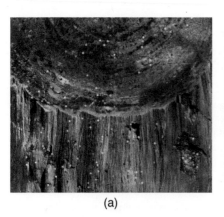 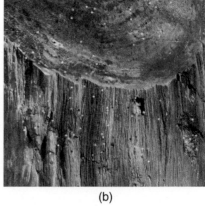

(a)   (b)

Figure 7.9 (a and b) The final homologous points obtained by Algorithm 7.2 when starting with the initial homologous points shown in Fig. 7.8. Homologous points are shown with the same color.

among the 1142 initial homologous points only 261 survive the outlier removal and, therefore, are considered the final homologous points. The parameters of an elastic transformation to register the images are then determined from the coordinates of the final homologous points shown in Fig. 7.9.

Parameter n depends on the severity of the local geometric difference between the images. The larger the local geometric differences between the images, the smaller the neighborhood size should be. Neighborhood size also depends on parameter N. When a large number of initial homologous points is given, n can be taken proportionately large. Parameter n should be large enough to contain at least three homologous points after removal of the outliers. Therefore, if it is anticipated that 50% of the initial homologous points are wrong, at least $n = 5$ points should be selected so that the median error will be that of a correct homologous pair.

How realistic is the assumption that local geometric difference between images taken from different views of a 3-D scene represent an affine transformation? To find the answer to this question, points in the reference image before outlier removal are shown in Fig. 7.10a. These points depict

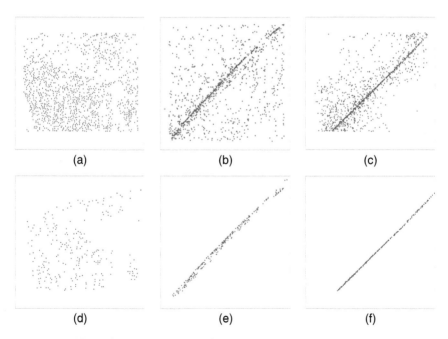

(a) (b) (c)

(d) (e) (f)

Figure 7.10 (a) Initial 1142 points in the reference image in Fig. 7.8a. (d) Final 261 points in the reference image in Fig. 7.9a. (b) Viewing of initial 3-D points $\{(x_i, y_i, X_i) : i = 1, \ldots, N\}$ after being projected in y-direction to the xX-plane. (c) Viewing of initial 3-D points $\{(x_i, y_i, Y_i) : i = 1, \ldots, N\}$ after being projected in x-direction to the yY-plane. (e and f) Same as (b) and (c) but after removal of the outliers.

$\{(x_i, y_i): i = 1, \ldots, N\}$ in Fig. 7.8a with $N = 1142$. After outlier removal, the 261 points shown in Fig. 7.10d are obtained.

The x and y components of the transformation to register the images are obtained from 3-D points $\{(x_i, y_i, X_i) : i = 1, \ldots, N\}$ and $\{(x_i, y_i, Y_i): i = 1, \ldots, N\}$, respectively, with $N = 261$. Figure 7.10e depicts 3-D points $\{(x_i, y_i, X_i): i = 1, \ldots, 261\}$ when viewed in y-direction (projected to the xX-plane), and Fig. 7.10f depicts 3-D points $\{(x_i, y_i, Y_i): i = 1, \ldots, 261\}$ when viewed in x-direction (projected to the yY-plane.

The y-component transformation when viewed in x-direction is locally nearly flat as all points with the same y when projected to the yY-plane fall on top of each other (Fig. 7.10f). This is because the images represent stereo images, with the cameras displaced horizontally when capturing the images. Therefore, corresponding points displace in x-direction and have about the same y values. Points in the x-component transformation when viewed in y-direction (projected to the xX-plane) do not quite fall on a plane, but the points locally fall near a plane. Therefore, locally again, the points can be approximated by a polynomial of degree 1, which is what each component of the affine transformation represents.

Figure 7.10b and c shows the initial homologous points when represented by two sets of 3-D points. Figure 7.10e and f shows the same points after outlier removal. Comparing the points in Fig. 7.10b and e and points in Fig. 7.10c and f, we see that many of the initial homologous points are incorrect that should be removed before using them to determine the transformation parameters.

Algorithm 7.2 has the ability to reduce the initial homologous points shown in Fig. 7.10b and c to the final homologous points shown in Fig. 7.10e and f from which the components of an elastic transformation to register the images can be computed. Various elastic transformation models suitable for nonrigid image registration are described next.

7.4 Elastic Transformation Models

Imagine printing a pattern on an elastic membrane and taking an image of the membrane while pulling it from different points in different directions. The transformation relating the geometry of the original pattern to the geometry of the pattern after the deformation is known as the nonlinear or elastic transformation.

When the geometric relation between the images to be registered is not known, the right transformation model to register the images cannot be chosen. In such a situation, a transformation model that can adapt to local geometric differences between the images should be used. Local geometric differences between two images are reflected in the coordinates of homologous points in the images. A transformation that maps points in the reference image to the corresponding points in the test image will also map other points in the reference image to the corresponding points in the test image, in effect, registering the images.

The registration of biomedical and industrial images taken of elastic surfaces requires a transformation that can account for local geometric differences between the images. Surface spline (SS) [5], also known as thin-plate spline [6], has been used to register images with local geometric differences. If the images to be registered represent different views of a 3-D scene composed of planar patches, the images can be registered by a piecewise affine (also known as piecewise linear, PWL) [7] or a piecewise homography [8, 9] transformation. Multiview images of a smoothly varying scene can be registered by moving least squares [10] and weighted local transformations [2, 11].

The problem of finding the transformation model for nonrigid registration can be described as follows. Given the coordinates of N homologous points in two images of a scene:

$$\{(x_i, y_i), (X_i, Y_i): i = 1, \dots, N\}, \tag{7.7}$$

we would like to find a transformation model with two components f_x and f_y that satisfy

$$X_i \approx f_x(x_i, y_i), \tag{7.8}$$
$$Y_i \approx f_y(x_i, y_i), \tag{7.9}$$

or

$$X_i = f_x(x_i, y_i), \tag{7.10}$$
$$Y_i = f_y(x_i, y_i), \tag{7.11}$$

for $i = 1, \dots, N$. The former defines an approximating transformation, while the latter defines an interpolating transformation.

f_x in Eq. (7.8) is a single-valued function approximating 3-D points

$$\{(x_i, y_i, X_i): i = 1, \dots, N\}, \tag{7.12}$$

and f_y in Eq. (7.9) is another single-valued function approximating 3-D points

$$\{(x_i, y_i, Y_i): i = 1, \dots, N\}. \tag{7.13}$$

Equations (7.10) and (7.11) define f_x and f_y as interpolating functions. When the homologous points are accurate, interpolation is preferred to approximation. However, when the homologous points contain inaccuracies, approximation is preferred because it treats the inaccuracies as noise and smoothes the noise while estimating the component of the transformation.

Each component of a transformation model is, therefore, a single-valued surface approximating/interpolating a set of 3-D points. A 3-D point is formed from the coordinates of a point in the reference image and the X-component or the Y-component of the corresponding point in the test image. f_x and f_y have the same form. Therefore, in the following, we will find single-valued function $F = f(x, y)$ that approximates/interpolates

$$\{(x_i, y_i, F_i) : i = 1, \dots, N\}. \tag{7.14}$$

The X-component of the transformation is obtained by letting $F_i = X_i$ and the Y-component of the transformation is obtained by letting $F_i = Y_i$.

7.4.1 Surface Spline (SS) Interpolation

Given a set of points in the plane with associating data values as described by (7.14), the SS interpolating the points is defined by [5]

$$f(x, y) = A_1 + A_2 x + A_3 y + \sum_{i=1}^{N} B_i r_i^2 \ln r_i^2, \tag{7.15}$$

where $r_i^2 = (x - x_i)^2 + (y - y_i)^2 + d^2$, and d^2 represents the stiffness of the surface. A SS is composed of a linear term and a weighted sum of radially symmetric (logarithmic) basis functions. In some literature, basis functions of form $r_i^2 \log r_i$ are used. Since $r_i^2 \log r_i^2 = 2 r_i^2 \log r_i$, by renaming $2B_i$ by B_i we obtain the same equation. $r_i^2 \log r_i^2$ is preferred to $r_i^2 \log r_i$ because it does not require the calculation of the square root of r_i^2.

SS also known as thin-plate spline describes the geometry of an elastic plate of infinite extent deforming under the imposition of vertical point loads at the data points: $\{(x_i, y_i) : i = 1, \dots, N\}$. The plate deforms under the point loads and assumes height values $\{F_i : i = 1, \dots, N\}$ at the points. As the stiffness parameter d^2 is increased, a smoother surface is obtained. When values at the points change sharply, a more elastic plate (a smaller stiffness parameter) is required to avoid the creation of fluctuations and overshoots in the surface.

Equation (7.15) contains $N + 3$ parameters. By substituting the coordinates of the N points in (7.14) into (7.15), N equations are obtained. Three more equations are obtained by imposing the following constraints:

$$\sum_{i=1}^{N} B_i = 0, \tag{7.16}$$

$$\sum_{i=1}^{N} x_i B_i = 0, \tag{7.17}$$

$$\sum_{i=1}^{N} y_i B_i = 0. \tag{7.18}$$

Constraint (7.16) ensures that the sum of the loads applied to the plate is 0 so that the plate will not move up or down. Constraints (7.17) and (7.18) ensure that moments obtained from the point loads with respect to the x- and y-axes are zero so that the plate will not rotate under the loads.

Since radial basis functions are symmetric, when feature points in the reference image are nearly uniformly spaced, SS will produce a smoothly varying mapping between the images. However, when spacing between the feature points in the reference image varies greatly across the image, SS may produce large fluctuations in the surface. To increase registration accuracy, either additional points should be selected in areas where density of points is low or some of the points in high density areas should be removed to produce nearly uniform spacing between the points.

An example of image registration using SS is given in Fig. 7.11. Using images (a) and (b) in Fig. 7.7 and the 261 homologous points obtained by Algorithm 7.2, SS produced the registration shown in Fig. 7.11a. Minor misregistration can be observed in areas where sparse homologous points are available. Because SS interpolates values at the points, it maps homologous points in the images to each other exactly. Therefore, when the points are well spread over the image domain and the homologous points are accurate, SS is expected to produce an accurate registration.

Fusion of the registered images is shown in Fig. 7.11b, enhancing the misregistered areas. The color image depicted in Fig. 7.11b is created by using the blue and green bands of the reference image and the red band of the resampled test image. Therefore, in areas where registration accuracy is high, the color of the reference image (Fig. 7.7a) is reproduced, while in misregistered areas, bluish/reddish colors are obtained. The light blue regions on the top and right side of the fused image show areas in the reference image that are out of view of the test image.

The monotonically increasing nature of logarithmic basis functions in SS ensures a smooth mapping between the images. In the presence of

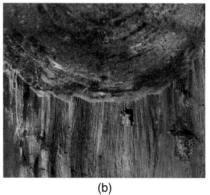

(a)   (b)

Figure 7.11 (a) Registration of images (a) and (b) in Fig. 7.7 by surface spline using the 261 homologous points in the images found by Algorithm 7.2. (b) Fusion of the registered images.

correspondence inaccuracies, however, a local inaccuracy can influence the entire registration. For that reason, when the homologous points are not accurate, transformation models that are defined in terms of monotonically decreasing basis functions are preferable. Examples of transformation models with monotonically decreasing basis functions are given below.

7.4.2 Piecewise Linear (PWL) Interpolation

If points in the reference image are triangulated, by knowing homologous points in the images, homologous triangles in the test image will be obtained. This makes it possible to compute an affine transformation from the vertices of homologous triangles and resample triangular regions in the test image one by one to the corresponding triangles in the reference image. The overall transformation becomes a composite of affine transformations. Each component of the transformation will be a PWL function.

To register images (a) and (b) in Fig. 7.7, the 261 points in the reference image were triangulated by the Delaunay triangulation. Knowing the correspondence between feature points in the images, homologous triangles were identified in the test image. Then, an affine transformation was computed from the coordinates of the vertices of corresponding triangles, and triangles in the test image were one by one mapped to the corresponding triangles in the reference image with the obtained affine transformations. This process produced the registration shown in Fig. 7.12a. The process can register image areas falling inside the convex hull of the points. Regions surrounding the convex hull of points cannot be registered by this method directly. Fusion of the registered images is shown in Fig. 7.12b.

 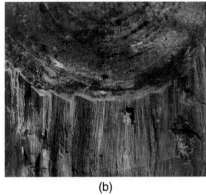

(a)   (b)

Figure 7.12 (a) Registration of images (a) and (b) in Fig. 7.7 by the piecewise affine transformation obtained from the 261 homologous points in the images. Only image areas within the convex hull of the points are registered. (b) Fusion of the registered images.

A factor that influences the registration accuracy of the piecewise affine transformation is the method used to triangulate the points. To avoid creation of elongated triangles, Delaunay triangulation [3, 4], which maximize the minimum angle in the obtained triangles is used. Improved accuracy in registration is possible if triangulation is carried out in 3-D using the points as well as the associating values. Such a triangulations is known as data-dependent triangulation and has been shown to produce smaller variations across triangle edges than Delaunay triangulation [12–18].

Although each component of the piecewise affine transformation is continuous, the transformation is not smooth across the triangle edges. The linear functions obtained over triangles that share an edge may have different gradients, producing an overall transformation that is continuous but is not smooth. This may be fine if local geometric differences between the images are small. If geometric differences between the images are not small, a transformation that can smoothly map points in the reference image to the corresponding points in the test image is required. The moving least-squares method described next can produce both approximating and interpolating functions that are smooth everywhere over the image domain and can handle large local geometric differences between the images.

7.4.3 Moving Least Squares (MLS) Approximation

If points $\{\mathbf{p}_i = (x_i, y_i): i = 1, \ldots, N\}$ with associating values $\{F_i: i = 1, \ldots, N\}$ are given, approximation by moving least squares involves finding a function $f(\mathbf{p})$ that minimizes [10]

$$\sum_{i=1}^{N} [f(\mathbf{p}_i) - F_i]^2 W_i(\mathbf{p}) \tag{7.19}$$

at each $\mathbf{p} = (x, y)$ in the approximation domain (the domain of the reference image). $W_i(\mathbf{p})$ is a nonnegative monotonically decreasing radial function, such as inverse distance or Gaussian, centered at $\mathbf{p}_i$. This weight function ensures that a data value closer to $\mathbf{p}$ will influence the value estimated at $\mathbf{p}$ more than a data value farther away.

If function $f(x, y)$ is a linear polynomial in x and y, the function approximating data in the neighborhood of (x, y) can be written as $f(x, y) = ax + by + c$. The unknown parameters a, b, and c are determined by finding the partial derivatives of the error

$$\sum_{i=1}^{N} [ax_i + by_i + c - F_i]^2 W_i(x, y) \tag{7.20}$$

with respect to a, b, and c, setting them equal to 0, and solving the equations for a, b, and c. Note that the value for $W_i(x, y)$ will be known once the location of point $\mathbf{p} = (x, y)$ is known.

Relation (7.19) is specific to point **p**; therefore, function f according to Eq. (7.19) is specific to point **p** and varies from point to point. Although a planar fit is considered locally, overall, the approximation is continuous and smooth everywhere in the approximation domain [19].

For moving least squares (MLS) to interpolate values at the points, the weight functions are taken such that $W_i(\mathbf{p})$ will assume a very large value at $\mathbf{p} = \mathbf{p}_i$, making the effect of weight functions associated with other points negligible. Some such weight functions are [20]

$$W_i(\mathbf{p}) = \frac{1}{||\mathbf{p} - \mathbf{p}_i||^2}, \tag{7.21}$$

$$W_i(\mathbf{p}) = \frac{1}{||\mathbf{p} - \mathbf{p}_i||^4} \tag{7.22}$$

$$W_i(\mathbf{p}) = \frac{\alpha \exp(-\beta||\mathbf{p} - p_i||^2)}{||\mathbf{p} - p_i||^k}, \quad \alpha, \beta, k > 0. \tag{7.23}$$

An example of image registration by approximating moving least squares with weight functions of form

$$W_i(\mathbf{p}) = \frac{1}{||\mathbf{p} - \mathbf{p}_i||^2 + d^2} \tag{7.24}$$

is given in Fig. 7.13. Parameter d^2 is meant to represent a positive number showing the stiffness of the approximating surface. When $d = 0$, the surface will be most elastic and will interpolate values at the points. As d is increased, the surface becomes smoother and will smooth noise in data. If some of the homologous points are not accurate and the inaccuracies are within a few pixels, $d=2$ pixels is appropriate. Registration of images (a) and (b) in Fig. 7.7 by MLS using the 261 homologous points obtained by Algorithm 7.2 is shown in Fig. 7.13a. Fusion of the registered images is shown in Fig. 7.13b.

 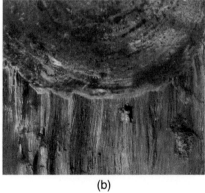

(a) (b)

Figure 7.13 (a) Registration of images (a) and (b) in Fig. 7.7 by moving least squares using the 261 homologous points in the images. (b) Fusion of the registered images.

7.4.4 Weighted Linear (WL) Approximation

The piecewise affine transformation also known as piecewise linear transformation described in Section 7.4.2 maps triangular regions in the reference image to the corresponding triangular regions in the test image. The mapping is not smooth, but it is continuous. The process is very fast and in many situations is sufficient, especially when the triangular regions are very small. However, when the triangles are large or the images have local geometric differences, inaccuracies can be observed in image registration by a piecewise linear transformation.

The MLS method discussed in the preceding section behaves locally similar to a linear function but produces an overall smooth mapping from the reference image to the test image. However, MLS becomes slow quickly as the number of homologous points in the images increases or the sizes of the images to be registered become large. MLS estimates the parameters of the best-fit linear function at each pixel in the reference image.

To speed up the computations, rather than finding the coefficients of the best-fit linear function at each pixel, the coefficients of the best-fit linear function over a small neighborhood are determined. The neighborhood can be triangular or rectangular. A weighted linear (WL) function blends local linear functions into a nonlinear function that smoothly maps points in the reference image to the corresponding points in the test image.

The local linear functions can be the linear polynomials obtained by the PWL method, or they can be the linear functions fitting to local data obtained by other means. The local functions are blended using monotonically decreasing weight functions. Therefore, locally, a WL function behaves similar to a linear function. But globally, it will be a smooth function that approximates data over the entire image domain.

Considering linear function

$$L(x, y) = ax + by + c \tag{7.25}$$

over a neighborhood of interest, parameters a, b, and c of the function are determined by using the coordinates of a minimum of three points in the reference image and one of the components of the homologous points in the test image. If points in the reference image are triangulated, the plane of the triangle with vertices

$$\{(x_k, y_k, F_k) : k = 1, 2, 3\} \tag{7.26}$$

will represent the local linear function. If $F_k = X_i$, the function will contribute to the X-component transformation, and if $F_k = Y_i$, the function will contribute to the Y-component transformation.

The linear functions can be obtained by subdividing the reference image into small regions and fitting a linear function to the points and associating values (the X-component or the Y-component of the homologous points) within each region and using a weighted sum of the linear functions as a component of the transformation.

A WL function is defined by

$$f(x, y) = \sum_{j=1}^{m} A_j W_j(x, y) L_j(x, y),$$ (7.27)

where $L_j(x, y) = a_j x + b_j y + c_j$ is the jth linear function, $W_j(x, y)$ is the jth monotonically decreasing weight function, and A_j is the coefficient of the jth function to ensure that $f(\bar{x}_j, \bar{y}_j) = L_j(\bar{x}_j, \bar{y}_j)$, for $j = 1, \ldots, m$. $(\bar{x}_j, \bar{y}_j)$ are the coordinates of the centroid of the jth neighborhood in the reference image. The number of linear functions, m, is much smaller than the number of points, N.

The jth linear and weight functions are computed over the jth neighborhood in the reference image. Therefore, if the reference image is subdivided into triangular regions, the coefficients of the jth linear function are estimated in such a way to best fit data within the jth triangle, and the weight function associated with the jth triangle is centered at $(\bar{x}_j, \bar{y}_j)$, the center of gravity of points within the jth triangle in the reference image. If reference image is subdivided into rectangular neighborhoods, the coefficients of the jth linear function are obtained to best fit data within the jth rectangle, and the jth weight function is centered at $(\bar{x}_j, \bar{y}_j)$, the center of gravity of points within the jth rectangle in the reference image.

Any monotonically decreasing radial function can be used as the weight function. If the inverse square distance weight function of Eq. (7.24) is used, that is, if

$$W_j(x, y) = \frac{1}{(x - \bar{x}_j)^2 + (y - \bar{y}_j)^2 + d^2},$$ (7.28)

coefficients $\{A_j : j = 1, \ldots, m\}$ are determined such that $f(\bar{x}_j, \bar{y}_j) = L_j(\bar{x}_j, \bar{y}_j)$ for $j = 1, \ldots, m$. Function $f(x, y)$ interpolates $L_j(x, y)$ at $(\bar{x}_j, \bar{y}_j)$ and approximates data from which the local linear functions were estimated. Therefore, function $f(x, y)$ approximates values at the points.

An example of image registration by WL approximation when using images (a) and (b) in Fig. 7.7 and the 261 homologous points found by Algorithm 7.2 is shown in Fig. 7.14. Points in the reference image are triangulated, a linear function is defined over each triangle in the reference image using the vertices of the triangle in the reference image and the X- or the Y-component of the corresponding triangle vertices in the test image. A weighted sum of the local linear functions is then used as a component of the transformation when registering the images. The monotonically decreasing function defined by Eq. (7.24) where $d = 2$ pixels is used to blend the local linear functions into two globally smooth surfaces that map points in the reference image to the corresponding points in the test image.

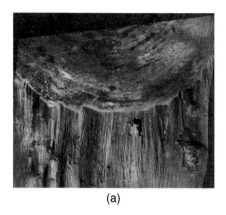

(a)   (b)

Figure 7.14 (a) Registration of images (a) and (b) in Fig. 7.7 by WL approximation using the weight functions defined by (7.24) with $d = 2$ pixels and the 261 homologous points found by Algorithm 7.2. (b) Fusion of the registered images.

To evaluate the quality of registrations obtained by SS, PWL, MLS, and WL transformations in registration of the images in Fig. 7.7, the correlation coefficient of red, green, and blue components of corresponding pixels in registered images is used. Registration by SS, PWL, MLS, and WL transformations produced correlation coefficients 0.831, 0.8333, 0.7353, and 0.6980, respectively. Excluding PWL since it uses areas within the convex hull of the points where errors are usually small, we see that SS has produced the most accurate registration. Next, registration accuracy of these transformation models will be determined using simulation data where true correspondence between points in the images is known.

7.4.5 Performance Evaluation

To provide a more objective evaluation of various transformation models in nonrigid registration, simulation data where true registration results are known were used. Performances of various elastic transformation models under changes in density and organization of points as well as the presence and absence of noise are determined. The performance measures considered are registration root-mean-squared error (RMSE) and computation time.

Consider selecting N random points in the reference image. Denoting the ith point by (x_i, y_i), the coordinates of the corresponding point in the test image, (X_i, Y_i), are computed from

$$X_i = (1 + (d/R)\sin(\pi r_i/R)(x_i - x_0) + X_0, \tag{7.29}$$
$$Y_i = (1 + (d/R)\sin(\pi r_i/R)(y_i - y_0) + Y_0, \tag{7.30}$$

where $r_i = \sqrt{(x_i - x_0)^2 + (y_i - y_0)^2}$, R is half the diameter of the reference image, and (x_0, y_0) are the coordinates of the reference image center. The deformation defined by Eqs (7.29) and (7.30) are similar to a lens' radial distortion.

Considering reference and test images of dimensions 513×513 and letting $x_0 = 256$, $y_0 = 256$, $X_0 = 240$, $Y_0 = 240$, and $d = 10$ pixels, the coordinates of $N = 20$ homologous points were determined in the images as shown in images (a) and (b) in Fig. 7.15. Adding uniformly distributed noise between -3 and $+3$

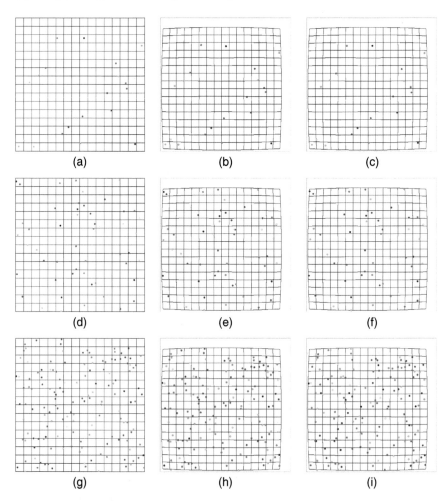

(a)   (b)   (c)

(d)   (e)   (f)

(g)   (h)   (i)

Figure 7.15 (a) A synthetically generated reference image with 20 randomly selected feature points. (b) The test image obtained by transforming the reference image using Eqs (7.29) and (7.30). (c) Same as (b) but adding noise to the feature points there. (d)–(f) Same as (a)–(c) but using 50 homologous points. (g)–(i) Same as (a)–(c) but using 150 homologous points. Homologous points in reference and test images are shown with the same color.

pixels to the coordinates of the points in the test image, the points shown in image (c) are obtained. The homologous points shown in (a) and (b) are accurate, while the homologous points shown in (a) and (c) contain inaccuracies of up to 3 pixels. By increasing N to 50, the homologous points shown in (d)–(f) are obtained, and by increasing N to 150, the homologous points shown in (g)–(i) are obtained.

Knowing Eqs (7.29) and (7.30) represent the true relation between the reference and test images, the coordinates of homologous grid points in the images are used to measure the registration RMSE using the transformation models described in the preceding sections. There are 17×17 grid points in the images. Denoting the coordinates of the ijth grid point in the reference image by (x_{ij}, y_{ij}) and the coordinates of the same grid point in the test image by (X_{ij}, Y_{ij}), registration RMSE at the grid points when using a particular transformation model is computed from

$$\text{RMSE} = \sqrt{\frac{1}{17 \times 17} \sum_{i=0}^{16} \sum_{j=0}^{16} [X_{ij} - f_x(x_{ij}, y_{ij})]^2 + [Y_{ij} - f_y(x_{ij}, y_{ij})]^2}, \quad (7.31)$$

where f_x and f_y are the x-component and the y-component of the transformation model registering the images.

Figure 7.15 shows the six images sets (a and b), (a and c), (d and e), (d and f), (g and h), and (g and i) used in the evaluation. Image sets (a and b), (d and e), and (g and h) contain accurate homologous points, while image sets (a and c), (d and f), (g and i) contain inaccurate homologous points. The coordinates of homologous points in the images were used to register the images using SS, PWL, MLS, and WL transformations. The registration results are shown in Figs 7.16, 7.17, and 7.18 for 20, 50, and 150 homologous points, respectively. The RMSE and the computation time of each transformation model using the six data sets are summarized in Table 7.1.

When the homologous points are accurate, by increasing the number of homologous points, all methods reduce the RMSE and at the same time increase the computation time. These results are expected. When noise is present and so the homologous points are not accurate, increasing the number of homologous points may not reduce RMSE.

PWL transformation has produced the lowest RMSE measures when using accurate homologous points, but that is partly due to calculating the errors at grid points that fall inside the convex hull of the points where errors are generally smaller than at grid points that fall outside the convex hull of the points.

When the homologous points are accurate, interpolation methods (SS and PWL) produce lower RMSE measures than approximation methods (MLS and WL). However, when the homologous points are not accurate, approximation methods produce lower RMSE measures than interpolation methods.

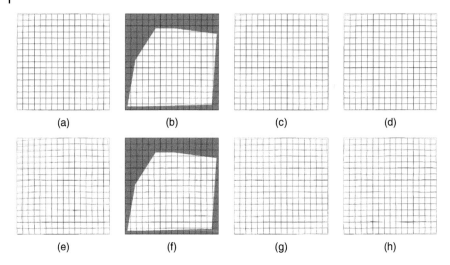

Figure 7.16 Registration of the grid images depicted in Fig. 7.15a and b by (a) surface spline, (b) piecewise linear, (c) moving least squares, and (d) weighted linear transformations when using the 20 accurate homologous points in the images. (e)–(h) The same as (a)–(d) but when using the 20 noisy (inaccurate) homologous points in the images.

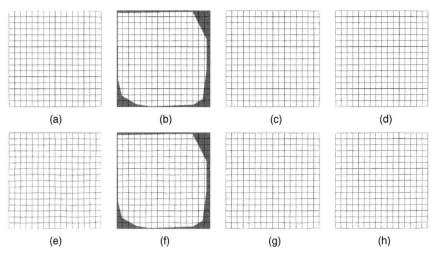

Figure 7.17 Similar to Fig. 7.16 but using 50 homologous points in the images.

The computation times included in Table 7.1 are in seconds, measured on a Windows PC with an Intel Centrino 2 processor. The computational requirements of the four methods are close although SS and WL require somewhat less time than PWL and MLS.

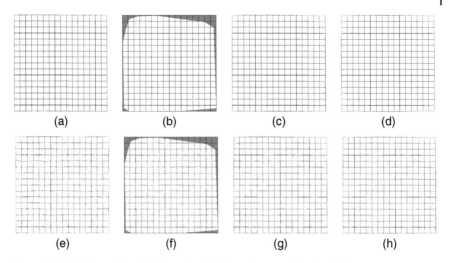

Figure 7.18 Similar to Fig. 7.16 but using 150 homologous points in the images.

Table 7.1 Registration root-mean-squared error (RMSE) in pixels measured at grid points when registering the image sets in Fig. 7.15 using surface spline (SS), piecewise linear (PWL), moving least squares (MLS), and weighted linear (WL) transformations. Results on noisy homologous points are signified by "Noisy" in the leftmost column. The computation times are in seconds shown under "TME."

Number of points	SS		PWL		MLS		WL	
	RMSE	TME	RMSE	TME	RMSE	TME	RMSE	TME
20	1.31	0.50	0.93	0.84	1.51	1.81	1.48	0.62
20 Noisy	4.02	0.49	1.99	0.83	2.84	1.23	2.63	0.61
50	0.71	1.11	0.60	2.06	1.16	2.36	1.26	1.52
50 Noisy	2.65	1.18	1.99	2.06	1.99	2.30	1.98	1.52
150	0.48	4.41	0.36	6.67	0.95	9.68	1.13	4.51
150 Noisy	2.68	4.56	2.10	6.68	1.62	7.38	1.60	4.50

7.4.6 Choosing the Right Transformation Model

If some information about the geometries of the images to be registered is available, a suitable transformation model to register the images can be chosen. Some transformation models adapt better than others to local geometric differences between the images. If no information about the geometries of the images to be registered is available, an adaptive transformation should be used to register the images. PWL, MLS, and WL are locally adaptive transformation models. Although SS can also represent nonlinear geometric difference between two images, because of its monotonically increasing basis functions, SS can spread a local inaccuracy over the entire image domain.

A required property of a transformation model is for it to preserve rigidity if the images have only translational and rotational differences. If two images are truly related by a rigid transformation, the adaptive transformation model used to register the images should closely follow the rigid transformation to register the images.

An adaptive transformation model should adapt to the spacing between the points in the reference image, which defines the domain of the approximation/interpolation. If density of points in the reference image is high in some areas and low in other areas, the local functions used to define local geometric differences between images should adapt to the density and organization of the points. By ensuring that sum of the weights everywhere in the image domain is 1, rational weights stretch the basis functions in areas where the density of points is low and shrink the basis functions in areas where the density of points is high. Therefore, when density of points vary greatly across the image domain, approximating/interpolating functions that use rational basis functions, such as rational Gaussians [21], are preferred to transformation models that use radial basis functions.

SS uses radially symmetric and monotonically increasing basis functions everywhere independent of the local density and organization of the points. Also, an inaccurate correspondence can influence the entire registration. Therefore, SS is not suitable when density of points across the reference image varies or some of the homologous points are inaccurate. However, if the density of points in the reference image does not change greatly and the homologous points are accurate, SS can produce a registration that is as accurate as any locally sensitive transformation models and in a shorter time.

7.5 Further Reading

Although Approximation Theory is a well-established area in mathematics, its results were unknown to image registration until the mid-1980s. A series of papers appearing during the 1980s demonstrated the power of approximation and interpolation methods in nonrigid registration [5, 7, 22–24]. During the 1990s, the desire to register medical images prompted the development of various nonrigid registration methods for medical images [6, 25–32]. During the 2000s, focus shifted to efficient and locally adaptive methods for the registration of images with local geometric differences [9, 11, 33–37].

Most recent approaches to nonrigid image registration have used WL approximation using Gaussian [38] and rational Gaussian weights [39], parametric Shepard interpolation [40], splines incorporating local gradients [41], functions that locally mimic homographies [42], nonradial basis functions

[43, 44], elastodynamics principles [45], local optimization [46], subdivision [1, 2, 47], conformal mapping [48], deconvolution of joint statistics [49], shape models [50, 51], graph cuts [52], and incorporation of information from image segmentation to image registration [53].

A great number of methods have been developed for the approximation and interpolation of scattered data in the plane. These methods can be used to elastically register images. Surveys of approximation/interpolation methods can be found in [54–60].

Readers interested in nonrigid registration may find the reviews and evaluations reported in [61–65] useful.

References

1 Y. Cai, X. Guoa, Z. Zhong, and W. Mao, Dynamic meshing for deformable image registration, *Computer-Aided Design*, **58**:141–150, 2015.

2 Z. Wu and A. Goshtasby, A subdivision approach to image registration, *IEEE Transactions on Image Processing*, **21**(5):2464–2473, 2012.

3 P. J. Green and R. Sibson, Computing Dirichlet tessellation in the plane, *Computer Journal*, **21**:168–173, 1978.

4 C. L. Lawson, Software for C^1 surface interpolation, in *Mathematical Software III*, J. R. Rice (Ed.), Academic Press, New York, 161–194, 1977.

5 A. Goshtasby, Registration of image with geometric distortion, *IEEE Transactions on Geoscience and Remote Sensing*, **26**(1):60–64, 1988.

6 F. L. Bookstein, Principal warps: thin-plate splines and the decomposition of deformations, *IEEE Transactions on Pattern Analysis and Machine Intelligence*, **11**(6):567–585, 1989.

7 A. Goshtasby, Piecewise linear mapping functions for image registration, *Pattern Recognition*, **19**(6):459–466, 1986.

8 D. Holtkamp and A. Goshtasby, Precision registration and mosaicking of multicamera images, *IEEE Transactions on Geoscience and Remote Sensing*, **47**(10):3446–3455, 2009.

9 M. Linger and A. Goshtasby, Aerial image registration for tracking, *IEEE Transactions on Geoscience and Remote Sensing*, **53**(4):2137–2145, 2015.

10 P. Lancaster and K. Šalkauskas, Surfaces generated by moving least squares methods, *Mathematics of Computation*, **37**(155):141–158, 1981.

11 B. Jackson and A. Goshtasby, Adaptive registration of very large images, in IEEE Conf. Computer Vision and Pattern Recognition, Columbus, OH, 351–356, June 2014.

12 M. Bertram, J. C. Barnes, B. Hamann, K. I. Joy, H. Pottmann, and D. Wushour, Piecewise optimal triangulation for the approximation of scattered data in the plane, *Computer Aided Geometric Design*, **17**:767–787, 2000.

13 J. L. Brown, Vertex based data dependent triangulations, *Computer Aided Geometric Design*, **8**:239–251, 1991.

14 N. Dyn, D. Levin, and S. Rippa, Algorithms for the construction of data dependent triangulation, in *Algorithms for Approximation II*, J. C. Mason and M. G. Cox (Eds.), Chapman and Hall Pub., New York, 185–192, 1988.

15 N. Dyn, D. Levin, and S. Rippa, Data dependent triangulation for piecewise linear interpolation, *IMA Journal of Numerical Analysis*, **10**:137–154, 1990.

16 N. Dyn, D. Levin, and J. A. Gregory, A butterfly subdivision scheme for surface interpolation with tension control, *ACM Transactions on Graphics*, **9**(2):160–169, 1990.

17 S. Rippa, Scattered data interpolation using minimum energy Powell-Sabin elements and data dependent triangulations, *Numerical Algorithms*, **5**:577–587, 1993.

18 L. L. Schumaker, Computing optimal triangulations using simulated annealing, *Computer Aided Geometric Design*, **10**:329–345, 1993.

19 P. Lancaster, Moving weighted least-squares methods, in *Polynomial and Spline Approximation*, B. N. Sahney (Ed.), NATO Advanced Study Institute Series C, Reidel, Dordrecht, 103–120, 1979.

20 P. Lancaster and K. Šalkauskas, *Curve and Surface Fitting: An Introduction*, Academic Press, New York, 55–62 and 225–244, 1986.

21 A. Goshtasby, Design and recovery of 2-D and 3-D shapes using rational Gaussian curves and surfaces, *International Journal of Computer Vision*, **10**(3):233–256, 1993.

22 A. Goshtasby, Piecewise cubic mapping functions for image registration, *Pattern Recognition*, **20**(5):525–533, 1987.

23 A. Goshtasby, Image registration by local approximation methods, *Image and Vision Computing*, **6**(4):255–261, 1988.

24 A. Goshtasby, Correction of image deformation from lens distortion using Bezier patches, *Computer Vision, Graphics, and Image Processing*, **47**:385–394, 1989.

25 J. Ashburner and K. J. Friston, Nonlinear spatial normalization using basis functions, *Human Brain Mapping*, **7**:254–266, 1999.

26 R. Bajcsy and S. Kovačič, Multiresolution elastic matching, *Computer Vision, Graphics, and Image Processing*, **46**:1–21, 1989.

27 G. E. Christensen and H. J. Johnson, Consistent image registration, *IEEE Transactions on Medical Imaging*, **20**(7):568–582, 2001.

28 R. Dann, J. Hoford, S. Kovacic, and M. Reivich, and R. Bajcsy, Evaluation of elastic matching system for anatomic (CT, MR) and functional (PET) cerebral images, *Journal of Computer Assisted Tomography*, **13**(4):603–611, 1989.

29 C. A. Davatzikos, J. L. Prince, and R. N. Bryan, Image registration based on boundary mapping, *IEEE Transactions on Medical Imaging*, **15**(1):112–115, 1996.

30 B. Likar and F. Pernuš, A hierarchical approach to elastic registration based on mutual information, *Image and Vision Computing*, **19**:33–44, 2001.

31 D. Rueckert, L. Sonoda, C. Hayes, D. Hill, M. Leach, and D. Hawkes, Non-rigid registration using free-form deformations: application to breast MR images, *IEEE Transactions on Medical Imaging*, **18**(8):712–721, 1999.

32 J. A. Schnabel, T. Christine, A. D. Castellano-Smith, et al., Validation of nonrigid image registration using finite-element methods: application to breast MR images, *IEEE Transactions on Medical Imaging*, **22**(2):238–247, 2003.

33 E. Ardizzone, O. Gambino, M. La Cascia, L. Lo Presti, and R. Pirrone, Multi-modal non-rigid registration of medical images based on mutual information maximization, in 14th International Conference on Image Analysis and Processing, 743–750, 2007.

34 C. Buerger, T. Schaeffer, and A. P. King, Hierarchical adaptive local affine registration for fast and robust respiratory motion estimation, *Medical Image Analysis*, **15**:551–564, 2011.

35 G. E. Christensen, X. Geng, J. G. Kuhl, et al., Introduction to the non-rigid image registration evaluation project, in *Biomedical Image Registration*, Lecture Notes in Computer Science, J. P. W. Pluim, B. Likar, and F. A. Gerritsen, (Eds.) Springer, Berlin, Heidelberg, Vol. **4057**, 128–135, 2006.

36 H. Park, P. H. Bland, K. K. Brock, and C. R. Meyer, Adaptive registration using local information measures, *Medical Image Analysis*, **8**:465–473, 2004.

37 Y.-T. Wu, T. Kanade, C.-C. Li, and J. Cohn, Image registration using wavelet-based motion model, *International Journal of Computer Vision*, **38**(2):129–152, 2000.

38 A. Goshtasby, A weighted linear method for approximation of irregularly spaced data, in *Geometric Modeling and Computing*, M. M. Lucian and M. Neamtu (Eds.), Nashboro Press, Brentwood, TN, 285–294, 2004.

39 A. Goshtasby, Registration of multiview images, in *Image Registration for Remote Sensing*, J. Le Moigne, N. Netanyahu, and R. Eastman (Eds.), Cambridge Press, 153–178, 2011.

40 A. Goshtasby, Suitability of parametric Shepard interpolation for nonrigid image registration, in *Approximation Theory XIV*, G. E. Fasshauer and L. L. Schumaker (Eds.), Springer, 1–18, 2014.

41 K. Rohr, M. Forenefett, and H. S. Stiehl, Spline-based elastic image registration: integration of landmark errors and orientation attributes, *Computer Vision and Image Understanding*, **90**:153–168, 2003.

42 D. Pizzarro, R. Khan, and A. Bartoli, Schwarp: locally projective image warps based on 2D Schwarzian derivatives, *International Journal of Computer Vision*, **119**:93–109, 2016.

43 S. Wörz and K. Rohr, Physics-based elastic registration using non-radial basis functions and including landmark localization uncertainties, *Computer Vision and Image Understanding*, **111**:263–274, 2008.

44 S. Wörz and K. Rohr, Spline-based hybrid image registration using landmark and intensity information based on matrix-valued non-radial basis functions, *International Journal of Computer Vision*, **106**:76–92, 2014.

45 S. Ahmad and M. S. Khan, Deformable image registration based on elasto-dynamics, *Machine Vision and Applications*, **26**:689–710, 2015.

46 X. Lu, H. Ma, and B. Zhang, A non-rigid medical image registration method based on improved linear elastic model, *Optik*, **123**:1867–1873, 2012.

47 G. Agam and R. Singh, Efficient subdivision-based image and volume warping, in IEEE Conference on Computer Vision and Pattern Recognition, 1–7, 2008.

48 S. Marsland, R. I. McLachlan, K. Modin, and M. Perlmutter, Geodesic warps by conformal mappings, *International Journal of Computer Vision*, **105**:144–154, 2013.

49 D. Pilutti, M. Strumia, and S. Hadjidemetriou, Bimodal nonrigid registration of brain MRI data with deconvolution of joint statistics, *IEEE Transactions on Image Processing*, **23**(9):3999–4009, 2014.

50 H. Hotani, Y. Tsunekawa, and Y. Sawada, Accurate and robust registration of nonrigid surface using hierarchical statistical shape model, in IEEE Conference on Computer Vision and Pattern Recognition, 2977–2984, 2013.

51 M. Taron, N. Paragios, and M.-P. Jolly, Registration with uncertainties and statistical modeling of shapes with variable metric kernels, *IEEE Transactions on Pattern Analysis and Machine Intelligence*, **31**(1):99–113, 2009.

52 R. W. K. So, T. W. H. Tang, and A. C. S. Chung, Non-rigid image registration of brain magnetic resonance images using graph-cuts, *Pattern Recognition*, **44**:2450–2467, 2011.

53 D. Mahapatra and Y. Sun, Integrating segmentation information for improved MRF-based elastic image registration, *IEEE Transactions on Image Processing*, **21**(1):170–183, 2012.

54 R. Franke, Scattered data interpolation: test of some methods, *Mathematics of Computation*, **33**(157):181–200, 1982.

55 R. Franke and L. L. Schumaker, A bibliography of multivariate approximation, in *Topics in Multivariate Approximation*, C. K. Chui, L. L. Schumaker, and F. I. Uteceras (Eds.), Academic Press, New York, 275–335, 1987.

56 E. Grosse, A catalogue of algorithms for approximation, in *Algorithms for Approximation II*, J. C. Mason and M. Cox (Eds.), Chapman and Hall, New York, 479–514, 1990.

57 C. A. Micchelli, Interpolation of scattered data: distance metrics and conditionally positive definite functions, *Constructive Approximation*, **2**:11–22, 1986.

58 M. A. Sabin, Contouring - a review of methods for scattered data, in *Mathematical Methods in Computer Graphics and Design*, K. Brodlie (Ed.), Academic Press, 63–86, 1980.

59 L. L. Schumaker, Fitting surfaces to scattered data, in *Approximation Theory II*, G. G. Lorentz, C. K. Chui, and L. L. Schumaker (Eds.), Academic Press, New York, 203–268, 1976.

60 V. Weiss, L. Andor, G. Renner, and T. Varady, Advanced surface fitting techniques, *Computer Aided Geometric Design*, **19**:19–42, 2002.

61 W. Crum, T. Hartkens, and D. Hill, Non-rigid image registration: theory and practice, *British Journal of Radiology*, **77**(2):140–153, 2004.

62 M. Holden, A review of geometric transformations for nonrigid body registration, *IEEE Transactions on Medical Imaging*, **27**(1):111–128, 2008.

63 A. Sotiras, C. Davatzikos, and N. Paragios, Deformable medical image registration: a survey, *IEEE Transactions on Medical Imaging*, **32**(7):1153–1190, 2013.

64 L. Zagorchev and A. Goshtasby, A comparative study of transformation functions for nonrigid image registration, *IEEE Transactions on Image Processing*, **15**(3):529–538, 2006.

65 B. Zitova and J. Flusser, Image registration methods: a survey, *Image and Vision Computing*, **21**(11):977–1000, 2003.

8

Volume Image Registration

8.1   Introduction

While a projective image represents a projection of a 3-D scene onto a plane and is represented by a 2-D array of numbers, a tomographic image is a 3-D array of numbers obtained from a sequence of 2-D cross sections of a 3-D object.

Volume elements (voxels) in a tomographic image are usually longer in the z direction than in the x and y directions. This is because the distance between adjacent pixels in a cross section is usually smaller than the distance between adjacent cross sections. To simplify various image registration steps, a tomographic volume is resampled to an isotropic volume with cubic voxels.

If voxels in a reference tomographic volume are of dimensions $d_1 \times d_1 \times d_2$ mm^3, and the volume is resampled to an isotropic volume with voxels of dimensions $d \times d \times d$ mm^3, the transformation required for this resampling will be

$$\mathbf{R} = \begin{bmatrix} d_1/d & 0 & 0 \\ 0 & d_1/d & 0 \\ 0 & 0 & d_2/d \end{bmatrix}. \tag{8.1}$$

If voxel $\mathbf{p}$ in the isotropic reference volume has coordinates (x, y, z), the intensity at the voxel will be the intensity at $\mathbf{p}' = (x', y', z')$ in the tomographic reference volume, where

$$\mathbf{p}' = \mathbf{Rp}. \tag{8.2}$$

Therefore, to resample a tomographic volume into an isotropic volume, the intensity at voxel $\mathbf{p}$ in the isotropic volume is set to the intensity at $\mathbf{p}'$ in the tomographic volume.

If the intensity at the voxel nearest to (x', y', z') in the tomographic volume is used as the intensity at (x, y, z) in the isotropic volume, the resampling method is called *nearest-neighbor*. If $\mathbf{p}' = (x', y', z')$ is obtained from Eq. (8.2), x', y', and z' are usually floating-point numbers; therefore, the intensity at $(\text{round}(x'), \text{round}(y'), \text{round}(z'))$ in the tomographic volume is read and saved

Theory and Applications of Image Registration, First Edition. Arthur Ardeshir Goshtasby.
© 2017 John Wiley & Sons, Inc. Published 2017 by John Wiley & Sons, Inc.

at (x, y, z) in the isotropic volume. Nearest-neighbor resampling preserves original intensities, keeping the original tissue properties in the resampled volume, avoiding introduction of partial volume effects [1].

Similarly, the tomographic test volume is resampled to an isotropic volume with voxels the same size as voxels in the isotropic reference volume. If voxels in the tomographic test volume are of dimensions $D_1 \times D_1 \times D_2$ mm^3, to resample it to an isotropic volume with voxels of dimensions $d \times d \times d$ mm^3, the following transformation is needed:

$$S = \begin{bmatrix} D_1/d & 0 & 0 \\ 0 & D_1/d & 0 \\ 0 & 0 & D_2/d \end{bmatrix}. \tag{8.3}$$

The intensity at voxel $\mathbf{P} = (X, Y, Z)$ in the isotropic test volume is set to the intensity at $\mathbf{P'} = (X', Y', Z')$ in the tomographic test volume, where

$$\mathbf{P'} = \mathbf{SP}. \tag{8.4}$$

Since X', Y', and Z' represent floating-point numbers, the intensity of the voxel closest to (X', Y', Z') is used as the intensity at (X, Y, Z). More specifically, the intensity at $(\text{round}(X'), \text{round}(Y'), \text{round}(Z'))$ in the tomographic test volume is taken and saved at (X, Y, Z) in the isotropic test volume.

Steps in registration of volumetric images are similar to steps in registration of 2-D images. In the remainder of this chapter, volumetric image will be referred to as *volume* or *image*. If two volumes are in the same modality, a set of points is detected in each volume, correspondence is established between the points, and from the coordinates of corresponding points in the volumes, a transformation model is determined to warp the test volume to the geometry of the reference volume, enabling spatial alignment of the volumes.

If the volumes are in different modalities, points are detected in the reference volume and the points are searched in the test volume by template matching using an appropriate similarity or distance measure.

Given a reference volume and a test volume with cubic voxels of the same size, in the following sections, the steps to register the volumes are provided. If the volumes are known to have translational and rotation differences, the volumes are registered by a rigid transformation. The rigidity constraint makes it possible to establish correspondence between points in the volumes by random sample consensus (RANSAC) [2] (Section 5.2.2).

If the volumes cannot be considered rigid bodies, information about the neighborhood of a point in the reference volume is used to find the same point in the test volume. Having a set of homologous points in the volumes, the parameters of an elastic transformation are determined and the test volume is resampled to the space of the reference volume, spatially aligning the volumes.

In the following sections, first, methods for detecting feature points in volumetric images are discussed. Then, methods for determining homologous points in images are detailed. Next, various transformation models for registration of volumetric images are described and examples of volume image registration are given. Finally, literature relating to volume image registration is reviewed.

8.2 Feature Point Detection

Many of the 2-D feature point detectors described in Chapter 3 can be extended to 3-D and used to detect feature points in volumes. In this section, extensions of some of the 2-D detectors to 3-D are discussed.

8.2.1 Central Moments

As discussed in Section 3.2.1, central moments are more useful when intensity gradients rather than raw intensities are used. Locally extremum central moments detect highly detailed neighborhoods in an image. The centroids of such neighborhoods can be used as points. Central moments of intensity gradients of order pqr in an $n \times n \times n$ region centered at (x_0, y_0, z_0) in a volumetric image is computed from

$$
\mu_{pqr}^{I_g(x,y,z)}(x_0, y_0, z_0)
$$

$$
= \sum_{x=x_0-n/2}^{x_0+n/2} \sum_{y=y_0-n/2}^{y_0+n/2} \sum_{z=z_0-n/2}^{z_0+n/2} (x - x_0)^p (y - y_0)^q (z - z_0)^r I_g(x, y, z), \quad (8.5)
$$

where

$$
I_g(x, y, z) = \{I_x^2(x, y, z) + I_y^2(x, y, z) + I_z^2(x, y, z)\}^{\frac{1}{2}} \quad (8.6)
$$

is the intensity gradient magnitude at (x, y, z). To compute central moments for a spherical region of radius R centered at (x_0, y_0, z_0), only values of x, y, and z in Eq. (8.5) that satisfy $R \geq \sqrt{(x - x_0)^2 + (y - y_0)^2 + (z - z_0)^2}$ are used.

Central moments characterize the geometric properties of the gradient pattern centered at (x_0, y_0, z_0). For each combination of $p \geq 0$, $q \geq 0$, and $r \geq 0$, where $p + q + r \geq 1$, a geometric property is obtained. By looking for local extrema of a property within a volume, locally unique gradient patterns are located in the volume.

Central moments are not rotation invariant. Therefore, they are suitable for registration of images with only translational differences. If the images are rotated with respect to each other, in order to detect the same physical points in the images, there is a need to use measures that are rotation invariant. Yang et al. [3] describe 3-D rotation-invariant Gaussian–Hermite moments that are independent of an image's orientation.

8.2.2 Entropy

The entropy of intensities in a region depends on the distribution of the intensities within the region. To determine the entropy of a spherical region centered at a voxel in an image, first, the probability distribution of intensities within the region is determined. If $p(i)$ is the probability that a randomly selected voxel in the region will have intensity i, the entropy of the region is computed from

$$E = -\sum_{i=\min}^{\max} p(i)\log_2 p(i). \tag{8.7}$$

Probability $p(i)$ is the number of voxels with intensity i divided by the total number of voxels in the region, and min and max in Eq. (8.7) are the minimum and maximum intensities in the region, respectively.

Points of locally maximum entropy represent centers of highly informative neighborhoods in a volume. This measure is rotationally invariant and can be used to detect the same points in images that are rotated with respect to each other.

8.2.3 LoG Operator

The Laplacian of Gaussian (LoG) operator in 3-D is defined by

$$\begin{aligned} \mathrm{LoG} &= \frac{\partial^2 G(x,y,z)}{\partial x^2} + \frac{\partial^2 G(x,y,z)}{\partial y^2} + \frac{\partial^2 G(x,y,z)}{\partial z^2}, \\ &= \frac{d^2 G(x)}{dx^2}G(y)G(z) + \frac{d^2 G(y)}{dy^2}G(x)G(z) + \frac{d^2 G(z)}{dz^2}G(x)G(y). \end{aligned} \tag{8.8}$$

The response of a LoG operator to a spherical blob reaches a peak when the scale of the LoG matches the size of the blob. The relation between the scale σ of the LoG and the diameter D of the blob is $D = 2\sqrt{3}\sigma$ by extending the result in [4] to 3-D.

Although the response of a LoG operator of scale σ to a blob of diameter D decreases as the difference between D and $2\sqrt{3}\sigma$ increases, the same LoG operator may produce locally peak responses for blobs with diameters quite different from D depending on the shape of the blob. For image registration purposes, one may let $\sigma = 2$ or 3 voxel units and mark voxels with locally maximum or minimum LoG responses as points. A voxel unit is considered to be the distance between adjacent voxels along the coordinate axes.

Centers of circular blobs make more reliable points than centers of irregularly shaped blobs. This is because by changing image resolution slightly, circular blobs and, therefore, their centers, remain stationary. An irregularly shaped or branching blob, however, may break into pieces when changing image resolution, displacing its center.

To detect stable points, those points that remain stationary under changes in σ are kept and the rest are discarded. Therefore, after detecting points with a LoG operator of scale σ, points are detected with LoGs of scales $\sigma \pm \delta\sigma$ and only those points that remain stationary under small changes in scale are kept and the rest are discarded. $\delta\sigma$ is typically 0.5 voxel units.

Note that, since the images under consideration are isotropic and in the same scale, there is no need to use a scale-invariant point detector when detecting points in volumetric images. When registering volumetric images, since the scales of the images are known, both images can be resampled to the same scale. Therefore, homologous points in images will represent centers of blobs of the same size, requiring LoG operators of the same scale to detect homologous points in the images.

The points detected by the LoG operator are rotationally invariant; therefore, they can be used to register images that are rotated with respect to each other.

8.2.4 First-Derivative Intensities

The square gradient matrix introduced by Förstner [5, 6] and used to detect corners in 2-D images [7, 8] can be extended to 3-D to detect corners in volumes.

The square gradient matrix in 3-D is defined by

$$\mathbf{N}(x,y,z) = \begin{bmatrix} \overline{I_x^2(x,y,z)} & \overline{I_x(x,y,z)I_y(x,y,z)} & \overline{I_x(x,y,z)I_z(x,y,z)} \\ \overline{I_y(x,y,z)I_x(x,y,z)} & \overline{I_y^2(x,y,z)} & \overline{I_y(x,y,z)I_z(x,y,z)} \\ \overline{I_z(x,y,z)I_x(x,y,z)} & \overline{I_z(x,y,z)I_y(x,y,z)} & \overline{I_z^2(x,y,z)} \end{bmatrix},$$

$$(8.9)$$

where the overline implies averaging in the neighborhood of (x,y,z). For example, if a neighborhood of size $n \times n \times n$ is taken, n being an odd number, $\overline{I_x^2(x,y,z)}$ is computed from

$$\overline{I_x^2(x,y,z)} = \frac{1}{n^3} \sum_{a=-n/2}^{n/2} \sum_{b=-n/2}^{n/2} \sum_{c=-n/2}^{n/2} I_x^2(x+a,y+b,z+c). \qquad (8.10)$$

Similarly, other terms in the square gradient matrix in Eq. (8.9) are computed. Local maxima of det(**N**) have been used [9, 10] as corners in volumetric images.

Local maxima of det(**N**)/trace(**N**), where N is a 2-D square gradient matrix, have been used as corners in 2-D images [5]. When N is a 3×3 square gradient matrix, local maxima of det(**N**)/(trace(**N**))^2 have been used as corners in volumetric images [11]. While maximizing det(**N**) detects neighborhoods where overall gradients in orthogonal directions are locally maximum, maximizing det(**N**)/(trace(**N**))^2 detects neighborhoods where not only overall gradients in orthogonal directions are locally high, but also the gradients in the three orthogonal directions are well balanced, detecting more well-defined corners.

8.2.5 Second-Derivative Intensities

The matrix of second-derivative intensities known as the Hessian matrix used by Beaudet [12] to detect corners in 2-D images can be extended to 3-D to detect corners in volumetric images. The Hessian matrix in 3-D is defined by

$$\mathbf{H}(x, y, z) = \begin{bmatrix} I_{xx}(x, y, z) & I_{xy}(x, y, z) & I_{xz}(x, y, z) \\ I_{yx}(x, y, z) & I_{yy}(x, y, z) & I_{yz}(x, y, z) \\ I_{zx}(x, y, z) & I_{zy}(x, y, z) & I_{zz}(x, y, z) \end{bmatrix}. \tag{8.11}$$

$I_{xx}(x, y, z)$ implies second-derivative image intensities in x direction at (x, y, z), $I_{xy}(x, y, z)$ implies derivative in x direction and then in y direction at (x, y, z), and so on. Since it is usually required to smooth an image to reduce noise before finding its derivatives, and since a 3-D Gaussian $G(x, y, z)$ can be split into three 1-D Gaussians $G(x)G(y)G(z)$, smoothing image $I(x, y, z)$ by a 3-D Gaussian $G(x, y, z)$ can be achieved by smoothing the image in x direction by 1-D Gaussian $G(x)$, then smoothing the result in y direction by 1-D Gaussian $G(y)$, and finally smoothing the result in z direction by 1-D Gaussian $G(z)$. Denoting the smoothing/convolution operation by $\star$, we have

$$I(x, y, z) \star G(x, y, z) = ((I(x, y, z) \star G(x)) \star G(y)) \star G(z). \tag{8.12}$$

The second derivative of a Gaussian smoothed image in x direction, I_{xx}, is obtained from

$$\frac{\partial^2 [I(x, y, z) \star G(x, y, z)]}{\partial x^2} = \left(\left(I(x, y, z) \star \frac{d^2 G(x)}{dx^2} \right) \star G(y) \right) \star G(z). \tag{8.13}$$

Similarly, I_{xy} is obtained from

$$\partial \left\{ \frac{\partial [I(x, y, z) \star G(x, y, z)]}{\partial x} \right\} / \partial y = \left(\left(I(x, y, z) \star \frac{dG(x)}{dx} \right) \star \frac{dG(y)}{dy} \right) \star G(z). \tag{8.14}$$

Other terms in the Hessian matrix are calculated in the same manner. Note that since convolution is performed over the entire image domain, the Hessian matrix is calculated at all image entries at the same time. Images representing $I_{xx}, I_{xy}, I_{xz}, I_{yy}, I_{yz}$, and I_{zz} are calculated first and then used to create the Hessian matrix at each voxel in the image. Then, an image is created with the value at each voxel showing the magnitude of the determinant of the Hessian matrix obtained at the voxel. Finally, entries with locally maximum values are identified and used as corners (the feature points).

8.2.6   Speed-Up Considerations in Feature Point Detection

Feature point detectors that use intensity gradients do not detect points where gradient magnitude is low. Detectors that do not use intensity gradients and look for locally maximum image properties may detect points at low-gradient areas. Points in low-gradient areas can be easily affected by noise and are not stable; therefore, when looking for feature points, image voxels where gradient magnitude is below a threshold value should be skipped. By skipping low-gradient voxels, speed-up factors from 2 to 10 can be achieved.

A coarse-to-fine approach can track points that persist from low to high resolution. Such points are stable under changes in image resolution. The coarse-to-fine approach not only will detect more stable points in a volume but also will considerably speed up the point detection process. By reducing the size of an image in each direction by a factor of 2, the number of voxels in the image is reduced by factor of 8. A point detected in low resolution needs to be accurately localized at high resolution by searching within a small neighborhood of the predicted location. A coarse-to-fine point detection that is implemented at three levels can speed up point detection by a factor of up to 64. The coarse-to-fine approach detects stable points that persist across resolutions and are useful when registering images acquired by scanners with different resolutions.

8.2.7   Evaluation of Feature Point Detectors

In addition to *speed, repeatability* and *accuracy* are important performance measures in a feature point detector. Speed is inversely proportional to computational complexity, repeatability determines the likelihood that a point detected in the reference image is detected in the test image, and accuracy is inversely proportional to the root-mean-squared (RMS) distance between homologous points in images after points in the reference image are mapped to the space of the test image.

To demonstrate evaluation of a point detector, a magnetic resonance (MR) brain image is used as the reference image. The brain image is slightly translated and rotated and then used as the test image. The reference and test images obtained in this manner are shown in red and light blue, respectively, in Fig. 8.1a. A second data set is created by translating and rotating the reference image some more. The second data set is shown in Fig. 8.1b. The MR image used in Fig. 8.1 is courtesy of Kettering Medical Center.

Knowing the translation and rotation of the test image with respect to the reference image, the rigid transformation matrix relating the test image to the reference image is used to transform points detected in the reference image to the space of the test image. After this transformation, reference points falling sufficiently close to test points are considered homologous points. Points without a correspondence are considered outliers and are discarded.

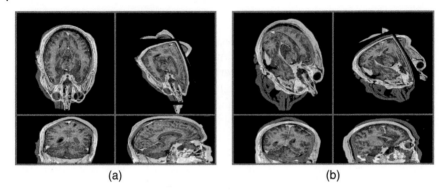

(a)   (b)

Figure 8.1 (a) A data set used to measure the speed, repeatability, and accuracy of various feature point detectors. This data set contains an MR brain volume (red) and its translated and rotated version (light blue). Upper-left, lower-left, and lower-right windows show axial, coronal, and sagittal cross sections of the reference and test volumes, and the upper-right window shows the relation between the cross sections within the volume. (b) Similar to data set (a) but with larger translational and rotational differences between the images. The MR image used in this experiment is courtesy of Kettering Medical Center.

One hundred points are detected in each volume. The points detected in the reference volume are transformed by the rigid transformation matrix obtained when creating the data set. To determine the repeatability of a method, the number of points in the reference volume after the rigid transformation that fall within a voxel distance of a point in the test image is counted and divided by the total number of points, which is 100 in this case, and used as the repeatability of the method.

To measure the accuracy of a point detector, the positional error of the method is determined. To achieve that, each point in the reference volume is transformed with the known rigid transformation and the point in the test volume closest to it is determined. If the distance between the two is within 3 voxels, the points are considered homologous points. After processing all points in the reference volume, the RMS distance between the transformed reference points and the homologous test points is determined and used as the positional error of the method. The larger the positional error, the less accurate the method will be.

In addition to repeatability and accuracy, the time required to detect 100 points in both images is measured and used to determine the computational requirement of a method. These performance measures were determined for four of the point detectors discussed in the preceding sections using the data sets shown in Fig. 8.1, and the results are summarized in Table 8.1.

The points detected by the four detectors when using the two data sets in Fig. 8.1 are shown in Figs 8.2 and 8.3. The points in red are those obtained in the reference image after being mapped to the test image with the known rigid

Table 8.1 The number of homologous points falling within a distance of 1 voxel of each other in data set 1 and in data set 2 are listed under NC 1 and NC 2, respectively. Root-mean-squared distance between homologous points falling within a distance of 3 voxels of each other in data set 1 and in data set 2 are listed under RMSD 1 and RMSD 2, respectively. The number of homologous points used to measure the RMSD in each case is shown within parentheses. The time in seconds needed to find 100 points in both images by each method on a Windows PC with an Intel Centrino 2 processor in data set 1 and in data set 2 are shown under Time 1 and Time 2, respectively.

Method	NC 1	NC 2	RMSD 1	RMSD 2	Time 1	Time 2
Central moments	10	0	1.29 (30)	1.85 (2)	65.084	65.418
Entropy	13	10	1.50 (29)	1.60 (29)	53.565	52.758
LoG operator	41	41	0.90 (51)	1.03 (56)	18.656	18.428
First derivative corners	4	10	1.18 (11)	0.93 (12)	11.862	11.905

transformation, and the points in green are those detected in the test image. Points falling within a distance of 1 voxel of each other are shown in yellow in these figures. The points in yellow are considered homologous points and are used to determine the repeatability measure. Points within a distance of 3 voxels of each other are used to determine the RMS positional error, which is inversely proportional to the accuracy. In Table 8.1, numbers within parentheses in columns RMSD 1 and RMSD 2 show the number of homologous points in a data set that fall within 3 voxels of each other after transforming points in the reference image by the known rigid transformation to the space of the test image.

Results from this limited experiment show that local extrema of LoG of an image are the most stable under changes in resolution and orientation of an image; therefore, LoG points are the most repeatable. Overall, they are also the most accurate. The first-derivative method is the fastest, but the detected points shift with change in resolution; therefore, the method is not highly repeatable. Entropy is not sensitive to an image's orientation; therefore, it can be used to register images with rotational differences. However, entropy is sensitive to an image's resolution. Central moments are sensitive to an image's orientation; therefore, they are not recommended when the images to be registered are rotated with respect to each other. The LoG point detector clearly stands out as the method of choice when the images to be registered have translation, rotation, and resolution differences.

8.3 Finding Homologous Points

Depending on the modalities of the given images, different methods may be used to find homologous points in the images. When the images are in the

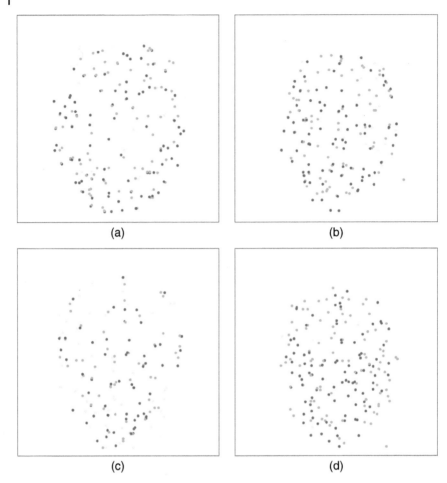

Figure 8.2 One hundred points detected in the images in data set 1 when using (a) central moments, (b) entropy, (c) LoG operator, and (d) first-derivative intensities. Points detected in the reference and test images are shown in red and green, respectively. Points in yellow are points in the reference image that fall within a distance of 1 voxel of points in the test image after being transformed with the known rigid transformation. Note that the feature points are in 3-D; shown above are the points after being projected to the *xy* plane.

same modality, feature points are detected in the images independently, initial correspondence is established between feature points in the images using intensity or gradient information in small neighborhoods of the points, and the correctness of the initial correspondences is verified using various geometric constraints holding between the images.

If the images are in different modalities, it is unlikely that the feature points detected in the reference image appear in the test image. In such a situation,

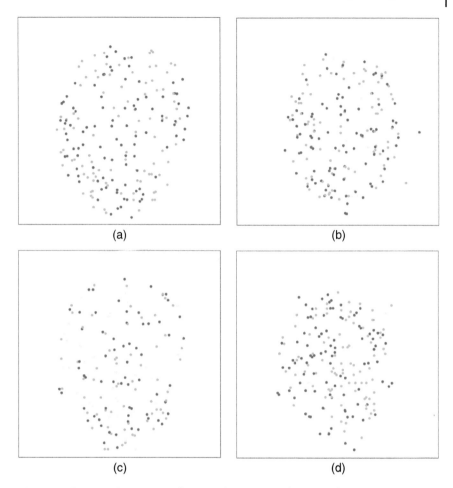

(a)   (b)

(c)   (d)

Figure 8.3 Same as Fig. 8.2 except for using the images in data set 2 shown in Fig. 8.1b.

feature points are detected in the reference image and searched for in the test image by template matching using an appropriate similarity or distance measure. The incorrect correspondences (outliers) are then removed using various geometric constraints holding between the images.

To account for local geometric differences between the given images, a coarse-to-fine search is taken. First, homologous points are obtained at low resolution where local geometric differences between the images are small and negligible. Knowing a set of homologous points in the images at low resolution, approximate locations of homologous points in the images at high resolution will be known. Having approximate locations of points in the images at high resolution, a search is made for each feature point in the reference image, in the neighborhoods of the estimated location in the test image, for its correspondence. The coarse-to-fine search strategy not only speeds up the correspondence process but also reduces the number of outliers.

8.3.1 Finding Initial Homologous Points Using Image Descriptors

When the images are in the same modality, some of the same points will be detected in both images. To determine an initial set of homologous points in the images, first a descriptor is computed for each point, characterizing the neighborhood of the point. Then, for each point in the reference image, the point in the test image with the most similar descriptor is identified and considered its correspondence. The correctness of the initial correspondences (the homologous points) is then verified using the geometric constraint holding between the images. The verification step is achieved via RANSAC [2]. Only those initial homologous points that satisfy the constraint are considered correct and kept. The remaining initial homologous points are considered outliers and discarded.

Intensities within a spherical region centered at a point is used to create a descriptor for the point. The histogram of intensities of voxels within the sphere describes the intensity distribution of the neighborhood of the point. An image's histogram is independent of the image's orientation.

After creating a histogram describing the intensity distribution of the neighborhood of each point, the correlation coefficient between the histograms associated with points in the images is used as the similarity between the neighborhoods of the points. Although the likelihood that two neighborhoods with different intensity patterns produce the same histogram is not 0, the likelihood is very low. When the images under consideration are in the same modality, it is not possible for two neighborhoods with different histograms to show the same intensity pattern; therefore, correlation of intensity histograms can be used to detect neighborhoods that do not correspond to each other with a very high confidence.

Since the likelihood exists that two neighborhoods with different intensity patterns produce very similar histograms, to improve the correspondence certainty, in addition to the intensity histogram, the intensity gradient magnitude histogram of a neighborhood is used. Neighborhoods that have similar intensity histograms and similar gradient magnitude histograms are considered homologous neighborhoods, and the points associated with them are considered initial homologous points.

If the correlation of intensity histograms of two neighborhoods is denoted by ρ_i and the correlation of gradient magnitude histograms of the neighborhoods is denoted by ρ_g, the product of the two is used as the similarity between the neighborhoods. Points where either ρ_i or ρ_g is smaller than a threshold value, such as 0.5, are dropped without further consideration as they are not likely to produce a correspondence. Otherwise, their product is used to determine the point in the test image that is most likely to correspond to the point in the reference image. The following algorithm summarizes the steps to be followed to find initial homologous points in the images.

Algorithm 8.1 Finding initial homologous points by local histogram matching

---

Given points $\{\mathbf{p}_i : i = 1, \ldots, m\}$ in reference image I_r and points $\{\mathbf{P}_i : i = 1, \ldots, n\}$ in test image I_s, this algorithm finds a set of initial homologous points by correlating intensity histograms and gradient magnitude histograms of spherical neighborhoods of radius R centered at the points. Parameters t_i and t_g denote the minimum correlation coefficient between intensity histograms of two windows and the minimum correlation coefficient between gradient magnitude histograms of two windows to be considered as homologous windows. Variable J shows the index of the feature point in the test image with a neighborhood that is most similar to the neighborhood of the feature point under consideration in the reference image.

1. Find intensity gradient magnitudes of image I_r and save them in image G_r. Also, find intensity gradient magnitudes of image I_s and save them in image G_s.
2. For $i = 1, \ldots, m$ repeat Steps 2.1–2.4.
   - 2.1. Take a spherical region of radius R centered at $\mathbf{p}_i$ in image I_r and call it w_{i_i}. Also, take a spherical region of radius R centered at $\mathbf{p}_i$ in image G_r and call it w_{g_i}.
   - 2.2. Let $\rho = 0$.
   - 2.3. For $j = 1, \ldots, n$ repeat Steps 2.3.1–2.3.3.
     - 2.3.1. Take a spherical region of radius R centered at $\mathbf{P}_j$ in image I_s and call it W_{i_j}. Also, take a spherical region of radius R centered at $\mathbf{P}_j$ in image G_s and call it W_{g_j}.
     - 2.3.2. Let ρ_i denote the correlation coefficient between w_{i_i} and W_{i_j} and let ρ_g denote the correlation coefficient between w_{g_i} and W_{g_j}.
     - 2.3.3. If $\rho_i > t_i$, $\rho_g > t_g$, and $\rho_i \rho_g > \rho$, let $\rho = \rho_i \rho_g$ and $J = j$.
   - 2.4. If $\rho > 0$, the neighborhood of point $\mathbf{P}_J$ in the test image is most similar to the neighborhood of point $\mathbf{p}_i$ in the reference image. Therefore, let reference point $\mathbf{p}_i$ correspond to test point $\mathbf{P}_J$.

Note that when $m > n$, Algorithm 8.1 may assign the same point in the test image to multiple points in the reference image. To reduce the likelihood of such cases, the reference and test images should be switched. After finding the initial homologous points, the images can be switched back. Switching the images may reduce the number of multiple assignments, but it may not completely remove them. Since multiple assignments show ambiguous matches, they are removed from the set of initial homologous points. Any remaining false homologous points are then removed by RANSAC using the geometric constraints holding between the images.

Detecting 100 points in each image in Fig. 8.1a using the LoG operator (Section 8.2.3) and finding initial correspondence between the points according to Algorithm 8.1, 74 homologous points are obtained as shown in Fig. 8.4a. Knowing that the images are related by a rigid transformation, from among

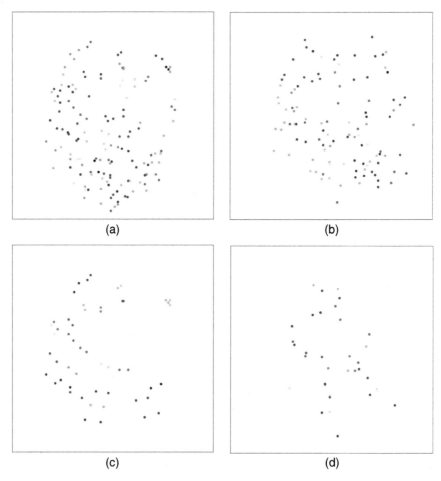

(a)

(b)

(c)

(d)

Figure 8.4 (a and b) The initial homologous points obtained between 100 points detected in the images in Fig. 8.1a and b, respectively. (c and d) Final homologous points in (a) and (b) after removal of the outliers by RANSAC using the rigidity constraint. Homologous points are shown with the same color. Note that the feature points are in 3-D; shown above are the points after being projected to the *xy* plane.

the 74 initial homologous points, only 26 are found to satisfy the rigidity constraint, as shown in Fig. 8.4c.

Starting with 100 points detected in the images in Fig. 8.1b, Algorithm 8.1 found 57 initial homologous points, as depicted in Fig. 8.4b. Removing the outliers by eliminating those homologous points that did not satisfy the rigidity constraint, 17 homologous points remain, as shown in Fig. 8.4d. To visualize the homologous points, points in the reference image are painted with random colors. Homologous points in the test image are painted with the same colors; therefore, homologous points in Fig. 8.4 are shown with the same color.

Results from the above experiments show that even for images with insignificant local geometric and intensity differences, only about one-sixth to one-fourth of the points detected in the image represent the same points in volumetric images. When the images to be registered have local geometric as well as intensity differences, there may be insufficient homologous points among the detected points to enable registration of the images. In the following section, a template matching correspondence method that can withstand considerable intensity differences as well as small geometric differences between images is described.

8.3.2 Finding Initial Homologous Points by Template Matching

Feature points detected in multimodality images often show different physical points in a scene; therefore, the likelihood of detecting the same physical points in multimodality images is very low. To find a sufficient number of homologous points in multimodality images, points are detected in the reference image and the points are searched for in the test image by template matching.

Template matching, however, requires that the images have the same orientation. Therefore, to make correspondence by template matching possible, it is required that the test image be brought to the approximate orientation of the reference image. This can be achieved either interactively or automatically. If interaction is allowed, the test image can be interactively transformed to approximately align with the reference image very quickly. Template matching can then be employed to find points in the test image that correspond to the points in the reference image.

Automatic determination of the rotational difference between images in different modalities requires an exhaustive search. The search involves determining three translation and three rotation parameters to rigidly transform the test image to align the reference image. To speed up search for the translation and rotation parameters, the sizes of the images are considerably reduced. Even when using 10 coarse rotational steps and 10 coarse translational steps, an exhaustive search requires on the order of 10^6 image comparisons by an appropriate similarity or distance measure. Therefore, the time required to automatically find the translation and rotation parameters between images in different modalities can be prohibitively long.

In medical imaging applications, often interaction with the registration software is allowed. By interactively translating and rotating the test image in the space of the reference image, the user can view and evaluate the registration. Since interactive alignment is subjective and often cannot guarantee a highly accurate alignment, once the images are approximately aligned, an automated template-matching process can be activated to find more accurate translation and rotation parameters by varying them within smaller ranges but in finer steps.

An example of interactive image alignment, which typically takes less than 10 s, is given in Fig. 8.5. An MR and PET brain image data set with large translational and rotational differences is shown in (a). The test image is interactively rotated in the space of the reference image until it approximately aligns with the reference image. The interactively obtained transformation is saved in a matrix and used later to relate the registration after the interactive alignment to the original images.

Template matching can establish correspondence between local neighborhoods/regions in two images that have the same orientation. To reduce the effect of small rotational and nonlinear geometric differences between the images, the distance of a voxel in a spherical region to the center of the region is used as a weight (Section 5.6.4) when computing the distance or similarity between two regions.

Detecting 100 points in the reference MR volume by the LoG operator (Section 8.2.3) as shown in Fig. 8.6a and using weighted mutual information (Section 7.2.2) as the similarity measure, the homologous points shown in Fig. 8.6b are obtained. Points in the reference image are painted with random colors. Corresponding points in the test image are painted with the same colors.

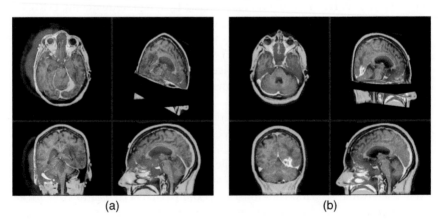

(a)   (b)

Figure 8.5 (a) An MR and PET brain image data set. This data set is courtesy of Kettering Medical Center. (b) Interactive translation and rotation of the test image to align with the reference image.

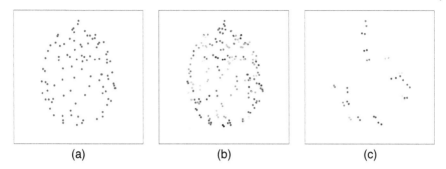

| (a) | (b) | (c) |

Figure 8.6 (a) 100 points detected in the reference MR volume. (b) Starting from the test PET volume that was interactively aligned to the MR volume in Fig. 8.5a, test points are found corresponding to the 100 reference points by template matching using mutual information as the similarity measure. Homologous points found for the images in Fig. 8.5b are shown with the same color. (c) From among the 100 initial homologous points obtained by template matching, only 19 satisfy the rigidity constraint, which are then considered true homologous points and kept. Shown are the 3-D homologous points after being projected to the xy plane.

Some of the homologous points in Fig. 8.6b are not correct. From among 100 homologous points, only 19 satisfy the rigidity constraint with a 2-voxel error tolerance, as shown in Fig. 8.6c. Increasing the error tolerance will increase the number of homologous points, but that will increase inaccuracies among the obtained homologous points. The 19 homologous points are sufficient to find the rigid transformation parameters needed to register the images.

Spherical templates of radius 18 voxels are used in template matching. Increasing the template radius will increase the number of detected homologous points, but that will increase the computation time. If the images have nonlinear geometric differences, increasing template size may actually reduce the number of homologous points; therefore, template radius should be chosen taking into consideration correspondence speed, correspondence accuracy, and nonlinear geometric differences between the images. A training data set should make it possible to choose the appropriate template size for a class of images where the developed methodology will be used.

Methods for distinguishing correct homologous points from incorrect homologous points (outliers) are discussed next.

8.3.3   Finding Final Homologous Points from Coarse to Fine

The initial homologous points obtained by matching image descriptors can contain outliers. To distinguish correct homologous points from the outliers, the geometric constraint holding between the images is used. Volumetric medical images are related globally by a rigid transformation, although local geometric differences may exist between the images.

To register images with local geometric differences, the resolution of the images is reduced sufficiently, so local geometric differences between the images become small and negligible. The low-resolution images are then aligned globally by a rigid transformation. After removing the global translational and rotational differences between the images, a search for homologous points is made in corresponding neighborhoods in high-resolution images.

If reference and test images have geometric differences that vary gradually, the reference image is divided into small blocks. If the blocks are small enough, homologous points can be found within corresponding blocks using the rigidity constraint. The homologous points obtained within corresponding blocks are then merged to produce homologous points over the entire image domain. The parameters of a transformation model to register the images are then determined from the coordinates of homologous points in the images.

To find corresponding blocks in images, first, the resolution of the images is sufficiently reduced, so entire images can be registered by a rigid transformation with a required tolerance. The primary objective of registration at low resolution is to determine the global translational and rotational differences between the images.

Initially, for each feature point in the low-resolution reference image, the corresponding feature point is determined in the low- resolution test image by matching image descriptors or by template matching. Only those homologous points that produce a sufficiently high similarity or sufficiently low distance measure are kept. Suppose n initial homologous points are obtained in the images at low resolution:

$$\{(\mathbf{p}_i, \mathbf{q}_i) : i = 1, \ldots, n\}, \tag{8.15}$$

where $\mathbf{p}_i = (x_i, y_i, z_i)$ and $\mathbf{q}_i = (X_i, Y_i, Z_i)$ are homologous points in low-resolution images.

To determine the rigid transformation that relates the geometries of the images at low resolution, four initial homologous points are randomly selected. If the four homologous points are correct, they satisfy the rigidity constraint. To test for rigidity, from the four random homologous points, parameters of the following linear transformation are determined by solving three systems of four linear equations

$$X_i = ax_i + by_i + cz_i + d, \tag{8.16}$$
$$Y_i = ex_i + fy_i + gz_i + h, \tag{8.17}$$
$$Z_i = ix_i + jy_i + kz_i + l, \tag{8.18}$$

for $i = 1, \ldots, 4$.

If the four homologous points satisfy the rigidity constraint,

$$\mathbf{R} = \begin{bmatrix} a & b & c \\ e & f & g \\ i & j & k \end{bmatrix} \tag{8.19}$$

will represent the rotational matrix, and that implies $\mathbf{R}$ should be a unitary matrix, requiring that the determinant of $\mathbf{R}$ be 1. Due to digital noise in point locations, $\det(\mathbf{R})$ may not be exactly 1, but if the four points truly correspond and the low-resolution images are related by a rigid transformation, $\det(\mathbf{R})$ will be close to 1. Allowing tolerance ε, we will consider the four randomly selected homologous points satisfying the rigidity constraint if $1 - \varepsilon < \det(\mathbf{R}) < 1 + \varepsilon$. ε is a small tolerance, such as 0.1. For example, when letting $\varepsilon = 0.1$, the homologous points shown in Fig. 8.6c are obtained.

Since a rigid transformation contains information about the translational and rotational differences between the images, if matrix R shows the rotation of the test image with respect to the reference image, parameters d, h, and l in Eqs (8.16)–(8.18) show translation of the rotated test image with respect to the reference image. After satisfying the rigidity constraint with a required tolerance, the rigid transformation that maps reference image points to the corresponding points in the test image in the homogenous coordinate system will be

$$\mathbf{M} = \begin{bmatrix} a & b & c & d \\ e & f & g & h \\ i & j & k & l \\ 0 & 0 & 0 & 1 \end{bmatrix}. \tag{8.20}$$

When a set of four initial homologous points satisfies the rigidity constraint with a required tolerance, homologous points in the images that satisfy transformation $\mathbf{M}$ with a required distance tolerance are determined, and only when the number of homologous points reaches a certain percentage (such as 10%) of the initial homologous points and the total number of homologous points is greater than a minimum number (such as 8), the process is stopped and the obtained homologous points is used to determine the rigid transformation parameters by the weighted least-squares method following the procedure outlined in Section 5.7.2 to register the images. The similarity measure obtained at a homologous pair is used as the weight of the homologous pair when finding the transformation parameters by the weighted least- squares method.

Feature point $\mathbf{p}_i = [x_i \ y_i \ z_i \ 1]^t$ in the low-resolution reference image is considered to correspond to feature point $\mathbf{q}_j = [X_j \ Y_j \ Z_j \ 1]^t$ in the low-resolution test image if

$$\|\mathbf{M}\mathbf{p}_i - \mathbf{q}_i\| < D, \tag{8.21}$$

where D is the required distance tolerance. For example, in Fig. 8.6c, the homologous points were obtained by letting $D = 1$ voxel in addition to rigidity tolerance $\varepsilon = 0.1$.

Rigid registration at low resolution enables approximate alignment of the images. This makes it possible to determine for each local neighborhood in the reference image, the corresponding local neighborhood in the test image. Knowing the rigid transformation that relates homologous points in the images at low resolution makes it possible to find approximate locations of homologous points in the images at high resolution.

If points (x, y, z) and (X, Y, Z) are related by rigid transformation $\mathbf{M}$ at low resolution, and scale ratio between the high- and low-resolution images is s, then if points (x', y', z') and (X', Y', Z') in high-resolution images approximately correspond to (x, y, z) and (X, Y, Z) in low-resolution images, respectively, we can write $x'/s \approx x$; $y'/s \approx y$; $z'/s \approx z$; $X'/s \approx X$; $Y'/s \approx Y$; and $Z'/s \approx Z$. The approximate relation allows some local geometric differences between the images at high resolution. The images at high resolution can be approximately related using the transformation obtained at low resolution as follows:

$$
\begin{bmatrix} X'/s \\ Y'/s \\ Z'/s \\ 1 \end{bmatrix} \approx \begin{bmatrix} a & b & c & d \\ e & f & g & h \\ i & j & k & l \\ 0 & 0 & 0 & 1 \end{bmatrix} \begin{bmatrix} x'/s \\ y'/s \\ z'/s \\ 1 \end{bmatrix} \tag{8.22}
$$

or

$$
\begin{bmatrix} X' \\ Y' \\ Z' \\ s \end{bmatrix} \approx \begin{bmatrix} a & b & c & d \\ e & f & g & h \\ i & j & k & l \\ 0 & 0 & 0 & 1 \end{bmatrix} \begin{bmatrix} x' \\ y' \\ z' \\ s \end{bmatrix}. \tag{8.23}
$$

If the reference image is subdivided into uniform blocks, for each corner of a block in the reference image the approximate corner of the same block in the test image can be determined from Eq. (8.23). This equation makes it possible to find correspondence between blocks or local neighborhoods in the images. This, in turn, makes it possible to search within small corresponding neighborhoods for homologous points.

If the geometric difference between two images is not locally sharp, correspondence between points within corresponding blocks in the images can be determined the same way homologous points were found in images at low resolution. Block size can be determined iteratively, starting with the entire image as a block and gradually reducing the block size until points within corresponding blocks in the images satisfy the rigidity constraint with a required tolerance. The steps of an algorithm finding homologous points in images with local geometric differences follow.

Algorithm 8.2   Finding homologous points in images from coarse to fine

Given the rigid transformation M relating the geometry of the reference volume to the geometry of the test volume at low resolution, feature points $\{\mathbf{p}'_i : i = 1, \ldots, N_1\}$ in high-resolution reference volume and feature points $\{\mathbf{P}'_i : i = 1, \ldots, N_2\}$ in high-resolution test volume, the scale ratio s between low- and high-resolution volumes, and distance tolerance D between two points (Eq. (8.21)) to consider them homologous points, this algorithm finds m or more homologous points in the images at high resolution. If the algorithm cannot find at least m homologous points in the images, it will report a failure.

1. For each point $\mathbf{p}' = (x', y', z')$ in the reference image, find the location of the homologous point $\mathbf{P}' = (X'Y'Z')$ in the test image using Eq. (8.23). If point $\mathbf{P}'$ falls within distance tolerance D of a point in the test image, consider them homologous points. Suppose overall n homologous points are obtained in this manner. If $n \geq m$, return the homologous points and stop. This happens when the images at high resolution are also related by a rigid transformation. Otherwise, let $i = 1$ and continue to Step 2.
2. Increment i by 1 and replace s with $s/2$. Then, subdivide the images into equal blocks as close to cubic as possible with the maximum of i blocks in each direction, and determine the coordinates of block corners in the test images from the coordinates of block corners in the reference image using Eq. (8.23). Find homologous points within corresponding blocks by assuming corresponding blocks are low-resolution images. If overall n homologous points are obtained from all corresponding blocks and $n \geq m$, return the homologous points and exit the program.
3. Repeat Step 2 until either the overall number of homologous points n is equal to or greater than the required number of homologous points m, at which time report the homologous points and exit. Otherwise, if the number of homologous points obtained at an iteration is smaller than the number of homologous points obtained in the previous iteration, report failure and exit.

Algorithm 8.2 subdivides the images into smaller and smaller blocks until the relation between corresponding blocks can be approximated by a rigid transformation. Homologous points are obtained within corresponding blocks using the rigidity constraint in a RANSAC paradigm, and the process is continued until the required number of homologous points is obtained or the blocks become too small to contain sufficient points to produce useful homologous points, at which time a failure is reported and program is terminated.

Use of the rigidity constraint in corresponding neighborhoods makes it possible to detect incorrect homologous points at high resolution. If geometric difference between corresponding blocks is sufficiently small, Algorithm 8.2 detects and removes outliers that do not satisfy the local rigidity constraint within the required tolerances.

8.3.4 Finding the Final Homologous Points by Outlier Removal

Many of the initial homologous points obtained by matching descriptors at the feature points or by template matching may be correct; however, there also may be outliers that are mixed with the correct homologous points. There is a need to distinguish the correct homologous points from the outliers and remove the outliers before finding the transformation parameters from the homologous points.

Following the outlier removal algorithm described for 2-D images (Algorithm 7.2), an algorithm to remove outliers in volumetric images is described.

Algorithm 8.3 Removing outliers in volumetric images

Given a set of initial homologous points $\{(x_i, y_i, z_i), (X_i, Y_i, Z_i) : i = 1, \dots, N\}$ in two volumes, this algorithm removes the incorrect homologous points (outliers).

1. For each initial homologous pair $(x_i, y_i, z_i), (X_i, Y_i, Z_i)$, do Steps 1.1–1.4.
   1.1. Find $n - 1$ points closest to (x_i, y_i, z_i) in the reference image. If point (x_j, y_j, z_j) in the reference image is initially found to correspond to point (X_j, Y_j, Z_j) in the test image for $j = 1, \dots, n - 1$, this step will determine the $n \leq N$ initial homologous points that are surrounding point (x_i, y_i, z_i) in the reference image.
   1.2. From the n initial homologous points obtained in Step 1.1, determine the parameters of a linear transformation model with components $X = ax + by + cz + d$, $Y = ex + fy + gz + h$, and $Z = ix + jy + kz + l$ relating the n homologous points by a robust estimator, such as the LMS estimator (Section 5.7.3).
   1.3. Let $\quad E_{x_i} = X_i - ax_i - by_i - cz_i - d, \quad E_{y_i} = Y_i - ex_i - fy_i - gz_i - h,$
        $E_{z_i} = Z_i - ix_i - jy_i - kz_i - l$, and compute $E_i = \sqrt{E_{x_i}^2 + E_{y_i}^2 + E_{z_i}^2}$.
   1.4. If E_i is smaller than the median error E_m in the LMS estimator and is also smaller than a required error tolerance E_t, keep the homologous pair $(x_i, y_i, z_i), (X_i, Y_i, Z_i)$. Otherwise, declare pair $(x_i, y_i, z_i), (X_i, Y_i, Z_i)$ an outlier, remove it, and decrement N by 1.
2. Repeat Step 1 on the remaining homologous points until no additional outliers are detected.

Parameter n shows the local neighborhood size and should be taken large enough to contain sufficient correct homologous points to enable computation of parameters $a - l$ of the local linear transformation model. Assuming 50% of the initial homologous points are incorrect, minimum seven initial homologous points are needed so that the homologous pair producing the median error will more likely represent a correct homologous pair than an outlier.

Algorithm 8.3 is easier to implement compared to Algorithm 8.2 as it does not involve a coarse-to-fine analysis. It can be applied to the initial homologous points obtained from the original images. The outlier removal process has the ability to remove inaccurate homologous points also by appropriately lowering the error tolerance E_t.

Once a set of homologous points free of outliers is obtained, the coordinates of the homologous points can be used to determine the parameters of an appropriate transformation model and register the images.

8.4 Transformation Models for Volume Image Registration

Given a set of points in the reference image

$$\{\mathbf{p}_i : i = 1, \dots, n\} \tag{8.24}$$

and the corresponding points in the test image

$$\{\mathbf{P}_i : i = 1, \dots, n\}, \tag{8.25}$$

we would like to determine transformation $\mathbf{T}$ such that

$$\mathbf{P}_i = \mathbf{T}(\mathbf{p}_i), \quad \text{for } i = 1, \dots, n \tag{8.26}$$

or

$$\mathbf{P}_i \approx \mathbf{T}(\mathbf{p}_i), \quad \text{for } i = 1, \dots, n. \tag{8.27}$$

The transformation satisfying (8.26) maps homologous points in the images exactly, while the transformation satisfying (8.27) maps homologous points in the images approximately. The former is more suitable when the homologous points are known to be very accurate, while the latter is more suitable when the homologous points are inaccurate. An approximating transformation not only smoothes noise among the locations of homologous points but is also more efficient as it does not require the solution of large systems of equations to find the transformation parameters.

If the images can be considered instances of the same rigid body, the coordinates of homologous points in the images can be related by the transformation described by Eqs (8.16)–(8.18), conditioned matrix (8.19) to approximate a unitary matrix.

A transformation model for registration of 3-D images has three components: $T_x, T_y,$ and T_z. For example, in a rigid transformation, Eq. (8.16) represents T_x, the x-component transformation, Eq. (8.17) represents T_y, the y-component transformation, and Eq. (8.18) represents T_z, the z-component transformation.

If a transformation is not rigid, it is called nonrigid. The nonrigid transformation used in registration of 2-D images can be extended to 3-D to register volumetric images. In the following section, the extension of the surface spline to volume spline and the extension of weighted linear approximation in 2-D to 3-D weighted rigid approximation for registration of volumetric images are shown. Volume spline represents an interpolating transformation, while weighted rigid is an approximating transformation. Weighted rigid rather than weighted affine is used because two medical images are rarely related by an affine transformation.

The problem of finding the parameters of a transformation for registration of two volumes can be converted into a volumetric data interpolation/approximation. Denoting the coordinates of point $\mathbf{p}_i$ by (x_i, y_i, z_i) and the coordinates of point $\mathbf{P}_i$ by (X_i, Y_i, Y_i), we can restate the problem of determining the transformation for registration of two volumes as follows. Given three sets of 4-D points:

$$\{(x_i, y_i, z_i, X_i) : i = 1, \dots, n\}, \tag{8.28}$$
$$\{(x_i, y_i, z_i, Y_i) : i = 1, \dots, n\}, \tag{8.29}$$
$$\{(x_i, y_i, z_i, Z_i) : i = 1, \dots, n\}, \tag{8.30}$$

we would like to find three functions, $T_x, T_y,$ and T_z, that satisfy

$$X_i = T_x(x_i, y_i, z_i), \tag{8.31}$$
$$Y_i = T_y(x_i, y_i, z_i), \tag{8.32}$$
$$Z_i = T_z(x_i, y_i, z_i), \tag{8.33}$$

or

$$X_i \approx T_x(x_i, y_i, z_i), \tag{8.34}$$
$$Y_i \approx T_y(x_i, y_i, z_i), \tag{8.35}$$
$$Z_i \approx T_z(x_i, y_i, z_i), \tag{8.36}$$

for $i = 1, \dots, n$. Equations (8.31)–(8.33) define the components of an interpolating transformation, while Eqs (8.34)–(8.36) define components of an approximating transformation. Since each component of a transformation can be determined independent of the other two, the same procedure can be followed three times to determine the three components of the transformation. Therefore, the common problem to be solved is as follows. Given a set of 3-D points

$$\{(x_i, y_i, z_i) : i = 1, \ldots, n\} \tag{8.37}$$

with associating values

$$\{F_i : i = 1, \ldots, n\} \tag{8.38}$$

we would like to find function f that satisfies

$$F_i = f(x_i, y_i, z_i) \quad \text{for } i = 1, \ldots, n \tag{8.39}$$

or

$$F_i \approx f(x_i, y_i, z_i) \quad \text{for } i = 1, \ldots, n. \tag{8.40}$$

A transformation model is a key component of an image registration system. Registration of medical images often requires an elastic transformation to warp the test image to the geometry of the reference image. Elastic transformations are needed in standardization of brain images [13] and estimation of cardiac motion [14].

In the following sections, volume spline and weighted rigid transformations are used to register volumetric images. A volume spline transformation uses three global interpolation functions, while a weighted rigid transformation uses three locally sensitive approximation functions.

8.4.1 Volume Spline

A volume spline interpolating values at n 3-D points is defined by

$$f(x, y, z) = A_1 + A_2 x + A_3 y + A_4 z + \sum_{i=1}^{n} B_i r_i^2 \ln{(r_i^2)}, \tag{8.41}$$

where $r_i^2 = (x - x_i)^2 + (y - y_i)^2 + (z - z_i)^2 + d^2$. d^2 is a positive number showing the rigidity of the volume. The smaller the rigidity parameter, the more elastic the volume will be, better reproducing sharper changes in the volume. A more elastic volume can accommodate larger local geometric differences between the images. If data point (x_i, y_i, z_i) has an associating value F_i, the interpolating volume spline should evaluate to F_i at (x_i, y_i, z_i), that is, $f(x_i, y_i, z_i) = F_i$.

Parameters $A_1 - A_4$ define a degree 1 polynomial within the volume, and parameters $B_1 - B_n$ are forces pushing/pulling the volume toward/away from the points to produce required values at the points. Parameters $A_1, \ldots, A_4$ and $B_1, \ldots, B_n$ are determined by substituting the n points given in (8.39) into (8.41) and letting $f(x_i, y_i, z_i) = F_i$. This will produce n linear equations in A's and B's.

Four more equations are obtained by imposing the following constraints:

$$\sum_{i=1}^{n} B_i = 0, \tag{8.42}$$

$$\sum_{i=1}^{n} x_i B_i = 0, \tag{8.43}$$

$$\sum_{i=1}^{n} y_i B_i = 0, \tag{8.44}$$

$$\sum_{i=1}^{n} z_i B_i = 0. \tag{8.45}$$

Equation (8.42) ensures that the sum of the forces is zero, so the volume will not move. Equation (8.43) ensures that the moment created by the forces with respect to the x-axis is 0, so the volume will not spin about the x-axis. Similarly, Eqs (8.44) and (8.45) ensure that the volume will not spin about the y- and z-axes.

Volume spline is defined in terms of radial basis functions of the same width; therefore, the best accuracy in interpolation is achieved when points in the interpolation domain (points in the reference image) are uniformly spaced. If the density of points varies greatly across the reference image, large errors may be obtained away from the points. If the spacing between the points varies greatly across the image domain, a more elastic (a smaller d^2) should be used to avoid creation of overshoots and fluctuations in interpolation.

Volume spline has all the characteristics of surface spline. It is computationally efficient and the matrix of coefficients obtained from the $n + 4$ linear equations never becomes ill conditioned [15]. Therefore, one can expect a solution under all arrangements of points, although an obtained interpolation may involve large errors away from the points when data values change sharply and spacing between the points varies greatly across the image domain.

It is important that the homologous points used to compute the parameters of a volume spline do not contain outliers. Otherwise, large errors may be obtained across the interpolation domain as all basis functions span over the entire interpolation domain. If homologous points are accurate, volume spline can represent rigid as well as nonrigid transformations, producing a continuous and smooth mapping from the reference image to the test image.

An example of volume spline transformation in the registration of multitemporal whole-body CT images is given in Fig. 8.7. These images are courtesy of Kettering Medical Center. The images are isotropic with cubic voxels of side 3 mm. The images before registration are shown in Fig. 8.7a. Lower-resolution images with cubic voxels of side 6 mm are created. One hundred feature points are detected in the lower-resolution reference image and the points are searched for in the lower-resolution test image by template matching using

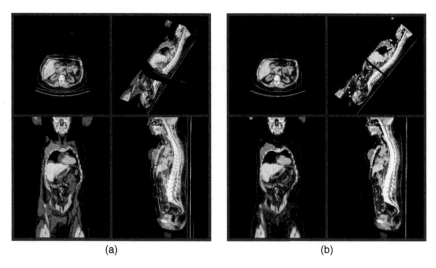

(a) (b)

Figure 8.7 (a) Multitemporal whole-body CT images with cubic voxels of side 3 mm. These images are courtesy of Kettering Medical Center. The reference image is shown in light blue (combination of green and blue) and the test image is shown in red. (b) Registration of the images by volume spline. Well-registered areas appear in gray, while misregistered areas appear in red or light blue.

correlation coefficient as the similarity measure. Some of the homologous points obtained by template matching are incorrect.

From among the 100 initial homologous points, 64 pass the rigidity test using rigidity tolerance $\varepsilon = 0.1$ and distance tolerance $d = 1$ voxel by Algorithm 8.2. Next, the original reference image with cubic voxels of side 3 mm is subdivided into $1 \times 2 \times 3$ equal blocks, and using the rigid transformation obtained at lower resolutions, homologous blocks are identified in the test image and homologous points are found within corresponding blocks by RANSAC.

Overall 53 homologous points as shown in the upper-right window in Fig. 8.7b are obtained by this method. Registration of the images by a volume spline of rigidity $d^2 = 0$ with its parameters determined from the 53 homologous points by the least-squares method is shown in Fig. 8.7b. The three orthogonal cross sections of the registered images are displayed. Some misregistration can be observed due to the lack of sufficient homologous points in areas with sharp local geometric differences.

8.4.2 Weighted Rigid Transformation

This transformation involves subdividing the reference image into blocks, finding the corresponding blocks in the test image, finding a rigid transformation to relate corresponding blocks in the images, and creating a transformation that is a weighted sum of the local rigid transformations. If corresponding blocks in the images are registered rigidly, a piecewise rigid transformation is obtained that may produce cracks or discontinuities between adjacent blocks in the resampled test image.

To provide a continuous and smooth mapping of the reference image to the test image, the local rigid transformations are blended using monotonically decreasing weight functions. Gaussians are used as the weight functions. If the center of the ith block in the reference image is $(x_{c_i}, y_{c_i}, z_{c_i})$, and if the rigid transformation mapping block i in the reference image to the corresponding block in the test image is denoted by $\mathbf{T}_i = (T_{x_i}, T_{y_i}, T_{z_i})$, then resampling using a Gaussian weighted sum of rigid transformations involves computation of

$$\mathbf{P} = \frac{\sum_{i=1}^{N} G_i \mathbf{T}_i(\mathbf{p})}{\sum_{i=1}^{N} G_i}, \tag{8.46}$$

where N is the number of blocks, $\mathbf{P} = (X, Y, Z)$ is a point in the test image, $\mathbf{p} = (x, y, z)$ is the homologous point in the reference image, $\mathbf{T}_i$ is the rigid transformation mapping points in the ith block in the reference image to the corresponding block in the test image, and G_i is a 3-D Gaussian of height 1 centered at the ith block $(x_{c_i}, y_{c_i}, z_{c_i})$ in the reference image. That is,

$$G_i = \exp\left\{ -\frac{(x - x_{c_i})^2 + (y - y_{c_i})^2 + (z - z_{c_i})^2}{2\sigma^2} \right\}. \tag{8.47}$$

Parameter σ is taken in such a way that the influence of a rigid transformation becomes negligibly small at the centers of blocks adjacent to it. To achieve this, σ is set to one-third the shortest side of a block. The denominator in Eq. (8.46) is to ensure that the sum of the weights everywhere in the reference volume is 1. The three components of $\mathbf{T}_i(\mathbf{p})$ in Eq. (8.46) are the right sides of Eqs (8.16)–(8.18).

The global transformation defined by Eq. (8.46) is not only continuous but also smooth over the entire approximation domain because the weight functions are continuous and smooth over the domain. Moreover, the global transformation evaluates to the rigid transformation at the center of the block the rigid transformation is computed for. Also, because Gaussians vanish exponentially, if σ is taken one-third the width of a block, the effect of a rigid transformation vanishes before reaching two blocks away. Consequently, a rigid transformation will need to be used in the calculations when resampling the block to which it belongs and the blocks adjacent to it. This property provides an efficient means for resampling the test image to the geometry of the reference image using only information about local homologous points.

Due to its local nature, an inaccurate correspondence within corresponding blocks will not affect resampling of distant blocks. When volume spline is used as the transformation model, due to its monotonically increasing logarithmic basis functions, a local inaccuracy can spread over the entire interpolation

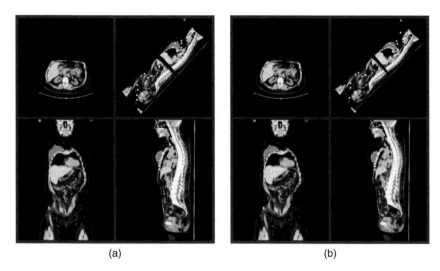

Figure 8.8 (a) Registration of the CT images in Fig. 8.7a by the weighted rigid transformation when subdividing the approximation domain into (a) $1 \times 2 \times 3$ equal blocks and (b) $2 \times 2 \times 4$ equal blocks.

domain. Therefore, volume spline is useful when the homologous points are accurate. Due to its monotonically decreasing weight functions, the weighted rigid transformation is preferred to volume spline when homologous points contain inaccuracies.

Using the CT images shown in Fig. 8.7a, the same homologous points used by volume spline, and using the rigid transformations obtained at homologous blocks, the weighted rigid transformation registered the images as shown in Fig. 8.8a. This result is slightly better than the result obtained by volume spline (Fig. 8.7b). Subdividing the reference image (the approximation domain) into $2 \times 2 \times 4$ blocks produced the registration shown in Fig. 8.8b. Similar results are obtained by the two subdivisions.

8.4.3 Computing the Overall Transformation

To register a test image to a reference image, there may be a need to carry out a sequence of transformations on each image before registering the images. Repeated transformation and resampling degrades the quality of the resampled image that is ultimately produced to register with the reference image. To avoid the unnecessary degradations, there is a need to obtain the final resampled test image from a single transformation that relates the original reference image to the original test image.

In medical applications, it is important to resample a provided test image to the geometry and resolution of the provided reference image. The reference image can be an atlas with all voxels labeled, showing the organ or tissue type

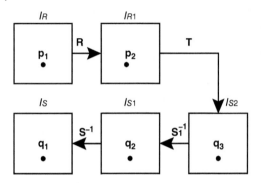

Figure 8.9 The sequence of transformations involved in resampling a provided test image to the geometry and resolution of a provided reference image.

each voxel belongs to. By resampling a test image to the reference image, labels of the reference can be transferred to voxels in the test image, finding the organ or tissue each voxel in the test image belongs to.

Given reference image I_R and test image I_S (Fig. 8.9), there is a need to first make the images isotropic so they have cubic voxels of the same size. Suppose transformation $\mathbf{R}$ resamples the provided reference image I_R into isotropic image I_{R_1} and transformation $\mathbf{S}$ resamples test image I_S into isotropic image I_{S_1} with voxels similar to those of image I_{R_1}. Transformations $\mathbf{R}$ and $\mathbf{S}$ represent the diagonal matrices shown by Eqs (8.1) and (8.3). Therefore, the relation between homologous points in images I_{R_1} and I_R can be written as

$$\mathbf{p}_2 = \mathbf{R}\mathbf{p}_1, \tag{8.48}$$

where $\mathbf{p}_2$ is the point in I_{R_1} corresponding to point $\mathbf{p}_1$ in I_R (Fig. 8.9). Similarly, the relation between homologous points in images I_{S_1} and I_S can be written as

$$\mathbf{q}_2 = \mathbf{S}\mathbf{q}_1, \tag{8.49}$$

where $\mathbf{q}_2$ is the point in I_{S_1} corresponding to point $\mathbf{q}_1$ in image I_S.

After making the reference and test images isotropic with cubic voxels of the same size, suppose the user interactively translates and rotates test image I_{S_1} to bring it closer to reference image I_{R_1}. Let us denote image I_{S_1} after this rigid transformation by I_{S_2}. Denoting this rigid transformation by $\mathbf{S}_1$, the relation between homologous points in images I_{S_1} and I_{S_2} can be written as

$$\mathbf{q}_3 = \mathbf{S}_1\mathbf{q}_2, \tag{8.50}$$

where $\mathbf{q}_3$ is the point in I_{S_2} corresponding to point $\mathbf{q}_2$ in I_{S_1}. Substituting $\mathbf{q}_2$ from Eq. (8.49) into Eq. (8.50), we obtain the relation between homologous points in images I_{S_2} and I_S:

$$\mathbf{q}_3 = \mathbf{S}_1\mathbf{S}\mathbf{q}_1. \tag{8.51}$$

Finally, suppose transformation $\mathbf{T}$ is found to relate reference image I_{R_1} to test image I_{S_2}:

$$\mathbf{q}_3 = \mathbf{T}\mathbf{p}_2, \tag{8.52}$$

where $\mathbf{q}_3$ is the point in test image I_{S_2} corresponding to point $\mathbf{p}_2$ in reference image I_{R_1}. This transformation $\mathbf{T}$ can be rigid or nonrigid. Substituting $\mathbf{p}_2$ from Eq. (8.48) into Eq. (8.51), we obtain

$$\mathbf{q}_3 = \mathbf{TRp}_1. \tag{8.53}$$

Since the left-hand sides of Eqs (8.51) and (8.53) are equal, their right-hand sides should also be equal. Therefore,

$$\mathbf{S}_1 \mathbf{Sq}_1 = \mathbf{TRp}_1, \tag{8.54}$$

from which we find

$$\mathbf{q}_1 = \mathbf{S}^{-1} \mathbf{S}_1^{-1} \mathbf{TRp}_1. \tag{8.55}$$

Equation (8.55) relates point $\mathbf{p}_1$ in the original (tomographic) reference image to the homologous point $\mathbf{q}_1$ in the original (tomographic) test image. The transformation defined by Eq. (8.55) makes it possible to directly resample the given nonisotropic tomographic test image to the geometry and resolution of the nonisotropic tomographic reference image.

To create the resampled test image, the original reference image is scanned, and for each point $\mathbf{p}_1$ in that image, the homologous point $\mathbf{q}_1$ is found in the original test image using Eq. (8.55). The intensity at $\mathbf{q}_1$ in the test image is then read and saved at $\mathbf{p}_1$ in the resampled image. The created resampled test image will have the geometry of the original reference image and the intensities of the original test image, spatially aligning the test image to the reference image.

Equation (8.55) makes it possible to avoid resampling reference image I_R to I_{R_1}, and resampling test image I_S to I_{S_1}, then to I_{S_2}, and finally to I_{R_1}. Each resampling step introduces digital errors to the process that can accumulate and noticeably reduce the quality of the created resampled image.

Note that if transformation $\mathbf{T}$ in Eq. (8.55) is a rigid transformation, it will be a 4×4 matrix so that $\mathbf{S}^{-1}\mathbf{S}_1^{-1}\mathbf{TR}$ will be a 4×4 transformation matrix. If $\mathbf{T}$ is a nonrigid transformation, for each point $\mathbf{p}_1$ in the original reference image, the location of the same point in image I_{R_1} is obtained from $\mathbf{Rp}_1$. Suppose this point is denoted by $\mathbf{p}_2$. Then, the point corresponding to $\mathbf{p}_2$ is found in image I_{S_3} from $\mathbf{T}(\mathbf{p}_2)$. This involves substituting the coordinates of point $\mathbf{p}_2$ into the three components of the volume spline, weighted rigid, or any other transformation that is used, and finding the coordinates of the homologous point in image I_{S_2}. Let us denote the location of the point in I_{S_2} by $\mathbf{q}_3$. Finally, the location of the point in the original test image corresponding to point $\mathbf{q}_3$ in I_{S_2} is obtained from $\mathbf{S}^{-1}\mathbf{S}_1^{-1}\mathbf{q}_3$. Note that although multiple transformations are performed to get from $\mathbf{p}_1$ to $\mathbf{q}_1$, only one resampling is performed at the end, minimizing degradation in the quality of the created resampled image.

8.5 Performance Evaluation

The key performance measures in a registration software are accuracy, reliability, and speed. Methods to determine these performance measures in volumetric image registration are described next.

8.5.1 Accuracy

Although measurement of the true accuracy of a registration method requires comparison of results obtained by the method with a gold standard, an estimation to the true accuracy is possible by various computational means without a gold standard. If the images are in the same modality, when the images are registered accurately, intensities of corresponding voxels in the images will correlate more than when the images are poorly registered. If the images are in different modalities, when the images are accurately registered, intensities of corresponding voxels in the images will depend on each other more than when the images are poorly registered. This dependency can be linear or nonlinear.

Treating intensities of corresponding voxels in registered images as two arrays of numbers, when the images are in the same modality, the quality of registration can be measured by the similarity between the two arrays using the Pearson correlation [16], also known as correlation coefficient. If the images are in different modalities, Shannon's mutual information [17, 18] can be used to measure the quality of registration. Alternatively, the dissimilarity or the distance between the two arrays can be measured by the normalized Euclidean distance if the images are in the same modality, and by Shannon's joint entropy [18, 19] if the images are in different modalities.

For example, in Fig. 8.7, the correlation coefficient between the images before and after registration are 0.74 and 0.86, respectively, while the normalized Euclidean distance between the images before and after registration are 58.20 and 42.90, respectively. Note that correlation coefficients fall between -1 and 1, and the closer the value is to 1, the more similar the two arrays are, showing a better registration. Normalized Euclidean distance is the Euclidean distance [20] between two arrays of numbers when divided by the dimension of the arrays. This value will be between 0 and 255 if intensities in the images vary between 0 and 255, and the closer the measure is to 0, the better the registration will be.

The quality of the registration cases shown in Fig. 8.8a and b when measured by the correlation coefficient are 0.85 and 0.86, respectively, and when measured by the normalized Euclidean distance are 43.57 and 43.39.

An example of multimodality volume registration is given in Fig. 8.10. The images in Fig. 8.10a have cubic voxels of side 1.5 mm and are courtesy of Kettering Medical Center. One hundred points are detected in the MR image, and

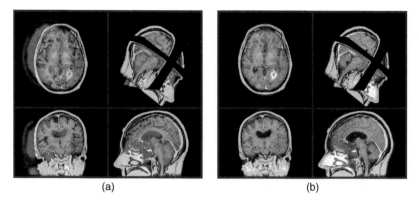

      (a)   (b)

Figure 8.10 (a) MR (light blue) and PET (red) brain images. These images are courtesy of Kettering Medical Center. (b) Rigid registration of the images by template matching using Shannon's mutual information as the similarity measure.

25 initial homologous points are obtained in the test image by template matching using Shannon's mutual information as the similarity measure. Among the 25 initial homologous points, 13 satisfy the rigidity constraint with tolerance $\varepsilon = 0.1$ and distance tolerance of $D = 1$ voxel. Using the 13 homologous points, the rigid parameters are determined by the least-squares method and the PET image is resampled and aligned with the MR image as shown in Fig. 8.10b. Registration RMSE measured at homologous points after this registration is 0.64 mm.

Similarities of the MR and PET images measured by Shannon's mutual information before registration (Fig. 8.10a) and after registration (Fig. 8.10b) are 0.16 and 0.40, respectively. The distance measures between the images before registration and after registration by Shannon's joint entropy are 1.42 and 1.33, respectively.

The registration quality measures obtained for Figs 8.7a, and b, 8.8a and b, 8.10a and b are summarized in Table 8.2. Generally, as the registration accuracy increases, Euclidean distance and joint entropy decrease while Pearson correlation and mutual information increase.

Note that although mutual information and joint entropy may be used to measure registration quality when the images are in the same modality or in different modalities, normalized Euclidean distance and Pearson correlation should be used only when the images are in the same modality. This is because normalized Euclidean distance and Pearson correlation quantify linear dependency between intensities of homologous voxels in registered images and intensities of registered multimodality images are usually nonlinearly dependent. The results in Table 8.2 show that mutual information has the ability to quantify linear as well as nonlinear dependencies between intensities of homologous voxels in registered images.

Table 8.2 Registration quality measures of Figs 8.7, 8.8, and 8.10.

Figure	NED	PC	SJE	SMI
8.7a	58.20	0.74	2.28	0.41
8.7b	42.90	0.86	1.60	0.56
8.8a	43.57	0.85	1.61	0.55
8.8b	43.39	0.85	1.59	0.56
8.10a	—	—	1.42	0.16
8.10b	—	—	1.33	0.40

Normalized Euclidean distance (NED), Pearson correlation (PC), Shannon's joint entropy (SJE), and Shannon's mutual information (SMI) are shown for each case. NED and PC measures are not reliable when images are in different modalities and so are not shown in the table.

Although a similarity/distance measure is helpful in telling which two registrations are more accurate, they may not be able to tell whether a registration is correct or incorrect. This is because similarity/distance measures tell how correlated or dependent intensities in two images are, while accuracy is a measure of geometric similarity between registered images.

A more suitable measure of accuracy can be obtained by creating a gold standard via simulation. Suppose taking a reference image and creating a test image from it by deforming it using a known transformation model. The transformation finds for each point in the reference image the corresponding point in the simulated test image. This correspondence will be exact, which can then be used as the gold standard.

Now suppose registering the reference image and the simulated test image by the method being evaluated, producing a transformation model. The transformation obtained by the method finds for each point in the reference image a corresponding point in the simulated test image. This correspondence will be approximate. The average distance between exact and approximate corresponding points obtained in the simulated test image from points in the reference image can be used as a measure of registration accuracy.

Although simulation data can produce a gold standard registration that can be compared with an actual registration, accuracy estimation using simulation data has its limits. When the images to be registered are in different modalities, mapping intensities of an image in one modality into intensities of another image in a different modality requires a deep understanding of the characteristics of the sensors generating the images and the true mapping that exists between intensities of corresponding voxels in the two modalities. For some image multimodalities, a unique mapping does not exist between intensities in the images, limiting the effectiveness of simulation data in evaluation of the accuracy of a registration method.

8.5.2 Reliability

Reliability measures the ability of a method in registering images with varying degrees and types of differences. If a registration is acceptable, it makes sense to find its accuracy. However, if the result of a registration cannot be used in the application under consideration, the registration is considered incorrect and is not used when evaluating the accuracy of the registration.

A method may have been designed to register images using a rigid transformation because the images to be registered have only translational and rotational differences. Two MR brain images of a subject taken a short time apart with the same scanner parameters have only translational and rotational differences. If a method has been designed to rigidly register images, it should be tested against images that have only translational and rotational differences. On the other hand, if a method is required to register the brain image of a subject to an atlas, it should have the ability to nonrigidly register two images. Such a method should be tested against images with the kind of geometric differences expected between various brain images and an atlas.

Reliability shows the ratio of image pairs correctly registered and the total number of registrations attempted. Correctly registered images can then be used to measure the registration accuracy.

8.5.3 Speed

Another performance measure that is important in image registration is computational speed. The time required for a method to register two images is the sum of the times required to find feature points in the reference image, find corresponding feature points in the test image, remove the possible outliers, determine a transformation from the obtained homologous points, and resample the test image with the obtained transformation to the geometry of the reference image.

If using local extrema of the LoG of an image as the feature points, the time required to find feature points in the reference image is a linear function of the number of voxels in the image. If the initial homologous points are obtained by template matching, the computation time will linearly depend on the number of points and a linear function of the search space used in the test image to find each point. If the product of the number of points and the number of voxels in a search area is about the same as the number of voxels in the test image, the computation time to find the initial homologous points will be a linear function of the number of voxels in the test image. Therefore, to speed up the computations, there is a need to reduce the sizes of both reference and test images. In the examples demonstrated earlier, the dimensions of the images were reduced by a factor of 2 when finding initial homologous points in the images, speeding up the computations by a factor of 8.

Determination of the final homologous points in the images requires removal of the outliers from among the initial homologous points by RANSAC. If the number of inliers over the number of initial homologous points is w, the likelihood that all four initial homologous points are correct is w^4. Therefore, the probability that at least one of the homologous pair is incorrect is $1 - w^4$. If four homologous pairs are randomly selected k times, the probability that all k cases contain at least one incorrect homologous pair is $(1 - w^4)^k$. Therefore, the probability that at least one of the k cases contain all correct homologous points is $1 - (1 - w^4)^k$. If we want this probability to be P, the number of iterations required to find a case that correctly registers the images will be

$$k = \frac{\log\,(1 - P)}{\log\,(1 - w^4)}. \tag{8.56}$$

For example, when $w = 0.2$ and $P = 0.999$, we find $k = 4314$. This is smaller than the number of voxels in a volume. Therefore, all calculations so far are a linear function of the number of voxels in the reference image, assuming the reference and test images are about the same size.

The time required to compute the parameters of the rigid transformation or volume spline is a quadratic function of the number of homologous points and a linear function of the number of voxels in the reference image. Since the square of the number of homologous points is usually smaller than the number of voxels in the reference image, this step is also a linear function of the number of voxels in the reference image. Therefore, computation time of the rigid registration as well as registration by volume spline is a linear function of the number of voxels in the reference image.

The weighted rigid transformation model requires determining for each voxel in the reference image the homologous voxel in the test image, which is a weighted sum of voxel coordinates determined not only by the rigid transformation of the block containing the voxel but also by the rigid transformations of the adjacent blocks, which can be up to 27 similar calculations. Therefore, the computation time for weighted rigid resampling can be a factor of up to 27 greater than resampling time required by a rigid registration.

Computation times for the registrations depicted in Figs. 8.7b, 8.8a and b, and 8.10b measured on a Windows PC with an Intel Centrino 2 processor are 43.403, 39.545, 101.817, and 21.290 s, respectively. Nonrigid registration by volume spline and weighted rigid transformations take about twice as much time as registration by a rigid transformation. Computation time considerably increases by subdividing the reference image (the domain of approximation) into smaller blocks. The registration depicted in Fig. 8.8a is obtained by subdividing the approximation domain into $1 \times 2 \times 3$ or six blocks, while the registration depicted in Fig. 8.8b is obtained by subdividing the approximation domain into $2 \times 2 \times 4$ or 16 blocks. We see that the time ratio of the two registrations by weighted rigid transformation is proportional to the ratio between the number of blocks or the number of local rigid transformations used to register the images.

8.6 Further Reading

Feature point detection methods: A number of feature point detectors start with 3-D edges. Methods developed by Thirion [21, 22] and Monga and Benayoun [23] start with digital surfaces representing zero-crossings of the LoG of a volumetric image. Principal curvatures [24, 25] at surface points are calculated and points where both principal curvatures become locally extremum are taken as points. Beil et al. [26] use local extrema of Gaussian and mean curvatures as points. Gaussian curvature at a point is the product of principal curvatures there, and mean curvature is the average of the principal curvatures at the point. Betke et al. [27] develop a method for detecting anatomically meaningful points in the trachea, sternum, and spine in CT images. Leong et al. [28] develop a method for detecting predefined anatomic points on laser range scans of the human body.

Frantz et al. [29] and Alker et al. [30] use parametric models to find points in volumetric images. The parameters of a model are determined by minimizing the error in fitting the model to local 3-D edges. Wörz and Rohr [31] extend this parametric model fitting method to volumes.

Liu et al. [32] create a model by segmenting the reference image and selecting points in the image manually. The model with known points is then initialized in the test image and the model is iteratively deformed to best fit the test image. The points obtained after model deformation are then used as the points corresponding to the points in the reference image.

Hartkens et al. [33, 34] and Rohr et al. [35] compare performances of various differential point detectors, finding that first-derivative detectors produce more repeatable points than second-derivative detectors.

Ho and Gibbins [36] and Ramos dos Santos et al. [37] use maximal curvature points on surface structures as points to align surfaces/volumes.

Methods finding homologous points: A point correspondence algorithm based on a combined local and global voting process is described by Buch et al. [38]. At the local level, initial homologous points are obtained and at the global level the initial homologous points satisfying a required constraint are detected and kept. A point correspondence method based on 3-D template matching using spherical templates is described by Ding et al. [39].

Many methods for finding homologous points in 2-D images can be extended to 3-D to find homologous points in image volumes. The methods include graph matching [40], appearance-based matching [41], Hough voting [42], group averaging [43], and coarse-to-fine matching [44].

Transformation models: The volume spline transformation described in Section 8.4.1 is an extension of surface spline [45], also known as thin-plate spline [46, 47], to 3-D. Volume spline does not require a regular grid of homologous points and, therefore, is very easy to use.

A transformation that requires a regular grid of homologous points is B-spline [48–51]. To determine a grid of homologous points in images, uniformly spaced templates are taken in the reference image and searched for in the test image. Templates are taken large enough so that if any of them fall in a homogeneous area, there will be sufficient details outside the homogeneous area but within the template to provide sufficient information to enable determination of reliable homologous points. Due to the requirement for the templates to be large, B-spline transformation is limited to images with slowly varying geometric differences.

A multilevel implementation of the B-spline transformation has been suggested to accommodate larger local geometric differences between the images [52]. However, lack of points in homogeneous areas in the reference image limits general use of B-splines in nonrigid registration. Transformations formulated as a fractional Euler–Lagrange equations [53], elastic warping of the Piola–Kirchhoff stress tensor [54], and Gaussian forces [55] are attempts to overcome some of the weaknesses of B-spline transformation and allow sharper local geometric differences between the images. To create discontinuity within the transformation field, Wu et al. [56] segment images, find a transformation model relating geometries of corresponding regions in the images, and then create a global transformation from a composite of local transformations to register the images. This method is found effective in registering 4-D CT lung images where the lungs, in addition to expanding/shrinking, slide against chest walls. Holden [57] provides an excellent review of various transformation models for nonrigid registration.

A great number of interpolation and approximation methods have appeared in Approximation Theory [58–63] that can be used in nonrigid registration of volumetric images. A bibliography of such methods is provided by Franke and Schumaker [64], and more recent works have appeared in collections of papers by Chui et al. [65], Dyn et al. [66], and Jetter et al. [67].

Other volumetric methods: While the focus of this chapter was on feature-based registration methods, a great number of intensity-based methods have appeared in the literature that achieve volumetric image registration by minimizing a cost function that is formulated in terms of intensity differences between images [68–70]. Methods that use both feature points as well as intensity patterns to register 2-D and volumetric images have also been proposed [71]. Sotiras et al. [72] provide a thorough review of intensity-based, as well as feature-based, nonrigid registration methods.

References

1 K. D. Toennies, *Guide to Medical Image Analysis*, Springer, 2012.

2 M. A. Fischler and R. C. Bolles, Random sample consensus: a paradigm for model fitting with applications to image analysis and automated cartography, *Communications of the ACM*, **24**(6):381–395, 1981.

3 B. Yang, J. Flusser, and T. Suk, 3D rotation invariants of Gaussian-Hermite moments, *Pattern Recognition Letters*, **54**:18–26, 2015.

4 D. Blostein and N. Ahuja, A multiscale region detector, *Computer Vision, Graphics and Image Processing*, **45**:22–41, 1989.

5 W. Förstner, A feature based correspondence algorithm for image matching, *International Archives of the Photogrammetry, Remote Sensing*, **26**:150–166, 1986.

6 W. Förstner and E. Gülch, A fast operator for detection and precise location of distinct points, corners and centers of circular features, in *Intercommission Conference on Fast Processing of Photogrammetric Data*, Interlaken, Switzerland, 281–305, 1987.

7 C. Harris and M. Stephens, A combined corner and edge detector, in *Proceedings of the 4th Alvey Vision Conference (AVC88)*, University Manchester, 147–151, 1988.

8 K. Rohr, Extraction of 3D anatomical point landmarks based on invariance principles, *Pattern Recognition*, **32**:3–15, 1999.

9 S. Frantz, K. Rohr, and H. S. Stiehl, Multi-step differential approaches for the localization of 3D point landmarks in medical images, *Journal of Computing and Information Technology*, **6**:435–447, 1998.

10 K. Rohr, On 3D differential operators for detecting point landmarks, *Image and Vision Computing*, **15**:219–233, 1997.

11 J. Ruiz-Alzola, R. Kikinis, and C. F. Westin, Detection of point landmarks in multidimensional tensor data, *Signal Processing*, **81**:2243–3347, 2001.

12 P. R. Beaudet, Rotationally invariant image operators, in *Proceedings of International Conference on Pattern Recognition*, 579–583, 1978.

13 D. Pilutti, M. Strumia, and S. Hadjidemetriou, Bimodal nonrigid registration of brain MRI data with deconvolution of joint statistics, *IEEE Transactions on Medical Imaging*, **23**(9):3999–4009, 2014.

14 W. Shi, X. Zhuang, H. Wang, et al., A comprehensive cardiac motion estimation framework using both untagged and 3-D tagged MR images based on nonrigid registration, *IEEE Transactions on Medical Imaging*, **31**(6):1263–1275, 2012.

15 I. R. H. Jackson, Convergence properties of radial basis functions, *Constructive Approximation*, **4**:243–264, 1988.

16 K. Pearson, Contributions to the mathematical theory of evolution, III, Regression, heredity, and panmixia, *Philosophical Transactions of the*

Royal Society of London, Series A: Mathematical, Physical and Engineering Sciences, **187**:253–318, 1896.

17 I. M. Gel'fand and A. M. Yaglom, Calculation of the amount of information about a random function contained in another such function, *American Mathematical Society Translations*, **2**(12):199–246, 1959.

18 C. E. Shannon, in *The Mathematical Theory of Communication*, C. E. Shannon and W. Weaver (Eds.), University of Illinois Press, Urbana, IL, 29–125, 1949, reprint 1998.

19 A. Rényi, *Probability Theory*, American Elsevier Publishing, North Holland, Amsterdam, 1970.

20 R. O. Duda, P. E. Hart, and D. G. Stork, *Pattern Classification*, Second Edition, Wiley-Interscience Publishing, New York, 2001.

21 J. P. Thirion, Extremal points: definition and applications to 3D image registration, in *Proceedings of IEEE Conference on Computer Vision and Pattern Recognition*, 587–592, 1994.

22 J. P. Thirion, New feature points based on geometric invariants for 3D image registration, *International Journal of Computer Vision*, **18**(2):121–137, 1996.

23 O. Monga and S. Benayoun, Using partial derivatives of 3D images to extract typical surface features, *Computer Vision and Image Understanding*, **61**(2):171–189, 1995.

24 M. E. Mortenson, *Geometric Modeling*, Wiley Press, New York, 1985.

25 L. Zagorchev and A. Goshtasby, A curvature-adaptive implicit surface reconstruction for irregularly spaced points, *IEEE Transactions on Visualization and Computer Graphics*, **18**(9):1460–1473, 2012.

26 W. Beil, K. Rohr, and H. S. Stiehl, Investigation of approaches for the localization of anatomical landmarks in 3D medical images, in *Computer Assisted Radiology and Surgery*, H. U. Lemke et al. (Eds.), Elsevier Science, 265–270, 1997.

27 M. Betke, H. Hong, D. Thomas, C. Prince, and J. P. Ko, Landmark detection in chest and registration of lung surfaces with an application to nodule registration, *Medical Image Analysis*, 7:265–281, 2003.

28 I.-F. Leong, J.-J. Fang, and M.-J. Tsai, Automatic body feature extraction from a marker-less scanned human body, *Computer-Aided Design*, **39**:568–582, 2007.

29 S. Franz, K. Rohr, and H. S. Stiehl, Localization of 3D anatomical point landmarks in 3D tomographic images using deformable models, in *Proceedings of the 3rd International Conference on Medical Image Computing and Computer-Assisted Intervention (MICCAI)*, Pittsburgh, PA, USA, 11–14, 2000.

30 M. Alker, S. Frantz, K. Rohr, and H. S. Stiehl, Improving the robustness in extracting 3D point landmarks from 3D medical images using parametric

deformable models, in *Lecture Notes in Computer Science*, Vol. **2191**, B. Radig and S. Florczyk (Eds.), Springer, Heidelberg, 108–115, 2001.

31 S. Wörz and K. Rohr, Localization of anatomical point landmarks in 3D medical images by fitting 3D parametric intensity models, *Medical Image Analysis*, **10**:41–58, 2006.

32 J. Liu, W. Gao, S. Huang, and W. L. Nowinski, A model-based, semi-global segmentation approach for automatic 3-D point landmark localization in neuroimages, *IEEE Transactions on Medical Imaging*, **27**(8):1034–1044, 2008.

33 T. Hartkens, K. Rohr, and H. S. Stiehl, Performance of 3D differential operators for the detection of anatomical point landmarks in MR and CT images, in *Medical Imaging—Image Processing (MI'99), Proceedings of SPIE International Symposium*, Vol. **3661**(1), K. M. Hanson (Ed.), San Diego, CA, 32–43, 1999.

34 T. Hartkens, K. Rohr, and H. S. Stiehl, Evaluation of 3D operators for the detection of anatomical point landmarks in MR and CT images, *Computer Vision and Image Understanding*, **86**:118–136, 2002.

35 K. Rohr, H. S. Stiehl, S. Frantz, and T. Hartkens, Performance characterization of landmark operators, in *Performance Characterization in Computer Vision, Computational Imaging and Vision Series*, Vol. **17**, R. Klette, H. S. Stiehl, M. A. Viergever, and K. L. Vincken (Eds.), Kluwer Academic Publishers, Dordrecht, Boston, MA, London, 285–297, 2000.

36 H. T. Ho and D. Gibbins, Curvature-based approach for multi-scale feature extraction from 3D meshes and unstructured point clouds, *IET Computer Vision*, **3**(4):201–212, 2009.

37 T. Ramos dos Santos, A. Seitel, T. Kilgus, et al., Pose-independent surface matching for intra-operative soft-tissue marker-less registration, *Medical Image Analysis*, **18**:1101–1114, 2014.

38 A. G. Buch, Y. Yang, N. Krüger, and H. G. Petersen, In search of inliers: 3D correspondence by local global voting, in *IEEE Conference on Computer Vision and Pattern Recognition*, 2075–2082, 2014.

39 L. Ding, A. Goshtasby, and M. Satter, Volume image registration by template matching, *Image and Vision Computing*, **19**(12):821–832, 2001.

40 M. Leordeanu and M. Hebert, A spectral technique for correspondence problems using pairwise constraints, in *International Conference Computer Vision*, Vol. **2**, 1482–1489, 2005.

41 G. Tolias and Y. Avrithis, Speeded-up, relaxed spatial matching, in *International Conference on Computer Vision*, 1653–1660, 2011.

42 H.-S. Chen, Y.-Y. Lin, and B.-Y. Chen, Robust feature matching with alternate Hough and inverted Hough transforms, in *International Conference on Computer Vision*, 2762–2769, 2013.

43 M. Temerinac-Ott, M. Keuper, and H. Burkhardt, Evaluation of a new point clouds registration method based on group averaging features, *International Conference on Pattern Recognition*, 2452–2455, 2010.

44 K. Grauman and T. Darrell, The pyramid match Kernel: discriminative classification with sets of image features, in *International Conference on Computer Vision*, Vol. **2**, 1458–1465, 2005.

45 A. Goshtasby, Registration of image with geometric distortion, *IEEE Transactions on Geoscience and Remote Sensing*, **26**(1):60–64, 1988.

46 F. L. Bookstein, Principal warps: thin-plate splines and the decomposition of deformations, *IEEE Transactions on Pattern Analysis and Machine Intelligence*, **11**(6):567–585, 1989.

47 K. Rohr, M. Forstner, and H. S. Stiehl, Spline-based elastic image registration: integration of landmark errors and orientation attributes, *Computer Vision and Image Understanding*, **90**:153–168, 2003.

48 H. Rivaz, S. J.-S. Chen, and D. L. Collins, Automatic deformable MR-ultrasound registration for image-guided neurosurgery, *IEEE Transactions on Medical Imaging*, **34**(2):366–380, 2015.

49 S. Lee, G. Wolberg, K.-Y. Chwa, and S. Y. Shin, Image metamorphosis with scattered feature constraints, *IEEE Transactions on Visualization Computer Graphics*, **2**:337–354, 1996.

50 D. Rueckert, L. I. Sonoda, C. Hayes, D. L. G. Hill, M. O. Leach, and D. J. Hawke, Nonrigid registration using free-form deformations: application to breast MR images, *IEEE Transactions on Medical Imaging*, **18**(8):712–721, 1999.

51 D. Rueckert, P. Aljabar, R. A. Heckermann, J. V. Hajnal, and A. Hammers, Diffeomorphic registration using B-Splines, in *Proceedings of Medical Image Computing and Computer-Assisted Intervention*, 1–8, 2006.

52 S. Lee, G. Wolberg, and S. Y. Shin, Scattered data interpolation with multilevel B-splines, *IEEE Transactions on Visualization Computer Graphics*, **3**:228–244, 1997.

53 J. Zhang and K. Chen, Variational image registration by a total fractional-order variation model, *Journal of Computational Physics*, **293**:442–461, 2015.

54 C. Davatzikos, Spatial transformation and registration of brain images using elastically deformable models, *Computer Vision and Image Understanding*, **66**(2):207–222, 1997.

55 S. Wörz and K. Rohr, Physics-based elastic registration using non-radial basis functions and including landmark localization uncertainties, *Computer Vision and Image Understanding*, **111**:263–274, 2008.

56 Z. Wu, E. Rietzel, V. Boldea, D. Sarrut, and G. C. Sharp, Evaluation of deformable registration of patient lung 4DCT with subanatomical region segmentations, *Medical Physics*, **35**(2):775–781, 2008.

57 M. Holden, A review of geometric transformations for nonrigid body registration, *IEEE Transactions on Medical Imaging*, **27**(1):111–128, 2008.

58 P. Alfeld, Scattered data interpolation in three or more variables, in *Mathematical Methods in Computer Aided Geometric Design*, T. Lyche and L. Schumaker (eds.), Academic Press, 1–33, 1989.

59 J. L. Brown and W. L. Etheridge, Local approximation of functions over points scattered in R^m, *Applied Numerical Mathematics*, **29**:189–199, 1999.

60 A. L. Mehaute, L. L. Schumaker, and L. Traversoni, Multivariate scattered data fitting, *Journal of Computational and Applied Mathematics*, **73**:1–4, 1996.

61 G. M. Nielson and J. Tvedt, Comparing methods of interpolation for scattered volumetric data, in *State of the Art in Computer Graphics: Aspects of Visualization*, D. Rogers and R. Earnshaw (Eds.), Springer-Verlag, 67–86, 1994.

62 A. Raviv and G. Elber, Three-dimensional freeform sculpting via zero sets of scalar trivariate functions, *Computer-Aided Design*, **32**:513–526, 2000.

63 R. J. Renka, Multivariate interpolation of large sets of scattered data, *ACM Transactions on Mathematical Software*, **14**(2):139–148, 1988.

64 R. Franke and L. L. Schumaker, *A Bibliography of Multivariate Approximation*, Topics in Multivariate Approximation, Academic Press, 275–335, 1987.

65 C. Chui, L. Shumaker, and F. Utrerus, *Topics in Multivariate Approximation*, Academic Press, New York, 1987.

66 N. Dyn, R. Schaback, M. D. Buchmann, et al. *Multivariate Approximation and Applications*, Cambridge University Press, 2001.

67 K. Jetter, M. D. Buhmann, W. Haussmann, et al. *Topics in Multivariate Approximation and Interpolation*, Elsevier, 2006.

68 M. P. Heinrich, I. J. A. Simpson, B. W. Papiez, Sir M. Brady, and J. A. Schnabel, Deformable image registration by combining uncertainty estimates from supervoxel belief propagation, *Medical Image Analysis*, **27**:57–71, 2016.

69 R. W. K. So, T. W. H. Tang, and A. C. S. Chung, Non-rigid image registration of brain magnetic resonance images using graph-cuts, *Pattern Recognition*, **44**:2450–2467, 2011.

70 R. B. Tennakoon, A. Bab-Hadiashar, Z. Cao, and M. de Bruijne, Nonrigid registration of volumetric images using ranked order statistics, *IEEE Transactions on Medical Imaging*, **33**(2):422–432, 2014.

71 S. Wörz and K. Rohr, Spline-based hybrid image registration using landmark and intensity information based on matrix-valued non-radial basis functions, *International Journal of Computer Vision*, **106**:76–92, 2014.

72 A. Sotiras, C. Davatzikos, and N. Paragios, Deformable medical image registration: a survey, *IEEE Transactions on Medical Imaging*, **32**(7):1153–1190, 2013.

9

Validation Methods

9.1 Introduction

Validation is the process of evaluating a claim. The designer of an image registration software builds the software from components aiming to deliver required performance measures. To validate the performance measures of each component of the system as well as the performance measures of the entire system, the designer carries out experiments using representative images the software is designed for and updates the theoretic performance measures with the actual ones. The user of the software may decide to validate the performance measures claimed by the designer using images available to the user.

The performance measures of a registration software are *accuracy, reliability*, and *speed*. Determination of accuracy requires comparison of results obtained by the software with true results. Reliability measures the ability of the software to register images under varying degrees of noise and geometric and intensity degradations. Speed is related to the computational complexities of the components of the software and the interaction between the components.

Accuracy, reliability, and speed are interdependent. If images used for registration contain very little noise and intensity and geometric differences, and if the images represent two instances of a rigid body in motion, registration will be highly accurate, highly reliable, and fast. However, if the images to be registered are noisy and contain intensity and geometric differences, registration will not be as accurate, reliable, or fast. If a software can register images even under noise and various intensity and geometric degradations, the software will be very reliable.

Evaluation of the performance measures of the components of a registration software were discussed in the preceding chapters. In this chapter, various methods for validating the accuracy of the entire registration software are discussed. This validation is mostly for the user of a registration software.

Theory and Applications of Image Registration, First Edition. Arthur Ardeshir Goshtasby.
© 2017 John Wiley & Sons, Inc. Published 2017 by John Wiley & Sons, Inc.

To determine the accuracy of a registration software, a set of perfectly registered images is needed. Perfect registration results can be created through simulation. This involves taking a reference image and converting it into a test image by appropriate intensity and geometry mapping. Knowing the exact geometric relation between the reference and test images, the accuracy with which the software finds the same relation is determined.

Simulation data, however, can be unrealistic. To create a data set that is as close as possible to a real data set, markers are placed at or attached to the scene before taking the images. These are reflective markers [1] left in a scene in remote sensing images or fiducial markers attached to a subject in medical images [2–4]. The geometric relation between two images of a scene/subject can be determined from the locations of the markers and the relation can be used as the gold standard to evaluate the accuracy of a registration software to find the same relation without the markers.

Because realistic images are obtained when using markers, the obtained accuracy will be more realistic than when using simulation data to measure the same. However, placement of markers in a scene or their attachment to a subject is not always possible. An immediate method for measuring the accuracy of a registration software is visual evaluation of the quality of the registration. For example, an expert may observe the result of an automatic registration and determine its suitability for use in a particular application.

Various methods for comparing registration accuracies of two or more software systems have been developed. An ideal validation method can produce an absolute accuracy measure; however, validation methods that can distinguish more accurate registration methods over less accurate ones are also useful. In the following sections, various methods for determining the accuracy of a registration software are described.

9.2 Validation Using Simulation Data

Simulation data involves using a reference image to create a test image with a known transformation model. When simulation data is used to determine a software's accuracy, the registration parameters are estimated from the reference and simulated test images. Then, either the parameters are directly compared with known transformation parameters or the distances of a number of homologous points in the images after registration are used to measure the registration accuracy.

If $\{\mathbf{p}_i : i = 1, \ldots, n\}$ are n points in the reference image, and if the test image is obtained with transformation F, the locations of the homologous points in the test image will be $\mathbf{P}_i = F(\mathbf{p}_i)$ for $i = 1, \ldots, n$. Note that the n points in the reference image do not have to be feature points, they can be any points;

therefore, they can be taken randomly or uniformly spaced over the reference image domain.

If a registration software finds F' to be the transformation relating the geometries of the images, registration error at point $\mathbf{p}_i$ will be

$$E_i = \|F(\mathbf{p}_i) - F'(\mathbf{p}_i)\|. \tag{9.1}$$

Average error

$$\text{AVGE} = \frac{1}{n} \sum_{i=1}^{n} E_i, \tag{9.2}$$

root-mean-squared (RMS) error

$$\text{RMSE} = \left\{ \frac{1}{n} \sum_{i=1}^{n} E_i^2 \right\}^{\frac{1}{2}}, \tag{9.3}$$

or maximum error

$$\text{MAXE} = \max_{i=1}^{n} \{E_i\} \tag{9.4}$$

can be used to measure the accuracy of the software.

If a software is supposed to register same modality images, the creation of a simulated test image from a reference image involves an appropriate warping of the reference image [5]. The more realistic the deformation model is, the more realistic the simulation data will be [6, 7].

The process of creating simulation data in different modalities is more challenging. A deep understanding of the characteristics of the sensors capturing the images is required to convert intensities in one modality to realistic intensities in another modality. Using the characteristics of the sensors capturing the images, Keibel et al. [8] created simulation PET images from magnetic resonance (MR) images, and Gholipour et al. [9] created simulated functional MR images from anatomic MR images for validation of registration accuracy.

9.3 Validation Using a Gold Standard

Gold standard validation involves creating registration results that are as close as possible to true results. If a software should find the translation and rotation parameters between two images that are related by a rigid transformation, markers are left in the scene and images of the scene are captured. The images are registered without the markers and the locations of homologous markers in the images is used to determine the registration accuracy. The markers should be large enough to be visible in the images but not so large that they hide critical parts of the scene.

When evaluating a 2-D registration software, the markers should not fall on a line, and when evaluating a 3-D registration software, the markers should not fall on a line or on a plane. The markers should be spread all over the scene. The best marker locations are those uniformly spaced and symmetric with respect to the scene center so that zero-mean errors among the markers can cancel each other out. If it is not possible to place the markers uniformly or symmetrically, the markers should be spread as much as possible over the scene.

Through simulation, Fitzpatrick [10] has shown that if the markers are randomly placed, marker localization error does not affect overall registration error. Errors at randomly placed markers tend to cancel each other out, having very little influence on the computed registration error. Since some randomly placed markers may fall near a plane, they can produce an inaccurate estimation of the gold standard transformation and, consequently, an unreliable accuracy measure. Seginer [11] has confirmed this using real marker positions. In practice, therefore, the arrangement of fiducial markers affects the measurement of registration accuracy. The smallest error measurements are expected when the markers are uniformly spaced and are symmetric with respect to the scene center.

The locations of homologous markers in reference and test images are used to determine the gold standard transformation. If the transformation is rigid, the translation and rotation parameters are the gold standard parameters that a registration software should find, and if the transformation model is nonrigid, the RMS distance between markers after registration by the software can be used to measure the registration accuracy. Note that the software is not aware of the markers and registers the images using image intensities/features. The locations of the markers are used to evaluate the registration accuracy.

Therefore, if $\{\mathbf{p}_i : i = 1, \ldots, n\}$ are n markers in the reference image and $\{\mathbf{P}_i : i = 1, \ldots, n\}$ are the same markers in the test image, if transformation F is obtained from the coordinates of homologous markers in the images and if a registration software registers the images with transformation model F' obtained without the markers, the registration error obtained at point $\mathbf{p}_i$ will be

$$E_i = \|F(\mathbf{p}_i) - F'(\mathbf{p}_i)\|. \tag{9.5}$$

Note that $\mathbf{P}_i \approx F(\mathbf{p}_i)$. If $n > 4$, the rigid transformation obtained from the n points will not be able to map all markers in the reference image exactly to the corresponding markers in the test image. The mapping will be approximate, involving some errors; therefore, the gold standard transformation used to estimate E_i itself will contain some error. If a nonrigid transformation model such as a volume spline is used as the transformation, function F will then be able to map all reference markers to the exact test markers and the gold standard transformation will not contain errors in relating homologous markers in the images.

Registration accuracy can again be expressed in terms of average, RMS, or maximum distance between markers in the test image and points obtained in the test image by the transformation obtained by the software when using the markers in the reference image.

In medical images, the markers are usually outside a subject's body, while registration is required inside the subject's body; therefore, use of marker locations to measure the software's accuracy may not be appropriate. Usually, a number of well-defined anatomic landmarks are selected in the reference image by an expert and the locations of homologous landmarks are obtained in the test image using the transformation computed from the locations of homologous markers in the images. The locations of homologous anatomic landmarks instead of the locations of the markers are then used as the gold standard to evaluate the accuracy of a registration software.

If two images are rotated with respect to each other, the distance between homologous points increases by moving away from the axis of rotation. In medical images, the axis of rotation is usually near the image center; therefore, homologous points farther from the image center are expected to have a larger distance between them than homologous points near the image center. If the markers are outside the subject's body, they are far from the image center and, therefore, the distances between homologous markers will be larger than the distances between homologous points inside the subject. Consequently, registration errors at markers outside the body will be higher than registration errors at anatomic landmarks that are inside the body. Errors computed at the markers by the transformation obtained by a software can be considered an upper limit on the registration error of the software.

Fiducial markers have been extensively used in validation of medical image registration accuracy. West et al. [4] used fiducial markers to evaluate registration of MR–computed tomography (CT) and MR–positron emission tomography (PET) brain images, and Barnden et al. [2] used fiducial markers to evaluate registration of MR and single-photon emission tomography (SPET) images.

A more suitable gold standard for validation of registration software may be obtained if the fiducial markers are placed inside the subject. But that may not be possible when the subject is a live human. Penney et al. [12] used a human cadaver, while Pawiro et al. [3], Yan et al. [13], and Zakariaee [14] used a pig cadaver to create suitable gold standards for the validation of rigid and nonrigid registration accuracy.

9.4   Validation by an Expert Observer

If the use of fiducial markers is not feasible in the evaluation of a registration software, homologous anatomic landmarks selected by an expert observer can be used instead. To reduce observer bias, the locations of homologous landmarks selected by an observer can be further optimized by an appropriate similarity or distance measure using the information surrounding the homologous landmarks.

When the images to be registered are in different modalities, the images are related by a rigid transformation, and realistic simulation data cannot be created to evaluate a registration software, an expert may register the images interactively by translating and rotating the test image with respect to the reference image. Once the images are registered, the transformation parameters interactively obtained can be used to determine the registration accuracy of the software. To reduce observer bias, after the interactive registration, a search in the parameter space in the neighborhood of the interactively determined parameters can be made to find parameters that minimize a distance measure.

Realistic data can be generated with the aid of an expert observer when simulation data are not realistic enough and the creation of data from fiducial markers is not feasible. Woods et al. [15] used manually selected anatomic landmarks in MR and PET brain images, while Vik et al. [16] and Murphy et al. [17] used landmarks in thoracic CT images manually selected by an expert to evaluate the accuracy of a nonrigid registration software.

A software that registers all images in an application is desired. However, that is usually not possible. Registration methods often find the registration parameters by minimizing a distance measure or a cost function. Due to noise and other image degradations, the lowest cost registration may not be the correct registration; therefore, when the result of a registration is critical in decision-making, the correctness of the result must be visually verified. Yin et al. [18] and Spampinato et al. [19] interactively registered images with the aid of an expert and used the results to distinguish a correct registration from an incorrect one obtained by a software.

Pietrzyk et al. [20] found multimodality image registration accuracy obtained by expert observers to be the same or higher than the accuracy obtained by available automatic registration software. By comparing registration accuracy of expert observers to gold standards obtained by fiducial markers, Fitzpatrick et al. [21] found interactive registration accuracy to be acceptable in clinical applications.

9.5 Validation Using a Consistency Measure

Given a reference image R and a test image T, if a rigid registration software produces transformation $\mathbf{M}_1$ when registering image T to image R and it produces transformation $\mathbf{M}_2$ when registering image R to image T, then the software is considered accurate if $\mathbf{M}_1 \mathbf{M}_2 \approx \mathbf{I}$, where $\mathbf{I}$ is the identity matrix. After transformation with $\mathbf{M}_2$ point $\mathbf{p}_i$ in the reference image will be a point $\mathbf{q}_i$ in the test image, and if after transformation by $\mathbf{M}_1$ point $\mathbf{q}_i$ in the test image is a point $\mathbf{r}_i$ in the reference image, the distance between $\mathbf{p}_i$ and $\mathbf{r}_i$ can be used as a measure of accuracy. Note that

$$\|\mathbf{p}_i - \mathbf{r}_i\| = \|\mathbf{p}_i - \mathbf{M}_1\mathbf{M}_2\mathbf{p}_i\|, \tag{9.6}$$
$$= \|\mathbf{p}_i(\mathbf{I} - \mathbf{M}_1\mathbf{M}_2)\|. \tag{9.7}$$

If n homologous points are available, the registration consistency measure (RCM) defined by

$$\text{RCM}_2 = \frac{1}{n}\sum_{i=1}^{n} \|\mathbf{p}_i - \mathbf{r}_i\| \tag{9.8}$$

can be used as the average distance between n points after forward transformation and then backward transformation. The closer RCM_2 is to 0, the more accurate the software is expected to be. Use of registration consistency in the measurement of registration accuracy was suggested by Woods et al. [22].

When evaluating the accuracy of a nonrigid registration software, transformations $\mathbf{M}_1$ and $\mathbf{M}_2$ become nonlinear. Applying transformation $\mathbf{M}_2$ to a point $\mathbf{p}_i$ in the reference image a point $\mathbf{q}_i$ in the test image is obtained. Then, point $\mathbf{q}_i$ is substituted into function $\mathbf{M}_1$ to obtain point $\mathbf{r}_i$ in the reference image. The distance between $\mathbf{p}_i$ and $\mathbf{r}_i$ is then used as a measure of registration error at $\mathbf{p}_i$. This shows that Eq. (9.8) can be used to measure consistency in nonrigid registration also.

The possibility exists that $\mathbf{M}_1$ and $\mathbf{M}_2$ are both incorrect but are nearly the inverse of each other. If point $\mathbf{p}_i$ in the reference image best matches point $\mathbf{q}_i$ in the test image based on information in the neighborhoods of the points, the likelihood exists that point $\mathbf{q}_i$ best matches point $\mathbf{p}_i$ in the reference image, and the likelihood can be high. To obtain a more robust consistency measure, use of three [23, 24] or more images [25, 26] have been suggested.

If three images of a scene, I_1, I_2, and I_3, are available, and if the transformation registering I_1 to I_2 is $\mathbf{M}_{12}$, the transformation registering I_2 to I_3 is $\mathbf{M}_{23}$, and the transformation registering I_3 to I_1 is $\mathbf{M}_{31}$, then, if all three registrations are accurate, $\mathbf{M}_{12}\mathbf{M}_{23}\mathbf{M}_{31}$ will be very close to an identity matrix, and a point $\mathbf{p}_i$ in I_1 after the three transformations will be a point $\mathbf{p}'_i$ that will be very close to $\mathbf{p}_i$. Therefore, $\|\mathbf{p}_i - \mathbf{p}'_i\|$ can be considered registration error at point $\mathbf{p}_i$. If n points are available, the RCM obtained from the three transformations will be

$$\text{RCM}_3 = \frac{1}{n}\sum_{i=1}^{n} \|\mathbf{p}_i - \mathbf{p}'_i\|, \tag{9.9}$$

where $\mathbf{p}'_i = \mathbf{M}_{12}\mathbf{M}_{23}\mathbf{M}_{31}\mathbf{p}_i$. When more than three images are available, either combinations of three images are used or the images are used in a sequence starting from an image and ending with the same image.

When various combinations of images are used, the average error obtained from the combinations can be used as the registration error. The consistency measures defined above are actually consistency errors. The larger a consistency measure, the less accurate the registration is expected to be. As the number of images used in the measurement of the consistency measure increases, the smaller the likelihood will be that two incorrect or inaccurate registrations cancel out each other's effects and produce a low registration error. Therefore, as more images are used, the confidence level of the obtained consistency measure as an indicator of registration error will increase.

The points $\{\mathbf{p}_i : i = 1, \dots, n\}$ used to measure the consistency measure can be all image pixels/voxels in the overlap area of the images after registration, or they can be uniformly spaced points within the area of overlap of the images after registration. It is important for the points to be uniformly spaced to capture errors in all areas in the domain of registration. This is especially important when validating the accuracy of a nonrigid registration software where geometric difference between the images varies across the transformation domain.

9.6   Validation Using a Similarity/Distance Measure

It is clear than when two images are in perfect alignment, corresponding intensities in the images will be very dependent. The dependency computed by a similarity measure, however, depends on many factors. Perfectly registered images may produce a low similarity measure if one or both images are noisy, have intensity differences, or contain occluded regions; therefore, although a very high similarity measure can indicate an accurate registration, a low similarity measure may falsely indicate an incorrect or inaccurate registration.

When validating the accuracy of a registration software by a similarity measure, the process must be aided by an expert observer. The expert observer can classify a registration into (A) highly accurate, (B) accurate, (C) acceptable, and (D) unacceptable, and also find the highest and lowest similarity measures in each category. The percentage of registrations obtained under each category can then be used to characterize the accuracy of the software in a particular case.

Suppose the highest and lowest similarity measures in the four categories are (A_h, A_l), (B_h, B_l), (C_h, C_l), and (D_h, D_l). The highest and lowest similarity measures in each category can be used to determine the accuracy of a registration software on new images. For example, if an *accurate* registration is needed in an application, the obtained similarity must be equal to or higher than B_l. Note that if $B_l < C_h$, C_h should be used instead of B_l to avoid classifying a possible *acceptable* registration as an *accurate* one. Therefore, if the similarities within adjacent categories overlap, the lowest similarity in a category that uniquely identifies that category should be used to separate that category from the category below it.

If instead of a similarity measure a distance measure is needed, the inverse of the distance measure can be treated as the similarity measure and registration accuracy can be determined in the same manner described above.

Note that since a similarity or a distance measured is calculated after a registration, correspondence between pixels/voxels in the images will be known. Corresponding pixel/voxel intensities are needed to determine a similarity/distance measure; therefore, the same process can be used to validate both rigid and nonrigid registration software.

Among the similarity/distance measures widely used in the validation of image registration accuracy are Pearson correlation, Shannon mutual information, and sum of squared intensity differences [27, 28].

9.7 Further Reading

Quantitative evaluation of software performance measures has been an area of active research from very early in software engineering [29]. Quantitative evaluation is particularly important when critical decisions are to be made based on the results produced by the software [30]. This is certainly true when dealing with medical images where the outcome of a registration could mean the success or failure of a diagnosis or treatment.

Since human subject data is not always possible to obtain, instead of using images of actual humans to evaluate a new medical image registration software, images of phantom humans have been used. Phantoms of the brain [31, 32], pelvic [14, 19], and other human organs have been created and used in validation of registration software systems. A phantom makes available to the researcher unlimited access to a synthetic human body for investigation.

A number of studies [33, 34] have determined the accuracy of a registration software via cross-validation [35]. Cross-validation involves using a subset of the homologous points to find the transformation parameters while using the remaining homologous points to evaluate the accuracy of the obtained transformation.

Evaluation of a software that registers images to an atlas requires the ability to work with labeled images. An atlas usually contains segmented regions with labels identifying different parts of an organ or different organs in an image. Therefore, the evaluation of the software that registers images to an atlas requires the ability to compare segmented regions in two images. The degree of overlap between regions of the same label, the mean distance [36], and the Hausdorff distance between surfaces delimiting the same labeled regions have been used to measure registration accuracy [37]. Hausdorff distance is the maximum of minimum distances between two surfaces [38].

Gonçalves et al. [39] provide various measures for evaluating a registration accuracy using homologous points in the images after registration. They include (1) the RMS distance between homologous points, (2) the change in RMS distance when registering the images by leaving out one homologous pair and repeating the same by leaving out other homologous pairs, (3) the number of homologous points that are farther than a threshold distance, (4) the distribution of the homologous distances, and (5) a scatter measure of the homologous distances.

References

1 K. Pathak, D. Bornmann, J. Elseberg, N. Vaskevcius, A. Birk, and A. Nüchter, Evaluation of the robustness of planar-patches based 3D-registration using marker-based ground-truth in an outdoor urban scenario, in *IEEE/RSJ International Conference on Intelligent Robots and Systems*, 5725–5730, 2010.

2 L. Barnden, R. Kwiatek, Y. Lau, B. Hutton, L. Thurfjell, K. Pilem, and C. Rowe, Validation of fully automatic brain SPET to MR co-registration, *European Journal of Nuclear Medicine*, **27**(2):147–154, 2000.

3 S. A. Pawiro, P. Markelj, F. Pernuš, et al., Validation for 2D/3D registration I: a new gold standard data set, *Medical Physics*, **38**(3):1481–1490, 2011.

4 J. West, M. Fitzpatrick, M. Y. Wang, et al., Comparison and evaluation of retrospective intermodality image registration techniques, *Journal of Computer Assisted Tomography*, **21**:554–566, 1997.

5 Y.-Y. Chou and O. Škinjar, Ground truth data for validation of nonrigid image registration algorithms, in *International Symposium on Biomedical Imaging: Nano to Macro*, vol. **1**, 716–719, 2004.

6 F. J. P. Richard, P. R. Bakić, and A. D. A. Maidment, Mammogram registration: a phantom-based evaluation of compressed Breast Thickness variation effects, *IEEE Transactions on Medical Imaging*, **25**(2):188–197, 2006.

7 J. A. Schnabel, C. Tanner, A. D. Castellano-Smith, et al., Validation of non-rigid image registration using finite-element methods: application to breast MR images, *IEEE Transactions on Medical Imaging*, **22**(2):238–247, 2003.

8 S. J. Keibel, J. Ashburner, J.-B. Poline, and K. J. Friston, MRI and PET coregistration—a cross validation of statistical parametric mapping and automated image registration, *Neuroimage*, **5**:271–279, 1997.

9 A. Gholipour, N. Kehtarnavaz, R. W. Briggs, et al., Validation of non-rigid registration between functional and anatomical magnetic resonance brain images, *IEEE Transactions on Biomedical Engineering*, **55**(2):563–571, 2008.

10 J. M. Fitzpatrick, Fiducial registration error and target registration error are uncorrelated, in *Proceedings of SPIE, Medical Imaging: Visualization, Image-Guided Procedures, and Modeling*, vol. **7261**, 2009.

11 A. Seginer, Rigid-body point-based registration: the distribution of the target registration error when the fiducial registration errors are given, *Medical Image Analysis*, **19**:397–413, 2011.

12 G. P. Penney, D. C. Barratt, C. S. K. Chan, M. Slomczykowski, et al., Cadaver validation of intensity-based ultrasound to CT registration, *Medical Image Analysis*, **10**:385–395, 2006.

13 C. X. B. Yan, B. Goulet, S. J.-S. Chen, D. Tampieri, and D. L. Collins, Validation of automated ultrasound-CT registration of vertebrae, *International Journal of Computer Assisted Radiology and Surgery*, 7:601–610, 2012.

14 R. Zakariaee, G. Hamameh, C. J. Brown, and I. Spadinger, Validation of non-rigid point-set registration methods using a porcine bladder pelvic phantom, *Physics in Medicine & Biology*, **61**:825–854, 2016.

15 R. P. Woods, S. T. Grafton, H. D. G. Watson, N. L. Sicotte, and J. C. Mazziotta, Automated image registration: II. Intersubject validation of linear and nonlinear models, *Journal of Computer Assisted Tomography*, **22**(1):153–165, 1998.

16 T. Vik, S. Kabus, J. von Berg, et al., Validation and comparison of registration methods for free-breathing 4D lung—CT, *Proceedings of SPIE, Medical Imaging 2008: Image Processing*, Vol. **6914**, 2008.

17 K. Murphy, B. van Ginneken, J. M. Reinhardt, et al., Evaluation of registration methods on thoracic CT: the EMPIRE10 challenge, *IEEE Transactions on Medical Imaging*, **30**(11):1901–1920, 2011.

18 L. S. Yin, L. Tang, G. Hammarneh, et al., Complexity and accuracy of image registration methods in SPECT-guided radiation therapy, *Physics in Medicine and Biology*, **55**:237–246, 2010.

19 S. Spampinato, A. M. Gueli, L. Raffaele, C. Stancampiano, and G. C. Ettorre, Validation of the CT–MRI image registration with a dedicated phantom, *Medical Physics Radiobiology and Safety*, **119**(12):942–950, 2014.

20 U. Pietrzyk, K. Herholz, G. Fink, et al., An interactive technique for three-dimensional image registration: validation for PET, SPECT, MRI, and CT brain studies, *Journal of Nuclear Medicine*, **35**(12):2011–2018, 1994.

21 J. M. Fitzpatrick, D. L. G. Hill, Y. Shyr, J. West, C. Studholme, and C. R. Maurer, Visual assessment of the accuracy of retrospective registration of MR and CT images of the brain, *IEEE Transactions on Medical Imaging*, **17**(4):571–585, 1998.

22 R. P. Woods, S. T. Grafton, C. J. Holmes, S. R. Cherry, and J. C. Mazziotta, Automated image registration: I. General methods and intrasubject, intramodality validation, *Journal of Computer Assisted Tomography*, **22**(1):139–152, 1998.

23 M. Holden, D. L. G. Hill, E. R. E. Denton, et al., Similarity measures for 3-D serial MR brain image registration, *IEEE Transactions on Medical Imaging*, **19**(2):94–102, 2000.

24 J. Pascau, J. D. Gispert, and M. Michaelides, et al., Automated method for small-animal PET image registration with intrinsic validation, *Molecular Imaging and Biology*, **11**:107–113, 2009.

25 R. Datteri and B. M. Dawant, Estimation of rigid-body registration quality using registration networks, in *Proceedings of SPIE, Medical Imaging: Image Processing*, Vol. **8314**, 2012.

26 R. D. Datteri, Y. Liu, P.-F. D'Haese, and B. M. Dawant, Validation of a non-rigid registration error detection algorithm using clinical MRI brain data, *IEEE Transactions on Medical Imaging*, **34**(1):86–96, 2015.

27 J. Bozek, M. Grgic, and J. A. Schnabel, Validation of rigid registration of mammographic images. in *53rd International Symposium ELMAR*, 11–16, 2011.

28 E. Heath, D. L. Collins, P. J. Keall, L. Dong, and J. Seuntjens, Quantification of accuracy of the automated nonlinear image matching and anatomical labeling (ANIMAL) nonlinear registration algorithm for 4D CT images of lung, *Medical Physics*, **34**(11):4409–4421, 2007.

29 R. J. Rubey, J. A. Dana, and P. W. Biché, Quantitative aspects of software validation, *IEEE Transactions on Software Engineering*, **1**(2):150–155, 1975.

30 D. R. Boccardo, R. C. S. Machado, S. M. Camara, et al., Software validation of medical instruments, in *IEEE International Symposium on Medical Measurements and Applications*, 1–4, 2014.

31 A. Isambert, B. Bonniaud, F. Lavielle, G. Malandain, and D. Lefkopoulos, A phantom study of the accuracy of CT, MR, and PET image registrations with a block matching-based algorithm, *Cancer Radiothérape*, **12**:800–808, 2008.

32 I. Reinertsen, M. Descoteaux, K. Siddiqi, and D. L. Collins, Validation of vessel-based registration for correction of brain shift, *Medical Image Analysis*, **11**:374–388, 2007.

33 L. Freire and F. Godinho, Registration by maximization of mutual information—a cross validation study, *Proceedings of IEEE International Symposium Bio-Informatics and Biomedical Engineering*, 322–329, 2000.

34 F. J. Sanchez, C. Pollo, R. Meuli, et al., A cross validation study of deep brain stimulation targeting: from experts to atlas-based, segmentation-based, and automatic registration algorithms, *IEEE Transactions on Medical Imaging*, **25**(11):1440–1450, 2006.

35 S. Geisser, *Predictive Inference*, Chapman and Hall, New York, 1993.

36 Z. Xu, C. P. Lee, M. P. Heinrich, et al., Evaluation of six registration methods for the human abdomen on clinically acquired CT, *IEEE Transactions on Biomedical Engineering*, **63**(8):1563–1572, 2016.

37 W. R. Crum, O. Camara, and D. L. G. Hill, Generalized overlap measures for evaluation and validation in medical image analysis, *IEEE Transactions on Medical Imaging*, **25**(11):1451–1461, 2006.

38 D. P. Huttenlocher, G. A. Klanderman, and W. J. Rucklidge, Comparing images using the Hausdorff distance, *IEEE Transactions on Pattern Analysis and Machine Intelligence*, **15**(9):850–863, 1993.

39 H. Gonçalves, J. A. Gonçalves, and L. Corte-Real, Measures for an objective evaluation of the geometric correction process quality, *IEEE Geoscience and Remote Sensing Letters*, **6**(2):292–296, 2009.

10

Video Image Registration

Edgardo Molina[1,2], Wai Lun Khoo[1,3], Hao Tang[1,4], and Zhigang Zhu[1,3]

[1] Department of Computer Science, The City College of New York, New York, NY, USA
[2] Vista Wearable, Inc., New York, NY, USA
[3] Department of Computer Science, The Graduate Center, CUNY, New York, NY
[4] Department of Computer and Information Systems, Borough of Manhattan Community College, CUNY, New York, NY, USA

10.1   Introduction

Video images have a temporal order or are temporally consecutive; therefore, we sometimes refer to video images as a video sequence. An image in a video sequence is also called a frame. Images in a video are typically captured at a rate of 24–30 frames per second (fps). However, a video sequence can have a much lower (e.g., 5 fps with a high-resolution camera) or a much higher (e.g., 1000 fps with a high-speed camera) frame rate.

The resolution and frame rate of a video sequence depending on the video camera hardware are chosen to satisfy a particular application's requirements. Unlike cameras for still photography, video cameras are designed to continuously capture and save images in a storage medium. Similar to still photography cameras, video cameras are available in a variety of resolutions and modalities (such as color and infrared, IR). The quality of captured images is dependent on illumination conditions, camera motion, and scene contents.

Registration of video images shares many steps with registration of still images. These steps include feature selection/detection, feature correspondence/matching, and image alignment/registration. However, video registration has its unique characteristics and requirements. First, the goal of video registration is often image mosaicing, the process of generating a composite image (mosaic) from video images. A mosaic image has a field of view (FOV) that is larger than the FOV of any of the individual images. This implies that video registration may involve the registration of a large number of images.

Theory and Applications of Image Registration, First Edition. Arthur Ardeshir Goshtasby.
© 2017 John Wiley & Sons, Inc. Published 2017 by John Wiley & Sons, Inc.

Second, the images in a video sequence are temporally consecutive and, therefore, their spatial relation (topology) is roughly known. For example, the relation is from left to right, or from top to bottom, and usually there are large overlaps between adjacent frames. This simplifies the correspondence and alignment when compared to general registration. Third, since video images usually represent three-dimensional (3-D) scenes, there is a need to consider the scene geometry as well as the camera geometry. This leads to a unique step in video registration – the use and estimation of the camera motion model, which typically includes both intrinsic camera parameters and extrinsic 3-D pose and structure information. Finally, due to the large area of coverage of a video sequence taken from different angles and perhaps under different illumination conditions, there is a need to solve the problem of blending overlapping images into one seamless composite image.

For the aforementioned reasons, a typical video registration method has the following three components: (1) motion modeling, (2) image alignment, and (3) image composition. In the following sections, first, these three components are discussed. Then, examples of a few real applications are provided, showing the uniqueness of video registration. Finally, additional literature in this area for readers who are interested in video registration research and development is pointed out.

10.2 Motion Modeling

10.2.1 The Motion Field of Rigid Objects

To better understand various types of motion models in video registration, let us start with the rigid camera motion model. A motion in 3-D can be characterized by a rotation matrix $\mathbf{R}$ and a translation vector $\mathbf{T}$, resulting from the motion of a camera viewing a static scene or from a stationary camera viewing a single object in motion. We can always use one rigid, relative motion between the camera and the scene (or object).

The image motion field is defined by the 2-D vector field of velocities of the image points induced by the relative motion. The input to a visual motion is an image sequence with frames captured at times $t = 0, 1, 2, \ldots$ For the basic visual motion, we will only consider two adjacent frames (i.e., a reference frame and the frame following it in a video). In this case, the image motion field can be viewed as a disparity map of two frames captured at two consecutive camera locations (assuming we have a moving camera).

To formally define the motion field, we use the following notations: Let $\mathbf{P} = [X\ Y\ Z]^t$ represent a point in a 3-D scene and $\mathbf{p} = [x\ y\ f]^t$ be the projection of the scene point to the reference image plane in the pinhole

Figure 10.1 Motion field of a rigid body.

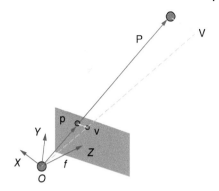

camera model. Then, we have

$$\mathbf{p} = \frac{f}{Z}\mathbf{P}. \tag{10.1}$$

The relative motion of $\mathbf{P}$ in the camera coordinate system is defined by (Fig. 10.1)

$$\mathbf{V} = -\mathbf{T} - \boldsymbol{\omega} \times \mathbf{P}, \tag{10.2}$$

where $\mathbf{T} = [T_x \ T_y \ T_z]^t$ is the translation component of the motion, and $\omega = [\omega_x \ \omega_y \ \omega_z]^t$ is the angular velocity, explained as follows.

In the above formulation, we assume the motion between two frames is small. For video registration, we would like to find the answer to the following two questions:

1. How can we extend the equation of the two-view geometry using $\mathbf{R}$ and $\mathbf{T}$ to a large motion?
2. How can the image velocity $\mathbf{v}$ be represented in terms of the location of 3-D point $\mathbf{P}$?

Answering the first question will help us to better understand 3-D motion and apply the visual motion concept to large motion between two frames. Angular velocity is defined by a rotation axis $\frac{\omega}{|\omega|}$ (a unit vector) and a rotation angle $|\omega|$. So, the cross product $\omega \times \mathbf{P}$ describes the rotational movement of the point $\mathbf{P}$. With this we have

$$\mathbf{P} - \mathbf{P}' = \mathbf{V} = -\mathbf{T} - \begin{bmatrix} 0 & -\omega_z & \omega_y \\ \omega_z & 0 & -\omega_x \\ -\omega_y & \omega_x & 0 \end{bmatrix} \mathbf{P}, \tag{10.3}$$

where $\mathbf{P}$ and $\mathbf{P}'$ represent the points before and after the motion. After some rearrangement, we have the following form:

$$\mathbf{P}' = \mathbf{R}\mathbf{P} + \mathbf{T}, \tag{10.4}$$

where the rotation matrix is

$$\mathbf{R} = \begin{bmatrix} 1 & -\omega_z & \omega_y \\ \omega_z & 1 & -\omega_x \\ -\omega_y & \omega_x & 1 \end{bmatrix}. \tag{10.5}$$

Recalling that a rotation matrix is generated by performing three rotations about $X, Y,$ and Z axes consecutively. This rotation can be written as

$$\begin{bmatrix} \cos\beta\cos\gamma & -\cos\beta\sin\gamma & \sin\beta \\ \sin\alpha\sin\beta\cos\gamma + \cos\alpha\sin\gamma & -\sin\alpha\sin\beta\sin\gamma + \cos\alpha\cos\gamma & -\sin\alpha\cos\beta \\ -\cos\alpha\sin\beta\cos\gamma + \sin\alpha\sin\gamma & \cos\alpha\sin\beta\sin\gamma + \sin\alpha\cos\gamma & \cos\alpha\cos\gamma \end{bmatrix}. \tag{10.6}$$

Equation (10.6) approaches Eq. (10.5) as angles α, β, and γ approach 0.

The answer to the second question will lead to the motion field equation of rigid body motion. Taking the time derivative of both sides of the projection Eq. (10.1), we obtain

$$\mathbf{v} = \frac{f}{Z^2}(Z\mathbf{V} - V_z\mathbf{P}). \tag{10.7}$$

Substituting the 3-D motion Eq. (10.2) into the above equation, we obtain the motion field equation:

$$\begin{bmatrix} V_x \\ V_y \end{bmatrix} = \underbrace{\frac{1}{f}\begin{bmatrix} xy & -(x^2+f^2) & fy \\ y^2+f^2 & -xy & -fx \end{bmatrix}\begin{bmatrix} \omega_x \\ \omega_y \\ \omega_z \end{bmatrix}}_{\text{Rotation part: no depth information}} + \underbrace{\frac{1}{Z}\begin{bmatrix} -f & 0 & x \\ 0 & -f & y \end{bmatrix}\begin{bmatrix} T_x \\ T_y \\ T_z \end{bmatrix}}_{\text{Translation part: depth } Z}$$

$$\tag{10.8}$$

Note that the motion field is the sum of two components: the translational component that includes the depth information and the rotational component that does not have any depth information. Here, we assume the intrinsic camera parameters are known.

10.2.2 Motion Models

In the following sections, we group motion models into four types depending on camera motion and the structure of the scene: (1) a pure camera rotation and a 3-D scene, (2) an arbitrary camera motion and a planar scene, (3) a translational camera motion and a 3-D scene, and (4) an arbitrary camera motion and a 3-D scene. While the last case is the most general, it makes video registration the most difficult. The first three cases are typical cases where video mosaics can be generated by video image alignment; therefore, we discuss only these three special cases in the following sections.

10.2.2.1 Pure Rotation and a 3-D Scene

The simplest case of video registration and mosaicing assumes a pure rotation model of the camera where the camera rotates about its center of projection (i.e., the optical center, also called the nodal point).

Under pure rotation $\mathbf{T} = 0$; therefore, the motion field equation can be written as

$$
\begin{bmatrix} V_x \\ V_y \end{bmatrix} = \frac{1}{f} \begin{bmatrix} xy & -(x^2 + f^2) & fy \\ y^2 + f^2 & -xy & -fx \end{bmatrix} \begin{bmatrix} \omega_x \\ \omega_y \\ \omega_z \end{bmatrix}. \tag{10.9}
$$

Clearly, the motion field of a pure rotation does not carry any 3-D information; Z is not included in the equation. The motion vector equation is a quadratic polynomial function of image coordinates $[x\ y\ f]^t$. Given two or more points with known velocities, we will have four or more linear equations from which the three angles can be estimated.

Note that, in practice, the motion field equation is an approximation when the motion is very small. For pure rotation, we can actually write an accurate image transformation between two frames, and the rotational motion can be large. A 3-D rotation transformation can be written as

$$
\mathbf{P}' = \mathbf{RP}, \tag{10.10}
$$

where $\mathbf{P}$ and $\mathbf{P}'$ are the 3-D points representing the points before and after the rotation. Since we can write the projections of the 3-D points before and after motion by

$$
\mathbf{p} = \frac{f}{Z}\mathbf{P} \tag{10.11}
$$

and

$$
\mathbf{p}' = \frac{f'}{Z'}\mathbf{P}', \tag{10.12}
$$

we have

$$
\mathbf{p}' \cong \mathbf{Rp} \tag{10.13}
$$

and $\cong$ implies a projective equality. Equation (10.13) can be implemented using pure image transformation; therefore, two images before and after a pure rotation can be precisely registered after finding at least four pairs of corresponding points between two images. This is the basic model for video mosaicing from a rotating camera creating. For example, a 360° panorama can be created from a video sequence captured by a camera rotating about its axis by 360°.

Depending on the FOVs of the mosaic, the projection model of the mosaic can be a perspective projection (FOV is less than 180°), a cylindrical projection (FOV is 360° in one direction), or a spherical projection (full 360° FOV in both directions). More details about these cases are provided in Section 10.4.1.

Applications of video mosaics from a camera pure rotation are limited to consumer applications such as personal photography, entertainment, and online maps. For more specialized applications such as surveillance, remote sensing, robot navigation, and land planning, the motion of the camera cannot be limited to a pure rotation. Translational motion usually cannot be avoided, resulting in the motion parallax problem. When the translational components are relatively small, the motion models can be approximated by a pure rotation. In this case, the generated mosaics lack geometric accuracy, but with some treatment for small motion parallax and moving targets, such as deghosting (Section 10.4.3), useful mosaics can be created. However, if the translational motion is large and dominant, we have to use one of the models described in the following sections.

10.2.2.2 General Motion and a Planar Scene

If the scene can be regarded as planar, for example, because the distance between the camera and the scene is much larger than the depth range of the scene, then the perspective motion model (homography) or, in some applications, a 2-D rigid motion model or an affine model can be used. In these cases, the problems are much simpler than general cases due to the 2-D scene assumption.

The relation defining the motion of a plane when the camera takes an arbitrary motion or when a moving plane is viewed by a stationary camera can be written as

$$\mathbf{n}^t \mathbf{P} = d, \tag{10.14}$$

where $\mathbf{n} = [n_x \ n_y \ n_z]^t$ is the normal to the plane, $\mathbf{P} = [X \ Y \ Z]^t$ is a 3-D point on the plane, and d is the distance of $\mathbf{P}$ to the camera. Using the camera projection equation, we have

$$\frac{1}{Z} = \frac{n_x x + n_y y + n_z f}{fd}. \tag{10.15}$$

Substituting Eq. (10.15) into the motion field Eq. (10.8) to eliminate Z, which is different from point to point, we will get a quadratic polynomial with only eight independent parameters. However, we again note that the motion field is only an approximation under small motion. If motion between two images is large, we can use a precise image transformation. For an arbitrary motion, we have

$$\mathbf{p}' \cong \mathbf{A}\mathbf{p}, \tag{10.16}$$

where $\mathbf{A}$ is the homography (a 3×3 matrix) for all points in which we have eight independent parameters. Note that Eq. (10.16) has the same form as Eq. (10.13); therefore, Eq. (10.13) can also be viewed as a special homography, which is a rotational matrix. Equation (10.16) is very useful for generating an image mosaic for a planar scene. Examples include generating wide FOV mosaics from an aerial image sequence or a video of a classroom blackboard. In many cases, affine transformation with only six parameters can be used instead of a homography that has eight parameters.

10.2.2.3 Translational Motion and a 3-D Scene

A 3-D camera motion model is considered when the translational components of the camera motion are large and the scene is truly 3-D. In this case, motion parallax cannot be ignored or eliminated. Examples include a camera mounted on an aircraft or a ground vehicle moving along a line over a long distance, or a camera's optical center moving on a circular path. Here, multiperspective projection models are used to generate the mosaics, enabling stereo mosaics or stereo panoramas to be created to preserve the 3-D information in the scene, and allowing the 3-D structures to be reconstructed and viewed. In this case, the accuracy of geometric modeling and image alignment is crucial for achieving the accuracy of 3-D reconstruction and viewing.

Under a pure translation (i.e., $\omega = 0$), the motion field simplifies

$$\begin{bmatrix} V_x \\ V_y \end{bmatrix} = \frac{1}{f} \begin{bmatrix} -f & 0 & x \\ 0 & -f & y \end{bmatrix} \begin{bmatrix} T_x \\ T_y \\ T_z \end{bmatrix}, \tag{10.17}$$

which can be further divided into the following two cases: radial motion field and parallel motion field.

1. **Radial motion field** ($T_z \neq 0$): We define the *vanishing point* $\mathbf{p}_0 = [x_0 \ y_0]^t$ as

$$\begin{bmatrix} x_0 \\ y_0 \end{bmatrix} = \frac{f}{T_z} \begin{bmatrix} T_x \\ T_y \end{bmatrix}, \tag{10.18}$$

which can be used to compute the 3-D motion direction. Then, we can write the motion field equation by

$$\begin{bmatrix} v_x \\ v_y \end{bmatrix} = \frac{T_z}{Z} \begin{bmatrix} x - x_0 \\ y - y_0 \end{bmatrix}. \tag{10.19}$$

From Eq. (10.19), we can easily see that the vanishing point $\mathbf{p}_0$ represents the focus of expansion (FOE) if $T_z < 0$, since all the motion vectors point away from $\mathbf{p}_0$ (Fig. 10.2); if $T_z > 0$, it is called the focus of contraction (FOC) since all the motion vectors move toward $\mathbf{p}_0$.

2. **Parallel motion field** ($T_z = 0$): The motion field of a translational motion when $T_z = 0$ can be written as

$$\begin{bmatrix} V_x \\ V_y \end{bmatrix} = -\frac{f}{Z} \begin{bmatrix} T_x \\ T_y \end{bmatrix}, \tag{10.20}$$

which shows that the motion field is a parallel field in the direction of the motion (T_x, T_y), as illustrated in Fig. 10.3.

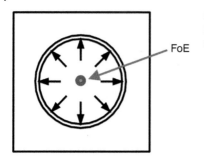

Figure 10.2 The optical flow radiating from the FOE when the camera optical axis is parallel to motion direction.

FoE

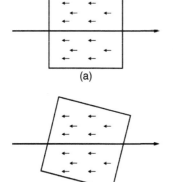

(a)

(b)

Figure 10.3 (a) The optical flow is parallel to the motion direction when the camera is viewing perpendicular to the motion direction. (b) The rotation (roll) of the camera about its optical axis does not affect the optical flow from remaining parallel to the motion.

When the dominant motion of the camera is translation, especially with a parallel motion field, the projection model of the mosaic can be a parallel-perspective projection, in that the projection in the direction of the motion is parallel, whereas the projection perpendicular to the motion remains perspective. This kind of a mosaic is also called pushbroom mosaic since the projection model of the mosaic, in principle, is the same as pushbroom imaging in remote sensing. Further details are provided in Section 10.5.1.

It is interesting to note that by selecting different parts of individual frames, a pair of stereo mosaics can be generated that exhibit motion parallax, while each of them represents a particular viewing angle of parallel projection. Parallel-perspective mosaics can be generated under a radial motion field, with some image warping present in the mosaics.

To generate a true parallel-perspective view in a mosaic for accurate 3-D reconstruction, pixel selection is carried out for a particular viewing angle, and the coordinate transformation is performed based on matches between at least two original images for each pixel. A similar principle can be applied to concentric mosaics under circular projection.

10.3   Image Alignment

A correlation approach is usually used to find the motion parameters. First, the images are divided into small blocks and then, each block in the first image is searched for over a predefined spatial domain in the second image. The best match is determined by finding the location of the maximum correlation value.

Steps in a correlation-based stereo matching approach can be summarized as follows. For each point (x_l, y_l) in the first image (a), a window centered at the point is taken and searched within a search area in the second image (b). The disparity (d_x, d_y) or displacement between images (a) and (b) where the correlation is maximum is determined. Figure 10.4 illustrates this matching approach.

There are three important issues to be worked out in correlation-based matching:

1. *Matching elements*: In the correlation-based approach, an image window of a fixed size centered at each pixel in image (a) is taken and used to find the corresponding pixel in image (b).
2. *Similarity/dissimilarity measure*: This is the measure of similarity or dissimilarity between windows in the two images. Corresponding windows are matching windows that produce the highest similarity or lowest dissimilarity measure; we provide more details about this below.
3. *Search area*: Since the motion parameters between the images under consideration are not known, we have to search for the point corresponding to a point in image (a) within a 2-D area in image (b). Due to the small motion assumption, this search area will be small.

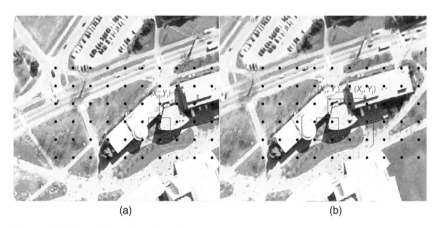

(a)   (b)

Figure 10.4 Correlation-based matching.

Considering these issues, we formally write the correlation between two windows of size $(2W + 1) \times (2W + 1)$ pixels in images (a) and (b) as

$$c(d_x, d_y) = \sum_{k=-W}^{W} \sum_{l=-W}^{W} \Psi(I_l(x_l + k, y_l + l), I_r(x_l + d_x + k, y_l + d_y + l)), \quad (10.21)$$

where Ψ is a similarity/dissimilarity measure. Popular similarity/dissimilarity measures used in image matching are

- Cross-correlation (similarity):

$$\Psi(u, v) = uv. \quad (10.22)$$

- Sum of square differences or SSD (dissimilarity):

$$\Psi(u, v) = (u - v)^2. \quad (10.23)$$

- Sum of absolute differences or SAD (dissimilarity):

$$\Psi(u, v) = |u - v|. \quad (10.24)$$

After calculating all similarity/dissimilarity values in a search area, the final disparity vector is defined as the one that maximizes $\{c(d_x, d_y)\}$ over all d_x and d_y if c is a similarity or the one that minimizes $\{c(d_x, d_y)\}$ over all d_x and d_y when c is a dissimilarity measure. This simple matching approach has the following strengths and weaknesses:

Strengths:

- It is easy to implement, both in software and hardware.
- It produces a dense map of image motion vectors within the image domain.
- It might be slow without optimization, but the algorithm can be implemented in parallel (e.g., using GPUs).

Weaknesses:

- It works well in only highly textured images.
- It is inadequate for matching image pairs from very different viewpoints for having radiometric and geometric differences.
- Windows may cover points with quite different disparities, blurring depth changes.
- It may produce inaccurate disparities along occluding boundaries.

A pair of images taken by a camera over a university campus (Fig. 10.5) illustrates the problems facing this approach, including regions with little to no texture, depth changes between adjacent objects, and occlusions caused by change in view. For example, centers of the blue boxes within the red ellipses represent corresponding points, but the rectangular windows cover three

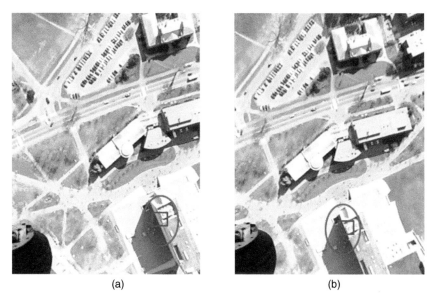

(a)   (b)

Figure 10.5 Problems in stereo correspondence.

planar surfaces in image (a) while covering only two surfaces in image (b). The side of the building is visible in image (a), but it is occluded in image (b). Even without this problem, the two windows cover multiple depths. This is a problem when the motion between the images is large, such as this example. However, in a video sequence, the motion between two consecutive frames is small, and we only need to find a sufficient number of correct matches to estimate motion. When the method based on correlation does not work well, a feature-based method should be used.

10.3.1 Feature-Based Methods

In a feature-based method, first, a feature detection operator such as the Harris corner or Scale-Invariant Feature Transform (SIFT) detector is used to find feature points in the images. Then, detected features in the images are matched to find the correspondences.

Primitives used in matching are (Fig. 10.6):

- *Edge points*: Points that have locally maximum gradient magnitudes in the gradient direction.
- *Lines*: Line segments extracted by linking edge points via either edge tracking or the Hough transform.
- *Corners*: Points on contours that have locally maximum curvatures.
- *Structures*: Higher-level structures that are formed by groups of edge points, lines, or corners.

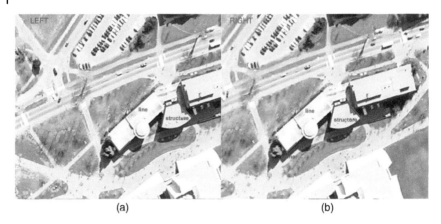

(a)   (b)

Figure 10.6 Feature-based matching.

A matching algorithm usually includes the following three steps:

1. *Extract features in the given image pair*: For example, if the matching primitives are line segments, an edge detector such as the Canny edge detector is used to detect the edges. Then, line segments are formed by a line tracking and fitting approach or by the Hough transform. A line segment can be defined by its endpoints, length, orientation, and average contrast.
2. *Define similarity measure*: If the features are line segments, the similarity between two line segments in the images can be formulated in terms of differences in orientations, lengths, and contrasts of the lines.
3. *Search correspondences*: We expect that only a few candidates for a primitive in image (a) will be within the search range in image (b). The candidate with the highest similarity value is taken as the correspondence.

For each primitive in image (a), a search is made in image (b) for its correspondence. The motion vector (d_x, d_y) is then set to the one that produces the largest similarity measure. Similar to the correlation-based approach, the feature-based approach also has strengths and weaknesses.

Strengths:

- It is relatively insensitive to illumination differences in images.
- It works well with man-made scenes where lines are abundant.
- It works well on occluding boundaries (edges).
- It is usually faster than the correlation-based approach.

Weaknesses:

- It only produces a small number of matches; therefore, many points in the reference image may not have motion vectors.

- Feature extraction may be difficult. For example, lines (edges) might be partially extracted in one image. It may also be difficult to find an effective means of measuring the similarity between two lines, since corresponding lines in images may have different endpoints and contrasts.

10.3.2 Mechanical-Based Methods

In a mechanical-based method, an accurately controlled platform is used to control the motion of the camera. For example, the camera may be moved on a straight line or rotated along a circle. The sensors used could be array cameras or 1-D cameras.

Next, we give an example of a mechanical-based method that not only can generate video mosaics with accurate camera motion control but can also align images from two different cameras. The schematic setup of a system with two cameras is shown in Fig. 10.7. It consists of a rotating platform, an electro-optical (EO) color camera, an IR thermal camera, and a personal computer (PC).

The rotating platform uses a DC motor that allows for rotational speeds up to $80°/s$ and has an ultrahigh resolution 8000 cts/rev rotary encoder with index pulse for precision homing. For the tightest position control, the rotary encoder is mounted directly on the worm screw. This eliminates most of the possible error sources associated with indirect read feedback devices. The controller is a single-axis motion controller for DC servo motors up to 48 VDC at 1.5 A rms, with an integrated RS-232-C interface for communication. The PC sends commands to the platform via the controller, such as setting and getting the velocity, position, and acceleration. Consequently, the platform provides precise $360°$ continuous motion with a minimum incremental motion of $0.002°$.

The EO color camera has a 720×480 pixel resolution with a focal length ranging from 6 to 72 mm, a shutter speed ranging from 1/60 to 1/10,000 s and

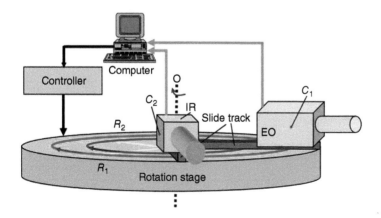

Figure 10.7 Setup of a rotating platform.

an IEEE-1394 firewire video output. The IR camera can detect temperature differences as small as 0.08 °C in the range from −40 to +500 °C, which can be digitally resampled to generate 640×480 pixel images at a refresh rate of 50/60 Hz via an IEEE-1394 firewire output.

Two slide tracks are placed on top of the rotation platform—one of their endpoints is the platform rotation center and the other is fixed on the edge of the platform. Referring to the schematic of Fig. 10.7, the EO and IR cameras are mounted on top of the two slide tracks and are looking outward from the rotation center (O). Due to physical limitations, the EO and IR cameras' two slide tracks are placed apart by an angle α, the paths of the cameras' optical centers are two concentric circles (C_1 and C_2) whose radii are R_1 and R_2. Each camera can also be precisely moved along the slide track so that its radius R_i can be adjusted (i.e., to have $R_1 = R_2$).

In order to build EO/IR coregistered multiview panoramic mosaics, the computer controls the platform to continually rotate with a constant speed, while the two cameras are continuously capturing images covering a 360° FOV, thus obtaining two image sequences. The multimodal, multiview panoramic imaging is mainly used to build a background model of static scenes for later target detection using motion, 3-D, and thermal signatures. Here, we want to emphasize two important points. First, we can achieve real-time processing by only using/storing the image columns of interest to build the panoramas for the background model. Second, in target detection applications where there are moving objects, current images will be registered and compared with the background model to detect any motion, 3-D, and thermal changes.

10.4 Image Composition

Image composition is the step of combining aligned images together to form a viewable mosaic. There are three important issues in this step: compositing surface determination, coordinate transformation and image sampling, and pixel selection and blending.

10.4.1 Compositing Surface

If the video sequence has only a small number of images, then one of the images can be selected as the reference image and all other images can be warped and aligned with the reference image. In this case, the reference image with a perspective projection is the compositing surface and, therefore, the final mosaic is a larger perspective image that represents an extension of the FOV of the reference image. In general, the compositing surface is the surface that the final mosaic will be rendered. Depending on the motion models (Section 10.2.2), the FOV, and the 3-D scene within the video sequence, different compositing surfaces including planar surface, cylindrical surface, and spherical surface are adopted to generate a mosaic.

A planar surface model is used to create a mosaic in the following cases:

- Camera motion is pure rotation and the FOV of video sequence is less than 180° (Section 10.2.2.1). Note that the final mosaic will have a large distortion at the border of the mosaic when the FOV is larger than 120°.
- The camera motion is arbitrary, but the 3-D scene captured in the video sequence can be approximated by a planar surface (Section 10.2.2.2). In other words, the 3-D variation in the scene is (approximately) constrained to a plane.
- The camera has translational motion (or approximately translational motion) while viewing a 3-D scene (Section 10.2.2.3). The composition surface is still a planar surface. However, the transformation used to generate a mosaic is different from that of the previous cases, and it is no longer a pure homography; instead, the composite image will be parallel-perspective. For the sake of easy discussion, details are given in one of the application examples in Section 10.5.1, together with the procedure of image warping. In the case of parallel-perspective projection, because of the 3-D scene, a planar surface is chosen to be a composite plane. In general, a planar surface with arbitrary depth can be used; however, a surface with similar depth in the majority of the 3-D scene (e.g., ground surface in an aerial video) is often chosen to minimize the distortion.

In addition to the planar compositing surface, cylindrical and spherical surfaces are adopted when FOV is large and distortions are severe when projecting the scene to a planar surface. Figure 10.8 illustrates the relation between the overlapping images, and the surface the images are projected to is planar, cylindrical, or spherical with a camera motion that is pure rotation.

A cylindrical mosaic surface should be used when the camera motion is of pure rotation (Section 10.2.2.1), but its FOV is large, usually from 180° to 360°, along one direction (in practice usually around the vertical axis). The mosaic is rendered onto a cylinder. The radius of the cylindrical surface is often the same as the focal length of the camera; hence, the mosaic (particularly the center area) and input video frames have similar resolutions.

A spherical mosaic surface should be used when the camera motion is of pure rotation, but the FOV is large in both directions, usually from 180° to 360°. Similar to cylindrical projection, the radius of the spherical surface is often the same as the focal length of the camera.

10.4.2 Image Warping

After a compositing surface is selected, the next issue is the coordinate transformation and resampling. This is also called image warping.

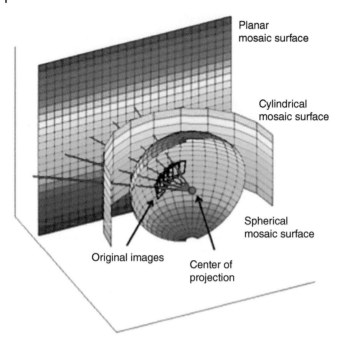

Planar
mosaic surface

Cylindrical
mosaic surface

Spherical
mosaic surface

Original images

Center of
projection

Figure 10.8 Mapping a set of overlapping images into a mosaic that is planar, cylindrical, or spherical.

Different coordinate transformations, under various projection models, are applied to transform video frames to generate a final mosaic, including perspective projection (homography), cylindrical projection, spherical projection, and parallel-perspective projection.

Perspective projection is used to warp video frames when (1) the camera motion is pure rotation and the FOV is small and (2) the camera motion is arbitrary, but the 3-D scene can be approximated by a planar surface. In both cases, video frames can be transformed to a common coordinate system on a flat surface using a homography matrix Eq. (10.16). Usually, one frame close to the center of an image sequence is selected as the reference frame, and the homography parameters between the reference image and any other image are then estimated by image alignment (Section 10.3). To generate a densely mosaiced image without holes, usually an inverse transformation (from the mosaic to the original image frame) is used. For each pixel in the mosaic, the corresponding pixels are located in one or more of the original image frames, and pixel intensities are blended.

The cylindrical or spherical mosaics are generated by projecting video frames onto the surface of a cylinder or a sphere. For the cylindrical mosaic, video frames are transformed to cylindrical coordinates and then are stitched together using a simple translational model. In other words, after transforming to the cylindrical coordinate, any two video frames captured at different panning angles are related by a horizontal translation (in angles), which can be estimated by the image matching method. Similarly for spherical mosaics, input video frames are first transformed to a spherical coordinate system and then they are stitched together using a translational model. Alternatively, similar to what we did for the perspective projection, an inverse transformation can be used in which every pixel in the final cylindrical (or spherical) mosaic is located in one or more original image frames and their pixel intensities are blended to obtain the value for the mosaiced pixel.

The parallel-perspective projection for translational motion with an arbitrary 3-D scene is sometimes called a pushbroom mosaic. This is more interesting and more complicated, and we discuss it in Section 10.5.1 using real data.

10.4.3 Pixel Selection and Blending

The third important issue to address in image composition is pixel selection and blending. When generating a mosaic, consecutive frames naturally overlap, creating two key problems:

1. *The pixel selection problem*: Where do we place the seam (i.e., the stitching line) in a mosaic?
2. *The pixel blending problem*: How do we select the values of overlapping pixels?

In practice, ghosting is a common problem in mosaic generation due to moving objects appearing in multiple images. The idea of pixel selection is to avoid placing seams in areas where images are not consistent (due to moving objects) to avoid ghosting artifacts. Therefore, potential ghosting areas need to be identified from all images, and only one image is used to contribute to such areas in the final mosaic, eliminating inconsistency.

In addition to the ghosting artifacts, color discrepancy (due to illumination changes or misalignment) of images affects the quality of a mosaic. Therefore, an image blending method, which can produce a smooth transition from one image to next, is required to reduce artifacts.

Simply averaging values at overlapping pixels cannot solve the problem of color discrepancy. A simple method, called feathering, finds a weighted average of overlapping intensities with the weight inversely proportional to the distance of the pixel from the border of the image. The method works well, but it sometimes oversmooths the mosaic because of the averaging operation, which applies the same transition function to the blended area regardless of the frequency (texture) of the area. The ideal remedy is to apply different blending transitions according to the spatial frequency (different resolutions) of the blending area. That is, apply high-frequency transition in high-frequency image regions, which are the high-texture areas, while applying a low- frequency blending transition in low-frequency image regions that represent textureless areas.

A Laplacian pyramid can be used to implement the aforementioned ideas in image blending. Assume a mosaic is generated from only two warped images using a three-step Laplacian pyramid blending. (1) First, Laplacian pyramids (with multilevels) of the warped images are generated as follows: the warped images are down-sampled by half and other levels after Gaussian smoothing, and then the Laplacian images are obtained by subtracting the smoothed images from the corresponding original images. (2) A Gaussian low-pass pyramid over the blended area is created and used as weights to apply blending (feathering) on each level of the two Laplacian pyramids, and hence a new Laplacian pyramid is generated by combining the two Laplacian pyramids. (3) The mosaic is finally generated by expanding and summing the levels of the new Laplacian pyramid.

10.5 Application Examples

10.5.1 Pushbroom Stereo Mosaics Under Translational Motion

A pinhole camera viewing in the direction perpendicular to the motion path is common when imaging from aerial or ground vehicles. Images are captured by placing the camera directly above, below, or on a side of the vehicle. When capturing images of a scene by this ideal camera, the optical flow between frames will be parallel to the direction of motion. Figure 10.3 illustrates parallel optical flow, regardless of the camera roll. This roll can happen either from a camera that is not aligned with respect to the vehicle's body or from a vehicle that moves diagonally rather than forward.

Construction of a mosaic requires that we first align the images in the sequence. This is typically done by taking the first frame as the reference frame and aligning the following frames with it. Image registration is used to compute a global transformation (typically affine) between frames by feature matching or correlation [1, 2, 3]. Basic matching methods were discussed in Section 10.3.

10.5.1.1 Parallel-Perspective Geometry and Panoramas

The panorama itself is constructed by taking a slit from each aligned frame (which has a parallel-perspective projection according to pinhole geometry) and stitching them together to create a panorama. This slit is taken perpendicular to the optical flow from each frame at the same location (Fig. 10.9). This procedure is similar to the pushbroom technique of scanning and mosaicing a 1-D sensor translating over a scene. This produces a *parallel-perspective*

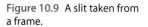

Figure 10.9 A slit taken from a frame.

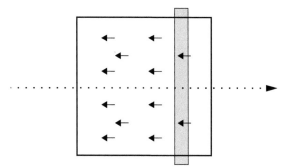

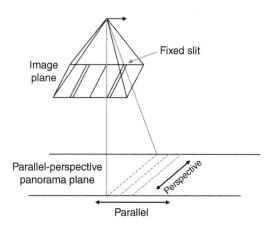

Figure 10.10 A parallel-perspective panorama constructed from a fixed slit.

panorama, which has a perspective projection along the slit (since the image comes from a normal array image under the pinhole geometry assumption) and it will have a parallel projection along the motion direction, since all slits come from the same fixed location in each image frame (Fig. 10.10).

PRISM (Parallel Ray Interpolation for Stereo Mosaics): Building a parallel-perspective panorama from a camera in motion is complicated by factors such as frame rate, speed of the camera, camera motion path, and amount of parallax caused by the 3-D features of the scene. This usually results in a scenario where the imagery between two captured frames is not dense enough to build a true parallel-perspective projection, where each panorama column comes from the same imaging angle. For this purpose, the parallel ray interpolation for stereo mosaics (PRISM) method [4] was developed to interpolate the missing parallel rays from neighboring rays.

Figure 10.11 illustrates the basic idea: we have two consecutive frames (frame 1 and frame 2) that image the scene after some translation. We can see here that a feature **P** in the scene is imaged in both frames but not with parallel rays (the bold black lines in the figure). Instead, we have a red line and a blue

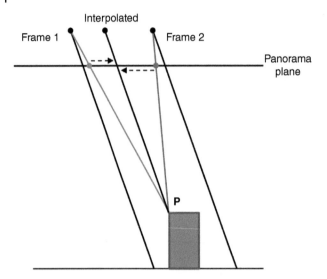

Figure 10.11 Interpolating parallel rays for parallel-perspective panoramas.

line depicting the differing angles (different slits) that would actually capture the feature. The PRISM algorithm finds these points along the slits in both frames and warps them by moving them along the dashed arrows so that the parallel-perspective panorama has a consistent parallel view on the scene and does not contain holes or wrong image data in-between consecutive views.

10.5.1.2 Stereo and Multiview Panoramas

Stereo images are typically captured as two images taken of the same scene from a slightly offset distance called the baseline, similar to the displacement of the human eyes. Stereo panoramas are constructed by creating two parallel-perspective panoramas that capture the same scene from a different baseline. Since we are following the pushbroom imaging model, this actually means capturing two slits that image the same scene from some offset. Since our slits come from a normal array image plane, these two slits will actually correspond to two different view angles of the scene. Figure 10.12 illustrates that a moving camera will capture the same scene point from two locations at two different slits for some baseline, a forward viewing slit and a backward viewing slit. We then construct a panorama from each of these slits, producing a stereo pair of panoramas. The depth, Z, of any point in the scene can then be calculated as

$$Z = \frac{B}{2 \tan \beta},$$
(10.25)

where 2β is the angle between the two viewing rays and B is the baseline of the displacement from where the two images were taken, as illustrated in Fig. 10.12.

Figure 10.12 Stereo
parallel-perspective
projection geometry.
A point imaged by a
forward-angle slit will be
viewed at a later time in
the frame sequence from
a backward-angle slit.

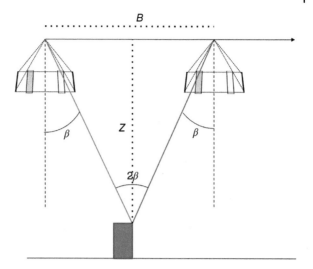

Note that in a pair of stereo panoramas, the angle 2β is fixed, whereas the baseline B varies from point to point. Having an adaptive baseline is actually advantageous in 3-D reconstruction [4], compared to a fixed baseline stereo camera.

We can extend this concept and construct a panorama from many slits from the original image frames (Fig. 10.13). Each panorama will have a different view angle on the scene and can be used to adaptively pick the two view-angle panoramas that are optimal for a given application. If the application under consideration is 3-D reconstruction, we pick two panoramas that provide a large baseline, and if the application is 3-D viewing, we pick two panoramas with a small baseline for viewing comfort (such that the baseline matches the viewer's eye separation). Another benefit of this representation is that the epipolar curves will be parallel lines along the camera motion path and aligned in all multiview panoramas.

Figure 10.13 Multiple slits can be used to
create different panoramas. This enables the
selection of adaptive baselines for improved
3-D viewing and reconstruction.

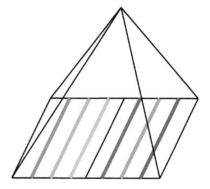

10.5.1.3   Results

The following results are from real-world aerial images captured by both EO and IR sensors, demonstrating the ability to use multimodality images.

The data sets used to obtain these results are publicly available data from Columbus Surrogate Unmanned Aerial Vehicles (CSUAV). Two UAVs flown over Columbus, Ohio, created these data sets. The EO UAV contained a high-resolution EO sensor, capturing 5 fps, at an altitude of 6500 ft. The IR UAV contained a mid-wave IR sensor capturing 30 fps at an altitude of 2500 ft. Each UAV made multiple back and forth passes over their designated linear route. In the results presented in Figs 10.14 and 10.15, we simply consider a single run along the route and use the PRISM algorithm to generate multiview panoramas, of which we show two for each run, a left-eye and right-eye stereo pair.

The panoramas were constructed using the following procedure:

1. *Motion estimation and image rectification*: Frame-to-frame local motion parameters were estimated for the sequence using a pyramid-based correlation match. Global motion parameters were then computed and frames were rectified so that the mosaics were aligned to linear motion.
2. *Stereo view selection*: $2N$ slits ($N = 4$ in the aforementioned examples) were selected for N pairs of stereo mosaics to provide multiple views of the scene.
3. *Mosaic generation*: A panorama was constructed for each slit across the entire sequence. The PRISM ray interpolation was applied when combining slits from neighboring frames to construct the dense panoramas without gaps or seams.

10.5.2   Stereo Mosaics when Moving a Camera on a Circular Path

In aerial imaging applications, such as surveillance and monitoring, it is often the case that there is some area of interest the aerial platform is required to continuously cover. A common way of achieving this is to have the aerial platform circle an area at a fixed altitude while its camera views down toward the ground,

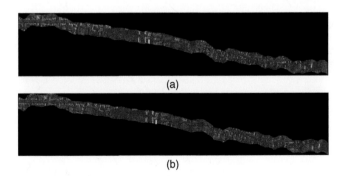

(a)

(b)

Figure 10.14 Two of 8 IR panoramas generated of a scene captured with linear motion.

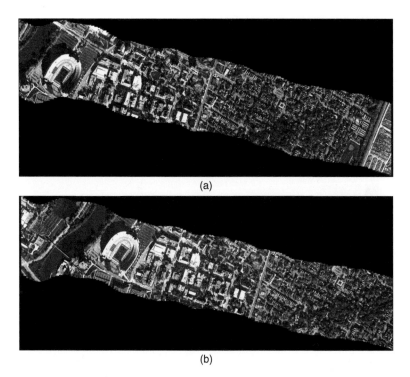

(a)

(b)

Figure 10.15 Two of 8 EO panoramas generated of a scene captured with linear motion.

perpendicular to the circular path. A large aircraft must make circles with a radius of many miles. While it is possible to capture all images and perform bundle adjustment and reconstruct the scenery, we have explored a method to create stereo mosaics from the scene that can be used for both 3-D reconstruction and real-time [5] visualization.

10.5.2.1 Circular Geometry

First we present the ideal geometry to generate circular mosaics from a push-broom sensor on a circular camera path. A 1-D camera with a single column off the center of an angle β moves along a circular path with a center C and a radius R. The camera's optical axis Z is perpendicular to the circular path. A circular panoramic image is generated by this scanning camera as illustrated in Fig. 10.16. The scanlines of the circular images are circles. Such an image is represented by $I(\alpha, r)$, where α is the angle of the pixel along the circle measured from a starting point and r is the distance along the column direction.

10.5.2.2 Stereo Geometry

Given two such circular scanning cameras moving on the same circular path with a center C and a radius R, both with a viewing angle β, one looking forward

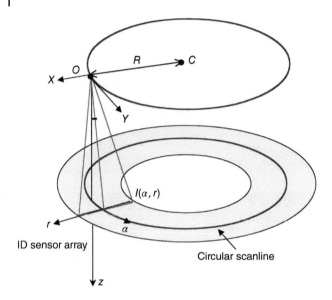

Figure 10.16 Circular flight geometry.

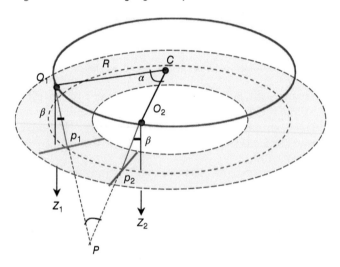

Figure 10.17 Stereo geometry for circular flight.

(O_1) and the other looking backward (O_2), a pair of circular stereo panoramas can be generated (Fig. 10.17). For any 3-D point **P**, its correspondences, $\mathbf{p}_1 = (\alpha_1, r_1)$ and $\mathbf{p}_2 = (\alpha_2, r_2)$, in the two panoramas are (approximately) along a circular scanline. Therefore, we have $r_1 = r_2$ and the angular disparity

$$\alpha = \alpha_2 - \alpha_1. \tag{10.26}$$

The baseline B between the two views O_1 and O_2 can be calculated as

$$B = 2R \sin \frac{\alpha}{2} = R\alpha, \tag{10.27}$$

where α is measured in radians, and the radius is much larger than the arc length B (this is typical of aerial images captured along large circular paths). Then, the distance from each view (O_1 or O_2) to the 3-D point can be calculated as

$$D = R \sin \frac{\alpha}{2} / \sin \beta = R\alpha/(2\beta), \tag{10.28}$$

where β is also measured in radians. Hence, the Z coordinate of the point $\mathbf{P}$ can be computed as

$$Z = D \cos \beta = R \sin \frac{\alpha}{2} / \tan \beta = 2R\alpha / \tan \beta. \tag{10.29}$$

We note here that pushbroom stereo mosaics under a circular motion path are different from multiperspective stereo panoramas with circular projections, as described below in Section 10.5.3. In stereo panoramas with circular projections, the optical axis of the camera points to (or away from) the center of the circular motion, while in pushbroom stereo panoramas with circular motion, the optical axis of the camera is perpendicular to the circular motion path. In fact, in all the cases where the optical axis is not pointing to (or away from) the center of the circular path, pushbroom stereo mosaics can be generated by applying image rectification before mosaicing, either to the former case (when the angle between the camera direction and the horizontal direction is smaller than 45°) or to the latter case (when the camera direction and the nadir direction is smaller than 45°).

Also, in circular pushbroom stereo mosaics, the depth error is independent of the depth in theory (Eq. (10.29)), which is the same as linear pushbroom stereo panoramas (Eq. (10.25)), whereas the depth error in stereo panoramas (either cyclographic or concentric) is proportional to the square of the depth.

The two types of pushbroom stereo panoramas (for linear and circular viewing down) can be combined into one model for a more general motion, characterized as piecewise linear and circular. Then, if a camera moves on a more general path, a generalized pushbroom panorama can be built along that path, in which the projection is perspective perpendicular to the direction of the motion. If the rates of changes of motion directions are slow, we can fit the motion parameters onto a smooth path that is piecewise linear and circular (with large radii), so that locally the epipolar geometry is still along scanlines.

10.5.2.3 Geometry and Results When Using PRISM

We have further observed that since matching image points in the stereo panoramas for 3-D scene points are found on circles with the same radius r about the center of rotation, we can apply the PRISM algorithm to interpolate in-between slits. Figure 10.18 illustrates the interpolation method. We

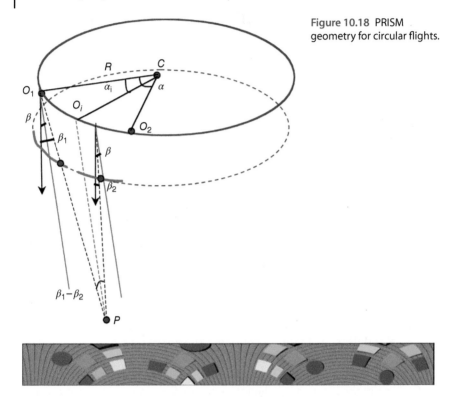

Figure 10.18 PRISM geometry for circular flights.

Figure 10.19 A 360° panorama for a circular simulation (in polar coordinates).

further observe that if we apply a polar transformation to the imagery with a center at C, the circles become horizontal parallel lines just like in the linear parallel-perspective case. In the following, we demonstrate the application of this method to a simulation (Figs 10.19 and 10.20) following an ideal circular path and to a real-world image data following a circular path (Fig. 10.21).

10.5.3 Multimodal Panoramic Registration of Video Images

A camera moving along a circular path and viewing outward can also be used to capture a 360° panorama. 360° views are desired in a wide range of applications including surveillance, robotics, and street-view and indoor mapping. Typically, the process involves implementing a circular path with a small enough radius R on a portable rotating platform that does not take up much space when mounted on a moving vehicle. An added benefit of creating a small rotating platform is that it can support multiple cameras of different modalities, such as EO and IR cameras commonly used in surveillance applications, discussed in Section 10.3.2. In these applications, it is useful to construct stereo panoramas for 3-D reconstruction as well as 3-D visualization. Since

Figure 10.20 Complete circular panorama (in Cartesian coordinates).

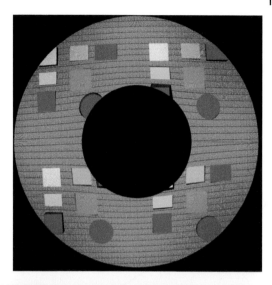

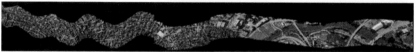

Figure 10.21 A circular panorama constructed from real imagery (in polar coordinates).

the cameras are typically offset and they have different intrinsic parameters (focal length, resolution, etc.), it is necessary to not only build stereo panoramas from all modalities but also analyze two modalities that are correctly aligned.

10.5.3.1 Concentric Geometry

Figure 10.22 illustrates the basic geometry of a single 1-D camera on a rotating platform. The camera's optical center follows the circular path around rotation axis O at a distance R, while viewing out from the rotation center. As in the case of the cyclograph geometry, if we consider two rays with angular distance 2β, we can construct a panorama for each ray on a virtual viewing circle, with radius r. The radius r can be computed from

$$r = R \sin \beta. \tag{10.30}$$

The images captured in this geometry are called concentric panoramas, which are essentially the same as those of the cyclograph geometry illustrated in Fig. 10.23.

We can compute the depth of a scene point $\mathbf{P}$ by matching the point in both stereo panoramas to their respective locations, $I_L(\phi_1, \nu_1)$ and $I_R(\phi_2, \nu_2)$. Figure 10.24 illustrates the way corresponding rays from the panoramas

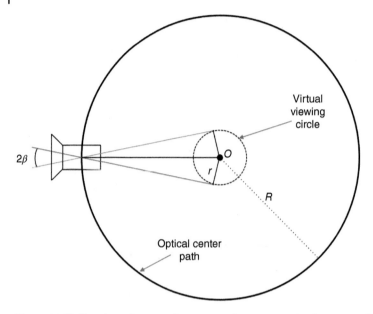

Figure 10.22 Top view of concentric geometry for a camera viewing outward from the center of the rotation path.

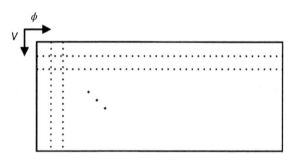

Figure 10.23 Image coordinates for circular projection panoramas.

converge. The depth D can then be computed from

$$D = \frac{r}{\sin \frac{\phi}{2}},$$ (10.31)

where $\phi = \phi_2 - \phi_1$. Once again, in the 2-D case, we note that the epipolar lines of the stereo panoramas are horizontal; therefore, $v_1 = v_2$ for all static features.

These 360° panoramas also have a circular projection in the horizontal direction and perspective projection in the vertical direction, but the flattened panoramas will be parallel-perspective projections; therefore, we can construct the panoramas using the PRISM algorithm as before. We are also able to construct multiple virtual viewing circles, except they will not have a perfect

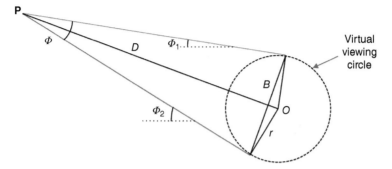

Figure 10.24 Computing depth of a scene point **P** using concentric stereo panoramas.

parallel epipolar line geometry as in the linear cases, because the radii of the viewing circles will be different, causing misalignments.

10.5.3.2 Multimodal Alignment
In surveillance applications where rotating platforms are used, it is often beneficial to include two or more multimodal sensors on the platform. Due to the availability and low cost of multimodal sensors, such as EO and IR cameras, it is often more practical and inexpensive to build a platform using off-the-shelf components. We can then apply the geometry outlined here to construct 360° panoramas for each sensor. But, when this is done, it is nearly impossible to obtain both EO and IR (or other modality) sensors with the same intrinsic parameters (focal length, resolution, pixel size, etc.) and it is also difficult (or inconvenient due to platform size) to precisely place both sensors at the same radius R. This is problematic because the sensors will have viewing circles of different radii, and their epipolar lines will not coincide. Therefore, it is ideal to be able to calibrate and align the panoramas in such a way that the viewing circles of both sensors coincide. In our work [6], we align multimodal panoramas according to the following four steps:

1. *Sensor alignment and calibration*: We install the two cameras in such a way that both of them point away from the rotation center. We then calibrate the platform to obtain values for R_1, R_2, f_1, and f_2, the distance from the rotation center and the focal length of each camera.
2. *Central panorama generation*: Since the cameras are placed next to each other at some distance, we must determine the angular distance α between the two cameras. We arrive at this by rotating the platform a complete 360°. We then build a *central panoramic view image* (CPVI) for each camera using the center slit, where the radius of the viewing circle is zero ($r = 0$). We determine α by finding feature points in both images and shifting the second one so that the distances between points become 0 (in reality, there will be some

differences between the points, so we aim to minimize the average distance between all corresponding feature points).

3. *Vertical alignment*: The vertical direction is scaled since the sensors have different FOVs.

4. *Off-center panorama generation*: We must align the panoramas for off-center slits by finding feature points in one sensor's panorama and then finding the column for which they best match in the second sensor's image.

Figure 10.25 illustrates the off-center panorama alignment geometry. Given column x_2 in one camera, we can obtain the corresponding column x_1 in the second camera and the additional shift α_{21} as follows:

$$x_1 = \frac{f_1}{f_2}\frac{R_2}{R_1}x_2, \tag{10.32}$$

$$\alpha_{21} = \arctan\left(\frac{x_2}{f_2}\right) - \arctan\left(\frac{R_2\,x_2}{R_1\,f_2}\right). \tag{10.33}$$

This procedure was developed to quickly align the multiview panoramas generated from each of the multimodal cameras. This method is particularly effective when a full intrinsic and extrinsic calibration is not available, such as when the same texture covers the entire scene, making matching of feature points difficult.

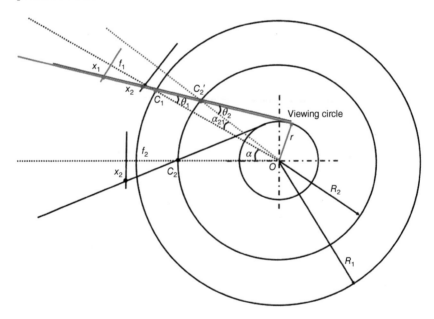

Figure 10.25 Multimodal alignment of two offset cameras on a rotating platform.

10.5.3.3 Results

The following results are from our real platform, outfitted with an EO camera and an IR camera on a controlled rotating platform with a constant speed. Each sensor took 3600 frames with the EO resolution at 720×480 and the IR resolution at 640×480. The images in Fig. 10.26 show the alignment results by using the IR images as the red channel of the color EO images. Due to channel mixing, cyan colors demonstrate cooler areas, while redder pixels show hotter areas. It can be observed that the hotter areas coincide with computer screens that are hotter than their surroundings. The images also illustrate that the vertical FOV of the two sensors was not equal, but the alignment procedure was able to align the two panoramas. This also shows the benefit of generating concentric panoramas. While the original EO and IR images cannot be globally aligned due to the motion parallax, the generated panoramas can be aligned. The generation of multiview panoramas also makes it possible to create multimodal stereoscopic images of the scene.

10.5.4 Video Mosaics Under General Motion

Images from cameras that move with general motion are not all handled at once. Typically, researchers [5, 7] have taken a divide-and-conquer approach, which segments the camera path into parts that conform to one of the previously described constraints in linear or circular motion. Figure 10.27 illustrates a simple example of a camera moving around a structure, such as an L-shaped building, and maneuvering the path in three consecutive parts, a circular path viewing in, followed by a linear path looking perpendicular to it, followed by a circular path viewing out.

Such methods have not been fully explored in the literature. Maneuvering general motion paths requires that the camera motion path be estimated first and then analyzed for circular and linear segments. The benefits of such an approach are that the PRISM and other mosaicing algorithms can then be used for each segment to construct panoramas. But this will require either manual input or an automated approach that can fit the constrained motion models to the general path in order to make it possible to segment it optimally. This method has two more problems: (1) the resulting panorama for each segment will not be continuous and (2) estimating the camera paths for long sequences will allow errors in motion estimation (drift) to significantly affect the creation of the panoramas.

To deal with these problems in large-scale scenes, we examined the applications where general motion is undertaken, particularly in aerial imaging. These paths are usually taken in surveillance and tracking applications, and typically these are all long and persistent captures (taking from hours to days), where the camera continuously cycles around an area of interest. The path is not

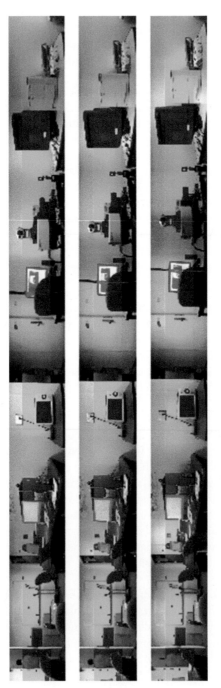

Figure 10.26 Multimodal alignment results for a platform with EO and IR cameras.

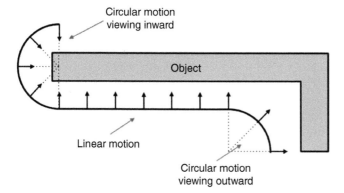

Figure 10.27 A general motion path that is segmented into three constrained paths.

necessarily circular, but it typically forms a cycle (after some time, the camera returns to an area previously imaged). We developed a new approach, the *Direct Layering approach*, to construct panoramas for general motion paths that can handle long cyclical motion paths while producing continuous stereo panoramas that are in alignment for the entire sequence.

10.5.4.1 Direct Layering Approach
This approach [8] proceeds as follows:

1. *Motion estimation from image registration*: First, interframe motion parameters for the sequence of images are estimated by frame-to-frame registration using either correlation or feature point matching. The sequence of images can be at a low frame rate (the only constraint is that consecutive frames contain sufficient overlap to enable matching).
2. *Motion modeling, base cycle registration, and error correction*: The next steps are to (a) compute the global motion path of the sequence, (b) identify where the cycle closes, and (c) correct drift errors from the base cycle path. In more detail, these steps involve the following:
   (a) The global motion is computed by making the first frame the reference frame and applying each subsequent interframe motion with respect to the previous frame. This gives each frame a global position on the path relative to the reference frame (frame 1).
   (b) Identifying the place where the cycle closes can be achieved through the analysis of the motion path (although it contains some error) or simply by matching every new frame with the first frame to detect the frame where the cycle closes.
   (c) Due to drift in global registration, it is necessary to perform some correction to the path. This is done by computing the total error accumulated at cycle closing, which is the amount of misalignment between the

last frame and the first frame. The total error is then redistributed in a weighted manner across all frames such that the global alignment is correct and the cycle closes. The weight for each frame is determined by computing the interframe error in registration using the SAD, SSD, MSE (mean squared error), or RMSE (root mean squared error) metric.

3. *Mosaic composition by the layering approach for fast multiview mosaicing*: After computing the camera motion and correcting its global drift, we can construct a set of multiview panoramas for the video scene. We use a layered approach for fast multiview mosaic generation with the following basic principle: Based on the global motion parameters, buffers for multiple empty layers are created and are laid out in the order of the first layer, the second layer, and so on, each below the previous one, as can be seen in Fig. 10.28. All of the original frames are warped based on their global motion parameters and the warped frames are laid out in the panorama space. Starting from the first layer at the top, pixels of each warped frame are placed down through all the layers until they hit the first empty layer and it gets drawn there. If it hits a layer (layer n) with existing pixels at its location, it continues onto the next layer (layer $n + 1$) until it falls on an empty layer.

The procedure GENERATEPANORAMAS in Fig. 10.29 outlines our approach to construct a set of multiview panoramic mosaics. The procedure takes as input an ordered sequence of the video images (along with its computed parameters), *Imgs*, and a reference to the ordered sequence of multiview panoramas, *Panos*.

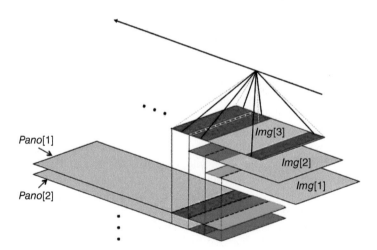

Figure 10.28 Illustration of the GENERATEPANORAMAS procedure (Fig. 10.29). Under ideal conditions, each multiviewpoint panorama *pano[i]* is constructed from a similar view angle of the scene.

Figure 10.29 Steps in the GENERATEPANORAMAS procedure.

Require: All *Panos* set to *empty*

1: **procedure** GENERATEPANORAMAS(*Imgs*,*Panos*)

2:    $N \leftarrow$ COUNT(*Imgs*)

3:    $L \leftarrow$ COUNT(*Panos*)

4:    **for** $t \leftarrow 1$ to N **do**

5:        $img \leftarrow Imgs[l]$

6:        **for** $l \leftarrow 1$ to L **do**

7:            $panos \leftarrow Panos[l]$

8:            **for all** $img(x, y) \neq empty$ **do**

9:                $(x', y') \leftarrow$ PROJECT $(img(x,y))$

10:                **if** $panos (x', y')$ is *empty* **then**

11:                    $panos(x', y') \leftarrow img(x,y)$

12:                    $img(x, y) \leftarrow empty$

Figure 10.28 illustrates drawing three image frames onto the first two multiview panoramas. Here, we see that *img*[3] paints its leading slit onto *pano*[1], and the following slit onto *pano*[2], and so on. Note that the slits contributing to a particular panoramic layer come from very similar perspective directions in the original images, thus minimizing misalignments between slits. In the ideal case, the camera performs a pure 1-D translation in the Y-direction and each image contributes a single X column to each panoramic layer. Therefore, it forms a perfect parallel-perspective (pushbroom) mosaic [4]. In more general cases, each layer approximates a multiperspective panorama with similar viewing directions. Thus, two layers can form a pair of multiperspective stereo panoramas.

Our goal with the Direct Layering method is to provide 3-D viewable results quickly without requiring the use of the PRISM algorithm. Warping and PRISM interpolation operations, in particular, can become computationally expensive as the imagery resolution keeps increasing. Blending operations can produce ghosting, which can make it distracting for some users when viewing the imagery on a 3-D display. Instead, we rely on the fact that our drift correction method has produced results with very minor local misalignments that the viewer can cope with, in particular, because we performed the layered construction approach where similar views align into each layer.

We understand that this is a subjective issue and will vary from user to user. Nevertheless, the multiview panoramas generated in this way naturally represent varying viewing angles (Fig. 10.28), and in an ideal case such as under a linear motion, the panoramas would be parallel-perspective.

10.5.4.2 Multiple Runs and Results

In addition to creating multiview panoramas for the base cycle, we use the base cycle as a reference panorama for subsequent cycles in the persistent imagery. For all frames in subsequent cycles, we developed a *spatiotemporal weighting method* to globally register each frame from its previous frame and from the base cycle, and we weight these two results once again using a distance metric such as SAD. This weighted result will handle drift as new frames arrive, allowing us to construct the panoramas in real time. Since the spatiotemporal method uses the base cycle, we are guaranteed to construct panoramas that are aligned across all cycles, and the panoramas are continuous.

The layered approach is used to generate sets of multiview mosaics from the base cycle as well as the subsequent cycles. Again, the multiperspective panoramic geometry here is the key factor that allows us to perform spatiotemporal alignment under obvious motion parallax, and the multiview panoramas preserve the motion parallax for 3-D reconstruction and visualization. Furthermore, the alignment of multiple runs also provides an efficient and effective way to detect changes over time, caused by movers (e.g., vehicles), illumination, and scene changes (such as new buildings). In fact, multiview mosaics can also be generated from aligned image frames that come from across all runs, providing dense imagery overlap for multiview mosaics. Work in this area is ongoing.

Figure 10.30a demonstrates the global motion path estimation of multiple cycles without our method (note the influence of drift on the path), while

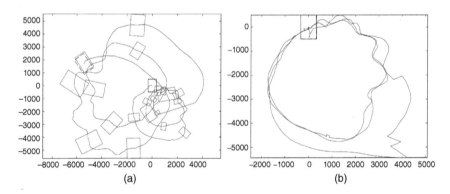

Figure 10.30 The CLIF 2007 sequence makes approximately four circular passes of an area. The units in both horizontal and vertical axes are in pixels. The dashed black box represents the last frame. Red boxes represent every 50th frame. (a) Image alignment without error correction. (b) Image alignment with error correction.

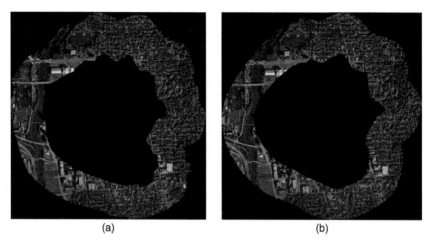

(a)	(b)

Figure 10.31 Panoramas for (a) base cycle and (b) second cycle.

Fig. 10.30b illustrates the path using our base cycle drift correction method and the spatiotemporal method applied to subsequent cycles. Figure 10.31 shows results for a base cycle and a second cycle after applying our method.

10.6   Further Reading

When collecting video images of a scene or object, each individual image in the video may have limitations in the FOV, dynamic range, or image resolution compared to the desired final product. Video registration and mosaicing aim to enhance the original images. The applications include enhancing video capture experience with a personal video camera [7, 9, 10], creating models for image-based rendering [11, 12, 13], increasing visualization capacity in aerial videography [4, 14, 15, 16, 17], and generating large format images in document digitization [18]. Generating mosaics with larger fields of view [4, 7, 10, 12, 18, 19], higher dynamic ranges [20], or higher image resolutions [21] also facilitates video viewing, video understanding, video transmission, and archiving. When the main objective of video registration and mosaicing is to generate a complete (e.g., 360°) view of an object (or a scene) by aligning and blending a set of overlapping images, the resulting image is also called a video panorama [10, 12, 13].

Many popular video mosaicing methods [22] assume a pure rotation model of the camera in which the camera rotates around its center of projection [13, 20]. For more accurate or consistent results, a global optimization can be applied among more than two frames. For example, global alignment may be applied to all the frames in a full 360° circle in order to avoid gaps between the first and the last frames [13]. However, the applications of video mosaics from a pure rotation camera are limited to mostly consumer applications, such as personal photography, entertainment, and online maps. For more specialized applications, such as surveillance, remote sensing, robot navigation, and land planning, the motion of the camera cannot be limited to a pure rotation.

Translational motion usually cannot be avoided, causing the motion parallax problem to arise. Using a pure rotation model, the generated mosaics lack geometric accuracy, but with some treatments for the small motion parallax and moving targets, such as deghosting [13], the mosaics generally look very natural. Under a general camera motion with large translation, the perspective motion model (homography), or in some applications a 2-D rigid motion model or an affine model, can be used [15, 17, 19] for planar scenes, such as those observed from a far distance. If motion parallax cannot be ignored or eliminated, multiperspective projection models have to be used to generate the mosaics, such as mosaics on an adaptive manifold [15], creating stitched images of scenes with parallax [14] and creating multiple-center-of-projection images [11]. Examples of a camera mounted on an aircraft or a ground vehicle translating a large distance can be found in [4, 7, 11, 14], while examples of a camera's optical center moving on a circular path can be found in [10, 12].

When the dominant motion of the camera is translation, the composite mosaic is also called pushbroom mosaic [23], since the projection model of the mosaic, in principle, is the same as pushbroom imaging in remote sensing. A more interesting case occurs when different parts of individual frames are selected, generating a pair of stereo mosaics that exhibit motion parallax while each mosaic represents a particular viewing angle of parallel projection [4, 8].

More sophisticated blending methods include Laplacian pyramid blending [24] and gradient domain blending [9]. The pixel selection problem is important when moving objects or motion parallax exist in the scene. For example, to avoid a person being cut in half or appearing twice in the mosaic, or to avoid cutting a 3-D object that exhibits obvious motion parallax, an optimal seam line can be selected at pixel locations where there are minimum misalignments between two frames [20].

Other considerations in image composition are high dynamic range imaging [20] and improved image resolution mosaicing [21]. A higher dynamic range mosaic is obtained by varying shutter speeds and exposures of the frames. A higher spatial resolution mosaic is obtained by camera motion.

In some applications such as surveillance and mapping, georeferencing mosaicing is also an important topic. This is usually done when geolocation metadata is available, for example, from GPS and IMU measurements [16, 17] taken with the video/images. Video mosaicing techniques are also used for dynamic scenes, to generate dynamic pushbroom mosaics for detection of moving targets [23], or to create animated panoramic video textures where different portions of a panoramic scene are animated with independently moving video loops [25, 26].

References

1 Y. Jeong, D. Nister, D. Steedly, R. Szeliski, and I.-S. Kweon, Pushing the envelope of modern methods for bundle adjustment, *IEEE Transactions on Pattern Analysis and Machine Intelligence*, **34**(8):1605–1617, 2012.

2 M. Montemerlo, S. Thrun, D. Koller, and B. Wegbreit, FastSLAM: a factored solution to the simultaneous localization and mapping problem, in *Proceedings of the 8th National Conference on Artificial Intelligence*, 593–598, 2002.

3 D. Scaramuzza and F. Fraundorfer, Visual odometry, *IEEE Robotics & Automation Magazine*, **18**(4):80–92, 2011.

4 Z. Zhu, A. R. Hanson, and E. M. Riseman, Generalized parallel-perspective stereo mosaics from airborne video, *IEEE Transactions on Pattern Analysis and Machine Intelligence*, **26**(2):226–237, 2004.

5 E. Molina, Z. Zhu, and O. Mendoza-Schrock, Mosaic-based 3D scene representation and rendering of circular aerial video, in *SPIE Defense, Security, and Sensing*, International Society for Optics and Photonics, 77040K, 2010.

6 Y. Qu, W. L. Khoo, E. Molina, and Z. Zhu, Multimodal 3D panoramic imaging using a precise rotating platform, in *IEEE/ASME International Conference on Advanced Intelligent Mechatronics (AIM)*, 260–265, 2010.

7 B. Rousso, S. Peleg, I. Finci, and A. Rav-Acha, Universal mosaicing using pipe projection, in *6th International Conference on Computer Vision*, 945–950, 1998.

8 E. Molina and Z. Zhu, Persistent aerial video registration and fast multi-view mosaicing, *IEEE Transactions on Image Processing*, **23**(5):2184–2192, 2014.

9 A. Agarwala, M. Dontcheva, M. Agrawala, et al., Interactive digital photomontage, *ACM Transactions on Graphics*, **23**(3):292–300, 2004.

10 S. Peleg and M. Ben-Ezra, Stereo panorama with a single camera, in *IEEE Computer Society Conference on Computer Vision and Pattern Recognition*, 1395–1401, 1999.

11 P. Rademacher and G. Bishop, Multiple-center-of-projection images, in *Proceedings of Computer Graphics, Annual Conference Series*, 199–206, 1998.

12 H.-Y. Shum and R. Szeliski, Stereo reconstruction from multiperspective panoramas, in *7th International Conference on Computer Vision*, 14–21, 1999.

13 H. Shum and R. Szeliski, Construction of panoramic image mosaics with global and local alignment, *International Journal of Computer Vision*, **36**(2):101–130, 2000.

14 R. Kumar, P. Anandan, M. Irani, et al., Representation of scenes from collections of images, in *IEEE Workshop on Representations of Visual Scenes*, 10–17, 1995.

15 S. Peleg, B. Rousso, A. Rav-Acha, and A. Zomet, Mosaicing on adaptive manifolds, *IEEE Transactions on Pattern Analysis and Machine Intelligence*, **22**(10):1144–1154, 2000.

16 C. N. Taylor and E. D. Andersen, An automatic system for creating geo-referenced mosaics from MAV video, in *IEEE/RSJ International Conference on Intelligent Robots and Systems*, 1248–1253, 2008.

17 Z. Zhu, E. M. Riseman, A. R. Hanson, and H. J. Schultz, An efficient method for geo-referenced video mosaicing for environmental monitoring, *Machine Vision and Applications*, **16**(4):203–216, 2005.

18 A. Iketani, T. Sato, S. Ikeda, et al., Video mosaicing for curved documents based on structure from motion, in *International Conference on Pattern Recognition*, (4):391–396, 2006.

19 M. Irani, P. Anandan, and S. C. Hsu, Mosaic based representations of video sequences and their applications, in *International Conference on Computer Vision*, 605–611, 1995.

20 A. Eden, M. Uyttendaele, and R. Szeliski, Seamless image stitching of scenes with large motions and exposure differences, in *IEEE Computer Society Conference on Computer Vision and Pattern Recognition*, 2498–2505, 2006.

21 R. Marzotto, A. Fusiello, and V. Murino, High resolution video mosaicing with global alignment, in *IEEE Conference on Computer Vision and Pattern Recognition*, Vol. 1, 692–698, 2004.

22 R. Szeliski, Image alignment and stitching: a tutorial, *Foundations and Trends in Computer Graphics and Vision*, **2**(1):1–104, 2006.

23 H. Tang and Z. Zhu, Content-based 3D mosaics for representing videos of dynamic urban scenes, *IEEE Transactions on Circuits and Systems for Video Technology*, **22**(2):295–308, 2012.

24 P. J. Burt and A. H. Adelson, A multiresolution spline with applications to image mosaics, *ACM Transactions on Graphics*, **2**(4):217–236, 1983.

25 A. Agarwala, C. Zheng, C. Pal, et al., Panoramic video textures, *ACM Transactions on Graphics*, **24**(3):821–827, 2005.

26 A. Rav-Acha, Y. Pritch, D. Lischinski, and S. Peleg, Dynamosaics: video mosaics with non-chronological time, in *IEEE Computer Society Conf. Computer Vision and Pattern Recognition*, 58–65, 2005.

11

Multitemporal Image Registration

11.1   Introduction

Aerial images of urban scenes are rich in line features. Lines are geometric features that remain stable under changes in camera view angle. They represent straight segments along the boundary between regions of different properties. Even when the properties of individual regions change over time, as long as properties of adjacent regions remain different, boundaries between the regions and, therefore, the straight segments along the boundaries remain unchanged.

The problem addressed in this chapter is as follows: Given two aerial images of a planar scene taken at different times, it is required to register the images using line features in the images. A planar scene is considered one where local changes in scene elevation are negligible compared to the distance of the camera to the scene center.

The relation between images of a planar scene can be most generally described by a 2-D projective or homography transformation. Due to radiometric differences between the images, some lines in the scene may be detected in only one of the images, and for the lines that are detected in both images, homologous lines may have different endpoints.

An example of the kind of images to be registered is given in Fig. 11.1. Figure 11.1a shows an aerial image of the O'Hare International Airport, and (b) shows another image of the same area taken in a different season. These images are courtesy of Microsoft Bing and Google Maps. Land-cover changes occurring due to change of season are visible; however, there are man-made structures that remain unchanged from one season to another. Lines detected in the images by a least-squares line-fitting method (Section 4.5) are shown. These lines will be used to register the images.

In the following sections, steps in the registration of multitemporal aerial images using lines in images are detailed and experimental results using various multitemporal images are provided. Throughout this chapter, line

Theory and Applications of Image Registration, First Edition. Arthur Ardeshir Goshtasby.
© 2017 John Wiley & Sons, Inc. Published 2017 by John Wiley & Sons, Inc.

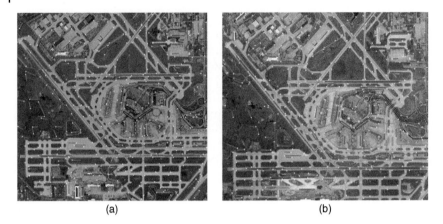

(a)   (b)

Figure 11.1 (a and b) Aerial images of the O'Hare International Airport, courtesy of Microsoft Bing and Google Maps, respectively. In image (a) 340 lines are detected, while in image (b) 354 lines are detected.

segment and line will be used interchangeably. A line segment in an image represents the projection of a straight edge or boundary segment in the scene to the image plane.

11.2 Finding Transformation Parameters from Line Parameters

In Section 6.2, the relation between two images of a planar scene in terms of the parameters of homologous lines in the images was determined. Images of a planar scene are most generally related by a 2-D *projective* or *homography* transformation. If point (x, y) in the reference image corresponds to point (X, Y) in the test images and the images are related by a homography transformation, coordinates of corresponding points in the images are related by

$$X = \frac{h_0 x + h_1 y + h_2}{h_6 x + h_7 y + 1}, \tag{11.1}$$

$$Y = \frac{h_3 x + h_4 y + h_5}{h_6 x + h_7 y + 1}. \tag{11.2}$$

From the results in Section 6.2, we know that if line $ax + by + 1 = 0$ in the reference image corresponds to line $AX + BY + 1 = 0$ in the test image, the same homography relates homologous lines in the images by the following equations:

$$Ah_0 - aAh_2 + Bh_3 - aBh_5 + h_6 = a, \tag{11.3}$$

$$Ah_1 - bAh_2 + Bh_4 - bBh_5 + h_7 = b. \tag{11.4}$$

Equations (11.3) and (11.4) show that if a minimum of four homologous lines in two images of a planar scene are available, the homography parameters to register the images can be determined by solving a system of eight linear equations. Note that no more than two of the lines can be parallel to enable determination of homography parameters from the coefficients of the homologous lines.

Having found the homography parameters, for each point (x, y) in the reference image, the corresponding point (X, Y) in the test image is determined from Eqs (11.1) and (11.2). The intensity at (X, Y) in the test image is then read and saved at (x, y) in a new image that has the intensities of the test image and the geometry of the reference image.

11.3   Finding an Initial Set of Homologous Lines

A set of lines $\{l_i : i = 1, \ldots, m\}$ in the reference image and a set of lines $\{L_i : i = 1, \ldots, n\}$ in the test image are given, and it is required to establish correspondence between the lines while determining the homography transformation that registers the images. Line l_i in the reference image in homogeneous coordinates is represented by $l_i = [a_i \quad b_i \quad 1]^t$ and line L_i in the test image in homogeneous coordinates is represented by $L_i = [A_i \quad B_i \quad 1]^t$, where t denotes transpose.

First, an approximate homography that establishes correspondence between a subset of lines in the images is determined. The approximate homography is then iteratively refined to maximize the number of homologous lines. The homography maximizing the number of homologous lines in the images is then used to register the images.

Determination of the homography parameters from Eqs (11.3) and (11.4) requires four homologous lines in the images. To find initial correspondence between lines in the images, according to the RANSAC paradigm [1, 2], four lines are randomly selected in each image and assumed homologous lines. The correctness of the assumption is then verified using all lines in the images.

If a sufficiently large number of lines in the images is found to match with the obtained homography, the homography is taken as an approximation to the homography to be determined. Otherwise, the process is repeated until either a homography is obtained that finds correspondence between a sufficiently large number of lines in the images or the maximum allowed number of iterations is reached.

If there are about the same number of lines in each image ($m = n$) and only about half of the lines in one image appear in the conjugate image, when a line is selected in the reference image, the probability that it appears in the test image is $\frac{1}{2}$. When a line is randomly selected in the test image, the probability that it corresponds to the line selected in the reference image is $\frac{1}{n}$. Therefore, when a line is randomly selected from each image, the probability that they correspond is $\frac{1}{2n}$, and when four lines are randomly selected in each image, the probability that they all correspond is $(\frac{1}{2n})^4$.

This shows that the probability that one, two, or three out of the four lines do not correspond is $1 - (\frac{1}{2n})^4$, and the probability that after k iterations four homologous lines are not obtained is $[1 - (\frac{1}{2n})^4]^k$. Therefore, the probability that at least one of the k iterations produces four lines in the images that correspond is $1 - [1 - (\frac{1}{2n})^4]^k$. If we want this probability to be P, we have

$$P = 1 - \left[1 - \left(\frac{1}{2n} \right)^4 \right]^k \tag{11.5}$$

from which we find

$$k = \frac{\log \, (1 - P)}{\log \, (1 - \frac{1}{16n^4})}. \tag{11.6}$$

For example, when $P = 0.99$ and $n = 10$, we find $k = 736{,}825$, and when $P = 0.99$ and $n = 20$, we find $k = 11{,}789{,}233$. Although computations may be affordable when $n \leq 10$, when $n > 10$, the process becomes too slow, rendering RANSAC impractical. Therefore, to make the computations manageable, lines in the images are grouped according to their local spatial properties and matching is performed between lines within the same group in the images.

When a line belongs to the boundary between two regions where each region has a nearly homogeneous property, the line is hardly affected by changing the resolution of the image. The same line will be detected at a wide range of resolutions. However, when regions on the two sides of a line are highly detailed, changing the resolution of the image slightly can break the line into pieces, displace the line, or cause it not to be detected. Spatial properties of regions on the two sides of a line determine whether a line will remain stationary, break, or disappear when the resolution is changed.

The stability of lines in an image under changes in the image's resolution can be used to group the lines; therefore, lines in homologous groups in two images of a scene will represent lines that have neighborhoods with similar spatial properties. Since homologous lines have neighborhoods that have similar spatial properties, by matching lines within homologous groups, wasteful matches that are not likely to find the transformation parameters are avoided.

Under considerable changes in image resolution, some lines persist while others disappear or new lines emerge. Starting from lines obtained at the highest resolution, each line is tracked from the highest to the lowest resolution until it disappears from the image. Lines that appear at the highest resolution are put in group 0 and lines in group 0 that appear at half the resolution are moved from group 0 to group 1. Lines in group 1 that also appear at 1/4 the resolution are moved to group 2. Lines in group 2 that also appear at 1/8 the resolution are

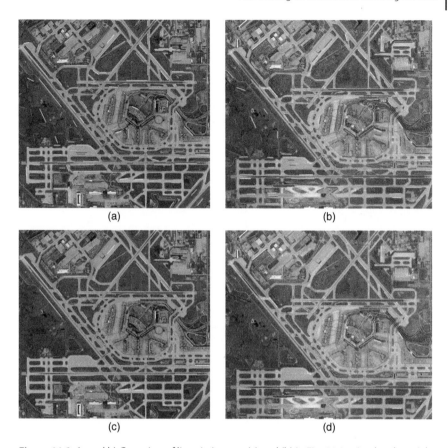

Figure 11.2 (a and b) Grouping of lines in images (a) and (b) in Fig. 11.1 using local spatial properties of the lines. Lines persisting from the highest resolution (red) to resolutions reduced by factors of 2 (green), 4 (blue), 8 (yellow), 16 (purple), and 32 (light blue) are shown. (c and d) The 10 longest lines in each group.

moved to group 3. Lines in group 3 that also appear at 1/16 the resolution are moved to group 4. Finally, lines in group 4 that also appear at 1/32 the resolution are moved to group 5.

Lines in Fig. 11.1a and b grouped in this manner are shown in Fig. 11.2a and b, respectively. Lines in groups 0, 1, 2, 3, 4, and 5 are shown in red, green, blue, yellow, purple, and light blue, respectively. When comparing the groups in Fig. 11.2a and b, we see that many homologous lines belong to the same group, and for a small percentage of homologous lines that do not appear in the same group, they appear in adjacent groups.

Grouping lines in this manner makes it possible to match lines that possess similar spatial properties. If there are too many lines in a group, a required number of the longest lines can be kept and the rest can be removed. Figure 11.2c and d shows the 10 longest lines in groups that contain more than 10 lines. If a group contains fewer than 10 lines, no change is made to the group. Lines in the same group are shown with the same color in these images. An algorithm that finds initial homologous lines in two images of a planar scene by grouping the lines in this manner is described next.

Algorithm 11.1 Line correspondence by line grouping

---

1. Group lines in the images based on their local spatial properties. Suppose lines at l levels (from 0 to $l - 1$) are obtained, and there are n_i lines at level i, where $0 \leq i < l$.
2. Let $i = l - 1$.
3. Find the initial homography parameters by matching lines in group i in the images by RANSAC.
4. If RANSAC was able to find the homography parameters, go to Step 6. Otherwise, decrement i by 1 and find the initial homography parameters by matching lines within groups i and $i + 1$ in the images by RANSAC.
5. If RANSAC was able to find the homography parameters, go to Step 6. Otherwise, decrement i by 1, and if $i \geq 0$, go to Step 3. Otherwise, report failure.
6. Return the obtained homography parameters and the homologous lines.

A line at level 0 is one that appears only at full resolution, and a line at level $0 < i < l$ is one that appears at all resolutions from the highest to $\frac{1}{2^i}$ resolution. An image at level i is obtained by reducing its dimensions by a factor of 2^i. The coordinates of the endpoints of a line detected at the $\frac{1}{2^i}$ resolution are then multiplied by 2^i so that lines in different groups can be matched.

In Step 3, matching is performed between lines in group i in the images. If the process fails to find an initial set of homologous lines, the process is repeated in Step 4, by decrementing i by 1 and matching lines in groups i, and $i + 1$ in the images. This is done so that if the images are in different scales, the process will still be able to find an initial set of homologous lines in the images.

When lines in Fig. 11.2c and d are matched according to Algorithm 11.1, the homologous lines shown in Fig. 11.3a and b are obtained. Note that while lines shown in Fig. 11.2c and d are used to find the approximate homography parameters, lines in Fig. 11.2a and b are used to verify the validity of the obtained parameters.

Although the majority of the homologous lines shown in Fig. 11.3a and b are correct, a small number of the homologous lines is incorrect. Such incorrect homologous lines are due to inaccuracies in the initial homography parameters.

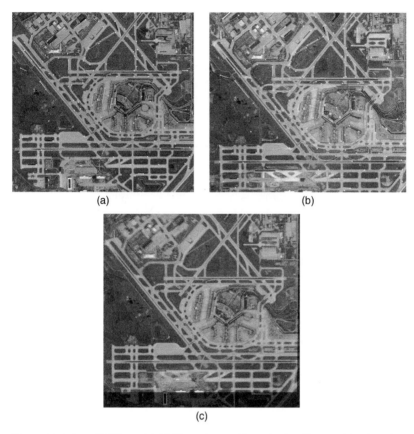

Figure 11.3 (a and b) The 110 initial homologous lines obtained by matching lines in Fig. 11.2c and d within small groups according to Algorithm 11.1. Homologous lines are shown with the same color. (c) Registration of the images by the initial (approximate) homography.

Registration of the images with the approximate homography obtained from the initial homologous lines is depicted in Fig. 11.3c. The initial homography parameters are iteratively refined while maximizing the number of homologous lines in the images. This is discussed next.

11.4 Maximizing the Number of Homologous Lines

Knowing an initial set of homologous lines in the images, four homologous line pairs are randomly selected and the correctness of the correspondence between the line pairs is verified using other homologous line pairs in the images. By testing various combinations of four homologous line pairs, whenever the combination producing more homologous lines than before is found, the initial set of homologous lines is replaced with the newly found homologous lines and the initial homography parameters are replaced with the newly found homography parameters. This process is repeated until the number of homologous lines can no longer be increased within a required number of iterations.

If n_I is the number of initial homologous lines, and assuming half of the initial correspondences are incorrect, if four homologous line pairs are selected from the set of initial homologous lines, the probability that they all correctly correspond to each other is $\frac{1}{16}$. Therefore, on average, every 16 iterations produces four homologous line pairs that truly correspond. Depending on the accuracy of detected lines, some homologous line pairs produce more homologous lines than others. The iterative process, in effect, identifies accurately positioned and oriented lines in the images and uses them to determine the homography parameters.

Since there is a limited number of homologous lines in the images, if the process is found not to increase the number of homologous lines after some iterations, the process is stopped and the homography transformation finding the most homologous lines is used to register the images. In the following experiments, the process is stopped whenever the number of homologous lines is not increased after N iterations, where N is the smaller of n_I^4 and 10,000.

The maximum 10,000 iterations is a compromise between speed and accuracy. As the number of iterations increases, it is possible to find more homologous lines but at an increasingly higher computational cost. The 10,000 iterations can be replaced by an error tolerance. For example, the process can be stopped whenever registration error falls below a required tolerance, such as 1 pixel. The number of iterations and the required error tolerance can both be used to stop the process if the required error tolerance is not reached after an afforded number of iterations.

Registration error is calculated using the root-mean-squared error (RMSE) measure. If n_c homologous lines are obtained in the images, RMSE is calculated using the following formula:

$$
\text{RMSE} = \left\{ \frac{1}{n_c} \sum_{i=1}^{n_c} \frac{d_{1_i}^2 + d_{2_i}^2}{2} \right\}^{\frac{1}{2}},
\tag{11.7}
$$

where d_{1_i} and d_{2_i} are orthogonal distances of the endpoints of line $\mathbf{l}_i$ in the reference image after the line is transformed with the obtained homography to the line corresponding to it in the test image.

Two lines are considered homologous under the obtained homography if (1) the mean of the orthogonal distances of the endpoints of the line in the reference image, after the line is transformed by the obtained homography, to the line in the test image is within a required distance tolerance ε_d pixels, and (2)

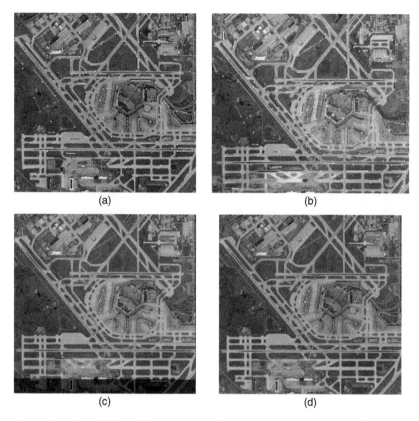

Figure 11.4 (a and b) The 161 homologous lines obtained in the images of Fig. 11.2a and b by the described iterative process. (c) Registration of the images with the obtained homography transformation. (d) Fusion of the registered images, visualizing the scene changes.

the angle between the line in the test image and the line in the reference image after transformation by the homography is within ε_θ degrees.

Letting $\varepsilon_d = 5$ pixels and $\varepsilon_\theta = 5°$, and starting from the 110 initial homologous lines shown in Fig. 11.3a and b, the refinement process finds 161 homologous lines in the images as shown in Fig. 11.4a and b. When the homography producing the 161 homologous lines is used to register the images, the result shown in Fig. 11.4c is obtained. RMSE in this registration is 0.83 pixels.

To visualize changes in the scene occurred between the times the images are obtained, a color image is created with the red band of the resampled test image and the green and blue bands of the reference image. In areas of the scene where there are no changes, the color of the reference image is reproduced. Areas of the scene where changes have occurred appear in colors that are different from those of the reference image. The red spots in the fused image in Fig. 11.4d identify new constructions at O'Hare that occurred between the times the images are obtained. The light blue region at the bottom of the fused image shows scene areas visible in the reference image but out of view of the test image.

11.5 Examples of Multitemporal Image Registration

In this section, registration results on a number of multitemporal images are given. Figure 11.5 shows two off-nadir-view images of an agricultural area taken from a rather low altitude. There are 120 lines in the reference image and 104 lines in the test image. The described method has found 62 homologous lines in the images. Homologous lines are shown with the same color in Fig. 11.5. Lines without a correspondence or lines that do not accurately correspond with the provided angular and distance tolerances are shown in black.

Figure 11.5c shows fusion of the registered images. The blue and green bands in this image are taken from the reference image and the red band is taken from the resampled test image. These aerial images are taken moments apart and, therefore, no scene changes are present. The light blue boundary regions in the fused image represent areas in the reference image that are out of view in the test image. The registration RMSE in this example computed according to Eq. (11.7) is 0.94 pixels.

(a) (b) (c)

Figure 11.5 (a and b) Low-altitude off-nadir-view images of an agricultural area. These images are courtesy of Image Registration and Fusion Systems. The line correspondence method has found 62 homologous lines in the images. Homologous lines are shown with the same color. Lines in black are those for which matching homologous lines could not be found with the provided angular and distance tolerances. (c) Registration and fusion of the images.

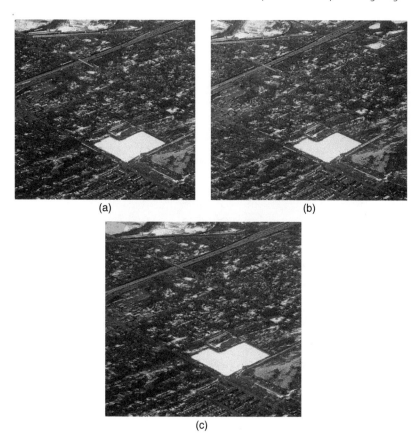

Figure 11.6 (a and b) High-altitude off-nadir-view images of an urban area. These images are courtesy of Image Registration and Fusion Systems. The described method has found 155 homologous lines in the images. (c) Registration and fusion of the images using the homologous lines.

Figure 11.6 shows a pair of off-nadir-view images of an urban scene taken from a rather high altitude. There are 289 lines in image (a) and 250 lines in image (b). The described line correspondence algorithm has found 155 homologous lines in the images. Registration and fusion of the images with the obtained homologous lines is shown in Fig. 11.6c. The registration RMSE in this example is 1.24 pixels.

Figure 11.7a and b shows Landsat 5 images of an area over Western Australia taken on January 8, 1990 and January 2, 2011, respectively. These images are courtesy of the US Geological Survey. There are 145 lines in image (a) and 136 lines in image (b). The described matching has found correspondence between 35 of the lines. Homologous lines are shown with the same color in these images.

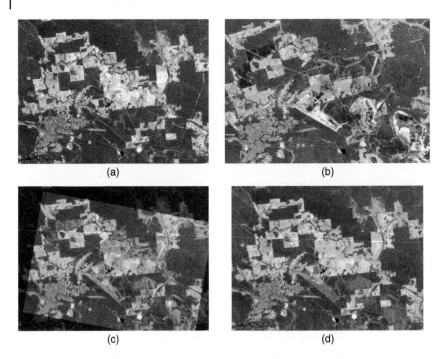

(a)　　　　　　　　　　　　　　　　(b)

(c)　　　　　　　　　　　　　　　　(d)

Figure 11.7 (a and b) Landsat 5 images of an area over Western Australia taken on January 8, 1990 and January 2, 2011, respectively. These images are courtesy of the US Geological Survey. The described correspondence algorithm has found 35 homologous lines in the images, producing the registration and fusion results shown in (c) and (d), respectively.

Registration of the images with the homography producing the 35 homologous lines is shown in Fig. 11.7c. The registration RMSE is 1.09 pixels. Fusion of the images visualizing changes occurring in the scene between January 8, 1990 and January 2, 2011 are shown in Fig. 11.7d. Red and light blue regions show scene areas where major changes have occurred during this period.

Next, examples demonstrating registration of images before and after a disaster where radiometric as well as geometric changes occur in the scene are given. Figure 11.8 shows satellite images of the New Jersey shore taken before and after the Hurricane Sandy destruction. These images are courtesy of the National Oceanic and Atmospheric Administration (NOAA). Not only have the reflectance properties of the scene changed, but also some buildings have been displaced or destroyed. There is also a resolution difference between the images. Despite these image differences, there are line segments that are well preserved and appear in both images. The process uses such lines as the main source of information to register the images.

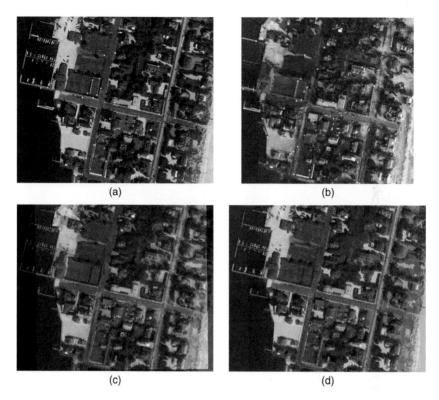

(a)   (b)

(c)   (d)

Figure 11.8 (a), (b) Images of a segment of the New Jersey shoreline before and after Hurricane Sandy. These images are courtesy of NOAA. The described method has found 47 homologous lines in the images, producing the registration and fusion results shown in (c) and (d), respectively.

Overall, 156 lines are detected in Fig. 11.8a, and 108 lines are detected in (b). Via the described line matching algorithm, correspondence is established between 47 of the lines. Homologous lines are shown with the same color in these images. Image (c) shows registration of the before and after images. The registration RMSE in this example is 1.44 pixels. Fusion of the images using the obtained homography is shown in Fig. 11.8d. Red and light blue regions in the fused image represent areas in the scene where changes have occurred due to the hurricane.

Figure 11.9a and b shows GeoEye satellite images of lake Onuma in Sendai, Japan, taken before and after the tsunami of 2011. These images are courtesy of Google. In addition to considerable radiometric differences between the images, there are geometric differences caused by the force of the tsunami. In spite of these differences, there are linear structures, such as roads and bridges, that have been preserved. Overall, 399 lines are detected in the before image

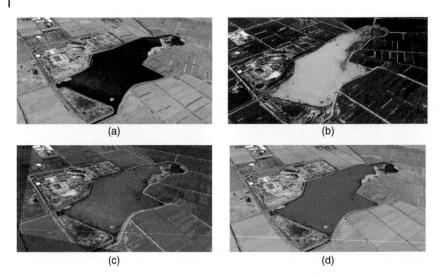

Figure 11.9 (a and b) GeoEye satellite images of Lake Onuma in Sendai, Japan, captured before and after the tsunami of 2011. These images are courtesy of Google. There are 97 homologous lines in the images, producing the registration and fusion results shown in (c) and (d), respectively.

and 389 lines are detected in the after image. Correspondence has been found between 97 of the lines by the described method, producing the registration and fusion results shown in Fig. 11.9c and d. The registration RMSE in this example is 1.16 pixels.

Another example demonstrating registration of the before and after tsunami images is given in Fig. 11.10. These images show the Yamamoto Town near Sendai, Japan, before and after the tsunami of 2011. These are Digital Globe and GeoEye images of the area and are courtesy of Google. The after image is covered by seawater due to the tsunami; however, some roads, bridges, and city structures remain above water and are visible. Overall, 166 lines are detected in the before image and 136 lines are detected in the after image.

Many of the lines represent edges of man-made structures that are not affected by the tsunami. Some lines belonging to small buildings are displaced due to the force of the tsunami. Overall, 34 homologous lines are found in the images, producing the registration and fusion results depicted in Fig. 11.10c and d. The registration RMSE in this example is 1.25 pixels. The main structures such as roads, bridges, and boundaries of agricultural fields have kept their geometric integrity and, therefore, are registered accurately. Changes have occurred across the scene, which appear in red or light blue in the fused image.

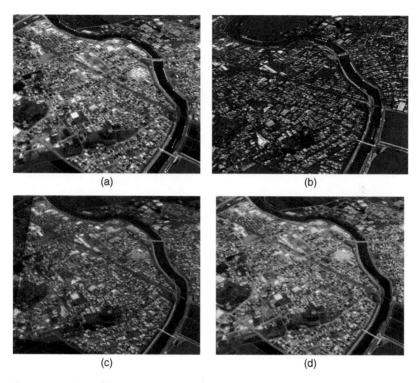

Figure 11.10 (a and b) Digital Globe and GeoEye images of Yamamoto Town near Sendai, Japan, captured before and after the tsunami of 2011. These images are courtesy of Google. Overall, 34 homologous lines are obtained in the images by the described method. (c) Registration and (d) fusion of the images.

Although the focus of this chapter has been on registration of multitemporal images, experiments have shown that line segments can also be used to register multimodal images. The procedure to register multitemporal images was followed when registering the multimodal images depicted in Fig. 11.11. There are 218 lines in the optical image, whereas141 lines in the IR image. The described line correspondence algorithm has found 55 homologous lines in the images. Homologous lines are shown with the same color in Fig. 11.11a and b. The obtained homologous lines have produced the registration and fusion results depicted in Fig. 11.11c and d, respectively. The registration RMSE in this example is 0.95 pixels.

Finally, registration of images of a terrain scene where man-made structures are absent is demonstrated. Figure 11.12a and b shows Landsat 5 and Landsat 8 images of a terrain in China taken on September 24, 1993 and on September 15, 2013. These images are courtesy of the US Geological Survey. There are 164 lines in image (a), while 106 lines in image (b). Although many of the lines are

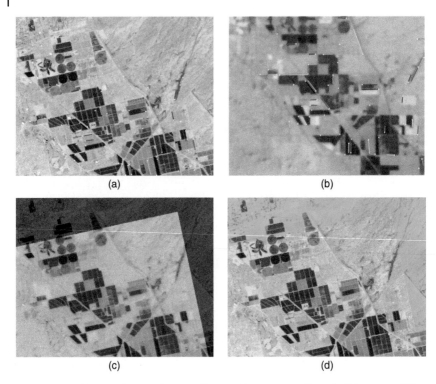

(a)   (b)

(c)   (d)

Figure 11.11 (a) A Landsat 5 reflectance image of an area over Phoenix, Arizona, and (b) a thermal IR image of the same area. These images are courtesy of the US Geological Survey. Overall, 55 homologous lines are obtained in the images, producing the registration and fusion results shown in (c) and (d), respectively.

short, the described method has been able to find correspondence between 48 of the lines. Registration of the images with the obtained homologous lines is depicted in Fig. 11.12c. The registration RMSE in this example is 1.19 pixels. Fusion of the images is depicted in Fig. 11.12d, showing no major changes in the scene during the 20-year period.

Multitemporal image registration is achieved by detecting lines in images and determining correspondence between the lines. Line correspondence is made faster by grouping the lines into subsets using spatial information about the regions on the two sides of each line. Line grouping reduces the number of line combinations that must be tested to find a sufficient number of homologous lines, enabling registration of the images. An earlier version of the method described in this chapter uses line endpoints to find initial homologous lines in the images [3]. Line grouping is found to speed up determination of the initial homologous lines by a factor of up to 100, depending on the number of lines in the images.

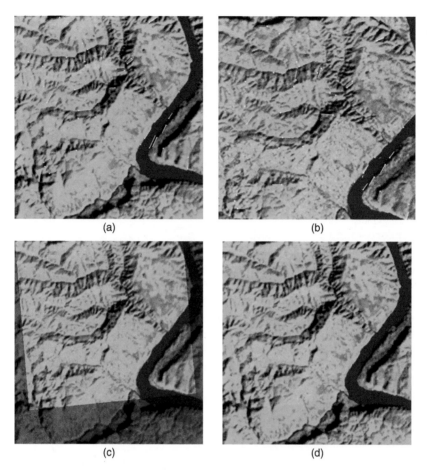

Figure 11.12 (a and b) Landsat 5 and Landsat 8 images of a terrain over China taken on September 24, 1993 and on September 15, 2013, respectively. These images are courtesy of the US Geological Survey. Overall, 48 homologous lines are obtained in the images, producing the registration and fusion results shown in (c) and (d), respectively.

11.6 Further Reading

Methods finding transformation parameters from line parameters: Methods that use lines to register images require that the parameters of the transformation to be determined from the parameters of the lines. Determination of rigid transformation parameters by clustering the orientational difference between randomly selected lines and clustering the intersections of randomly selected line pairs in images is described by Stockman et al. [4].

Extension of the clustering idea to the affine transformation is described by Habib and Kelley [5].

Use of intersections of randomly selected line triples in finding the affine parameters is described by Coiras et al. [6] and Li et al. [7], and use of endpoints of randomly selected line pairs in the computation of homography parameters is described by Krüger [8].

Determination of the rotational difference between two images from the difference of orientations of homologous lines in images is described by Tang et al. [9]. The translational difference between the images is determined by template matching using Rènyi mutual information [10] as the similarity measure. Computation of rigid and affine transformation parameters from unit vectors obtained from homologous lines and homologous checkpoints is described by Shekar [11] and Teo et al. [12].

Line correspondence methods: The main difficulty in the use of lines in image registration is the determination of correspondence between the lines. A method that first finds an initial correspondence between the lines using their angular difference and the distance between the midpoints of nearest lines is described by Li et al. [7]. Intersections of homologous line triples are used to hypothesize an affine transformation, and the correctness of the hypothesis is verified using other lines in the images. If the hypothesized transformation produces a sufficient number of homologous lines, the transformation and the homologous lines are considered correct. A method that uses the average color difference of pixels around lines and minimizes the sum of average color differences between lines in images to determine the correspondence between the lines is described by Volegov and Yurin [13] .

A method that represents lines in polar form, maps lines in two images to two sets of points in the polar space, and matches point patterns in the polar space to establish correspondence between the lines in the images is described by Wang et al. [14]. An expectation maximization method that estimates the affine registration parameters from lines in two images is described by Long et al. [15]. The method starts with a plausible initial affine transformation. It then refines the affine parameters iteratively in such a way to increase the number of homologous lines. The process of increasing the number of homologous lines and refining the affine parameters is repeated until a maximum is reached in the number of homologous lines.

Multitemporal image registration methods: Due to radiometric differences between multitemporal images, raw image intensities have not been used to register such images from very early. Anuta [16] used intensity gradients, Dai and Khorram [17] used zero-crossing edges representing region boundaries, and Eugenio et al. [18] used coastlines detected by a gradient energy function to register multitemporal images. By matching boundaries of land-cover patches, Cao et al. [19] and Han et al. [20] found correspondence between the boundaries. The centroids of homologous closed boundaries were then used as homologous points to register the images.

The need to use geometric features in order to avoid radiometric differences between multitemporal images was recognized by Li and Davis [21] and Hu et al. [22]. They suggested using points in multitemporal images and the descriptors associated with the points to find the correspondence between them. A descriptor for a point characterizes these gradient properties of the neighborhood of the point. In addition to points, Coulter et al. [23] used information from the global positioning system to capture new images that had the same center as an image previously captured to reduce the geometric difference between the images to be registered.

Chen et al. [24] and Moorthi et al. [25] showed that the effect of radiometric differences between multitemporal images can be reduced by using mutual information as opposed to cross-correlation as the similarity measure when registering the images.

Most recently, Murphy et al. [26] demonstrated use of shearlet features in the registration of multitemporal images. To register two images by a rigid transformation, a distance measure was used to relate homologous features in the images. Then, by minimizing the distance measure through an iterative process, the rigid transformation parameters were determined.

References

1 M. A. Fischler and R. C. Bolles, Random sample consensus: a paradigm for model fitting with applications to image analysis and automated cartography, *Communications of the ACM*, **24**(6):381–395, 1981.

2 A. Goshtasby, *Image Registration: Principles, Tools, and Methods*, Springer, 2012.

3 C. Zhao and A. Goshtasby, Registration of multitemporal aerial optical images using line landmarks, *Photogrammetric Engineering and Remote Sensing*, **117**:149–160, 2016.

4 G. Stockman, S. Kopstein, and S. Benett, Matching images to models for registration and object detection via clustering, *IEEE Transactions on Pattern Analysis and Machine Intelligence*, **4**(3):229–241, 1982.

5 A. Habib and D. Kelley, Automatic relative orientation of large scale imagery over urban areas using modified iterated Hough transform, *Photogrammentry & Remote Sensing*, **56**:29–41, 2001.

6 E. Coiras, J. Santamaria, and C. Miravet, A segment-based registration technique for visual-infrared images, *Optical Engineering*, **39**:282–289, 2000.

7 Y. Li, R. L. Stevenson, and J. D. Gai, Line segment based image registration, in *SPIE Proceedings of Visual Communications and Image Processing*, Vol. 6822, 68221H-1-8, 2008.

8 W. Krüger, Robust and efficient map-to-image registration with line segments, *Machine Vision and Applications*, **13**:38–50, 2001.

9 J. Tang, X. Yang, C. Liu, and X. Wu, Image registration based on fitted straight lines of edges, in *Proceedings of the 6th World Congress on Intelligent Control and Automation*, 9782–9785, 2006.

10 A. Rènyi, On measures of entropy and information, in *Proceedings of the 4th Berkeley Symposium on Mathematical Statistics Probability*, Vol. 1, 547–561, 1961.

11 A. Shekar, The line-based transformation model (LBTM): a new approach to the rectification of high-resolution satellite imagery, *International Archives of Photogrammetry, Remote Sensing, and Spatial Information Sciences*, **35**:850–856, 2004.

12 T.-A. Teo, Line-based rational function model for high-resolution satellite imagery, *International Journal of Remote Sensing*, **34**(4):1355–1372, 2013.

13 D. B. Volegov and D. V. Yurin, Preliminary coarse image registration by using straight lines found on them for constructing super resolution mosaics and 3D scene recovery, *Programming and Computer Software*, **34**(5):279–293, 2008.

14 K. Wang, T. Shi, G. Liao, and Q. Xia, Image registration using a point-line duality based line matching method, *Journal of Visual Communication and Image Representation*, **24**:615–626, 2013.

15 T. Long, W. Jiao, G. He, and W. Wang, Automatic line segment registration using Gaussian mixture model and expectation-maximization algorithm, *IEEE Journal of Selected Topics in Applied Earth Observation and Remote Sensing*, **7**(5):1688–1699, 2014.

16 P. E. Anuta, Spatial registration of multispectral and multitemporal digital imagery using fast Fourier transform techniques, *IEEE Transactions on Geoscience Electronics*, **8**(4):353–368, 1970.

17 X. Dai and S. Khorram, Development of a feature-based approach to automated image registration for multitemporal and multisensor remotely sensed imagery, *Geoscience and Remote Sensing (IGARSS)*, **1**:243–245, 1997.

18 F. Eugenio, F. Marqeés, and J. Marcello, A contour-based approach to automatic and accurate registration of multitemporal and multisensor satellite imagery, *IEEE International Symposium Geoscience and Remote Sensing*, **6**:3390–3392, 2002.

19 S. Cao, X. Zhu, Y. Pan, and Q. Yu, A stable land cover patches method for automatic registration of multitemporal remote sensing images, *IEEE Journal of Selected Topics in Applied Earth Observations and Remote Sensing*, **7**(8):3502–3512, 2014.

20 Y. Han, F. Bovolo, and L. Bruzzone, Fine co-registration of VHR images for multitemporal urban area analysis, in *8th International Workshop on the Analysis of Multitemporal Remote Sensing Images (Multi-Temp)*, 1–4, 2015.

21 Y. Li and C. H. Davis, Pixel-based invariant feature extraction and its application to radiometric co-registration for multi-temporal high-resolution satellite imagery, *IEEE Journal of Selected Topics Applied Earth Observation and Remote Sensing*, 4(2):348–360, 2011.

22 L. Hu, J. Ye, Y. Feng, and Y. Zhang, Registration for long-term multi-temporal remote sensing images under spatial constraints from historical data, in *IEEE International Symposium Geoscience and Remote Sensing (IGARSS)*, 4836–4839, 2015.

23 L. I. Coulter, D. A. Stow, and S. Baer, A frame center matching technique for precise registration of multitemporal airborne frame imagery, *IEEE Transactions on Geoscience and Remote Sensing*, 41(11):2436–2444, 2003.

24 H.-M. Chen, P. K. Varshney, and M. K. Arora, Performance of mutual information similarity measure for registration of multitemporal remote sensing images, *IEEE Transactions on Geoscience and Remote Sensing*, 41(11):2445–2454, 2003.

25 S. M. Moorthi, R. K. Gambhir, I. Misra, and R. Ramakrishnan, Adaptive stochastic gradient descent optimization in multi temporal satellite image registration, in *Recent Advances in Intelligent Computational Systems (RAICS)*, 373–377, 2011.

26 J. M. Murphy, J. Le Moigne, and D. J. Harding, Automatic image registration of multimodal remotely sensed data with global shearlet features, *IEEE Transactions on Geoscience and Remote Sensing*, 54(3):1084–1087, 2015.

12

Open Problems and Research Topics

In the preceding chapters, fundamentals of feature-based image registration were described and a number of applications of image registration were discussed. In this final chapter, open problems in image registration are identified and some of the problems are suggested as topics of research for students and researchers interested in gaining further expertise in image registration.

To register two images, a number of steps must be completed. If any of the steps fails, the entire process fails. A robust image registration system should have redundant and alternate methods so that if one method fails another method can take its place and complete the process. It is possible to find an image pair where none of the methods reported in the literature can satisfactorily register them. Following are some of the causes of image registration failures for which there are no satisfactory solutions.

12.1 Finding Rotational Difference between Multimodality Images

Since images in different modalities have different structures, homologous features are rarely detected in the images. For this reason, template matching becomes the method of choice in finding homologous points in multimodality images. For template matching to work, however, images must have the same scale and orientation. Scale difference between images is not a problem if pixel dimensions are known. By resampling the test image to the scale of the reference image, both images can be made the same scale; however, rotational difference between the images remains a problem, which should be solved before finding homologous points in the images by template matching.

In Chapter 2, a method for determining the rotational difference between images in the same modality was described. The method may work for some multimodality images, but it may fail for others. There is a need to develop a robust method that can determine the rotational difference between images of a scene captured by different sensors.

Theory and Applications of Image Registration, First Edition. Arthur Ardeshir Goshtasby.
© 2017 John Wiley & Sons, Inc. Published 2017 by John Wiley & Sons, Inc.

It is possible to rotate one image with respect to the other in small steps, find the translational difference between the images at each rotational step, and find the rotation amount where the images produce the highest match rating. When registering 2-D images, an exhaustive search is required in the 3-D parameter space: one dimension representing the rotation angle and the remaining two dimensions representing translations along x and y.

Are there rotation-invariant similarity/distance measures that can be calculated between images in different modalities?

12.2 Designing a Robust Image Descriptor

Establishing initial (putative) correspondence between feature points in two images is essential in achieving the speed required to register the images within a reasonable time. The larger the true positive rate of initial homologous points, the more reliable will be the final homologous points from which the transformation parameters are determined.

When the images to be registered are in the same modality, feature points can be detected in the images and image descriptors centered at the points can be used to find initial correspondence between the points. When the images are in the same modality, but the scene has gone through radiometric changes, descriptors generated at the same point in the images may be quite different because the descriptors capture local information about intensity gradients in the images.

Many of the so-called rotation-invariant descriptors do not produce similar descriptors for homologous neighborhoods in images taken from different views of a scene. Intensity gradients are used to determine the dominant orientation of a local neighborhood, and from the results in Chapter 2, we know that intensity gradients do not provide accurate directional information about a neighborhood and scan direction can greatly influence the outcome.

Dominant orientations determined from intensity gradients for the same neighborhood in two images will likely be different, especially when the images have radiometric differences. This inaccuracy in estimation of the dominant orientation of a neighborhood results in a reduction in the number of correct homologous points and, consequently, an increase in the false-negative rate.

Even when dominant orientations for a neighborhood in two images are correctly determined, when the images have radiometric differences, corresponding pixels have different intensity gradients. That means, when the histogram of intensity gradients is computed within each sector of a descriptor of the kind shown in Fig. 12.1, different histograms are obtained for corresponding sectors, producing a poor match rating at homologous points. This contributes to an increase in the false-negative rate. By having a high false-negative rate,

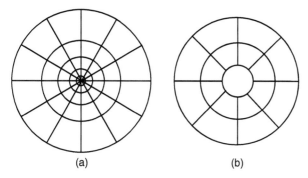

Figure 12.1 Log-polar grids used in design of rotationally invariant descriptors called (a) shape context [1] and (b) gradient location and orientation histogram [2].

current image descriptors miss many correct homologous points, leaving too few homologous points to register the images.

To produce a high true-positive rate, a descriptor is required that is truly rotation invariant. Descriptors that rely on intensity gradients to determine the dominant orientation of a neighborhood quantize the neighborhood into sectors that partition the rotation angle into multiples of 30° or 45°. Any inaccuracy in determining the orientation of a neighborhood results in a description that does not accurately portray the properties of the neighborhood. Descriptors are needed that are composed of rotation-invariant features. In Section 5.3.4, a number of features suitable for the design of a rotation-invariant descriptor was described. *There is a need to find more rotation-invariant features. Also, there is a need to find an effective means of measuring the similarity/distance between descriptors that are composed of features of different types and magnitudes.*

12.3 Finding Homologous Lines for Nonrigid Registration

In Chapter 7, algorithms for finding homologous feature points for nonrigid registration was described. It should also be possible to find homologous lines in images with nonlinear geometric differences and use the homologous lines to elastically register the images. The line correspondence algorithms described in Chapter 6 require that the geometries of the images be related by a global homography. The algorithms are restricted to images taken from about the same view direction of a 3-D scene or from different view directions of a 2-D scene. To register images taken from different views of a 3-D scene using lines, algorithms that can establish correspondence between lines within local neighborhoods in images are required.

If two images cannot be related by a single homography, first, homologous neighborhoods in the images that can be related by a homography should be identified. Then, homologous lines should be determined within homologous neighborhoods in the images.

To find homologous neighborhoods in images with nonlinear geometric differences, the images should be sufficiently reduced in size so that homologous lines in the images can be related by a global homography. By having a global homography that relates the geometries of the images at low resolution, the homography to approximately relate the images at high resolution can be determined by appropriately scaling the homography parameters (Section 7.2.1). Then, a homography can be computed by RANSAC or a robust estimator to find homologous lines within each corresponding neighborhood in the images.

This process is demonstrated in Fig. 12.2. The green circular neighborhoods in the images show corresponding neighborhoods determined by matching lines in the images at low resolution. At high resolution, there is only a need to find homologous lines within homologous neighborhoods. Then, the images can be registered by a composite or a weighted sum of local homographies.

Rather than having a neighborhood of a fixed size, the size of a neighborhood can be taken in such a way as to include sufficient lines, such as 10 or 15. Once neighborhoods in the reference image, each containing a required number of lines is selected, the corresponding local neighborhoods in the test image can be determined from the global homography obtained by matching lines at low resolution. *Details of the algorithm to find homologous neighborhoods in images to enable determination of homologous lines in them need to be worked out and its performance in nonrigid registration should be evaluated.*

 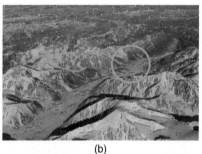

| (a) | (b) |

Figure 12.2 (a and b) The lines detected in two aerial images of a mountainous area. These images are courtesy of Image Registration and Fusion Systems. Green circular regions show homologous neighborhoods in the images that were estimated by matching the images at a lower resolution. The task is to find homologous lines in homologous regions.

12.4 Nonrigid Registration Using Homologous Lines

Although various nonrigid registration methods using homologous points were described in Chapter 7, no nonrigid registration method based on homologous lines was mentioned. This is because a method that can find the parameters of an elastic transformation from homologous lines is not available.

By knowing that each component of a transformation model represents an approximation, if the ability to approximate data lines can be developed, it will become possible to nonrigidly register images using homologous lines in images.

In [3], a method for recovering the geometry of a 3-D scene from 3-D line segments obtained by computer vision techniques was described. The method, in effect, approximates data lines by a 3-D surface, which can be treated as a component of an elastic transformation model. An example of this line approximation is given in Fig. 12.3.

Consider the range image shown in Fig. 12.3a. Intensities in the image show the elevations of points in a terrain scene. Lines detected in the image are shown in Fig. 12.3b. Elevations along each line segment make it possible to fit a 3-D line to points with coordinates (x, y, F), with F being the elevation of point (x, y). A surface is then fitted to the 3-D lines. Views from the front and back of the approximating surface are shown in Fig. 12.3c and d, respectively. The 3-D lines from which the surface was obtained are also shown.

There is a need to evaluate the suitability of elastic transformations defined in terms of surfaces approximating 3-D lines in this manner. *Are transformations obtained from homologous lines more accurate than transformations obtained from homologous points in nonrigid registration? What are the strengths and weaknesses of transformation models obtained from homologous lines when compared to transformation models obtained from homologous points?*

12.5 Transformation Models with Nonsymmetric Basis Functions

The transformation models described in Chapter 7 for nonrigid registration are defined in terms of radial basis functions. Radial basis functions are symmetric and have a fixed shape and size. Surface (thin-plate) spline uses monotonically increasing (logarithmic) functions while moving least squares and weighted linear use monotonically decreasing (inverse squared distance) functions. Because basis functions of the same size are used everywhere in the approximation/interpolation domain, when density of feature points varies greatly across the reference image, the obtained transformation can produce large errors in areas where a low density of points is available.

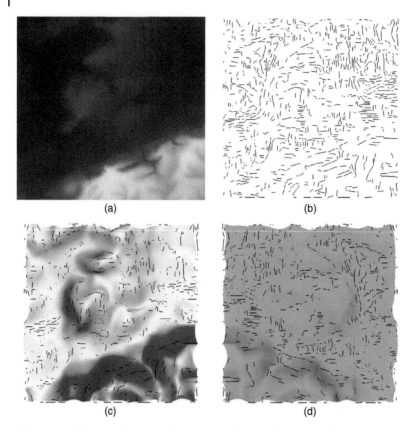

Figure 12.3 (a) A range image with intensities showing elevations. This image is courtesy of NASA. (b) Lines detected in the range image. (c) Front and (d) back views of a surface approximating the of 3-D line segments.

Rational basis functions adjust the size and shape of a basis function to the local density and organization of the points; therefore, rational basis functions are expected to approximate data better than radial basis functions when the density of points varies greatly across the approximation domain.

Consider points $\{\mathbf{p}_i = (x_i, y_i) : i = 1, \dots, N\}$ with associating data values $\{F_i : i = 1, \dots, N\}$. Approximation of the data by a function defined by rational Gaussian (RaG) basis functions [4] can be written as

$$F(x, y) = \sum_{i=1}^{N} g_i(x, y) F_i, \tag{12.1}$$

where

$$g_i(x, y) = \frac{G_i(x, y)}{\sum_{j=1}^{N} G_j(x, y)} \tag{12.2}$$

is the ith RaG basis function and $G_i(x, y)$ is a Gaussian of height 1 centered at (x_i, y_i). When data points are irregularly spaced, rational basis functions stretch toward large gaps and shrink within small gaps to ensure that the sum of the basis functions everywhere in the approximation domain is 1.

To make the function defined by Eq. (12.1) interpolate data, the heights of the Gaussians $\{A_i : i = 1, \dots, N\}$ are computed by solving the following system of N linear equations:

$$\sum_{i=1}^{N} g_i(x_j, y_j) A_i = F_j \quad \text{for} \quad j = 1, \dots, N. \tag{12.3}$$

In Eq. (12.1), if instead of N data values $\{F_i : I = 1, \dots, N\}$ we use M linear polynomials $\{L_j(x, y) : j = 1, \dots, M\}$, each fitting to local data, the following weighted linear approximation will be obtained:

$$F(x, y) = \sum_{i=1}^{M} g_j(x, y) L_j(x, y). \tag{12.4}$$

$L_j(x, y)$ can be considered a plane fitting to data points and associating data values in the jth neighborhood by the least squares method. $G_j(x, y)$ in $g_j(x, y)$ is a Gaussian of height 1 and standard deviation equal to the radius of the jth neighborhood containing n points, with $n \geq 3$.

When $n = 3$, the centroid of the triangle is taken as the location of the basis function and the scale of the Gaussian is taken equal to the radius of the circumcircle of the triangle. Therefore, if data points are triangulated into M triangles, Eq. (12.4) describes the function approximating the data values by a weighted linear approximation.

An example of RaG basis functions obtained from two triangulated data sets is shown in Fig. 12.4. A basis function adjusts to the shape and size of the triangle over which the basis function is defined. In this manner, a RaG basis function expands in areas where the density of points is low and shrinks in areas where the density of points is high.

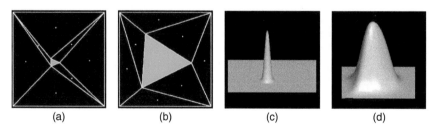

(a) (b) (c) (d)

Figure 12.4 (a and b) Triangulation of two sets of points in the approximation domain. The centroid of each triangle is also shown. (c and d) RaG basis functions defined over the shaded triangles in (a) and (b), respectively. RaG basis functions adapt to the local density and organization of the points.

Note that local function $L_i(x, y)$ does not have to be linear. It can be any function that is simple and approximates local data well. For instance, it can be a component of a homography transformation, relating corresponding neighborhoods in two images.

There is a need to determine the accuracy and speed of transformation models defined by rational basis functions and compare the results with transformation models defined by radial basis functions. *Does the additional computational cost of rational basis functions justified when compared to radial basis functions? When should we use rational basis functions against radial basis function in nonrigid registration?*

12.6 Finding Homologous Points along Homologous Contours

Edge contours in an image are the least influenced by radiometric changes in a scene. Consider taking two images from different views of a well-defined region in the scene and determining region boundaries in the images by an edge detector. Due to the dependency of the foreshortening distortion on the imaging view angle, the segment of the region boundary nearer to the camera will be scaled more than a segment of the region boundary farther away from the camera. This dependency of scale on distance in the imaging process causes different segments of the region boundary in the images to have different scale ratios. To ensure that homologous points along the region boundaries in the images align well when the images are registered, there is a need to find homologous points along homologous region boundaries in the images and use the homologous points to register the images.

Suppose the edge contours in Fig. 12.5a and b represent the same region boundary in two images. Also, suppose the images are globally aligned, so they do not have global translational and rotational differences. Under these assumptions, we would like to find homologous points along homologous edge contours.

To find homologous points along homologous contours, the distance transforms [5, 6] of the edge contours are determined as depicted in Fig. 12.5c and d, the distance transform images are subtracted, and the zero crossings are located within the difference image. The zero-crossing contour obtained in this example is shown in Fig. 12.5e. Overlaying of the edge contours (a) and (b) and the zero-crossing contour (e) is shown in (f) in Fig. 12.5. Each zero-crossing point is of the same distance to the two edge contours; therefore, each point on the zero-crossing contour can be considered identifying a pair of homologous points on the edge contours. *Are correspondences obtained in this manner correct?* Unique homologous points obtained from the zero crossings are connected by line segments in Fig. 12.5f. *How accurate are the unique correspondences obtained from the zero crossings?*

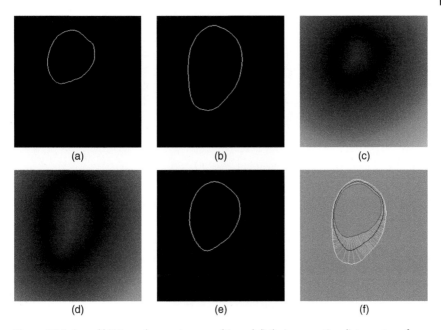

Figure 12.5 (a and b) Two edge contours, and (c and d) their respective distance transform images. (e) The zero crossings of the difference of the distance transform images. (f) Overlaying of edge contours (a) and (b) and the zero-crossing contour (e). Each zero-crossing point produces a correspondence. The unique homologous points obtained from the zero crossings are connected with line segments in (f).

An example of edge matching, where one edge contour does not completely fall inside another edge contour, is given in Fig. 12.6. In addition to the true zero crossings, false zero crossings are obtained. Contour segments A and B in Fig. 12.6e are the true zero crossings and segments C, D, and E are the false zero crossings. True zero crossings are closer to the two edge contours than the false zero crossings. This provides a means to distinguish true from false zero crossings and filter out the false zero crossings. Figure 12.6f shows the overlaid edge contours and the obtained homologous points.

The same procedure can find homologous points along open edge contours. An example is given in Fig. 12.7. Three edge contours are shown in the figure. If it is not known which edge contour in one image corresponds to which edge contour in another image, but there is sufficient space between the contours such that when the images are overlaid, homologous contours fall closer to each other compared to nonhomologous contours, the process can find correspondence between edges in two images without explicit knowledge about homologous contours.

If after overlaying the images, the closest contours do not represent homologous contours, there is a need to find correspondence between the contours before attempting to find homologous points along homologous contours. *The*

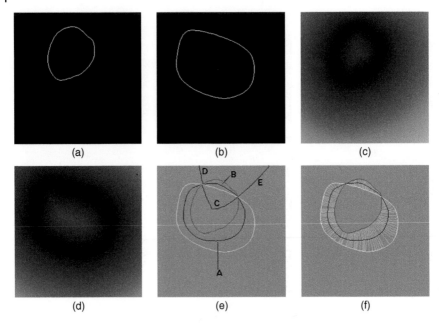

Figure 12.6 (a and b) Corresponding edge contours in two images. (c and d) Distance transforms of the edge contours. (e) Zero crossings of the difference of distance transform images when overlaid with the edge contours. Segments A and B are the true zero crossings while segments C, D, and E are the false zero crossings. (f) Homologous points along contours (a) and (b) are considered points that are of the same distance to the zero-crossing contour (e).

challenge is to find correspondence between individual edge contours in two images of a scene. A coarse-to-fine approach may be able to find correspondence between the edge contours at low resolution where a small number of them is available. Once correspondence is established between the contours at low resolution, the edge contours can be tracked from low to high resolution by a process known as edge focusing [7, 8]. Although an edge contour can be tracked from low to high resolution by edge focusing, as the resolution is increased, new edge contours can emerge in the image. *How should we determine correspondence between edge contours at high resolution using information from homologous edge contours at lower resolution?*

Having solved the problem of finding homologous contours in images and finding homologous points along homologous contours, how can we determine the remaining homologous points in the images? The elastic transformation models described in Chapter 7 require that the density of points across the reference image not change greatly. The rational basis functions defined by Eq. (12.2) allow the density of feature points to vary somewhat, but even rational basis functions cannot satisfactorily handle dense points along contours with large

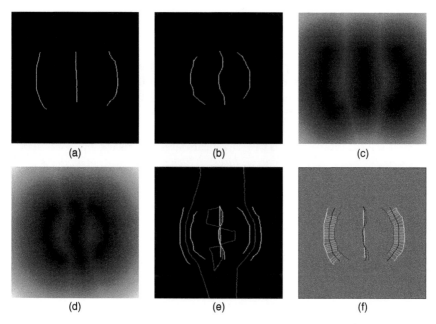

Figure 12.7 (a and b) Open edge contours in two images of a scene. (c and d) Distance transforms of the edge images. (e) Detected true and false zero crossings. The true zero crossings together with the edge contours are shown in (f). Unique homologous points obtained from the true zero crossings are connected with line segments, showing homologous points along homologous contours.

gaps between contours. *A new class of transformation models is required that can use homologous points along homologous contours to register images. This problem is similar to that of using data (intensities) along edge contours in an image to recover intensities everywhere within the image.* Some preliminary results relating to this problem have been provided by Hummel and Moniot [9].

12.7 4-D Image Registration

Extension of 2-D registration methods to 3-D to register volumetric images was for the most part straightforward. 4-D images are becoming more and more available in medicine for diagnosis and treatment planning [10–12]. It should be possible to extend 3-D registration methods to 4-D with some effort. By registering temporal 4-D intrasubject images, it becomes possible to detect not only local tissue shape changes but also detect changes in the direction and magnitude of local tissue motion [13–16].

To register two 4-D images, it is required to detect a set of 4-D feature points in the reference image, find the homologous feature points in the test image, and from the homologous points in the images, determine an appropriate transformation model to register the images. *How can 3-D feature point detection methods be extended to 4-D?* Note that three of the dimensions in 4-D represent space, while the fourth dimension represents time. Extension of 3-D point detectors to 4-D requires converting the time dimension into space.

Determination of homologous points in 4-D images *requires development of 4-D template matching methods, and design of 4-D rotation-invariant descriptors.*

Extension of volume splines to 4-D appears straightforward, but *what about weighted linear, and moving least squares? Which transformation model is most suitable for registering 4-D images?*

References

1 S. Belongie, J. Malik, and J. Puzicha, Shape matching and object recognition using shape contexts, *IEEE Transactions on Pattern Analysis and Machine Intelligence*, **24**(4):509–522, 2002.

2 K. Mikolajczyk and C. Schmid, A performance evaluation of local descriptors, *IEEE Transactions on Pattern Analysis and Machine Intelligence*, **27**:1615–1630, 2005.

3 A. Goshtasby, Surface approximation to scattered lines, *Computer-Aided Design and Applications*, **4**(1–4):277–286, 2007.

4 A. Goshtasby, Surface reconstruction from scattered measurements, *Curves and Surfaces in Computer Vision and Graphics III*, Boston, MA, 247–256, 1992.

5 G. Borgefors, Distance transforms in digital images, *Computer Vision, Graphics, and Image Processing*, **34**:344–371, 1986.

6 P. E. Danielsson, Euclidean distance mapping, *Computer Graphics and Image Processing*, **14**:227–248, 1980.

7 F. Bergholm, Edge focusing, *IEEE Transactions on Pattern Analysis and Machine Intelligence*, **9**:726–741, 1987.

8 A. Goshtasby, On edge focusing, *Image and Vision Computing*, **12**(4):247–256, 1994.

9 R. T. Hummel and R. Moniot, Reconstructions from zero crossings in scale space, *IEEE Transactions on Acoustics, Speech, and Signal Processing*, **37**(12):2111–2130, 1989.

10 J. M. Blackall, S. Ahmad, M. E. Miquel, J. R. McClelland, D. B. Landau, and D. J. Hawkes, MRI-based measurements of respiratory motion variability and assessment of imaging strategies for radiotherapy planning, *Physics in Medicine and Biology*, **51**(17):4147–4169, 2006.

11 P. Keal, 4-dimensional computed tomography imaging and treatment planning, *Seminars in Radiation Oncology*, **14**(1):81–90, 2004.

12 K. Murphy, B. van Ginneken, J. M. Reinhardt, et al.,, Evaluation of registration methods on thoracic CT: the EMPIRE10 challenge, *IEEE Transactions on Medical Imaging*, **30**(11):1901–1920, 2011.

13 V. Boldea, G. C. Sharp, S. B. Jiang, and D. Sarrut, 4-D-CT lung motion estimation with deformable registration: quantification of motion nonlinearity and hysteresis, *Medical Physics*, **35**(3):1008–1018, 2008.

14 R. I. Ionasec, I. Voigt, B. Georgescu, et al.,, Patient-specific modeling and quantification of the aortic and mitral valves from 4-D cardiac CT and TEE, *IEEE Transactions on Medical Imaging*, **29**(9):1636–1651, 2010.

15 Z. Wu, E. Rietzel, V. Boldea, D. Sarrut, and G. C. Sharp, Evaluation of deformable registration of patient lung 4DCT with subanatomical region segmentations, *Medical Physics*, **35**(2):775–781, 2008.

16 H. Zhang, A. Wahle, R. K. Johnson, T. D. Scholz, and M. Sonka, 4-D cardiac MR image analysis: left and right ventricular morphology and function, *IEEE Transactions on Medical Imaging*, **29**(2):350–364, 2010.

Glossary

affine An *affine transformation* relates the geometries of two images of a planar scene taken from very far. An affine transformation preserves parallelism, but it does not preserve distances and angles.

blob A *blob* is a blurred image region containing very little details.

corner A *corner* is the point where two linear segments intersect. It is a geometric feature where the product of gradients in directions normal to each other is locally maximum. Corners of buildings and intersections of roads are example of corners.

correlation *Correlation* between two sequences of numbers measures the dependency of the sequences on each other. When respective numbers within the sequences change together, the sequences are said to correlate highly. When the sequences represent unit vectors, correlation values falls between -1 and 1. In such a situation, the correlation is called *correlation coefficient*.

dissimilarity *Dissimilarity* represents the distance between two points in n dimensions.

distance Given two points in n dimensions, the distance between them can be determined in different manners. Examples of *distance measures* are L_1 norm or Manhattan distance, L_2 norm or Euclidean distance, and L_∞ norm.

edge An *edge* is a point in an image where gradient magnitude in the gradient direction becomes locally maximum. An edge also appears at a location in an image where the second-derivative intensity in the gradient direction becomes 0. An *edge contour* is a sequence of connected edges, representing the boundary of an object or separating regions of different properties from each other.

elastic An *elastic transformation* is a transformation that can represent local geometric differences between two images of a scene.

Theory and Applications of Image Registration, First Edition. Arthur Ardeshir Goshtasby.
© 2017 John Wiley & Sons, Inc. Published 2017 by John Wiley & Sons, Inc.

entropy *Entropy* measures the inability to correctly guess an outcome. In an image with very little variation, the likelihood that a guessed intensity will be correct is high, while in a highly detailed image, the likelihood that a guessed intensity will be correct is low.

feature A *feature* is a property that can be measured and represented by a number. Examples are intensity, gradient, distance, roundness, and so on.

filter A *filter* is an image operation that preserves image properties at some pixels while modifying image properties at other pixels. For example, a low-pass filter is an operation that preserves intensities in areas where there is very little variation and modifies intensities in areas where there is high variation, producing intensities in the output that are smoother than intensities in the input.

gradient *Gradient* is the same as the first derivative. *Intensity gradient* is the first-derivative intensity. In two and higher dimensions, gradient becomes a vector, which has magnitude and direction.

homography *Homography transformation*, also known as 2-D projective transformation, shows the relation between a planar scene and its image, or the relation between two images of a planar scene. The homography transformation preserves linearity. That is, lines in one image map to lines in another image. Homography does not preserve parallelism, angles, or distances.

line A *feature line*, or a *line* for short, is a geometric feature in an image that has position and orientation. The position of a line is the point on the line closest to the origin, and the orientation of the line is the angle the normal to the line makes with the x-axis. A line segment is a line that is delimited by two endpoints.

mean *Mean* is the same as average. A *mean filter* is an image operation that replaces the intensity at a pixel with the average of intensities at the neighboring pixels.

median *Median* is the mid-value. Having a sequence of values, ordered from the smallest to the largest, the median of the sequence is the mid-value in the sequence. A *median filter* is an image operation that replaces the intensity at a pixel with the median of intensities in a small patch centered at the pixel.

noise Noise can be radiometric or geometric. *Radiometric noise* is the uncertainty a sensor adds to captured intensities. Sensor noise is usually zero-mean (i.e., if intensity at a pixel is measured over a long period, the average intensity at the pixel will be close to the true intensity at the pixel). *Geometric noise* depends on the resolution of an image. Displacement of a scene point from its true position when projected to the image plane represents geometric noise. Geometric noise is also known as digital noise.

nonrigid Nonrigid means something that is not rigid, and *nonrigid registration* is the process of spatially aligning two images with an elastic transformation.

outlier An *outlier* is something that is out of the ordinary. When homologous points or homologous lines are involved, an outlier means an incorrect correspondence.

point A *feature point*, or *point* for short, is a geometric feature that represents the center of a locally unique neighborhood.

reference A *reference image* is one of the two images used in image registration. The other image is called the test image. The reference image is the image that is kept unchanged. An image registration method transforms the geometry of the test image to resemble the geometry of the reference image.

registration *Image registration* is the process of spatially aligning two images of a scene taken at different times, by different sensors, or from different viewpoints. The process finds correspondence between all scene points appearing in the images.

resampling *Image resampling* is the process of finding intensities at locations within the test image that correspond to pixel locations in the reference image. By image resampling, an image is created that has the geometry of the reference image and the intensities of the test image.

rigid *Rigid transformation*, also known as Euclidean transformation, is a transformation that preserves angles and distances.

robust *Robust* implies reliable. A *robust estimator* is an estimator that determines a reliable output from a corrupted input. Robust estimation of transformation parameters from homologous points that contain outliers implies having the ability to identify the outliers, remove them, and use the inliers to determine the transformation parameters.

segmentation *Segmentation* is a partitioning operation. *Image segmentation* is the process of partitioning an image into meaningful or predefined parts, and *edge segmentation* is partitioning edge contours into segments that have predefined properties, such as line segments or conic sections.

similarity A *similarity measure* determines the dependency between two sequences of numbers. *Similarity transformation* is a transformation that relates images with translational, rotational, and scaling differences. Under the similarity transformation, angles are preserved, but distances are not.

smoothing *Image smoothing* is a filtering operation that reduces high spatial frequency in an image. Image smoothing reduces image noise, but it also blurs image details. Image smoothing has the same effect as reducing image resolution.

test A *test image* is one of the two images used in image registration. The other image is called the reference image. Image registration involves transforming the test image to take the geometry of the reference image.

transformation Transformation can be radiometric or geometric. *Radiometric or intensity transformation* refers to the process of converting intensities of one image to resemble the intensities of another image, and *geometric transformation* is the process of transforming the geometry of one image to resemble the geometry of another image. A *transformation model* is the mathematical formulation used to resample the test image to the geometry of the reference image.

Acronyms

ACC	Accuracy
ADE	Average directional error
AFRL	Air Force Research Laboratory
ALL	Average line length
APE	Average positional error
CR	Correlation ratio
CT	(X-ray) computed tomography
Det	Determinant
DoG	Difference of Gaussians
EFI	Exclusive F-information
FN	False negative
FNR	False negative rate
FP	False positive
FPR	False positive rate
GLOH	Gradient location and orientation histogram
IRV	Intensity-ratio variance
JPD	Joint probability distribution
Landsat	Land satellite
LMS	Least median of squares
LoG	Laplacian of Gaussian
MAD	Median of absolute differences
MRI	Magnetic resonance imaging
NASA	National Aeronautics and Space Administration
NIH	National Institutes of Health
NSF	National Science Foundation
OLS	Ordinary least squares
OM	Ordinal measure
PET	Positron emission tomography
RaG	Rational Gaussian

Theory and Applications of Image Registration, First Edition. Arthur Ardeshir Goshtasby.
© 2017 John Wiley & Sons, Inc. Published 2017 by John Wiley & Sons, Inc.

RANSAC	Random sample consensus
RD	Rank distance
RMSE	Root-mean-squared error
SAD	Sum of absolute differences
SIFT	Scale-invariant feature transform
SJE	Shannon joint entropy
SMI	Shannon mutual information
SSD	Sum of square differences
TME	Time
TMI	Tsallis mutual information
TN	True negative
TNR	True negative rate
TP	True positive
TPR	True positive rate
TPS	Thin-plate spline
Tr	Trace of a matrix
USGS	United States Geological Survey
WLS	Weighted least squares

Symbols

σ	standard deviation
σ^2	variance
μ	mean
κ	curvature
$\times$	vector cross product, scalar multiplication
∇^2	Laplacian
ρ	distance of a line in polar form to the origin, also denotes Spearman's Rho

Theory and Applications of Image Registration, First Edition. Arthur Ardeshir Goshtasby.
© 2017 John Wiley & Sons, Inc. Published 2017 by John Wiley & Sons, Inc.

A

Image Registration Software

The results reported in this monograph can be reproduced with the accompanying software packages. The software package for each chapter implements the various algorithms described in that chapter.

The software packages are intended as learning tools for readers of the book to learn the algorithms through practice. They are not intended for commercial use.

The software packages use the OpenCV [1] library functions to read and save images and use the OpenGL [2] library functions to display images.

The software packages have been compiled with Visual Studio on a computer running the Microsoft Windows Operating System (OS); therefore, the software packages run only on computers running Windows OS.

The following sections serve as the user's guide to the software packages. The software packages and sample images can be downloaded from http://www .imgfsr.com/WileyRegistrationBook.html. If the website cannot be reached for some reason, contact the author directly at arthur.goshtasby@gmail.com for the software and the images.

A.1 Chapter 2: Image Orientation Detection

A.1.1 Introduction

An image of a natural scene will very likely have a preferred or dominant orientation. Since image orientation is a property of the scene, when two images of a scene are taken, by finding the orientation of each image, the images can be brought to the same orientation. Just like humans that can find an object in an image more easily if the object appears upright than at an angle, computer algorithms can more easily find an object (template) in the test image if the object is in the orientation it is seen in the reference image. This software finds the orientation of an image and shows the orientation by a yellow line over the image.

If two images (reference and test) are available, this software will determine the rotational difference between the images, print the rotational difference to the screen, resample the test image to orientation of the reference image, and display the resampled test image.

A.1.2 Operations

To start, double-click **Chapter2.exe**. A file-selection window will appear on the screen; select an image filename. The software will load the image file into memory and display it on the screen. To select operations of the software, use the menu attached to the right mouse button. Move the cursor inside the image and press the right mouse button. The menu shown in Fig. A.1 will appear.

To find the orientation of the loaded image using geometric gradients, choose **Find image orientation using** from the menu and then **geometric gradients** from the submenu (Fig. A.2). The orientation of the image will be determined and displayed by a yellow line in the image (Fig. A.3). Also, the angle between the yellow line and the x-axis will be printed to the command window. Since gradient directions are calculated using edge contours without knowledge about the direction an edge contour is traced, computed orientations will be between 0 and π. Therefore, no distinction is made between images with orientations θ and $\theta \pm \pi$.

The orientation of an image can be determined using directions of lines in the image and vanishing points in the image also. These methods are discussed in Sections A.3 and A.5.

To find the rotational difference between two images using geometric gradients, choose **Find rotational difference between images using** from the menu and then **geometric gradients** from the submenu (Fig. A.4). A file- selection window will appear. Choose the filename of the test image. The image already in memory will be used as the reference image. The software will determine the orientations of both images, resample the test image to the orientation of the reference image, and display the resampled test image.

Load another image
Find image orientation using ▶
Find rotational difference between images using ▶
Quit

Figure A.1 Appearance of the menu after loading an image into memory.

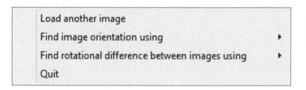

Load another image	
Find image orientation using ▶	geometric gradients
Find rotational difference between images using ▶	line directions
Quit	vanishing point

Figure A.2 Finding the orientation of the displayed image.

Figure A.3 The orientation of an image is shown by a yellow line in the image.

Load another image		
Find image orientation using	▸	
Find rotational difference between images using	▸	geometric gradients
Quit		line directions
		vanishing points

Figure A.4 Finding the rotational difference between two images.

An example is given in Fig. A.5. Assuming images (a) and (b) are the reference and test images, the software resamples the test image to the orientation of the reference image and displays the resampled image (Fig. A.5c). To cut a rectangular area out of the resampled test image, choose **Crop image** from the new menu (Fig. A.6a). Then place the cursor at the upper-left-hand corner of the desired area, press the left mouse button, and drag the cursor to the lower-right-hand corner of the area. Releasing the left mouse button will crop the selected area and display it (Fig. A.5d). To undo this operation, choose **Restore image** from the new menu (Fig. A.6b), and to replace the original image with the selected subimage, choose **Replace image** from the new menu (Fig. A.6b).

To save the cropped subimage, choose **Save displayed image** from the menu. A file-selection window will appear. Provide a filename to save the image. The extension of the filename determines the format of the file. For example, if *image.jpg* is provided, the displayed image will be saved in file *image.jpg* in jpeg format.

In addition to the rotated test image, which is initially displayed, the reference image, the test image, the overlaid reference and rotated test, and absolute color/intensity difference of reference and the resampled test can be displayed

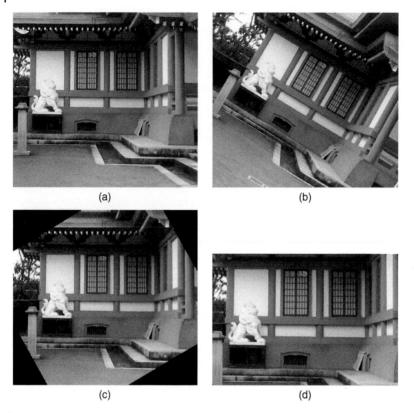

(a)   (b)

(c)   (d)

Figure A.5 (a and b) Reference and test images. (c) The test image after being resampled to the orientation of the reference image. (d) Cutting a subimage out of image (c).

by choosing an appropriate entry of the **Display** submenu (Fig. A.7). This software does not register the images, it only rotates the test image about its center so its orientation aligns with the orientation of the reference image.

Note that if the true rotational difference between the images $\theta \geq \pi$, the rotational difference determined by the software will be $\theta - \pi$. In such a situation, choose **Rotate by PI** from the **Display** submenu (Fig. A.7) to correct the orientation of the resampled test image.

To exit the software, choose **Quit** from the menu.

A.2 Chapter 3: Feature Point Detection

A.2.1 Introduction

Feature points are the most basic geometric features in an image. They represent centers of locally unique neighborhoods. If rotation- and scale-invariant

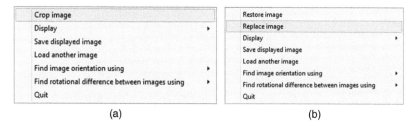

Crop image		Restore image	
Display	▸	Replace image	
Save displayed image		Display	▸
Load another image		Save displayed image	
Find image orientation using	▸	Load another image	
Find rotational difference between images using	▸	Find image orientation using	▸
Quit		Find rotational difference between images using	▸
		Quit	

(a)   (b)

Figure A.6 (a) The appearance of the menu after rotating the test image to the orientation of reference image. (b) The appearance of the menu after cropping an area out of the resampled test image.

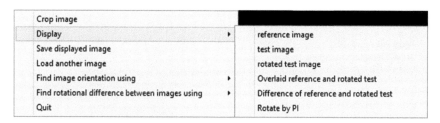

Crop image		
Display	▸	reference image
Save displayed image		test image
Load another image		rotated test image
Find image orientation using	▸	Overlaid reference and rotated test
Find rotational difference between images using	▸	Difference of reference and rotated test
Quit		Rotate by PI

Figure A.7 Various display options.

properties are used to detect them, the points will be rotation- and scale-invariant, representing ideal features for image registration.

This software implements a number of feature point detection methods, including (1) local extrema of central moments of order $pq = 11$, (2) local maxima of a uniqueness measure, (3) local extrema of the LoG of an image, (4) local maxima of image entropy, (5) local maxima of Hu invariant moment ϕ_2, (6) Harris corners, and (7) local maxima of the determinant of the Hessian matrix of 3×3 neighborhoods in an image.

A property is measured at each pixel using intensities/gradients within a circular neighborhood of a desired radius centered at the pixel. Points in an image where the property becomes locally minimum or maximum are detected and used as feature points. Among all the detected points, a desired number of the strongest points that are apart by at least the radius of the neighborhood are returned.

A.2.2 Operations

To start the software, double-click **Chapter3.exe**. A file-selection window will appear on the screen. Select an image filename. The selected image file will be loaded into memory and displayed on screen. To select an operation of the software, put the cursor inside the image and press the right mouse button. If the loaded image is small enough to fit the screen, the menu shown in Fig. A.8a

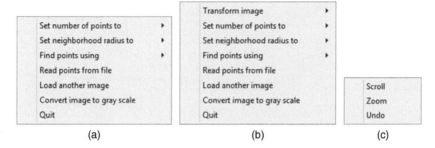

Figure A.8 Contents of the menu after loading (a) a small image and (b) a large image into memory. (c) The submenu associated with **Transform image**.

will appear. Otherwise, the menu shown in Fig. A.8b will appear. If the image is too large to fit the screen, it will be scaled down sufficiently to fit the screen. To view the large image in full resolution, choose **Transform image** from the menu. The submenu shown in Fig. A.8c will appear. Choose **Zoom** to zoom the image by moving the mouse to right and choose **Scroll** to translate the zoomed image within the display window. To return to the original display, choose **Undo** in the submenu.

To choose the number of feature points to be detected in an image, choose **Set number of points to** and then the desired number of points from the submenu (Fig. A.9). If the desired number is not in the submenu, choose **?** and then enter the desired number from the command window. Note that if the number of desired points is larger than the number of all points detected in an image, only the detected points will be returned.

To change the default neighborhood of radius 15 pixels inside which an image property is computed, choose **Set neighborhood radius to** and then the desired radius from the displayed list (Fig. A.10). If the desired radius is not in the list, choose **?** and then enter the desired radius from the command window.

To find feature points in the displayed image, choose **Find points using** and then a method from the submenu (Fig. A.11). The software will then detect the desired number of points, if possible, and display the points.

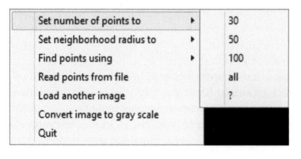

Figure A.9 Choosing the number of feature points to be detected in an image.

Figure A.10 Choosing the desired radius of neighborhoods.

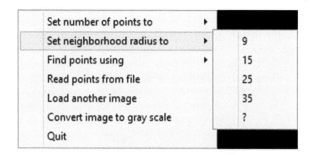

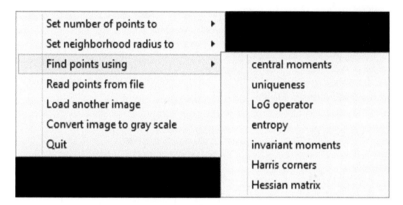

Figure A.11 Choosing a feature point detection method.

If a method is selected that finds local extrema of a property within the image, points with locally maximum values will be displayed in red and points with locally minimum values will be displayed in blue. If a method is chosen that finds local maxima of property values, then the detected points will be displayed all in red. For example, if **central moments** is chosen, local extrema of the central moments will be detected, as shown in Fig. A.12a. However, if **uniqueness** is chosen, local maxima of calculated uniqueness measures are detected, as shown in Fig. A.12b.

To save the coordinates of the detected points, choose **Save points to file** from the menu (Fig. A.13). A file- selection window will appear. Enter a filename to save the points. The extension of the provided filename should be .txt as the created file will be in ASCII form. To read the saved points at a later time, load the same image and choose **Read points from file** from the menu.

The feature point detection process can be repeated by loading another image and detecting points in it as mentioned above. To replace the image in memory with a new image, choose **Load another image** from the menu.

Finally, if the loaded image is in color and you would like to find feature points in a gray-scale version of the image, first convert the image into gray

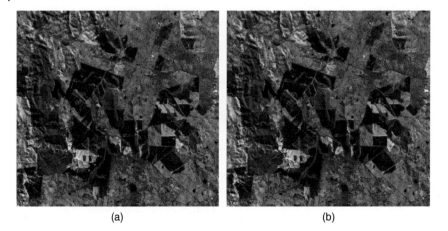

(a)   (b)

Figure A.12 Fifty feature points detected by (a) central moments and (b) the uniqueness measure. These images are courtesy of NASA.

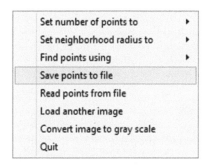

Set number of points to	▶
Set neighborhood radius to	▶
Find points using	▶
Save points to file	
Read points from file	
Load another image	
Convert image to gray scale	
Quit	

Figure A.13 Saving the coordinates of detected points to a file.

scale by choosing **Convert image to gray scale** from the menu and then find points in the displayed gray-scale image. To exit the program, choose **Quit** from the menu.

A.3   Chapter 4: Feature Line Detection

A.3.1   Introduction

Feature lines are geometric features useful in image registration. Scenes that go through radiometric changes often preserve the boundary between regions of different properties. Linear segments along region boundaries make robust features that can be used to register images independent of their radiometric differences. A line is defined by its position and orientation. The position of a line is the intersection of the line with a line a normal to it from the origin, and the orientation of the line is the angle the normal to the line makes with the x-axis.

Although a line in an image is actually a line segment, but because noise and various image degradations can displace the endpoints of a line segment, the endpoints of a line segment are usually not used in image registration; only its position and orientation are used. The orientation of a line can vary between 0 and 2π. Therefore, the tip and the tail of a line are distinct points. Direction is assigned to a line in such a way that when moving from the tail to the tip, the right side of the line is brighter than its left side.

This software implements eight different line detection methods. Methods 1 and 2 are based on the Hough transform. While method 1 works with the polar equation of lines, method 2 works with the slope and y-intercept equation of lines. Method 3 is a RANSAC-based line detector that works with the parametric equation of lines. Method 4 detects edges and clusters them according to their gradient magnitudes and directions and uses points in a cluster to form a line. Method 5 detects edges in an image and finds linear segments along the edges, and method 6 fits a parametric curve to each edge contour and partitions the curve into linear segments using curvatures along the curve. Methods 7 and 8 are two versions of a region subdivision method that segment an image into regions of similar gradient directions and fits a line to high gradient pixels in each region. Method 8 is a fast version of the region subdivision method and is due to Grompone von Gioi et al. [3].

A.3.2 Operations

To start the line detection software, double-click **Chapter4.exe**. A file-selection window will appear. Select an image filename. The selected image file will be loaded into memory and displayed on screen. To choose an operation of the software, move the cursor inside the image and press the right mouse button. The menu shown in Fig. A.14 will appear.

To select a line detector, choose **Detect lines by** from the menu and then the desired method from the submenu (Fig. A.15).

The software will detect directed lines in the image with the selected method and display the lines within the image. Figure A.16 shows lines detected in an image by (a) the Hough transform using polar equation of lines, (b) Hough transform using slope and y-intercept equation of lines, (c) RANSAC using parametric equation of lines, (d) clustering, (e) edge tracing, (f) curve fitting, (g) region subdivision, and (h) fast region subdivision methods.

Figure A.14 Contents of the menu after loading an image into memory.

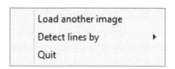

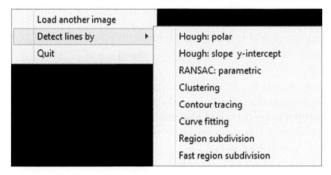

Load another image	
Detect lines by ▶	Hough: polar
Quit	Hough: slope y-intercept
	RANSAC: parametric
	Clustering
	Contour tracing
	Curve fitting
	Region subdivision
	Fast region subdivision

Figure A.15 Selecting a line detection method.

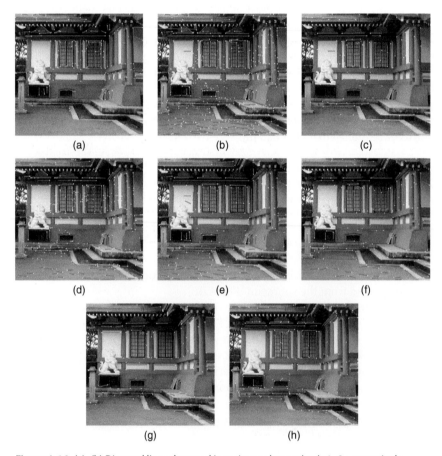

(a) (b) (c)

(d) (e) (f)

(g) (h)

Figure A.16 (a)–(h) Directed lines detected in an image by methods 1–8, respectively.

Figure A.17 Saving the detected lines to a file.

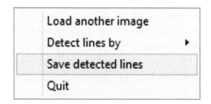

To save the detected lines in a file, choose **Save detected lines** from the menu (Fig. A.17) and then provide a filename with extension .txt. Each row in the created file will contain the (x, y) coordinates of the tip and the tail of a line followed by the polar coordinates (ρ, θ) of the line. ρ shows the distance of the line to the image center and θ shows the angle the normal to the line makes with the x-axis.

To quit the program, choose **Quit** from the menu.

The functions that determine the orientation of an image and the rotational difference between two images using line directions are included in the software for Chapter 2. To find the orientation of the image in memory using line directions, choose **Find image orientation using** from the menu and then **line directions** from the submenu (Fig. A.18).

To determine the rotational difference between the image in memory and a new image, choose **Find rotational difference between images using** from the menu and then **line directions** from the submenu (Fig. A.19). A file-selection window will appear. Provide the filename of the image in external memory. The image in internal memory will be used as the reference image and the new image will be used as the test image. Then, the orientation of the test image with respect to the reference image will be determined and the test

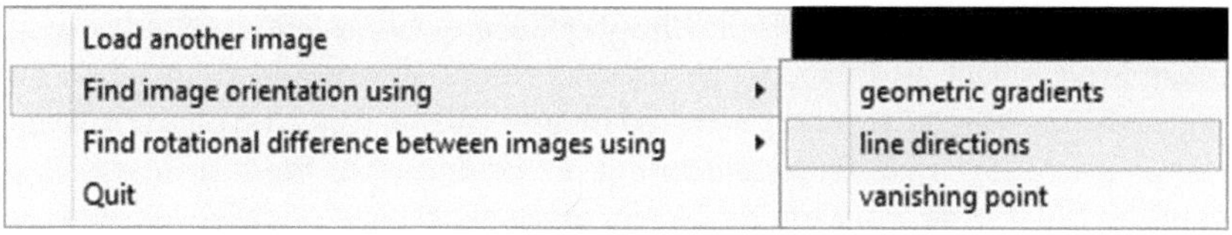

Load another image		
Find image orientation using	▶	geometric gradients
Find rotational difference between images using	▶	line directions
Quit		vanishing point

Figure A.18 Finding the orientation of an image using line directions.

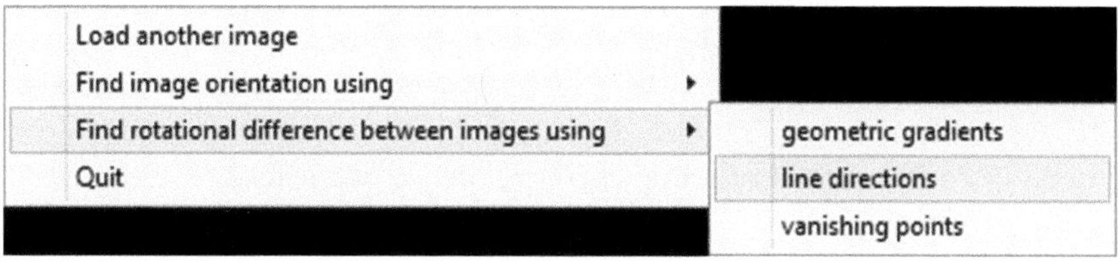

Load another image		
Find image orientation using	▶	
Find rotational difference between images using	▶	geometric gradients
Quit		line directions
		vanishing points

Figure A.19 Finding the rotational difference between the image in memory and a new image.

image will be rotated to the orientation of the reference image and displayed on screen. Also, the rotational difference between the images will be printed to the command window.

Determination of the orientation of an image and the rotational difference between two images using vanishing points is discussed in Section A.5.

A.4 Chapter 5: Finding Homologous Points

A.4.1 Introduction

The most important step in image registration is the determination of a set of homologous points in the images. To find a sufficient number of homologous points in the images, many of the same feature points must be detected in the images. This requires that the images be in the same modality.

Given two same-modality images of a planar scene, correspondence is established between feature points in the images in three steps. First, a set of feature points is detected in each image. Then, using information about the neighborhoods of the points, a set of initial homologous points are identified in the images. Finally, the incorrect homologous points are removed by an outlier removal process.

It is assumed that the scene appearing in the images is flat so that the geometries of the images can be related by a rigid, similarity, affine, or homography transformation. Only those initial homologous points that satisfy one of these constraints are retained and the rest are considered outliers and removed.

A.4.2 Operations

To start the software, double-click **Chapter5.exe**. A file-selection window will appear. First, select an image to be used as the reference and then select an image to be used as the test. The selected images will be displayed on the screen. Image registration involves transforming the geometry of the test image so it resembles the geometry of the reference image.

To select an operation of the software, move the cursor inside the Reference Image or the Test Image and press the right mouse button. One of the menus shown in Fig. A.20 will appear depending on whether the cursor is inside the Reference Image or the Test Image.

To register the images automatically, choose **Register images automatically** from either of the menus. This will select 50 feature points (Harris corners) in each image, find initial correspondence between the points using rotation-invariant composite descriptors, remove the outliers by RANSAC using the affine constraint, and find the affine transformation parameters to register the images using the least median of squares (LMS) estimator. Finally, it will resample the test image to the geometry of the reference image, overlay

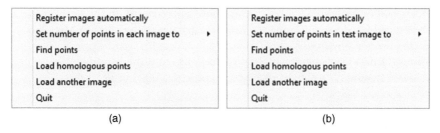

Register images automatically		Register images automatically	
Set number of points in each image to	▶	Set number of points in test image to	▶
Find points		Find points	
Load homologous points		Load homologous points	
Load another image		Load another image	
Quit		Quit	

(a)	(b)

Figure A.20 The menu initially appearing in (a) the Reference Image and (b) the Test Image.

the reference and resampled test images, and display the overlay in a new window. For example, given images (a) and (b) in Fig. A.21, the process will display the overlaid image shown in Fig. A.21c.

To visually examine the registration quality, various display options are provided. To select a display option, move the cursor inside the Overlay View and press the right mouse button. The menu shown in Fig. A.22 will appear. To display the resampled test image, choose **Display resampled**; to display the overlaid reference and resampled test images (Fig. A.21c), choose **Display overlaid**; to display the absolute intensity/color difference between the reference and the resampled test images, choose **Display difference**; to display a color image with its red band taken from the resampled test image and its green and blue bands taken from the reference image (Fig. A.21d), choose **Display fused**; to display the registered images in checkered form (Fig. A.21e), choose **Display checkered**; and to overlay boundary contours of the reference image over the resampled test image (Fig. A.21f), choose **Overlay boundaries**.

To save a displayed registration result into a file, choose **Save displayed image** from the menu. A file-selection window will appear. Provide a filename to save the displayed image. The extension of the file will show the format of the saved image. For example, if the provided filename is *image.jpg*, the contents of the Overlay View will be saved in file *image.jpg* in jpeg format.

To evaluate the registration result, choose **Evaluate registration using** from the menu and then either **Correlation coefficient** or **Mutual information** from the submenu. The similarity between the overlapping areas in the images will be determined with correlation coefficient or mutual information and displayed in the command window. The higher the similarity between the registered images, the higher is expected to be the registration accuracy. If the images do not have radiometric differences, correlation coefficient is preferred; however, if the images have some radiometric differences, mutual information is more suitable in measuring the registration accuracy.

To save the obtained homologous points in a file for later use, choose **Save homologous points** from the menu associated with the Reference Image or

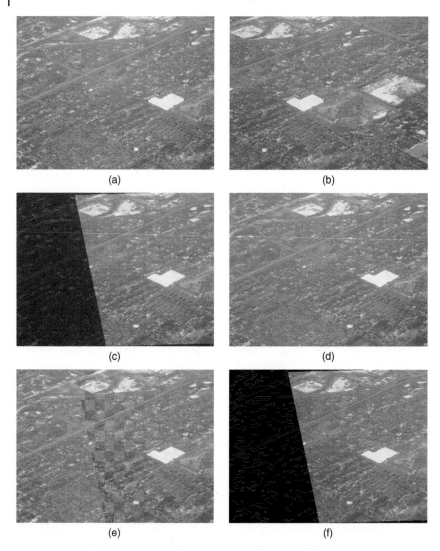

Figure A.21 (a) Reference image, (b) test image, and (c) automatic registration of the reference and test images. 17 homologous points are obtained in the reference and test images. (d) Fused, (e) checkered, and (f) boundary overlaid views of the registered images.

the Test Image (Fig. A.23). A file-selection window will appear. Provide a file-name with extension .txt to save the coordinates of homologous points in ASCII form.

Automatic registration finds homologous points in the images assuming the images are related by an affine transformation. If the view angle between the

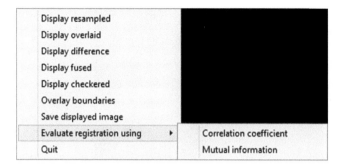

Figure A.22 The menu associated with the Overlay View, providing various display and evaluation options.

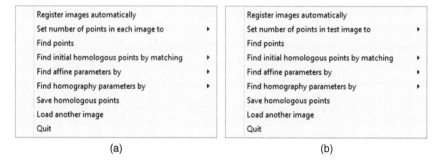

Figure A.23 Contents of menus associated with (a) the Reference Image and (b) the Test Image, after image registration.

images is large, a better transformation model for registration of the images is homography. To register the images using the homologous points obtained by automatic registration with the homography transformation, choose **Find homography parameters by** from the menu and then either **OLS estimator** or **LMS estimator** from the submenu (Fig. A.24). This will use the existing homologous points in the images to find the homography parameters by the ordinary least squares (OLS) method or the LMS estimator.

To interactively register the images, first specify the number of feature points to be detected in each image by choosing **Set number of points in each image to** in the menu associated with the Reference Image and then the number of desired points from the submenu (Fig. A.25a). If the desired number of points is not in the list, choose **provide no.** and then provide the desired number from the command window. If you want a different number of points in the reference and test images, after setting the number of points in each image from the menu associated with the Reference Image, choose **Set number of test points to** from the menu associated with the Test Image and then select the desired number

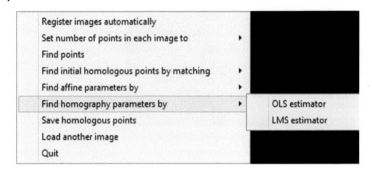

Register images automatically		
Set number of points in each image to	▶	
Find points		
Find initial homologous points by matching	▶	
Find affine parameters by	▶	
Find homography parameters by	▶	OLS estimator
Save homologous points		LMS estimator
Load another image		
Quit		

Figure A.24 Choosing an estimator to calculate the homography parameters from homologous points in the images.

Register images automatically		
Set number of points in each image to	▶	30
Find points		50
Load homologous points		100
Load another image		all
Quit		provided no.

(a)

Register images automatically		
Set number of points in test image to	▶	30
Find points		50
Load homologous points		100
Load another image		all
Quit		provided no.

(b)

Figure A.25 (a) Selecting the same number of points in both images. (b) Selecting the number of points in the test image different from the number of points in the reference image.

from the submenu (Fig. A.25b). The default number of points in each image is 50.

To find the specified number of feature points in the images, choose **Find points** from either of the menus. This will select the specified number of points in the images and display the points in the images. For example, in Fig. A.26, if 50 points are specified for each image, the points shown in images (a) and (b) are detected.

To find an initial set of homologous points in the images, choose **Find initial homologous points by matching** from the menu and then either **histograms** or **composite descriptors** from the submenu (Fig. A.27). By matching histograms of regions of radius 25 pixels centered at the points, or by matching composite descriptors calculated within neighborhoods of radius 25 pixels centered at the points, initial correspondence is established between the points. Ambiguous homologous points are removed and only the unique ones are retained. For example, for points in (a) and (b) in Fig. A.26, the homologous points shown in (c) and (d) are obtained by histogram matching, while the initial homologous points shown in (e) and (f) are obtained by matching the composite descriptors. Homologous points are shown with the same color in these images.

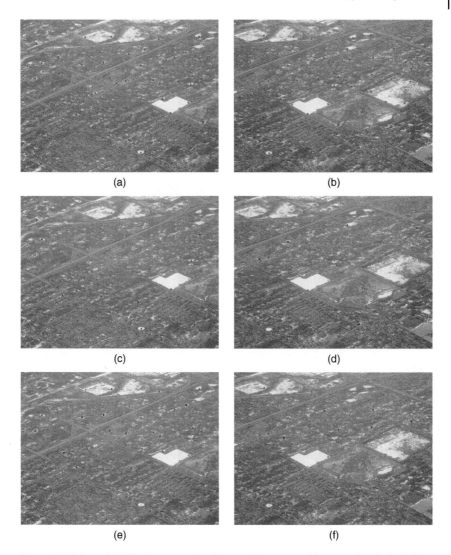

Figure A.26 (a and b) Fifty feature points detected in two aerial images of a relatively flat scene. Initial homologous points obtained by (c and d) histogram matching, and (e and f) by matching the composite descriptors at the points. Homologous points are shown with the same color.

To remove the outliers, choose **Use RANSAC with initial corr. to find** from the menu and then **rigid parameters, similarity parameters**, or **affine parameters** from the submenu (Fig. A.28). For example, when the initial homologous points are obtained by histogram matching, 17 inliers are obtained with the

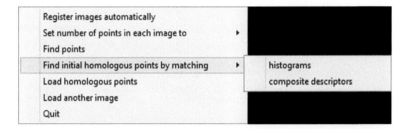

Figure A.27 Finding an initial set of homologous points.

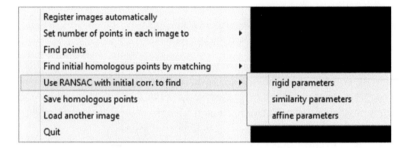

Figure A.28 Removing outliers by RANSAC using different geometric constraints.

affine constraint, and if the initial homologous points are obtained by matching the composite descriptors associated with the points, 19 inliers are obtained with the affine constraint. Calculation of histograms is much faster than calculation of composite descriptors, but generally fewer false homologous points are obtained by matching composite descriptors than by matching histograms.

The affine parameters obtained by removing the outliers may not be optimal. To remove the inaccurate homologous points, various robust estimators are provided. To refine the parameters of an affine transformation obtained by RANSAC, choose **Find affine parameters by** from the menu and then one of the robust estimators from the submenu (Fig. A.29). OLS, WLS, LMS, and LTS stand for ordinary least squares, weighted least squares, least median of squares, and least trimmed squares, respectively.

After finding the initial homologous points, rather than using the affine constraint, rigid or similarity constraint can also be used to remove the outliers. If one image is a translated and rotated version of another, rigid transformation can be used to register the images, and if the images have scale differences in addition to having translational and rotational differences, similarity transformation should be chosen to register the images. Outlier removal using rigid or similarity constraint is much faster than affine constraint. This is because point pairs are used by RANSAC to find the rigid and similarity transformation parameters, while point triples are needed to find the affine parameters.

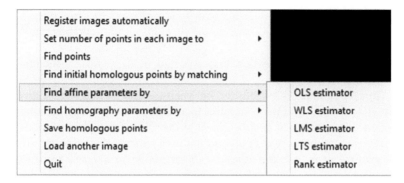

Register images automatically		
Set number of points in each image to	▶	
Find points		
Find initial homologous points by matching	▶	
Find affine parameters by	▶	OLS estimator
Find homography parameters by	▶	WLS estimator
Save homologous points		LMS estimator
Load another image		LTS estimator
Quit		Rank estimator

Figure A.29 Choosing a robust estimator to find the parameters of an affine transformation from the coordinates of homologous points in the images.

It takes a larger number of iterations to hit three random homologous points, all of which are correct, than hitting two random homologous points, both of which are correct. If angles are not preserved from one image to another but parallelism is preserved, affine must be chosen because rigid and similarity constraints cannot identify and remove outliers in such images.

To load a new reference image, choose **Load another image** from the menu associated with the Reference Image, and to load a new test image, choose the same from the menu associated with the Test Image. This will reset all detected feature points, homologous points, and the transformation parameters, allowing registration of the images from the beginning. To exit the program, choose **Quit** from the menu associated with any of the windows.

A.5   Chapter 6: Finding Homologous Lines

A.5.1   Introduction

When lines are used as features, homologous lines are needed to register the images. It is assumed that the images to be registered contain region boundaries with straight segments that appear in both images. Homologous lines in the images are not required to have the same endpoint.

To speed up the process of finding homologous lines in images, lines in each image are grouped, and information about each group is used to facilitate search for the homologous lines. One method groups lines according to the vanishing points the lines belong to, and another method groups lines using spatial information on the two sides of each line.

This software works best on nadir-view aerial and satellite images. Homologous lines are determined in two steps. First, the images are reduced in size to reduce possible local geometric differences between the images. Then correspondence is established between lines in the images assuming the images are related by a rigid transformation. Then, correspondence is established between lines in the images at high resolution using a rigid, affine, or homography transformation.

Both automatic and interactive methods are provided. The automatic method first detects lines in the images and then finds the correspondence between the lines. Correspondence is established between the lines using the rigidity constraint. Then, by relaxing the constraint to affine and then to homography, correspondence is established between lines in the images at high resolution. In the interactive method, the user detects lines in the images, finds correspondence between the lines with the desired transformation model, and registers the images with the obtained transformation.

A.5.2 Operations

To start the software, double-click **Chapter6.exe**. A file-selection window will open. First, select the reference image filename and then the test image filename. The selected images will be loaded into memory and displayed on the screen. To select an operation of the software, move the cursor inside one of the image windows and press the right mouse button. The menu shown in Fig. A.30a will appear.

To register the images automatically, choose **Register images automatically** from the menu. The software will find homologous lines in the images and display the homologous lines with the same color. It also finds the parameters of the rigid, affine, or homography capable of finding the most homologous lines in the images. It then registers the images with the obtained transformation. An example is given in Fig. A.31. Images (a) and (b) show the homologous lines obtained in the images, and image (c) shows registration of the images with the obtained homologous lines. Homologous lines in the images are shown with the same color. The red band in image (c) shows the red band of the resampled test image and the green and blue bands in image (c) show the respective bands

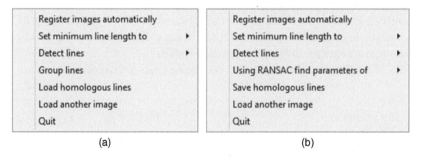

(a)   (b)

Figure A.30 (a) The menu appearing in the Reference Image and Test Image after loading two images into memory. (b) The menu appearing in the images after registering the images.

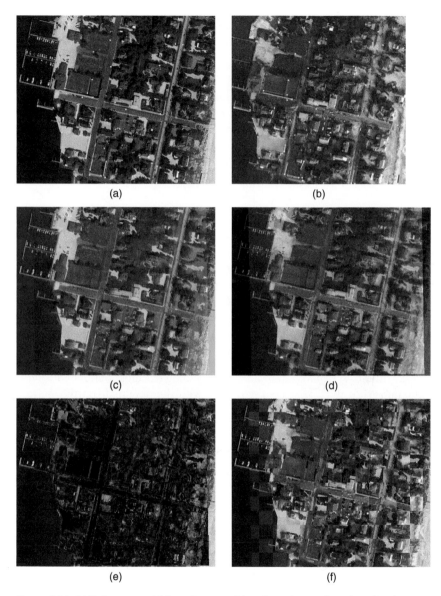

(a)

(b)

(c)

(d)

(e)

(f)

Figure A.31 (a) Reference and (b) test images with 47 homologous lines found in the images. The original images are courtesy of NOAA and show images before and after the Hurricane Sandy disaster. Homologous lines are shown with the same color. (c) Fusion, (d) overlaid, (e) absolute difference, and (f) checkered displays of the registered images.

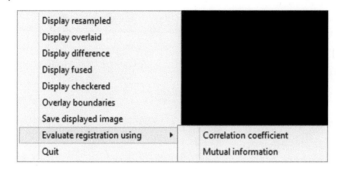

Figure A.32 The menu associated with the Overlay View.

in the reference image. This fused image enhances changes in the scene that have occurred in the scene between the times the images are obtained. Regions in red or light blue in the fused image show the changes.

To show the registered images in different forms, place the cursor inside the Overlay View and press the right mouse button. The menu shown in Fig. A.32 will appear. Choose one of the options shown. Choosing **Display overlaid** produces image (d), choosing **Display difference** produces image (e), and choosing **Display checkered** produces image (f) in Fig. A.31. To overlay reference region boundaries over the test image, choose **Overlay boundaries** from the menu. Any of the displayed images can be saved by choosing **Save displayed image** from the menu (Fig. A.32).

In addition to evaluating the quality of registration by visual examination of the various display options, it is possible to measure registration accuracy. First, choose **Evaluate registration using** from the menu and then either **Correlation coefficient** or **Mutual information** from the submenu. The similarity between overlapping areas in the images after registration will be determined with the selected similarity measure and displayed within the command window. The higher the similarity measure, the higher is expected to be the registration accuracy.

To save the obtained homologous lines, choose **Save homologous lines** from the menu (Fig. A.30b). A file-selection window will appear. Provide a filename with extension .txt to save the coordinates of the endpoints of the lines in ASCII form. Along with the coordinates of homologous lines, the parameters of the obtained transformation will be saved. To read the contents of a saved file later, first load the two images into memory and then choose **Load homologous lines** from the menu (Fig. A.30a). This will restore the state of the software to the point the homologous lines were saved.

To find homologous lines in the images and register the images interactively, first specify the minimum length of the lines to be detected. To avoid detection of very short line segments, specify the desired minimum line length by

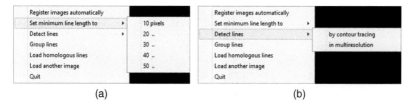

Figure A.33 (a) Specifying the minimum line length in line detection. (b) Specifying the line detection method.

choosing **Set minimum line length to** from the menu and then one of the numbers in the submenu as shown in Fig. A.33a. The default minimum line length is 16 pixels.

To detect lines in the images, choose **Detect lines** from the menu and then either **by contour tracing** or **in multiresolution** from the submenu (Fig. A.33b). The former method finds lines in the images by finding image edges, tracing the edge contours, and extracting straight segments within the contours. An example is given in images (a) and (b) in Fig. A.34. The latter method uses the same line detection method but finds the lines at various resolutions. An example is given in images (c) and (d) in Fig. A.34. Lines in different resolutions are shown with different colors. Lines detected in the same resolution in images (c) and (d) are shown with the same color.

To speed up the computation of homologous lines, the number of lines detected in each image is reduced. To reduce the number of lines detected by contour tracing, the lines are grouped according to the vanishing points they belong to. This is achieved by choosing **Group lines** from the menu (Fig. A.33). The grouping for images (a) and (b) in Fig. A.34 are, respectively, shown in images (a) and (b) in Fig. A.35. Lines in different groups are shown with different colors. Lines in the same group in the images are shown with the same color. To further reduce the number of lines in a group, a required maximum value is specified. To specify the maximum number of lines in a group, choose **Reduce group size to** from the menu and then the required number from the displayed list (Fig. A.36). This will remove the shorter line segments in a group, ensuring that the number of lines in a group does not exceed the required maximum. For example, by requiring a maximum of 10 lines per a group, the lines detected in images (a) and (b) in Fig. A.35 are reduced to the lines shown in images (c) and (d) in the same figure.

Many of the lines in images (c) and (d) in Fig. A.34 are obtained by processing the images in different resolutions. Some of the same lines are detected in different resolutions and so are redundant. If the same line is detected more than once, only the line detected at the lowest resolution is kept and lines at higher resolutions are removed. Removal of redundant lines in images

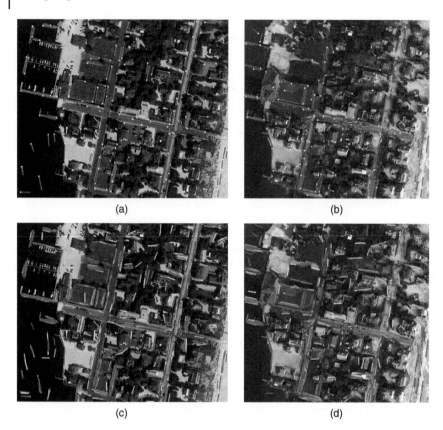

(a)

(b)

(c)

(d)

Figure A.34 (a and b) Lines detected by contour tracing. (c and d) Lines detected in multiresolution. Lines appearing in the same resolution in the images are shown with the same color.

(c) and (d) in Fig. A.34 in this manner produces the lines shown in images (a) and (b) in Fig. A.37. The number of lines detected in an image can be further reduced by discarding the shorter segments in each group. This is again achieved by choosing **Reduce group size to** from the menu and then the desired number from the submenu (Fig. A.36). The lines in (c) and (d) in Fig. A.37 are obtained by limiting the number of lines in each group to 10.

The next step in the registration process is to find homologous lines in the image. This can be achieved by choosing **Find rigidly related initial homologous lines** from the menu (Fig. A.38a). Using the lines in (c) and (d) in Fig. A.34, the registration shown in Fig. A.39a is obtained from the 42 homologous lines in Fig. A.40a and b, while if using the lines shown in (c) and (d) in Fig. A.37, the registration shown in Fig. A.39b is obtained from 31 homologous lines shown in

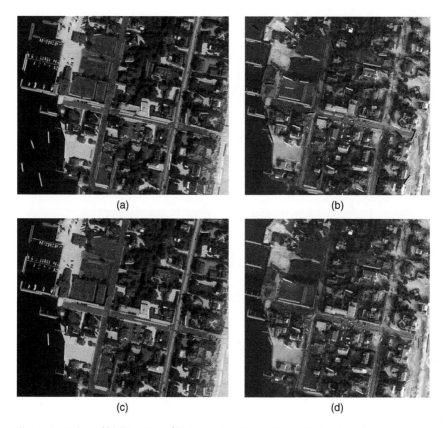

Figure A.35 (a and b) Grouping of lines in (a) and (b) in Fig. A.34. Lines in different groups are shown in different colors. (c and d) Elimination of shorter line segments in each group to reduce the number of lines in each group to 10.

Register images automatically		
Set minimum line length to	▶	
Detect lines	▶	
Reduce group size to	▶	10
Find rigidly related initial homologous lines		15
Load homologous lines		20
Load another image		30
Quit		

Figure A.36 Specifying the maximum number of lines in a group.

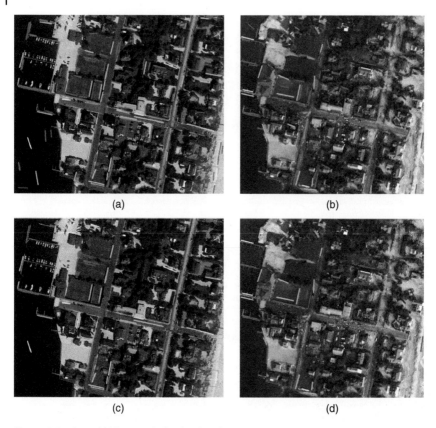

(a)   (b)

(c)   (d)

Figure A.37 (a and b) Removal of redundant lines in images (c) and (d) in Fig. A.34. (c and d) Removal of short segments within each group in (a) and (b) to limit the number of lines in each group to 10.

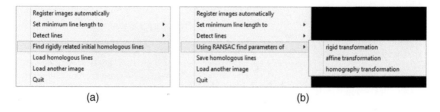

(a)   (b)

Figure A.38 (a) Finding initial homologous lines. (b) Finding final homologous lines.

Fig. A.40c and d. Grouping using vanishing points has produced more homologous lines than grouping using spatial information in the neighborhoods of the lines. This is anticipated in this particular case due to various changes in the scene that have occurred between the times the images are obtained.

(a)   (b)

Figure A.39 Image registration when grouping lines (a) according to vanishing points and (b) according to local spatial information.

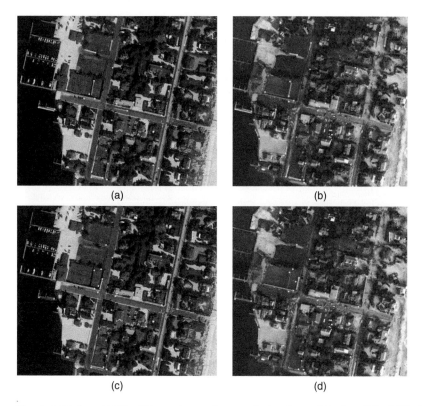

(a)   (b)

(c)   (d)

Figure A.40 (a and b) The 42 homologous lines producing the registration of Fig. A.39a. (c and d) The 31 homologous lines producing the registration of Fig. A.39b. Homologous lines are shown in the same color in these images.

Once the images are initially registered, the menus associated with the Reference Image and Test Image change to that shown in Fig. A.38b. To see if improvement to the initial registration is possible, choose **Using RANSAC find parameters of** from the menu and **rigid transformation, affine transformation,** or **homography transformation** from the submenu. In this particular example, no additional homologous lines are obtained by using affine or homography as both images show nadir views of a relatively small area captured from a high altitude.

If registration fails for a selected group size, the process may be repeated using a larger group size. For that, choose **Detect lines** from the menu again, choose a larger group size, and follow the procedure outlined above to find enough homologous lines to register the images.

To replace the reference image with a new image, choose **Load another image** from the menu associated with the Reference Image, and to replace the test image with a new image, choose the same from the menu associated with the Test Image. Finally, to exit the program, choose **Quit** from the menu associated with any of the windows.

The functions to determine the orientation of an image and the rotational difference between two images using vanishing points are included in the software accompanying Chapter 2. To determine the orientation of the image in memory from the dominant vanishing point in the image, choose **Find image orientation using** from the menu and then **vanishing point** from the submenu (Fig. A.41a). To determine the rotational difference between the image in memory and a new image, choose **Find rotational difference**

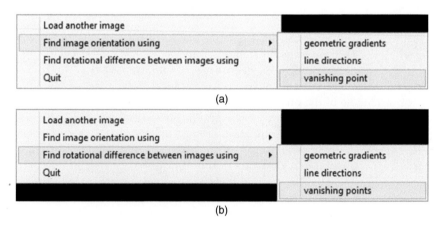

(a)

(b)

Figure A.41 (a) Finding the orientation of the image in memory from its dominant vanishing point. (b) Finding the rotational difference between the image in memory and a new image using the orientations of the images obtained from their dominant vanishing points.

between images using from the menu and then vanishing points from the submenu (Fig. A.41b).

A.6 Chapter 7: Nonrigid Image Registration

A.6.1 Introduction

When no information about the scene geometry or the imaging view angles is available, a set of homologous points is determined in each image and from them an appropriate transformation model is determined to register the images.

Both automatic and interactive registration methods are provided. The automatic method finds homologous points in the images and uses the coordinates of the points to find the parameters of an elastic transformation model to register the images. The interactive method achieves the same with the aid of the user.

Since a single outlier can break a registration, an outlier removal capability is also provided to find and remove the outliers. Correspondence is established between local neighborhoods in the images by reducing the resolution of the images sufficiently so that nonlinear geometric differences between the images can be considered small and negligible.

In addition to affine and homography transformations, elastic transformations, including surface (thin-plate) spline, moving least squares, and weighted linear transformations are provided to elastically register the images.

A.6.2 Operations

To start this software, double-click **Chapter7.exe**. A file-selection window will appear. First, select the filename of the reference image and then select the filename of the test image. The selected image files will be loaded into memory and displayed on the screen. To choose an operation of the software, place the cursor inside one of the images and press the right mouse button. The menu shown in Fig. A.42a or b will appear depending on whether the cursor is inside the Reference Image or the Test Image.

To register the images automatically, choose **Register images automatically** from the menu and then one of the transformation models from the submenu (Fig. A.42c). This method finds homologous points in homologous neighborhoods in the images in a coarse-to-fine fashion. It then determines a homography transformation for each homologous neighborhood. If **piecewise homography** is chosen, homologous neighborhoods in the images will be registered by a homography transformation. If **RaG approximation** is chosen, the local homography transformations will be blended into a globally smooth elastic transformation, and if **RaG interpolation** is chosen, the blending

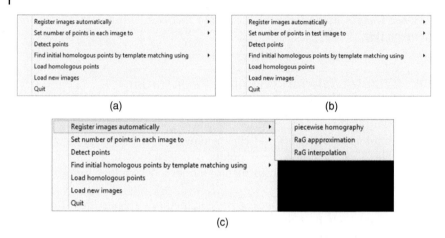

Figure A.42 The menu associated with (a) the Reference Image and (b) the Test Image. (c) Choosing a transformation model for automatic registration.

functions will be weighted in such a way that the global transformation converges to each local transformation at the center of the neighborhood the local transformation is defined.

An example of automatic registration is given in Fig. A.43. The reference and test images are shown in (a) and (b), and registration of the images by the three transformation models are shown in (c)–(e).

To interactively register two images, first find a set of homologous points in the images. To specify the number of points to be detected in each image, choose **Set number of points in each image to** from the menu associated with the Reference Image and then the desired number from the submenu (Fig. A.44). If the desired number is not in the list, choose **provided no.** from the submenu and then enter the desired number from the command window. The default number of points to be detected in each image is 50. Changing this default value will change the number of points used to automatically register the images.

To detect the specified number of points in each image, choose **Detect points** from the menu. If there are fewer points in an image than the specified number, all detected points will be returned. If there are more points in an image than the specified number, the required number of the strongest points will be selected from among the detected points and returned. The returned points will be displayed in the images. For example, when 200 points are required in each image, the points shown in (a) and (b) in Fig. A.45 are obtained when using images (a) and (b) in Fig. A.43.

Homologous points in images are determined in two steps. First, a set of initial homologous points is determined using information from the neighborhoods of the points. Then, the incorrect homologous points (outliers) are

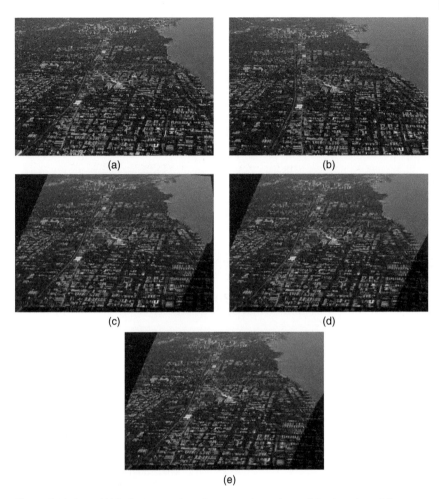

Figure A.43 (a and b) Reference and test images to be registered. Registration of the images by (c) piecewise homography, (d) RaG approximation, and (e) RaG interpolation.

removed by an outlier removal algorithm. To find a set of initial homologous points in the images, choose **Find initial homologous points by matching** from the menu and then either **histograms** or **composite features** from the submenu (Fig. A.46).

If the **histograms** option is chosen, the intensity/color histogram of a circular neighborhood of radius 20 pixels centered at each feature point in each image is determined. Then, for each feature point in the reference image, the feature point in the test image with the most similar histogram is found and the two feature points are considered homologous points. Finding homologous

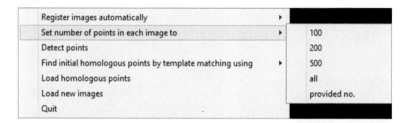

Register images automatically	▶	
Set number of points in each image to	▶	100
Detect points		200
Find initial homologous points by template matching using	▶	500
Load homologous points		all
Load new images		provided no.
Quit	-	

Figure A.44 Specifying the number of feature point to be detected in each image.

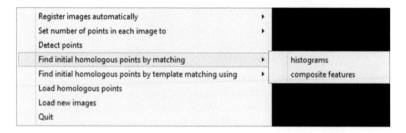

(a)   (b)

Figure A.45 (a and b) Two hundred feature points detected in images (a) and (b) in Fig. A.43.

Register images automatically	▶	
Set number of points in each image to	▶	
Detect points		
Find initial homologous points by matching	▶	histograms
Find initial homologous points by template matching using	▶	composite features
Load homologous points		
Load new images		
Quit		

Figure A.46 Choosing a method for determining an initial set of homologous points in the images.

points in this manner may assign a test point to multiple points in the reference image, causing ambiguity in the homologous points. Ambiguous assignments are removed and the remaining homologous points are considered initial homologous points.

If the **composite features** option is chosen, a set of rotationally invariant features is computed within a circular neighborhood of radius 20 pixels centered at each feature point, defining a rotation-invariant descriptor for the point. Matching is performed using image descriptors rather than histograms at the points to find the initial homologous points. Examples of initial homologous points obtained by histogram matching and descriptor matching using the

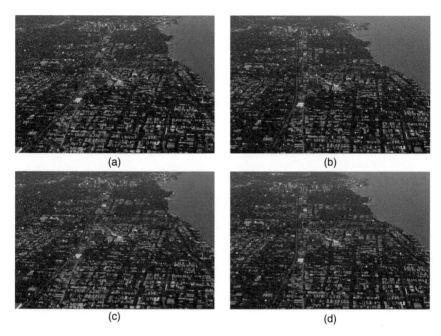

(a) (b)

(c) (d)

Figure A.47 Initial homologous points obtained in the images (a and b) when matching histograms at the points and (c and d) when matching composite descriptors at the points. Homologous points in conjugate images are shown with the same color.

feature points shown in Fig. A.45 are given in Fig. A.47. One hundred and twenty-five initial homologous points are obtained by histogram matching, while 134 initial homologous points are obtained by matching the descriptors at the points. Homologous points are shown with the same color in these images.

Many of the initial homologous points obtained in this manner are incorrect. Incorrect homologous points are outliers that need to be removed before determining the transformation parameters. To remove the outliers, choose **Remove outliers** from the menu (Fig. A.48). A robust estimator with affine constraint is applied to the neighborhood of each point to determine whether the point is an inlier or an outlier. The size of the neighborhood is adjusted to the local density of points. Removing outliers in this manner from among the initial homologous points shown in Fig. A.47, the final homologous points shown in Fig. A.49 are obtained. Thirty-seven final homologous points are obtained by histogram matching, while only 14 final homologous points are obtained by matching image descriptors. The images appear to be more different geometrically than radiometrically. Since histograms contain radiometric information and the descriptors contain geometric information, in this particular example, matching the color histograms produces more

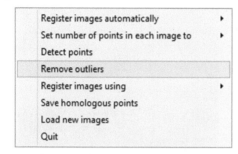

Register images automatically	▶
Set number of points in each image to	▶
Detect points	
Remove outliers	
Register images using	▶
Save homologous points	
Load new images	
Quit	

Figure A.48 Removing outliers from the initial homologous points.

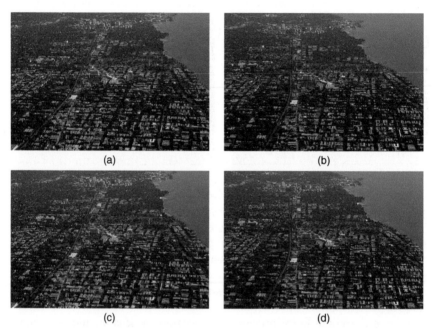

(a)   (b)

(c)   (d)

Figure A.49 Final homologous points obtained after removing outliers from the initial homologous points shown in Fig. A.47.

homologous points than matching the composite descriptors associated with the points.

Instead of finding initial homologous points among already chosen feature points in the images, feature points can be selected in the reference image and then searched for in the test image by template matching. To use template matching, choose **Find initial homologous points by template matching using** from the menu and then either **cross-correlation** or **mutual information** from the submenu (Fig. A.50). Cross- correlation is preferred when the images are radiometrically very similar, and mutual information is preferred when the images are from different sensors or there are radiometric

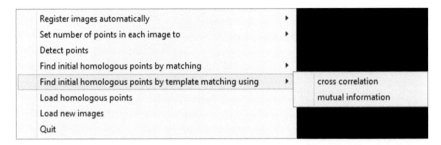

Register images automatically	▶	
Set number of points in each image to	▶	
Detect points		
Find initial homologous points by matching	▶	
Find initial homologous points by template matching using	▶	cross correlation
Load homologous points		mutual information
Load new images		
Quit		

Figure A.50 Finding the initial homologous points in the images by template matching.

(a)   (b)

Figure A.51 Initial homologous points obtained by cross-correlation template matching.

differences between the images. Using cross-correlation template matching, the 160 homologous points shown in Fig. A.51 are obtained. The outlier removal process does not find any outliers from the initial homologous points obtained by template matching.

Having found a set of homologous points in the images, the next step is to use the homologous points to determine the parameters of an appropriate transformation model to register the images. To select a transformation model, choose **Register images using** from the menu and then one of the transformation models from the submenu (Fig. A.52).

If **affine OLS** is chosen, the parameters of an affine transformation will be determined by the OLS method using the coordinates of homologous points in the images. If **affine LMS** is chosen, the parameters of the affine transformation will be determined by the LMS estimator. This is a robust estimator that is capable of removing the outliers while calculating the affine parameters. Therefore, after finding the initial homologous points, this option can be used to remove the outliers and determine the affine parameters simultaneously. The process also removes the inaccurate homologous points that are left by the outlier removal process.

Options **homography OLS** and **homography LMS** are similar to affine OLS and affine LMS except that homography rather than affine is used.

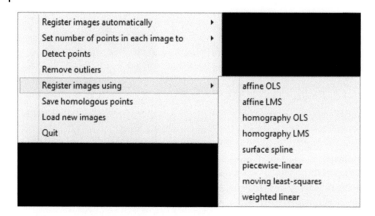

Figure A.52 Choosing a transformation model for image registration.

Affine should be chosen when registering high-altitude aerial images, while homography should be chosen when registering low-altitude aerial images of a scene that can be considered flat. If the scene is not flat, one of the other transformation models should be used to register the images. Registration results of the aerial images in Fig. A.43a,b by the various transformation models when using the 37 homologous points in Fig. A.49a and b are shown in Fig. A.53.

To evaluate the quality of a registration, choose one of the options in the menu associated with the Overlay View (Fig. A.54). Choosing **Display overlaid** will display the overlaid images shown in Fig. A.53. Figure A.55 shows some of the other display options. Choosing **Display difference** will display an image that represents the absolute difference of intensities/colors of homologous pixels in the images (Fig. A.55a). Larger differences are shown brighter, indicating a poorer registration or a change in the scene.

Choosing **Display fused** will create an image with its red band taken from the resampled test image and its green and blue bands taken from the reference image (Fig. A.55b). If the images are registered accurately and the images do not have radiometric differences, the fused image will look like the reference image. Otherwise, red and light blue regions will appear in areas where registration is poor or changes have occurred in the scene between the times the images are obtained. Choosing **Overlay boundaries** will find edges in the reference image and overlay them with the resampled test image (Fig. A.55c). This method of display makes it possible to visually assess the registration accuracy by concentrating on region boundaries in the images.

To measure the quality of registration, choose **Evaluate registration using** from the menu associated with the Overlay View and then **correlation coefficient** or **mutual information** from the submenu (Fig. A.54). Use correlation coefficient when the images are obtained by the same sensor and the scene has

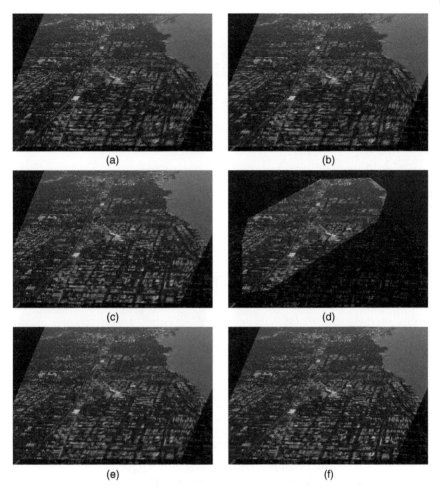

(a)

(b)

(c)

(d)

(e)

(f)

Figure A.53 Registration of images (a) and (b) in Fig. A.43 using the 37 homologous points in Fig. A.49a and b by (a) affine LMS, (b) homography LMS, (c) surface spline, (d) piecewise linear, (e) moving least squares, and (f) weighted linear transformations.

not gone through radiometric changes. Otherwise, use mutual information to determine the similarity between overlapping areas in the images after registration. The higher the obtained similarity measure, the more accurate is expected to be the registration.

Finally, to save the resampled test image or any one of the displayed images, first choose the desired **Display** option and then choose **Save displayed image** from the menu associated with the Overlay View (Fig. A.54). To save the coordinates of the homologous points obtained thus far, choose **Save homologous points** from the menu associated with the Reference Image or the Test Image

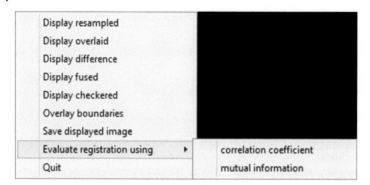

Display resampled	
Display overlaid	
Display difference	
Display fused	
Display checkered	
Overlay boundaries	
Save displayed image	
Evaluate registration using ▸	correlation coefficient
Quit	mutual information

Figure A.54 Measuring the registration quality using a similarity measure.

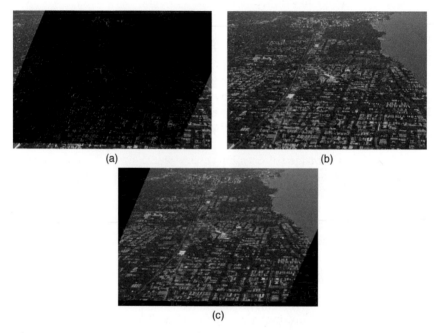

(a)

(b)

(c)

Figure A.55 Display of (a) absolute difference, (b) fused, and (c) boundary overlaid registered images.

(Fig. A.52). A file-selection window will appear. Provide a filename with extension .txt to save the coordinates of the homologous points in ASCII form. To read back the homologous points at a later date to register the same images again, first load the images into memory and then choose **Load homologous points** from the menu associated with the Reference Image or the Test Image (Fig. A.42a and b).

To exit the program, choose **Quit** from the menu associated with any one of the windows.

A.7 Chapter 8: Volume Image Registration

A.7.1 Introduction

Volumetric images come in different forms. Some scanners produce isotropic volumes, while others produce a sequence of cross-sectional images. In the latter case, an isotropic volume must be created from the cross-sectional images before attempting to register the images. This software can register isotropic as well as nonisotropic images. It will use voxel dimensions to convert a non-isotropic volume into an isotropic one. After finding the registration parameters, it then resamples the original test volume to the resolution and geometry of the original reference volume.

Volumetric images are generally saved in formats different from those of remote sensing images. Medical images are generally in DICOM [4] format, while remote sensing images are generally in JPEG format. Occasionally, other formats are also used. This software uses the most basic file formats that can be created using MATLAB [5] or other image analysis programming environments. The file formats used by this software are described in the following section.

After loading two image volumes into memory, the software automatically registers the images and provides tools to evaluate the registration quality. A set of feature points is detected in the reference image. The corresponding feature points are located in the test image by template matching, and the coordinates of homologous feature points in the images are used to determine the parameters of a rigid/nonrigid transformation to register the images.

A.7.2 I/O File Formats

This software accepts image files in the following formats:

1. One byte per voxel, showing values in the range [0, 255]. Files in this format have extension **.bin**.
2. Two bytes per voxel, showing values in the range [0, 65,535] or in the range [−32,768, 32,767]. Files in this format have extension **.img**.

A file in **.bin** format has a header followed by voxel intensities in 8-bit unsigned integers. The first 6 bytes in the header show the number of columns, the number of rows, and the number of slices, each as a 16-bit unsigned integer. The next 12 bytes in the header show voxel dimensions in x, y, and z directions in millimeters. Each dimension is saved as a 32-bit floating-point number. Voxel intensities follow the header. Voxels within each slice are saved in raster order, each by an 8-bit unsigned integer. After saving the first slice, voxel intensities in the second slice are saved, and this is continued until voxel intensities in the last slice are saved. A volumetric image with c columns, r rows, and s slices when saved in **.bin** format will have $c \times r \times s + 18$ bytes.

Files in **.img** format are similar to files in **.bin** format except that they use 2 bytes per voxel. Both signed and unsigned numbers can be used. An image with c columns, r rows, and s slices in **.img** format will have $2 \times c \times r \times s + 18$ bytes, with the 18 bytes representing the header. To use this software, therefore, the images must be converted from DICOM, JPEG, or other formats to **.bin** or **.img** format. A MATLAB program (dcm2img.m) to convert DICOM image slices into **.img** format is included within the software package for this chapter.

A.7.3 Operations

To start the software, double-click **Chapter8.exe**. A file-selection window will appear. First, choose the filename of the reference volume and then the filename of the test volume. Files can be in **.bin** or **.img** format. Files in **.bin** format use one byte per voxel while files in **.img** format use two bytes per voxel. Since intensities between 0 and 255 can be displayed on a screen, if a 2-byte per voxel volume is loaded, it will be converted into a 1-byte per voxel volume. Two-byte intensities are mapped to one-byte intensities in such a way to maximize entropy of displayed image volume. Since some medical images show noise outside the body, intensities that appear near volume borders are attenuated. Specify a percentage of the lower intensities that should be attenuated by selecting a number between 0 and 70 when loading an image volume in **.img** format.

The image volumes read into memory are displayed on the screen. The reference volume will be shown in light blue and the test volume in red. An example is given in Fig. A.56a. Orthogonal cross sections of a volume appear in the

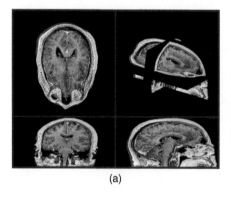
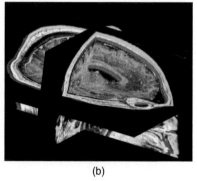

(a) (b)

Figure A.56 (a) Display of reference and test volumes in three orthogonal views and a 3-D view. (b) The magnified 3-D view.

upper-left (axial), lower-left (coronal), and lower-right (sagittal) windows, and the locations of the orthogonal cross sections within the volume appear in the upper-right window. The user may navigate through the volume by moving the mouse to left–right while pressing the left mouse button in any one of the cross-sectional views.

Operations of the software can be chosen from the menu associated with the cross-sectional views. To choose an operation, move the cursor inside one of the cross-sectional views and press the right mouse button. One of the menus shown in Fig. A.57 will appear depending on whether isotropic or nonisotropic volumes are loaded.

Depending on the scan direction when capturing an image sequence, displayed slices may appear upside down. If both volumes appear upside down, choose **Reverse scan** from the menu. If only reference/test volume is upside down, first display the reference/test volume and then choose **Reverse scan** from the menu. This will correct the display, showing the slices right-side up. To only display the reference image volume, choose **Display reference image** from the menu (Fig. A.57). This will change the **Display reference image** entry to **Display overlaid images**. To display the overlaid image volumes again, choose **Display overlaid images** from the menu. In the same manner, to only display the test image volume, choose **Display test image** from the menu.

The menu that is associated with the upper-right window is shown in Fig. A.58a. Choosing the **Magnify view** from the menu will replace the four-window display with a single-window display, showing the contents of the upper-right window (Fig. A.56b). This makes it possible to see details within the slices better. To navigate through the axial, coronal, and sagittal slices while in magnified view, press keys **a/A**, **c/C**, and **s/S** on the keyboard. To return to the four-window display, select **Minify view** from the menu (Fig. A.58b).

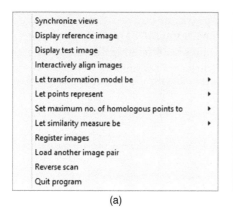

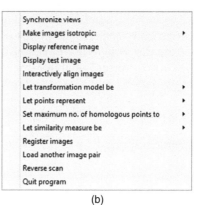

(a)   (b)

Figure A.57 Contents of the menu associated with the axial, coronal, and sagittal views after loading (a) isotropic volumes and (b) nonisotropic volumes.

Figure A.58 (a), (b) Menus associated with the 3-D view.

To synchronize the three orthogonal views, choose **Synchronize views** from the menu associated with one of the orthogonal views (Fig. A.57). This method of display ensures that the point of interest within the volume appears in all views, making it possible to see the point's surroundings. While in this viewing mode, the **Synchronize views** entry will change to **Normal view**. To return to the original viewing mode, choose **Normal view** from the menu. The normal viewing mode makes it possible to go through the slices in the three orthogonal directions independently.

To register the images, first choose the tools to be used in the registration. To select the desired transformation model, choose **Let transformation model be** from the menu and then one of the options from the submenu (Fig. A.59a). **Rigid** is the default transformation. If the images should be registered nonrigidly, choose either **Local weighted linear** or **Volume spline**. Local weighted linear is a blending of local rigid transformations and is an approximation method. Volume spline is a global interpolation method.

Two feature point detection methods are provided. One method finds centers of 3-D dark and bright blobs and another method finds 3-D corners. To select a feature point detection method, choose **Let points represent** from the menu (Fig. A.57) and then either **3-D blob centers** or **3-D corners** from the submenu (Fig. A.59b). The default method is **3-D corners**.

To select the number of homologous points to be used to determine the transformation parameters, choose **Set maximum no. of homologous points to** from the menu (Fig. A.57) and then one of the numbers in the submenu (Fig. A.59c). The default number is 100. The larger the number of homologous points, the longer it takes to find them.

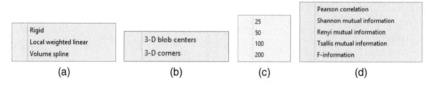

Figure A.59 Various options for (a) image transformation, (b) feature point detection, (c) number of homologous points, and (d) the similarity measure used by template matching to find homologous points in the images.

Finally, a number of similarity measures are provided to find homologous points in images by template matching. To select a desired similarity measure, choose **Let similarity measure be** from the menu (Fig. A.57) and then one of the options from the submenu (Fig. A.59d). **Pearson correlation**, also known as correlation coefficient, should be used only when the images are in the same modality. **Shannon mutual information**, **Renyi mutual information**, **Tsallis mutual information**, and *F*-**information** can be used when the images are in the same modality or different modalities. *F*-**information** is the default similarity measure.

To register the image volumes with the selected parameters, choose **Register images** from the menu. Registering the image volumes in Fig. A.56 with the default parameters produces the result shown in Fig. A.60. Forty-four homologous points are found, from which the parameters of a rigid transformation to register the volumes are obtained. Registration RMSE at homologous points using the obtained rigid transformation is 0.65 mm. Voxel dimensions in both images are 1 mm. The 3-D view shows the overlaid volumes as well as the homologous points. Feature points in the reference volume are shown in green and feature points in the test volume are shown in red. When homologous points after registration fall within 3 voxel units of each other, the points are shown in yellow. Otherwise, homologous points are shown in green (reference) and red (test). Feature points in Fig. A.60 are drawn with spheres of radius 5 voxels. If the volumes are nonisotropic, they are made isotropic to have cubic voxels before registering the volumes.

After this registration, the menu entry **Register images** (Fig. A.57) will change to **Refine registration** (Fig. A.61a). To further refine the registration, choose **Refine registration** from the menu. This will repeat the registration process starting from the registered volumes. If the volumes before registration have a rotational difference that is greater than 15°, template matching

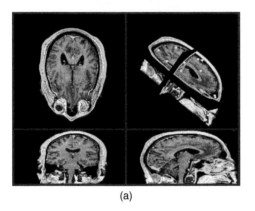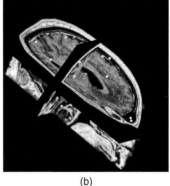

(a)   (b)

Figure A.60 (a and b) Result of rigid registration of image volumes in Fig. A.56.

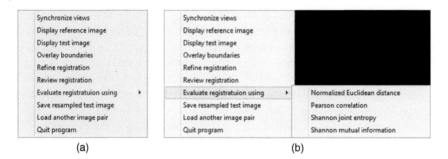

Synchronize views		Synchronize views		
Display reference image		Display reference image		
Display test image		Display test image		
Overlay boundaries		Overlay boundaries		
Refine registration		Refine registration		
Review registration		Review registration		
Evaluate registratuion using ▸		Evaluate registratuion using ▸		Normalized Euclidean distance
Save resampled test image		Save resampled test image		Pearson correlation
Load another image pair		Load another image pair		Shannon joint entropy
Quit program		Quit program		Shannon mutual information

(a)   (b)

Figure A.61 (a) Contents of the menu associated with the three orthogonal views after completion of a registration. (b) Choosing a measure to evaluate the quality of the registration.

may not be able to produce accurate homologous points in the first try. By registering the volumes again, the rotational difference between the volumes is reduced. The refinement step, by finding more homologous points in the volumes, improves the registration accuracy. If the volumes do not have a large rotational difference, the refinement process may not find additional homologous points to produce a more accurate registration. In that case, the software will print an appropriate message in that effect in the command window.

To visually evaluate the quality of a registration, choose **Review registration** from the menu. This option will make it possible to examine the registered volumes within cross-sectional slices along horizontal and vertical lines. An example showing review of axial slices along horizontal and vertical lines is given in Fig. A.62. Review along horizontal lines is made possible by pressing the left mouse button while moving the mouse up–down, and review along vertical lines is made possible by moving the mouse to left–right. When in review mode, navigation through the orthogonal slices can be achieved by pressing **a/A**, **c/C**, and **s/S** on the keyboard. After entering the review mode, the entry **Review registration** in the menu (Fig. A.61a) will change to **Stop review**. To get out of the review mode, choose **Stop review** from the menu.

To measure the registration quality, choose **Evaluate registration using** from the menu and then one of the options in the submenu (Fig. A.61b). If **Normalized Euclidean distance** is chosen, the root-mean-squared intensity differences between homologous voxels within the overlap area in the volumes after registration will be determined and displayed in the command window. The smaller this measure, the more accurate the registration is expected to be. If **Pearson correlation** is chosen, the similarity between overlapping areas in the volumes will be measured using the correlation coefficient between intensities of homologous voxels in the volume after registration. The larger the correlation measure, the more accurate is expected to be the registration. These two measures are suitable when the volumes are in the same modality.

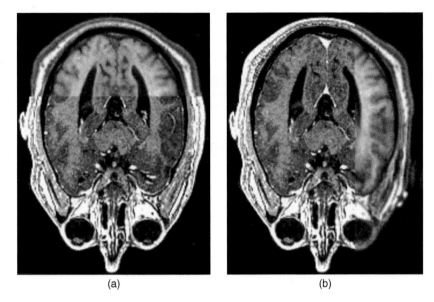

Figure A.62 Reviewing the registration quality within the axial view (a) along horizontal lines and (b) along vertical lines.

When the volumes are in different modalities, either **Shannon joint entropy** or **Shannon mutual information** should be used to measure the registration quality. Shannon joint entropy is a distance measure and, therefore, the smaller the obtained value, the more accurate is expected to be the registration. Shannon mutual information is a similarity measure and, therefore, the larger the obtained value, the more accurate should be the registration.

The registration process resamples the test image volume to the resolution and geometry of the reference volume. To save the resampled test volume, choose **Save resampled test image** from the menu (Fig. A.61a). A file-selection window will open. Provide a filename with extension **.bin** or **.img** to save the resampled test volume.

The image volumes to be registered cannot have very large translational and/or rotational differences. This is due to the use of template matching in finding homologous points in the volumes. If the image volumes have large translational and/or rotational differences, first bring the images close to each other interactively. To do that, choose **Interactively align images** from the menu (Fig. A.57a). If the image volumes are nonisotropic, there is a need to first make them isotropic. This is done by choosing **Make images isotropic** from the menu and then one of **High resolution**, **Mid resolution**, or **Low resolution** (Fig. A.63a). The lower the selected resolution, the more responsive the interaction will be, and the higher the selected resolution, the more accurate the alignment will be.

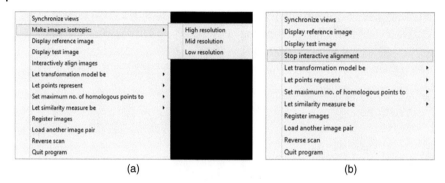

Figure A.63 (a) Making the image volumes isotropic for interactive alignment. (b) Stopping the interactive alignment.

To interactively align images, after choosing **Interactively align images** from the menu, use the mouse to drag the test image close to the reference image. To rotate the test image, first press 2 on the keyboard and then move the mouse up/down or left/right to rotate the test image volume about an axis. If the axial slice is selected, image volume will be rotated about the z-axis, if coronal slice is selected, image volume will be rotated about the y-axis, and if the sagittal slice is selected, image volume will be rotated about the x-axis. To go back to the translation mode, press 1 on the keyboard. Translating the axial slice will translate test image volume with respect to x- and y-axes. Similarly, translating the coronal and sagittal slices will translate the test image volume with respect to yz-axes and xz-axes, respectively. To stop the interactive alignment, choose **Stop interactive alignment** from the menu (Fig. A.63b). The approximately aligned images can now be more accurately registered by selecting **Register images** from the menu (Fig. A.63a).

In addition to the menu operations, the software provides a number of keyboard operations. To view the available keyboard operations, press **h** on the keyboard. The available commands will be printed to the command window.

To go through axial, coronal, and sagittal slices at any time, press keys **a/A**, **c/C**, and **s/S**, respectively. To increase slice numbers use keys **a**, **c**, and **s** and use keys **A**, **C**, and **S** to decrease slice number.

To zoom in/out of the displayed images, press key **z/Z**. To view the portion of an image slice that falls out of view due to image zooming, press **p** on the keyboard and then press the left mouse button and move the slice within its window with the motion of the mouse. To reset or undo the pan and zoom operations performed so far, press **r** on the keyboard.

When image volumes in different modalities are displayed, intensities in one modality may be much higher than intensities in the other modality, creating an overlay that is dominated by one modality. To increase/decrease intensities in a modality, use keys **i**, **I**, **j**, and **J**. Use keys **i/I** to multiply/divide intensities in the reference volume by 1.1 and keys **j/J** to multiply/divide intensities in the test volume by 1.1. If by multiplying an intensity by 1.1 the intensity becomes larger than 255, it will be set to 255.

Finally, to exit the program, choose **Quit program** from one of the menus.

References

1 http://opencv.org/

2 https://www.opengl.org/

3 R. Grompone von Gioi, J. Jakubowicz, J.-M. Morel, and G. Randall, LSD: a line segment detector, *Image Processing On Line*, **2**:35–55, 2012.

4 http://dicom.nema.org/

5 http://www.mathworks.com/products/matlab/

Index

Theory and Applications of Image Registration, First Edition. Arthur Ardeshir Goshtasby.
© 2017 John Wiley & Sons, Inc. Published 2017 by John Wiley & Sons, Inc.